Psychosocial Treatments for
CHILD AND ADOLESCENT DISORDERS
Empirically Based Strategies for Clinical Practice

Psychosocial Treatments for
CHILD AND ADOLESCENT DISORDERS

Empirically Based Strategies for Clinical Practice

Edited by

EUTHYMIA D. HIBBS &
PETER S. JENSEN

American Psychological Association
Washington, DC

First printing April 1996
Second printing December 1996
Third printing November 1997

Published by
American Psychological Association
750 First Street, NE
Washington, DC 20002

Copies may be ordered from
APA Order Department
PO Box 92984
Washington, DC 20090-2984

In the UK and Europe, copies may be ordered from
American Psychological Association
3 Henrietta Street
Covent Garden, London
WC2E 8LU England

Typeset in Goudy by PRO-IMAGE Corporation, Techna-Type Div., York, PA

Cover designer: Paul Purlow, New York, NY
Printer: United Book Press, Inc., Baltimore, MD
Technical/production editor: M. Liliana Riahi

Library of Congress Cataloging-in-Publication Data
Psychosocial treatments for child and adolescent disorders :
  empirically based strategies for clinical practice / edited by
  Euthymia D. Hibbs and Peter S. Jensen.
      p.   cm.
  Includes bibliographical references and index.
  ISBN 1-55798-330-5 (acid-free paper)
    1. Child psychotherapy.   2. Adolescent psychotherapy.   I. Hibbs,
Euthymia D.   II. Jensen, Peter S.
  RJ504.P75   1996
  618.92′8914—dc20   96-1003
                                                                      CIP

British Library Cataloguing-in-Publication Data
A CIP record is available from the British Library.

Printed in the United States of America

CONTENTS

v

CONTRIBUTORS

Howard B. Abikoff, PhD
Associate Professor of Psychiatry
Director of Research
Division of Child and Adolescent Psychiatry
Schneider Children's Hospital
Long Island Jewish Medical Center
Albert Einstein College of Medicine
New Hyde Park, New York

Anne Marie Albano, PhD
Assistant Director
Phobia and Anxiety Disorders Clinic
Center for Stress and Anxiety Disorders
The University at Albany
State University of New York
Albany, New York

Arthur D. Anastopoulos, PhD
Associate Professor of Psychiatry and Pediatrics
Department of Psychiatry
Chief, Attention Deficit Hyperactivity Disorders Clinic
University of Massachusetts Medical Center
Worcester, Massachusetts

Joseph Angelelli, MA
Graduate Resident Assistant
Department of Human Development and Family Sciences
Oregon State University
Corvallis, Oregon

Russell A. Barkley, PhD
Professor of Psychiatry and Neurology
Department of Psychiatry
Director of Psychology
University of Massachusetts Medical Center
Worcester, Massachusetts

David H. Barlow, PhD
Distinguished Professor and Director
Phobia and Anxiety Disorders Clinic
Center for Stress and Anxiety Disorders
The University at Albany
State University of New York
Albany, New York

Marquita Bedway, PhD
Assistant Professor of Psychiatry
Associate in Pediatrics
Wayne State University School of Medicine
Detroit, Michigan

Guillermo Bernal, PhD
Clinical Psychologist
Professor, Psychology Department
University of Puerto Rico
Rio Piedras, Puerto Rico

Boris Birmaher, MD
Director, Child and Adolescent Outpatient Services
Director, Child and Adolescent Mood Disorders Clinic
Western Psychiatric Institute and Clinic
Associate Professor of Psychiatry
University of Pittsburgh
Pittsburgh, Pennsylvania

Blair Bowen, PhD candidate
Department of Educational Psychology
University of Texas
Austin, Texas

David A. Brent, MD
Chief, Division of Child and Adolescent Psychiatry
Director, Services for Teens at Risk
Western Psychiatric Institute and Clinic
Professor of Psychiatry
University of Pittsburgh
Pittsburgh, Pennsylvania

Dennis P. Cantwell, MD
Joseph Campbell Professor of Child Psychiatry
School of Medicine
University of California Los Angeles
Los Angeles, California

Patricia Chamberlain, PhD
Research Scientist
Oregon Social Learning Center
Eugene, Oregon

Gregory N. Clarke, PhD
Assistant Professor of Psychiatry
Department of Child Psychiatry
Oregon Health Sciences University
Portland, Oregon

Giuseppe Costantino, PhD
Sunset Park Mental Health Center of Lutheran Medical Center
Hispanic Research Center
Fordham University
St. John's University
New York, New York

Peter Fonagy, PhD
Freud Memorial Professor of Psychoanalysis
University College London
Research Director
The Anna Freud Center
London, England

Fred Frankel, PhD
Associate Professor, School of Medicine
University of California Los Angeles
Los Angeles, California

Marcia Gilroy, PhD
Assistant Professor of Psychiatry
Associate in Pediatrics
Wayne State University School of Medicine
Detroit, Michigan

Howard Goldstein, PhD
Professor, Communication Disorders
University of Pittsburgh
Pittsburgh, Pennsylvania

Lily Hechtman, MD, FRCP
Professor of Psychiatry and Pediatrics
Director of Research, Division of Child Psychiatry
McGill University
Montreal, Canada

Stephen P. Hinshaw, PhD
Associate Professor of Psychology
Director, Attention Deficit Disorders Program
University of California at Berkeley
Berkeley, California

Diane Holder, MSW
Associate Administrator, Clinical Administration
Western Psychiatric Institute and Clinic
Associate Professor of Psychiatry
University of Pittsburgh
Pittsburgh, Pennsylvania

Hyman Hops, PhD
Research Scientist
Oregon Research Institute
Eugene, Oregon

Betsy Hoza, PhD
Assistant Professor, Department of Psychiatry
University of Pittsburgh
Attention Deficit Disorders Program
Western Psychiatric Institute and Clinic
Pittsburgh, Pennsylvania

Barbara A. Johnson, MD
Co-Director, Child and Adolescent Mood Disorders Clinic
Western Psychiatric Institute and Clinic
Assistant Professor of Psychiatry
University of Pittsburgh
Pittsburgh, Pennsylvania

Alan E. Kazdin, PhD
Professor of Psychology and Psychiatry
Department of Psychology
Yale University
New Haven, Connecticut

Philip C. Kendall, PhD, ABPP
Professor and Head, Division of Clinical Psychology
Department of Psychology
Temple University
Philadelphia, Pennsylvania

Lynn Kern Koegel, PhD
Clinic Director, Autism Research Center
Graduate School of Education
University of California Santa Barbara
Santa Barbara, California

Robert L. Koegel, PhD
Director, Autism Research Center
Professor of Clinical Psychology
Head, Development and Disability Specialization
University of California Santa Barbara
Santa Barbara, California

Frank W. Kohler, PhD
Research Scientist
Allegheny–Singer Research Institute
Pittsburgh, Pennsylvania

David J. Kolko, PhD
Associate Professor of Child Psychiatry and Psychology
University of Pittsburgh School of Medicine
Director, Child and Parent Behavior Clinic
Western Psychiatric Institute and Clinic
Pittsburgh, Pennsylvania

Cynthia Kurowski, PhD candidate
Department of Educational Psychology
University of Texas
Austin, Texas

William M. Kurtines, PhD
Professor and Director of Graduate Studies
Department of Psychology
Florida International University
Miami, Florida

Peter M. Lewinsohn, PhD
Research Scientist
Oregon Research Institute
Professor Emeritus of Psychology
University of Oregon
Eugene, Oregon

Robert G. Malgady, PhD
Program in Quantitative Studies
New York University
Hispanic Research Center
Fordham University
New York, New York

John S. March, MD, MPH
Assistant Professor and
Director of the Program in Child and Adolescent Anxiety Disorders
Departments of Psychiatry and Psychology
Duke University Medical Center
Durham, North Carolina

Donna Moreau, MD
Research Scientist
New York Psychiatric Institute
Associate Professor of Psychiatry
Director of the Children's Anxiety and Depression Clinic
Presbyterian Hospital
New York, New York

Laura Mufson, PhD
Research Scientist
New York State Psychiatric Institute

Assistant Professor of Clinical Psychology in Psychiatry
College of Physicians and Surgeons
Columbia University
Assistant Clinical Director
Children's Anxiety and Depression Clinic
Presbyterian Hospital
New York, New York

Karen Mulle, BSN, MTS
Clinical Research Nurse Specialist
Department of Psychiatry
Duke University Medical Center
Durham, North Carolina

Robert Myatt, PhD
Assistant Professor, Olive View Medical Center
University of California Los Angeles
Los Angeles, California

William E. Pelham, PhD
Professor of Psychiatry and Psychology
University of Pittsburgh
Director, Attention Deficit Disorders Program
Western Psychiatric Institute and Clinic
Pittsburgh, Pennsylvania

Paul A. Pilkonis, PhD
Associate Professor of Psychiatry and Psychology
Department of Psychiatry
Western Psychiatric Institute and Clinic
University of Pittsburgh School of medicine
Pittsburgh, Pennsylvania

Arthur L. Robin, PhD
Professor of Psychiatry
Associate in Pediatrics
Wayne State University School of Medicine
Detroit, Michigan

Paul Rohde, PhD
Research Scientist
Oregon Research Institute
Eugene, Oregon

Jeannette Rosselló, PhD
Clinical Psychologist
Associate Professor
Psychology Department
University of Puerto Rico
Rio Piedras, Puerto Rico

Claudia Roth, MSW
Associate Clinical Administrator
Division of Child and Adolescent Psychiatry
Western Psychiatric Institute and Clinic
Pittsburgh, Pennsylvania

Laura Schreibman, PhD
Professor of Psychology
Department of Psychology
University of California, San Diego

Joy Schweers, MEd
Research Principal/Project Coordinator,
Family and Individual Resources for Suicidal Teens
Western Psychiatric Institute and Clinic
Associate Professor of Psychiatry
University of Pittsburgh
Pittsburgh, Pennsylvania

John R. Seeley, MS
Research Analyst
Oregon Research Institute
Eugene, Oregon

Terri L. Shelton, PhD
Associate Professor of Psychiatry and Pediatrics
Department of Psychiatry
University of Massachusetts Medical Center
Worcester, Massachusetts

Patricia T. Siegel, PhD
Associate Professor of Psychiatry
Associate in Pediatrics
Wayne State University School of Medicine
Detroit, Michigan

Wendy K. Silverman, PhD
Professor, Department of Psychology
Child and Family Psychosocial Research Center
Florida International University
Miami, Florida

Dawn Sommer, PhD candidate
Department of Educational Psychology
University of Texas
Austin, Texas

Kevin D. Stark, PhD
Associate Professor and Program Director
Department of Educational Psychology
University of Texas
Austin, Texas

Phillip S. Strain, PhD
Assistant Executive Director
Research, Training, and Evaluation Division
Early Learning Institute
Pittsburgh, Pennsylvania

Susan Swearer, MA, PhD candidate
Department of Educational Psychology
University of Texas
Austin, Texas

Jose Szapocznik, PhD
Professor and Director
Center for Family Studies
Department of Psychiatry
University of Miami
Miami, Florida

Mary Target, PhD
Senior Research Fellow
The Anna Freud Center
University College of London
London, England

Kimberli R. H. Treadwell, PhD
Clinical Psychology
Department of Psychology
Temple University
Philadelphia, Pennsylvania

Samuel Vuchinich, PhD
Associate Professor
Department of Human Development and Family Sciences
Oregon State University
Corvallis, Oregon

Carolyn Webster-Stratton, PhD, FAAN
Professor and Director, Parenting Clinic
University of Washington
Seattle, Washington

Myrna M. Weissman, PhD
Professor of Epidemiology in Psychiatry
Columbia University College of Physicians
Chief, Department of Clinical-Genetic Epidemiology
New York State Psychiatric Institute
New York, New York

Barbara Wood, MA
Instructor
Department of Human Development and Family Sciences
Oregon State University
Corvallis, Oregon

PREFACE

The field of psychosocial treatment research for children and adolescents is still in its early childhood. Although in the past two decades research has been burgeoning, methodologies have improved, and public awareness has been raised concerning children's mental health issues, the field is still far away from the level reached in other areas of study, such as biological, pharmacological, and treatment research, with adult populations. We felt compelled to put this volume together because there is not, to our knowledge, a comprehensive document that recapitulates ongoing research of the psychosocial treatments for children and adolescents that examines, in detail, several therapeutic approaches for different disorders and that, at the same time, can be used for teaching, research, and clinical practice.

Research on psychosocial treatments for young people was a major priority mandated by the *National Plan for Research on Child and Adolescent Disorders* (1990), a plan that was generated as a response to a congressional request. This plan charged the scientific community with developing a coherent national strategy of mental health research on child and adolescent disorders and called for the expansion of the entire spectrum of research related to these disorders, with special focus on the development of optimal approaches to defining, assessing, diagnosing, and treating young people's mental disorders. The plan also called for the development of clinical services research and services systems research to evaluate and improve the efficacy, organization, delivery, and accessibility of treatment and prevention services to young people with mental disorders.

Since then, the psychosocial treatment research field has made improvements. The Institute of Medicine's *"Report Card" on the National Plan*

(1994) indicated that, although overall funding has fallen short of that envisioned originally, psychosocial treatment research has shown greater growth in comparison with many other areas, and that the number of grants has doubled between 1987 and 1993.

This is not the time for psychosocial treatment investigators to become complacent, however. There is an urgent need to learn and document what type of treatments are most appropriate for which conditions; which psychosocial treatments are effective; and how developmental family, school, and contextual factors can influence treatment outcomes. Also, there is a need to disseminate existing research in the field of psychosocial treatments to clinical health care providers and to academic institutions for the training of future professionals.

Dissemination of research findings is even more critical at this juncture in health care system reform because many questions are being raised regularly concerning the usefulness, validity, intensity, and especially the length of psychosocial treatments. Therefore, additional research is needed urgently to examine the usefulness of these treatments and to inform clinicians, educators, other investigators, policy makers, and insurance companies of the benefits, limitations, and the transferability of psychosocial treatments.

In this book, we have chosen to present mostly work funded by the National Institute of Mental Health (NIMH). Most of the research reported here has undergone the scrutiny of the peer review system within NIMH and expert review again when the chapters were written for publication in this volume. We believe that the research presented here is among the soundest and most supported theoretically and empirically in the literature, and that it is based on the most promising treatments that now exist for children and adolescents.

We hope that this volume will serve as an overview and a guide to contemporary research and practice in the field and as a model and catalyst for future psychosocial treatment research and intervention. Although many would have us wait until the field matures more before creating a handbook such as this, we feel that our nation's youths cannot wait. They need those who provide their health and mental health care to know about the latest treatment techniques and methods that have actually been shown to work. Moreover, many practitioners need to know that this work exists and that it can be useful in their practice.

One of the aims of NIMH is to promote state of the art research on psychosocial treatments for children and adolescents, with the ultimate goal of securing appropriate health and mental health care for our nation's youth. We designed this volume, under its auspices, to contribute to this goal by making available and accessible to those who provide this health care and to those who are making health care decisions the most current and empirically supported psychosocial treatments for children and adolescents in the field.

We wish to thank our contributors for their willingness to share their work with colleagues and for surviving the editors' push for meeting the deadlines. We want to thank the NIMH for encouraging and supporting our endeavor.

In the process of preparing this volume, our enthusiasm has been rekindled by the chapter authors many times. We trust that the final product will enthuse you as much as it has us.

Euthymia D. Hibbs
Peter S. Jensen

I

INTRODUCTION

1

ANALYZING THE RESEARCH: WHAT THIS BOOK IS ABOUT

EUTHYMIA D. HIBBS and PETER S. JENSEN

It is estimated that between 17 and 22% of children aged 6 to 18 years exhibit some form of behavioral, emotional, or developmental disorder. The majority of such youth who seek help receive some form of psychosocial intervention. Helping young children and adolescents to overcome these difficulties early in life offers the possibility of alleviating their suffering, permitting them to reach their full potential, reducing conflict and distress in their families, and diminishing the overall health-care costs to the nation.

Although the need has been great, research on the psychosocial treatment of children and adolescents has not received as much attention as that of adults. It is estimated that more than 200 treatment modalities are actually practiced with this population, and research has examined only a few of these. Therefore, a situation exists in which many treatments are practiced on children without scientific verification of their efficacy. One example of this would be the psychodynamic treatments (including play therapy) that are used extensively with children and adolescents. Although clinicians using this modality often undergo rigorous training, and case studies of their interventions are published, there is little scientific research to testify to their efficacy.

Recently, however, methodologically sound research has been conducted with other modalities and, although it is preliminary, it provides a

3

useful base of knowledge for both child and adolescent treatment research-ers and practitioners. For instance, there is evidence, also preliminary, that cognitive behavior therapy (CBT) is an effective treatment for adolescent major depressive disorder and anxiety disorders, such as generalized anxiety and phobias. There is also preliminary evidence that training parents and teaching problem-solving skills to youth and their families is highly useful in the treatment of externalizing disorders, such as oppositional–defiant and conduct disorders. More research to support these treatment modalities is needed, but investigators also need to expand their repertoire to include, in their experiments, play and other forms of psy-chodynamic therapy, family therapy, and emerging modalities that are just beginning to be practiced (see, for example, chapters 25 to 28, this vol-ume). Although interventions with these theory bases and techniques may be more complex to research, scientists are encouraged to brave engaging in new endeavors and develop appropriate methodologies to examine such commonly practiced treatment modalities.

AIMS OF THIS VOLUME

This volume was written for several audiences: practitioners, treat-ment researchers, students, health care administrators, and others who make decisions about the services to be provided for our nation's youth. One of the aims of this volume is to address an issue that we have been troubled by while attempting to foster research on psychosocial treatments for children and adolescents at the National Institute of Mental Health and that is the lack of communication that has occurred between clinical researchers in the child and adolescent treatment field and the practitioners who are the front line of service for most children and adolescents.

It is our perception that clinicians frequently see researchers as fo-cusing only on highly specific disorders in middle-class environments with families that are unlike those seen in day-to-day practice. What do data on treatment of these "pure" disorders in a hospital or university clinic setting have to do with treating the multiproblem children and families who are weighted down with economic survival issues, family violence, parental psychopathology, and poor neighborhoods and school environ-ments? The jargon-filled journal articles focusing on design questions and multivariate statistical methods seem to have little to offer to them in the scant time that is left for professional development at the end of their work day.

Researchers, on the other hand, are rightfully concerned with veri-fying basic knowledge about treatment efficacy, given the stage of the field of child and adolescent treatment research. They must focus on method-ology and, as they struggle to corroborate the efficacy of psychosocial treatments, they must start with the simpler cases first and have enough participants to attain the statistical power needed to support their results (therefore accounting for much research taking place in university- and hospital-based settings). This is not because they do not understand the complexity of presenting problems in the community, but because they are creating new methodologies and measurement techniques or applying known ones to a childhood or adolescent disorder for the first time. At this early juncture of research, their funding depends on innovative research designs in carefully controlled experiments for clearly defined problems. When they are subjected to the cynicism and criticism of their practitioner colleagues, they feel isolated and misunderstood.

As a result of this, we have perceived both groups as becoming more insular, tending to communicate among themselves but not with each other. Researchers who are studying the efficacy of interpersonal therapy for adolescents suffering from depression know about the research that is being conducted on cognitive–behavioral therapy for adolescents with depression; but the clinician who is treating 12–15 depressed teens a week may not be aware of either research program or of some of the innovative treatment techniques on which they are based.

In actuality, there has never been a time in which these professionals were so dependent on one another for survival. Under the managed care umbrella, practitioners will need research data to show insurers that child and adolescent psychosocial therapy actually works. In increasingly complex social environments, treatment researchers need the practitioners' feedback to develop treatments that meet the real-life demands of clinical practice and to persuade policy makers to provide the resources to study complex issues.

In reporting their research, chapter authors in this book have tried to bridge, in part, the gap between researchers and practitioners by describing their treatment strategies more fully than usually occurs in journal articles on treatment research, by presenting these treatments in their environmental and theoretical contexts, and by making available source information on the manuals and guidelines that will help practitioners to translate interventions in a different practice context.

The psychosocial treatment researchers and graduate students, who aspire to become scientists and practitioners working with children and adolescents, must become aware that conducting psychosocial treatment research with children and adolescents requires making choices of methodologies that may be more complicated than those used in research on treatments of adults. In making assessment and sampling decisions, for example, the research reported in this volume indicates that the child and adolescent treatment researcher–practitioner may need to consider comorbidity much more carefully than their adult treatment counterparts. Which comorbid conditions to include in the treatment protocol and which to exclude, and why, have important implications for the general-izability of the research and the applicability of the interventions tested for community populations. Assessment instruments and interventions must be designed to address the level of the child's developmental abilities, no easy task, and a determination of whether the same treatment methodologies could be applied to a wider range of ages must be considered. For example: To what extent, if any, should parents be involved in the treatment? Should parents of adolescents be as involved as parents of prepubertal children? At what age, if any, does parent training become less effective than the problem-solving treatment for the entire family? What about parental psychopathology? How is that handled in designing effective treatments and in interpreting the results?

How can treatment research address the mosaic of diverse ethnic and cultural backgrounds in the United States? Recruitment strategies for studies may have to be adjusted to take into account cultural norms about seeking and accepting treatment. So far, little research has been done to understand how individuals from various cultures experience psychopathology, much less how investigators should measure and treat mental illness across various cultural groups. The need for culturally sensitive psychosocial treatment research, tailored to address specific groups, looms very large indeed. How can we innovate our treatment and our research designs to begin to address this issue? In this volume, for example, a sample of treatments tailored to Hispanic populations are provided that could serve as catalysts for the development of other culturally sensitive treatment approaches.

Our final audience includes health care administrators (e.g., in HMOs, hospital clinics and community clinics, health insurance companies) who make decisions about which services are offered for whom and for how long. One aim of psychosocial treatment research is to provide answers to these questions that grow more pressing as the funds available for health care continue to decline. In the research reported here, important questions concerning being penny wise and pound foolish are broached. For example, most of the treatments documented in this book show significant efficacy *after* 12 to 20 sessions delivered in consecutive weeks. Yet, some managed care guidelines for a disorder allow only 8 to 10 sessions for treating a particular problem, and practitioners are often advised to budget these sessions such that youth are seen over a longer period of time. Is this really the wisest or most fiscally sound way to proceed?

A medical analogy may be useful to think about here. In the case of certain infections, a patient is asked to take an antibiotic 4 times a day for 10 consecutive days. Imagine for a moment that a limited amount of the antibiotic is available to a physician who has to treat a number of patients. A new shipment is to arrive in six weeks. Would it make sense to give each patient a reduced dose of the antibiotic over a longer period of time (at least until the next shipment comes in)? It is clear, in this case, that because of the nature of how the antibiotic works, it would not make sense. The scarce amount of antibiotic available would be wasted and none of the patients would be likely to get better. When a treatment has been shown to work effectively under certain conditions, it may be highly wasteful, over the long run, to deliver it in a different manner. But research on such questions is just beginning, and investigations, such as the ones reported here, need to be followed up to see how much effectiveness is compromised (or not compromised) when treatments are altered. Health care administrators who want to make the most intelligent managed care decisions, based in part on the most cost-effective "dose" and duration of treatment for children, youth, and their families struggling with specific psychological disorders, need to follow the treatment research field carefully. This book may serve as a beginning.

ORGANIZATION OF THE VOLUME

Chapter 2 provides a more detailed and substantive critique of the issues involved in developing effective psychosocial treatments for children and adolescents and in evaluating those treatments. The remainder of the book is arranged into six sections; each of the first 5 represent a major disorder commonly seen in practice with children and adolescents: anxiety disorders, affective disorders, attention deficit disorder with hyperactivity, conduct disorders, and autism. The sixth section describes treatments, not specific to a particular disorder, that have begun to be investigated or appear highly promising and thus deserve research attention. (Each of these sections is described in greater detail in the section openers.)

In each chapter, the authors describe the nature and characteristics of the disorder, their program of research, their research and intervention strategies, and the results. The research strategies discuss such issues as target population, sampling, assessment instruments, follow-up, and other salient methodological issues. Descriptions of interventions include theory, technique, timing and order of interventions, and, depending on the particular chapter, session outlines, case examples, session dialogue, checklists, and other information of particular interest to therapists who want to integrate all or part of the treatment described into their practice. Many of the chapters contain additional source information for treatment manuals, assessment instruments, and the like. Outcome data are provided, some more preliminary than others, and authors discuss the limitations, issues of generalizability, and future directions of research and practice in their area.

In closing, our goals in this volume are to disseminate the emerging findings on child and adolescent treatment research to investigators and practitioners alike, to demystify the research milieu, to generate increased linkages among specialists working in different areas of the field, and to kindle the motivation of students who would consider venturng into the new world of psychosocial treatment research and empirically based practice for child and adolescent disorders. We invite you to join us.

2

DEVELOPING EFFECTIVE TREATMENTS FOR CHILDREN AND ADOLESCENTS

ALAN E. KAZDIN

The mental health of children and adolescents has come into sharp focus within the past decade for several reasons. Epidemiological research has demonstrated that a high proportion of youths experience significant impairment. Although estimates vary, prevalence studies indicate that between 17–22% of youth under 18 years of age suffer developmental, emotional, or behavioral problems (Costello, 1989; Institute of Medicine, 1989; Zill & Schoenborn, 1990). This might be an underestimate if one broadens the definition of dysfunction to include at-risk behaviors such as substance use, isolated antisocial acts, or running away (Dryfoos, 1990; U.S. Congress, 1991). Also, research has demonstrated that many forms of dysfunction such as attention deficit–hyperactivity disorder, conduct disorder, and depression that are identified in childhood and adolescence can have life-term consequences (see Robins & Rutter, 1990; Weiss & Hechtman, 1986). The continuity of many dysfunctions across the life span, beginning in childhood, heightens the significance of early intervention, not only to reduce the suffering of children and adolescents but also to prevent or to attenuate impairment in adulthood.

Completion of this chapter was facilitated by a Research Scientist Award (MH00353) and by grant MH35408 from the National Institute of Mental Health. Correspondence concerning this chapter should be directed to Alan E. Kazdin, Department of Psychology, Yale University, P. O. Box 208205, New Haven, CT 06520-8205.

9

Development of effective treatments is critically important. Treatments provided on an outpatient basis, including alternative forms of psychotherapy and psychopharmacological interventions, are particularly critical so that services can be provided on a much larger scale than in more restrictive, costly, and disruptive interventions, such as hospitalization and residential care. Psychosocial intervention, the central focus of this book, includes a wide range of interventions designed to decrease or eliminate symptoms and maladjustment and to improve adaptive and prosocial functioning. The interventions are referred to as *psychosocial* because they rely on psychological processes (e.g., learning, movitation) and interpersonal influences as the means of improving how persons feel (affect), think (cognition), and act (behavior). Interventions can take place in diverse settings (at a clinic, at home, at school) and involve a variety of individuals (e.g., clinician, parents, teacher, peers) in an effort to achieve change.

Psychotherapy has come to serve as a general term to refer to the broad range of psychosocial treatments for clinical dysfunction. Traditionally, a variety of conceptual views, interventions, therapeutic agents, and settings are included. For example, conceptual views encompass psychoanalytic, psychodynamic, client-centered, behavioral, cognitive, and family approaches. Techniques within and among alternative approaches can vary greatly depending on who is receiving treatment (e.g., youth, parents, family), the medium of treatment (e.g., talk, play), the central therapeutic focus (e.g., the individual, family), and the setting in which the intervention takes place (e.g., clinic, home, school).

THE EFFECTIVENESS OF PSYCHOTHERAPIES

The question that has evoked the greatest interest is whether psychotherapy is effective. The question, in its broad form, is rejected in contemporary work because of its inherent oversimplicity. There are many types of treatment, clinical problems, and conditions (e.g., characteristics of the child, parent, family; conditions of treatment administration; competence of the therapist) that influence the outcome. One cannot discuss the effectiveness of therapy in a meaningful manner without specifying these different conditions more precisely.

Concerns with the more simplified version of the question have prompted research and development of the field. Well-known in the therapy literature are the galvanizing reviews of psychotherapy research by Eysenck (1952, 1966). The central conclusion drawn from these reviews was that the rates of improvement for those who received psychotherapy and for those who did not were no different. Similar reviews of psychotherapy research that focused specifically on children and adolescents followed and reached the same verdict (Levitt, 1957, 1963). Only a small number of studies (18 and 22 studies, respectively) were available for these latter reviews. Also, the studies encompassed diverse interventions and "youth" of very different ages (preschoolers to 21 years of age). The paucity of controlled studies was as much a problem as the suggestion that treatment did not work well. In the past 15 years in particular, the quantity and quality of evidence on treatment for children and adolescents have proliferated. Hundreds of controlled outcome studies have been completed and have permitted more positive conclusions about treatment.

The evaluation of treatment has been aided by the development of meta-analysis, a quantitative method of delineating a common metric (effect size) to combine studies. From several meta-analyses of child and adolescent therapy and extensive empirical literature on treatment (e.g., Casey & Berman, 1985; Hazelrigg, Cooper, & Borduin, 1987; Kazdin, Bass, Ayers, & Rodgers, 1990; Shadish et al., 1993; Weisz & Weiss, 1993), the following conclusions seem to be warranted (see Kazdin, 1993):

- The changes achieved with psychotherapy are greater than those that emerge without treatment. This finding has been consistent across reviews, cited previously.
- The magnitude of treatment effects parallels closely the effects obtained from outcome research with adults (Brown, 1987). Effect sizes for treatment versus no treatment tend to hover within the range of .7–.8, even though treatment technique, problem domain, and age of the youths are among the many influences on effect size.
- Classes of treatment (e.g., behavioral vs. nonbehavioral) and individual treatment techniques within a given class of treatments do not vary consistently in effectiveness, although some reviews have favored behavioral and cognitive–behavioral treatments (see Weisz & Weiss, 1993).
- The effects of treatment are not clearly different for internalizing problems (e.g., anxiety, depression, withdrawal) and externalizing problems (e.g., hyperactivity, aggression).

Reviews of psychotherapy for children and adolescents have been useful in culling the available studies, identifying the strength of effects among various classes of treatment, and characterizing how treatment is conducted and evaluated. Reviews have yielded general conclusions (e.g., psychotherapy is better than no treatment). Broad conclusions are important as a response to initial concerns of whether the effectiveness of psychotherapy surpass in impact those changes that occur without treatment. Despite the progress, fundamental questions remain to be addressed. These questions constitute priorities for current research and many of the themes that have served as impetus for the programs of research presented in this book.

PRIORITIES IN CURRENT RESEARCH: BRIEFLY NOTED

Expansion in the Range of Treatments Investigated

Treatment research for children and adolescents has focused on a narrow range of treatment techniques. For example, behavior modification and cognitive–behavioral techniques account for approximately one half of the treatment research (Kazdin, Bass, et al., 1990). Other "more traditional" approaches, such as psychodynamic therapy, psychoanalysis, client-centered therapy, and family therapy, and combinations of these as part of eclectic approaches are rarely studied, although they are commonly used in clinical practice (e.g., Kazdin, Siegel, & Bass, 1990; Koocher & Pedulla, 1977; Silver & Silver, 1983). The dearth of research on commonly used treatments identifies an obvious research priority.

When one considers treatment techniques more concretely, rather than broad approaches, the research task appears enormous. Well over 200 interventions are in use for children and adolescents (Kazdin, 1988). The vast majority of these have not been studied empirically. A priority of research is not necessarily to investigate each technique, but rather to consider how treatments effect change and whether different treatments operate in a similar fashion, that is, through the same mechanisms or processes.

A related issue pertains to the use of treatment combinations. Separate movements within the field of psychotherapy generally have helped spawn the combination of treatments. Integration of different approaches and the search for common factors reflect a broad conceptual movement within psychotherapy research (see Norcross & Goldfried, 1992). This movement, referred to as *integrationism*, has fostered an ecumenicism among varied treatments conducive to their combined application. Also, eclecticism in clinical treatment (e.g., "I use whatever works") or drawing on many different treatments has suffered perennial criticism for the lack of an empirical base. Nevertheless, more studies have become available that combine multiple treatments "as needed," as often discussed in clinical work (e.g., Henggeler, Melton, & Smith, 1992; Satterfield, Satterfield, & Schell, 1987). Finally, characteristics of childhood and adolescent dysfunction, such as the frequent presence of comorbid conditions and the possible long-term effects of dysfunction, have prompted efforts to maximize the impact of treatment. Perhaps, treatment effects may be bolstered if multiple interventions are provided in combination. Research on many constituent techniques is sparse; even more rare is research on combinations of these treatments.

Expansion in the Range of Research Questions

Treatment technique is one source of influence and is likely to operate in conjunction with other factors that also contribute toward the outcome. Other sources of influence including characteristics of youth and their families, therapist factors, treatment processes, and traditional foci that underlie many advances in adult psychotherapy have been neglected (Kazdin, Bass, et al., 1990). Developing and identifying effective treatments require evaluation of the impact of alternative techniques as well as the conditions that influence their outcomes. In general, we wish to find out the:

- impact of treatment in relation to no-treatment;
- components of the treatment that contribute to change;
- parameters of treatment (e.g., duration) that can be varied to improve outcome;
- relative effectiveness of alternative treatments;
- treatment combinations that can improve outcome;
- role of various treatment processes (e.g., therapeutic alliance) in therapy; and
- impact of patient, family, or therapist characteristics alone and in combination with alternative treatments.

In general, scant attention is accorded to evaluation of nontechnique variables (e.g., classification variables to divide the groups) that may moderate treatment outcome. Among the questions that warrant attention, special emphasis might be placed on efforts to match children and treatment. A given treatment is likely to vary in effectiveness as a function of child, parent, and family characteristics. Research relating these domains to outcome would greatly advance our knowledge.

Long-Term Follow-Up of Treatment

Many of the gains demonstrated in psychotherapy have been tested within a relatively brief time frame without consideration of the long-term effects. The majority of studies of child and adolescent therapy omit follow-up assessment. Among studies that do, assessment takes place typically 5–6 months after treatment (Kazdin, Bass, et al., 1990). Follow-up studies are critically important because the outcomes evident immediately after treatment are not always the same as those evident over time. Indeed, some treatments that appear to be effective in the short run do not show sustained effects; other treatments that produce little or no effect immediately after treatment occasionally show significant improvements one to two years later; and treatments that appear equally effective immediately after treatment occasionally vary systematically in outcomes at follow-up (see Kazdin, 1988).

If we are to understand fully the extent to which treatments are effective, further research is needed to evaluate the long-term impact of diverse therapies on various clinical problems. Different time periods reflect different questions, each of which is important in its own right. For example, we wish to know if therapy can produce change, whether gains are maintained, and whether long-term adjustment (e.g., adulthood) is affected. Knowledge about the short- and long-term impact of treatment may help to guide both the interventions that are selected and when and how they are deployed during the course of development.

Expansion of Clinical Samples and Problem Domains

The majority of child and adolescent psychotherapy research has been conducted with nonreferred populations, primarily recruited from school settings (Kazdin, Bass, et al., 1990). Much can be learned in this fashion because youths with significant impairment can be identified. Also, integration of psychosocial services in the context of schools raises its own interesting prospects. At the same time, there is a need to evaluate clinically referred samples and youths whose dysfunction represents significant impairment. Clinically referred samples often are characterized by conditions that can attenuate the benefits of treatment (e.g., greater severity of impairment than volunteer samples, comorbid disorders, parent and family dysfunction). The scope and nature of dysfunction of clinic samples and the associated features regarding parent and family functioning can affect materially the conclusions made about treatment. Consequently, a priority for research is the study of clinical samples.

A related sampling issue pertains to the problem domains studied in treatment research. Reviews, including several meta-analyses, have indicated that treatment is effective across a range of problem domains. To draw conclusions, reviews often combine symptom domains into broad classes such as internalizing and externalizing disorders and show that treatments are effective for both classes. The development of broad classes that combine different problems may be helpful for general conclusions, but not for identifying whether effective treatments exist within more circumscribed types of dysfunctions.

Within the broad categories, major areas of dysfunction remain in which few controlled studies exist. For example, anxiety, depression, and adjustment disorder are seen frequently in clinical practice in children and adolescents (Kazdin, Siegel, & Bass, 1990) but are studied infrequently in outcome research (Kazdin, Bass, et al., 1990). Other domains of dysfunction may be added to these, such as physical abuse, sexual abuse, anorexia and bulimia, gender identity, obsessive–compulsive disorder, tic disorders, and substance abuse, each with few outcome studies in its behalf (see Ammerman, Last, & Hersen, 1993). To be sure, outcome studies in each of these areas can be identified, but the numbers are small. A few studies in an area represent an important beginning, but the range of variations required to elaborate the effects of therapy under different conditions requires more programmatic efforts.

Another sampling issue worthy of special mention as a priority pertains to research on minority samples (e.g., African-American, Hispanic-American, Asian-American, and American-Indian). Minority youths are underrepresented in clinical practice as well as in treatment research. Providing and evaluating treatments for minorities are multifaceted because ethnic and racial status have impact on when and how youths are identified for treatment, manifestations of symptoms, help-seeking patterns, and treatment use (Gaw, 1993; Tharp, 1991). Research designed to address the mental health of minorities requires scrutiny at each step of case identification and treatment delivery.

General Comments

Priorities for research highlighted earlier are designed to redress deficits in the knowledge base. In each area identified, one can cite noteworthy studies. As one example, little follow-up data and short-term follow-up effects are the dominant characteristics of contemporary treatment outcome research with children and adolescents. Nevertheless, there are noteworthy exceptions of controlled studies that have evaluated the impact of treatment close to a decade or more after treatment (e.g., Long, Forehand, Wierson, & Morgan, 1994; McEachin, Smith, & Lovaas, 1993; Satterfield et al., 1987). The issue for research is not to provide isolated and exemplary examples but, rather, to establish a firm foundation for clinical work. This foundation requires a sustained and concentrated effort to understand and to treat clinical dysfunction.

PROGRAMMATIC RESEARCH

Programmatic research on child and adolescent therapy is a primary means of addressing research priorities and ensuring progress. Such research refers to consecutive studies by an individual investigative team that explores and develops a particular treatment approach. The advantages of programmatic treatment research warrant mention here as a preview to the remaining chapters in this volume. First, and most obvious, a sequence of studies leads to an accretion of findings about treatment of a clinical problem. No single study, nor two or three isolated studies, can be so helpful as an ongoing program of research. In a program of studies, an investigator can learn from experience and codify the new learning in the next investigation. The iterative, evolutionary, and cumulative facets of treatment development are optimal within a programmatic series of studies.

Second, the questions that are addressed can build in a systematic way, moving from basic questions about efficacy to those related to process and youth × treatment modality interactions. Also, additional questions that emerge from initial studies can be pursued in a research program. In this way, along the main stream of work, tributaries of related questions emerge as well. The accretion of data in a research program permits exploration of basic research questions about the nature of clinical function, long-term prognosis, and so on, all in the context of a treatment trial.

Third, programs of research often develop methods that make their own contribution to the field. In a research program, inadequacies of available methods cannot be ignored and must be redressed for the program of studies to provide the needed information. New assessment devices, observational codes, treatment manuals, follow-up procedures, and manners of evaluating therapeutic change are examples of contributions that programmatic research has made, apart from the substantive findings on specific treatment questions.

Finally, programmatic research serves critical training functions. Individuals in training (graduate students, postdoctoral students, residents) have direct opportunities to learn treatments and to learn about treatment research. This is not a trivial contribution. If programmatic research makes a contribution, then its continuation is critical as well. There are few places to learn about treatment research. The demands of clinical treatment studies are usually outside the boundaries of what individuals in training can conduct within a feasible period. Involving trainees in programmatic research provides opportunities that they themselves can use after training.

This volume provides chapters that address several of the priorities noted earlier. In the process, the multiple advantages of programmatic studies are conveyed concretely. From many of the programs described, palpable advances have been achieved in demonstrating the effectiveness of specific techniques for specific clinical problems. The broader contributions of programmatic research are evident as well. What follows is a rich buffet of different lines of work that hold great promise for improving the mental health of children and adolescents. The editors of the volume deserve special credit for their vision in bringing this work together and for crafting the form in which it is conceptualized and presented, and for their own direct contributions to the development and evaluation of interventions for children and adolescents.

REFERENCES

Ammerman, R. T., Last, C. G., & Hersen, M. (Eds.). (1993). *Handbook of prescriptive treatments for children and adolescents*. Needham Heights, MA: Allyn & Bacon.

Brown, J. (1987). A review of meta-analyses conducted on psychotherapy outcome research. *Clinical Psychology Review, 7*, 1–23.

Casey, R. J., & Berman, J. S. (1985). The outcome of psychotherapy with children. *Psychological Bulletin, 98*, 388–400.

Costello, E. J. (1989). Developments in child psychiatric epidemiology. *Journal of the American Academy of Child and Adolescent Psychiatry, 28*, 836–841.

Dryfoos, J. G. (1990). *Adolescents at risk: Prevalence and prevention*. New York: Oxford University Press.

Eysenck, H. J. (1952). The effects of psychotherapy: An evaluation. *Journal of Consulting Psychology, 16*, 319–324.

Eysenck, H. J. (1966). *The effects of psychotherapy*. New York: International Science Press.

Gaw, A. C. (Ed.). (1993). *Culture and ethnicity and mental illness*. Washington, DC: American Psychiatric Press.

Hazelrigg, M. D., Cooper, H. M., & Borduin, C. M. (1987). Evaluating the effectiveness of family therapies: An integrative review and analysis. *Psychological Bulletin, 101*, 428–442.

Henggeler, S. W., Melton, G. B., & Smith, L. A. (1992). Family preservation using multisystemic therapy: An effective alternative to incarcerating serious juvenile offenders. *Journal of Consulting and Clinical Psychology, 60*, 953–961.

Institute of Medicine. (1989). *Research on children and adolescents with mental, behavioral, and developmental disorders*. Washington, DC: National Academy Press.

Kazdin, A. E. (1988). *Child psychotherapy: Developing and identifying effective treatments*. Elmsford, NY: Pergamon.

Kazdin, A. E. (1993). Psychotherapy for children and adolescents: Current progress and future research directions. *American Psychologist, 48*, 644–657.

Kazdin, A. E., Bass, D., Ayers, W. A., & Rodgers, A. (1990). Empirical and clinical focus of child and adolescent psychotherapy research. *Journal of Consulting and Clinical Psychology, 58*, 729–740.

Kazdin, A. E., Siegel, T. C., & Bass, D. (1990). Drawing upon clinical practice to inform research on child and adolescent psychotherapy: A survey of practitioners. *Professional Psychology: Research and Practice, 21*, 189–198.

Koocher, G. P., & Pedulla, B. M. (1977). Current practices in child psychotherapy. *Professional Psychology, 8*, 275–287.

Levitt, E. E. (1957). The results of psychotherapy with children: An evaluation. *Journal of Consulting Psychology, 21*, 189–196.

Levitt, E. E. (1963). Psychotherapy with children: A further evaluation. *Behaviour Research and Therapy, 60,* 326–329.

Long, P., Forehand, R., Wierson, M., & Morgan, A. (1994). Does parent training with noncompliant children have long-term effects? *Behaviour Research and Therapy, 32,* 101–107.

McEachin, J. J., Smith, T., & Lovaas, O. I. (1993). Outcome in adolescence of autistic children receiving early intensive behavioral treatment. *American Journal of Mental Retardation, 97,* 359–372.

Norcross, J. C., & Goldfried, M. R. (Eds.). (1992). *Handbook of psychotherapy integration.* New York: Basic Books.

Robins, L. N., & Rutter, M. (Ed.). (1990). *Straight and devious pathways from childhood to adulthood.* Cambridge: Cambridge University Press.

Satterfield, J. H., Satterfield, B. T., & Schell, A. M. (1987). Therapeutic interventions to prevent delinquency in hyperactive boys. *Journal of the American Academy of Child and Adolescent Psychiatry, 26,* 56–64.

Shadish, W. R., Montgomery, L. M., Wilson, P., Wilson, M. R., Bright, I., & Okwumabua, T. (1993). Effects of family and marital psychotherapies: A meta-analysis. *Journal of Consulting and Clinical Psychology, 61,* 992–1002.

Silver, L. B., & Silver, B. J. (1983). Clinical practice of child psychiatry: A survey. *Journal of the American Academy of Child Psychiatry, 22,* 573–579.

Tharp, R. G. (1991). Cultural diversity and treatment of children. *Journal of Consulting and Clinical Psychology, 59,* 799–812.

United States Congress, Office of Technology Assessment. (1991). *Adolescent health* (OTA-H-468). Washington, DC: U.S. Government Printing Office.

Weiss, G., & Hechtman, L. T. (1986). *Hyperactive children grown up.* New York: Guilford.

Weisz, J. R., & Weiss, B. (1993). *Effects of psychotherapy with children and adolescents.* Newbury Park, CA: Sage.

Zill, N., & Schoenborn, C. A. (1990, November). Developmental, learning, and emotional problems: Health of our nation's children, United States 1988. *Advance Data: National Center for Health Statistics* (No. 190).

II

ANXIETY DISORDERS

INTRODUCTION

Anxiety is a debilitating disorder, especially for young children who need all their faculties to achieve academically and to acquire the social skills necessary to function in the community. It is estimated that about 8 to 10% of the child population suffers from some form of anxiety. Yet, children do not always recognize when they are anxious or when their fears are excessive, and they rarely report distress about their anxiety. Instead, they usually express their disquietude by crying, clinging, etc. It is important, therefore, for parents, teachers, and health care providers to recognize anxiety early and refer the children for treatment.

The term *anxiety disorders* encompasses a variety of conditions, such as generalized anxiety, panic, obsessive compulsive disorder, separation anxiety, and specific phobias, such as anxietal, social, animal, or situational phobias. Although anxiety disorders impair functioning, there is a dearth of treatment research in this area. Of the few types of treatments studied empirically, cognitive–behavioral (CBT) and behavioral treatments (BT) seem to be especially promising and offer reasonable hope for reasonable outcomes. This section discusses studies conducted using these techniques in treating children and adolescents with anxiety disorders.

Using CBT, Philip C. Kendall and Kimberli R. H. Treadwell have developed an impressive research program to test the efficacy of treatments for children with overanxious, separation anxiety, and avoidance disorders. Posttreatment assessments indicate that short-term improvements are sustained at one-year follow-up assessment; these improvements are supported by parent and teacher reports. In their hands, CBT has also proven to be beneficial to the comorbid condition of anxiety–depression. Especially noteworthy is the evidence that ethnicity did not influence outcomes.

Highlighting future directions, the authors recommend that future studies include interventions with parents as clients, and that such research incorporate the interpersonal and social contexts into the child-oriented treatments.

Anne Marie Albano and David H. Barlow report on a CBT-group treatment study with adolescents suffering from social phobia, and they describe in detail their assessment and outcome measures. Treatment is divided into two phases: Phase 1 addresses cognitive restructuring, and Phase 2 consists of in vivo use of learned materials. Although preliminary results support the treatment's effectiveness, the generalizability of this treatment remains to be evaluated.

Wendy K. Silverman and William K. Kurtines have designed a model based on theory-driven procedures (from CBT and BT). Their evidence suggests that this treatment model is efficacious for the treatment of childhood anxiety and phobias, has a pragmatic and contextual orientation, and can be of use to practitioners. It is currently being tested with groups in school-based settings to treat posttraumatic stress disorder in multiethnic populations. The authors note a range of obstacles and limitations of their research and recommend that future studies address parent–child relational processes and focus on reducing parental psychopathology.

John S. March and Karen Mulle present a CBT treatment for children with obsessive–compulsive disorders (OCDs). They developed a manualized treatment, titled *How I Ran OCD Off My Land*©, using selective CBT procedures. Outcomes from a pilot study appear promising. The authors offer several ideas for future research, among others, the comparison of medication, BT, and combined treatments. They recommend that follow-up studies evaluate the relapse rates, examine the usefulness of CBT booster sessions, and compare individual and family treatments.

It should be noted that, in all the research programs described in this section, parents are involved as essential parts of the treatment protocol. Also, male, female, and minority children are included in all programs presented here. Comparisons of outcomes among ethnic groups are provided only in one chapter because the other three report only preliminary results. Nonetheless, the studies included in this section indicate that CBT treatments may be effective in alleviating anxiety disorders in children and adolescents. They all recommend that parental involvement in the treatment of children with anxiety disorders should be more vigorous, even in treating concurrent parental psychopathology. Although other therapies currently used by clinicians may be just as efficacious as CBT approaches, empirical data are lacking. Future research, in addition to refining CBT, should examine other treatment modalities that may be useful for the subdiagnostic categories of the anxiety disorders.

3

COGNITIVE–BEHAVIORAL TREATMENT FOR CHILDHOOD ANXIETY DISORDERS

PHILIP C. KENDALL and KIMBERLI R. H. TREADWELL

The Child and Adolescent Anxiety Disorders Clinic (CAADC) represents the scientist–practitioner model of clinical psychology in the integration of clinical and research pursuits. The CAADC was founded by Philip C. Kendall, PhD, ABPP, in 1986, as a combination research and service-provision clinic. Initially, the CAADC was supported by the Department of Psychology at Temple University. Soon after its inception, however, external funding for research was provided by the National Institute of Mental Health (NIMH) in the form of research grants. Through collaboration with graduate students in clinical psychology, the CAADC grew from its initial "pilot clinic" situation to its current full-functioning and active status.

The overall aim of the CAADC is to conduct a series of randomized clinical trials and systematic single-subject analyses to evaluate the effectiveness of psychosocial interventions for anxiety-disordered youth. Currently, following the development of a cognitive–behavioral intervention for anxiety-disordered children, outcome evaluations are ongoing. An out-

Funding for the CAADC is provided by grant MH44042 from the National Institute of Mental Health, with additional support provided by the Department of Psychology of Temple University in the form of research assistantships. Correspondence concerning this chapter should be addressed to Dr. Philip C. Kendall, Department of Psychology, Weiss Hall, Temple University, Philadelphia, PA 19122.

patient service for children 9–13 years of age, the CAADC is housed within the Division of Clinical Psychology, Weiss Hall, at Temple University. Dr. Kendall and a team of clinical psychology graduate students—who serve as therapists, diagnosticians, and research assistants—compose the staff.

Since 1986, the CAADC has experienced expansion in the number of (a) children referred, (b) children who have completed treatment, (c) the graduate student staff, (d) the research projects completed, and (e) the size of the participating geographic region. As a result of numerous efforts (e.g., successful treatment of initial cases, newspaper articles about the clinic, seminars provided for school personnel), the CAADC currently provides treatment for anxiety-disordered youth from a wide variety of backgrounds. In a recent 12-month period for example, 111 referral patients participated in a 3–4 hour intake evaluation; 80 children were accepted into the clinic and received treatment. The socioeconomic status of the patients' families was varied (e,g., from poverty to upper-middle-class levels), as was the geographic distribution (e.g., Delaware, New Jersey, Pennsylvania), the presence of boys and girls, and the inclusion of ethnic minority groups. The referrals came from various sources, including school counselors, school psychologists, practicing professionals, and concerned parents.

The first randomized clinical trial testing the effectiveness of a psychosocial (cognitive–behavioral) treatment protocol was completed in 1992. The CAADC received a grant renewal from NIMH to conduct a further full-scale, randomized clinical trial. In this study, in addition to examining the effectiveness of the manualized intervention, which compares a no-treatment 8-week waiting-list control group to a treated group, a midtreatment assessment was added and the effect of comorbidity on treatment will be examined. In conjunction with this clinical trial, such variables as behavioral observations of children in anxious distress, predictors of treatment outcome, the influence of anxiety and depression on parental report, family problem solving, self-report in a normal comparison group, and the development of several in-house assessment measures have been studied.

METHOD

Participants and Selection

Children who received a diagnosis of primary childhood anxiety disorder were accepted into the program. These diagnoses, as described in the *Diagnostic and Statistical Manual of Mental Disorders* (3rd. ed., rev.; DSM-III-R; American Psychiatric Association, 1987) include overanxious disorder (generalized anxiety disorder in *DSM-IV*), separation anxiety disorder, and avoidance disorder (social phobia in *DSM-IV*). Primary diagnoses of simple phobia were not accepted, although children with a secondary diagnosis of simple phobia were included. Exclusion criteria included psychotic symptoms, a disabling physical condition, or current use of antianxiety medication.

In the first treatment outcome study, 47 children (20 of whom first completed the wait-list control) completed the treatment protocol. Of the 47 participants, 28 were boys and 19 were girls. Thirty-six children were White and 11 were Black. Twenty-two of the 47 children were 9–10 years old, and 27 were 11–13 years old (Kendall, 1994). Treatment and wait-list children did not differ significantly on these variables. In this sample, 30 children received a primary diagnosis of overanxiety disorder, 8 of separation anxiety, and 9 of avoidant disorder. Fifteen percent were comorbid for ADHD, 30% for depression, 2% for conduct disorder, and 60% for simple phobia (Kendall & Brady, 1995).

In the second clinical trial, 68 children were accepted into treatment. Of these, 52 were White, and 16 were Black. Forty-six children were boys and 22 were girls. Thirty-four were 9–11 years of age, and 34 were 12–13 years of age. Thirty-six children received a primary diagnosis of overanxiety disorder, 19 of separation anxiety, and 13 of avoidant disorder. A midtreatment assessment was added to this trial so that the effects of each section of treatment could be evaluated (i.e., the first half, which was mainly cognitive and educational, could be compared to the second half, which added behavioral experiences). Also, the effects of comorbidity, such as children with anxiety-disorder and with secondary diagnoses of ADHD or depression, on treatment effectiveness were analyzed.

Procedure

Following referral to CAADC, the parents were contacted to set up an intake evaluation with a staff diagnostician. The parents and child signed informed consents and participated in separate structured diagnostic interviews. Self-report measures for the child and parents, as well as reports of child functioning from the parents and teachers were completed prior to acceptance. The child also participated in a videotaped behavioral observation after the structured interview was completed. Each child was asked to speak about him- or herself for five minutes in front of a video camera; then the tape was coded for behavioral manifestations of anxiety. Following the taping session, the children participated in a thought-listing procedure, during which she/he responded to a semistructured interview about the cognitions, or self-statements, that passed through his/her mind during the videotaping. Diagnosis is determined by the diagnostician based on the information obtained during the diagnostic interview. Children who met diagnostic criteria for one of the childhood anxiety disorders were accepted into treatment.

At the time of acceptance, each child was assigned randomly either to the treatment or to the wait-list control condition. An eight-week wait-list was chosen as an optimal length of time to serve as a control condition, because it was considered to be a sufficient period of time to control for the passage of time and any transitory aspects of anxious symptomatology. Although a 16-week (4-month) waiting-list would provide methodological soundness, this option was rejected for clinical reasons. Given the stress caused by an anxiety disorder to both the child and the family, a shorter interval between the original diagnosis and treatment was determined to be more appropriate. At the end of the waiting-list period, children and parents participated in another diagnostic evaluation prior to the beginning of treatment. At the end of the first diagnostic interview, the appropriate children were guaranteed treatment. Even if a child no longer meets diagnostic criteria for a childhood anxiety disorder after the 8-week wait-list, the child continues treatment if the family still desires it. However, after the waiting-list period, only those children who still met diagnostic criteria for an anxiety disorder were retained for evaluation of treatment effects. Children to receive treatment were assigned randomly to a therapist.

Assessment

Assessments for the second, current clinical trial are completed at the initial intake, following the wait-list condition, at midpoint and the completion of treatment, and one year following treatment completion. The investigation includes a comprehensive battery of outcome measures, assessed at repeated intervals; outcome is assessed in terms of diagnostic status and psychiatric symptoms based on child, parent, and teacher reports. Areas of assessment include anxiety, fears, depression, perceived coping abilities, internalizing and externalizing distress, parental involvement, perceptions of the therapeutic relationship, and behavioral observations. The battery includes standardized instruments and specific measures believed to be sensitive to therapeutic changes associated with the cognitive–behavioral approach. Brief descriptions of the assessment instruments are listed in Appendix A.

Treatment

Therapists work individually with each child, tailoring the content of the structured protocol to the individual child's needs. The 16–20-session treatment program is divided into two segments: the first segment (8 sessions) involves an educational focus, teaching the child to identify somatic, cognitive, and behavioral components of anxiety; the second segment involves application of the newly learned skills in vivo (exposure) situations selected and designed to be tailored to the child's specific anxieties. (For additional information, see Kendall, Kane, Howard, & Siqueland, 1990.)

As part of the educational process, the first segment gradually builds to a four-step coping plan for managing anxious distress. Initially, the child learns to discriminate between different feelings. Specific somatic reactions to anxiety are examined, and the child begins to discern the various signals of his or her own anxious arousal. The child learns that the first signal for using coping skills is to ask, "Feeling frightened?" Each child is taught relaxation exercises to help cope with tense bodily sensations, and an audiotape of these exercises and relaxing imagery is produced and given to the child to listen to at home.

The next skill that is taught focuses on identifying and modifying anxious cognitions in the internal dialogue. The child asks, "Expecting bad things to happen?" as a way to identify anxious cognitions. These cognitions are discussed, and the child is encouraged to ask him- or herself what else might happen in a given situation, focusing on a number of different possibilities.

Once the child can successfully dispute anxious cognitions, basic problem-solving skills are thought to assist the child in devising a behavioral plan to cope with the anxiety. The child develops "actions and attitudes that help," generating alternate solutions to manage the anxiety, weighing the consequences of each action, then choosing and following through with an appropriate plan.

Finally, the idea of judging the effectiveness of the coping plan and fulfilling the self-reward is implemented. The children "rate and reward" themselves for complete as well as partial successes. This step culminates the four-step coping plan symbolized by the acronym FEAR, involving the first letters of each coping step (see Exhibit 1).

As noted earlier, the second segment of the treatment concerns preparing the child for and exposing the child to anxiety-arousing events, giving him or her opportunities to practice using the FEAR steps. The child begins by being exposed to imaginary and low-anxiety situations and then progresses to being a participant in moderate and then highly anxiety-provoking events. The therapist helps prepare the child for the exposure, assists the child in coping with the stress, and facilitates the child's postexperience processing of the exposure. This latter effort helps to frame the child's experience in a pattern toward future coping.

Homework assignments are used throughout treatment as a means to promote the rehearsal of the steps and the use of the skills outside of the treatment context. Each child completes "show that I can," or STIC, tasks, in a personal notebook. To encourage completion of STIC tasks, rewards (e.g., stickers) are provided on completion of STIC assignments. After

EXHIBIT 1
The FEAR plan: Steps toward mastering unwanted anxious arousal

F	Feeling frightened?	Clients ask themselves this question as they begin learning to recognize their internal and/or physical signs of unwanted anxious arousal. They also learn relaxation skills.
E	Expecting bad things to happen?	Clients ask themselves about the potential catastrophes that they worry about. Also, clients think about other likely outcomes. Clients learn to identify anxiety-related cognition.
A	Actions and attitudes that help	Clients are given a variety of actions and/or attitudes that they can use to reduce and master unwanted anxious arousal. Clients learn to use strategies to manage anxiety.
R	Rate and reward	After completion of the **F**, **E**, and **A** steps, clients learn to rate the outcome and to reward themselves for progress. Successful coping includes movement toward the goal.

completing four assignments, the child can earn bigger rewards (e.g., base-ball cards, magic tricks).

During the last session, each child makes a videotaped commercial describing the FEAR steps and their use in an anxiety-provoking situation that was mastered during treatment. This is done to help the child (a) organize and crystallize his or her experience, (b) "go public" with the new skills, (c) recognize the accomplishment, and (d) allow creative expression of his or her ideas. Each child receives a copy of the videotaped commercial to take home.

In the program, therapists function as coping models when new skills are introduced. A therapist might first describe a personal anxiety-provoking incident to the child, and then discuss the coping strategies used that managed the anxiety effectively. The therapist may then describe an-other situation, this time asking the child to help identify possible physical arousals, cognitive beliefs and expectations, and action plans. This allows the child to increase involvement gradually in discussing anxious distress as the therapist decreases input.

Developmentally sensitive materials are used to encourage the child's participation and facilitate learning. The *Coping Cat Workbook* (see sample in Figure 1) contains exercises that are coordinated with treatment sessions and that assist the child in mastering the skills (Kendall, 1992a). For ex-ample, the child writes dialogue for characters in vignettes, draws pictures, and creates personal coping stories. As part of the *Coping Cat Workbook*,

Figure 1. Sample page from the *Coping Cat Workbook*, in which the children use blank thought bubbles to help identify their self-talk.

the child is given a notebook to take home in which to complete the STIC tasks. These exercises help the child to generalize each session's message to home or school.

The ultimate goal—the child continues to use the coping skills after treatment—requires therapist attention. Therapeutic intervention is seen as a first step in the process of realigning anxiety-disordered children's maladaptive developmental trajectories to better them for the inevitable challenges experienced later in life (Kendall, 1992b). Several strategies are used to guide children toward consolidation of treatment-produced gains. The first involves shaping and encouraging "effort" attributions regarding the management of anxiety. Children are encouraged to reward their efforts at coping, including partial successes. Also, children are introduced to the concept of "lapses in efforts," rather than "relapses." Partial successes and mistakes are framed constructively as a vital and inevitable part of the learning process rather than as evidence of incompetence. The goal is for the children to identify, label, and accept setbacks as temporary and to move forward and return to problem solving. Mistakes are not excuses to throw in the towel nor are they confirmation of anxious thought processes—they are learning experiences, and children are shown how to frame them in this coping fashion.

RESEARCH ACCOMPLISHMENTS

The CAADC serves as a center in which many research activities have been completed or are currently underway, revolving around four areas. The first area of research involves randomized clinical trials of the cognitive–behavioral treatment protocol. Second, the nature of anxiety disorders in children has been explored. Additionally, a focus on the family of anxiety-disordered youth, such as parental pathology and expectations, is underway. Finally, several assessment measures have been developed in the context of the ongoing research projects at the CAADC.

Treatment Outcome

A cornerstone of the CAADC's activities is assessing treatment outcomes for anxiety-disordered youth. A series of single-case designs were conducted initially to assess the potential of a psychosocial treatment intervention for childhood anxiety that combined demonstrated behavioral techniques with a cognitive component. Four children, between the ages of 9 and 13 years and diagnosed with overanxious disorder, served as subjects in a multiple-baseline evaluation of the treatment protocol. Assessments were completed across baseline and at pre-, mid-, and posttreatment, and later at a 3–6 month follow-up.

The effects of the intervention were positive (Kane & Kendall, 1989). Child internalizing behavior problems assessed by parent and teacher reports were brought to within normal limits following the completion of treatment. Clinicians' ratings of the children's anxiety, children's self-reported trait anxiety, and specific changes in each clients' targeted symptoms (e.g., fear of sleeping in the dark), decreased at posttreatment. At follow-up, two children's self-reported anxious symptoms remained within normal ranges, but parent reports indicated some return of anxious symptoms. For the other two cases, the treatment gains were maintained, and anxious behaviors remained within normal ranges.

Given the initially supportive findings, and following further developments of the treatment manual and therapy materials, the first randomized clinical trial for the treatment of anxiety disordered children was undertaken. The investigation involved 47 children who met diagnostic criteria (from a larger pool of referred children). Following the treatment protocol, and judged against a wait-list control condition, treated cases showed significant treatment gains from pretreatment to posttreatment on child self-reports (e.g., state and trait anxiety, specific fears, perceived coping abilities, anxious self-talk, depression) and on behavioral observations of children's anxious distress (all $ps < .05$). Gains were also reported for parent reports of child internalizing behavior problems, social and health problems, and trait anxiety, and for teacher reports of child internalizing behavior problems (Kendall, 1994). In addition, two thirds of the children who received treatment no longer met diagnostic criteria at posttreatment, and diagnostic changes were maintained 1 year after treatment. An extended follow-up (3.5-years' average) indicated that the positive outcomes were maintained (Kendall & Gerow, in press).

Process and pretreatment predictors of treatment outcome were also studied during the first randomized clinical trial. Variables, examined as pretreatment predictors that might potentially influence treatment outcome, included maternal depression, maternal anxiety, comorbidity with a DSM-III-R disorder (e.g., ADHD, conduct disorder), and symptom severity. Process variables were obtained from therapist session summaries and from audiotapes of therapeutic sessions, including variables such as the child's level of participation and the explication of the treatment model by the therapist. Neither pretreatment nor process variables were related consistently to treatment outcome.

A second clinical trial is underway using an additional midtreatment assessment to address any differential impact of the first or second segment of treatment to treatment gains. Additionally, the effects of comorbidity will be assessed as it impacts treatment outcome.

Nature of the Disorder

As research projects evolve at the CAADC, the nature of anxiety disorders in children has received empirical and theoretical attention. Topics examined include comorbidity, cognitive functioning, social behavior, gender and ethnic differences, and behavioral manifestations of anxiety. For example, several theoretical works regarding the comorbidity of anxiety and depression have been published. Factors influencing the rate of comorbidity of anxiety and depression in children have been examined at the symptom and syndrome level (Brady & Kendall, 1992). A large percentage of anxious children (16%–60%) was noted to be comorbid for depression. Additionally, comorbidity rates tended to increase with age and with the severity level of the disorder. Research suggested that cognitive–behavior frameworks for treatment of anxiety or depression could be integrated effectively to meet the demands of comorbid cases (Kendall, et al., 1992). Restructuring cognitive distortions, improving problem-solving skills, emphasizing reinforcement, and using systematic desensitization and graduated exposure were common to therapies of each disorder and could be integrated successfully when treating comorbid cases.

Self-statements in the internal dialogue of anxiety-disordered children have received preliminary attention (Kendall & Chansky, 1991). Surprisingly, clinic-referred children reported significantly greater frequencies of what may be considered to be coping self-statements (e.g., saying to oneself "Just stay calm") rather than positive (e.g., "I like it") or negative (e.g., "I can't do it") thoughts, regardless of specific diagnostic status. Although the anxiety-disordered youth reported coping self-talk, they did not believe it or use it functionally in their efforts to cope. The self-statement data were elicited from a semistructured thought-listing task following a behavioral task. A study examined the relationship between positive and negative self-statements in anxiety-disordered and normal control groups of children, as well as the effects of the cognitive–behavioral intervention on self-statements.

Anxious children's behaviors and expectations with the peer groups were also investigated. A measure was developed and validated, consisting of 40 specific social behaviors (e.g., initiates conversations with other children, gives compliments to other children) that children may exhibit in a peer setting. Items that differentiate anxious from nonanxious children were retained (Panichelli, Kendall, Callahan, Levin, & Gerow, 1993). Anxious children's management of social situations was also explored. Cognitions, anxiety, and expectations that anxious youth report when entering an unknown peer group were the variables investigated.

Ethnicity and gender were examined as they impact self-reported functioning, diagnostic status, and response to treatment for anxiety-disordered children (Treadwell, Flannery, & Kendall, 1995). For the most part, no systematic differences were noted, suggesting that standardized measures accurately assessed child functioning. In addition, the treatment protocol was effective for anxious youth, regardless of gender or ethnicity.

Behavioral manifestations of anxiety in youth were assessed after the structured diagnostic interviews during assessments. Individually, six specific behaviors (gratuitous movements, gratuitous verbalizations, trembling voice, avoiding task, absence of eye contact, fingers in mouth) were not successful in differentiating anxious from normal control children (Gosch et al., 1991). However, three global behavior ratings (e.g., overall anxiety, overall performance, and fearful facial expressions) rated on a 5-point Likert Scale differentiated anxiety-disordered children from normal children, and the total of the specific behavioral observations was sensitive to treatment (Kendall, 1994).

Focus on the Family

Family characteristics that might impact the manifestation of anxiety disorders in children or that might assist in the remediation of anxiety received attention at the CAADC. For instance, the relationship between maternal distress (anxiety and depression) and the report of child functioning was studied. Mothers reporting elevated anxiety and depression viewed their children more negatively than mothers who did not report distress, as compared to the child's self-reported symptoms (Treadwell & Kendall, 1993). The extent to which maternal stress (e.g., depression, life experiences) influences maternal expectations about her child's coping ability in a stressful situation is receiving attention. Fathers of anxiety-disordered youth, as well as family problem solving, are also being studied.

Anxiety-disordered and normal children's families were compared on parenting dimensions and style (Siqueland, 1993). The family environment was assessed by child and parental perceptions, and by independent observers during a family interaction task. Anxious children's parents granted them less psychological autonomy than normal control children's parents as judged by independent observers. Anxious children rated their parents as less accepting than did normal control children. In addition, children's self-reported anxiety and depression was associated with children's perceptions of greater parental psychological control and less parental acceptance.

A multiple-baseline treatment outcome study involving a family-based intervention was completed recently. Six children diagnosed with a childhood anxiety disorder and their parents participated in a cognitive–behavioral treatment that was based on the CAADC protocol, with an additional parental component. Parents and their child were treated together by a therapist, who tailored the 16-session treatment to helping the parents assist the child in identifying and coping with anxious distress. Although the parents were involved, the treatment was still child-focused, and the parents were viewed as collaborators or "coaches," rather than as clients. Outcomes were favorable (see Howard & Kendall, in press) and comparable to the outcomes produced by the individual treatment.

Instruments Developed

A review revealed that, with the exception of a few instruments assessing specific fears and anxious predispositions in youth, the literature did not contain instruments designed to measure several of the more specific features of anxiety needed for treatment evaluation. Therefore, efforts at the CAADC have focused on the assessment of changes in children's internal dialogue (self-talk), their self-perception (and parental perception) of their coping abilities, and their satisfaction with the therapist and the program.

Coping Questionnaire

This questionnaire assesses a child's ability to cope with targeted problematic symptoms that are identified for each child during a structured diagnostic interview. There are two forms: a child (CQ-C) and a parent (CQ-P) form (Kendall, 1994). The three most prominent anxiety-producing situations are determined by the diagnostician and the child, and the child rates his or her perceived ability to cope with that situation on a 7-point Likert Scale. The CQ-P is administered to the parents, who rate their perceptions of the child's ability to cope in each of three identified situations. Common situations include giving a speech in front of the class, sleeping in one's own room, and meeting new children. The CQ-C and CQ-P evidenced test–retest reliability (8-weeks; .46 and .62, respectively, $p < .01$) as assessed by children assigned to the wait-list condition and sensitive to therapeutic change (Kendall, 1994).

Negative Affectivity Self-Statement Questionnaire (NASSQ)

This 70-item questionnaire assesses children's self-statements associated with their negative affectivity (Ronan, Kendall, & Rowe, 1994). Children endorse the frequency of each thought as it was experienced over the prior week on a 5-point Likert Scale. Within the NASSQ, two subscales were developed containing anxious and depressive thoughts, and are scored separately for 7–10 year-olds and for 11–15 year-olds. The depression subscale evidenced .94 coefficient alpha and a test–retest reliability of .91. The anxious subscale evidenced .86 coefficient alpha and a test–retest reliability of .86 (Ronan et al., 1994).

CBCL-Anxiety Scale (CBCL-A)

Nineteen of the existing 118 items from the Child Behavior Checklist (CBCL) were chosen to represent specific child anxiety symptoms that were observed by parents. The CBCL-A pulls for anxiety-disorder symptoms based on the DSM-III-R rather than the broad-band internalizing factor. This subscale differentiated anxiety-disordered children from normal control children and was sensitive to cognitive–behavior treatment gains (Kendall & MacDonald, 1993).

Child's Perception of Therapeutic Relationship (CPTR)

The CPTR was developed to assess each child's perception of the therapeutic relationship and to examine if such relationship factors account for outcome. Seven items of 10 are scored on a 5-point scale; 4 items pertain to the child's liking and feeling comfortable with the therapist, and 3 items refer to the quality of the relationship. The remaining 3 filler items are not scored.

Consumer Satisfaction Questionnaire

This 10-item questionnaire was designed to assess the parents' global satisfaction with the treatment program at the CAADC. It is completed at the posttreatment assessment and 1-year follow-up.

Parental Involvement Rating

Therapists assess the level and degree of interaction between parents and the client on this three-item scale. The first item concerns the amount of contact the therapist had with the parents regarding their child's treatment. Second, the amount of positive interactions between the parents and child is assessed. Finally, the amount of parental interference with the child's treatment is estimated by the therapist.

FUTURE CONSIDERATIONS

The activities of the CAADC were summarized recently by Kendall, et al. (1992) and, because of the experience gained, future areas of examination became apparent. For instance, the treatment protocol has been demonstrated to be an effective alternative to a wait-list condition, and alternate comparisons would now be fruitful. The cognitive–behavioral approach should be compared with alternate treatment interventions, such as family-based and psychopharmacological, to assess differential impact in alleviating clinical levels of child anxiety. Also, although the effectiveness of the treatment protocol has been supported, the impact of the cognitive component on treatment remains unclear. The two halves of treatment differ, and it is not yet clear whether the beneficial effects result from the sequencing of the treatment segments or from either segment alone. Future research is needed to address specifically the question of the contribution of the cognitive versus the behavioral treatment components.

Several extensions of the protocol intervention remain to be explored, including its effectiveness with alternate ages, with comorbid cases, in small peer groups, and with parental involvement. One question to be answered is the extent to which children younger than 9 years of age have the cognitive sophistication to use the cognitive treatment component. Also, the effectiveness of this treatment intervention with adolescents awaits empirical research. Overall, the impact of treatment effects on children at various cognitive, behavioral, and emotional developmental stages must be explored (Kendall & Morris, 1991). In addition, given the comorbidity of anxiety and depression and the reported decrease in child self-reported depressive scores after treatment, the question remains whether a similar treatment would benefit diagnosed depressed children, or whether addressing anxious symptoms is sufficient to alleviate depressive symptoms.

Finally, the role of parents in therapy has not been addressed fully. Although the CAADC is child-focused, numerous parent contacts are involved, with a base-level protocol involving two parent meetings. However, in some treatments multiple parental contacts and meetings were necessary to help implement in vivo situations. The effects of these contacts on treatment outcome suggested a meaningful relationship, and additional research on family-based interventions or parental collaboration is needed. Also, parent training may be helpful as a supplement to a child-focused therapy.

NATURE OF THE RESEARCH ORGANIZATION

CAADC Staff

The staff of the CAADC currently comprises the director, Philip C. Kendall, PhD, ABPP and a number of advanced graduate students in clinical psychology, who hold primary responsibilities and function as therapists, diagnosticians, or both, with secondary responsibilities such as data analysis, staff training, and community contact.

Relation to Other Research Programs

Although the CAADC is not involved directly with investigations at other institutions, its cognitive–behavioral intervention has been adapted and evaluated by a team of psychologists in Australia (e.g., Barrett, Dadds, & Rapee, in press). This group revised the *Coping Cat Workbook* to the *Coping Koala* (adjusting the language to fit Australian youth) and conducted an outcome evaluation.

A team of clinical psychologists and graduate students from Japan visited the program to extend their knowledge of cognitive–behavioral treatment of childhood disorders. They returned to Japan with methods and materials to implement in their country. One Japanese doctoral student from this group (M. Ichii) recently completed a 1-year Fullbright fellowship at the CAADC. Descriptions of psychosocial treatment for child and adolescent disorders (i.e., Kendall, 1991) have been translated into Japanese.

The work of the CAADC has also resulted in an Italian program for the treatment of anxiety-disordered youth (Kendall & Di Pietro, 1995).

REFERENCES

Achenbach, T. M. (1991a). *Manual for the Child Behavior Checklist/4–18 and 1991 Profile*. Burlington, VT: University of Vermont.

Achenbach, T. M. (1991b). *Manual for the Teacher's Report Form and 1991 Profile*. Burlington, VT: University of Vermont.

American Psychiatric Association. (1987). *Diagnostic and statistical manual of mental disorders* (3rd ed., rev.). Washington, DC: Author.

American Psychiatric Association. (1994). *Diagnostic and statistical manual of mental disorders* (4th ed.). Washington, DC: Author.

Barrett, P., Dadds, M., & Rapee, R. (in press). Treatment of childhood anxiety: A controlled trial. *Journal of Consulting and Clinical Psychology*.

Beck, A. T., Rush, A., Shaw, B., & Emery, G. (1979). *Cognitive therapy of depression*. New York: Guilford Press.

Brady, E. U., & Kendall, P. C. (1992). Comorbidity of anxiety and depression in children and adolescents. *Psychological Bulletin, 111*, 244–255.

Gosch, E., Kendall, P. C., Panas, J., & Bross, L. (1991, November). *Behavioral observations of anxiety-disordered children*. Paper presented at the convention of the Association for the Advancement of Behavior Therapy, New York.

Howard, B., & Kendall, P. C. (in press). Cognitive–behavioral family therapy for anxiety-disordered children: A multiple-baseline evaluation. *Cognitive Therapy and Research*.

Kane, M. T., & Kendall, P. C. (1989). Anxiety disorders in children: A multiple-baseline evaluation of a cognitive–behavioral treatment. *Behavior Therapy, 20*, 499–508.

Kendall, P. C. (Ed.). (1991). *Child and adolescent therapy: Cognitive–behavioral procedures*. New York: Guilford Press.

Kendall, P. C. (1992a). *Coping Cat Workbook*. Admore, PA: Workbook Publishing.

Kendall, P. C. (1992b). Childhood coping: Avoiding a lifetime of anxiety. *Behavioural Change, 9*, 1–8.

Kendall, P. C. (1994). Treating anxiety disorders in youth: Results of a randomized clinical trial. *Journal of Consulting and Clinical Psychology, 62*, 100–110.

Kendall, P. C., & Brady, E. U. (1995). Comorbidity in the anxiety disorders of childhood. In K. D. Craig & K. S. Dobson (Eds.), *Anxiety and depression in adults and children*. Newbury Park, CA: Sage Publications.

Kendall, P. C., & Chansky, T. E. (1991). Considering cognition in anxiety disordered children. *Journal of Anxiety Disorders, 5*, 167–185.

Kendall, P. C., Chansky, T. E., Kane, M., Kane, R., Kortlander, E., Ronan, K., Sessa, F., & Siqueland, L. (1992). *Anxiety disorders in youth: Cognitive–behavioral interventions*. Needham Heights, MA: Allyn & Bacon.

Kendall, P. C., & Di Pietro, M. (1995). *Terapia scolastica dell'ansia: Guida per psicologi e insegnanti* [Anxiety therapy at school: Guide for psychologists and teachers]. Trento, Italy: Edizioni Erickson.

Kendall, P. C., & Gerow, M. (in press). Long-term follow-up of a cognitive–behavioral therapy for anxiety-disordered youth. *Journal of Consulting and Clinical Psychology.*

Kendall, P. C., & Hollon, S. D. (1989). Development of the Anxious Self-Statement Questionnaire. *Cognitive Therapy and Research, 13,* 81–93.

Kendall, P. C., Kane, M., Howard, B., & Siqueland, L. (1990). *Cognitive–behavioral therapy for anxious children: Treatment manual.* Ardmore, PA: Workbook Publishing.

Kendall, P. C., Kortlander, E., Chansky, T. E., & Brady, E. U. (1992). Comorbidity of anxiety and depression in youth: Treatment implications. *Journal of Consulting and Clinical Psychology, 60,* 869–880.

Kendall, P. C., & MacDonald, J. P. (1993). *Parent ratings of anxiety in children: Development and validation of the CBCL-A.* Unpublished manuscript.

Kendall, P. C., & Morris, R. J. (1991). Child therapy: Issues and recommendations. *Journal of Consulting and Clinical Psychology, 59,* 777–784.

Kovacs, M. (1981). Rating scales to assess depression in school aged children. *Acta Paedopsychiatrica, 46,* 305–315.

Ollendick, T. (1978). *Fear survey schedule: Revised.* (Available from the author, Virginia Polytechnic Institute and State University, Blacksburg, VA.)

Panichelli, S., Kendall, P. C., Callahan, S., Levin, M., & Gerow, M. *Social behavior scale for anxious children: Initial development and validation* (1993, November). Paper presented to the Association for Advancement of Behavior Therapy Convention, Atlanta, GA.

Reynolds, C. R., & Richmond, B. O. (1978). A revised measure of children's manifest anxiety scale. *Journal of Abnormal Child Psychology, 6,* 271–280.

Ronan, K., Kendall, P. C., & Rowe, M. (1994). Negative affectivity in children: Development and validation of a self-statement questionnaire. *Cognitive Therapy and Research, 18,* 509–528.

Silverman, W. (1987). *Anxiety Disorders Interview Schedule (ADIS) for Children.* SUNY Albany, NY: Graywind Publications.

Siqueland, L. (1993). *Anxiety in children: Perceived family environments and observed family interaction styles.* Unpublished doctoral dissertation, Temple University, Philadelphia, PA.

Spielberger, C. (1973). *Manual for State-Trait Anxiety Inventory for Children.* Palo Alto, CA: Consulting Psychologists Press.

Strauss, C. (1987). *Modification of trait portion of State-Trait Anxiety Inventory for Children—Parent form.* (Available from the author, Western Psychiatric Institute and Clinic, Pittsburgh, PA 15213.)

Treadwell, K. R. H., Flannery, E., & Kendall, P. C. (1995). Ethnicity and gender in clinic-referred children: Functioning, diagnostic status, and treatment outcome. *Journal of Anxiety Disorders, 9,* 373–384.

Treadwell, K. R. H., & Kendall, P. C. (1993). *The relationship of maternal negative affectivity and perceptions of child internalizing and externalizing behavior problems.* Manuscript submitted for publication.

APPENDIX

DIAGNOSTICIAN REPORT

Anxiety Disorder Interview Schedule (ADIS) for Children

The ADIS is a structured interview schedule for the diagnosis of *DSM-III-R* disorders, designed primarily to assess childhood anxiety disorders. It also includes questions about other disorders (Silverman, 1987).

Behavioral Observations

After the structured diagnostic interview, children are asked to speak about themselves for five minutes in front of a video camera. Their behaviors are coded by reliable independent raters for three global and six specific behaviors that are hypothesized to be indicative of anxiety.

CHILD SELF-REPORT

Children's Depression Inventory (CDI)

The CDI includes 27 items related to the affective, behavioral, and cognitive signs of depression (Kovacs, 1981).

Child's Perception of the Therapeutic Relationship (CPTR)

The CPTR assesses the child's perception of the therapeutic relationship, and was described earlier.

Coping Questionnaire–Child (CQ-C)

The CQ-C was designed by the CAADC to assess change in children's perceived ability to manage specific anxiety-provoking situations. Three items are rated on a 7-point Likert Scale.

Fear Survey Schedule for Children–Revised (FSSC-R)

The FSSC-R is an 80-item inventory assessing specific fears in children on a 3-point scale, with 8 fear content categories measured (Ollendick, 1978).

Negative Affectivity Self-Statement Questionnaire (NASSQ)

This questionnaire assesses children's self-statements associated with negative affectivity, and was described earlier.

Revised Children's Manifest Anxiety Scale (RCMAS)

The RCMAS is a standardized instrument, and contains 37 items to measure chronic anxiety in children (Reynolds & Richmond, 1978). Four subscales assess physiological symptoms, worry and oversensitivity, concentration, and a lie scale.

State-Trait Anxiety Inventory for Children (STAIC)

The STAIC is a standardized scale that includes two 20-item scales that measure the enduring tendency to experience anxiety (A-Trait) and the temporal and situational variations in anxiety (A-State; Spielberger, 1973).

PARENT MEASURES

Automatic Thoughts Questionnaire

This 32-item inventory assesses the frequency of anxious self-talk experienced during the past two weeks. Responses are reported on a 5-point scale representing the frequency that each thought occurred. Reliability and validity were supported (Kendall & Hollon, 1989).

Beck Depression Inventory (BDI)

This 21-item inventory measures depressive symptomatology, and has acceptable reliability and validity (see Beck, Rush, Shaw, & Emery, 1979).

Child Behavior Checklist (CBCL)

The CBCL contains 118 items that assess an array of behavioral problems and can be scored by internalization and externalization factors (Achenbach, 1991a).

Coping Questionnaire–Parent (CQ-P)

The CQ-P is the parent version of the CQ-C, and assesses changes in parents' perceptions of their child's ability to cope with three problematic situations.

State-Trait Anxiety Inventory, State-Trait Anxiety Inventory for Children–Modification of Trait Version for Parents (STAIC-P)

This modified version of the Trait scale of the STAIC assesses parents' ratings of their child's trait anxiety (Strauss, 1987).

TEACHER REPORT

CBCL-Teacher Report Form (TRF)

The TRF is completed by the teacher to report on the child's behavioral problems, and is similar in format to the CBCL (Achenbach, 1991b). It is scored for internalization and externalization factors.

4

BREAKING THE VICIOUS CYCLE: COGNITIVE–BEHAVIORAL GROUP TREATMENT FOR SOCIALLY ANXIOUS YOUTH

ANNE MARIE ALBANO and DAVID H. BARLOW

In 1904, G. Stanley Hall described the period of adolescence as one of "storm and stress," characterized by rapid and intense emotional and physical changes. During this period, adolescents are challenged by physical maturation and puberty, occurring concurrently with the task of defining a personal identity and self-concept. Confusion and conflict abound as pubertal and cognitive–developmental processes combine in a synergistic manner, and thus exert reciprocal influences on the adolescent and his or her environment.

For most adolescents, the impact of stage-specific challenges are buffered by the awareness of their own emerging autonomy, and by accessing reinforcement and support from the social environment. Consider, for example, what one would hear if eavesdropping on a "typical" conversation between teens. Parties, crushes, shopping, sports, food, and music, to name a few, are the usual "hot" topics of the day. Hence, for the typical adolescent, this stage of life is generally considered a time of excitement over dating, parties, and proms. However, for the socially phobic adolescent, this period of life is characterized by continuous dread and misery. Feeling too anxious to even make eye contact with peers or socialize in school

Research for this chapter was supported by grant MH49691 from the National Institute of Mental Health. Correspondence concerning this chapter should be addressed to Dr. Anne Marie Albano, Department of Psychology, University of Louisville, KY 40292.

hallways, these teenagers risk increasing isolation and anxiety that may last a lifetime. Research has indicated that although social fears are considered a transient part of the normal developmental process, for some adolescents, such fears are unrelenting and of sufficient magnitude to negatively influence mastery of skills and emotional growth (Francis, 1990; Kendall et al., 1991; Rubin, LeMare, & Lollis, 1990). Investigators have demonstrated that socially anxious children display inadequate social skills and maintain a negative self-evaluative focus (Rubin et al., 1990). Moreover, these children have difficulty in peer relationships and tend to have limited involvement in mainstream social activities (Albano, DiBartolo, Heimberg, & Barlow, 1995; Francis, 1990). Hence, for the social phobic adolescent, the "storm and stress" of this period is unending and may yield a lifetime of struggle.

Current epidemiological data estimate the prevalence of social phobia at 1.1% for the general child and adolescent population (Kashani & Orvaschel, 1990). Rates reported in the literature range from 0.9% among 11-year-old children (Anderson, Williams, McGee, & Silva, 1987) to 1.1% for 15-year-old adolescents (McGee et al., 1990). The rate reported in the McGee et al. study is most likely an underestimate, because fear of public speaking was diagnosed as a specific (simple) phobia. The most recent published data on adult social phobia indicates a prevalence of 13.3% for the general adult population in the United States (Kessler et al., 1994), and establishes social phobia as the third most common mental disorder among adults. This large discrepancy between the child and adult estimates most likely reflects an overall under-reporting and under-recognition of internalizing disorders in children, and speaks to the necessity of education programs and means to promote access to services for childhood emotional disorders overall. Published reports of clinic-referred samples of children and adolescents receiving a principal diagnosis of social phobia (*Diagnostic and Statistical Manual of Mental Disorders* [3rd ed., rev.]; [*DSM-III-R*]; American Psychiatric Association [APA], 1987) range from 9% to 17.9% (Albano et al., 1995; Last, Perrin, Hersen, & Kazdin, 1992; Strauss & Francis, 1989).

In this chapter, we review briefly our clinical research program, describe social phobia in cognitive–behavioral terms, and present in detail our psychosocial treatment program for social phobic adolescents.

THE CHILD AND ADOLESCENT ANXIETY DISORDERS PROGRAM

The Center for Stress and Anxiety Disorders (CSAD) was established in 1982 by the State University of New York at Albany, under the codirection of David H. Barlow and Edward B. Blanchard. The Center is recognized in the Albany area as the resource center for anxiety and stress disorders. The Phobia and Anxiety Disorders Clinic (PADC), a major division within the CSAD, has been in operation since 1979 and is widely recognized as a major treatment and research center for panic disorder and other anxiety disorders. Within the clinic, the Child and Adolescent Anxiety Disorders Program is concerned with research and treatment of childhood anxiety disorders, such as separation anxiety disorder, overanxious disorder, specific phobia, school refusal, obsessive–compulsive disorder, and social phobia. In the past four years, clinic staff have assessed and treated more than 200 children presenting with anxiety complaints. Among the current research efforts are the validation of the revised Anxiety Disorders Interview Schedule for the *Diagnostic and Statistical Manual of Mental Disorders* (4th ed.) (*DSM-IV*; APA, 1994), Child and Parent Versions (ADIS-IV-C/P; Silverman & Albano, 1996), evaluation of a new psychosocial treatment protocol for childhood obsessive–compulsive disorder, and the examination of comorbid anxiety disorders on treatment outcome.

SOCIAL PHOBIA FROM A COGNITIVE–BEHAVIORAL PERSPECTIVE

DSM-IV defines social phobia as fear of a variety of social and performance situations because of concern that one may become embarrassed or humiliated by performing inadequately or by others' noticing visible anxiety symptoms. Social phobics may become anxious in situations ranging from simple one-on-one conversations and writing in front of others, to performing motor tasks such as those called for in athletics or the performing arts. Social phobics have also been known to avoid using public bathrooms (Holt, Heimberg, Hope, & Liebowitz, 1992). Most social phobics fear and avoid two or more social situations rather than a discrete, single situation. As such, *DSM-IV* requires the specifier to be generalized if the fears include most social situations.

Unfortunately for the typical adolescent, there is no escape from the daily scrutiny of peers and teachers, and thus by definition, adolescence is a series of social–evaluative situations. Public presentation is an expected part of every school curriculum. Oftentimes pupils are "called to the board" to work out a mathematics problem, to read aloud, or to give oral reports in front of the class. Physical education classes, music or dance lessons, and team sports also place the adolescent directly in the spotlight for evaluation by peers and adults. Moreover, adolescents are continually barraged by the latest fashion requirements that may involve "minimal peer-accepted standards" for clothing, hair styles, and makeup. Overall, the adolescent is expected to look cool, act cool, and interact with smooth social skills as he or she climbs the ladder to popularity. It is no wonder then that social fears are part of the normal developmental process for adolescents. But, for a substantial proportion of children and adolescents, social fears are not a mere transient developmental phenomenon, but remain fixed and progress to disruptive levels.

Current cognitive–behavioral conceptualizations of social phobia view the disorder as a negative interaction of cognitive processes, physiological arousal, and behavioral products in response to social–evaluative situations. According to Barlow (1988), for reasons of evolutionary significance, humans are sensitive to anger, criticism, or other means of social disapproval. For the adolescent, such disapproval may take the form of a low test grade, being laughed at while giving a talk, or being teased and bullied. Although all persons encounter such situations during the course of development, social phobia occurs in persons who are biologically and psychologically vulnerable to the development of anxious apprehension. Consequently, relatively minor negative life events involving performance or interpersonal interactions can lead to anxiety, particularly if panic (alarm) sensations are associated with these social events. Social anxiety is generally not considered to be readily acquired by vicarious means (Ohman, 1986), such as observing a classmate being teased by peers or admonished by an adult. However, in our clinical experience some adolescents will report never having had the experience of being teased or of faltering during an oral presentation, but they recall in detail the observation of their peers in such situations and a fear that "I may be next!"

Thus, the adolescent's biological and psychological vulnerabilities to develop anxiety, coupled with stressful social–evaluative experiences, set the stage for the onset of social anxiety. Self-focused attention, expressed through self-deprecatory statements, and awareness of physiological arousal interfere with adequate functioning and contribute to social performance deficits. Behavioral avoidance of social situations may serve to decrease anxiety in the short term; however, in the long term the adolescent misses the opportunity to learn corrective information about his or her own coping abilities and the realistic probability of experiencing a truly negative outcome. Consequently, a vicious cycle of negative thoughts and feelings and behavioral avoidance serve to maintain the social phobia and perpetuate the adolescent's misery. A summary of this model is presented in Figure 1. The reader interested in a comprehensive review of the model is directed to Barlow (1988) and Heimberg and Barlow (1991).

The challenge for the cognitive–behavioral therapist is to intervene at all levels of the vicious cycle and assist the adolescents in acquiring corrective information regarding social situations and their own cognitive and behavioral abilities and resources.

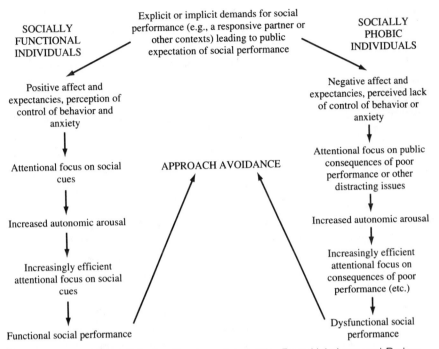

Figure 1. Model of social dysfunction in social phobia. From Heimberg and Barlow (1991). Reprinted with permission.

COGNITIVE–BEHAVIORAL GROUP TREATMENT FOR SOCIAL PHOBIC ADOLESCENTS (CBGT-A)

The purpose of the CBGT-A program is to assist social phobic adolescents with ways to reduce anxiety and increase effective social functioning. The program is designed to be delivered to adolescents between the ages of 13 and 17 years, in group format, by a team of trained cotherapists. It is essential that therapists be familiar with the relatively complex concepts underlying the therapeutic techniques and exercises, in addition to having a solid understanding of the complex behavior and cognitive–developmental abilities of the group members. This program is not indicated for individual application. Given the nature of social phobia, treatment in a social context is recommended. CBGT-A is presented in 16 sessions, each taking approximately 90 minutes. Parent involvement may be required in selected treatment sessions.

Issues and Goals

CBGT-A is designed for adolescents who suffer from social phobia. It is ideal for teenagers who meet *DSM-III-R* or *DSM-IV* criteria for the diagnosis, but is also useful for teens who suffer from excessive anxiety in social or evaluative situations but do not meet criteria for social phobia. It is not uncommon for social phobic adolescents to present with comorbid psychiatric diagnoses, such as an additional anxiety disorder or mood disorder. These problems do not preclude treatment using this program as long as the social phobia is the principal diagnosis. If, for example, it is determined that an affective disorder or an additional anxiety disorder is the most interfering and disabling condition, then the principal disorder should be treated first.

Clinical experience suggests that this program may be inappropriate for patients who present with severe family dysfunction. Early in the development of the program, we accepted adolescent patients with extremely limited or absent parental support. These parents presented with active substance abuse problems, severe anxiety disorders, or interfering Axis II (personality) psychopathology. Consequently, the adolescents' treatment was compromised by missed sessions and preoccupation with worry about the family. Hence, we suggest that family system problems be the principal target of intervention in such cases, as these problems appear to warrant more immediate treatment for the adolescent. Similarly, adolescents with substance abuse problems or principal diagnosis of an externalizing disorder (e.g., conduct disorder) may not benefit from this program for similar clinical reasons. Thus far, we have modified the program to meet the special needs of adolescents presenting with pervasive developmental disorder (PDD). The information component in the program and adjunctive aids were modified to meet the educational and cognitive–developmental level of the PDD group members. We expect that, for groups with mentally retarded or learning disabled teenagers, the program may be applied similarly with appropriate modifications, however, empirical validation of such applications are necessary. We suggest that groups be structured to included members who are similar on these cognitive–developmental dimensions.

The CBGT-A treatment program is based on the successful adult social phobia program developed by Richard Heimberg and colleagues (Heimberg et al., 1990; Hope & Heimberg, 1993) and incorporates specific skill-building components for increasing social functioning and prosocial behaviors. The treatment program allows for the range of the members' skill levels to be addressed. The overall goals of the CBGT-A program are to teach adolescents to master their social phobia by learning to (a) identify the triggers to their anxiety; (b) recognize and examine anxious responses across the three components of anxiety (cognitive, physiological, behavioral); (c) learn and apply appropriate anxiety management skills across the three components; and (d) accept and cope with normal, expected levels of social anxiety.

Assessment Methods

Prior to the first treatment session, each adolescent participates in a pretreatment assessment focused on defining individual target behaviors and goals. Establishing pretreatment markers of functioning and behavioral limits permits a microscopic examination of the three components of anxiety, allows patterns of responding to be examined for both individual members and the group, and increases our understanding of the phenomenology of social phobia in adolescents. Moreover, periodic follow-up assessments provide a rigorous test of the efficacy of the treatment program. For the CBGT-A project, assessments are completed at pre- and posttreatment, and at 6-, 12-, and 24-month follow-up. A summary of the assessment methods follows.

Diagnostic Interview

Patients are diagnosed using the ADIS-IV-C/P (Silverman & Albano, 1996). The ADIS-IV-C/P allows for the accurate differential diagnosis among the anxiety disorders, affective disorders, and externalizing disorders of childhood (e.g., conduct disorder, oppositional defiant disorder), while also screening for additional problems, such as psychotic symptomatology, eating disorders, and somatoform disorders. Diagnoses are derived separately for the child interview, parent interview, and then combined based on specific guidelines to form the composite diagnosis. In addition to identifying a principal diagnosis (most severe/disabling condition), additional comorbid disorders may be assigned and tracked. The Clinician Severity Rating (CSR) is based on a 9-point scale (0–8), serving to anchor diagnostic severity. Diagnoses assigned a CSR of four or above are considered to be of clinical severity and warrant intervention.

Questionnaire Measures

A number of self-report measures are suitable for assessing social phobic adolescents, and the reader is directed to Albano, DiBartolo, et al. (1995) for a comprehensive review. A battery of questionnaires may be compiled for the assessment of social anxiety and avoidance and related constructs. For example, our battery includes the Fear of Negative Evaluation (FNE) and Social Avoidance and Distress (SAD) scales (Watson & Friend, 1969), the State–Trait Anxiety Inventory for Children (STAIC; Spielberger, 1973), and the Children's Depression Inventory (CDI; Kovacs, 1982). Each questionnaire taps specific features of social anxiety, general anxiety, and depressive ideation, respectively.

Behavioral Approach Task (BAT)

Standardized individual behavioral tests are used to assess the behavioral limits of the adolescent and to provide an observable index of clinical change. In our clinic, adolescents participate in two tasks designed to re-create realistic social–evaluative situations, during which measures of behavioral, cognitive, and physiological reactivity are accessed. For the first task, the adolescent is instructed to give a brief, 6-minute impromptu talk in front of a group of four confederates. Topics are chosen at random and may include talking about favorite hobbies, family, or vacations. The second task is an interpersonal interaction, where the adolescent engages in a 6-minute conversation with a same-gender confederate. Specific guidelines for the interaction are given to the confederates, such as to allow a specified time period of silence to elapse prior to initiating conversation and to refrain from leading the conversation with questions. During the BAT, heart rate and blood pressure ratings are taken using an ambulatory monitor. Subjective units of distress scale (SUDS) ratings are taken on a 0 (none) to 100 (extreme) scale at 1-minute intervals during each task of the BAT. Immediately following each task, the adolescent is asked to list up to six thoughts that he or she recalls having during the task, to complete the state form of the STAIC, and to rate his or her overall performance. Such measures allow changes within the specific anxiety response domains to be tracked.

Treatment Measures

In addition to the pretreatment assessment battery, several specific indices of change are taken throughout the treatment process.

Self-Monitoring

Adolescents are instructed in the use of a continuous self-monitoring diary, where they track social situations encountered in their everyday lives and their responses to such situations across the three components of anxiety. SUDS ratings are assigned for each incident noted on the diary. The diary provides a method of direct and immediate feedback to the adolescents and therapists, whereby treatment effectiveness can be assessed continually and problems addressed immediately.

Self-Report

Prior to the start of each treatment session, the CDI and the STAIC are administered to the participants. Again, these measures provide a continual index of levels of depressive symptomatology and general anxiety and alert the therapists to any potential difficulties deserving further evaluation.

Fear and Avoidance Hierarchies (FAH)

Each adolescent completes an individualized FAH at the beginning of each session. The FAH defines operationally the "top 10" social phobic situations for the adolescent, which serve as a measure of treatment progress and provide specific targets for the behavioral exposure phase of treatment. Each item is rated by the adolescent separately for level of fear and degree of avoidance on a 0 (not at all) to 8 (extreme) scale. The FAH provides an ecologically valid method of defining the behavioral limits of the adolescent's social phobia. Parents also complete the FAH, providing an observer's impression of the adolescent's degree of fear and avoidance.

The FAH is constructed prior to the first treatment session. Each member's individual goals and specific behavioral targets are identified and rank-ordered according to assigned SUDS ratings. Parent input is also solicited for external validation of the individual hierarchy items, as parents can often provide important observations about the behavioral limits of their child. A completed hierarchy will have 10 situations rated for fear and avoidance by the participant, on a 0–8 SUDS rating. The adolescents rate each hierarchy item prior to the start of each treatment session, and ratings are solicited from the parents at selected points in the program. Thus, the FAH provides an ongoing measure of therapeutic change.

Parent Input

In addition to the measures described earlier, parent input is solicited at all assessment points and throughout treatment. Parents are administered the Parent Version of the ADIS-IV-C/P, lending their observations to the diagnostic process. A battery of parent-report questionnaires is also used, including measures such as the Child Behavior Checklist-Parent Report Form (CBCL; Achenbach & Edelbrock, 1987). Throughout treatment parents complete Problem Situation Forms and return them to the therapists as indicated. The Problem Situation Form requests the parent(s) to document "critical incidents" relating to social situations, and how the adolescent and parent responded to each incident. In addition to providing important information for assessing the external validity of the treatment, the Problem Situation Form provides a measure of reliability of the adolescent's diary forms. And, last, the parents and their adolescent participate in a Family Behavioral Test (FBAT) by which they are given two social situations that may be encountered by an adolescent and are asked to discuss how to manage the situations. Videotaped discussions are then coded for communication patterns, emotional expression, and problem solving.

Treatment Components and Procedures

The basic treatment protocol for CBGT-A incorporates education, skill building, modeling and role-playing, cognitive-restructuring, and both within- and between-session exposure to anxiety-provoking social situations. Specific details of the program may be found in the treatment manuals (Albano, Marten, & Holt, 1991; Marten, Albano, & Holt, 1991). A brief description of the individual treatment components and rationale is presented here.

Psychoeducation

Information about the nature of anxiety and tripartite model (cognitive, physiological, behavioral) is presented to increase the adolescents' awareness and understanding about the initiation and maintenance of anxiety. Self-monitoring, in the form of a daily diary and additional specific homework assignments, is assigned to facilitate the identification of anxiety triggers and reactions.

Skill Building

The following skills are presented to the adolescents with the rationale that the group setting provides a "safe" environment to practice and refine skill deficits.

Cognitive Restructuring. Adolescents are taught to identify cognitive distortions (errors in thinking) that perpetuate the vicious cycle of anxiety. Systematic rationale responses, based on realistic appraisal of social situations, are developed and replace the distorted cognitions. Modeling, role-playing, and systematic exposure exercises are utilized to develop this skill.

Social Skills. Often, social phobic adolescents present with deficient social skills because of lack of practice, insufficient opportunity to learn and practice the skill, or both, stemming from behavioral avoidance. Specific social skills for interpersonal interactions, maintenance of relationships, and assertiveness are identified and taught through modeling and role-playing.

Problem Solving. A model for identifying problems and developing realistic goals is presented and practiced. Again, because of behavioral avoidance and escape from aversive situations, the adolescents have limited experience in dealing with difficult situations through proactive plans. Problem solving plans are developed in the group context for situations relevant to present group members (e.g., dealing with teasing, managing school assignments).

Exposure

Items from each adolescents' individual fear and avoidance hierarchy become the focus of within-session simulated exposures. During these exposures, the hierarchy item is simulated, using either group members or trained confederates as participants. Exposures target the cognitive component and behavioral avoidance of anxiety directly, while demonstrating to the adolescents that the sensations of anxiety will dissipate through habituation. Adolescents progress through their hierarchies in a graduated manner. "Double exposure" is accomplished by having the adolescents participate in other members' exposures. Maintenance and generalization are promoted through the assignment of between-session homework exposures.

Snack Time Practice

A structured snack time is scheduled midway through each treatment session. The majority of adolescents assessed at our clinic identify difficulty in eating in public situations, including the school cafeteria and restaurants. Snack time provides a natural activity for shaping social behavior and social anxiety while serving refreshments (soda, snacks) and fostering group cohesion. Initially, therapists model prosocial behaviors and coping behaviors by giving short presentations in an informal manner (e.g., discussing an embarrassing moment). Adolescents' behaviors are shaped in a graduated manner through structured tasks (e.g., reading aloud a paragraph, preparing a paragraph, giving an impromptu talk). Later in the program, snack time is used for extra "mini-exposures" (e.g., giving or receiving compliments) and group process activities.

Parent Involvement

Parents are actively involved in selected treatment sessions to receive education about the model of anxiety and maintenance of social phobia, to address realistic and appropriate expectations for their son's or daughter's treatment, and to receive specific feedback on how to encourage the adolescents in applying their skills between sessions and after termination. Additional exercises in perspective taking, examining expectations and goals, and effective communication are employed. We include parents in the protocol to target the feelings and behavioral reactions of the adolescents and their parents in their family interactions affected by social phobia.

Session Plans

CBGT-A is divided into two 8-session phases. Sessions 1 through 8 are focused on the introduction and review of various skills to reduce anxiety and facilitate social interactions. Throughout treatment, self-monitoring is emphasized and specific homework assignments reviewed. Sessions 1 through 4 are conducted within a 2-week period. The remaining sessions in phase one are conducted weekly. A session outline is written on a flipchart prior to the beginning of each session. Parents attend sessions 1, 2, and 8 during phase one. A summary of the focus of each session and corresponding intervention techniques is provided in Table 1.

Sessions 1 and 2 present the treatment rationale and introduce the participants to working within the group format. Ground rules are described, including confidentiality, punctuality, and attendance. A group confidentiality contract is signed by all participants and the therapists. The three-response model of anxiety is described, and social phobia is defined in cognitive–behavioral terms. Therapists solicit the participants' descriptions of anxiety-provoking situations and cues. Group members may initially be hesitant to participate; however, the sharing of problem situations typically results in nods of recognition and acknowledgment, culminating in a group member declaring, "I thought I was the only one who felt this way!" Expectations regarding treatment for both adolescents and their parents are solicited and shared.

Sessions 3 and 4 target cognitive restructuring. Therapists introduce the concept of automatic thoughts (ATs), which serve to magnify and maintain anxiety. A 4-step process of cognitive restructuring is presented, with a focus on producing rational responses to the chain of ATs. Sessions 5 and 6 review problem solving strategies targeted to expand the adolescents' repertoire of coping behaviors. Social skills are identified and targeted for remediation through a systematic plan of action. Therapists rely heavily on modeling and shaping behavior through guided participation.

A review of skills and coping strategies is presented in Session 7, in addition to discussion of support systems. The adolescents prepare for their parents to attend the next session, and identify any specific and relevant issues for discussion in the next session. Parents attend Session 8, which focuses on communication between parents and adolescents and outlines appropriate parental involvement in the second phase of treatment.

During the second phase of treatment, adolescents are exposed to both simulated within-session exposures and in vivo personally relevant anxiety provoking situations. The skill modules introduced during phase one are essential to the adolescents' ability to cope with these exposure practices.

Sessions 9 through 14 are devoted primarily to simulated exposures, cognitive restructuring, and assigned homework exposures. Typically, two adolescents are targeted for exposure during each session, with snack time practice reserved for mini-exposures and group process activities. Each adolescent, in turn, selects a target situation from their individual fear and avoidance hierarchy. The particular situation is then simulated within session by other group members or with the assistance of trained confederates

TABLE 1

CBGT-A Treatment Protocol and Strategies

Session	Focus	Strategy/Techniques
Phase One		
Sessions 1 and 2 (with parents)	Cognitive–behavioral model of social anxiety	Psychoeducation/Didactic presentation
	Treatment rationale, expectations for treatment	
	Sharing of problems and goals	
Sessions 3 and 4	Cognitive component	Psychoeducation, therapist modeling and role playing, Socratic method, shaping participation through social reinforcement (e.g., smiles, nods)
	Automatic thoughts and rational responses	
	Four steps to cognitive restructuring	
Sessions 5 and 6	Problem-solving strategies and building coping plans	Psychoeducation, modeling, role playing, guided participation, increased use of social reinforcers to shape and encourage participation
	Identification and training of appropriate social and assertiveness skills	
Session 7	Review of skills and coping strategies	Psychoeducation, Socratic method, role playing
	Expectations for treatment progress	
	Accessing and using support systems	
Session 8 (with parents)	Communication with support systems	Role-reversal and perspective-taking experiment with adolescents and parents
	Preparation for Phase 2 of treatment	
	Parents coach their adolescents in managing anxiety-provoking situations	
Phase Two		
Sessions 9–14	Simulated experiences for gathering evidence to refute automatic thoughts and to habituate to anxiety-provoking situations	Simulated exposures, cognitive restructuring, and systematic homework assignments
Session 15 (with parents)	Maintenance of gains and preparation for termination	Simulated exposures, relapse prevention strategies
Session 16	Treatment progress and termination issues	Final simulated exposures

Note. Table from A. M. Albano (1995). Adapted with permission.

(research assistants or graduate students). Staging of the situation is directed by the therapists, with instructions given to participants to "get tougher" and challenge the target adolescent as treatment progresses. For example, we may ask the participants not to respond to the target adolescent unless he or she speaks first and asks two questions. Typically, we rely on confederates for the more sensitive and challenging situations, such as being teased by peers, handling rejection in dating situations, and being laughed at during oral presentations. However, the program relies largely on the participation of the adolescents in these exposures, and as such, participants receive double doses of exposure by acting in each other's situations.

Exposures are structured such that the adolescent specifies observable behavioral goals (e.g., ask four questions, introduce self), identifies ATs, and constructs a rational response for the situation. SUDS ratings are taken each minute during the 10-minute exposure, followed by the recitation of the rational response. Following the exposure, goals are reviewed and performance is critiqued. An individual exposure curve is drawn on a flipchart, graphing the habituation of the adolescent's SUDS ratings taken during the exposure. In situations in which SUDS do not decrease, an analysis of performance is discussed and obstacles to habituation identified. It is expected that initial curves should peak early and maintain high levels of anxiety (SUDS) for a significant portion of the exposure. However, as treatment proceeds and the adolescent gains experience with mastering anxiety, the overall SUDS levels of the curve should drop, and habituation is expected to occur more quickly.

Session 15 involves simulated exposures executed in front of the parents. In several groups conducted to date, parents were privileged to see their children achieving tasks such as oral reading or musical performance for the first time! Additionally, parents and adolescents discuss the treatment gains made thus far as well as plans for the future. A model of "relief" is presented, such that the adolescents learn to recognize relief as a marker for social anxiety. Situations that may be canceled or postponed, to which the adolescent responds with "Whew, I'm glad I didn't have to go there (do that)," serve as triggers for exploring thoughts and expectations related to social anxiety. The adolescents are encouraged to construct exposure plans for such episodes to prevent the escalation of anxiety and avoidance. Finally, Session 16 is devoted to processing termination issues, final exposures, and a group farewell party.

TREATMENT EFFECTIVENESS

In Albano, Marten, Holt, Heimberg, and Barlow (1995), 1-year follow-up data are reported for five adolescents treated with the

CBGT-A protocol. The sample consisted of three boys and two girls (ages 13–16 years), each receiving principal *DSM-III-R* diagnoses of social phobia, generalized type. In addition, all five adolescents presented with various comorbid conditions, including overanxious disorder and mood disorders. At the 3-month follow-up, social phobia was subclinical for all but one adolescent. By the 12-month follow-up, four participants were completely remitted of all mental disorders and, in the remaining participant, social phobia was at subclinical levels. BAT task results indicate that participants' cognitions changed from a negative self-focus to a nonthreatening, non-anxious presentation during socially challenging tasks. SUDS ratings likewise dropped to minimal levels. These results are interesting when compared to the heart rate data, which revealed continued physiological arousal. Such data suggest that the adolescents are able to tolerate arousal much like the average person challenged by a novel social–evaluative task.

OUTCOMES

We have been conducting a controlled clinical evaluation of the CBGT-A program and, as such, have preliminary evidence that supports the program's effectiveness (Albano, Marten, et al., 1995). The objective of our project, supported by the National Institute of Mental Health (NIMH), is threefold: (a) to evaluate the effectiveness of treatment versus no treatment of adolescent social phobia; (b) to evaluate whether the inclusion of parents enhances (or detracts from) treatment efficacy; and (c) to determine the long-term impact of these treatments on adolescent social phobia through follow-up analyses. Adolescents meeting diagnostic criteria for social phobia are randomly assigned either to a self-monitoring control condition, the CBGT-A protocol without parent involvement, or to the CBGT-A protocol with parent participation. We anticipate 20 participants in each group for a total sample of 60 adolescents by the conclusion of the study.

We fully expect the CBGT-A protocol to be a potent intervention for adolescent social phobia. We hypothesize that the inclusion of parents will be an additive curative factor and will enhance treatment effectiveness, as compared to delivery of the protocol without parent involvement. In the pilot study, parent involvement was minimal; but we expect that, by enlisting parents as active change agents (through assigned practice and feedback), the intervention will be maximally effective. Furthermore, we expect that the adolescents treated without parental involvement will show a significant decrease in social phobia as compared to the self-monitoring control group.

In addition to questions of overall treatment effectiveness and impact of parent participation, this project will enable us to explore a multitude of questions pertaining to social phobia and anxiety in youth. Our plans include the explication and examination of factors that impact on treatment outcome. For example, variables such as diagnostic severity, patterns of comorbidity, and parent pathology (assessed through self-report methods) will be evaluated. In addition, we seek to evaluate the usefulness of the individual and family behavioral test paradigms in the assessment of social phobia. Data generated from the BAT protocols will also allow us to examine, in detail, anxiety on a physiological, cognitive, and behavioral level in the adolescents. And last, the data generated from this study may allow comparison with data gathered in our adult social phobia program and, thus, provoke some interesting questions and answers concerning the longitudinal course of this disorder.

GENERALIZABILITY AND FUTURE DIRECTIONS

Issues regarding the generalizability of CBGT-A remain to be evaluated. Because the CBGT-A protocol incorporates specific skill training components and behavioral exposure, an examination of the relative contribution of specific components to treatment outcome may be undertaken. It remains to be seen whether both treatment phases (skill building and exposure) are necessary in the treatment of adolescents. Similarly, the length of each phase of treatment may be manipulated to maximize the effects of treatment.

The generalizability and effectiveness of the protocol for adolescents with complex clinical presentations should be evaluated in future studies. As discussed earlier, the CSR provided by the ADIS-IV-C/P interview defines the diagnostic severity of the adolescent's presenting disorder. Thus far, adolescents receiving CSRs that indicate very serious and disabling levels of social phobia have been treated with this protocol (e.g., 7–8 range) with good results (see Albano, Marten, et al., 1995). Although we offer this program to all social phobic youth, it is possible that an adolescent with extreme social phobia could find the group program too threatening and refuse treatment. Although we have not as yet encountered such a case, a course of individual therapy would be indicated with the goal of having the adolescent eventually enter into the group program.

Anxious adolescents comorbid with selective mutism and severe school refusal behavior present for treatment with extreme complications that place them at a greater disadvantage than their peers (Albano, 1995). Adolescents with selective mutism have failed to speak in social situations for an extended period of time (usually many years) and, typically, are not conversing with anyone outside of the immediate family. Thus, the group therapy format may be perceived as an overwhelming threat to the adolescent with selective mutism, much more so than the average group member. Likewise, adolescents with serious school refusal behavior (more than 1 month of continuous absence) are often confronting the possibility of court supervision because of their absences, along with compromised academic progress. Moreover, whereas the average group member develops individualized plans for increasing social interactions in school-related situations, the school-refusing adolescent with social phobia does not have ready access to such situations. Adolescents with selective mutism or school refusal randomized to the CBGT-A program typically require much more individualized intervention and therapeutic support than the average group member, often involving coordinated services with school personnel and behavioral programs directly targeting the additional problematic behavior (mutism or school refusal). Thus, the CBGT-A program may not be the first line of intervention for adolescents with selective mutism or school refusal but may be appropriate after a trial of individual therapy or pharmacologic treatment designed to target these severe concomitant conditions (see Albano, 1995; Albano, Marten, et al., 1995).

Thus far, we have administered the protocol to younger children (ages 9–12 years) in our clinical practice and have adapted the protocol for adolescents presenting with comorbid pervasive developmental disorder. Although we have not collected systematic outcome data on either trial, the reports of the children and parents lend preliminary support to the program's generalizability to these samples. It is our hope that the program will prove to be clinically useful for a broad age range and easily adapted for both clinical and educational settings. Manuals and participant workbooks are currently being adapted for widespread dissemination, with the intention that the program be evaluated with culturally and developmentally diverse populations in a variety of settings.

Questions regarding the effectiveness of psychotropic medications in the treatment of adolescent social phobia remain unanswered. To date, only a limited number of uncontrolled investigations have been reported in the literature (Beidel & Morris, 1993). However, data from controlled pharmacological and psychosocial clinical trials with adult social phobics have burgeoned in recent years (see Heimberg, Hope, Leibowitz, & Scheier, 1995, for a comprehensive review). These data have demonstrated the individual effectiveness of both treatment modalities. At present, a controlled clinical trial examining separate and combined effects of psychosocial and drug treatments with adults is currently underway in our setting. Future studies will undoubtedly be directed toward examining the efficacy of combined medication–CBGT protocols in the treatment of adolescent social phobia. In addition, future plans also involve conducting a clinical trial of the program in a mental health services setting. The distinction between our clinical research center and a mental health services center is that patients must meet specific inclusion criteria for entrance into our protocols. Hence, questions regarding generalization of the protocol to more heterogeneous patient samples will be answered better through a services research evaluation.

CONCLUSIONS

The purpose of this chapter was to review the cognitive–behavioral conceptualization of social phobia and to provide an overview of the Cognitive–Behavioral Group Treatment for Social Phobia in Adolescents program. We have found the program to be enjoyable for therapists and participants alike, and preliminary data suggest that the program is a promising intervention strategy for socially anxious youth. Further research is necessary to evaluate the generalizability of the program with minority youth, in a variety of clinical and educational settings and to assess the differential effectiveness of the specific components of treatment.

REFERENCES

Achenbach, T. M., & Edelbrock, C. (1987). *Manual for the Child Behavior Checklist and Revised Child Behavior Profile.* Burlington: University of Vermont.

Albano, A. M. (1995). Treatment of social anxiety in adolescents. *Cognitive and Behavioral Practice, 2,* 271–298.

Albano, A. M., DiBartolo, P. M., Heimberg, R. G., & Barlow, D. H. (1995). Children and adolescents: Assessment and treatment. In R. G. Heimberg, M. R. Leibowitz, D. A. Hope, & F. Schneier (Eds.), *Social phobia: Diagnosis, assessment, and treatment* (pp. 387–425). New York: Guilford Press.

Albano, A. M., Marten, P. A., & Holt, C. S. (1991). *Cognitive–behavioral group treatment of adolescent social phobia: Therapist's manual.* Unpublished manuscript, State University of New York at Albany.

Albano, A. M., Marten, P. A., Holt, C. S., Heimberg, R. G., & Barlow, D. H. (1995). Cognitive–behavioral group treatment for social phobia in adolescents: A preliminary study. *Journal of Nervous and Mental Disease, 183,* 649–656.

American Psychiatric Association. (1987). *Diagnostic and statistical manual of mental disorders* (3rd ed., rev.). Washington, DC: Author.

American Psychiatric Association. (1994). *Diagnostic and statistical manual of mental disorders* (4th ed.). Washington, DC: Author.

Anderson, J. C., Williams, S., McGee, R., & Silva, P. A. (1987). DSM-III disorders in preadolescent children. *Archives of General Psychiatry, 44,* 69–76.

Barlow, D. H. (1988). *Anxiety and its disorders.* New York: Guilford Press.

Beidel, D. C., & Morris, T. L. (1993). Social phobia and avoidant disorder. *Child and Adolescent Psychiatric Clinics of North America, 2,* 623–638.

Francis, G. (1990). Social phobia in childhood. In C. G. Last & M. Hersen (Eds.), *Handbook of child and adult psychopathology: A longitudinal perspective* (pp. 163–168). Elmsford, NY: Pergamon Press.

Hall, G. S. (1904). *Adolescence: Its psychology and its relations to physiology, anthropology, sociology, sex, crime, religion, and education.* New York: Appleton-Century-Crofts.

Heimberg, R. G., & Barlow, D. H. (1991). New developments in cognitive–behavioral therapy for social phobia. *Journal of Clinical Psychiatry, 52,* 21–30.

Heimberg, R. G., Dodge, C. S., Hope, D. A., Kennedy, C. R., Zollo, L. J., & Becker, R. J. (1990). Cognitive behavioral group treatment for social phobia: Comparison with a credible placebo control. *Cognitive Therapy and Research, 14,* 1–23.

Heimberg, R. G., Hope, D. A., Liebowitz, M. L., & Scheier, F. (1995). *Social phobia: Diagnosis, assessment, and treatment.* New York: Guilford Press.

Holt, C. S., Heimberg, R. G., Hope, D. A., & Liebowitz, M. L. (1992). Situational domains of social phobia. *Journal of Anxiety Disorders, 6,* 63–77.

Hope, D. A., & Heimberg, R. G. (1993). Social phobia and social anxiety. In D. H. Barlow (Ed.), *Clinical handbook of psychological disorders: A step-by-step treatment manual* (pp. 99–136). New York: Guilford Press.

Kashani, J. H., & Orvaschel, H. (1990). A community study of anxiety in children and adolescents. *American Journal of Psychiatry, 147,* 313–318.

Kendall, P. C., Chansky, T. E., Freidman, M., Kim, R., Kortlander, E., Sessa, F. M., & Siqueland, L. (1991). Treating anxiety disorders in children and adolescents. In P. C. Kendall (Ed.), *Child and adolescent therapy: Cognitive–behavioral procedures* (pp. 131–164). New York: Guilford Press.

Kessler, R. C., McGonagle, K., Zhao, S., Nelson, C. B., Hughes, M., Eshleman, S., Wittchen, H.-U., & Kendler, K. (1994). Lifetime and 12-month prevalence of DSM-III-R psychiatric disorders in the United States. *Archives of General Psychiatry, 51,* 8–19.

Kovacs, M. (1982). *The Children's Depression Inventory: A self-rated depression scale for school-aged children.* Unpublished manuscript, University of Pittsburgh.

Last, C. G., Perrin, S., Hersen, M., & Kazdin, A. E. (1992). DSM-III-R anxiety disorders in children: Sociodemographic and clinical characteristics. *Journal of the American Academy of Child and Adolescent Psychiatry, 31,* 1070–1076.

Marten, P. A., Albano, A. M., & Holt, C. S. (1991). *Cognitive–behavioral group treatment for adolescent social phobia with parent participation: Therapist's manual.* Unpublished manuscript, State University of New York at Albany.

McGee, R., Fehan, M., Williams, S., Partridge, F., Silva, P. A., & Kelly, J. (1990). DSM-III disorders in a large sample of adolescents. *Journal of the American Academy of Child and Adolescent Psychiatry, 29,* 611–619.

Ohman, A. (1986). Face the beast and fear the face: Animal and social fears as prototypes for evolutionary analysis of emotion. *Psychophysiology, 23,* 123–145.

Rubin, K. H., LeMare, L. J., & Lollis, S. (1990). Social withdrawal in childhood: Developmental pathways to peer rejection. In S. R. Asher & J. D. Coie (Eds.),

Peer rejection in childhood (pp. 217–249). Cambridge, England: Cambridge University Press.

Silverman, W. K., & Albano, A. M. (1996). *The anxiety disorders interview schedule for DSM-IV, child and parent versions.* Albany, NY: Graywind Publications.

Spielberger, C. (1973). Manual for the State–Trait Anxiety Inventory for Children. Palo Alto, CA: Consulting Psychologists Press.

Strauss, C. C., & Francis, G. (1989). Phobic disorders. In C. G. Last & M. Hersen (Eds.), *Handbook of child psychiatric diagnosis* (pp. 170–190). New York: Wiley.

Watson, D., & Friend, R. (1969). Measurement of social-evaluative anxiety in junior high school students. *Adolescence, 19,* 643–648.

5

TRANSFER OF CONTROL: A PSYCHOSOCIAL INTERVENTION MODEL FOR INTERNALIZING DISORDERS IN YOUTH

WENDY K. SILVERMAN and WILLIAM M. KURTINES

Internalizing disorders such as excessive anxiety, social withdrawal, and shyness are pervasive in many children and adolescents. Unfortunately, however, because youth with externalizing disorders such as conduct or attentional difficulties are likely to have a direct and disruptive effect on other individuals and institutions, these are the youth who have been more likely to be referred to mental health professionals, and who have been the primary focus of research attention. As a consequence, researchers' conceptual and practical knowledge pertaining to internalizing disorders of youth have lagged far behind. Only recently have these disorders become a primary interest of psychosocial intervention researchers. This interest was fueled in part by the formal recognition of many internalizing disorders in youth with the publication of the third edition of the *Diagnostic and Statistical Manual of Mental Disorders* (DSM-III; American Psychiatric Association, 1980).

The *transfer of control* approach to prevention and intervention described in this chapter, which is grounded in an ongoing program of

This research was funded by grants 44781 and 49680 from the National Institute of Mental Health. Correspondence concerning this chapter should be addressed to Dr. Wendy K. Silverman, Florida International University, Child and Family Psychosocial Research Center, Department of Psychology, University Park, Miami, FL 33199.

research, is guided by what we have termed a *pragmatic orientation*[1] (see Silverman & Kurtines, 1996, for details). This orientation grew out of our recognition that effective interventions can draw on many traditions, and that rigid adherence to a particular tradition is not necessarily the most useful way to treat children and their families. Thus, in developing interventions, we seek to integrate and combine, in useful ways, the most efficacious procedures previously identified by psychosocial research and to modify and adapt these procedures for use with particular populations in particular contexts. Furthermore, we seek to design formats that render them usable by practitioners. Our interest in developing user–clinician friendly procedures is a response to the growing recognition that a substantial hiatus exists between clinical research and clinical practice and to the need to close this hiatus (e.g., Kazdin, Siegel, & Bass, 1990; Silverman & Kearney, 1992; Silverman & Wallander, 1993; Weisz, Weiss, & Donenberg, 1992).

PROGRAM DESCRIPTION

The Child and Family Psychosocial Research Center at Florida International University in Miami, Florida, comprises a number of programs and laboratories and provides multifaceted child and family interventions that include both clinic- (individual and group) and school-based services. As noted, the pragmatic orientation of the Center guides our clinical and research activities as well as our efforts to bridge the gap between these activities. Also, this pragmatic orientation is incorporated into the graduate training activities of the Center and the clinical training of professionals in the community.

The work described in this chapter draws mainly on the activities of the Childhood Anxiety and Phobia Program (CAPP) at the Center. Within the Center, CAPP has the distinctive mission of developing and evaluating approaches to assessment and intervention specific to the phobic and anxiety disorders of youth. In terms of assessment, we have spent many years in developing, testing, and refining methods of assessment, particularly child- and parent-structured interview schedules (i.e., the Anxiety Disorders Interview Schedule for Children, Silverman & Eisen, 1992; Silverman & Nelles, 1988; Silverman & Rabian, 1995), including the most recent *DSM-IV* version of the schedules (Silverman & Albano, 1996). In

---

[1]*Pragmatic* is sometimes interpreted as meaning simple and expedient—and sometimes that is what pragmatic means. It can, however, mean much more. The pragmatic tradition in modern thought, for example, has played a key role in shaping the way in which we think about many issues, including complex theoretical and philosophical issues. This pragmatic tradition is distinctly American in origin—its best known exponents (Pierce, James, and Dewey) were American. The pragmatic tradition continues to have a strong influence on contemporary thought (e.g., Rorty, 1979, 1992). The concept of pragmatic that defines our orientation draws, in part, on this tradition.

addition, we have devoted considerable effort to developing self-report instruments for assessing dimensions relevant to childhood phobic and anxiety disorders (i.e., anxiety sensitivity, Silverman, Fleisig, Rabian, & Peterson, 1991; school refusal behavior, Kearney & Silverman, 1993; and worry, Silverman, La Greca, & Wasserstein, 1995). The instruments that have emerged from this work have since been adopted by a number of investigators and practitioners interested in working with youth with anxiety and its disorders.

The focus of this chapter, however, is on the transfer of control approach that grew out of CAPP's efforts to develop and refine a transfer of control psychosocial intervention approach for use with youth with phobic and anxiety disorders. These efforts have been supported by the National Institute of Mental Health (NIMH), which only in recent years has launched controlled clinical trials on these disorders in youth in various clinical research settings across the country. CAPP is currently conducting two such funded projects (no. 44781 and no. 49680), with other grant applications under review or in preparation for projects that seek to extend and refine the intervention.

TREATING YOUTH WITH PHOBIC AND ANXIETY DISORDERS: THE TRANSFER OF CONTROL APPROACH

This section describes our transfer of control approach and the key change-producing procedures and therapeutic strategies that we use in our work. The transfer of control approach explicitly recognizes that internalizing disorders of youth (including anxiety and phobic disorders) are complex, multifaceted, and multidetermined. Four basic, interrelated types of processes—behavioral, cognitive, affective, and relational—are at the core of our approach. These four processes have long been central to conceptualizations of the etiology of all psychopathology (including internalizing disorders) as well as being the cornerstone of many effective and distinguished treatment approaches. Our efforts in developing the transfer of control approach focused on delineating the links among the types of interrelated maladaptive processes or symptoms (behavioral, cognitive, affective, and relational) that provide the basis for a diagnosis of an anxiety or phobic disorder and the types of interventions (therapeutic procedures and strategies) that can be used to modify those processes or symptoms.

The transfer of control approach holds that effective long-term psychotherapeutic change in youth involves a gradual transfer of control, in which the sequence is generally from therapist to parent to youth. Within this approach, the therapist is viewed as an expert consultant who possesses the knowledge of the skills and methods necessary to produce therapeutic change. Furthermore, it is the therapist who initially controls the use of these skills and methods, but then transfers the use of these skills and methods to the parent, who subsequently transfers the use of these skills and methods to the youth. We use this transfer of control approach as an organizational framework for all of our work with youth with phobic and anxiety disorders because it provides guidelines for implementing specific procedures and strategies in particular contexts.

We note that transfer of control notions of behavior change efforts have been demonstrated in work with other populations such as obese children (e.g., Israel, Guile, Baker, & Silverman, 1994; Israel, Stolmaker, Sharp, Silverman, & Simon, 1984). In treating phobic and anxiety disorders, the primary focus of the transfer of control is on controlling the occurrence and on successfully implementing key change-producing procedures. The approach further assumes that the most critical task of a psychosocial treatment of youth, if it is to be effective, is allowing for the adequate transfer of control from the therapist to the youth. Within this frame, we view the main task in constructing and implementing youth treatments as the identification of efficient and clear pathways for transferring this control, and the identification of pathways that are available and accessible to therapists (Silverman & Kurtines, 1996).

Key Change-Producing Procedure

Exposure is the key therapeutic ingredient or change-producing procedure in all of our interventions for phobic and anxiety disorders. We use exposure as a specific change-producing procedure because of the growing research evidence that shows it to be the most effective way to reduce phobic and anxious symptomatology. Exposure is central to any effective psychosocial treatment and is the procedure of choice of most clinical researchers (Barlow, 1988; Marks, 1969). Although there are varying views among theorists and investigators as to why exposure works, all of these views involve, in various ways, the modification of behavioral, cognitive, and affective processes (see Barlow, 1988).

The forms of direct therapeutic exposure that we use in the intervention to modify these maladaptive processes require the youth to confront anxious–phobic objects or events so that reductions in anxious–phobic symptomatology can occur. These exposures involve both in vivo and imaginal forms. Because exposure is the primary change-producing procedure, all of the participants involved in our treatment programs are told, at the onset, that they will learn how to handle their fears or anxiety through exposure—"facing your fear–anxiety." Because it is difficult for youth to engage in exposures that involve fear- or anxiety-provoking stimuli, in our work (as in the work of others), the exposures are conducted gradually. Most participants are reassured when they learn that the program takes a gradual approach to exposure; thus, they will not be expected to face their worst fear or anxiety immediately. It is further explained that gradual exposure is used so that they can obtain step-by-step success experiences with the anxious or phobic event or object, thereby increasing their confidence and ability to face increasingly fearful events or objects.

Facilitative Strategies

We also have developed or adapted a number of therapeutic strategies (e.g., contingency management, self-control training) for facilitating the occurrence of exposure. A brief description of contingency management and self-control training is presented here.

Contingency Management

On the basis of behavioral processes of change, *contingency management* strategies emphasize the training of the parents in the use of appropriate contingencies to facilitate the youth's exposure or approach behavior toward feared objects or situations. A key element of contingency management is contingency contracting.

In our work, we have found it useful to use relatively formal and detailed contracts that are completed each week by both the parent and the youth, with the assistance of the therapist. In particular, the contract details the specific exposure or approach behavior task that the youth is to engage in each week, when he or she should conduct the task, the specific reward that the parent is to give to the youth—contingent on that behavior—and when the reward should be given. We have found that having an explicit contract with this level of detail helps to reduce the conflict and negotiation necessary to implement successful exposure. These contracts also help instill in parents the notion that they have a primary role in reducing their child's fear or anxiety.

To help parents implement contingency contracting successfully, we give them detailed instruction and training in child behavior management during the individual parent sessions. Principles such as reinforcement, extinction, consistency, following through, and so on are taught to the parents during these sessions. The parents also receive training and practice in implementing these principles in both in-session and out-of-session activities via the contracts.

Self-Control

Based on cognitive processes of change, self-control strategies emphasize the training of the youth in the use of appropriate cognitive strategies to facilitate exposure or approach behavior toward feared objects or situations. A key element of self-control training is cognitive restructuring and self-reward.

In our work, we have also found it useful to use relatively formal and structured methods to help the youth learn and use self-control strategies. Thus, in implementing self-control training, we use the STOP model (STOP fear) that we have developed. STOP refers to S (recognizing when you are "Scared," anxious, worried, nervous, or afraid), T (what are my "Thoughts?" what am I thinking?), O (what are "Other" thoughts or things that I can do?), and P ("Praise" myself for controlling my fear). The participants receive weekly practice in using STOP in specific exposure or approach behavior tasks (both in- and out-of-session), thereby instilling in the youth the notion that they have a primary role in reducing their own fear or anxiety.

USING A TRANSFER OF CONTROL APPROACH FOR IMPLEMENTING AN EXPOSURE-BASED INTERVENTION

The transfer of control approach thus provides guidelines for the general sequence for the administration of the behavioral and cognitive strategies in working with youth with phobic and anxiety disorders. Specifically, this sequence involves first training the parents in contingency management and in using these skills to encourage the youth's exposure (parent control). This is followed by a gradual fading of parental control, while the youth is taught to use self-control strategies to encourage his or her own exposure (youth control). In other words, parental (or external) control is gradually reduced, while the child learns cognitive self-control strategies in contexts specific to his or her anxiety problems.

EVOLUTION OF THE TRANSFER OF CONTROL APPROACH

This section describes how the transfer of control approach evolved out of our clinical work and our research. It shows how our activities in these areas provided us with the opportunity to articulate and refine the transfer of control approach that has become central to all our intervention efforts.

Individual Treatment with a Clinic-Based Population of Youth with Phobic and Anxiety Disorders

The origins of the transfer of control approach can be found in our early work on using exposure-based interventions with children with phobic and anxiety disorders. We first began by adopting a developmental perspective and conducting several single-case studies that used an exposure-based procedure and cognitive and behavioral strategies (Eisen & Silverman, 1991, 1993; Kearney & Silverman, 1990a, 1990b). The results were encouraging and provided the impetus for seeking support from the NIMH for conducting a controlled clinical trial. Our first funded effort thus involved a controlled test of the components of our psychosocial intervention (i.e., exposure facilitated by contingency management versus exposure facilitated by self-control training versus an education-support comparison group) with a clinic-based population of youth with phobic and anxiety disorders.

Although analyses of the data for the full sample are not yet completed, our preliminary examination of some of the primary outcome data suggests that facilitating exposure through the use of either contingency management or self-control strategies is effective (e.g., Silverman, 1993). However, the effectiveness of each strategy depends on whom we ask (i.e., the youth or the parent). That is, in examining the outcome measures obtained from the youth (e.g., anxiety and fear self-rating questionnaires), the youth in the self-control condition show greater improvements than the youth in the contingency management condition. On the other hand, in examining the outcome measures obtained from the parents (e.g., parent ratings of child anxiety and fear), the youth in the contingency management condition show greater improvements than the youth in the self-control condition.

Although preliminary, these results, coupled with our clinical experiences in implementing these strategies, serve to refine further our conceptualization of the transfer of control approach. More specifically, they enable us to extend and articulate more fully how this approach provides guidelines for developing and implementing psychosocial interventions. Thus, in this initial project, we implemented interventions that involved single and direct pathways or lines for the transfer of control—either from therapist to parent (contingency managment) or from therapist to youth (self-control training). However, our clinical and research experiences in the systematic implementation of interventions based on these single and direct lines of transfer highlighted both the strengths and weaknesses of using only one of these two lines of transfer exclusively. On the one hand, single and direct lines of transfer provide the most parsimonious means for implementing interventions. On the other hand, single and direct lines of transfer do not address fully (or adequately) the full range of clinical issues and problems that frequently arise in implementation. Single and direct lines of transfer may also not provide the youth and the parent with the sense of empowerment that may be necessary for both to view that change has occurred. For example, in the case of a young child and competent parent, it may be sufficient to work directly with the parent (i.e., a line from therapist to parent), or in the case of an adolescent and a competent parent, it may be sufficient to work directly with the adolescent (i.e., a line from therapist to adolescent). In a majority of cases, however, it is necessary to work directly with both the parent and the youth (i.e., a line from therapist to parent to youth), as both are frequently essential to the change process, as well as for both of them to view the occurrence of change.

Thus, as our conceptualization of the transfer of control approach evolved (and continues to evolve), it has helped to crystallize our understanding of effective change processes. As our work progressed, we came to the view that the concept of single and direct lines of transfer of control (i.e., using either the parent or the youth as the primary agent of change) is more restrictive (and in many instances, probably less effective) than a more comprehensive view that includes multiple pathways of transfer of control. This view, in turn, has provided focus and direction for all of our work in constructing psychosocial interventions, including those for use with youth with phobic and anxiety disorders. To continue the effort, we once again sought the support of the NIMH.

Group Treatment with a Clinic-Based Population of Youth with Phobic and Anxiety Disorders

Our second funded project was designed to provide a controlled test of a more integrated transfer of control approach using a group format, which we refer to as Group Cognitive Behavioral Treatment (GCBT). GCBT uses exposure as a key change-producing procedure as well as contingency management and self-control training as facilitative therapeutic strategies—all of which we refined in the previous project. However, consistent with our extended and more fully articulated transfer of control model, this intervention included additional pathways (i.e., group processes) for facilitating the transfer of control as well as including both the youth and the parent as agents of change via the concept of transfer of control. GCBT also applied the transfer of control approach to a broader spectrum of DSM-III-R disorders (i.e, overanxious disorder, social phobia, and avoidant disorders), thereby rendering the intervention more usable by clinicians.

In implementing GCBT, we find it useful to use a relatively structured format that involves a sequence of 10 to 12 treatment sessions. As in our previous project, this project includes youth and parent involvement, with separate group sessions for each. The transfer of control approach provides a framework for the general sequence for the administration of the behavioral and cognitive strategies. This sequence is depicted in Table 1.

As Table 1 indicates, this sequence involves first the training of parents in contingency management (Education Phase A) and their use of these skills to facilitate the youth's exposure (Application Phase A). This

TABLE 1
Sequence for Administration of the Behavioral and Cognitive Strategies

Sequence	Activity
Education Phase A	Parent training in contingency management
Application Phase A	Parental application of contingency management to facilitate youth's exposure
Education Phase B	Youth training in self-control
	Gradual fading of contingency management–parental control
Application Phase B	Youth application of self-control to facilitate youth's exposure

is followed by a gradual fading of parental control, while the youth is trained in self-control skills (Education Phase B) and in the use of these skills to facilitate his or her own exposure (Application Phase B).

The transfer of control approach also provides a framework for incorporating group processes as an additional pathway for the transfer of control (i.e., from therapist to group to youth). These processes include peer modeling, peer reinforcement, feedback, support, and social comparison. For example, the group can provide peer reinforcement to the youth for successful change efforts, thereby assuming some of the functions provided by the parents and facilitating the fading of parental control. In addition, when the participants in the group observe a group peer perform a successful in vivo exercise, it provides the opportunity for positive modeling to occur. The successful completion of the exposure task, in turn, results in peer reinforcement for the group member who completed the exercise. The group also provides a context for corrective or instructive peer feedback (e.g., as when a group member shares with the others his or her method for engaging in exposure or in approaching an anxiety-provoking situation). (For further discussion of GCBT and its implementation, see Ginsburg, Silverman, & Kurtines, 1995a.)

The early returns on GCBT are encouraging and suggest that it may be an effective intervention approach, and it appears to be viewed as such by both the youth and the parent. For example, for the first 28 children and parents who completed the treatment, scores on both the child and the parent questionnaires showed considerable improvement. Similar improvements were also found on the parents' and clinicians' ratings of severity and interference. Clinically, we are also encouraged: All GCBT participants were highly committed to the treatment, attendance was excellent, and change in the children was apparent.

Because GCBT allows for multiple pathways, it has the additional advantage of possessing characteristics that render it usable by practitioners. Incorporating group process as one of the pathways, for example, enhances cost-effectiveness in that it makes more efficient use of the therapist's time. It also makes the intervention more cost-effective for the clients because in actual clinical practice, group treatment is a less expensive format than individual treatment. Moreover, an intervention that includes group process for youth who present with differing primary problems is consistent with the clinical reality of the practitioner. That is, youth who present for treatment are likely to display a range of disorders such as social phobia, overanxious disorder, and so on (both within and between individuals). An intervention that targets a range of disorders (rather than one specific disorder) is more in keeping with this clinical reality.

Group Cognitive Treatment with a School-Based Population of Youth with Posttraumatic Stress Disorder

As noted earlier, our pragmatic orientation enables us to adapt the transfer of control intervention approach for use with a wide range of internalizing disorders in diverse contexts. In this section, we describe our efforts to adapt the approach for use in a school setting with multi-ethnic urban youth who have been exposed to crime or violence. An NIMH grant proposal currently is under review for this project.

Our interest in adapting the intervention for use in this context stems from the growing reports of how the rate of violent crime in the United States has increased dramatically in recent years, and how the probability of exposure, either as a witness or a victim, has also increased dramatically among our country's youth. Moreover, such youth are at significant risk for developing subsequent psychopathology, including internalizing symptomatology of anxiety, depression, phobia, and posttraumatic stress.

Inner city urban youth are not likely to present, however, for treatment in mental health clinics for exposure to crime or violence. Indeed, crime and violence have become so much a part of the culture of modern American life that exposure to such traumatic events among many youth has become the norm. Consequently, the effects of this exposure (such as internalizing symptoms) are frequently not recognized by youth as problems in need of mental health services. Therefore, we felt that it would be important to adopt our group psychosocial intervention for use in a school-based setting. Because the parents are not readily available in school-based contexts to serve as a line of transfer of control (i.e., from therapist to parent to youth), peer group process becomes a central line (i.e., from therapist to peers to youth). Thus, as noted earlier, although the transfer of control approach evolved into a more comprehensive view of the usefulness of multiple pathways, our pragmatic orientation dictated that we use the most efficient and effective pathways that are available—which in this case, ironically, was a single pathway.

In planning the psychosocial intervention for use with inner city urban youth exposed to severe trauma, our pragmatic orientation also dictated that we broaden the scope of the intervention to include adjunctive strategies (coping skills enhancement and social support enhancement) as well as our key change-producing procedure (exposure) and our core facilitative strategies (contingency management and self-control). We have thus extended the transfer of control approach to include the concept of *layering*. The phases of the intervention planned for this project, therefore, involve the sequential implementation in layers of the exposure tasks via the facilitative strategies, supplemented with the adjunctive strategies. For example, as we plan to implement the intervention, the exposure exercises will begin in Session 3. Session 4 will begin the layering process by initiating the group-based coping skills enhancement training. Session 5 will continue the layering process by initiating the group-based social support enhancement training. This type of layering process is planned throughout the 12-week program.

Finally, our plan to adapt the intervention for use with inner city urban youth in a school-based context will help us to achieve the goal of developing a psychosocial intervention with characteristics that are usable by practitioners. The development of a cost- and time-effective group intervention that can be readily implemented in a school-based setting makes available to school counselors and other mental health professionals the potential for providing a psychosocial treatment for a multiethnic population of urban youth not likely to present for treatment in mental health clinics.

OBSTACLES TO THE TRANSFER OF CONTROL

Although we are encouraged by our preliminary work with the transfer of control approach as well as its potential usefulness for implementing an exposure-based intervention with youth with phobic and anxiety disorders, we note that obstacles may arise that may impede a successful transfer of control. A full discussion of these obstacles and suggestions for handling them is not possible here (but see Silverman, Ginsburg, & Kurtines, 1995; Silverman & Kurtines, 1996); however, a few of the major obstacles are briefly mentioned.

One obstacle that may arise is what we refer to as the *protection trap*. Alluded to earlier in the chapter, the protection trap refers to parents' instincts to protect their offspring in anxious or fearful situations. How the protection trap may serve to block the transfer of control is illustrated in the following dialogue that occurred between a therapist and the mother of one of our child patients:

Therapist (T): How did things go this past week with you leaving the house for one hour while Pam stayed home with your older daughter?

Mother: Not so good. I didn't go.

T: You didn't go? What happened?

Mother: I just didn't go. Things got busy at home so I did not have a chance to leave the house.

T: Did something happen at home that made it difficult for you to leave Kim at home, as we discussed last week?

Mother: Pam told me that she would rather I not go, so I decided not to go.

T: It is hard sometimes to be a parent, isn't it? Its especially hard when we have to put our kids into situations that we know are hard for them. It is probably just as hard for us as it is for our kids.

Mother: I just knew Pam would get really upset by my leaving her. So I didn't.

T: It is not unusual for parents to have a hard time putting their children in situations that we know are hard for them—that we know may make our kids feel uncomfortable and maybe even get them upset. As parents our instincts are to protect our children from these uncomfortable feelings. I wonder if this is what happened here with you?

Mother: What do you mean?

T: Well, sometimes parents try to "protect" their children by keeping them away from situations that they know will make their children feel anxious or uncomfortable. In this program, we see parents doing this a lot. They "give up" very easily when their children show any hesitation about doing their exposure. Do you think something like this might have been going on this week with you and might partially explain why the exposure didn't take place?

Mother: Well, I guess I didn't push it too much.

T: I understand you wanted to "protect" Pam from feeling uncomfortable or getting too upset.

Mother: I just know how terrible I would feel if someone would try that with me. You know, I am a very anxious person myself. I know I could never handle it, so why should I expect Pam to do so?

T: But you understand that that was the next step on the hierarchy, and Pam was feeling like she was ready for this step. It might have been hard for Pam and for you, but Pam was at least ready to try it.

Mother: I guess I shouldn't have given in so easily.

T: That's right. You see, giving in and not encouraging the exposure because you are concerned that Pam might get too upset is sort of like a "trap." It is a trap because in the short term you and Pam come to feel better. You feel better because you are protecting Pam from feeling uncomfortable or scared, and Pam feels better because she will not have to feel uncomfortable or scared. But you see, keeping Pam away from doing this is completely against what we try to do in this program. That is, what we try to do in the program is to get children to expose themselves to what they are afraid of, not to stay away. So in the long term, keeping Pam away is not going to solve anything, and may even make the problem worse.

Usually, once we point out to parents, as we did to Pam's mother, that the protection trap is counter-therapeutic, most parents are able to modify this unwanted parental behavior. Unfortunately, however, there are those parents who, no matter how much we emphasize the dangers of engaging in the protection trap, continue to engage in this behavior. As noted, these are the parents in whom the pathway of transfer of control is "blocked." This might be caused by a number of factors, including the parents' own anxiety problems, as was the case with Pam's mother. Therapeutic progress is unlikely to occur unless more thorough probing and correcting of these parental problems occur. In the next section, we elaborate briefly on how this issue has shaped our future research interests.

Another reason why there might have been a failure in following through with the contingency contracts is because of problems or difficulties with what the parent was "supposed to do" in terms of giving the child the reward, even though the child did the exposure task. A common reason why parents do not give the reward to the child is because the reward listed on the contract is viewed by the parents as being inappropriate (i.e., too extravagant), but the parent did not mention this during the writing up of the contract in session. In our work, when we suspect that parents are feeling this way, or when rewards being agreed on are too extravagant (e.g., a trip to Disney World, a compact disc player, etc.), we intervene, emphasize social (e.g., special time with a relative or friend) and activity (e.g., playing a game, going bowling) rewards, and highlight the need for collaboration between child and parent to achieve the program's goals.

However, we have worked with children and parents who, in spite of our protests and our attempts to intervene, agree in the session on extravagant and expensive rewards. This may occur because for some child–parent dyads, agreeing on a weekly reward escalates into a weekly power struggle and, in turn, to the parent giving in to the child's demand for an inappropriate reward. Once again, the pathway of transfer or control is blocked in these families, and positive change is unlikely to occur unless the pathway is unblocked, and parents and children define and clarify their respective roles in the family. This too is briefly discussed in the next section.

In addition to obstacles such as these that generally pertain to parental difficulties in implementing control, obstacles also may arise that pertain to youth difficulties in implementing self-control. The following dialogue illustrates an example of difficulties that 12-year-old Jim had in learning and using the STOP procedure. In addition to Jim's anxiety problems, Jim also exhibited many oppositional tendencies.

> Therapist (T): Let's practice STOP as though you were in the school cafeteria.
>
> Jim: I walk into the cafeteria and say stop to myself.
>
> T: I mean, let's practice each letter of STOP and go over what it stands for and how you can use it to help you not feel so scared in the cafeteria.
>
> Jim: I just say "stop," "stop," "stop."
>
> T: Yes, you say "stop" to remind you what to do . . . but what does each letter stand for? What does S stand for?
>
> Jim: Scared.
>
> T: Right. And how do you know you are feeling scared before you walk into the cafeteria?
>
> Jim: Oh, when I have to go into the cafeteria I feel sick to my stomach, like I'm going to throw up—that's how I know I'm scared.
>
> T: Great, so that is your S. Let's write this on the board. Okay, now what does T stand for?
>
> Jim: Thinking, but I know all this. I don't need to say it out loud. I'll just practice it on my own.

T: I'm glad you want to practice on your own. The more you practice, the better you'll get. Let's practice together now and you can practice alone at home.

Jim: I already know how to do it. I don't need any more practice and I don't want to say it out loud. I'll just do it in my head.

T: I guess you think that I might think something bad about you if I hear your thoughts.

Jim: Yeah, you're going to think it's stupid.

T: Being scared isn't stupid, everyone feels scared about something. But your scary feelings are messing things up for you, stopping you from being with other kids and making friends. To stop feeling so scared we need to practice together.

Jim: But I don't see why I just can't do it all in my head. Why do I have to say it out loud?

T: If I was teaching you how to play the piano we couldn't just spend the lesson having you *think* about playing notes to a piece. I would need to hear how you play out loud. This way I can tell for sure whether you are playing all the right notes. Same here—practicing out loud is like making sure you are hitting the right notes. Okay? So let's hear the T note. What is your T?

Jim: I'm thinking that the other kids are staring at me and everyone will tease me and laugh at me and I want to leave. That's my T note.

T: Great! You did the S and T part of STOP really well. Now what about the O? What are the O or other thoughts or things you can do?

Jim: Everyone is eating their lunch so they are probably not staring at me and if I hear them laugh it doesn't mean they are laughing at me; no one has teased me before. But even if they do I can handle it. I can face it. I'm brave. The cafeteria may have something good to eat too! That's my O.

T: You're hitting all the right notes! What about other things that you can do—do you have an action plan that you can do when you are in the cafeteria?

Jim: I can ask Billy to eat lunch with me or I can bring a book and read if I don't have anyone to eat lunch with.

T: Very good. Now what about the P? How can you praise yourself?

Jim: My P is great job! I did it! I'm really doing good!

SUMMARY AND FUTURE DIRECTIONS

In this chapter, we have described our programmatic efforts in developing a scientifically grounded and clinically relevant psychosocial intervention approach that is usable by practitioners. Drawing on our pragmatic orientation, we have developed a transfer of control approach for implementing an exposure-based intervention for use with youth with phobic and anxiety disorders. We are currently in the process of rendering the intervention more user–clinician friendly and in conducting controlled clinical trials to provide evidence of its scientific validity.

In our future work, we intend to shift to the challenge of removing the major obstacles that impede the pathways for a successful transfer of control. One example of how we will attempt to render the pathways clearer and more direct is to target systematically the parent–child relational processes and parental anxiety–phobic disorders–symptoms in a dyadic format. It is hypothesized that treatment outcome (and maintenance) will be enhanced because training that improves these processes will serve to unblock the pathways, thereby maximizing the likelihood that the change-producing procedure will occur (and be maintained).

In particular, when relational processes, such as child management, parent–child communication, and parent–child problem solving, are maladaptive, pathways of transfer of control may be obstructed. For example, when parents and children are given an out of session exposure task and a problem arises that the child and the parent cannot solve, the opportunity for a transfer of control from therapist to the parent to the child is lost. In addition, if the problem is serious enough, the exposure may not be completed and the opportunity for a therapeutic gain may be lost.

Similarly, interventions that target the reduction of parent symptoms are likewise hypothesized to enhance treatment outcome effectiveness (and maintenance) because symptom relief in parents is likely to render pathways of transfer of control clearer and more direct. Specifically, parents who suffer from anxiety and phobic symptoms may display avoidant behavior, distorted cognitions, and subjective distress. These symptoms may make it difficult for the parent to be actively involved in his or her child's treatment program. For example, a parent who displays avoidant behavior may not be able to engage in activities (e.g., transport the child) that facilitate his or her child's exposure to objects or situations that the parent personally finds anxiety- or fear-provoking. The case of Pam's mother, presented above, provides yet another example of how parental anxiety may interfere with the child's exposure efforts. (See Ginsburg, Silverman, and Kurtines, 1995b, for additional details.)

Working with children and parents in dyads to improve their relational processes and parental symptomatology is just one example of where we see our clinical research activities heading. To the extent that these activities help to bridge the gap between research and practice, then we will have made substantial strides toward accomplishing our goals.

REFERENCES

American Psychiatric Association. (1980). *Diagnostic and statistical manual of mental disorders* (3rd ed.). Washington, DC: Author.

Barlow, D. H. (1988). *Anxiety and its disorders: The nature and treatment of anxiety and panic.* New York: Guilford Press.

Eisen, A. R., & Silverman, W. K. (1991). Treatment of an adolescent with bowel movement phobia using self-control therapy. *Journal of Behavior Therapy and Experimental Psychiatry, 22,* 45–51.

Eisen, A. R., & Silverman, W. K. (1993). Should I relax or change my thoughts?: A preliminary study of the treatment of overanxious disorder in children. *Cognitive Psychotherapy Research: An International Quarterly, 7,* 265–280.

Ginsburg, G. S., Silverman, W. K., & Kurtines, W. M. (1995a). Cognitive–behavioral group therapy. In A. R. Eisen, C. A. Kearney, & C. E. Schaefer (Eds.), *Clinical handbook of anxiety disorders in children and adolescents* (pp. 521–549). Northvale, NJ: Jason Aronson.

Ginsburg, G. S., Silverman, W. K., & Kurtines, W. M. (1995b). Family involvement in treating children with phobic and anxiety disorders: A look ahead. *Clinical Psychology Review, 15,* 457–473.

Israel, A. C., Guile, C. A., Baker, J. E., & Silverman, W. K. (1994). An evaluation of enhanced self-regulation training in the treatment of childhood obesity. *Journal of Pediatric Psychology, 19,* 737–749.

Israel, A. C., Stolmaker, L., Sharp, J. P., Silverman, W. K., & Simon, L. G. (1984). An evaluation of two methods of parental involvement in treating obese children. *Behavior Therapy, 15,* 266–272.

Kazdin, A. E., Siegel, T. C., & Bass, D. (1990). Drawing on clinical practice to inform research on child and adolescent psychotherapy: Survey of practitioners. *Professional Psychology, 21,* 189–198.

Kearney, C. A., & Silverman, W. K. (1990a). Treatment of an adolescent with obsessive–compulsive disorder by alternating response prevention and cognitive therapy. *Journal of Behavior Therapy and Experimental Psychiatry, 21,* 39–49.

Kearney, C. A., & Silverman, W. K. (1990b). A preliminary analysis of a functional model of assessment and treatment for school refusal behavior. *Behavior Modification, 14,* 340–366.

Kearney, C. A., & Silverman, W. K. (1993). Measuring the function of school refusal behavior: The School Refusal Assessment Scale. *Journal of Clinical Child Psychology, 22,* 85–96.

Marks, I. M. (1969). *Fears and phobias.* New York: Academic Press.

Rorty, R. (1979). *Philosophy and the mirror of nature.* Princeton, NJ: Princeton University Press.

Rorty, R. (1992). *Consequences of pragmatism: Essays 1972–1980.* Minneapolis: University of Minnesota Press.

Silverman, W. K. (1993, June). Behavioral treatment of childhood phobias: An update and preliminary research findings. In E. Hibbs (Chair), *Psychosocial and combined treatment for childhood disorders: Development and issues.* Symposium conducted at the meeting of the New Clinical Drug Evaluation Unit Program, Boca Raton, FL.

Silverman, W. K., & Albano, A. M. (1996). *The Anxiety Disorders Interview Schedule for Children-IV* (child and parent version). Albany, NY: Greywind Publications.

Silverman, W. K., & Eisen, A. R. (1992). Age differences in the reliability of parent and child reports of child anxious symptomatology using a structured interview. *Journal of American Academy of Child and Adolescent Psychiatry, 32,* 117–124.

Silverman, W. K., Fleisig, W., Rabian, B., & Peterson, R. A. (1991). Childhood anxiety sensitivity index. *Journal of Clinical Child Psychology, 20,* 162–168.

Silverman, W. K., Ginsburg, G. S., & Kurtines, W. M. (1995). Clinical issues in the treatment of children with anxiety and phobic disorders. *Cognitive and Behavioral Practice, 2,* 93–117.

Silverman, W. K., & Kearney, C. A. (1992). Listening to our clinical partners: Informing researchers about children's fears and phobias. *Journal of Behavior Therapy and Experimental Psychiatry, 23,* 71–76.

Silverman, W. K., & Kurtines, W. M. (1996). *Anxiety and phobic disorders: A pragmatic approach.* New York: Plenum Press.

Silverman, W. K., La Greca, A. M., & Wasserstein, S. (1995). What do children worry about? Worry and its relation to anxiety. *Child Development, 66,* 671–684.

Silverman, W. K., & Nelles, W. B. (1988). The Anxiety Disorders Interview Schedule for Children. *Journal of the American Academy of Child and Adolescent Psychiatry, 27,* 772–778.

Silverman, W. K., & Rabian, B. (1995). Test–retest reliability of the *DSM-III-R* childhood anxiety disorders symptoms using the Anxiety Disorders Interview Schedule for Children. *Journal of Anxiety Disorders, 9,* 1–12.

Silverman, W. K., & Wallander, J. L. (1993). Bridging research and practice in interventions with children: An introduction to the special issue. *The Clinical Psychologist, 46,* 165–168.

Weisz, J. R., Weiss, B., & Donenberg, G. R. (1992). The lab versus the clinic: Effects of child and adolescent psychotherapy. *American Psychology, 47,* 1578–1585.

6

BANISHING OCD: COGNITIVE–BEHAVIORAL PSYCHOTHERAPY FOR OBSESSIVE–COMPULSIVE DISORDERS

JOHN S. MARCH and KAREN MULLE

At any given time, between 1 in 100 and 1 in 200 children and adolescents suffers from obsessive–compulsive disorder (OCD; Flament, 1990). Among adults with OCD, one third to one half develop the disorder during childhood or adolescence (Rasmussen & Eisen, 1990). Because most clinicians do not see that many children with OCD, a large number of them must be suffering in silence. Consistent with this picture, the National Institute of Mental Health (NIMH) epidemiologic OCD survey suggested that few adolescents with OCD receive a correct diagnosis and even fewer receive appropriate treatment (Flament et al., 1988). This is unfortunate because effective cognitive–behavioral and pharmacological treatments are now available (March, Leonard, & Swedo, 1995a, 1995b; Rapoport, Swedo, & Leonard, 1992).

As in the third edition, revised of the *Diagnostic and Statistical Manual of Mental Disorders* (*DSM-III-R*; American Psychiatric Association, 1987), in the fourth edition (*DSM-IV*; American Psychiatric Association, 1994) OCD is characterized by recurrent obsessions, compulsions, or both that cause marked distress, interfere in one's life, or both. *Obsessions* are recur-

This work was supported in part by a Scientist Development Award for Clinicians (1 K20 MH00981-01) from the National Institute of Mental Health. Correspondence concerning this chapter should be addressed to Dr. John S. March, Department of Psychiatry, Duke University Medical Center, Box 3527, Durham, NC 27710. Internet: jsmarch@acpub.duke.edu.

rent and persistent thoughts, images, or impulses that are ego-dystonic, intrusive, and, for the most part, senseless. Obsessions are generally accompanied by dysphoric affects, such as fear, disgust, doubt, or a feeling of incompleteness and, as such, are distressing to the affected individual. Not surprisingly, young persons with OCD typically attempt to ignore, suppress, or neutralize obsessive thoughts and associated feeling by performing *compulsions*, which are repetitive, purposeful, and intentional behaviors that are performed in response to an obsession, and often conform to certain rules such as counting, or are performed in a stereotypical fashion. Generally then, *compulsions*, which can be observable repetitive behaviors such as washing, or covert mental acts such as counting, serve to neutralize or alleviate anxious discomfort or to prevent a dreaded event.

To obtain a diagnosis of OCD, an affected youth may have either obsessions or compulsions, although most have both, and the symptoms must "cause marked distress, be time-consuming (take more than an hour a day), or significantly interfere with the person's normal routine, occupational functioning, or usual social activities or relationships with others" (American Psychiatric Association, 1987, p. 245). The *DSM-IV* specifies that affected individuals recognize, at some point in the illness, that obsessions originate within the mind and are not simply excessive worries about real problems; similarly, compulsions must be seen as excessive or unreasonable. The requirement that insight be preserved is waived for children; however, persons of all ages who lack insight receive the appellation of "Poor insight type." Despite the common impression that poor insight is more common among children than adults, there is little empirical support for this view, and our clinical impression suggests the opposite, namely that young persons with OCD, like adults with OCD, generally recognize their obsessions as senseless and their compulsions as excessive.

GOALS AND ISSUES

Flexible, empirically supported cognitive–behavioral treatments have been around for many years (Kendall, 1991), and cognitive–behavioral psychotherapy (CBT) is routinely described as the psychotherapeutic treatment of choice for children and adolescents with OCD (March, 1995; Rapoport et al., 1992; Wolff & Rapoport, 1988). Because antiexposure instructions (in which patients are encouraged not to resist their obsessions and rituals) seem to attenuate the benefits of drug treatment (Marks et al., 1988), the combination of medication and CBT may be the treatment of choice for OCD in patients requiring medication (Greist, 1992), although empirical evidence favoring this proposition is lacking.

Clinicians routinely complain that children will not comply with behavioral treatments and parents routinely complain that clinicians are poorly trained in CBT. Both critiques may avoidable, given an increased understanding regarding the implementation of CBT with child and adolescents with OCD. In this chapter, we review our approach to the cognitive–behavioral treatment of children and adolescents with OCD as implemented in *How I Ran OCD Off My Land: A Guide to the Treatment of Obsessive–Compulsive Disorder in Children and Adolescents©* (March & Mulle, 1994). We begin with a brief review of the principles that inform CBT for OCD, discuss our OCD protocol, summarize our results using this protocol, and conclude by discussing directions for future research in the context of specific treatment recommendations.

PRINCIPLES OF TREATMENT

Until recently, most of the published literature concerning the cognitive–behavioral treatment of youth with OCD mixed and matched poorly defined behavioral therapies with nonbehavioral interventions, such as family therapy or supportive psychotherapy (March, 1995). Because precise specification of the goals and process of treatment, usually via a written manual or protocol, is essential to the empirical evaluation of treatment efficacy, we now turn to a discussion of the building blocks of psychotherapy for OCD: exposure-based treatments, anxiety management training, operant treatments, and nonbehavioral psychotherapies, bearing in mind that elements of each compose most treatment programs, including ours (March, Mulle, & Herbel, 1994).

Exposure

As applied to OCD, the exposure principle relies on the fact that anxiety usually attenuates after sufficient duration of contact with a feared stimulus (Dar & Greist, 1992). Thus a child with phobic symptoms regarding germs must come into and remain in contact with "germy" objects until his or her anxiety extinguishes. Repeated exposure is associated with decreased anxiety across exposure trials until the child no longer fears contact with a particular phobic stimulus. Exposure in child patients is typically implemented in a gradual fashion (sometimes termed *graded exposure*), with exposure targets under either therapist or patient control (March et al., 1994).

Response Prevention

Adequate exposure frequently depends on blocking rituals or avoidance behaviors, a process termed *response prevention* (Dar & Greist, 1992).

For example, a child with germ worries must not only touch "germy things," but must refrain from ritualized washing until his or her anxiety diminishes substantially. Many children cannot realistically avoid exposure to specific phobic stimuli, such as bathrooms for the child with contamination fears, and response prevention targets frequently can be selected independently of contrived exposure targets.

Extinction

Because blocking rituals or avoidance behaviors remove the negative reinforcement effect of the rituals or avoidance, exposure and response prevention (E/RP) technically is an extinction procedure. By convention, however, extinction is usually defined as the elimination of OCD-related behaviors through removal of parental positive reinforcement. For example, a child with reassurance-seeking rituals may ask parents to refrain from reassurance seeking. Extinction frequently produces rapid effects, but can be hard to implement when the child's behavior is bizarre or very frequent. As with E/RP, placing extinction targets under the child's control leads to increased compliance and improved outcomes (March et al., 1994).

Anxiety Management Training

Anxiety management training (AMT)—defined here as a combination of relaxation training, breathing control, and cognitive restructuring—appears to be an effective treatment for overanxious children and adolescents (Kendall, 1991). In studies with adults, however, cognitive interventions appear weak (Emmelkamp & Beens, 1991) and relaxation has been used as an active placebo (Marks, 1987). Our clinical experience suggests that AMT may contribute to the successful cognitive–behavioral treatment of younger persons with OCD by (a) targeting comorbidities that might interfere with OCD treatment, (b) facilitating exposure through reducing the amplitude of exposure-related anxiety, and (c) making exposure predictable and controllable through cognitive training (March et al., 1994).

Operant Techniques

Although operant procedures are technically defined by their effects, in clinical practice, they reduce to the application of rewards, punishments, and negative reinforcement. Positive reinforcement does not alter OCD symptoms directly, but may help encourage exposure and produce a noticeable if indirect clinical benefit. Thus, we routinely use within-session prizes and between-session rewards to recognize and solidify treatment gains (March et al., 1994). In contrast, punishment (imposition of an aversive event) or response-cost (removal of a positive event) procedures have shown themselves to be uniformly not helpful in the treatment of OCD (Harris & Wiebe, 1992). The same may be said for negative reinforcement procedures, namely the removal of an aversive event to increase a desired behavior. Conversely, the process of negative reinforcement almost always characterizes successful treatment in that a reduction in aversive OCD symptoms produces an increase in adaptive E/RP and consequent symptom reduction. Thus, children in the NIMH cohort who did well seemed to have spontaneously discovered the value of saying "no" to OCD (Flament et al., 1990), and we explicitly rely on the negative reinforcement value of OCD to negotiate graded exposure (March et al., 1994).

Modeling and Shaping

Therapist modeling—whether overt (the child understands that the therapist is demonstrating more appropriate or adaptive behavior) or covert (the therapist informally models a behavior)—helps improve compliance with in-session E/RP and generalization to between-session E/RP homework. Similarly, shaping involves the positive reinforcment of successive approximations to a desired target behavior. Modeling and shaping also reduce anticipatory anxiety and provide an opportunity for constructive self-talk before and during E/RP tasks respectively (Thyer, 1991). Because E/RP has not proven to be particularly helpful with obsessional slowness, modeling and shaping procedures may be the CBT of choice in children with this OCD subtype (Ratnasuriya, Marks, Forshaw, & Hymas, 1991). Unfortunately, relapse often occurs when therapist-assisted shaping, limit setting, and temporal speeding procedures are withdrawn (Wolff & Rapoport, 1988).

Habit Reversal

For patients with complex tic-like repeating rituals, habit reversal procedures, in which patients and their families are taught thought stopping, visualization, relaxation, competing motoric responses, and relapse prevention strategies, sometimes prove helpful alone or in combination with E/RP (Baer, 1992; Vitulano, King, Scahill, & Cohen, 1992). Habit reversal, frequently in combination with a serotonin reuptake inhibitor, can be particularly helpful in patients with OC-spectrum disorders, such as trichotillomania.

Individual and Group Psychotherapy

Insight-oriented psychotherapy appears to be an ineffective treatment for both younger (Hollingsworth, Tanguay, & Grossman, 1980) as well as older persons (Esman, 1989) with OCD. When aimed at comorbidities such as depression, or Axis II traits such as excessive dependency needs, focused psychotherapy may benefit patients by increasing compliance with E/RP. Similarly, when normal development has been adversely impacted by OCD, insight-oriented psychotherapy and focused cognitive–behavioral interventions such as assertiveness training or anger coping (Lochman, Lampron, Gemmer, & Harris, 1987) frequently become more important as OCD diminishes. Group social skills training can be helpful in those OCD patients for whom a comorbid nonverbal learning disability interferes with the pragmatics of social–emotional communication (March et al., 1990; Voeller, 1990).

Family Therapy

Despite the fact that OCD runs in families, and probably shares a genetic diathesis with Tourette's syndrome in some children (Lenane et al., 1990; Riddle et al., 1990), family psychopathology of any variety is neither necessary nor sufficient for the onset of OCD (Lenane, 1989). Nonetheless, families affect and are affected by OCD, especially if more than one family member is affected. For example, high expressed emotion may exacerbate OCD; in contrast, a calm, supportive family atmosphere facilitates improvement (Hibbs et al., 1991). Although cognitive–behavioral treatment for OCD is more commonly administered in an individual rather than in a family setting, the combination of individual and family sessions may prove best for most patients (March et al., 1994). Specific family therapy or marital therapy is appropriate only when family dysfunction or marital discord impedes the application of cognitive–behavioral interventions directed at OCD.

HOW I RAN OCD OFF MY LAND©

History

As noted earlier, practicing clinicians routinely complain that children will not comply with behavioral treatments and parents complain that clinicians do not know how to apply CBT to young persons with OCD. In part, these justifiable lamentations reflect the fact that research in this area greatly lags behind that for both CBT and pharmacotherapy in adults (Greist, 1992; Marks, 1987) and pharmacotherapy in children (March et al., 1995b; Rapoport et al., 1992). To address these and other concerns, we developed and piloted a treatment manual for children and adolescents with OCD explicitly designed to facilitate compliance, exportability, and empirical evaluation (March & Mulle, 1994). To enhance treatment outcome and to ensure reproducibility across divergent clinical settings, we also incorporated "clinical pearls" that in our experience make CBT work for young persons with OCD.

Initial Evaluation

Accurate assessment is essential to the skillful application and evaluation of cognitive–behavioral treatments (Stallings & March, 1995; Thyer, 1991). Prior to initiating CBT, every child should have an extensive neuropsychiatric evaluation. In the Program for Child and Adolescent Anxiety Disorders at Duke University, a typical evaluation includes the following: a semi-structured clinical interview of the child and his or her parents covering Axis I through V of *DSM-III-R*; multiple parent and self-report rating scales; review of school and previous mental health treatment records; and a series of computerized and pencil and paper neuropsychological tests. We also carefully consider previous psychiatric history, treatment history regarding OCD, potential interactions between specific externalizing and internalizing comorbidities (including learning disabilities), level of knowledge regarding OCD, wishes and expectations regarding treatment, and parental psychopathology.

The Treatment Protocol

Treatment takes place in four steps spread over 16 weekly sessions (Table 1). Vagueness is anathema to accomplished cognitive–behavioral therapists. Consequently, each session includes a statement of goals, review of the preceding week, provision of new information, selection of E/RP targets, therapist-assisted practice, homework for the coming week, and monitoring procedures.

TABLE 1
Treatment Protocol

Week Number	Goals
1	Establish a neurobehavioral framework
2	Making OCD the problem
3	Mapping OCD
4–15	Anxiety management training
	Exposure and response prevention
1, 6, and 12	Parent sessions
16	Graduation ceremony
22	Booster session

Session 1: Establishing a Neurobehavioral Framework

Many patients and their families come to treatment with limited or even erroneous knowledge regarding OCD, especially if they have been through an unsuccessful course of individual or family psychotherapy or have received only pharmacotherapy. Inasmuch as patient enthusiasm for CBT depends in part on careful psychoeducation, we devote most of Session 1 to placing OCD securely within a medical model, including making analogies to medical illnesses such as asthma or diabetes. Simple metaphors such as "brain hiccups" or "problems with the volume control" work well with children. In addition to discussing OCD as a medical illness, we describe our treatment program in some detail, and in so doing, we also address the indications, risks, and benefits of CBT for OCD. The intent is to link OCD, specific cognitive–behavioral interventions, and a desired outcome (namely symptom reduction), within a neurobehavioral framework. For example, a conversation between a therapist and a parent and child might go something like this:

> There are two aspects of OCD I want to tell you about. The first is that OCD is a problem in the brain. If the brain were a computer, OCD would be one small chip that kept sending out the wrong message, loudly, to the rest of the computer. In other words, one part of the brain sends thoughts or urges or feelings of fear to the rest of the body and you when it's not supposed to. Or it might send a BIG fear message instead of a small fear message when something unusual but normal occurs. Many times though, OCD will give a BIG fear message or feeling for normal everyday experiences. For example, when you go into public restrooms, your brain might tell you to be EXTRA, EXTRA careful and wash your hands many times, instead of gently reminding you to wash before you leave. These fear messages are called obsessions. The second aspect of OCD is the action you do to get the fear message to go away like washing your hands over and over again. These actions are called compulsions, and they actually make OCD stronger because you are doing what OCD wants you to do. Medication can help the first aspect of OCD by turning down the volume a little in that part of the brain. YOU can help the second aspect of OCD by bossing OCD back. During our sessions together, I will be like a coach to teach you how to boss back OCD.

Session 2: Making OCD the Target of Treatment

Reframing OCD as a neurobehavioral disorder corrects the pejorative connotation that many people associate with mental illness in general and OCD in particular. Unless carefully presented, however, the medical model has the potential to underemphasize the behavioral aspects of the illness, possibly closing the window to treatments founded on the principle that the patient must assume responsibility for undertaking exposure-based interventions. Moreover, OCD symptoms turn up in some settings and not in others, can sometimes be suppressed, and usually remain isolated from areas of normal personality functioning, all of which render the relationship between OCD and "motivation" confusing to the child and his or her parents. Hence, even when OCD is viewed as an illness children are still brought to treatment because of "troublesome behavior" in which OCD is affectively framed as a "bad habit" that the child could resist if he or she wanted.

To further emphasize the child's responsibility for resisting OCD without inviting additional "blaming" by family members, teachers, and friends, session two introduces a very simple but effective intervention: We ask the child to give OCD a nasty nickname. For example, an 8-year-old girl with contamination fears and washing rituals, who was treated successfully with CBT alone, chose to refer to OCD as "germy" (March & Mulle, manuscript in preparation). By always using a disparaging nickname to refer to OCD, the therapist externalizes OCD (White, 1984) so that OCD becomes a discrete enemy and not a bad habit. Approaching OCD in this manner allows everyone to ally with the child to "boss back" OCD. Sessions 1 and 2 also place OCD in a narrative context, opening the possibility that the child can create a new story in which he or she "authors" out OCD. Using story metaphors helps establish a therapeutic conversation between therapist and child (White & Epston, 1990), and allows the progress of treatment to be monitored through the use of informal symptom diaries.

Using the child's nickname for OCD, sample externalizing questions that a therapist might ask include:

> How has OCD bossed you around this week?
> How does OCD mess things up at home? At school? With your friends?
> How have you "Said No" to OCD?
> Please give me an example how you "beat up" on OCD this week.
> When you beat up OCD, how did it feel? What did you say to yourself?
> Who helps you boss back OCD?
> How would "name hero" boss around OCD?
> Who do you most want to know about your success in writing OCD out of your story?
> What will your life without OCD look like?

Session 3: Mapping OCD

Session 2 begins, and Session 3 completes, the process of mapping the child's experience with OCD, including specific obsessions and compulsions, triggers, avoidance behaviors, and consequences. Using a fear thermometer to generate subjective units of discomfort scores (SUDS), the child ranks his or her OCD symptoms from the easiest to hardest to "boss back," thereupon generating a stimulus hierarchy, albeit within a narrative context.

After OCD symptoms are ranked, we rely on cartographic metaphors to understand where the child's life territory is free from OCD, where OCD and the child each "win" some of the time, and where the child cedes control to OCD (see Figure 1). "Standing" with the child on territory free from "nasty nickname" allows us to strengthen the twin beliefs that we are, first, on his or her side in the struggle against OCD, and second, interested in him or her as a person who wants desperately to write OCD out of the story. In this process, we are chiefly concerned with identifying the region where the child is sometimes able to successfully "boss back" OCD, which we term the *transition zone*. In practice, the transition zone is usually defined by the lower end of the stimulus hierarchy. As treatment proceeds, the transition zone provides a dependable guide for the child to use when selecting targets for graded E/RP. With this in mind, the second and third sessions also include easy AMT and E/RP tasks designed to gauge the patient's tolerance for anxiety, level of understanding, and willingness

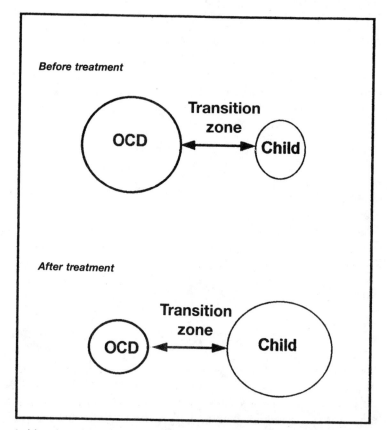

Figure 1. Mapping obsessive–compulsive disorder (OCD)

or ability to comply with treatment, and at the same time instilling the idea that it is possible to successfully resist and then "win" against OCD.

At this point in the treatment, the conversation between therapist and child might go something like this:

> When bossing back OCD, it is important that we first know what OCD looks like and how much of your life is under the control of OCD. Therefore, today and over the next few weeks, we will work together to map out OCD. We want to find out what part of your life OCD controls, what part you control, and what part is half and half. I call this half-and-half part the transition zone. Does this mapping idea make sense to you? If you have any questions, please stop me and I'll explain some more.
>
> Kids with OCD try to make their fears, feelings, and urges go away mostly by doing a ritual or by avoiding OCD's territory. To know how to beat up on OCD, we need to identify OCD's territory and what rituals or habits help out OCD. This week and next week we are going to draw a map of GERMY. There are three parts to this map. The first part is where GERMY always wins and has control (draw a large circle to indicate OCD's territory). The second part is where YOU always win, or where GERMY almost never tries to boss you around (draw a smaller circle next to the large one). The third part is in the middle and I call it the transition zone. This is where sometimes GERMY wins and sometimes YOU win (draw an arrow between the two circles). (In addition, at this point other analogies may be used to further explain the transition zone, such as the image of playing tug-of-war).
>
> Tell me about a time when GERMY tried to boss you around, but you did not do the usual ritual or habit. In other words, a time when you bossed back GERMY. What would you like to call the transition zone?

Sessions 4–16: Anxiety Management Training and Exposure and Response Prevention

The remaining sessions, covering weeks 4 through 16, rely on implementing AMT and E/RP as the child moves up the stimulus hierarchy by "bossing back" OCD. Stated differently, we explicitly frame AMT and E/RP as *the strategies* and the therapist and parents (and sometimes teacher or friends) as *the allies* in the child's "battle" against OCD. Having a strategy and allies increases confidence that treatment will be successful; confidence increases compliance with E/RP, which in turn brings about the desired outcome.

Anxiety management training, which includes relaxation, diaphragmatic breathing, and constructive self-talk ("bossing OCD"), provides the child with a "tool kit" to use during E/RP tasks. E/RP includes therapist-assisted imaginal and in vivo exposure and response prevention exercises coupled to weekly homework assignments. Because only the child can complete E/RP tasks, having the child choose E/RP targets from the transition zone maximizes compliance and avoids disruptions in treatment associated with misdirected E/RP targets. The transition zone is updated each session as the child becomes more competent and successful at resisting OCD. Positive reinforcement, modeling, shaping, and habit reversal play a supporting role, depending on the particular needs of the child. Because the therapist controls the structure of the treatment while leaving the initiative for change in the hands of the child, all parties remain intransigent against OCD, and it is difficult for the treatment itself to become an excuse for avoiding E/RP tasks.

The following dialogue gives the flavor of mapping and initiating AMT and E/RP with children and adolescents:

> I will be your coach over the next four months, and will teach you about bossing back OCD. We will work together each week and you will get to practice what you learn and choose in between sessions. How does that sound so far?
>
> While we are mapping OCD, I will give you some tools to help you boss OCD off your map. There are two big tools, and these are the most important. One is called *exposure*, and the second is called *response prevention*. Before I tell you what these two tools are, I want to assure you that you are in charge of when and how you use them. We will always boss OCD back at your pace. Now, exposure happens when you do the thing OCD is telling you not to do, like going into a public bathroom and touching the toilet or sink. Response prevention happens when you allow yourself to feel anxious without doing any of the compulsions or rituals, like washing your hands over and over again. You might think this will make your fear go up higher and higher, but actually what happens is gradually your fear and anxiety goes down until it's gone or very, very small. It is a little like riding a roller coaster, the first time you ride one it can feel scary, but if you ride the same roller coaster over and over again, after the third or fourth time, it's no longer scary. What do you think about this so far?
>
> I have some other tools to teach you that will help you during exposure and response prevention. The fear thermometer is one tool, which will help you know both how high your fear goes and how low it comes down. I will also teach you some relaxation exercises that will help your body's fear and tension. Talking back to OCD is the tool that will help your mind's fear and tension.
>
> Now there's one more tool that is very, very important, and that is a sense of humor. OCD likes to be taken very seriously, so the more we can laugh at OCD the better. Remember, as I said before, we will go at your pace, but it is important that we "go." It's okay to tackle OCD slowly, little by little, but if you stand still, then OCD wins. That's why I'm here as your coach to encourage you to keep on, so that you can beat OCD. You'd like to do that, right?

Sessions 1, 6, and 12: Involving Parents

Parents are centrally involved at Sessions 1, 6, and 12, with the latter two sessions devoted to incorporating targets for parental response prevention or extinction. Parents check in with the therapist at the beginning of each session; we also provide written feedback describing the goals of each session and the child's progress in treatment. For example, parents receive a self-help instruction booklet, incorporating written tips on how to manage themselves with respect to their child's OCD, that is keyed to the weekly homework assignments. Because treatment depends on leaving the initiative for change to the child (i.e., graded E/RP, with the child in charge of choosing E/RP targets), we work with parents to cease insisting on inappropriate E/RP tasks. We encourage parents to praise their child for resisting OCD, and strongly suggest that they pay more attention to positive elements in the child's life than to OCD, an intervention technically termed differential reinforcement of other behavior (DRO). Finally, we invite families to join the Obsessive–Compulsive Foundation, which provides a variety of useful materials for families with a member suffering from OCD.

During Sessions 6 and 12, the child works with his or her parents and the therapist to select E/RP targets from the transition zone that are specific to parental involvement with OCD. When children are simply unwilling or unable to disengage parents from OCD rituals, parents are asked to select E/RP targets, even when the child protests. This strategy requires that the therapist (a) choose manageable E/RP targets (especially when parents desire too rapid improvement) and (b) provide parents with a strategy for managing the child's distress. Although attractive to therapists who incorrectly believe that CBT involves telling patients what to do, this strategy is considerably less likely to be successful than leaving the choice of E/RP targets to the child, and should be avoided unless absolutely necessary. Drawbacks include the inevitable distress suffered by the child and the family; inability to target OCD symptoms that occur "out-of-sight" of parents; and most important, the failure of extinction-rated strategies to provide the child with a strategy for resisting OCD effectively.

To promote positive reinforcement and to extinguish punishment for OCD-related behaviors, we also endeavor to make friends and significant adults (such as teachers or grandparents) aware of the child's progress by using ceremonies of notification. Treatment ends with a graduation ceremony at week 16, followed by a booster session at week 22.

Format for Each Session

Although the time allocated to each segment will vary somewhat with the specific content of the individual sessions, a general format for conducting the session is presented in Table 2.

TABLE 2
Session Format

Session Goals	Time Allocated
Check in with child and parents	5 minutes
Review homework	5 minutes
Teach/learn tasks for week	20 minutes
Therapist-assisted practice	10 minutes
Discuss and agree on homework	10 minutes
Parent review of session and homework	10 minutes

Monitoring Outcome

We typically approach each patient as a single-subject design (Kazdin, 1982), carefully distinguishing insofar as possible the targets for psychosocial and pharmacological therapies (Maletic, March, & Johnston, 1994). All patients are assessed for specific OCD symptomatology using the symptom checklist from the Yale–Brown Obsessive–Compulsive Scale (YBOCS)—currently considered the instrument of choice for rating OCD symptoms (Goodman et al., 1989; Wolff & Wolff, 1991)—after which they are assigned a baseline score on the YBOCS, the NIMH Global Obsessive–Compulsive scale (Leonard et al., 1989), and clinical global measures of impairment, the CGI Impairment, and improvement, the CG Improvement. Young persons with OCD vary widely with respect to the impact of the disorder on the level of functioning and associated distress, and these scales provide a quantitative measure of symptom severity that permits reliable and valid assessment of treatment outcome across time. We also use a visual analogue scale—the fear thermometer—to measure expected or actual SUDS ratings to imaginal or in vivo E/RP targets. A single patient's SUDS ratings in turn define symptom baselines for evaluating outcome using single-subject designs (Kendall, 1991).

DOES IT WORK?

We recently reviewed the published literature on CBT for children and adolescents with OCD, and identified 32 investigations, most of them single case reports (March, 1995). Despite wide variations in terminology and theoretical framework, all but one showed some benefit for cognitive–behavioral interventions. Taken as a whole, the evidence to date suggests that exposure is the nugget at the heart of treatment; graded E/RP is the most effective means of guaranteeing exposure; anxiety management training and family therapy may play an adjunctive role (March, 1995).

In our initial case series, we treated 15 consecutive child and adolescent patients with OCD, most of whom were stably treated with medications at the point in which CBT was initiated (March et al., 1994). Statistical analyses showed significant benefit immediately posttreatment and at six-month follow-up. Nine patients showed at least a 50 percent reduction in symptoms on the YBOCS at posttreatment, and fell in the asymptomatic range on the NIMH Global OC Scale. Twelve patients were defined as responders—as indicated by a greater than 30% improvement on the YBOCS; not one relapsed at follow-up intervals as long as 18 months, although several had "hiccups" requiring additional CBT sessions. Booster behavioral treatment allowed medication discontinuation in six of nine asymptomatic patients, again without relapse after six months or more of follow-up observation. Clinically, patients and parents alike reported that the treatment approach was understandable, inspired confidence, and was relatively easy to implement.

Because these 15 patients represented all patients who came to us for treatment (excluding consults, hospitalized patients, those living at extended distances, and patients treated by other therapists), we concluded that our protocol-driven implementation of CBT represents a safe, effective, and acceptable treatment program for young persons with OCD. We have since initiated a series of single-subject designs with much the same results (March & Mulle, 1995), and are evaluating the question of exportability through a clinical replication study in which mental health providers from a wide variety of settings are using the *How I Ran OCD Off My Land©* manual with their clinical patients.

Even though we used reliable and valid measures of treatment outcome in a large number of patients, systematically assessed OCD symptoms pre- and posttreatment and at follow-up, and used a novel treatment manual, clinical verities inevitably constrained methodological purity. For example, patients were not always treated identically, not all patients received all measures, and we did not use structured interviews to assess comorbidity. To maximize the probability of success, we included several discrete cognitive–behavioral components in the treatment protocol, making it impossible to disentangle the relative contribution of any single component. More important, no control condition was available, and all but one patient received concurrent treatment with medications, so that the effect of behavioral psychotherapy and medication could not be evaluated independently. Thus, while this first instance of successful protocol-driven treatment for young persons with OCD is a notable advance, considerable work remains to be done.

FUTURE DIRECTIONS

It should be clear by now that the empirical evidence favoring CBT as a treatment for young persons with OCD is strong if not definitive, especially when contrasted with the ample evidence favoring pharmacotherapy in child patients (March, Leonard, & Swedo, 1995b; Rapoport et al., 1992) or CBT in adults (Dar & Greist, 1992). Future research will of necessity focus on eight areas: (a) controlled trials comparing medications, behavior therapy, and combination treatment to controls to determine whether medications and behavior therapy are synergistic or additive in their effects on symptom reduction; (b) follow-up studies to evaluate relapse rates, including examining the utility of booster CBT in reducing relapse rates in patients treated with medications, alone or in combination with CBT; (c) component analyses, such as a comparison of E/RP, AMT, and the combination, to evaluate the relative contributions of specific treatment components to symptom reduction and treatment acceptability; (d) comparisons of individual- and family-based treatments to determine which is more effective in which children; (e) development of innovative treatments for OCD subtypes, such as obsessional slowness, primary obsessional OCD, and tic-like OCD, that do not respond well to E/RP; (f) targeting treatment innovations to factors such as nonverbal learning disabilities (March et al., 1990) or family dysfunction (Hand, 1988), that constrain the application of CBT to patients with OCD; and (g) exporting research treatments such as *How I Ran OCD Off My Land©* to divergent clinical settings and patient populations to judge the acceptability and effectiveness of CBT as a treatment for child and adolescent OCD in real-world settings.

CONCLUSIONS AND RECOMMENDATIONS FOR TREATMENT

Despite conspicuous limitations in the research literature, CBT, alone or in combination with pharmacotherapy, is the psychotherapeutic treatment of choice for children and adolescents with OCD. Unlike other psychotherapies, CBT affords a logically consistent and compelling relationship among the disorder, the treatment, and the specified outcome. Moreover, as Baer points out, arguments advanced against CBT for OCD, such as symptom substitution, danger of interrupting rituals, uniformity of learned symptoms, and incompatibility with pharmacotherapy, have all proven unfounded (Baer, 1992). Perhaps the most insidious myth is that CBT is a simplistic treatment that ignores "real problems." We believe that the opposite is true. Helping patients make rapid and difficult behavior change over short time intervals takes both clinical savvy and focused treatment.

Young persons with OCD should first receive CBT that has been optimized for treating childhood-onset OCD, and if not rapidly responsive, begin pharmacotherapy with a serotonin reuptake inhibitor. To avoid the need for medication and the side effects that may accompany pharmacotherapy, however, some may prefer to begin with CBT. Others will choose medication, trying to avoid the time, effort, expense, and anxiety associated with behavior therapy. Because CBT, including booster treatments during medication discontinuation, may improve both short- and long-term outcome in medication-responsive patients, the majority will likely combine the two approaches, even in those patients for whom ongoing pharmacotherapy proves necessary.

For the clinician seeking to address the needs of his or her child and adolescent patients with OCD, we feel confident in making the following recommendations:

- Describing OCD in a medical context, that is as a neurobehavioral disorder, and not as a bad habit, improves compliance with treatment.
- Externalizing OCD helps to keep the focus on OCD as the identified problem.
- Graded E/RP is the foundation of treatment; AMT and family interventions serve an important if adjunctive function.
- E/RP and AMT are strategies in the child's struggle with OCD; the therapist, family, teacher, and friends then become the child's "allies."
- The choice of E/RP targets is best left to the child, with the caveat that the child must make progress.
- Many, if not most, patients will likely benefit from pharmacotherapy with a serotonin reuptake inhibitor.
- Multimodality OCD treatments are more precisely delivered by a multidisciplinary team, preferably but not necessarily located in a subspecialty clinic setting.

In summary, CBT for children and adolescents with OCD is emerging from the hinterland of clinical lore to the realm of efficacy and effectiveness research. Further work is clearly necessary before the empirical database concerning the application of CBT to child and adolescent subjects with OCD even remotely approximates that for adults. The availability of a manual of time-limited treatment protocols such as *How I Ran OCD Off My Land*©[1] should drive this process forward to the benefit of children and adolescents with OCD.

---

[1]*How I Ran OCD Off My Land*© is still a research tool. With additional replication studies addressing the twin issues of efficacy and exportability, we plan to revise the manual for publication as both a self-help and a therapist treatment manual.

REFERENCES

American Psychiatric Association. (1987). *Diagnostic and statistical manual of mental disorders* (3d ed., revised). Washington, DC: Author.

American Psychiatric Association. (1994). *Diagnostic and statistical manual of mental disorders* (4th ed.). Washington, DC: Author.

Baer, L. (1992). Behavior therapy for obsessive–compulsive disorder and trichotillomania: Implications for Tourette syndrome. *Advances In Neurology, 58*(333), 333–340.

Dar, R., & Greist, J. (1992). Behavior therapy for obsessive–compulsive disorder. *Psychiatric Clinics of North America, 15,* 885–894.

Emmelkamp, P. M., & Beens, H. (1991). Cognitive therapy with obsessive–compulsive disorder: A comparative evaluation. *Behaviour Research and Therapy, 29,* 293–300.

Esman, A. (1989). Psychoanalysis in general psychiatry: Obsessive–compulsive disorder as a paradigm. *Journal of the American Psychoanalytical Association, 37,* 319–336.

Flament, M. (1990). Epidemiology of obsessive–compulsive disorder in children and adolescents [Fre]. *Encephale, 11,* 311–316.

Flament, M. F., Koby, E., Rapoport, J. L., Berg, C. J., Zahn, T., Cox, C., Denckla, M., & Lenane, M. (1990). Childhood obsessive–compulsive disorder: A prospective follow-up study. *Journal of Child Psychology and Psychiatry and Allied Disciplines, 31,* 363–380.

Flament, M. F., Whitaker, A., Rapoport, J. L., Davies, M., Berg, C. Z., Kalikow, K., Sceery, W., & Shaffer, D. (1988). Obsessive compulsive disorder in adolescence: An epidemiological study. *Journal of the American Academy of Child and Adolescent Psychiatry, 27*(6), 764–771.

Goodman, W. K., Price, L. H., Rasmussen, S. A., Mazure, C., Delgado, P., Heninger, G. R., & Charney, D. S. (1989). The Yale–Brown Obsessive Compulsive Scale. II. Validity. *Archives of General Psychiatry, 46,* 1012–1016.

Greist, J. H. (1992). An integrated approach to treatment of obsessive–compulsive disorder. *Journal of Clinical Psychiatry, 53,* 38–41.

Hand, I. (1988). Obsessive–compulsive patients and their families. In M. Halloon (Ed.), *Handbook of behavioral family therapy* (pp. 231–256). New York: Guilford Press.

Harris, C., & Wiebe, D. (1992). An analysis of response prevention and flooding procedures in the treatment of adolescent obsessive–compulsive disorder. *Journal of Behavior Therapy and Experimental Psychiatry, 23,* 107–115.

Hibbs, E. D., Hamburger, S. D., Lenane, M. C., Rapoport, J. L., Kruesi, M. J., Keysor, C. S., & Goldstein, M. J. (1991). Determinants of expressed emotion in families of disturbed and normal children. *Journal of Child Psychology and Psychiatry and Allied Disciplines, 32,* 757–770.

Hollingsworth, C., Tanguay, P., & Grossman, L. (1980). Long-term outcome of obsessive–compulsive disorder in childhood. *Journal of the American Academy of Child Psychiatry, 19,* 134–144.

Kazdin, A. (1982). *Single-case research designs: Methods for clinical and applied settings.* New York: Oxford University Press.

Kendall, P. (1991). *Child and adolescent therapy.* New York: Guilford Press.

Lenane, M. C. (1989). Families in obsessive–compulsive disorder. In J. L. Rapoport (Ed.), *Obsessive–compulsive disorder in children and adolescents* (pp. 237–249). Washington, DC: American Psychiatric Press.

Lenane, M. C., Swedo, S. E., Leonard, H. L., Pauls, D. L., Sceery, W., & Rapoport, J. L. (1990). Psychiatric disorders in first degree relatives of children and adolescents with obsessive–compulsive disorder. *Journal of the American Academy of Child and Adolescent Psychiatry, 29,* 407–412.

Leonard, H. L., Swedo, S. E., Rapoport, J. L., Koby, E. V., Lenane, M. C., Cheslow, D. L., & Hamburger, S. D. (1989). Treatment of obsessive–compulsive disorder with Clomipramine and Desipramine in children and adolescents: A double-blind crossover comparison. *Archives of General Psychiatry, 46,* 1088–1092.

Lochman, J., Lampron, L., Gemmer, T., & Harris, S. (1987). Anger coping intervention with agressive children: A guide to implementation in school settings. In P. Keller & S. Heyman (Eds.), *Innovations in clinical practice: A source book* (pp. 339–356). Sarasota, FL: Professional Resource Exchange.

Maletic, V., March, J., & Johnston, H. (1994). Child and adolescent psychopharmacology. In J. Jefferson & J. Greist (Eds.), *Psychiatric clinics of North America: Annual of drug therapy* (pp. 101–124). Philadelphia: W. B. Saunders.

March, J. (1995). Behavioral psychotherapy for children and adolescents with obsessive–compulsive disorder: A review of the literature and recommendations for treatment. *Journal of the American Academy of Child and Adolescent Psychiatry, 34,* 7–18.

March, J., Johnston, H., Jefferson, J., Greist, J., Kobak, K., & Mazza, J. (1990). Do subtle neurological impairments predict treatment resistance in children and adolescents with obsessive–compulsive disorder? *Journal of Child and Adolescent Psychopharmacology, 1,* 133–140.

March, J., Leonard, H., & Swedo, S. (1995a). Obsessive–compulsive disorder. In J. March (Ed.), *Anxiety disorders in children and adolescents* (pp. 217–236). New York: Guilford Press.

March, J., & Leonard, H., & Swedo, S. (1995b). Pharmacotherapy of obsessive–compulsive disorder. In M. Riddle (Ed.), *Child psychiatric clinics of North America* (pp. 217–236). Philadelphia: W. B. Saunders.

March, J., & Mulle, K. (1994). *"How I Ran OCD Off My Land": A cognitive–behavioral program for the treatment of obsessive–compulsive disorder in children and adolescents* (Rev. 1.8). Unpublished manuscript.

March, J., & Mulle, K. (1995). Behavioral psychotherapy for obsessive–compulsive disorder: A preliminary single-case study. *Journal of Anxiety Disorders, 9,* 175–184.

March, J., Mulle, K., & Herbel, B. (1994). Behavioral psychotherapy for children and adolescents with obsessive–compulsive disorder: An open trial of a new protocol-driven treatment package. *Journal of the American Academy of Child and Adolescent Psychiatry, 33,* 333–341.

Marks, I. M. (1987). *Fears, phobias, and rituals.* New York: Oxford Unversity Press.

Marks, I. M., Lelliott, P., Basoglu, M., Noshirvani, H., Monteiro, W., Cohen, D., & Kasvikis, Y. (1988). Clomipramine, self-exposure and therapist-aided exposure for obsessive–compulsive rituals. *British Journal of Psychiatry, 152*(522), 522–534.

Rapoport, J. L., Swedo, S. E., & Leonard, H. L. (1992). Childhood obsessive–compulsive disorder. *Journal of Clinical Psychiatry, 56,* 11–16.

Rasmussen, S. A., & Eisen, J. L. (1990). Epidemiology of obsessive compulsive disorder. *Journal of Clinical Psychiatry, 53*(Suppl), 3–10.

Ratnasuriya, R. H., Marks, I. M., Forshaw, D. M., & Hymas, N. F. (1991). Obsessive slowness revisited. *British Journal of Psychiatry, 159*(273), 273–274.

Riddle, M. A., Scahill, L., King, R., Hardin, M. T., Towbin, K. E., Ort, S. I., Leckman, J. F., & Cohen, D. J. (1990). Obsessive–compulsive disorder in children and adolescents: Phenomenology and family history. *Journal of the American Academy of Child and Adolescent Psychiatry, 29,* 766–772.

Stallings, P., & March, J. (1995). Assessment of anxiety in children and adolescents. In J. March (Ed.), *Anxiety disorders in children and adolescents* (pp. 125–127). New York: Guilford Press.

Thyer, B. A. (1991). Diagnosis and treatment of child and adolescent anxiety disorders. *Behavior Modification, 15,* 310–325.

Vitulano, L. A., King, R. A., Scahill, L., & Cohen, D. J. (1992). Behavioral treatment of children and adolescents with trichotillomania. *Journal of the American Academy of Child and Adolescent Psychiatry, 31,* 139–146.

Voeller, K. (1990). Right hemisphere deficit syndrome in children: A neurological perspective. *International Journal of Pediatrics, 5,* 163–170.

White, M. (1984). Marital therapy—Practical approaches to longstanding problems. *Australian Journal of Family Therapy, 5,* 27–44.

White, M., & Epston, D. (1990). *Narrative means to therapeutic ends.* New York: Norton.

Wolff, R. P., & Rapoport, J. L. (1988). Behavioral treatment of childhood obsessive–compulsive disorder. *Behavior Modification, 12*(2), 252–266.

Wolff, R. P., & Wolff, L. S. (1991). Assessment and treatment of obsessive–compulsive disorder in children. *Behavior Modification, 15*(3), 372–393.

III

AFFECTIVE AND RELATED DISORDERS

INTRODUCTION

Depression in youth is a severely disabling illness. Because of chronicity and associated impairments, it may result in life-long struggles and, in some cases, it may even be lethal. It is estimated that 0.4 to 5.9% of children suffer from some form of depression. Rates may increase 2- or 3-fold during adolescence to approximate those of adults, with estimates suggesting 1-year prevalence rates as high as 13%. Yet, depression in children is an elusive condition. Children often cannot verbalize their distress and may express only it through somatic symptoms, irritability, withdrawal, etc. As a consequence, the child with depressive symptoms may be dismissed simply as being quiet or irritable. Many children with depression will not necessarily be troublesome to parents and teachers and, because adults may not recognize any overt symptoms, such a child can easily "fall through the cracks." In fact, the best informants in reporting depressive symptomatology are usually the children and adolescents themselves.

Depression in children and adolescents is commonly comorbid with other childhood disorders and, as such, is a very impairing disorder, both through its own symptoms and also by virtue of its associated conditions. Yet, empirically tested treatments for the condition are sparse. In this section, we present six studies using various modes of treatment for childhood and adolescent depression, including cognitive–behavioral therapy (CBT), systemic—behavioral family therapy (SBFT), and interpersonal psychotherapy for adolescents (IPT-A), as well as psychodynamic treatments.

Also in this section, we have included the treatment of a different but related disorder, anorexia nervosa. Because depression frequently cooccurs with anorexia, and because recent family genetic studies have indicated links between depression and anorexia, we have included it here. Anorexia nervosa affects .5 to 1.5 of the adolescent population, mostly girls. This can also be a lethal disorder and more treatment studies are needed to combat this illness.

Peter M. Lewinsohn and his colleagues have a long history of studying CBT for adolescents with depression. They have developed a group-administered course on adolescents coping with depression (CWD-A), based on a cognitive model of depression, and they provide good evidence of the effectiveness of the treatment. The components of this treatment—course are delineated in the chapter, and limitations and exportability of this treatment modality are discussed.

Laura Mufson and her colleagues present preliminary research on the IPT-A with depressed adolescents. This treatment was adapted from adult IPT. The treatment elements and measures used, as well as vignettes of illustrative cases, are described. Their preliminary results indicate significant decrease in symptomatology and improvement in functioning. The limitations of the study are discussed as well as the issues of generalizability of this treatment.

Jeanette Rosselló and Guillermo Bernal present a comparative study of CBT and IPT, adapted for the treatment of Puerto Rican adolescents suffering from depression. They discuss the cultural, developmental, and practical and technical issues that guided them in the adaptation of the treatments, and the step-by-step manualized treatment procedures for both modalities. Preliminary results indicate that both CBT and IPT conditions promise to be beneficial to this group of adolescents. The authors recommend that more studies be conducted to examine treatment efficacy and the factors influencing outcome, as well as to explore group modalities as potential vehicles for successful interventions.

David A. Brent and his coauthors have undertaken an ambitious program to compare three treatment modalities in adolescents with depression: cognitive—behavioral therapy (CBT), systemic—behavioral family therapy (SBFT), and nondirective supportive therapy (NST). All three treatment modalities have been manualized. Patients who experienced only partial remission received additional booster sessions. Preliminary results indicate that patients respond to all three treatments. The authors suggest that future research should develop family-based assessments and treatments, and that new therapeutic techniques must address the comorbid conditions of adolescent depression.

Kevin D. Stark and his colleagues present their work using CBT for depressed children in school settings. This treatment is tailored to address children's individual expression of the disorder and its comorbid conditions through a combination of techniques, including group and individual therapy. Procedures based on the CBT theoretical model are considered. Their studies of treatment outcomes indicate that treatments reduced depressive symptoms significantly and that gains were sustained at follow-up. The authors note the limitations of their studies, but their results provide evidence for the generalizability of CBT beyond the laboratory setting.

Arthur L. Robin and his colleagues used BFST for the treatment of anorexia nervosa. The treatment plan, which blends behavior modification, cognitive therapy, and FST, is described in detail and includes the assessment phase, the control phase (during which parents establish control over the youth's eating), weight gain management phase, and the weight maintenance phase (during which control shifts to adolescent). The results of this study seem encouraging for the younger adolescent group and for those living in two-parent households. Treatments may be less successful with older adolescents, with those living in chaotic or troubled families, or those with parents suffering from severe psychopathology.

The authors in this section use a number of treatment modalities and combination techniques for the treatment of depression and its comorbid conditions in children and adolescents. They unanimously note the need for more research in this area. In addition, more refined tools are needed to detect and differentiate aspects and risks for the disorder, because it is often difficult to diagnose depression in young children and differentiate adolescent moodiness from disorder. Furthermore, future research must examine differences in treatment effectiveness as a function of the severity of the condition and the setting in which it is identified and treated (e.g., school vs. clinic vs. inpatient setting). Although parents were involved to a varying extent in the treatment protocols of the studies presented in this section, future research may need to include parents as clients more systematically because affective disorders seem to be familial. Minority and female participants were included in all studies, but no separate gender and cultural differences were reported here.

7

A COURSE IN COPING: A COGNITIVE–BEHAVIORAL APPROACH TO THE TREATMENT OF ADOLESCENT DEPRESSION

PETER M. LEWINSOHN, GREGORY N. CLARKE, PAUL ROHDE, HYMAN HOPS, and JOHN R. SEELEY

Study of the treatment of depression in adolescents has moved from being a relatively neglected area to being a very active area of research and clinical attention (e.g., Clarizio, 1989; Matson, 1989; Mufson, Moreau, Weissman, & Klerman, 1993; Stark, 1990). A contributing factor to this increased interest is the fact that epidemiologic studies, including our own (Lewinsohn, Hops, Roberts, Seeley, & Andrews, 1993), indicate that the point and lifetime prevalence rates of affective disorders in this age group are surprisingly high and comparable to adult levels (e.g., Robins & Regier, 1991). The goal of this chapter is to describe our program of research on adolescent depression, especially the evaluation of a cognitive–behavioral treatment approach.

Our efforts in this area have consisted of a three-pronged approach. First, our group completed a large two-wave epidemiologic study, the Oregon Adolescent Depression Project (OADP; Lewinsohn, Hops, et al., 1993). The OADP is based on a representative sample of 1,709 high school adolescents (ages 14 to 18 years) who, beginning in 1987, completed a diagnostic interview and a wide array of psychosocial measures on entry into the study. After an interval of approximately one year, most of the

This research was supported by National Institute of Mental Health grants MH41278 and MH40501. Correspondence concerning this chapter should be addressed to Dr. Peter M. Lewinsohn, Oregon Research Institute, 1715 Franklin Boulevard, Eugene, OR, 97403-1983.

participants (1,507; 88.1% of the sample) returned for a second assessment. Also, the group has been involved in a major research effort to develop and test the efficacy of the Adolescent Coping With Depression Course (CWD-A; Clarke, Lewinsohn, & Hops, 1990). Since 1982, we have conducted two randomized, controlled clinical trials to evaluate the efficacy of this cognitive–behavioral group intervention for adolescent depression. In addition, we have completed a controlled pilot investigation of a school-based, group cognitive therapy prevention program to reduce the incidence of depression in adolescents who are at elevated risk for future depression.

We begin this chapter by summarizing some of the findings pertaining to adolescent depression that have emerged from our research with the OADP. Next, we review the rationale and theoretical background for our treatment approach, describe the CWD-A course for adolescents and the companion course for the parents of the depressed adolescents, and summarize results from two randomized clinical trials with 24-month follow-up. For a better understanding of the mechanisms of therapeutic change in depressed adolescents, we address additional issues, such as variables that mediate treatment seeking and the characteristics of those depressed adolescents who did not respond well to the CWD-A course. We conclude by describing initial results from a project evaluating the efficacy of a school-based intervention aimed at preventing depressive episodes in at-risk adolescents.

WHAT IS KNOWN ABOUT ADOLESCENT DEPRESSION?

On the basis of the findings of the OADP, we have been able to provide information about the point prevalence (2.9%) and the total annual incidence (7.7%) of depression in the 14-to-18-years age group (Lewinsohn, Hops, et al., 1993). The duration of major depressive disorder (MDD) episodes in adolescents is highly skewed and, in general, shorter than MDD episodes in adults (mean and median durations of 26.4 and 8.0 weeks, respectively; Lewinsohn, Clarke, Seeley, & Rohde, 1994).

Comorbidity

As is true with adults (Weissman, Bruce, Leaf, Florio, & Holzer, 1991), MDD is much more prevalent in adolescents than dysthymia: Approximately 85% of depressed adolescents have a pure MDD episode, 10% have pure dysthymia, and approximately 5% have comorbid MDD and dysthymia (Lewinsohn, Rohde, Seeley, & Hops, 1991). On the other hand, the comorbidity of depression with other psychiatric disorders (both lifetime and concurrent) is higher in adolescents than in adults (Rohde, Lewinsohn, & Seeley, 1991). The disorders most often comorbid with adolescent depression were anxiety disorders (18% in the depressed group vs. 3% in the nondepressed control group), disruptive behavior disorders (8% vs. 2%), and substance use disorders (14% vs. 2%). Temporally, depression was more likely to occur after the other disorder rather than precede it. Although adolescents whose depression was comorbid with another disorder did not have longer lasting or more severe episodes of depression, they were more likely to have a history of a suicide attempt (25% vs. 18%) and to have received treatment (45% vs. 24%) than were adolescents with a pure episode of depression.

Psychosocial Problems Associated With Being Depressed

Depression in the OADP study (operationalized either by the third edition, revised, of the *Diagnostic and Statistical Manual of Mental Disorders* [DSM-III-R; American Psychiatric Association, 1987] criteria or by elevated scores on the Center for Epidemiological Studies-Depression Scale [CES-D; Radloff, 1977]) was associated with a majority of the psychosocial measures we assessed (Lewinsohn, Roberts, et al., 1994). Specifically, the depressed middle-to-older adolescent tends to be an individual who (a) has a history of current and past psychopathology (especially substance abuse and anxiety disorders); (b) has elevated levels of problematic (including suicidal) behaviors as well as physical symptoms and illnesses; (c) manifests a depressotypic cognitive style (e.g., pessimism and internal, global, and stable attributions for failure); (d) has a negative body image and low self-esteem; and (e) is excessively emotionally dependent on others. The depressed adolescent also (a) is more self-conscious; (b) uses less effective coping mechanisms; (c) reports less social support from friends and family; (d) reports more frequent and more angry discussions with parents regarding common parent–teen issues (e.g., choice of friends); and (e) is likely to be smoking more cigarettes than are his or her nondepressed peers. Self-esteem and self-image may be more closely associated with depression in girls than in boys (Allgood-Merten, Lewinsohn, & Hops, 1990). Our results indicate that, in general, depressed adolescents manifest the same pattern of psychosocial problems associated with depression in adults.

Risk Factors for Future Depression

Many of the depression-related psychosocial variables also acted as risk factors for a future depressive episode in the OADP sample (Lewinsohn, Roberts, et al., 1994). Risk factors included past depression and anxiety disorders, current depression symptoms, internalizing and externalizing behavior problems, suicidal behavior and past suicide attempt, being female, an elevated number of major life events and daily hassles, excessive emotional reliance on others, low social support from one's family and increased conflict with parents, dissatisfaction with grades and failure to complete homework, poor physical health, poor appetite, low energy level, and an elevated number of lifetime physical symptoms. In contrast to our research with adults (Lewinsohn, Hoberman, & Rosenbaum, 1988; Lewinsohn, Steinmetz, Larson, & Franklin, 1981), the depressotypic cognitive variables made strong contributions to predicting future depression, especially pessimism, attributions, self-esteem, and to a weaker extent, self-consciousness and coping skills.

Characteristics of the Formerly Depressed

Depressed adolescents in the OADP sample who have fully recovered from their episode were found to differ from never-depressed control adolescents (Lewinsohn, Roberts, et al., 1994; Rohde, Lewinsohn, & Seeley, 1994a). The formerly depressed adolescents continued to show an elevated level of depression symptoms (e.g., mean Beck Depression Inventory [BDI; Beck, Ward, Mendelson, Mock, & Erbaugh, 1961] score = 9.3 vs. mean BDI of 5.8 for the never-depressed control adolescents). In addition, formerly depressed adolescents continued to exhibit most of the characteristics of currently depressed individuals, albeit to a reduced extent. These results stand in marked contrast with studies of adults in which these variables have not been found to characterize formerly depressed persons (e.g., Lewinsohn, Steinmetz, et al., 1981; Rohde, Lewinsohn, & Seeley, 1990). Interestingly, the formerly depressed adolescents from the OADP sample who did not receive treatment for depression continued to show a higher level of difficulties (higher levels of depression symptoms and, controlling for differences in depression level, a greater level of dysfunctional attitudes and more problems and anxiety and worry) than formerly depressed adolescents from the second clinical trial.

Relationship of Depression and Suicide Attempts

We have conducted a series of studies looking at the occurrence of suicidal behavior, especially attempts, in adolescents from the OADP sample (Andrews & Lewinsohn, 1992; Lewinsohn, Rohde, & Seeley, 1993, 1994). More girls in the OADP had a past suicide attempt (10%) than boys (4%). A history of past attempt was highest in the currently depressed (36%) compared with 21% in those with a disorder other than depression and 2% in the never mentally ill group. In our treatment samples, 30% to 40% of the adolescents reported a past suicide attempt. Treated teenagers with a past attempt had significantly ($p < .05$) higher BDI scores than the adolescent patients with no previous attempt.

RATIONALE FOR TREATMENT

Our treatment approach is rooted in behavioral as well as cognitive formulations of depression. As we have noted elsewhere (Clarke & Lewinsohn, 1989; Lewinsohn, Clarke, & Rohde, 1994), what is now being referred to as *cognitive–behavioral therapy for depression* has two sources that, at least initially, represented separate approaches: one stemming from the cognitive theories of Beck (1967), Ellis & Harper (1961), Rehm (1977), and Seligman (1975), and the other stemming from behavioral formulations such as those by Coyne (1976), Ferster (1966), and Lewinsohn (e.g., Lewinsohn, Weinstein, & Shaw, 1969).

The primary goal of cognitive therapy is to help the depressed patient become aware of what are often unconscious pessimistic and negative thoughts, depressotypic beliefs and biases, and causal attributions by which the person blames him or herself for failures but does not take credit for successes. Given the ability to recognize such depressotypic patterns, the patient is then taught how to substitute more constructive cognitions for these destructive ones. The primary goal of behavior therapy for depression is to increase engagement in behaviors that elicit positive reinforcement and that avoid negative reinforcement from the environment. This may involve teaching social and other coping skills. The Adolescent Coping With Depression (CWD-A) course combines cognitive and behavioral strategies aimed at the amelioration of the types of problems that have been shown to be problematic for depressed individuals (e.g., pessimism; internal, global, and stable attributions for failure; low self-esteem; low engagement in pleasant activities; anxiety and tension; low social support). The treatment incorporates other elements shared by cognitive–behavioral treatments such as the focus on specific and current behavior/cognitions as targets for change, homework assignments, structured intervention sessions, repeated practice of skills, use of rewards and contracts, and a relatively small (typically under 20) number of therapy sessions.

The CWD-A course is based on the premise that teaching adolescents new coping skills and strategies will allow them to counteract the putative causal factors that contribute to their depressive episodes and deal more effectively with the problems posed by their environment. Treatment is intended to help adolescents overcome their depression and to enable them to effectively deal with future occurrences of the putative risk factors.

Our approach rests on an underlying theoretical model of depression: to wit, the multifactorial model proposed by Lewinsohn, Hoberman, Teri, and Hautzinger (1985). This model assumes that there are several putative risk or etiological factors that can contribute to the final outcome of depression, none of which by themselves are necessary or sufficient preconditions. Depression is hypothesized to be the result of multiple causal elements acting either in concert or in combination; the exact mix or combination of contributory factors differs in individual cases. Depression is seen as occurring within the person–environment context, with person and environmental variables in reciprocal and continuous interaction. The model assumes the existence of vulnerabilities (person characteristics that increase the probability of becoming depressed, such as depressotypic cognitions or living in a stressful and conflictual environment) and immunities (person characteristics that reduce the probability of becoming depressed, such as effective coping, social, and other skills; engagement in pleasant activities; high self-esteem).

The model hypothesizes that the depressogenic process begins with a disruption of important adaptive behavior patterns. Undesirable life events, at the macro (major life events) and micro (daily hassles) levels, are good examples of events that can cause serious disruptions of behavior patterns that are important for the individual's everyday interactions with the environment. If such disruptions lead to increased aversive experience, they result in a negative shift of the quality of the person's life. The inability to reverse such disruptions is hypothesized to lead to dysphoria and to other cognitive (e.g., pessimism) and behavioral (e.g., passivity) manifestations.

THE TREATMENT INTERVENTION

The CWD-A is a cognitive–behavioral group intervention for depressed adolescents, adapted from the adult version of the CWD course (Lewinsohn, Antonuccio, Steinmetz-Breckenridge, & Teri, 1984). The relevance of the CWD course for depressed adolescents is suggested by research indicating that depressed adolescents show a pattern of psychosocial problems that is very similar to that manifested by depressed adults (Lewinsohn, Roberts, et al., 1994). Unique and important aspects of the course as a form of therapy include (a) its psychoeducational, nonstigmatizing nature, (b) its emphasis on skills training to promote control over one's moods and to enhance one's ability to cope with problematic situations, (c) the use of group activities and role-playing, and (d) its cost-effectiveness. In modifying the course for use with adolescents, the material was simplified with a greater emphasis on experiential learning. Homework assignments were shortened and, in contrast with the adult CWD course, no between-session reading assignments were required.

The CWD-A course includes 16 two-hour sessions conducted over an 8-week period for groups of up to 10 adolescents. Each participant receives a workbook that provides brief readings, short quizzes, structured learning tasks, and forms for the homework assignments for each session. At the end of each session, the participants are given homework assignments that are reviewed at the beginning of the subsequent session. The intent is for the skills to be practiced outside the treatment setting, thereby increasing the likelihood of generalization to everyday situations. Although evaluated in a group format, the CWD-A can be used in individual therapy.

Parent Participation

A parallel course for the parents of depressed adolescents (Lewinsohn, Rohde, Hops, & Clarke, 1991) is derived from the concepts that parents are an integral part of an adolescent's social system, and that unresolved parent–adolescent conflicts contribute to the onset, and to the maintenance, of depressive episodes. The goal of the parent course is to help parents accelerate the learning of the adolescents' new skills with support and positive reinforcement and assist in the use of these skills in everyday situations. Parents meet with their therapist weekly for 2 hours, during which the skills being taught in the adolescent course are described to them. The parents are also taught the communication and problem-solving skills being taught to the adolescent. Two joint sessions are held during which the adolescents and the parents practice these skills on issues that are salient to each family. Workbooks have been developed to guide the parents through the sessions.

COMPONENTS OF THE ADOLESCENT COURSE

In the first session, the group guidelines, the rationale for treatment, and the "social learning" view of depression (Lewinsohn, Hoberman, et al., 1985) are presented. From the very beginning, the participants are taught to monitor their moods to provide a baseline and a method for demonstrating changes in mood as a result of learning new skills and engaging in activities. The remaining sessions focus on teaching the various skills. As shown in Figure 1, although specific skills are introduced in specific sessions, discussion and practice continue throughout to facilitate the acquisition of the behavior.

Increasing Social Skills

Training in social skills, a basic deficiency in many depressed individuals (e.g., Libet & Lewinsohn, 1973), is spread throughout the course to provide a foundation on which to build other essential skills (e.g., communication). Included in social skills training are conversation techniques, planning social activities, and strategies for making friends.

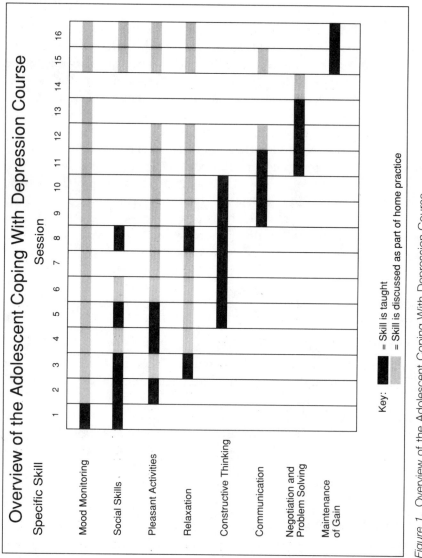

Figure 1. Overview of the Adolescent Coping With Depression Course.

Increasing Pleasant Activities

Sessions designed to increase pleasant activities are based on the assumption that relatively low rates of positive reinforcement (e.g., positive social interactions, participation in enjoyable activities) are critical antecedents of depressive episodes (see Lewinsohn, Biglan, & Zeiss, 1976). Thus, depressed individuals are urged to increase pleasant activities. To accomplish this goal, the participants are taught basic self-change skills such as self-monitoring to establish a baseline, setting realistic goals, developing a plan and a contract for behavior change, and self-reinforcement for achieving the goals of the contract. The Pleasant Events Schedule (PES, MacPhillamy & Lewinsohn, 1982), a comprehensive list of potentially pleasant activities, which has been adapted for use with adolescents, provides each participant with an individualized list of activities to be targeted for increase.

Decreasing Anxiety

Relaxation training with the Jacobson (1929) procedure is provided. This technique requires participants to alternatively tense and relax major muscle groups throughout the body. A less conspicuous method is subsequently taught that does not require progressive tension and relaxation (Benson, 1975), for use in public settings such as classrooms. Relaxation training is provided because many depressed individuals are also anxious (e.g., Maser & Cloninger, 1990), which may reduce the potential enjoyability of many pleasant activities. Furthermore, tension and anxiety often interfere with performance in social situations. Relaxation skills are taught early in the course because they are easy to learn and thus provide participants with an early success experience.

Reducing Depressogenic Cognitions

Sessions focused on depressotypic cognitions are included on the assumption that depression is caused and maintained by negative or irrational cognitive schema. The course includes adapted and simplified elements of the interventions developed by Beck and his colleagues (e.g., Beck, Rush, Shaw & Emery, 1979), Ellis and Harper (1961), and Kranzler (1974) for identifying, challenging, and changing negative thoughts and irrational beliefs. Cartoon strips with popular characters that appeal to adolescents (e.g., Garfield the cat, Bloom County) are used to illustrate depressotypic negative thoughts and positive thoughts that may be used to counter them.

TABLE 1
Measures Assessed in Clinical Trials 1 and 2

Measure	Clinical Trial	Number of Items[a]	Reference
Beck Depression Inventory	1, 2	21	Beck et al., 1961
Center for Epidemiologic Studies—Depression Scale	1, 2	7, 20	Radloff, 1977
Self-Rated Depression Scale	2	1	
Child Behavior Checklist	1, 2	113	Achenbach & Edelbrock, 1983
Conduct Disorder Scale	2	6	Unpublished measure
State Anxiety Questionnaire	1, 2	10	Spielberger, 1970
Worry Scale	2	5	Unpublished measure
Hypomanic Personality Scale	2	15	Eckblad & Chapman, 1986
Hypochondriasis	2	8	Pilowsky, 1967
Suicidal Ideation Scale	2	4	Lewinsohn, Garrison, et al., 1989
Subjective Probability Questionnaire	1, 2	5	Muñoz & Lewinsohn, 1988
Dysfunctional Attitude Scale	1, 2	10	Weissman & Beck, 1978
Personal Beliefs Inventory	1	5	Muñoz & Lewinsohn, 1976
Frequency of Self-Reinforcement Attitudes Scale	1, 2	5, 10	Heiby, 1982
Perceived Control	2	3	Pearlin & Schooler, 1978
Self-Consciousness Scale	2	9	Fenigstein et al., 1975
Physical Appearance Evaluation Subscale of the Body Self-Relations Questionnaire	2	3	Winstead & Cash, 1984
Body Parts Satisfaction Scale	2	3	Berscheid et al., 1973
Rosenberg Self-Esteem Inventory	2	3	Rosenberg, 1965
Coping Skills	2	17	Rohde, Lewinsohn, et al., 1990
Pleasant Events Schedule	1, 2	320	MacPhillamy & Lewinsohn, 1982
Interpersonal Events Schedule	1	20	Youngren et al., 1976
Unpleasant Events Schedule	2	20	Lewinsohn, Mermelstein, et al., 1985

TABLE 1 (*continued*)
Measures Assessed in Clinical Trials 1 and 2

Measure	Clinical Trial	Number of Items[a]	Reference
Major Life Events Schedule	2	15	Holmes & Rahe, 1967; Sandler & Block, 1979
Issues Checklist	1, 2	45	Robin & Weiss, 1980
Perceived Competence Scale	1	7	Harter, 1982
Moos Family Environment Scale	2	5	Moos, 1974
Conflict Behavior Questionnaire	2	11	Prinz et al., 1979
Parent Attitude Research Instrument	2	6	Schaefer, 1965
Parental Criticism	2	1	
UCLA Loneliness Scale	2	8	Russell et al., 1980
Self-Perceived Competence Scale	2	21	Lewinsohn, Mischel, et al., 1980
Expected BDI	2	21	Steinmetz et al., 1983
Marlowe-Crowne Social Desirability Scale	1, 2	6, 2	Crowne & Marlowe, 1960
MMPI Lie Scale	1, 2	5, 10	Hathaway & McKinley, 1951
Infrequency Scale	1, 2	5	Jackson, 1976
Shipley-Hartford Vocabulary Test	1, 2	20, 10	Zachary, 1986

Note. [a]When two numbers are given, they refer to the number of items in Clinical Trials 1 and 2, respectively.

Resolving Conflict

Six sessions involve teaching communication, negotiation, and conflict-resolution skills for use with parents and peers. Parent–adolescent conflict increases as adolescents assert their independence (Steinberg & Silverberg, 1986). Unsuccessful problem resolution paired with increased intrafamilial conflict may contribute to the occurrence of depression within this age group. The specific techniques used in the course were derived from techniques used in behavioral marital therapy (e.g., Gottman, 1979; Jacobson & Margolin, 1979; Weiss, Hops, & Patterson, 1973) and their adaptations for use with parents and children (e.g., Forgatch, 1989; Robin & Foster, 1989). Communication training focuses on the acquisition of positive behaviors, such as paraphrasing to verify the message, active responding, appropriate eye contact, and the deletion and correction of nonproductive behaviors such as accusations, interruptions, and put-downs. The participants are taught negotiation and problem-solving techniques, such as defining the problem without criticism, brainstorming alternative solutions, evaluating and mutually agreeing on a solution, and specifying the agreement with the inclusion of positive and negative consequences for compliance and noncompliance, respectively. All of these techniques are practiced during the two joint parent–adolescent sessions in which the adolescent and parent leaders participate as facilitators.

Planning for the Future

The final two sessions focus on the integration of skills, the antici-pation of future problems, the development of a life plan and goals, and the prevention of relapse. Aided by the group leader, each adolescent de-velops a written, personalized "emergency plan" detailing the steps he or she will take to counteract renewed feelings of depression in the future.

BOOSTER SESSIONS

A difficult and unresolved problem in the treatment of depressed adults is the high probability of a recurrence of depression (Lewinsohn, Zeiss, & Duncan, 1989). Consequently, treatment programs should include procedures aimed at relapse prevention. Our initial assumption was that the high rate of relapse noted in adults also characterizes depressed ado-lescents. Therefore, for the second clinical trial, we adapted relapse pre-vention procedures derived from the meager published literature on de-pression (e.g., Wilson, 1992) and the larger number of studies conducted on relapse prevention in the addictive disorders (e.g., Marlatt & Gordon, 1985). From this literature, it appears that three factors affect the main-tenance of treatment gains: (a) the continued self-monitoring of behaviors and of situations that may affect this maintenance; (b) relatively pervasive and persistent lifestyle changes designed to cope with future stressful events; and (c) the level of social support. Thus, depressed individuals who are treated successfully should be provided with coping skills that allow them to be aware of situations that are likely to cause dysphoria, recognize the early manifestations of depression, and reinstitute the appropriate tech-niques from the intervention to cope with the situation.

In view of these considerations, we prepared a relapse prevention protocol, part of which includes booster sessions offered at 4-month inter-vals over a 2-year period. Because individuals may vary in their level of functioning and types of continuing problem situations, the booster sessions are individualized. Each booster may include up to two weekly 2-hour ses-sions. Prior to the first booster session, the participant completes a brief paper-and-pencil questionnaire designed to provide information on his or her current mood level and psychosocial functioning, current target complaints, and recollection and use of specific skills taught during the course. The latter includes information about the level of the adolescent's knowledge of specific course components, the adolescent's use of these skills during the previous 4 months, and a more general assessment of their functioning.

During the first booster session, the therapist meets separately with the parents and with the adolescent to gather more information on the adolescent's functioning, including how well he or she dealt with stressful situations. This session is also used to present some of the findings from the assessment, and to present plans for use of the rest of the session and Session 2. On the basis of all of the information, the therapist determines whether the booster should include the parents and which specific skills will be emphasized. The rest of the first session focuses on how specific skills learned in class can be used to cope with the specific problematic situations that have come up. Specific techniques and their purposes are reviewed with special reference to specific problem areas. For example, if parent–adolescent conflict remains a problem, the conflict resolution skills are discussed and practiced again. If anxiety remains a problem, the therapist reviews the relaxation procedures. As in the regular class, homework assignments are made and reviewed at the beginning of Session 2. The second session is completed with the formulation of a plan of action to cope with problems for the adolescent and the parents.

TREATMENT EFFECTIVENESS

The First Clinical Trial

Our first controlled clinical trial (Lewinsohn, Clarke, Hops, & Andrews, 1990) included 59 adolescents meeting Research Diagnostic Criteria/DSM-III (American Psychiatric Association, 1980) criteria for MDD or intermittent depression who were assigned randomly to one of three treatment conditions: (a) a group for adolescents only ($n = 21$); (b) an identical group for adolescents, but with their parents enrolled in a separate parent group ($n = 19$); and (c) a wait-list condition ($n = 19$). Participants and their parents completed extensive diagnostic and psychosocial measures at intake, posttreatment, and at 1-, 6-, 12-, and 24-month posttreatment. Overall multivariate analyses demonstrated significant pre- to posttreatment change on all dependent variables across treatment conditions. Subsequent planned comparisons indicated that all significant subject improvement was accounted for by the two active treatment conditions (mean scores on the BDI for the two active treatments dropped from 21.5 to 8.3; effect size = 1.18). Contrary to expectation, with only one exception, differences between the Adolescent Only and the Adolescent and Parent conditions on diagnostic and other outcome variables failed to attain statistical significance. The one exception was that parents assigned to active treatment reported fewer problems on the Child Behavior Checklist (Achenbach & Edelbrock, 1983) at the end of therapy. Forty-six percent of the treated adolescents no longer met *DSM-III* criteria for an affective disorder by the end of the CWD-A course (compared with 5% in the waitlist condition). By 6 months posttreatment, the rate of recovery for the treated adolescents increased to 83%. Two-year follow-up data indicated that treatment gains were maintained for the adolescents in the two active interventions, with very few adolescents relapsing.

The Second Clinical Trial

Our second clinical trial (Lewinsohn, Clarke, & Rohde, 1994) involved 96 adolescents meeting *DSM-III-R* (American Psychiatric Association, 1987) criteria for MDD or dysthymia. The goals of this trial were similar to the first clinical trial, with two modifications. First, the treatment protocol was revised to be more user friendly, with skills training interwoven throughout the course rather than presented in monolithic segments. Second, we evaluated the impact of a second independent variable; at the end of treatment, the patients were randomly assigned to one of three 24-month follow-up conditions. In the first follow-up condition, assessments and subsequent booster sessions, as described earlier in the chapter, occurred every 4 months. The second condition consisted of the 4-month follow-up assessments only, without boosters. The third condition consisted of two annual assessments, also without boosters. The design of the study made it possible to evaluate the three treatments through the end of treatment and to compare the three follow-up conditions.

As in the first clinical trial, recovery rates at posttreatment in the two treatments were superior to those of the wait-list control. Likewise, the two active treatments did not significantly differ (mean BDI change for the two active treatment dropped from 26.4 to 11.6; effect size = .39). A total of 67% of the treated teenagers no longer met criteria at posttreatment versus 48% in the wait-list (65% in the Adolescent Only condition vs. 69% in the Adolescent plus Parent condition). Recovery and relapse rates in the three follow-up conditions did not differ. Similarly, rates of recovery and relapse for girls and boys did not differ. By 12-months posttreatment, 81.3% of the adolescents had recovered; 97.5% had recovered by 24 months. Among the adolescents who had recovered, the rate of relapse at 12 months was 9.4%; at 24 months, 20.4%.

The Role of Booster Sessions

Unexpectedly, the booster sessions failed to impact outcome (i.e., recovery and relapse rates). We suggest several potential explanations for this outcome. First, the majority of treated adolescents were functioning well during the follow-up period. Given the high recovery and relatively low relapse rates associated with the initial intervention, it was difficult for the booster sessions to improve on this rate. Second, the time interval between the end of treatment and the first booster (4 months) may have been too long to maintain the interest of adolescents and parents in the booster sessions. The delay until the first booster session was likely most difficult to endure for the teenagers who were still depressed or having other difficulties immediately posttreatment. Third, if adolescents did not respond to the initial treatment, it is possible that the family, the adolescent, or both sought treatment elsewhere rather than wait 4 months for "more of the same" booster sessions.

In spite of the negative findings, we are still committed to the idea that the provision of booster sessions to maintain therapy gains is important. Based on our experience, we propose the following solutions:

1. Have group leaders end the course with individual sessions for each adolescent, to get his or her perceptions of the course and provide closure and perhaps some continuity for those who will be involved in individual booster sessions. This would change the emphasis from prevention to a continuation of treatment.
2. Limit individual booster sessions to those adolescents who are still experiencing depression symptoms even though they no longer meet diagnostic criteria.
3. Have boosters begin at monthly intervals and reduce frequency as appropriate for individuals.
4. Adjust the frequency of sessions as a function of each adolescent's level of problematic behaviors.
5. As an alternative, conduct group boosters with the same membership as the original treatment groups, which will capitalize on the positive group relationships formed during the CWD-A course sessions.

What Stimulates Treatment Seeking?

In an effort to determine the factors that lead patients to treatment, participants in the second clinical treatment trial were compared with 42 nontreated adolescents with depression from the OADP data set on assessed constructs. Although both groups met criteria for MDD, the treated patients had, on average, higher Hamilton Rating Scale for Depression scores and reported greater levels of major stressful events, heightened self-consciousness, less social self-confidence, less perceived social support from their friends, and more conflicts with parents. These findings suggest the hypothesis that treatment seeking in depressed teens is triggered by stressful life events in the context of low social support. In other words, it appears that the circumstances surrounding a depressive episode set the stage for treatment seeking in adolescents with depression.

What do Depressed Teenagers Want from Therapy?

As part of the intake interview, teenagers and their parents reported independently on the specific difficulties that they wanted to address most in therapy. The four most common complaint categories reported by teenagers were (a) dysphoric mood (45%), (b) poor self-esteem (33%), (c) interpersonal difficulties (e.g., problems with schoolmates, conflict with parents, 32%), and (d) decreased effectiveness and coping (32%). The same four problem categories were also the most frequent problems reported by the parents (percentages were 33%, 62%, 38%, and 54%, respectively). Although the treated boys and girls did not differ on the average number of reported target complaints, girls reported significantly more problems with poor self-esteem (42% of the girls vs. 21% of the boys), whereas boys reported significantly more problems with reduced effectiveness and coping (39% of the boys vs. 21% of the girls).

Who Responds to Treatment?

Using data from the first clinical trial, we identified variables that predict change in self-reported depression levels (Clarke et al., 1992). Greater change in BDI from pre- to posttreatment had a significant univariate association with a greater number of past diagnoses, a younger onset age of first depression, parent involvement in treatment, being female, fewer dysfunctional attitudes, and living in single-parent or blended family homes. In a simultaneous multivariate regression analysis predicting BDI change, the multiple R was .84 ($p < .0001$). Improvement was associated significantly with (a) a greater number of past psychiatric diagnoses, (b) parent involvement in treatment, and (c) younger age at onset of first depressive episode. The significance of parental involvement in treatment seems to contradict the earlier findings that outcome for the Adolescent plus Parent condition did not differ from the Adolescent Only condition. It needs to be kept in mind that multivariate analyses were conducted in the original report, whereas only the BDI was used for predicting change. This finding is tentative pending cross validation.

In a discriminant function analysis with posttreatment recovery, as per diagnosis as the dependent variable, the overall canonical correlation was $R = .63$ ($p < .005$). Better outcome (i.e., no diagnosis of affective disorder at posttreatment) was associated with (a) lower initial levels of self-reported depression, (b) lower initial state anxiety, (c) higher initial enjoyment and frequency of pleasant activities, and (d) more rational thoughts at intake. The differences in prediction for two somewhat different but basically related dependent measures is intriguing. Analyses to clarify this difference are in progress.

In the second clinical trial, the dependent variable was represented by an aggregate of BDI and Hamilton Depression Rating Scale (Hamilton, 1960). Pretreatment variables with significant univariate associations with lower scores on the depression aggregate at posttreatment included higher enjoyment and frequency of pleasant activities, no past history of suicide attempt, younger age, being male, lower intake depression levels, and more rational thoughts. In a simultaneous multiple regression analysis predicting the depression measure at posttreatment, the multiple $R = .57$ ($p < .001$). Variables chosen in the multivariate analyses indicated that improvement was uniquely associated with (a) younger age, (b) higher initial enjoyment and frequency of pleasant activities, and (c) being male. A lower initial level of depression, greater enjoyment and frequency of pleasant activities, and more frequent endorsement of rational thoughts predicted positive treatment response in both samples. Unfortunately, the lack of cross-validation for the remaining variables is not uncommon in treatment outcome research (e.g., Garfield & Bergin, 1986).

Impact of Initial Severity

We also evaluated the impact of pretreatment depression severity level on outcome in the two clinical trials (Rohde, Lewinsohn, & Seeley, 1994b). Based on the findings of Elkin et al. (1989), our hypotheses were that differences between the two active treatments and between active treatment conditions versus a wait-list control condition would be greater in the more severely depressed group. In the second clinical trial, improvement for the two active treatment conditions in comparison with the control condition was greater in the more severely depressed group than in the less severely depressed group. This finding was not present in the first clinical trial. Our prediction that the relative effectiveness of the two treatments would be accentuated in the more severely depressed group was not supported in either clinical trial. It would therefore be premature to advise that treatment outcome studies be restricted to only the more severely depressed individuals.

LIMITATIONS

Although highly encouraging, there are several limitations of our research that need to be recognized. For one, the CWD-A course needs to be evaluated with adolescents who have other disorders comorbid with their depression. At this point, we cannot generalize our results to adolescents who, in addition to depression, also exhibit serious delinquency or substance abuse problems. In addition, this treatment approach needs to be evaluated and modified for use with racial and ethnic minorities. Research also needs to evaluate whether the CWD-A intervention can be used in conjunction with other modes of therapy (e.g., family therapy). When used in conjunction with other treatment, the clinician should be sensitive to the time demands of the CWD-A intervention (i.e., 4 hours of group per week plus home practice assignments).

TREATMENT APPLICATIONS

We recognize that in its current form, the CWD-A intervention may be difficult for many clinicians to implement. In a clinic setting, the material can be presented to a group either as it currently exists (i.e., 16 2-hour group sessions), or as 30 to 35 50-minute sessions. This material can also be used with individual clients, in which case the material covered in most 2-hour group sessions will be covered in a single hour (because of time saved from not having to review homework assignments for 6 to 10 adolescents). One advantage to the use of individual therapy is that clinicians can personalize treatment to the adolescent rather then administering the entire intervention. In selecting the modules for use, a therapist might consider building on strengths rather than focusing on deficits. Our research with adults (Zeiss, Lewinsohn, & Muñoz, 1979) has shown that various forms of depression treatment have nonspecific improvement effects (e.g., cognitive therapy resulted in improved cognitive functioning but so did therapy focused on interpersonal skills). Given our emphasis on in-session role-play involving multiple group members, one disadvantage to individual therapy is that the clinician will need to assume a dual role of therapist and role-play partner.

The group format appears to play a powerful role for many of our clients, who often have had little or no opportunity to talk candidly with other adolescents who are wrestling with the same types of difficulties. The group, psychoeducational format also appears to be less stigmatizing and threatening than standard psychotherapy. To be used in a group format, the clinician probably needs to have some ongoing relationship with an institution, which could be a school district, clinic, health maintenance organization (HMO), or county or state facility (e.g., county juvenile detention center). One alternative is to run a semi–open-ended group, in which an introductory session is conducted individually with adolescents, who are then incorporated into an ongoing group that is working its way through the various modules. New members are introduced into the group only at the time of changing treatment modules. Adolescents may "graduate" at different times, as they complete an individual cycle through all the personally relevant skill modules. However, they could remain in the group at the therapist's discretion to repeat modules that were either especially difficult or useful.

Given that the majority of depressed adolescents neither seek nor receive treatment, an active outreach component is necessary. The therapist should pursue a vigorous, multifaceted outreach approach, which may include approaches to school personnel (teachers and counselors), health care professionals (pediatricians, family practitioners, child psychiatrists), and the media. We distribute brochures and posters to schools and make presentations to school counselors. Our experience has been that school and health care professionals are very receptive to short presentations at staff meetings and training sessions.

AN ALTERNATIVE TO PSYCHOTHERAPY: SCHOOL-BASED PREVENTION

Following the success of our tertiary treatment outcome research (Lewinsohn, Clarke, et al., 1990), we initiated a randomized trial to examine the efficacy of a school-based, group cognitive therapy prevention program in reducing the prospective incidence of unipolar affective disorders and symptomatology in high school adolescents at risk for future depression (Clarke et al., 1995). Ninth grade adolescents in three suburban high schools were identified as being potentially at risk for depression through a 2-stage procedure: (a) a schoolwide administration of the CES-D (Radloff, 1977) to 1,652 adolescents in 9th grade health classes; and (b) a subsequent confirmatory structured diagnostic interview (the K-SADS) for the 222 adolescent with an adolescent-appropriate CES-D cutoff score of 24 or greater. Forty-six adolescents (22.2%) were currently depressed and were thus not appropriate candidates for prevention. The 172 adolescents identified as not currently depressed but with elevated CES-D scores, who were judged to be at risk for future depression (Roberts, 1987), were invited to participate in the prevention study; 150 accepted and were assigned randomly to either (a) a 15-session, after-school, cognitive–behavioral preventive intervention ($n = 76$); or (b) a usual care control condition ($n = 74$). The active intervention (Clarke & Lewinsohn, 1990) consisted of 15 45-minute sessions in which at-risk adolescents were taught cognitive therapy techniques to identify and challenge negative or irrational thoughts that may contribute to the development of future affective disorder. The intervention was modified from the relevant sessions of the CWD-A course (Clarke et al., 1990).

Survival analysis results indicate significantly fewer cases of either MDD or dysthymia in the experimental group (Mantel-Cox $\chi^2 = 2.72$, p

< .05) at 12-month follow-up, with affective disorder total incidence rates of 14.5% for the active intervention versus 25.7% for the control condition. To our knowledge, this is the first published report of the prevention of unipolar affective disorder in high school adolescents.

CONCLUSION

Although adolescent depression is common and has a serious impact on functioning, it is often unrecognized and untreated. A cognitive–behavioral intervention, the Adolescent Coping With Depression course has been shown to be an effective, nonstigmatizing, and cost-efficient treatment for depression. We believe that with relatively minor modifications, this form of therapy can be successfully implemented in clinical practice. We are very interested in hearing about the results of efforts of clinical psychologists to implement the intervention in clinics, private practice, or schools.

REFERENCES

Achenbach, T. M., & Edelbrock, C. S. (1983). *Manual for the Child Behavior Checklist and Revised Child Behavior Profile*, Burlington: University of Vermont, Department of Psychiatry.

Allgood-Merten, B., Lewinsohn, P. M., & Hops, H. (1990). Sex differences and adolescent depression. *Journal of Abnormal Psychology, 99*, 55–63.

American Psychiatric Association. (1980). *Diagnostic and statistical manual of mental disorders* (3rd ed.). Washington, DC: Author.

American Psychiatric Association. (1987). *Diagnostic and statistical manual of mental disorders* (3rd ed., rev.). Washington, DC: Author.

Andrews, J. A., & Lewinsohn, P. M. (1992). Suicidal attempts among older adolescents: Prevalence and co-occurrence with psychiatric disorders. *Journal of the American Academy of Child and Adolescent Psychiatry, 31*, 655–662.

Beck, A. T. (1967). *Depression: Clinical, experimental, and theoretical aspects.* New York: Harper & Row.

Beck, A. T., Rush, A. J., Shaw, B. F., & Emery, G. (1979). *Cognitive therapy of depression.* New York: Guilford Press.

Beck, A. T., Ward, C. H., Mendelson, M., Mock, J. E., & Erbaugh, J. K. (1961). An inventory for measuring depression. *Archives of General Psychiatry, 4*, 561–571.

Benson, H. (1975). *The relaxation response.* New York: William Morrow.

Berscheid, E., Walster, E., & Bohrnstedt, G. (1973). The happy American body: A survey report. *Psychology Today, 7*, 119–131.

Clarizio, H. R. (1989). *Assessment and treatment of depression in children and adolescents.* Brandon, VT: Clinical Psychology Publishing.

Clarke, G. N. (1990a). *Chasing the blues* [Videotape]. Eugene, OR: Independent Video Services.

Clarke, G. N. (1990b). *Reversing the spiral of the blues* [Videotape]. Eugene, OR: Independent Video Services.

Clarke, G. N., Hawkins, W., Murphy, M., Sheeber, L. B., Lewinsohn, P. M., & Seeley, J. R. (1995). Targeted prevention of unipolar depressive disorder in an at-risk sample of high school adolescents: A randomized trial of a group cognitive interview. *Journal of American Academy of Child and Adolescent Psychiatry, 34,* 312–321.

Clarke, G. N., Hops, H., Lewinsohn, P. M., Andrews, J. A., Seeley, J. R., & Williams, J. A. (1992). Cognitive–behavioral group treatment of adolescent depression: Prediction of outcome. *Behavior Therapy, 23,* 341–354.

Clarke, G. N., & Lewinsohn, P. M. (1989). The Coping with Depression Course: A group psychoeducational intervention for unipolar depression. *Behaviour Change, 6,* 54–69.

Clarke, G. N., & Lewinsohn, P. M. (1990). *Instructor's manual for the Adolescent Coping with Stress Course for the secondary prevention of depression.* Unpublished manuscript, Oregon Health Sciences University.

Clarke, G. N., & Lewinsohn, P. M. (1991a). *The adolescsent coping with stress class: Leader manual.* Unpublished manuscript, Child Psychiatry Clinic, Portland, OR.

Clarke, G. N., & Lewinsohn, P. M. (1991b). *Adolescent depression health class curriculum.* Unpublished manuscript, Child Psychiatry Clinic, Portland, OR.

Clarke, G. N., & Lewinsohn, P. M. (1991c). *The Coping with Stress Course adolescent workbook.* Unpublished manuscript, Child Psychiatric Clinic, Portland, OR.

Clarke, G. N., Lewinsohn, P. M., & Hops, H. (1990). *Instructor's manual for the Adolescent Coping with Depression Course.* Eugene, OR: Castalia Press.

Coyne, J. C. (1976). Toward an interactional description of depression. *Psychiatry, 39,* 28–40.

Crowne, D. P., & Marlowe, D. (1960). A new scale of social desirability independent of psychopathology. *Journal of Consulting Psychology, 24,* 349–354.

Eckblad, M., & Chapman, L. J. (1986). Development of a scale for hypomanic personality and validation. *Journal of Abnormal Psychology, 95,* 214–222.

Elkin, I., Shea, M. T., Watkins, J. T., Imber, S. D., Sotsky, S. M., Collins, J. F., Glass, D. R., Pilkonis, P. A., Leber, W. R., Docherty, J. P., Feister, S. J., & Parloff, M. B. (1989). National Institute of Mental Health Treatment of Depression Collaborative Research Program: General effectiveness of treatments. *Archives of General Psychiatry, 46,* 971–982.

Ellis, A., & Harper, R. A. (1961). *A guide to rational living.* Hollywood, CA: Wilshire Book.

Fenigstein, A., Scheier, M. F., & Buss, A. H. (1975). Public and private self-consciousness: Assessment and theory. *Journal of Consulting and Clinical Psychology, 43*, 522–527.

Ferster, C. B. (1966). Animal behavior and mental illness. *Psychological Record, 16*, 345–356.

Forgatch, M. S. (1989). Patterns and outcome with family problem solving: The disrupting effect of negative emotions. *Journal of Marriage and the Family, 51*, 115–124.

Garfield, S. L., & Bergin, A. E. (1986). *Handbook of psychotherapy and behavior change.* New York: John Wiley & Sons.

Gottman, J. M. (1979). *Marital interaction: Empirical investigations.* San Diego, CA: Academic Press.

Hamilton, M. A. (1960). A rating scale for depression. *Journal of Neurology and Neurosurgical Psychiatry, 23*, 56–62.

Harter, S. (1982). The Perceived Competence Scale for Children. *Child Development, 53*, 87–97.

Hathaway, S. R., & McKinley, J. C. (1951). *The Minnesota Multiphasic Personality Inventory Manual.* New York: Psychological Corporation.

Heiby, E. M. (1982). A self-reinforcement questionnaire. *Behaviour Research and Therapy, 20*, 347–401.

Holmes, T. H., & Rahe, R. H. (1967). *Schedule of recent experiences.* Seattle: University of Washington Press.

Jackson, D. N. (1976). *Jackson Personality Inventory Manual.* Port Huron, MI: Research Psychologists Press.

Jacobson, E. (1929). *Progressive relaxation.* Chicago: University of Chicago Press.

Jacobson, N. S., & Margolin, G. (1979). *Marital therapy: Strategies based on social learning and behavior exchange principals.* New York: Brunner/Mazel.

Kranzler, G. (1974). *You can change how you feel.* Eugene, OR: RETC Press.

Lewinsohn, P. M., Antonuccio, D. O., Steinmetz-Breckenridge, J., & Teri, L. (1984). *The coping with depression course: A psychoeducational intervention for unipolar depression.* Eugene, OR: Castalia Press.

Lewinsohn, P. M., Biglan, A., & Zeiss, A. (1976). Behavioral treatment of depression. In P. Davidson (Ed.) *Behavioral management of anxiety, depression, and pain* (pp. 91–146). New York: Brunner/Mazel.

Lewinsohn, P. M., Clarke, G. N., Hops, H., & Andrews, J. (1990). Cognitive-behavioral group treatment of depression in adolescents. *Behavior Therapy, 21*, 385–401.

Lewinsohn, P. M., Clarke, G. N., & Rohde, P. (1994). Psychological approaches to the treatment of depression in adolescents. In W. M. Reynolds & H. F. Johnston (Eds.), *Handbook of depression in children and adolescents* (pp. 309–344). New York: Plenum Press.

Lewinsohn, P. M., Clarke, G. N., Seeley, J. R., & Rohde, P. (1994). Major depression in community adolescents: Age at onset, episode duration, and time to recurrence. *Journal of the American Academy of Child and Adolescent Psychiatry, 33,* 809–818.

Lewinsohn, P. M., Garrison, C. Z., Langhinrichsen, J., & Marsteller, F. (1989). *The assessment of suicidal behavior in adolescents: A review of scales suitable for epidemiologic and clinical research.* Unpublished manuscript.

Lewinsohn, P. M., Hoberman, H. M., & Rosenbaum, M. (1988). A prospective study of risk factors for unipolar depression. *Journal of Abnormal Psychology, 97,* 251–264.

Lewinsohn, P. M., Hoberman, H., Teri, L., & Hautzinger, M. (1985). An integrative theory of depression. In S. Reiss & R. Bootzin (Eds.), *Theoretical issues in behavior therapy* (pp. 331–359). San Diego, CA: Academic Press.

Lewinsohn, P. M., Hops, H., Roberts, R. E., Seeley, J. R., & Andrews, J. (1993). Adolescent psychopathology: I. Prevalence and incidence of depression and other *DSM-III-R* disorders in high school students. *Journal of Abnormal Psychology, 102,* 133–144.

Lewinsohn, P. M., Mermelstein, R. M., Alexander, C., & MacPhillamy, D. (1985). The Unpleasant Events Schedule: A scale for the measurement of aversive events. *Journal of Clinical Psychology, 41,* 483–498.

Lewinsohn, P. M., Mischel, W., Chaplin, W., & Barton, R. (1980). Social competence and depression: The role of illusory self-perceptions. *Journal of Abnormal Psychology, 89,* 203–212.

Lewinsohn, P. M., Roberts, R. E., Seeley, J. R., Rohde, P., Gotlib, I. H., & Hops, H. (1994). Adolescent psychopathology: II. Psychosocial risk factors for depression. *Journal of Abnormal Psychology, 103,* 302–315.

Lewinsohn, P. M., Rohde, P., Hops, H., & Clarke, G. (1991). *Leaders's manual for parent groups: Adolescent Coping with Depression Course.* Eugene, OR: Castalia Press.

Lewinsohn, P. M., Rohde, P., & Seeley, J. R. (1993). Characteristics of adolescents with past suicide attempt. *Journal of the American Academy of Child and Adolescent Psychiatry, 32,* 60–68.

Lewinsohn, P. M., Rohde, P., & Seeley, J. R. (1994). Psychosocial risk factors for future adolescent suicide attempts. *Journal of Consulting and Clinical Psychology, 62,* 297–305.

Lewinsohn, P. M., Rohde, P., Seeley, J. R., & Hops, H. (1991). The comorbidity of unipolar depression: Part 1. Major depression with dysthymia. *Journal of Abnormal Psychology, 100,* 205–213.

Lewinsohn, P. M., Steinmetz, J. L., Larson, D. W., & Franklin, J. F. (1981). Depression related cognitions: Antecedents or consequences? *Journal of Abnormal Psychology, 90,* 213–219.

Lewinsohn, P. M., Weinstein, M., & Shaw, D. (1969). Depression: A clinical research approach. In R. D. Rubin & C. M. Frank (Eds.), *Advances in behavior therapy* (pp. 231–241). San Diego, CA: Academic Press.

Lewinsohn, P. M., Youngren, M. A., & Grosscup, S. J. (1980). Reinforcement and depression. In R. A. Depue (Ed.), *The psychobiology of depressive disorders: Implications for the effects of stress*. New York: Academic Press.

Lewinsohn, P. M., Zeiss, A. M., & Duncan, E. M. (1989). Probability of relapse after recovery from an episode of depression. *Journal of Abnormal Psychology, 98*, 107–116.

Libet, J., & Lewinsohn, P. M. (1973). Concept of social skill with special reference to the behavior of depressed persons. *Journal of Consulting and Clinical Psychology, 40*, 304–312.

MacPhillamy, D. J., & Lewinsohn, P. M. (1982). The pleasant events schedule: Studies on reliability, validity, and scale intercorrelations. *Journal of Consulting and Clinical Psychology, 50*, 363–380.

Marlatt, G. A., & Gordon, J. R. (1985). *Relapse Prevention: Maintenance strategies in the treatment of addictive behaviors*. New York: Guilford Press.

Maser, J. D., & Cloninger, C. R. (1990). *Comorbidity in anxiety and mood disorders*. Washington, DC: American Psychiatric Press.

Matson, J. L. (1989). *Treating depression in children and adolescents*. Elmsford, NY: Pergamon Press.

Moos, R. H. (1974). *Family Environment Scale and preliminary manual*. Palo Alto, CA: Consulting Psychologists Press.

Muñoz, R. H., & Lewinsohn, P. M. (1976). *The Subjective Probability Questionnaire*. Unpublished manuscript, University of Oregon, Eugene.

Muñoz, R. F., & Lewinsohn, P. M. (1988). Personal Beliefs Inventory. In M. Hersen & A. S. Bellack (Eds.), *Dictionary of Behavioral Assessment Techniques* (pp. 342–344). Elmsford, NY: Pergamon Press.

Mufson, L., Moreau, D., Weissman, M. M., & Klerman, G. L. (1993). *Interpersonal psychotherapy for depressed adolescents*. New York: Guilford Press.

Pearlin, L. I., & Schooler, C. (1978). The structure of coping. *Journal of Health and Social Behavior, 19*, 2–21.

Pilowsky, I. (1967). Dimensions of hypochondriasis. *British Journal of Psychiatry, 113*, 89–93.

Prinz, R. J., Foster, S., Kent, R. N., & O'Leary, K. D. (1979). Multivariate assessment of conflict in distressed and nondistressed mother-adolescent dyads. *Journal of Applied Behavior Analysis, 12*, 691–700.

Radloff, L. S. (1977). The CES-D Scale: A self-report depression scale for research in the general population. *Applied Psychological Measurement, 1*, 385–401.

Rehm, L. P. (1977). A self-control model of depression. *Behavior Therapy, 8*, 787–804.

Roberts, R. E. (1987). Epidemiologic issues in measuring preventative effects. In R. F. Muñoz (Ed.), *Depression prevention: Research directions* (pp. 45–75). New York: Hemisphere Publishing Co.

Robin, A. L., & Foster, S. L. (1989). *Negotiating parent-adolescent conflict: A behavioral family systems approach*. New York: Guilford Press.

Robin, A. L., & Weiss, J. G. (1980). Criterion-related validity of behavioral and self-report measures of problem-solving communication skills in distressed and nondistressed parent-adolescent dyads. *Behavioral Assessment, 2,* 339–352.

Robins, L., & Regier, D. (1991). *Psychiatric disorders in America.* New York: Free Press.

Rohde, P., Lewinsohn, P. M., & Seeley, J. R. (1990). Are people changed by the experience of having an episode of depression: A further test of the scar hypothesis. *Journal of Abnormal Psychology, 99,* 264–271.

Rohde, P., Lewinsohn, P. M., & Seeley, J. R. (1991). Comorbidity with unipolar depression II: Comorbidity with other mental disorders in adolescents and adults. *Journal of Abnormal Psychology, 100,* 214–222.

Rohde, P., Lewinsohn, P. M., & Seeley, J. R. (1994a). Are adolescents changed by an episode of major depression? *Journal of the American Academy of Child and Adolescent Psychiatry, 33,* 1289–1298.

Rohde, P., Lewinsohn, P. M., & Seeley, J. R. (1994b). Response of depressed adolescents to cognitive–behavioral treatment: Do differences in initial severity clarify the comparison of treatment? *Journal of Consulting and Clinical Psychology, 62,* 851–854.

Rohde, P., Lewinsohn, P. M., Tilson, M., & Seeley, J. R. (1990). Dimensionality of coping and its relation to depression. *Journal of Personality and Social Psychology, 58,* 499–511.

Rosenberg, M. (1965). *Society and the adolescent self-image.* Princeton, NJ: Princeton University Press.

Russell, D., Peplau, L. A., & Cutrona, C. E. (1980). The Revised UCLA Loneliness Scale: Concurrent and discriminant validity evidence. *Journal of Personality and Social Psychology, 39,* 472–480.

Sandler, I. N., & Block, M. (1979). Life stress and maladaptation of children. *American Journal of Community Psychology, 7,* 425–439.

Schaefer, E. S. (1965). Children's reports of parental behavior: An inventory. *Child Development, 36,* 413–424.

Seligman, M. E. P. (1975). *Helplessness: On depression, development, and death.* San Francisco: Freeman Press.

Spielberger, C. D., Gorsuch, R. L., & Lushene, R. E. (1970). *Manual for the State-Trait Anxiety Inventory.* Palo Alto, CA: Consulting Psychologists Press.

Stark, K. D. (1990). *Childhood depression: School-based intervention.* New York: Guilford Press.

Steinberg, L., & Silverberg, S. (1986). The vicissitudes of autonomy in adolescence. *Child Development, 57,* 841–851.

Steinmetz, J. L., Lewinsohn, P. M., Antonuccio, D. O. (1983). Prediction of individual outcome in a group intervention for depression. *Journal of Consulting and Clinical Psychology, 51,* 331–337.

Weiss, R. L., Hops, H., & Patterson, G. R. (1973). A framework for conceptualizing marital conflict, a technology for altering it, some data for evaluating it.

In L. A. Hamerlynck, L. C. Handy, & E. J. Mash (Eds.), *Behavior change: Methodology, concepts, and practice* (pp. 299–342). Champaign, IL: Research Press.

Weissman, A. N., & Beck, A. T. (1978, November). *Development and validation of the Dysfunctional Attitude Scale.* Paper presented at the annual meeting of the Association for the Advancement of Behavior Therapy, Chicago.

Weissman, M. M., Bruce, M. L., Leaf, P. J., Florio, L. P., & Holzer, C. (1991). Affective disorders. In L. N. Robins & D. A. Regier (Eds.), *Psychiatric disorders in America: The Epidemiologic Catchment Area Study* (pp. 53–80). New York: Free Press.

Wilson, P. H. (1992). *Principles and practice of relapse prevention,* New York: Guilford Press.

Winstead, B. A., & Cash, T. F. (1984). *Reliability and validity of the Body Self-Relationship Questionnaire: A new meassure of body image.* Paper presented at the meeting of the Southeastern Psychological Association, New Orleans, LA.

Youngren, M. A., Lewinsohn, P. M., & Zeiss, A. M. (1976). *The Interpersonal Events Schedule.* Eugene: University of Oregon.

Zachary, R. A. (1986). *Shipley Institute of Living Scales: Revised manual.* Los Angeles: Western Psychology Corporation.

Zeiss, A., Lewinsohn, P. M., & Muñoz, R. F. (1979). Nonspecific improvement effects in depression using interpersonal skills training, pleasant activity schedules, or cognitive training. *Journal of Consulting and Clinical Psychology, 47,* 427–439.

APPENDIX

ADOLESCENT COPING WITH DEPRESSION COURSE (CWD-A) MANUALS

The CWD-A Course (Clarke et al., 1990) materials consist of (a) a therapist's manual, providing a scripted outline for each of the 16 2-hour sessions; and (b) an associated adolescent's workbook, providing short explanations of key concepts, quizzes on the knowledge presented in each session, structured in-session exercises, and homework assignments forms.

A therapist's manual and parent's workbook were developed for the complementary, but separate, 9-session parent group (Lewinsohn, Rohde, Hops, & Clarke, 1991). These materials provide an overview of the skills and techniques taught in the adolescent group sessions. Portions of the parent's and adolescent's workbooks are similar because there are combined parent and adolescent sessions in which families practice problem-solving techniques.

Adolescents entering the CWD-A course are recommended to complete a 320-item PES, originally developed for adults (MacPhillamy & Lewinsohn, 1982) and recently modified for adolescents. A computer scoring program is available to score the PES.

CURRICULUM FOR THE PRIMARY PREVENTION OF ADOLESCENT DEPRESSION

A depression primary prevention curriculum, designed for administration in high school health classes, was developed (Clarke & Lewinsohn, 1991b) and evaluated (Clarke et al., 1995). The curriculum package consists of three 50-minute class sessions, consisting of three structured lectures and two 20-minute videotapes (Clarke, 1990a, 1990b) covering the symptoms, causes, and treatments of depression. Lectures and discussions emphasize the treatable nature of depression and encourage adolescents to seek intervention when appropriate. Based on the behavioral theory of depression (Lewinsohn, Youngren, & Grosscup, 1980), the curriculum also encourages adolescents to increase their daily rates of pleasant activities to help prevent the onset or exacerbation of depressive mood. However, no specific behavioral skill-training is provided.

THE COPING WITH STRESS (CWS) CLASS MANUAL

A therapist's manual and an adolescent's workbook (Clarke & Lewinsohn, 1990) were developed for this 15-session preventive intervention targeting adolescents at risk for future depression. The manual and workbook introduce and provide training in cognitive therapy techniques for identifying and challenging irrational or depressogenic thoughts.

OBTAINING MANUALS

Materials for the CWD-A adolescent and parent groups, the PES scoring program, and the primary prevention curriculum and videotapes may be obtained from: Castalia Publishing Co., P.O. Box 1587, Eugene, Oregon 97440; (503) 343-4433.

A therapist's manual and adolescent's workbook for the CWD-A booster sessions are available from the authors. The Coping with Stress preventive intervention materials have not yet been published, but advance copies will be made available to researchers by Dr. Clarke.

8

FOCUS ON RELATIONSHIPS: INTERPERSONAL PSYCHOTHERAPY FOR ADOLESCENT DEPRESSION

LAURA MUFSON, DONNA MOREAU, and MYRNA M. WEISSMAN

Interpersonal psychotherapy (IPT) is a brief treatment specifically developed and tested for depressed adults (Klerman, Weissman, Rounsaville, & Chevron, 1984). IPT places the depressive episode in the context of interpersonal relationships and focuses on currrent interpersonal conflicts. The goals of IPT are (a) to decrease depressive symptomatology, and (b) to improve interpersonal functioning. IPT has been adapted to treat outpatient adolescents who are suffering from a nonbipolar, nonpsychotic, depressive episode.

DESCRIPTION OF IPT-A

The modifications of IPT for depressed adolescents (IPT-A) address issues that present themselves in adolescent treatment cases, using the IPT framework. The overall goals and problem areas of IPT (grief, interpersonal

This work was supported by a grant to Dr. Weissman from the John D. and Catherine T. MacArthur Foundation Network I (Psychobiology of Depression and Other Affective Disorders) and by a NARSAD Young Investigators Award, and by a FIRST Award to Dr. Mufson and by the University of Chicago—Anne Pollock Lederer Foundation for the Study of Depression in Young Adults Award. Case material has been altered to prevent identification. Correspondence concerning this chapter should be addressed to Dr. Laura Mufson, New York State Psychiatric Institute, 722 West 168th Street, Unit 14, New York, NY 10032.

role disputes, role transitions, and interpersonal deficits) are similar in IPT-A. A fifth problem area, the single-parent family, has been added because of its frequent occurrence, its association with depression, and the conflicts it engenders for adolescents. It is generally possible to identify one of these areas as the treatment focus; however, if not, then the treatment may not be appropriate for the adolescent. The treatment has been adapted to address developmental issues most common to adolescents, including separation from parents, exploration of authority in relation to parents, development of dyadic interpersonal relationships with members of the opposite sex, initial experience with the death of a relative or friend, and peer pressures. Strategies were developed for including family members in various phases of the treatment as needed and for addressing special issues that arise in the treatment of adolescents such as school refusal, physical or sexual abuse, suicidality, aggression, and involvement of child protective service agency. All of the modifications were organized into a treatment manual specifically designed for depressed adolescents (Mufson, Moreau, Weissman, & Klerman, 1993).

This chapter focuses on the development of IPT-A, published IPT-A research protocols as well as those in progress, and preliminary speculation about the implications of the project for both future research and wider clinical application. Preliminary experience with depressed adolescents treated with IPT-A are presented, and case histories are used to illustrate the application of IPT-A.

Rationale for Developing IPT-A: History of Adolescent Depression

The rationale for developing IPT-A is based on our current understanding of the nature of depression in adolescents. It is well established that major depression does occur in adolescents and that the most frequent age at first onset is in adolescence and young adulthood (Christie et al., 1989; Weissman, Gammon, et al., 1987). The symptom pattern of childhood depression is similar to that of adults as described in the third edition of the *Diagnostic and Statistical Manual of Mental Disorders* (DSM-III; American Psychiatric Association, 1980; see also Ryan et al., 1987; Strober, Green, & Carlson, 1981). These findings have been confirmed in clinical, epidemiologic, family-genetic, and high-risk studies.

The epidemiologic and clinical data point out the need for increased attention to adolescent depression because of its significant prevalence and associated morbidity, chronicity, recurrence, and persistence into adulthood. Major depression is associated with significant enduring impairments including increased substance abuse, peer relationship problems, high-risk behaviors, declining school performance, and mortality from suicide (Kandel & Davies, 1982; Kovacs & Goldston, 1991). Depressive symptoms have been found to be associated with significant family dysfunction and are comorbid with other psychiatric disorders (Geller et al., 1985; Kashani, Burbach, & Rosenberg, 1988; Kovacs et al., 1988). Puig-Antich et al. (1993) found that depressed adolescents had significant psychosocial impairment in multiple domains in comparison to a normal control group. While the symptoms of depression in adolescents may be transient, adolescents with major depression have been shown to be at high risk for recurrent episodes (Garber, Kriss, Koch, & Lindholm, 1988; Harrington, Fudge, Rutter, Pickles, & Hill, 1990; Keller, Beardslee, Lavori, & Wunder, 1988), and the accompanying interpersonal impairments tend to persist (Angst, Merikangas, Scheidegger, & Wicki, 1990).

Despite the high prevalence and social morbidity of early onset depression, little research has been conducted on the efficacy of treatments for depressed adolescents. The results of psychopharmacological trials on the use of antidepressants with depressed adolescents have been disappointing. Researchers have found a significant placebo response in depressed adolescents (Kramer & Feiguine, 1981; Ryan, Puig-Antich, Cooper, et al., 1986; Strober, Freeman, & Rigali, 1990). Individual clinicians' experiences suggest some efficacy for antidepressants with an adolescent population, but more research with larger numbers of adolescents is needed to better evaluate their true efficacy.

Given the successful use of psychopharmacology in the treatment of numerous adult disorders such as depression, the past decade has been characterized by the application of this knowledge to the treatment of children and adolescents. However, the results have been far more equivocal for children and adolescents than they have been for adults (see Campbell & Spencer, 1988, for review), especially with the use of antidepressant medication with children and adolescents who are depressed. The reluctance of clinicians to use medication as the initial treatment has spurred a renewed interest in exploring the efficacy of psychosocial treatments for children and adolescents with depressive disorders. Moreover, researchers who were using psychopharmacological interventions for adult affective disorders recognized the importance of combining psychopharmacological treatments with a form of psychosocial treatment to achieve the best outcome (Klerman, DiMascio, Weissman, Prusoff, & Paykel, 1974; Paykel, DiMascio, Klerman, Prusoff, & Weissman, 1976; Weissman, Jarrett, & Rush, 1987; Weissman, Klerman, Prusoff, Sholomskas, & Padian, 1981). These findings were the impetus to initiate studies on psychosocial interventions to treat adolescent major depression.

Because of the growing evidence for the social morbidity of the disorder and the findings of the pharmacology trials, it is important to begin to empirically test the efficacy of psychotherapy for depressed adolescents. Although psychotherapy is a widely used treatment for depressed adolescents, there have been no controlled clinical trials of individual psychotherapy with a sample of adolescents with a major depression. There have been several trials of group psychotherapy and individual psychotherapy with a more heterogeneous sample of depressed adolescents (Lewinsohn, Clarke, Hops, & Andrews, 1990; Reynolds & Coats, 1986; Robbins, Alessi, & Colfer, 1989). Wilkes and Rush (1988) suggested methods for adapting cognitive therapy (CT) for the treatment of nonpsychotic depressed adolescents and proposed a treatment model of CT for this age group.

In light of IPT's proven efficacy for depressed adults, it has been adapted for use with depressed adolescents for the following reasons: (a) there is a similarity between adolescent and adult symptoms; (b) its brief nature would appeal to the adolescents' reluctance to be in therapy for an unspecified duration; and (c) its focus on interpersonal issues is compatible with adolescents' developmental task of negotiating relationships with both family and peers. The final reason is that a therapy that focuses on interpersonal issues might impede the development of significant long-term impairments in social functioning and the concomitant social withdrawal that result from depression.

Development of the Manual

Prior to conducting a controlled clinical trial, it was necessary to develop a manual of the modified IPT to train therapists and to ensure that the treatment being tested was standardized so that the results could be replicated in future studies. The revised techniques were used with depressed adolescents seeking treatment at an outpatient clinic at a university hospital. Therapy sessions, conducted by an experienced child clinical psychologist under the supervision of the developer of IPT, were videotaped. The final manual (Mufson et al., 1993) is intended to be used to train experienced child and adolescent therapists in the specific IPT-A principles. The modified manual for adolescents should be read in conjunction with the manual for adults (Klerman et al., 1984).

Specific Treatment Techniques

IPT-A is designed as a once weekly, 12-week treatment. If there is a crisis, therapist and patient may meet for an additional session. The goals of the treatment are to reduce depressive symptoms and to address the interpersonal problems associated with the onset of the depression. The two main approaches for achieving these goals are to identify one or two problem areas as the focus of treatment and to emphasize the interpersonal nature of the problem as it occurs in current relationships. The treatment is divided into three phases: (a) the initial phase, (b) the middle phase, and (c) the termination phase.

Initial Phase

The initial phase, sessions 1 through 4, deals with the depressive symptoms, identifies the problem areas, and establishes the treatment contract. Six tasks need to be accomplished: (a) conduct a diagnostic assessment, which includes reviewing the symptoms with the patient, giving the syndrome a name, explaining depression and its treatment, giving the patient the sick role, and evaluating the need for medication; (b) assess the type and nature of the patient's social and familial relationships (the interpersonal inventory) and relate the depression to the interpersonal context; (c) identify the problem area(s); (d) explain the rationale and intent of the treatment; (e) set a treatment contract with the patient; and (f) explain the patient's expected role in the treatment.

The therapist reviews current and past interpersonal relationships as they relate to current depressive symptoms. The therapist clarifies the nature of interactions with significant others, the expectations of the adolescent and significant others for the relationships, the satisfying and unsatisfying aspects of the relationships, and the changes the patient wants in the relationships.

The responsible parent is brought into the diagnostic process and is educated about the depression, its nature, its course, and treatment options. Both the parent and the adolescent are involved in discussing the various treatment options as part of the education about depression. The initial phase is also an important time for the therapist to develop an alliance with the school system (see Mufson et al., 1993, for more detailed explanation).

The adolescent is encouraged to think of him- or herself as "in treatment" and is given a limited sick role. Despite the tendency to withdraw socially or avoid usual social expectations when depressed, the adolescent is encouraged to maintain his or her usual social roles in the family, at school, and with friends. The parent is advised to be supportive and to encourage the adolescent to engage in as many normal activities as possible. Together, the assignment of the sick role and psychoeducation can help reverse negative behaviors by family members.

At the end of the initial phase, the therapist and patient together make an explicit treatment contract. The contract specifies which of the five problem areas they will focus on in the treatment, as well as confidentiality, frequency of sessions, rules regarding missed appointments, level of parental involvement in treatment, and the patient's role in the treatment. The therapist discusses the hope that the adolescent will be feeling better at the end of the 12 weeks, but that if this is not the case, further treatment can and will be arranged. The middle phase begins once agreement is reached on the treatment plan.

Middle Phase

During the middle phase, Sessions 5–8, the therapist and patient begin to work directly on one or two of the designated problem areas. The goals of the middle phase are to alleviate the symptoms, clarify the problem, identify effective strategies to attack the problem, implement the interventions, and improve interpersonal functioning. The therapist encourages the patient to bring in feelings, monitors the depressive symptoms, and continues to work with the family to support the treatment. Techniques vary depending on the problem area being addressed. A variety of techniques are employed, including exploratory questioning, encouragement of affect, linkage of affect with events, clarification of conflicts, communication analysis, and behavior change techniques such as role playing. The therapist gives continuous feedback about the use of strategies and observed changes in the patient's functioning, in efforts to improve the patient's self-esteem.

Therapist and patient work as a team. Together, they assess the accuracy of the initial formulation of the problem area and shift the focus of the treatment to events occurring outside of the session that appear related to the patient's depressive symptomatology. Interpersonal style in the session is discussed as it relates to interactions that may be occurring outside of the session. The middle phase also may involve other family members as needed to address situations both in and outside of the sessions. Education about depression and interpersonal relationships continues.

Termination Phase

The termination phase is approximately sessions 9 through 12. Termination is addressed at the beginning of treatment and periodically during the course of therapy. The adolescent's two main tasks of termination are (a) to give up the relationship with the therapist and (b) to establish a sense of competence to deal with future problems. Many patients are unaware of having any feelings about the end of treatment; others may hesitate to acknowledge that they have come to value the relationship with the therapist. Patients and families are advised that a slight recurrence of symptoms is common as termination approaches, and that it is not unusual for patients to have feelings of apprehension, anger, or sadness, but that the appearance of such feelings does not necessarily portend a relapse. To support the patient's ability to cope with problems, the therapist highlights the patient's skills and external supports.

The IPT-A therapist conducts a final termination session with the adolescent alone and then with the family members who have been involved in the treatment, usually a parent. The sessions conducted during this phase include an explicit discussion of feelings engendered by the end of treatment, a review of strategies learned and goals accomplished, recognition of the adolescent's areas of competence, and goal-directed antic-ipation of possible future episodes. Termination with family members ad-dresses the same issues. In addition, the therapist and family discuss any changes that occurred in the family as a result of the treatment. The ther-apist assists the family in anticipating the possibility of future episodes of depression and educates them as to warning signs of possible recurrence and appropriate management of recurrent episodes.

There may be occasions when therapist and adolescent together de-cide there is a need for further treatment. This can occur for several rea-sons: (a) the depression has not fully remitted, (b) the adolescent may now be able to work on other issues since the depression has remitted, or (c) the therapy is serving as a stabilizing force in an otherwise chaotic envi-ronment. If there is uncertainty about whether to continue treatment, the therapist advises the adolescent to wait a few weeks without treatment and then to call the therapist to reassess the need for further treatment. If it is clear at termination that the adolescent needs further treatment, an ap-propriate referral is arranged. Long-term treatment may be indicated for patients with long-standing personality problems and chronic or recurrent depression, and for nonresponders.

Problem Areas

Grief

Grief is only a problem if it is prolonged or becomes abnormal. IPT-A can be used to treat abnormal grief or prevent it from developing. There are three types of pathological mourning (distorted grief, delayed grief, or chronic grief) that can lead to depression either immediately following the loss or at some later time when the patient is reminded of the loss (Raph-ael, 1983). Loss of a parent during adolescence necessitates premature sep-aration and individuation in addition to the usual tasks of mourning. Com-mon reactions include withdrawal and depressed feelings, a display of pseudo-maturity, identification with the deceased, or regression to earlier developmental stages (Krupnick, 1984). The adolescent also may experi-ence feelings of abandonment. The difficulties may manifest themselves in behavioral problems rather than affective symptoms. The therapist must be alerted to problems of drug or alcohol abuse, sexual promiscuity, or truancy (Raphael, 1983).

The role of IPT in the treatment of normal grief reactions in adoles-cents is to assist the adolescent in separating from the deceased by helping him or her to accept the actual loss of and dependency on the deceased (Raphael, 1983). It similarly addresses the depression associated with path-ological grief reactions.

In treating a grief reaction, the therapist helps the patient discuss the loss, as well as identify and experience the associated feelings. As the patient begins to grieve appropriately and the symptoms dissipate, the loss should be better understood and accepted and the patient freed to pursue new relationships. One must consider the adolescent's role in the family system, the nature of the relationship lost, the remaining social support network, and the adolescent's psychological maturity in addressing the impact of the loss.

Interpersonal Role Disputes

An interpersonal role dispute is defined as a situation in which an individual and at least one significant other person have nonreciprocal expectations about their relationship. Adolescents' role disputes commonly occur with parents over issues of sexuality, authority, money, and life values (Miller, 1974). A common interpersonal role dispute that occurs between adolescents and parents is the conflict between a parent with traditional values and an adolescent responding to peer pressure. Often these conflicting values lead to different expectations for the adolescent's behavior. This conflict also can be seen frequently in the normal adolescent rebellion against parental authority.

The general strategies for treating adolescent interpersonal role disputes are essentially the same as they are for adults: identify the dispute; make choices about negotiations; reassess expectations for the relationship; and clarify role changes, modify communication patterns, or both, for resolution of the dispute. What differs in treating adolescent role disputes is the nature of the problems and the involvement of the parents. The therapist needs to explain to the adolescent and the parents how the interpersonal role disputes contribute to depressive symptoms and how resolution of these disputes can alleviate the symptoms. It is useful to involve the parent (or parents) with whom there is a dispute and to facilitate the negotiations of the relationship in the session with the therapist. Improvements may take the form of a change in the expectations and behavior of the patient, the other person, or both. The goal of IPT-A is to help the adolescent clarify his or her expectations for the relationship, evaluate which expectations are realistic, and find strategies for coping with the immutable expectations.

Role Transitions

Role transitions are defined as the changes that occur as a result of progression from one social role to another. A person can experience depression when he or she has difficulty coping with the life changes associated with a role change. The transition may result in impaired social functioning if it occurs too rapidly or is experienced by the individual as a loss.

Normal role transitions are expected and anticipated by adolescents and their families as rites of passage and are typically handled successfully (Miller, 1974). Normal role transitions for adolescents include: (a) passage into puberty, (b) shift from group to dyadic relationships, (c) initiation of sexual relationships or desires, (d) separation from parents and family, and (e) work, college, or career planning. Problems arise when parents are unable to accept the transition or when the adolescent is unable to cope with the changes. Role transitions also can be thrust on adolescents as a result of unanticipated circumstances. Unforeseen or imposed role transitions include parenthood or a change in family role because of divorce, remarriage, death, illness, impairment in parent, or separation from parent. Problems that occur with expected and unexpected role transitions include loss of self-esteem, failure to meet one's own and others' expectations, increase in pressures and responsibilities, and inability to separate from family or family's inability to allow that separation (Erikson, 1968).

An adolescent's ability to cope with unforeseen circumstances rests on prior psychological functioning and social supports. Role transitions can be perceived as a loss to the adolescent, particularly if he or she felt more competent in his or her old role and is uncertain about his or her ability to fill the new role. Consequently, the psychological reaction to the transition can resemble that of mourning.

If the role transition problems involve changes in family roles, the therapist may include the parents in several sessions to help support the adolescent or, if necessary, help the family adjust to the normative role transition so that they do not restrict the adolescent's development and impair his or her functioning. If the family is having an easier adjustment to the transition, it is hoped that they will facilitate an easier transition for the adolescent.

The Case of F. S. F. S., a 15-year-old girl in the 10th grade, was the second of three children who lived with her mother and siblings. Although her parents had never lived together, her father lived nearby and she enjoyed a good relationship with him. F. S. presented to the outpatient depression clinic with symptoms of sad mood, increased irritability, social withdrawal, decreased concentration, decreased grades, loss of interest in friends, loss of appetite, early and middle insomnia, increased heart rate, and tingling in hands periodically when at home. Her symptoms had been present for approximately two months and had been precipitated by a break-up with a boyfriend that resulted in conflict with her mother. She met *DSM-III-R* criteria for major depression.

F. S. described her parents, particularly her mother, as very old-fashioned in regard to dating. F. S. had been dating a boy, but decided that she did not like him and ended the relationship. Her mother became angry about the way F. S. conducted her social life and increased restrictions on her. While her mother was away for 2 weeks, F. S. met and began to date another boy. She was afraid to discuss her new relationship and her views on dating with her mother. Concealing her relationship increased her anxiety and feelings of depression about her deceitful behavior. F. S. anticipated that her mother would not understand other dating practices.

The identified problem area was role transitions. The therapist focused on F. S.'s transition from a little girl to an adolescent girl who was beginning to date. Discussion focused on examining her mother's concerns, what mother's expectations were for dating, and how to communicate with her mother about her need for increasing independence while still remaining under her mother's guidance and supervision. The therapist and F. S. frequently role played how she might tell her mother about her new boyfriend, elicit her mother's concerns, and discuss them rationally so they could work out a mutually agreeable plan. Although her mother was unable to attend sessions, F. S. was able to communicate with her mother about her desire for a relationship. F. S. told her mother that she felt the relationship should not preclude her from remaining a part of the family, she expressed her views on dating, and they worked out a compromise that was acceptable to her mother as well as to her. As F. S.'s communication with her mother improved, the conflict and anxiety decreased, and her concentration, mood, and grades improved.

Interpersonal Deficits

Interpersonal deficits are identified when an individual appears to lack the requisite social skills to establish and maintain appropriate relationships within and outside the family. Interpersonal deficits can impede an adolescent's achievement of developmental tasks, which are primarily social and include making same-age friends, participating in extracurricular activities, becoming part of a peer group, beginning to date, and learning to make choices regarding exclusive relations, career, sexuality (Hersen & Van Hasselt, 1987). As a result of interpersonal deficits, the adolescent may be socially isolated from peer groups and relationships, which can lead to feelings of depression and inadequacy. These feelings of depression can in turn lead to increased social withdrawal and result in a lag in interpersonal skills when the depression resolves.

The focus of treatment is on those interpersonal deficits that are more a consequence of the depression rather than personality traits that result in isolation. The strategies for treating adolescents include reviewing past significant relationships and exploring repetitive or parallel interpersonal problems. New strategies for approaching situations are identified and discussed. The patient is encouraged to apply these strategies to current issues. The therapist may utilize role-playing of problematic interpersonal situations, enabling the adolescent to explore and practice new communication skills and interpersonal behaviors, and engendering a sense of social competence in the adolescent that can generalize to other situations.

Single-Parent Families

Single-parent homes arise for a variety of reasons. Each situation presents unique emotional conflicts for the adolescent and the custodial parent. Depending on the circumstances, children of single-parent families can function without significant problems, or they can experience a myriad of problems, including depression. The intensity of the depressive reaction is likely to be related to the degree of separation, its abruptness, and whether it has happened before (Jacobson & Jacobson, 1987). Not only is the child's relationship with the absent parent affected, but the relationship with the remaining parent also is frequently altered.

IPT-A identifies several tasks for the treatment of such adolescents: (a) acknowledging that the departure of the parent was a significant disruption in their lives, (b) addressing feelings of loss, rejection, abandonment, punishment, or a combination of feelings by the departed parent, (c) clarifying remaining expectations for the relationship with the absent parent, (d) negotiating a working relationship with the remaining parent, (e) establishing a relationship with the removed parent, if possible, and (f) accepting the permanence of the current situation. It can be helpful to have the custodial parent participate in a session to discuss the feelings associated with the other parent's departure. The focus of the session is to discuss the parent's recollection of the spouse and to correct any misconceptions the adolescent may have about the parents. It may also be helpful to have a session with the parent alone, specifically to discuss adolescent parenting issues, including appropriate discipline and restrictions on behavior.

The Case of P. Z. P. Z. was a 15-year-old girl living alone with her mother. Her parents divorced when she was three years old. Her father lived nearby and visited regularly. P. Z. presented with decreased concentration and poor school performance, increased irritability and crying, headaches, depressed mood, suicidal ideation, social withdrawal, loss of appetite, and early and middle insomnia, in addition to panic attacks.

When she presented to the outpatient clinic, P. Z. and her mother were sharing a room in her grandmother's apartment because of financial troubles. P. Z. was getting into increasing conflict with both her mother and grandmother. She felt as though she never had any quiet or a place to herself. During this time, P. Z. continued contact with her father and told him about the stress of so many people living in a small space. In the fourth week of treatment, P. Z. and her mother moved to their own apartment, but she was very worried about how they could afford it and what that pressure was going to do to her mother. She felt guilty about complaining to her mother. She expressed a lot of anger at her father because he would always want to come over and joke around with her, but he had not been making his child support payments or giving her an allowance as had been mandated by the courts. She felt the need to stand up for her mother and to try to convince him to make the payments. He would respond by telling her that she favored her mother over him. She felt very trapped in her relationship with him and guilty that she had angry feelings toward him.

The therapist identified her problem area as related to living in a single-parent family with a father who did not provide for her financially or emotionally but still demanded allegiance to him over the mother. P. Z.'s father refused to participate in the treatment. P. Z. wanted to pull away from her relationship with him because of the conflicting feelings she had toward him. The therapist focused on discussing and clarifying P. Z.'s expectations for her relationship with her father and what she perceived were her mother's expectations for her own relationship with her ex-husband. P. Z.'s mother participated in these sessions to help clarify for P. Z. her feelings about her ex-husband, what type of relationship she wished for P. Z. to have with her father, and to relieve P. Z. of the need to defend her mother's needs to the father. Different ways of communicating her feelings to her parents were explored. P. Z. was able to delineate more realistic expectations for her relationship with her father and to resume her visits with him with these new terms in mind. With increased clarification of the issues between her and her parents and improved communication and negotiation of her place in regard to her parents' custody arrangement, P. Z.'s depression and anxiety symptoms resolved.

APPLICATION OF IPT-A IN RESEARCH

The aim of the IPT-A project is to develop a detailed training program and to conduct a pilot-controlled clinical trial of IPT-A with random assignment to determine treatment efficacy. The current study is an outgrowth of the preliminary open clinical trial of IPT-A. This section includes a discussion of both the completed open clinical trial and the ongoing controlled clinical trial.

Therapist Training

In preparation for conducting the open clinical trial, the author trained as an IPT therapist, created videotapes of IPT-A to use to train other therapists, and tested a battery of outcome assessments in depressed adolescents. The training in IPT was conducted in accordance with the methods used in the National Institute of Mental Health (NIMH) Collaborative Study of the Treatment of Depression (Elkin et al., 1989; Weissman, Rounsaville, & Chevron, 1982). The IPT manual was modified and adapted for use with adolescents and a clinic was identified within which to conduct the study. These procedures are the model for the IPT-A training program being used in the controlled clinical trial.

Open Clinical Trial

The purpose of the open clinical trial was similar to that of a Phase II psychopharmacology trial. The goal was to gain experience with the therapy, look at dose response, and assess the feasibility of using IPT-A with an adolescent population. The sample included 14 adolescents with depression between the ages of 12 and 18 years old who were referred for treatment to the Babies Hospital—Child Anxiety and Depression Clinic or who responded to an advertisement to participate in a research project on treatment for adolescent depression sponsored by the Department of Child Psychiatry Clinical Research Center.

Prior to entering the open clinical trial, patients underwent a two- to three-week evaluation by a research nurse, child psychiatrist, and child psychologist. Information was obtained from both the adolescent and a parent. The following tests were administered: the Schedule for Affective Disorders and Schizophrenia for School-Aged Children—Epidemiologic Version (K-SADS-E) (Orvaschel, Puig-Antich, Chamber, Tabrizi, & Johnson, 1982), the Hamilton Rating Scale for Depression (HRSD) (Carroll, Fielding, & Blashki, 1973), the Global Assessment Scale for Children (C-GAS) (Shaffer et al., 1983), the Social Adjustment Inventory for Children and Adolescents (SAICA) (John, Gammon, & Prusoff, 1987), and the Beck Depression Inventory (BDI) (Strober et al., 1981). Demographic, medical, social, and family histories were also collected.

The patient was enrolled in the study if found to meet the inclusion criteria. The patients then had 12 weekly therapy sessions. During the trial, all patients were seen by a clinical research nurse at weeks 0, 2, 4, 8, and 12. The research nurse administered assessments of clinical status including the HRSD, BDI, Symptom Checklist (SCL-90) (Derogatis, 1977), Social Adjustment Scale—Self-Report (SAS-SR) (Weissman & Bothwell, 1976; Garber et al., 1988), and a Treatment History Form. At week 12, the patients were again administered the K-SADS, Present State Version (Ambrosini, Metz, Prabucki, & Lee, 1989) and treatment was terminated. At termination, patient and therapist decided whether any further treatment was needed.

Preliminary Outcome

The mean age of the patients was 15.4 years old. The participants attended an average of 10 therapy sessions in 12 weeks. In general, the results indicated a significant decrease in adolescents' depressive symptomatology and symptoms of psychological and physical distress, as well as a significant improvement in functioning over the course of treatment. At the end of the protocol, none of the subjects met *DSM-III-R* criteria for any depressive disorder (Mufson, Moreau, Weissman, Wickramaratne, Martin, & Samoilov, 1994).

Limitations

Although the preliminary results are certainly encouraging for the use of IPT-A in the treatment of depressed adolescents, the results must be viewed in light of their limitations. First, all the IPT-A treatment has been conducted by the one therapist who developed the treatment, therefore, it is unclear whether the patients' improvement was due to the specific therapist or the techniques of the treatment. To address this issue, treatment in the controlled clinical trial will be conducted by four other therapists who have been trained in IPT-A. Second, because of the small sample size and lack of a control group, we do not know how many of the patients would have gotten better over time without treatment. Despite these limitations, the results were encouraging enough to proceed with a controlled clinical trial of IPT-A.

Controlled Clinical Trial

The controlled clinical trial is currently underway with patients enrolled in both an experimental and control treatment group. The therapist training program consisted of two components: a didactic seminar using the training manual (Mufson et al., 1993) and a clinical practicum. Training was designed to modify the practices of fully trained child and adolescent clinicians to conform to IPT-A, not to train them to become therapists.

Following completion of the didactic program, the therapists entered the clinical practicum. Each therapist consecutively treated two cases for 12 weeks each. All sessions were videotaped and discussed in supervision that occurred weekly for 1 hour. Therapists' videotapes were also reviewed by clinical IPT experts who decided whether they were competent to be certified as IPT-A therapists. Rating forms designed for the NIMH Collaborative Study were used to document the competency criteria.

The four trained therapists are participating in the randomized controlled clinical trial of IPT-A. The experimental treatment group is IPT-A and the control group is a nonscheduled treatment group. The latter has been used in controlled clinical trials for the treatment of acute depression in adults and has been discussed in the literature as an ethical control group (DiMascio et al., 1979; Richman, Weissman, Klerman, Neu, & Prusoff, 1980). The patients are being evaluated using the same measures as in the open clinical trial at weeks 0, 2, 4, 6, 8, 10, and 12. Therapists continue to videotape their sessions and the videotapes are regularly reviewed to ensure against therapist drift from the prescribed treatment.

The goal of the project is to gain experience and efficacy data on using interpersonal psychotherapy to treat depressed adolescents. The findings of the pilot controlled clinical trial will assist in designing future studies, in considering appropriate controls, and in updating the manual for dissemination to other research groups interested in conducting similar studies.

It is premature to generalize to a larger population based on so small and select a sample. Although the results are promising, true statements about the efficacy of the treatment and target populations must await the results of the controlled clinical trial that is currently underway.

SUMMARY AND RECOMMENDATIONS

The IPT-A project, including an open clinical trial and a randomized controlled clinical trial, will make significant contributions to the small body of research available on treatments for adolescents with depression. Based on the information gathered from the controlled clinical trial, further studies on psychosocial treatments for depressed adolescents will be planned. Further standardization of treatments and more studies are recommended to better inform clinicians in the field about treatment efficacy for particular populations. IPT-A does not create new therapeutic techniques, but rather seeks to organize effective techniques into a coherent treatment package that can be used successfully as a brief treatment. In this manner, therapists would likely benefit from adopting some of the strategies of IPT-A, but the definitive research data on its efficacy are not yet complete.

REFERENCES

Ambrosini, P. J., Metz, C., Prabucki, K., & Lee, J. C. (1989). Videotape reliability of the third revised edition of the K-SADS. *Journal of the American Academy of Child and Adolescent Psychiatry, 28,* 723–728.

American Psychiatric Association. (1980). *Diagnostic and statistical manual of mental disorders* (3rd. ed.) Washington, DC: Author.

American Psychiatric Association. (1987). *Diagnostic and statistical manual of mental disorders* (3rd ed., rev.). Washington, DC: Author.

Angst, J., Merikangas, K., Scheidegger, P., & Wicki, W. (1990). Recurrent brief depression: A new subtype of affective disorder. *Journal of Affective Disorders*, *19*, 87–98.

Campbell, M., & Spencer, E. K. (1988). Psychopharmacology in child and adolescent psychiatry: A review of the past five years. *Journal of the American Academy of Child and Adolescent Psychiatry*, *27*, 269–279.

Carroll, B. J., Fielding, J. M., & Blashki, T. G. (1973). Depression rating scales: A critical review. *Archives of General Psychiatry*, *28*, 361–366.

Christie, K. A., Burke, J. D., Regier, D. A., Rae, D. S., Boyd, J. H., & Locke, B. Z. (1989). Epidemiologic evidence for early onset of mental disorders and higher risk of drug abuse in young adults. *American Journal of Psychiatry*, *145*, 971–975.

Derogatis, L. (1977). *The SCL-90 Manual I. Scoring, administration, and procedures for the SCL-90*. Baltimore: Johns Hopkins University School of Medicine, Clinical Psychometrics Unit.

DiMascio, A., Klerman, G. L., Weissman, M. M., Prusoff, B. A., Neu, C., & Moore, P. (1979). A control group for psychotherapy research in acute depression: One solution to ethical and methodological issues. *Journal of Psychiatric Research*, *15*, 189–197.

Elkin, I., Shea, M. T., Watkins, J. T., Imber, S. D., Sotsky, S. M., Collins, J. F., Glass, D. R., Pilkones, P. A., Lebee, W. R., Docherty, J. P., Ferster, S. F., & Parloff, M. B. (1989). National Institute of Mental Health Treatment of Depression Collaborative Research Program: General effectiveness of treatments. *Archives of General Psychiatry 46*, 971–982.

Erikson, E. H. (1968). *Identity, youth, and crisis*. New York: Norton.

Garber, J., Kriss, M. R., Koch, M., & Lindholm, L. (1988). Recurrent depression in adolescents: A follow-up study. *Journal of the American Academy of Child and Adolescent Psychiatry*, *27*(1), 49–54.

Geller, B., Chestnut, E. C., Miller, D., Price, D. T., & Yates, E. (1985). Preliminary data on *DSM-III* associated features of major depression disorder in children and adolescents. *American Journal of Psychiatry*, *142*, 643–645.

Harrington, R., Fudge, H., Rutter, M., Pickles, A., & Hill, J. (1990). Adult outcomes of childhood and adolescent depression. *Archives of General Psychiatry*, *47*, 465–473.

Hersen, M., & Van Hasselt, V. B. (1987). *Behavior therapy with children and adolescents: A clinical approach*. New York: Wiley.

Jacobson, G., & Jacobson, D. S. (1987). Impact of marital dissolution on adults and children: The significance of loss and continuity. In J. Bloom-Feshbach, & S. Bloom-Feshbach (Eds.), *The psychology of separation and loss: Perspectives on development, life transitions, and clinical practice* (pp. 316–344). San Francisco: Jossey-Bass.

John, K., Gammon, D., & Prusoff, B. A. (1987). The Social Adjustment Inventory for Children and Adolescents (SAICA): Testing of a new semi-structured interview. *Journal of the American Academy of Child and Adolescent Psychiatry, 26,* 898–911.

Kandel, D. B., & Davies, M. (1982). Epidemiology of depressive mood in adolescents: An empirical study. *Archives of General Psychiatry, 39,* 1205–1212.

Kashani, J. H., Burbach, D. J., & Rosenberg, T. K. (1988). Perception of family conflict resolution and depressive symptomatology in adolescents. *Journal of the American Academy of Child and Adolescent Psychiatry, 27,* 42–48.

Keller, M. B., Beardslee, W. R., Lavori, P. W., & Wunder, J. (1988). Course of major depression in nonreferred adolescents: A retrospective study. *Journal of Affective Disorders, 15,* 235–243.

Klerman, G. L., DiMascio, A., Weissman, M. M., Prusoff, B., & Paykel, E. S. (1974). Treatment of depression by drugs and psychotherapy. *American Journal of Psychiatry, 131,* 186–194.

Klerman, G. L., Weissman, M. M., Rounsaville, B. H., & Chevron, E. S. (1984). *Interpersonal Psychotherapy of Depression.* New York: Basic Books.

Kovacs, M., & Goldston, D. (1991). Cognitive and social cognitive development of depressed children and adolescents. *Journal of the American Academy of Child and Adolescent Psychiatry 30,* 388–392.

Kovacs, M., Paulauskas, S., Gatsonis, C., & Richards, C. (1988). Depressive disorder in childhood: Part 3. A longitudinal study of comorbidity with and risk for conduct disorders. *Journal of Affective Disorders, 15,* 205–217.

Kramer, A. D., & Feiguine, R. J. (1981). Clinical effects of amitriptyline in adolescent depression: A pilot study. *Journal of the American Academy of Child and Adolescent Psychiatry, 20,* 636–644.

Krupnick, J. (1984). Bereavement during childhood and adolescence. In M. Osterweis, F. Solomon, & M. Green (Eds.), *Bereavement: Reactions, consequences, and care* (pp. 99–141). Washington, DC: National Academy Press.

Lewinsohn, P. M., Clarke, G. N., Hops, H., & Andrews, J. (1990). Cognitive–behavioral treatment for depressed adolescents. *Behavioral Therapy, 21,* 385–401.

Miller, D. (1974). *Adolescence: Psychology, psychopathology, psychotherapy.* Northvale, NJ: Jason Aronson.

Mufson, L., Moreau, D., Weissman, M. M., & Klerman, G. L. (1993). *Interpersonal psychotherapy for depressed adolescents.* New York: Guilford Press.

Mufson, L., Moreau, D., Weissman, M. M., Wickramaratne, P., Martin J., & Samoilov, A. (1994). The modification of interpersonal psychotherapy with depressed adolescents (IPT-A): Phase I and Phase II studies. *Journal of the American Academy of Child and Adolescent Psychiatry, 33,* 695–705.

Orvaschel, H., Puig-Antich, J., Chamber, W., Tabrizi, M. A., & Johnson, R. (1982). Retrospective assessment of prepubertal major depression with the Kiddie-SADS-E. *Journal of the American Academy of Child and Adolescent Psychiatry, 21,* 392–397.

Paykel, E. S., DiMascio, A., Klerman, G. L., Prusoff, B. A., & Weissman, M. M. (1976). Maintenance therapy of depression. *Pharmakopsychiatrie Neuropsycho-pharmakologie, 9,* 27–136.

Puig-Antich, J., Kaufman, J., Ryan, N. D., Williamson, D. E., Dahl, R. E., Lukens, E., Todak, G., Ambrosini, P. J., Rabinovich, H., & Nelson, B. (1993). The psychosocial functioning and family environment of depressed adolescents. *Journal of the American Academy of Child and Adolescent Psychiatry 32,* 244–253.

Raphael, B. (1983). *The anatomy of bereavement.* New York: Basic Books.

Reynolds, W. M., & Coats, K. I. (1986). A comparison of cognitive–behavioral therapy and relaxation training for the treatment of depression in adolescents. *Journal of Consulting and Clinical Psychology, 44,* 653–660.

Richman, J., Weissman, M. M., Klerman, G. L., Neu, C., & Prusoff, B. A. (1980). *Ethical issues in clinical trials: Psychotherapy research in acute depression: Vol. 2, IRB: A review of human subjects research.* New York: The Hastings Center, Institute of Society, Ethics, and the Life Sciences.

Robbins, D. R., Alessi, N. E., & Colfer, M. V. (1989). Treatment of adolescents with major depression: Implications of the DST and the melancholic clinical subtype. *Journal of Affective Disorders, 17,* 99–104.

Ryan, N. D., Puig-Antich, J., Ambrosini, P., Rabinovich, H., Robinson, D., Nelson, B., Iyengar, S., & Twomey, J. (1987). The clinical picture of major depression in children and adolescents. *Archives of General Psychiatry, 44,* 854–861.

Ryan, N. D., Puig-Antich, J., Cooper, T., Rabinovich, H., Ambrosini, P. J., Davies, M., King, J., Torres, D., & Fried, J. (1986). Imipramine in adolescent major depression: Plasma level and clinical response. *Acta Psychiatrica Scandinavica 73,* 275–288.

Shaffer, D., Gould, M. S., Brasic, J., Ambrosini, P., Fisher, P., Bird, H., & Aluwahlia, S. (1983). A Children's Global Assessment Scale (C-GAS). *Archives of General Psychiatry, 40,* 1228–1231.

Strober, M., Freeman, R., & Rigali, J. (1990). The pharmacotherapy of depressive illness in adolescence: Part 1. An open label trial of imipramine. *Psychopharmacological Bulletin, 26,* 80–84.

Strober, M., Green, J., & Carlson, G. (1981). Utility of the Beck Depression Inventory with psychiatrically hospitalized adolescents. *Journal of Consulting and Clinical Psychiatry, 49,* 482–483.

Weissman, M. M., & Bothwell, S. (1976) Assessment of social adjustment by patient self-report. *Archives of General Psychiatry, 33,* 1111–1115.

Weissman, M. M., Gammon, D., John, K., Merikangas, K. R., Warner, V., Prusoff, B. A., & Sholomskas, D. (1987). Children of depressed parents: Increased psychopathology and early onset of major depression. *Archives of General Psychiatry, 44,* 847–853.

Weissman, M. M., Jarrett, R. B., & Rush, A. J. (1987). Psychotherapy and its relevance to the pharmacotherapy of major depression: A decade later

(1976–1985). In H. Meltzer (Ed.), *Psychopharmacology: The Third Generation of Progress*. New York: Raven Press.

Weissman, M. M., Klerman, G. L., Prusoff, B. A., Sholomskas, D., & Padian, N. (1981). Depressed outpatients: Results one year after treatment with drugs and/or interpersonal psychotherapy. *Archives of General Psychiatry, 38,* 52–55.

Weissman, M. M., Rounsaville, B. J., & Chevron, E. (1982). Training psychotherapists to participate in psychotherapy outcome studies: Identifying and dealing with research requirements. *American Journal of Psychiatry, 139,* 1442–1446.

Wilkes, T. C. R., & Rush, A. J. (1988). Adaptations of cognitive therapy for depressed adolescents. *Journal of the American Academy of Child and Adolescent Psychiatry, 27,* 381–386.

9

ADAPTING COGNITIVE–BEHAVIORAL AND INTERPERSONAL TREATMENTS FOR DEPRESSED PUERTO RICAN ADOLESCENTS

JEANNETTE ROSSELLÓ and GUILLERMO BERNAL

Within the United States, minorities have grown in number over the last three decades. Minority youth will constitute 30% of the nation's youth population by the year 2000 and 38% by 2020 (Ho, 1992). This population is at risk for mental health problems because of "low socioeconomic status, the stressful life events of these environments, and the limited access to mental health services" (Ho, 1992). When minorities do have access to services, these seem to be inappropriate (Acosta, Yamamoto, & Evans, 1982; Aponte, Rivers, & Wahl, 1995; Dana, 1993; Ghali, 1977; Inclán & Herron, 1985; Smith, Burlew, Mosley, & Whitney, 1978; Yamamoto & Sasaki, 1968). Sue (1977) found that Asians and Hispanics were underrepresented in mental health centers, and that ethnic minority clients had a higher (50%) drop out rate than whites (30%).

Sue and Zane (1987) explain the underrepresentation of minorities in mental health services by the failure of therapists to provide culturally appropriate forms of treatment. They reported that the most frequent reason that minority patients drop out of treatment was a negative reaction

Preparation of this chapter was supported in part by the National Institute of Mental Health grant 49368 and by Fondos Institucionales para la Investigación (FIPI) from the University of Puerto Rico, Río Piedras Campus. Correspondence concerning this chapter should be addressed to Jeannette Rosselló, Department of Psychology, Centro Universitario de Servicios y Estudios Psicológicos (CUSEP), P.O. Box 23174, San Juan, PR 00931.

to the therapist. To simply apply therapeutic interventions created for White, middle class Anglo-Americans to minorities without considering language, cultural, and socioeconomic issues is not effective (Aponte, 1990; Board of Ethnic Minority Affairs, 1990; Canino & Spurlock, 1994; Dana, 1993; Ho, 1992; Inclán & Herron, 1985; Malgady, Rogler, & Constantino, 1990; Sue & Zane, 1987; Szapocznik, Scopetta, & Aranalde, 1978).

The role of culture and ethnicity has been an important consideration of clinicians from different theoretical positions (Mays & Albee, 1992; Tharp, 1991). A variety of cultural models for individual psychotherapy (Comas-Díaz & Griffith, 1988; Jones & Korchin, 1982) and family therapies (McGoldrick, Pearce, & Giordano, 1982) have been proposed. Others have developed culturally sensitive frameworks (Bernal, Bonilla, & Bellido, 1995; López et al., 1989) to inform clinicians about cultural and minority issues in conducting psychotherapy.

Although there have been important clinical advances in the consideration of cultural and ethnic minority issues for a wide range of psychotherapies, treatment research has not kept up with these developments. Most treatment outcome research with adults and children are not generalizable to ethnic minority populations. In fact, treatment outcome research with minority populations is almost nonexistent. The literature shows few studies with minority participants (Mays & Albee, 1992), and even fewer studies include Hispanics (Bernal, 1993; Navarro, 1993). Clearly there is a need to adapt, develop, and test treatment approaches that show empirical promise with minority populations.

This chapter offers clinical guidelines for the treatment of Puerto Rican adolescents with depression. We present our preliminary work aimed at adapting and testing two promising treatments for depressed adolescents: a cognitive–behavioral therapy (CBT) and an interpersonal psychotherapy treatment (IPT) for depression, which follow ecological validity and culturally sensitive criteria (Bernal et al., 1995). We present a brief description of the problem of depression in Puerto Rico, followed by the guidelines used in the adaptation of the two treatments. Next, we present the basic steps employed in both CBT and IPT. Finally, the chapter closes with a description of our research still in progress to test the two treatment interventions.

DEPRESSION IN PUERTO RICAN CHILDREN AND ADOLESCENTS

Nationally representative epidemiological studies of depression in the U.S. adolescent population have not been reported in the literature (Petersen et al., 1993). Therefore, there is no reference about the incidence of depression comparing ethnic groups and social classes.

However, epidemiological data have revealed that depression among children and adolescents is not as rare as previously thought by investigators (Kanner, 1972; Rie, 1966). Given the different definitions of depression in youth, measurement instruments (self-report, interview), and populations (clinical, community, age ranges, sex, special education groups), there are widely varying prevalence figures. The prevalence rates of depression ranges between 1%–2% among children and adolescents, when *Diagnostic and Statistical Manual of Mental Disorders*, third edition (*DSM-III*; American Psychiatric Association, 1980) criteria are used, to 1.3%–52.4%, when self-report depression scales are used (Albert & Beck, 1975; Chien & Chang, 1985; Fleming, Offord, & Boyle, 1989; Gibbs, 1985; Kandel & Davies, 1982; Kaplan, Hong, & Weenhold, 1984; Kashani, Holcomb, & Orvaschel, 1986; Kashani & Simonds, 1979; Reynolds, 1983; Schoenbach, Kaplan, Grimson, & Wagner, 1982; Siegel & Griffin, 1984; Sullivan & Elgin, 1986; Teri, 1982; Weinberg & Emslie, 1988; Wells, Klerman, & Deykin, 1987).

A recent epidemiological study in Puerto Rico (Bird et al., 1988) estimated a prevalence of 5.9% of depression and dysthymia in children 4–16 years old, using *DSM-III* criteria in combination with the Children's Global Assessment Scale. Depression and dysthymia were found to be the third most frequent disorder in Puerto Rican children (after oppositional and attention deficit disorders). This study also revealed that 15% of the Puerto Rican population in this age group manifest moderate to severe psychopathology. In numerical terms, this means that between 125,000 and 150,000 children are in need of professional services. Because fewer than 10,000 individual children received mental health services as reported by the Puerto Rican Division of Mental Health (during the time the study was conducted), the authors concluded that there is a "major public health problem in the treatment of mental disorders for children in Puerto Rico" (p. 1126).

When one considers that sometimes oppositional and attention deficit disorders may mask or co-exist with depressive characteristics (Carlson & Cantwell, 1980), the importance of the study of depression and its treatment in the Puerto Rican youth population becomes significant. As mentioned earlier, it is critical to adapt, develop, and test treatments that show positive empirical results with other populations and hold promise as therapeutic interventions.

ADAPTATIONS OF THE TREATMENTS TO THE PUERTO RICAN CONTEXT

The present project is an attempt to contribute to the development of effective interventions for depression in Puerto Rican adolescents. Drawing on the adult treatment outcome literature for depression as a starting point, two psychosocial treatment approaches were selected. For theoretical and practical reasons CBT and IPT, which have been shown to be effective with adults, were adapted to the Puerto Rican adolescent population. Developmental, cognitive, linguistic, and cultural factors were considered in the translation and adaptation of these therapeutic modalities.

One of the considerations in developing cultural sensitivity is when to apply specific norms versus universal norms for a particular cultural group. This issue is known as the etic–emic conflict. Draguns (1981) has defined etic as the universal norms and emic as the group specific norms. Lopez et al. (1989) have proposed that cultural sensitivity is the "ability to entertain both etic and emic views within the context of the individual" (p. 375). From our experience there are some dimensions that have to be culturally adapted to Puerto Rican adolescents and others that are more "universal" or generic that could apply to other adolescents as well.

In the treatment of culturally diverse populations, ecological validity has been signaled as an important aspect to consider (Bernal et al., 1995). This refers to the congruence between the client's experience imbedded in his or her ethnic context and the properties of that treatment assumed by the clinician or investigator. Therefore, the ecological validity of a therapeutic intervention is related to its cultural sensitivity: What is implicit for one normative group must be explicit for another. This understanding has motivated the development of culturally sensitive treatments (López et al., 1989; McGoldrick et al., 1982; Rogler, Malgady, Constantino, & Blumenthal, 1987; Tharp, 1991).

Using the framework of cultural sensitivity developed by Bernal et al. (1995), the treatment manuals were adapted for Puerto Rican adolescents. This framework identified eight elements or dimensions that must be considered to guarantee ecological validity: (a) language, (b) persons, (c) metaphors, (d) content, (e) concepts, (f) goals, (g) methods, and (h) context. In addition, developmental, technical, and theoretical issues were considered in the adaptation process.

Language

Language must be culturally appropriate and syntonic. Because language is often the carrier of the culture, a treatment delivered in the language of the target population assumes an integration of culture. The matching of ethnic backgrounds increases the therapist's cultural knowledge of the client and thus augments his or her "credibility" (Sue & Zane, 1987), which in turn may contribute to treatment effectiveness. In our project, because treatment was delivered in Spanish by native Spanish-speaking therapists to native Spanish-speaking patients, the criteria of a language-appropriate intervention was met.

Although the CBT manual was in Spanish, adaptations were made to the words and syntax to make it syntonic with the Puerto Rican manner of speech. Through case studies (Rosselló 1993), language was evaluated and was adapted to the populations. Words, phrases, or concepts that were not understood by test cases were changed. School personnel, graduate and undergraduate students, and expert translators were consulted. Language more appropriate to adolescents was introduced. For example, throughout the manual, the informal (tu) rather than the formal (usted) manner of speech is used in reference to the adolescents. The informal form of language serves to reduce interpersonal distance and is more characteristic of Caribbean Spanish. Alternatively, when dealing with parents the formal form is used as a means of acknowledgment of parental authority and respect for the parent's position. Also, words in the original manual were simplified to clarify concepts. For example: "Porque rompí este vaso soy una *nulidad*" (Because I broke this glass I am worthless). The word *nulidad*, although conceptually equivalent to "worthless," is too sophisticated to be understood by the average adolescent, so it was changed to: "Porque rompí este vaso *no sirvo para nada*" (Because I broke the glass I am *not worth anything*), which is the conceptual equivalent of *nulidad* and a simpler version of the same idea.

The IPT manual was translated into Spanish. Therapists were reminded in the manual to keep the language simple in the sessions so that the adolescents would be able to understand the concepts presented in therapy. Examples and illustrative cases were substituted for our population and context (Rosselló, 1993; Rosselló, Guisasola, Ralat, Martínez, & Nieves, 1992). These examples and case studies were used in the therapists' training.

Persons

This dimension of the culturally sensitive model refers to the role that racial/ethnic similarities play in the shaping of the therapy relationship. Research supports the notion of culturally matching therapist–client psychotherapy dyads (Sue & Zany, 1987). In our project, therapists were sensitized during training and supervision to socio-economic, racial, and cultural aspects and the exploration of accepting different ways of living as valid. Treatment was delivered by Puerto Rican therapists to Puerto Rican adolescents. However, socioeconomic and racial differences could surface in certain dyads and these differences were to be discussed and accepted. In the adaptation of the intervention models, flexibility was allowed to accommodate different solutions, alternatives, and examples of the contents to be presented.

Metaphors

This dimension refers to the use of symbols and concepts shared by the cultural group. Suggestions made by Muñoz (1982) and Zuñiga (1992) were incorporated. The adolescents and their parents were received in the waiting room and office with objects and symbols of the Puerto Rican adolescent culture. It was suggested that posters with positive Puerto Rican role models and messages be placed in the clinic. In addition, culturally consonant ideas, sayings, and images were used as metaphors in the therapy to communicate ideas more effectively.

Content

Content issues—cultural knowledge and handling information about values, customs, and traditions—were considered equally for both CBT and IPT. The literature has identified some of these values and traditions as familism, respeto, simpatía, personal space, parental authority, present time orientation, etc.

For example, familism is one of the strongest cultural values of Puerto Ricans and Hispanics (Sabogal, Marín, & Otero-Sabogal, 1987). It refers to a strong identification and attachment to the family group with strong feelings of solidarity, loyalty, and reciprocity. The family is the most important unit for meeting psychological needs and enhancing the identity and emotional security of its members. Even in the midst of poverty, discrimination, racism, and isolation, minority families survive and handle problems (Smith et al., 1978). Familism has been related to healthy psychological adjustment and mental health by protecting against stressors and providing a natural support system (Mannino & Shore, 1976). Therefore, issues of family obligation, support, and referent for self-esteem must be evaluated. The therapist has to be sensitive to this value and must try to strenghten its positive aspects. Because Puerto Rican adolescents depend on their parents for solutions, alternatives, and even to attend therapy sessions, parents were interviewed before and after the therapy in a climate of utmost respect. If needed, therapists were allowed to discuss issues related to treatment with the parents individually or together with the adolescent. Confidentiality with the adolescent was guaranteed and is explained to both parents and adolescents.

Because Puerto Rican parents often adopt cultural values of absolute parental authority and respect, the period of dependence on parents is somewhat longer in the Puerto Rican culture. Therapists need to be aware of these values and address such issues in ancillary meetings with parents.

The issues of family dependence and interdependence has to be understood.

In one case, we had the mother of an adolescent boy say that she was withdrawing her son from therapy as a punishment for his drop in grades. A meeting with the mother helped clarify the reasons for the decrease in grades and the objectives of the therapy. This had to be discussed in an atmosphere of respect so that the mother did not feel that her authority was threatened or questioned.

In another case, parents of another adolescent boy were extremely overprotective of their son because an older son had drug-related problems. This adolescent was permitted to go only to school and could not attend any activities or have any friends. Without affecting the family unit, the therapist respectfully explored alternatives with the parents and the adolescent. After-school karate classes seemed acceptable to all.

Therapists meet with parents and the adolescent before the first session begins. This gives the therapist one open session to explore in detail the adolescent's condition within the family context and initiate the building of rapport with the adolescent and the parent(s).

Concepts

This dimension refers to a consonance with the culture and context and how constructs are used within the intervention model. The underlying concepts of the cognitive–behavioral and interpersonal therapies were examined within the concepts and belief systems of the Puerto Rican culture. Congruence was established in the present orientation and in the interpersonal components of both therapeutic models. These two factors make these constructs consonant to Puerto Rican cultural concepts. Family dependence and interdependence also were considered and integrated in the therapies' deliveries.

Goals

This dimension of the model refers to the establishment of an agreement of the goals of treatment between the therapist and client. In our adaptation of the models within the first session for the CBT and within the first four sessions for the IPT models, goals must be defined. Parents' goals are also evaluated and taken into consideration.

Methods

This dimension refers to the procedures for achieving the goals defined for the treatment. Considering culturally sensitive methods requires incorporating cultural knowledge into the treatment procedures. As explained earlier, the family unit is a very important component of the Puerto Rican culture. This component can be incorporated into both the CBT and IPT as needed. The Puerto Rican depressed adolescent is, among other processes, struggling to find an acceptable balance between dependence, interdependence, and independence. Defining this balance is part of the therapy and is consonant with the possibility of parents or other family members participating before and after the 12 sessions, and in some of the sessions if necessary. The short-term nature and present-time orientation of both CBT and IPT are also consonant with the Puerto Rican culture where long-term commitments to therapy are difficult to achieve.

Context

This dimension of cultural sensitivity considers elements such as daily stress; developmental stages; the availability of social support; and the social, economic, and political context of the presenting problem. A very large percentage of the Puerto Rican population live within the definition of poverty. This had to be considered in both treatment models. Therapists were trained to identify resources in the community available in case they are needed (i.e., free-of-charge after school programs or classes, organizations that support youth employment, health services).

Developmental Issues

In the CBT model, examples of the different types of thoughts and mistakes in thinking were selected from actual thoughts of Puerto Rican adolescents identified in a pilot study (Rosselló, 1993). Therapists also were encouraged to use examples from the intake interview to make the material more relevant to each adolescent. Exercise materials were revised to make homework assignments more relevant (e.g., lists of thoughts and pleasant activities). For example, some thoughts that were identified included: "If I don't do well in school, I'm a failure;" "I can't concentrate, so I'm stupid." Some pleasant activities that were identified included going to the shopping mall, going to the movies, cooking, and playing with pets.

Some adolescents resist doing the homework or assigned exercises. To deal with this, the therapist can choose between two alternatives: work with the thoughts related to the homework (for example, "This is not going to help me") or do the homework with the adolescent at the beginning of the session. Puerto Rican adolescents reacted positively to role playing exercises.

For the IPT model, because the original manual had examples that applied mostly to adults, the manual was revised to present situations that would be relevant and typical of Puerto Rican adolescents. For example, cases from our population were used in the manual to illustrate four problem areas: (a) grief, (b) interpersonal disputes, (c) role transitions, and (d) interpersonal deficits. For the grief interpersonal problem area, the case of a 15-year-old girl was described in which she was adopted by her aunt and uncle because her mother could not raise her. The girl's adoptive mother was sick with terminal brain cancer and had deteriorated rapidly to the point that she could not identify the people around her. This represented a loss of a relationship that was meaningful to the girl and that was evidently related to her depressive symptoms. During the course of therapy, the adopted mother died and a process of mourning as well as role transition were addressed in the subsequent sessions.

For both models, therapists were trained to speak in terms that the adolescent could understand and to give concrete examples of the principles and ideas that were communicated in the sessions. Some adolescents may have more limited skills in abstract thinking, verbal knowledge, psychological mindedness, and capacity to form a therapeutic relationship.

Because of their ages and dependence on parents, some of the adolescents are "brought" into therapy constituting a nonvoluntary and sometimes resistant participation. This is evaluated and addressed in both therapies. In both models, the adolescent, the parents, or both meet for one session before the therapy starts to establish rapport, therapeutic alliance, and work on motivational issues.

Technical Issues

For the CBT model, the group format was adapted to an individual treatment modality because the individual modality concentrates more on the adolescent's particular problems and on his or her experiences, thoughts, actions, and relationships as examples for the material that is taught and presented. Because adolescents usually do not like to be lectured or to be treated as though they were in school, the model was made more interactive between the therapist and adolescent. At the beginning of each session, time was devoted to the adolescent's free expression of feelings, reports of what had changed or happened since the last session, or any spontaneous communication that he or she wanted to make.

The IPT manual establishes the possibility of 16 sessions. The interventions were adapted to 12 sessions to make both treatment approaches equivalent in quantity of sessions (dosage).

Theoretical Issues

The concept of the "sick role" was eliminated from the IPT manual to help the adolescents assume more responsibility over their interpersonal relationships and therapy and because it was determined that this concept had negative implications for the adolescent's self-esteem and evaluations.

The medical model's implication of the "sick role" did not seem compatible with the psychosocial nature of IPT.

DESCRIPTION OF THE PSYCHOTHERAPEUTIC APPROACHES

The two psychotherapeutic approaches adapted for the treatment of depression in Puerto Rican adolescents are summarized below. For a more detailed description of the treatments and case studies, reference can be made to the original manuals (Klerman, Weissman, Rounsaville, & Chevron, 1984; Muñoz & Miranda, 1986) or the revised manuals in Spanish (Rosselló, 1993, 1994).

Cognitive–Behavioral Therapy (CBT)

The CBT was based on the cognitive–behavioral model developed by Muñoz and Miranda (1986), based on concepts of cognitive–behavioral therapy (Lewinsohn, Antonuccio, Steinmetz-Beckenridge, & Teri, 1984; Lewinsohn, 1975, 1976), cognitive therapy (Beck, Rush, Shaw, & Emery, 1979), and rational–emotive therapy (Ellis, 1962; Ellis & Bernard, 1983). Because CBT is based on the interrelationship of thoughts, actions, and feelings, this model attempts to identify the thoughts and actions that influence depressive feelings. The primary goals of this therapy are to diminish depressive feelings, to shorten the time that the person feels depressed, to teach alternative ways of preventing depression, and to increase the person's sense of control over his or her life. This model is a group intervention for depressed adults, which has been used with an adult Hispanic population in the San Francisco area. The model was adapted for adolescents and modified to an individual treatment format.

CBT is a short-term intervention that consists of 12 weekly sessions. The sessions are divided into three major themes: (a) how thoughts influence mood (sessions 1–4); (b) how daily activities influence mood (sessions 5–8); and (c) how interactions with other people affect mood (sessions 9–12).

Working with Cognitions (Sessions 1–4)

The initial session establishes the structure and purpose of the therapy. Therapist and client discuss issues of scheduling weekly appointments and confidentiality. The therapist asks the adolescent about what is troubling him or her and how he or she is feeling, and explains that the depression will be treated by teaching alternative ways to control feelings. The specific goals of treatment are to reduce feelings of depression; to shorten the periods of depression; to learn new ways of preventing depression; and to develop more control over the adolescents' life. The definition of depression and its symptoms are reviewed, which are then related to how the adolescent has been feeling and which symptoms apply to his or her experience. The adolescent elaborates on how he or she feels with his or her depression. The adolescent is told how thoughts affect mood. Thoughts are then defined as "things we tell ourselves." Examples are given on how thoughts affect body, actions, and mood. The adolescent is asked to provide his or her own examples (or the therapist can provide them from what he or she already knows about the adolescent).

The first session ends with the introduction of "The Daily Mood Scale," which provides a scale to select the mood that characterizes each day of the week (best, very good, good, better than average, average, worse than average, low, very low, worst). The adolescent is asked to fill out the scale every day of the following week and to bring it to the next session. The purpose of this exercise is to help the adolescent identify his or her mood and its fluctuations throughout the week.

The focus of treatment of the next three sessions is cognitions. Depressed thinking is defined as inflexible and judgmental. Examples of inflexible thoughts related to depression include: "Nothing I do comes out right," or "I'll never find a boyfriend." Examples of flexible thoughts include: "Although I didn't do well on this test, I have done well in the past and I can do better next time," or "I don't have a boyfriend now but I'll try to meet new boys and I'll probably meet someone who wants me as a girlfriend." An example of a judgmental thought is: "I'm a failure". The nondepressed counterpart could be: "Although I didn't succeed in math class, I do better in literature and sports. I will try to do better in math next time." Nondepressed thinking is changeable, specific, and hopeful. For example, "I'll always be rejected," can be transformed into a more flexible thought: "I have been rejected in some situations, sometimes, or by some people." Another example is: "Nothing will ever change," which can be transformed into a more specific and hopeful thought: "Nothing I have tried yet has helped, but there are more alternatives to try that might help change my situation."

The adolescent is taught to identify types of thinking:

1. *Constructive versus destructive.* Constructive thinking helps build up a person. For example, "I'll study a little harder and ask Mary for help in math, so that I can pass the class with an acceptable grade." Destructive thoughts tear down: "I'm no good at all," or "I'll never pass math class."
2. *Necessary versus unnecessary.* Necessary thinking refers to things that must be done. For example: "I have to finish my homework before I go to bed." Unnecessary thinking is irrelevant and does not change things except to make the per-

son feel bad and worry about things that he or she can not control. Some unnecessary thoughts are: "There's going to be a hurricane soon," and "Everything will be ruined."

3. *Positive versus negative.* Positive thoughts reflect optimism, hope, and make the person feel better. For example, "Although I'm the youngest and least experienced member of the team, I will try to do my best in the game." Negative thinking makes the person feel bad about him- or herself: "All the other players are better than me. I will never be able to make it." To convey this concept a Puerto Rican saying is used: "Todo se ve a través del cristal con que se mira [Everything is as seen through the glass of one's choosing]."

Mistakes in thinking that relate to depressive feelings are explained to the adolescent. Definitions and examples of 9 thinking errors are given and discussed: (a) all or none thinking, (b) seeing one example of something bad as if everything will be bad, (c) mental filter, (d) discounting the positive, (e) jumping to conclusions (e.g., mind reading and fortune telling), (f) making more or less of things than is appropriate, (g) taking feelings too seriously, (h) labeling, and (i) self-blame. Exercises are assigned to be carried out during the week to help the adolescent identify his or her errors in thinking.

By the third session, techniques to increase healthy thinking and to decrease unhealthy thinking are introduced: Increase the number of good thoughts about yourself, recognize and give yourself credit for the good things you do, take time to relax, and make projections in time when things will be different and better. To decrease negative thoughts, the following activities are suggested: Stop negative thoughts, set up worry time for no longer than 30 minutes a day, make fun of problems by exaggerating them, consider the worst that could happen, and be your own coach. These activities are then related to the adolescent's own thoughts.

Also, the A-B-C-D cognitive technique is introduced. The adolescent is taught that "A" is the activating event, "B" is the belief or thought about the event, "C" is the consequence, and "D" is the way to dispute or talk back to the thought. A 13-year-old adolescent in our project followed the exercise illustrating an incident that affected her during the week: "A: I prepared dinner and the food was too salty. I ruined the dinner; B: As a consequence I felt angry; C: I told myself that I don't know how to cook and that I'm a failure; D: This is only a small incident during the week, other things came out OK. I was in a hurry and was not careful about the salt, I can learn so that next time I'll be more careful. I have cooked nice dinners before. One mistake doesn't make me a failure. I don't have to be perfect all the time. Nobody is perfect."

Finally, common thoughts related to depression are presented: "I should be loved and approved of by everyone," "I should always be able to do things well and work hard all the time to feel good about myself," "Some people are bad and should be punished," "I will feel awful if things don't go the way that I want them to go", "Other people and things I cannot change make me unhappy," "I should worry about bad things that could happen," "I can never be happy if I don't have someone to love me," "I can't change the way I am, I was raised or born this way," "I must feel sad when people I care about are having bad times," and "It will be awful if I don't do the right thing."

Pleasant Activities (Sessions 5–8)

In this second phase of treatment, the adolescent is introduced to the concept that "the fewer pleasant activities people do, the more depressed they feel." The therapist explains the vicious cycle that ensues between depression and activities: "The less you do, the more depressed you feel; the more depressed you feel, the less you do," and that to break this cycle, it is necessary to increase pleasant activities. To this end, a list of pleasant activities (activities that the adolescent finds pleasant, rewarding, or inspiring) is discussed with the adolescent. The adolescent is asked to fill out the daily mood graph and to use the pleasant activities list to check those activities he or she did during each day of the week.

Subsequently, the adolescent is introduced to the notions that pleasant activities: (a) are different for different people; (b) do not have to be special events although they can be special; (c) help develop a sense of well being; (d) do not have to be expensive or involve spending money; (e) help with keeping a healthy balance between pleasures and obligations; and (f) can be planned.

The adolescent is then asked to consider different activities in his or her community that do not necessarily involve spending money and obstacles that affect carrying out pleasant activities. The therapist explains two ways to deal with obstacles: making a contract and predicting pleasure. The adolescent is told that he or she does not have to wait until he or she feels like doing something—he or she can choose to do something and then do it—and that activities can be enjoyable even if he or she did not think they would be.

The adolescent learns that another aspect of pleasant activities entails creating a plan to overcome depression: setting reasonable goals, noticing positive things he or she does, and planning rewards. The therapist teaches that goals should be clear, concrete, and realistic. Examples of goals are presented; for instance, an unclear goal is "to be less bored on weekends," a clear goal is "to go to the movies Sunday afternoon." The adolescent learns that large goals must be made specific and broken down into smaller goals; for example, if the goal is to become a dancer, smaller steps in that direction must be taken into account such as finding a good dance school and teacher, and attending daily classes after school. Finally, the adolescent is taught that goals can change and they may need to be revised periodically.

The adolescent is asked to define his or her goals and the obstacles in attaining them. The concept of short-term, long-term, and life goals are explained and an exercise on time management is introduced: making a list of what he or she wants to accomplish the following week and assigning priorities to each goal. The adolescent is taught to schedule the high priority goals and pleasant activities into his or her weekly plans.

The last component of pleasant activities is healthy management of reality and depression. The adolescent is taught ways to develop more control, and that the more alternatives a person learns to identify, the more freedom he or she will have. The therapist works to generate more alternatives with the adolescent and continues identifying new pleasant activities.

Contacts with People (Sessions 9–12)

The last four sessions focus on how contacts with people affect mood. The therapist discusses the question: Does depression cause people to be less sociable or does being less sociable cause depression in people? The answer to both questions is likely to be true where both elements affect each other. The importance of social support (the network of people a person has available, including family, friends, neighbors, teachers, teammates, and acquaintances) is discussed: The stronger the social support system, the better and easier it is to face tough situations.

The adolescent is then asked to describe his or her support system. The therapist suggests that if the support system is weak, it would help to strengthen or enlarge it. If the support system is adequate, it is important to find ways to maintain its strength.

Ways to meet people are also discussed. The therapist explains that the best way to meet people is to do something pleasant with other people because when a person does something he or she likes, he or she will be in a better mood and will be friendlier. The therapist introduces an exercise: "Places or activities where one can meet others." This exercise generates ideas of places to go or things to do in the company of others.

Next, the therapist discusses ways to keep a support system healthy (stay in contact by phone or in person, and share activities with others) and also ways to strenghten family ties and keep healthy relationships with others. Here the therapist defines assertive behavior, and discusses the differences among passive, assertive, and aggressive behaviors.

Therapy then focuses on the thoughts, expectations, behavior, and feelings of the adolescent when he or she is with other people. The therapist explains that there are thoughts that help a person to be comfortable with other people and that there are thoughts that get in the way of developing a good relationship; examples are provided with the help of the adolescent. The therapist also discusses that expectations can also facilitate or get in the way of positive relationships—if expectations are too high, disappointment and frustration will probably follow; if expectations are too low, a fair chance might not be given to the relationship.

The actions of the adolescent in his or her personal relationships are examined. The following questions are asked to examine the adolescent's actions: How often do you smile at other people? Do you make eye contact? Do you look tired or angry? How do you dress? Is your speech too slow or too soft? Do you show interest in what others say? Do you complain a lot? The therapist then explores how the adolescent feels when he or she interacts with others. The therapist emphasizes the importance of recognizing one's feelings and learning to communicate what he or she feels in an appropriate manner. The therapist teaches the adolescent ways to be more assertive. An exercise of practicing in the mind is performed: Imagine the scene as though it were a photograph, imagine the action starting as if it were a movie, imagine yourself saying something assertively, and imagine the response you get.

The thoughts of the adolescent when he or she is with others are examined. Questions about contact with people are asked: Do you find you cannot trust others? Do you find that you are intolerant of others? Do you feel frightened in the presence of others? Do you feel others expect too much of you? The therapist asks the adolescent to consider how he or she appears to others: How can you help others feel comfortable with you? Do you behave assertively? Feelings are then explored by identifying feelings the adolescent has before and after being with others. Also, the adolescent is asked to practice, first by thinking differently about others and then by behaving differently with others. The daily mood graph, the weekly activities schedule, and the practice of thinking and behaving differently with others continue to be recorded.

In the closing session, concepts from the prior sessions are reviewed. The therapist explains the importance of people, such as the ways they can help increase rewarding experiences, provide support values, provide companionship and a sense of stability, and serve as a reflection of one's own image. The adolescent learns that if a relationship is not working, it is helpful to ask: "Do you both want the same thing from the relationship?"; "Are your interests sufficiently similar?"; and "Can you tell each other what you think and feel?" Then the therapist helps the adolescent understand that relationships are worth working on. Finally, an evaluation of the adolescent's progress during the 12 sessions of the therapy is made and recommendations are shared with the adolescent.

Clinical Vignette

Angela is a 14-year-old adolescent who was referred to our project by her school's social worker, who had observed that her academic performance and participation in school activities had diminished. Upon initial evaluation, Angela also presented with symptoms of depressed affect, feelings of unworthiness and hopelessness, and recurrent wishes to be dead. Symptoms appeared as a result of various stressful events such as a change in school, which was very demanding, and communication problems with her parents, especially her father. Angela is the oldest of three sisters (she has two sisters aged 11 and 6 years), and she lives with both parents, who work full time outside the home.

Angela was randomly assigned to CBT and she attended the 12 programmed sessions. During the first 4 sessions, the thoughts related to her depression were identified: "I will never be anything in the future;" "I used to be intelligent, now I am not;" "I'm stupid;" and "Nothing is going right." Angela became aware of the multiple thoughts that were affecting her mood and that did not allow a better performance. She also worked with the thought: "When I feel a lot of pressure from my parents about my school work, I think that I would be better off dead." Through the daily mood scale and the A-B-C-D method she was able to relate her thoughts to her depression, to analyze her errors and inflexible thinking, and to produce alternative thoughts.

During the following 4 sessions, Angela continued working with her thoughts. At that time, she learned that her best friends were leaving the island. Her thoughts about losing her friends were: "I will always be alone;" and "I will never have friends again." Angela was able to understand that she could keep contact with her friends and that she had the ability to make new friends or get closer to other adolescents at school and in her neighborhood. She also continued working with the thoughts that she was no good and that her sister was more intelligent than she was. Her activities during the week were analyzed and she realized that apart from school she was not involved in other activities. The importance of pleasant activities were discussed and she was able to identify that she enjoyed playing volleyball and spending time with her pet. Angela started to incorporate these activities into her weekly schedule. She also identified her goals. Her immediate goal was to graduate from intermediate school and start high school. Long-term goals included a university education.

During the last 4 sessions, Angela was able to understand the relationship between her depressed mood and contacts with people. She talked about ways to make her family relationships better and how to have a larger and stronger support system. Assertive behavior was explained to Angela and she was able to assume an active position in strengthening her relationships.

In the last session, Angela was able to identify changes in her life and feelings. Postevaluations revealed elimination of depressive symptomatology and a more positive self-concept.

Interpersonal Psychotherapy (IPT)

The IPT intervention is based on the Klerman, Weissman, Rounsaville, & Chevron (1984) model, which was developed for the treatment of depressed adults. Mufson (1991, 1993) adapted IPT to an Anglo-adolescent population based on the original model. For the purpose of this study, an adaptation and translation of the original model was made for depressed Puerto Rican adolescents. The present study was started in 1991; at that time the original IPT manual (Klerman et al., 1984) and a draft of the IPT-A manual (Mufson, 1993) were available. We decided to base our adaptation and translation on the original model to maintain a stronger theoretical and practical fidelity.

IPT maintains that depression can be explained by difficulties in interpersonal relationships. These difficulties are associated with the symptoms of depression and constitute the main focus of this intervention. With the improvement of the quality of the person's current interpersonal relationships, IPT facilitates recovery by alleviating depressive feelings and by helping the person develop more satisfying and healthy relationships. Emphasis is placed on the immediate and current problems, important interpersonal relations, evaluating the present situation, and solving the problematic situation.

IPT is a short-term psychotherapy adapted to 12 weekly sessions. Sessions are divided into approximately three groups of four sessions each. The initial sessions (1 to 4) have these objectives: Obtain information about the depression and its development, explain what IPT is, evaluate interpersonal relationships, identify the main problems, establish a treatment plan, and explain what is expected of the patient in therapy. The intermediate sessions (5 to 8) deal with helping the patient work the problematic interpersonal relationship, monitoring the patient's depressive feelings, facilitating a positive therapeutic relationship so that communication is maximized, and preventing the patient's parents' sabotaging treatment. The last four sessions (9 to 12) are oriented toward termination and address the following issues: discussion of termination, acknowledgment of feelings related to separation, a review of the course of treatment and symptoms, and a recognition of the patient's competence and new ways of coping in interpersonal contexts.

Primary Interpersonal Problem Areas

Because IPT is a short-term treatment, it is necessary to identify and focus on one or two problem areas. The problem areas do not exclude each other and are usually present in combinations. The therapist may use precipitating events as a guide to define the main problem area, realizing that the problem to be focused on may change as therapy progresses. The problem areas targetted in IPT are: (a) grief, (b) interpersonal disputes, (c) role transitions, and (d) interpersonal deficits.

Grief. The feelings that follow the death or loss of a loved and significant person are considered grief. If the depression is associated with grief reactions resulting from the loss of a loved one, this will be the focus of the intervention. The therapy facilitates the mourning process and helps the adolescent establish new interests and relationships to substitute for the lost one. IPT uses the following strategies to deal with grief reactions: elicitation of feelings, nonjudgmental exploration, reassurance, reconstruction of the adolescent's relationship with the lost person, development of awareness, and behavioral change.

Interpersonal Disputes. These are situations where the adolescent and at least one other important person in his or her life have nonreciprocal expectations about their relationship. Although interpersonal disputes can happen with almost anyone in the adolescent's life, those that seem related to the depression will be considered in depth. Disputes that are recurrent, continuous, and that seem to increase in frequency lead to loss of self-esteem, lack of control, and a threat of losing the relationship. The adolescent may feel helpless and hopeless, sensing that nothing can be done to change the situation. With adolescents, the most frequent role disputes occur with one or both parents.

The treatment goals with regard to interpersonal disputes are to identify the dispute, elaborate a plan of action, encourage better communication patterns, and reassess expectations. The satisfactory resolution of an interpersonal dispute may involve a change in the expectations and behavior of the adolescent or the significant other, a more accepting attitude of the adolescent with or without attempts to satisfy needs outside the relationship, or a satisfactory dissolution of the relationship. The therapist may use the following strategies: analysis and exploration of role disputes and its stages (renegotiation, impasse, and dissolution); discussion of how nonreciprocal role expectations relate to disputes and depression; and exploration of the adolescent's expectations, values, options, and resources. Parallels between the present problematic relationship and other relationships may also be explored. Communication patterns and problems are identified to encourage more adequate communication styles. Once the adolescent has a clear picture of the interpersonal dispute and the role he or she plays in it, decision making can be undertaken by encouraging the adolescent to evaluate and choose between the possible alternatives to solve the dispute.

Role Transitions. Sometimes depression in adolescents is related to life changes of some kind that can be perceived as losses. Some examples of life changes in an adolescent are: the divorce of parents, the birth of a sibling, changes in schools, parent unemployment and subsequent change in social status, migration, and physical changes. Some of the issues that make coping with role transitions difficult are loss of familiar social support or other support systems, management of new affects like anger or fear, demands for new social skills, and loss of self-esteem and sense of belonging. Recent life events and changes should be evidenced as related to the depression. The therapist should explore the changes produced in the life of the adolescent and his or her lifestyle. The goal for the treatment of depression associated to role transitions is to enable the adolescent to perceive the new role as positive and as an opportunity to grow and to restore self-esteem by encouraging a sense of competence to deal with the new demands. The therapist may use the following strategies: encourage an examination of positive and negative aspects of the old and new role; facilitate a realistic evaluation of what has been lost; encourage release of affect related to the change; and explore with the adolescent the development of new social support systems and additional social skills to deal with the new role.

Interpersonal Deficits. These become evident when an adolescent presents a history of poor interpersonal relationships. The adolescent may describe feelings of loneliness and severe social isolation. Interpersonal deficit may involve an absence of lasting, intimate, and satisfying relationships. IPT establishes three types of interpersonal deficits: (a) those who are socially isolated, (b) those who are socially unfulfilled with their relationships, and (c) those who are chronically depressed. The goal of the treatment of interpersonal deficits is to reduce the social isolation. The strategies are used to explore past relationships and the relationship with the therapist, and to encourage the development of new relationships. The therapist may analyze communication styles and may use role playing.

Initial Phase (Sessions 1–4)

During the first 4 sessions, the therapist obtains a history of the depressive condition, explains the nature and objectives of IPT, makes an evaluation of the interpersonal relationships and problems, identifies the main problem areas, sets up a treatment contract, and lets the adolescent know what is expected of him or her in therapy. The first session elicits from the adolescent a description of what brings him or her to therapy, a history of the depressive conditions and its interpersonal context, and an enumeration and elaboration of the depressive symptoms. Special attention is given to the appearance of symptoms and to the precipitating events that led to therapy. A review of past episodes, interpersonal context, and consequences of the depression is elaborated. Suicidal ideation and intent are assessed. The relationship between the depressive phenomena and the adolescent's interpersonal functioning is explained to the adolescent. The therapist offers information about IPT—that most of the work will center on present events and relationships, that the focus will be on significant relationships and relevant past ones, and that the emphasis of treatment is to clarify the problems and search for solutions. The adolescent is told that therapy consists of 12 sessions that will be held once per week and is given other practical information about appointment times and cancellations. Issues concerning confidentiality are discussed. The therapist can then proceed with a detailed exploration of the interpersonal relationships: nature of the interactions, frequency of contact, activities shared, expectations, satisfactory and unsatisfactory aspects of the relationship, detailed examples of interactions, changes that the adolescent would like to see, when and what kind of problems develop, if any, and what the adolescent has tried in the past to solve difficulties. The therapist identifies the primary problem area, which can usually be categorized in one of the four areas.

After the primary problem areas have been defined, the therapist proceeds to establish therapeutic goals. The main goal is to improve interpersonal relationships. Symptom reduction and emotional well-being are other goals that can be accomplished as consequences of the first. The adolescent is asked to define what could be the best possible outcome, the most likely outcome, and the worst possible outcome to the problem presented. The setting of goals and evaluation of outcomes should be a collaborative effort between therapist and adolescent. The therapist will explain that the first 4 sessions require active participation of the therapist whereas in the following sessions the therapist will be less active, allowing the adolescent to talk about things that are relevant to him or her and what his or her feelings are. The therapist will work on developing a therapeutic alliance with the adolescent during these sessions. The initial phase is completed when the treatment goals and the problem area have been defined.

Intermediate Phase (Sessions 5–8)

The next 4 sessions concentrate on the assessment and problem solving of each particular case: grief, role dispute, role transition, or interpersonal deficit. The therapist has five tasks to accomplish in each of these sessions: (a) helping the adolescent open up and discuss topics relevant to the problem area; (b) stimulating the adolescent's self-disclosure by creating a climate of trust; (c) attending to the adolescent's feelings; (d) strengthening the therapeutic relationship; and (e) preventing the adolescent or his or her parents from sabotaging the treatment.

The adolescent is encouraged to express him- or herself freely and to present topics spontaneously. This allows new material to be introduced, which could represent unrecognized or suppressed problems that have not been discussed previously. Sometimes because of mistrust of the therapist or a genuine misunderstanding of his or her problems, the adolescent does not present the most important problem during the first 4 sessions. If not, then it will probably come forth in the following four sessions. If the adolescent elaborates on the problem area or treatment goals, the therapist need not focus the session. However, if irrelevant or avoidance material is presented, the therapist should allow some time to discuss it so that he or she can determine if it is truly irrelevant. If avoidance material is present, the therapist needs to focus the session back to the problem area or treatment goals. Each problem area is worked in the following sequence: general exploration of the problem, definition of the maladaptive behavior or demands, analysis of options to solve the problem, and encouragement of new behavior.

The therapist encourages self-disclosure and trust by being aware of timing issues. When the adolescent brings emotionally relevant material, the therapist encourages further elaboration and a fuller expression and exploration of feelings. If the adolescent discusses irrelevant material, the therapist may re-focus the session to emotionally important and relevant issues. By accepting and understanding the adolescent's feelings, the therapist is strengthening the relationship.

The therapist must be aware of signs of negative and counter-therapeutic feelings to prevent the adolescent or his or her parents from sabotaging treatment. Behaviors such as lateness, missed appointments, silence, evasion of significant material, uncooperativeness, acting out, or suicidal attempts should be discussed. The therapist should try to curb the behavior and relate it to the problems of interpersonal relationships outside of the therapy. Resolving problems within the therapeutic session can be an example for the adolescent to handle other problems in other relationships.

Termination Phase (Sessions 9–12)

To the adolescent, termination means having to give up a valued relationship and to develop a sense of competence to solve further problems on his or her own. If the adolescent is not able to address these issues successfully, depressive symptoms and maladaptive behavior could reappear at the end of treatment or afterward. The resurgence of feelings of hopelessness should be avoided.

To help the adolescent deal with termination, the therapist openly discusses the end of treatment and the adolescent's feelings with regard to termination, acknowledges that termination is a time of potential grieving, and recognizes the adolescent's new found competence to solve interpersonal difficulties. The therapist and the adolescent review the course of treatment and new options discovered through therapy. If a need for further treatment is identified, the therapist discusses the alternatives with the adolescent and his or her parents. A session with parents at termination is helpful to summarize the course accomplishments of therapy.

Clinical Vignette

Elena is a 13-year-old adolescent who was referred to our project by her school's psychologist. He observed that she was depressed and that her academic performance was affected.

Elena had been reared by an aunt and uncle. Her mother's addiction to heroin incapacitated her from caring for Elena. Elena had a younger brother, 8 years old, who was being reared by her grandmother, who also lived with her mother. This brother was born with a chronic illness. Elena's father was also addicted to drugs and had never taken care of her. In fact, she could not remember her father.

Elena said that she had felt sad since the age of 7 years. She felt sad over her separation from her mother and brother. Her aunt did not like Elena to visit her grandmother's house because her mother's addiction could be a "bad" influence on Elena. Her aunt also worried about Elena's safety in her grandmother's house. Nevertheless, Elena longed for more frequent visits with her mother and brother. Elena felt sorry for her mother and brother. She felt that she had a better life than they had in terms of economic resources.

One day, Elena discovered that her mother has the human immunodeficiency virus (HIV). She did not want her aunt to find out because her aunt would be more strict with her visits to her mother and brother. Elena also worried that her aunt and uncle were making arrangements to adopt her legally. She did not want to be adopted and feared that her aunt would have more power over her, prohibiting contacts with her mother and not allowing her participation in after school activities or accepting invitations from her friends. This atmosphere was the extreme opposite of that at her grandmother's house, where there were few rules and no clear structure. However, Elena did not want to hurt her aunt and uncle's feelings. She still wished to live with them and did not want them to abandon her. Elena appreciated what they had done for her but felt she would feel happier if she could have the liberty to spend more time with her mother, brother, and grandmother. She felt that her aunt was more inflexible than her uncle. Many conflicts had arisen between Elena and her aunt, with her uncle assuming conciliatory postures but finally allying himself with his wife. Elena felt that to avoid conflicts with her aunt she had to lie to her, which made Elena feel uncomfortable.

In interpersonal terms, Elena had two areas of difficulties: grief over the psychological loss of her mother, brother, and father (her biological family); grief over her mother's illness (drug addiction and HIV) and brother's illness; and interpersonal disputes with her aunt. These issues were identified as related to her depression. Elena was able to express her feelings of sadness, anger, and guilt related to the situations in her biological family. Elena was able to develop better communication with her aunt and was able to express her feelings and fears. They were able to agree on the postponement of the adoption, on a more acceptable visitation schedule with her mother and brother, and on getting permission to attend activities with her friends. This helped Elena to feel better and to perform better in school. After 12 sessions of the interpersonal psychotherapy, Elena's depressive symptomatology was markedly reduced.

TESTING THE EFFICACY OF CBT AND IPT WITH PUERTO RICAN ADOLESCENTS

The development of these two approaches has been funded by the National Institute of Mental Health for a pilot test of the efficacy of CBT and IPT with depressed Puerto Rican adolescents. Our plan is to develop and adapt the manuals, develop the instrumentation, and conduct a preliminary test of 12 sessions of CBT and IPT in comparison with a no treatment control condition.

To date, we have entered 63 subjects into the clinical trial. The CBT, IPT, and wait-list control (WLC) conditions each have 22, 23, and 18 participants, respectively, who have completed the pre- and postevaluation.

The research team provided an orientation to nearby school principals, social workers, and counselors about depression and its symptoms in adolescents. They also explained the treatment that could be provided through the research project. Referrals with parental approval were received from seven schools. Adolescents were then interviewed and evaluated by a clinical psychologist. Parents were also interviewed and asked to fill out the Child Behavior Checklist. Subjects who scored over 11 on the Children's Depression Inventory (CDI; Kovacs, 1983) and who met *DSM-III-R* criteria for depression (DISC-2, parent and/or adolescent versions) were invited to participate in the study. Exclusionary criteria included: (a) serious imminent suicidal risk; (b) psychotic features; (c) organic brain syndrome; (d) marked hyperaggresion; (e) currently on psychopharmacological medication or psychotherapy; and (f) legal or court proceedings. Informed consent was necessary and obtained from parents and adolescents.

Measures

Pre-, post-, and follow-up evaluations (3 months after treatment) were made using the following instruments:

1. CDI (Kovacs, 1983, 1992; Rosselló, Guisasola, Ralat, Martínez, & Nieves, 1992);
2. Piers-Harris Children's Self Concept Scale (Piers, 1972);
3. Social Adjustment Measure (Beiser, 1990);
4. Stressful Life Events (Coddington, 1972a, 1972b);
5. Child Behavior Checklist (Achenback & Edelbrock, 1983); and
6. Family Emotional Involvement and Criticism Scale (Shields, Franks, Harp, McDaniel, & Campbell, 1992).

At present, results on only the CDI have been analyzed and will be presented here. The CDI is a 27-item self-rated symptom-oriented scale suitable for school aged children and adolescents. Kovacs (1983) reported a reliability coefficient of .86 for the scale and has found it to be a valid measure when compared with other instruments. Rosselló et al. (1992) translated the CDI into Spanish and adapted the instrument to Puerto Rican culture and youth population.

Preliminary Results

We conducted early analyses of the pre-to-post completers on the depression (CDI) measure, and the data are promising. Analysis of variance results show that time (pre–post) has a significant effect on depression ($F(1,54) = 26.75$, $p < .0001$). The effect of the interaction between time and treatment was also significant ($F(2,53) = 3.03$, $p < .05$). Effect sizes were calculated for the treatment groups. So far, the IPT reflects an effect size of .71 while the CBT group reflects an effect size of .36. These effect sizes can be interpreted as moderate effects for both treatments. We are encouraged by these early findings.

CONCLUSIONS AND FUTURE DIRECTIONS

Preliminary findings suggest that both CBT and IPT treatment approaches as adapted for the Puerto Rican adolescent population appear to be promising methods of interventions. Although further analysis must be performed, a reduction of depressive symptomatology seems to be accomplished by the interventions.

Cultural and developmental adaptations of successful adult therapeutic interventions for minority adolescents are possible and effective, and should be considered as alternatives to the creation of new models. Technology transfer and careful adaptation are possibilities that can guide and nurture interventions with different populations, which permit further transcultural studies.

Our data need to be expanded and additional analysis performed to answer questions about the relative efficacy of the CBT and IPT treatment approaches. Future studies should explore a group format of these treatments versus individual modalities to test cost-effectiveness issues. Process questions also should be addressed to better understand the characteristics of successful interventions.

REFERENCES

Achenbach, T. M., & Edelbrock, C. S. (1983). *Manual for the Child Behavior Checklist and Revised Child Behavior Profile*. Burlington: University of Vermont.

Acosta, F. X., Yamamoto, J., & Evans, L. A. (1982). *Effective psychotherapy for low-income and minority patients*. New York: Plenum Press.

Albert, N., & Beck, A. T. (1975). Incidence of depression in early adolescence: A preliminary study. *Journal of Youth and Adolescence, 4*, 301–305.

American Psychiatric Association. (1980). *Diagnostic and statistical manual of mental disorders* (3rd ed.). Washington, DC: Author.

American Psychiatric Association. (1987). *Diagnostic and statistical manual of mental disorders* (3rd ed., rev.). Washington, DC: Author.

Aponte, H. (1990). Ethnicity dynamics important in therapeutic relationship. *Family Therapy News, 21*, 3.

Aponte, J. F., Rivers, R. Y., & Wahl, J. (1995). *Psychological Interventions and cultural diversity*. Boston: Allyn & Bacon.

Beck, A. T., Rush, A. J., Shaw, B. F., & Emery, G. (1979). *Cognitive therapy of depression*. New York: Guilford Press.

Beiser, M. (1990). *Final Report Submitted in Fulfillment of Requirements for the Grants of the United States National Institute of Mental Health (5-R01-MH36678-04) and the Canada Health and Welfare National Health Research Directorate Program (NHRDP 6610-1322-04)*.

Bernal, G. (1993). Psychotherapy research: An introduction to the special issues. *Interamerican Journal of Psychology, 27*, 127–130.

Bernal, G., Bonilla, J., & Bellido, C. (1995). Ecological validity and cultural sensitivity for outcome research: Issues for the cultural adaptation and development of psychosocial treatments with Hispanics. *Journal of Abnormal Child Psychology, 23*, 67–87.

Bird, H. R., Canino, G., Rubio-Stipec, M., Gould, M. S., Ribera, J., Sesman, M., Woodbury, M., Huertas-Goldman, S., Pagan, A., Sánchez-Lacay, A., & Moscoso, M. (1988). Estimates of the prevalence of childhood maladjustment in a community survey in Puerto Rico. *Archives of General Psychiatry, 45,* 1120–1126.

Board of Ethnic Minority Affairs. (1990). *Guidelines for providers of psychological services to ethnic, linguistic, and culturally diverse populations.* Washington, DC: American Psychological Association.

Canino, I. A., & Spurlock, J. (1994). *Culturally diverse children and adolescents: Assessment, diagnosis, and treatment.* New York: Guilford Press.

Carlson, G., & Cantwell, D. P. (1980). Unmasking masked depression in children and adolescents. *American Journal of Psychiatry, 137,* 445–449.

Chien, C., & Change, T. (1985). Depression in Taiwan: Epidemiological survey utilizing the CEOS-D. *Sunshine Shank Gaku Zasshi, 87,* 355–358.

Coddington, R. (1972a). The significance of life events as etiologic factors in the diseases of children: Part 1. A survey of professional workers. *Journal of Psychosomatic Research, 16,* 7–18.

Coddington, R. (1972b). The significance of live events as etiologic factors in the diseases of children: Part 2. A study of a normal population. *Journal of Psychosomatic Research, 16,* 205–213.

Comas-Díaz, L., & Griffith, E. E. H. (Eds.). (1988). *Clinical guidelines in cross-cultural mental health.* New York: Wiley.

Dana, R. H. (1993). *Multicultural assessment perspectives for professional psychology.* Boston: Allyn & Bacon.

Draguns, J. G. (1981). Counseling across cultures: Common themes and distinct approaches. In P. B. Pedersen, W. J. Lonner, & S. E. Trimble (Eds.), *Counseling across cultures* (pp. 3–21). Honolulu: University of Hawaii Press.

Ellis, A. (1962). *Reason and emotion in psychotherapy.* New York: Lyle Stuart.

Ellis, A., & Bernard, M. (1983). *Rational-emotive approaches to the problems of childhood.* New York: Plenum Press.

Fleming, J. E., & Offord, D. R. (1990). Epidemiology of childhood depressive disorders: A critical review. *Journal of the American Academy of Child and Adolescent Psychiatry, 29,* 571–580.

Fleming, J. E., Offord, D. R., & Boyle, M. H. (1989). Prevalence of childhood and adolescent depression in the community: Ontario Child Health Study. *British Journal of Psychiatry, 155,* 647–654.

Ghali, B. (1977). *Ethnic America.* New York: Basic Books.

Gibbs, J. T. (1985). Psychological factors associated with depression in urban adolescent females: Implications for treatment. *Journal of Youth and Adolescence, 14,* 47–60.

Ho, M. K. (1992). *Minority children and adolescents in therapy.* Newbury Park, CA: Sage.

Inclán, J., & Herron, D. G. (1985). Ecologically oriented therapy with Puerto Rican adolescents and their families. In J. T. Gibbs & L. N. Hung (Eds.), *Psychological treatment of minority children and adolescents* (pp. 251–277).

Jones, E. E., & Korchin, S. J. (Eds.). (1982). *Minority mental health.* New York: Praeger.

Kandel, D. B., & Davies, M. (1982). Epidemiology of depressive mood in adolescents. *Archives of General Psychiatry, 39,* 1205–1212.

Kanner, L. (1972). *Child Psychiatry.* Illinois: Charles C. Thomas.

Kaplan, N. J., Hong, G. H., & Weenhold, C. (1984). Epidemiology of depressive symptomatology in adolescents. *Journal of the American Academy of Child Psychiatry, 23,* 91–98.

Kashani, J. H., Holcomb, W. R., & Orvaschel, H. (1986). Depression and depressive symptoms in preschool children from the general population. *American Journal of Psychiatry, 143,* 1138–1143.

Kashani, J. H., & Simonds, J. F. (1979). The incidence of depression in children. *American Journal of Psychiatry, 136,* 1203–1205.

Klerman, G. L., Weissman, M. M., Rounsaville, B. J., & Chevron, E. S. (1984). *Interpersonal psychotherapy of depression.* New York: Basic Books.

Kovacs, M. (1983). *The Children's Depression Inventory: A self-report depression scale for school-aged youngsters.* Unpublished manuscript, University of Pittsburgh School of Medicine.

Kovacs, M. (1992). *Children's Depression Inventory.* New York: Multi-Health Systems.

Lewinsohn, P. M. (1975). The behavioral study and treatment of depression. In M. Hersen, R. Isler, and P. Miller (Eds.), *Progress in behavior modification* (Vol. 1). San Diego, CA: Academic Press.

Lewinsohn, P. M. (1976). Activity schedules in treatment of depression. In J. Krumholtz and C. Thoresen (Eds.), *Counseling Methods.* New York: Holt, Rinehart, & Winston.

Lewinsohn, P. M., Antonuccio, D. O., Steinmetz-Breckenridge, J., & Teri, L. (1984). *The coping with depression course.* Eugene, OR: Castalia Press.

Lewinsohn, P. M., & Libet, J. (1972). Pleasant events, activity schedules, and depression. *Journal of Abnormal Psychology, 79,* 291–295.

López, S. R., Grover, P., Holland, D., Johnson, M. J., Kain, C. D., Danel, D., Mellins, C. A., & Culkin-Rhyne, M. (1989). Development of culturally sensitive psychotherapists. *Professional Psychology: Research and Practice, 20,* 369–376.

Malgady, R. G., Rogler, L. H., & Constantino, G. (1990). Culturally sensitive psychotherapy for Puerto Rican children and adolescents: A program of treatment outcome research. *Journal of Consulting and Clinical Psychology, 58,* 704–712.

Mannino, F. V., & Shore, M. F. (1976). Perceptions of social support by Spanish-speaking youth with implications for program development. *The Journal of School Health, 46,* 471–474.

Mays, V. M., & Albee, G. W. (1992). Psychotherapy and ethnic minorities. In D. K. Freedheim (Ed.), *History of psychotherapy: A century of change* (pp. 552–570). Washington, DC: American Psychological Association.

McGoldrick, M., Pearce, J. K., & Giordano, J. (1982). *Ethnicity and family therapy.* New York: Guilford Press.

Mufson, L. (1991). Interpersonal psychotherapy for depressed adolescents (IPT-A): Description of modification and preliminary application. *Journal of the American Academy of Child and Adolescent Psychiatry, 30*(4), 624–651.

Mufson, L. (1993). *Interpersonal psychotherapy for depressed adolescents.* New York: Guilford Press.

Muñoz, R. F. (1982). The Spanish speaking consumer and the community mental health center. In E. E. Jones & S. Korchin (Eds.), *Minority mental health* (pp. 362–398). New York: Praeger.

Muñoz, R. F., & Miranda, J. (1986). *Group therapy manual for cognitive–behavioral treatment of depression.* San Francisco: University of California.

Navarro, A. (1993). The effectiveness of psychotherapy with Latinos in the United States: A metanalytic review. *Interamerican Journal of Psychology, 27*, 131–146.

Petersen, A. C., Compas, B. E., Brooks-Gunn, J., Stemmler, M., Ey, S., & Grant, K. E. (1993). Depression in adolescence. *American Psychologist, 48*, 155–168.

Piers, E. V. (1972). Prediction of children's self-concepts. *Journal of Consulting and Clinical Psychology, 38*, 428–433.

Reynolds, W. M. (1983). *Depression in adolescents: Measurement, epidemiology, and correlates.* Paper presented at the annual meeting of the National Association of School Psychologists, Detroit, MI.

Rie, H. E. (1966). Depression in childhood: A survey of pertinent contributions. *Journal of the American Academy of Child Psychiatry, 4*, 653–686.

Rogler, L. H., Malgady, R. G., Constantino, G., & Blumenthal, R. (1987). What do culturally sensitive mental health services mean? The case of Hispanics. *American Psychologist, 42*, 565–570.

Rosselló, J. (1993). Acercamientos terapéuticos para la depresión en adolescentes puertorriqueñas: Dos estudios de casos [Therapeutic approaches to depression in Puerto Rican adolescents: Two case studies]. *Revista Interamericana de Psicología, 27*, 163–180.

Rosselló, J. (1994). *Manuales para las terapias interpersonal y cognoscitiva-conductual para el tratamiento de la depresión en adolescentes puertorriqueños* [Manuals for interpersonal and cognitive–behavioral treatments for depression in Puerto Rican adolescents]. Río Piedras, Universidad de Puerto Rico. Unpublished manuscript.

Rosselló, J., Guisasola, E., Ralat, S., Martínez, S., & Nieves, A. (1992). La evaluación de la depresión en un grupo de jóvenes puertorriqueños [Evaluation of depression in a group of Puerto Rican youths]. *Revista Puertorriqueña de Psicologia, 8*, 155–162.

Sabogal, F., Marín, G., & Otero-Sabogal, R. (1987). Hispanic familism and acculturation: What changes and what doesn't. *Hispanic Journal of Behavioral Sciences, 9*, 397–412.

Schoenbach, V. J., Kaplan, B. H., Grimson, R. C., & Wagner, E. H. (1982). Use of a symptom scale to study the prevalence of a depressive syndrome in young adolescents. *American Journal of Epidemiology, 116,* 791–800.

Shields, C., Franks, P., Harp, J., McDaniel, S., & Campbell, T. (1992). Development of the Family Emotional Involvement and Criticism Scale (FEICS): A self-report scale to measure expressed emotion. *Journal of Marital and Family Therapy, 18,* 395–407.

Siegel, L., & Griffin, N. J. (1984). Correlates of depressive symptoms in adolescents. *Journal of Youth and Adolescence, 10,* 475–487.

Simon, F. B., Stierlin, H., & Wynne, L. C. (1988). *Vocabulario de terapia familiar* [Dictionary of family therapy]. Buenos Aires, Argentina: Editorial Gedisa.

Smith, W. D., Burlew, A. K., Mosley, M. H., & Whitney, W. M. (1978). *Minority issues in mental health.* Reading, MA: Adison-Wesley.

Sue, S. (1977). Community mental health services to minority groups: Some optimism, some pessimism. *American Psychologist, 32,* 616–624.

Sue, S., & Zane, N. (1987). The role of culture and cultural techniques in psychotherapy: A critique and reformulations. *American Psychology, 42,* 37–45.

Sullivan, H. S. (1986). Adolescent depression: Its prevalence in high school students. *Journal of School Psychology, 24,* 103–109.

Sullivan, H. S., & Elgin, A. W. (1986). Adolescent depression: Its prevalence in high school students. *Journal of School Psychology, 24,* 103–109.

Szapocznik, J., Scopetta, M. A., & Aranalde, M. A. (1978). Cuban value structure: Treatment implications. *Journal of Consulting and Clinical Psychology, 46,* 961–970.

Teri, L. (1982). Depression in adolescence: Its relationship to assertion and various aspects of self-image. *Journal of Clinical Child Psychology, 11,* 101–106.

Tharp, R. G. (1991). Cultural diversity and treatment of children. *Journal of Consulting and Clinical Psychology, 59,* 799–812.

Weinberg, W. A., & Emslie, G. J. (1988). Weinberg Screening Affective Scales (WSAS and WSAS-SF). *Journal of Child Neurology, 3,* 294–296.

Wells, V., Klerman, G. L., & Deykin, E. Y. (1987). The prevalence of depressive symptoms in college students. *Social Psychology, 22,* 20–28.

Yamamoto, J., & Sasaki, Y. (1968). Cultural problems in psychiatric therapy. *Archives of General Psychiatry, 19,* 45–49.

Zuñiga, M. E. (1992). Using methapors in therapy: Dichos and Latino clients. *Social Work, 37,* 55–60.

10

PSYCHOSOCIAL INTERVENTIONS FOR TREATING ADOLESCENT SUICIDAL DEPRESSION: A COMPARISON OF THREE PSYCHOSOCIAL INTERVENTIONS

DAVID A. BRENT, CLAUDIA M. ROTH, DIANE P. HOLDER, DAVID J. KOLKO, BORIS BIRMAHER, BARBARA A. JOHNSON, and JOY A. SCHWEERS

This chapter describes a clinical trial comparing three psychosocial interventions (cognitive–behavioral treatment, systemic–behavioral family treatment, and nondirective supportive treatment) for depressed adolescents. The trial is still ongoing, and therefore no conclusive data on the final results of the trial are available. This chapter emphasizes the salient psychosocial factors associated with onset, course, and recurrence of depression; the rationale for the design; and methodological issues that emerged in the course of conducting the trial.

OVERVIEW

Depression in Adolescents

Major depression is a common and serious disorder in adolescents, with a point prevalence of 2.9%–8.3% (Fleming & Offord, 1990; Lewinsohn & Hops, 1993). This disorder is recurrent and associated with significant role impairment, including early parenthood, divorce, work and

This work was supported by National Institute of Mental Health Grant MH46500. Correspondence concerning this chapter should be addressed to Dr. David A. Brent, Western Psychiatric Institute and Clinic, 3811 O'Hara Street, Suite 112, Pittsburgh, PA 15213.

legal difficulties, and substance abuse (Harrington, Fudge, Rutter, Pickles, & Hill, 1990; Kandel & Davies, 1986; Kovacs, Feinberg, Crouse-Novak, Paulauskas, & Finklestein, 1984a; Kovacs, Feinberg, Crouse-Novak, Paulauskas, Pollock, & Finklestein, 1984b; Rao et al., 1995). Finally, this condition is associated with significant risk for both suicidal behavior and suicide (Brent, Perper, et al., 1993; Garrison, Jackson, Addy, McKeown, & Waller, 1991; Kovacs, Goldston, & Gatsonis, 1993; Lewinsohn, Rohde, & Seeley, 1994; Shaffer, Garland, Gould, Fisher, & Trautman, 1988; Shafii, Steltz-Lenarsky, Derrick, Beckner, & Whittinghill, 1988).

Onset of Depression

Studies of risk factors for the onset of depression are relatively rare, because they require a longitudinal design. Several studies have identified cognitive distortion as a risk factor for depressive symptomatology, particularly in the adolescent age group (Garber & Hilsman, 1992; Nolen-Hoeksema, Seligman, & Girgus, 1992). Both dysthymic disorder and anxiety disorder are risk factors for the development of depression (Kovacs et al., 1984a, 1984b, 1989, 1994; Reinherz et al., 1993). Family history of depression is associated with onset in the offspring, particularly when the pedigree shows affective disorder in multiple generations, and the age of onset of disorder in parents is under 20 years of age (Orvaschel, 1990; Orvaschel, Walsh-Allis, & Ye, 1988; Weissman et al., 1987; Weissman, Warner, Wickramaratne, & Prusoff, 1988). Family history of depression also predicts the onset of depression in the face of a severe psychosocial stressor (Brent, Poling, McKain, & Baugher, 1993). Poor perceived support and parent–child discord are also associated with the onset of depression (Fendrich, Warner, & Weissman, 1990; Garrison, Jackson, Addy, McKeown, & Waller, 1991; Reinherz et al., 1993; Rutter & Quinton, 1984).

Course of Depression

The severity of depression in the parent is associated with greater impairment in the child (Keller et al., 1986). Early age of onset in the child, exposure to more than one parental depressive episode, and exposure to divorce are all associated with more prolonged depressive episodes (Warner et al., 1992), as was comorbid dysthymic disorder (Kovacs et al., 1994).

Recurrence of Depression

A longitudinal study indicates that as many as 40% of early onset depressives may suffer a recurrence in 2 years, and more than 70% will have a recurrence in 5 years (Kovacs et al., 1984b). From this longitudinal study came the observation that earlier age of onset and comorbid dysthymic disorder were associated with increased risk of recurrence. A related observation comes from Clarke et al. (1995) and Warner et al. (1992), who found that subsyndromal symptoms of depression are a risk factor for either onset or recurrence. In addition, social impairment and expressed emotion, as measured by the Five Minute Speech Sample (FMSS), have been found to predict recurrence of depression (Asarnow et al., 1993, 1994; Warner et al., 1992).

Summary of Risk Factor Research

In summary, factors associated with the onset, course, or recurrence of depression can be grouped into two types of categories. First are intrapersonal factors such as early age-of-onset, dysthymia, anxiety, and cognitive distortion. Second are interpersonal, often familial, factors, such as family discord, poor support, divorce, "expressed emotion," and parental psychopathology. Although these two sets of factors clearly interact, the findings suggest two types of interventions, one aimed at intrapersonal factors, and one aimed at interpersonal, familial factors. We will now review the extant intervention trials in adolescent depression utilizing standard psychosocial approaches.

Psychosocial Intervention Studies for Adolescent Depression
Nonreferred Participants

Most psychosocial intervention studies for depressed adolescents have been performed in nonreferred samples. Reynolds and Coates (1986) compared two group interventions (cognitive–behavioral treatment [CBT] vs. relaxation therapy) to a wait-list control in high school students who were screened for depression using a self-report inventory. Both experimental conditions were superior to the wait-list control in the reduction of depressive symptomatology, and not different from one another. Lewinsohn and Clarke (1990) compared a CBT group intervention to a wait-list control in nonreferred high school students who met research diagnostic criteria (Feighner, Robins, & Guze, 1972) for major or minor depression. The CBT group was superior to the wait-list control; these differences persisted over a 2-year follow-up. Kahn, Kehle, Jenson, and Clark (1990) used Lewinsohn and Clarke's methodology and compared this intervention to "self-modelling," relationship therapy, and a wait-list control, and, similar to Reynolds and Coates (1986), found that all three active treatments were superior, with trends favoring CBT. Lerner and Clum (1990) compared a problem-solving group to a supportive group for depressed, suicidal college students and found the experimental treatment superior at termination and at the 9-month follow-up.

Two studies focused on the prevention of depression in children and adolescents who were at high risk. Beardslee et al. (1993) reported on a comparison of a clinician-based and a lecture-based preventive intervention for families with parental affective disorder. The clinician-based group resulted in more participant satisfaction and led to more parental changes in behaviors and attitudes toward illness, but no changes affecting offspring have yet been reported. Clarke et al. (1995) reported on the effectiveness of a 15-session group CBT group session in youth with subsyndromal depression, and found that the CBT intervention was superior to the wait-list control in the prevention of depression.

As noted, these studies did not include referred subjects, although they were carefully characterized by use of standard self-report assessments, and, in the case of Lewinsohn and Clarke (1990), by research psychiatric interviews. All studies found active treatments to be most effective, usually a cognitive–behavioral type of intervention. None of the studies reported the predictors of treatment response, specifically within the above-noted domains that theoretically contribute to the pathogenesis of depression. Also, none of the treatments dealt with the family as a unit, despite the wealth of literature finding a relationship between family variables and the onset, course, and recurrence of depression. Lewinsohn and Clarke (1990) did have a parent group augment their cognitive–behavioral group treatment in one cell, but the addition of this intervention did not result in a more efficacious treatment than group CBT alone.

Psychosocial Interventions for Adolescent Depressions: Clinically Referred Subjects

Much less work has focused on psychosocial interventions in referred patients. Mufson et al. (1994) reported on an open label trial of interpersonal therapy (IPT) for depressed adolescents, and reported that the treatment can be delivered with fidelity to the treatment model, is acceptable, and appears efficacious. A clinical trial of IPT is now ongoing by Mufson and colleagues. Case reports suggest that cognitive–behavior therapy for children and adolescents may be effective (Wilkes & Rush, 1988). A brief cognitive–behavioral family model for female minority suicide attempters (many of whom were depressed) has been described, is reportedly well-accepted, and a clinical trial is ongoing using this model of treatment (Rotheram-Borus et al., 1994). No definitive results of these trials are yet available to guide clinicians and researchers.

Psychopharmacologic Treatment of Adolescent Major Depression

The majority of published clinical trials addressing the treatment of adolescent major depression have compared antidepressant and placebo, usually finding no difference between active medication and placebo. This has been true of amitriptyline (Kramer & Feiguine, 1981; Kye et al., in press), desipramine (Kutcher et al., 1994), nortriptyline (Geller et al., 1990), and fluoxetine (Kye et al., in press). One study (Emslie et al., 1995) demonstrated the superiority of fluoxetine over placebo for child and adolescent major depression. However, in the medication cell, the response rate was only 58%, and differences between groups were reported only on the clinical global improvement scale and not on depressive symptoms.

In summary, at the present time, there are no known effective treatments for clinically referred patients with adolescent depression, either psychosocial or psychopharmacological. However, cognitive–behavioral interventions show promise on the basis of the existing literature. Moreover, given the strength of evidence implicating familial factors in the onset, course, and recurrence of adolescent depression, there is strong reason to hypothesize that family-based treatments would also be effective. Therefore, we embarked on a study comparing individual and family approaches to adolescent depression. Furthermore, we endeavored to assess critical psychosocial variables that we thought might predict onset, course, recurrence, or differential response to different types of treatment.

CONDUCT OF THE STUDY

Design

This study, still ongoing, compares the efficacy of three psychosocial treatments: cognitive–behavioral treatment (CBT), systemic–behavioral family treatment (SBFT), and nondirective supportive treatment (NST). Treatment consists of 12 to 16 1-hour sessions delivered over 12 to 16 weeks, followed by up to 4 booster sessions over the following 4 months. Subjects and their families are followed for 2 years after the termination of treatment.

Rationale

CBT and SBFT were chosen as interventions because they both target problem areas associated with the onset, course, and recurrence of adolescent depression. NST was chosen as a comparison treatment that controls for the attention and support that are central to psychotherapeutic interventions, without targeting specific domains associated with adolescent depression. The duration of treatment was consistent both with other reported clinical trials (e.g., Lewinsohn & Clarke, 1990), and with our own clinical experience. Boosters were added to the basic treatment package because of the knowledge that many of the attendant stressors, as well as depression, are recurrent. Subjects and their families were followed-up for 2 years after termination because of the high risk of recurrence during this period (Kovacs et al., 1984b). Extensive assessments were performed at the beginning and end of treatment, and on follow-ups. These assessments focused on domains thought to be associated with onset, course, and recurrence of treatment, and thereby enabled us to assess the specificity of treatment effect, and the roles of these variables in both treatment response and in depressive recurrence.

Sample

Patients for this study presented to the Child and Adolescent Mood and Anxiety Disorder Clinic. About one fourth were responding to advertisements; the remainder were self-, parent-, or professional-directed referrals. Patients are between the ages of 13 and 18 years of age, of at least normal intelligence, living with at least one parent or guardian, with a Beck Depression Inventory (BDI) (Beck et al., 1961) score greater or equal to 13, and fulfilling *Diagnostic and Statistical Manual of Mental Disorders*, third edition revised (*DSM-III-R*; American Psychiatric Association, 1987) criteria for major depressive disorder. Patients on psychotropic medication were excluded as were those with psychosis, bipolar I or II disorder, substance abuse or dependence, eating disorders, obsessive–compulsive disorder, pregnancy, ongoing physical or sexual abuse, or chronic medical illness. Thus far, of those offered the opportunity to participate in the study, more than 90% have accepted.

Assessment

Each patient admitted to the study receives an in-depth research assessment covering several domains. Psychiatric symptomatology is assessed by use of the BDI (Beck et al., 1961), the School Aged Schedule for Affective Disorders and Schizophrenia, Epidemiologic and Parent Versions (K-SADS-E and P; Chambers et al., 1985; Orvaschel et al., 1982), and the Child Behavior Check List (CBCL; Achenbach & Edelbrock, 1983). The CBCL is also utilized to assess social competency. Cognitive distortion is assessed by the Beck Hopelessness Scale (BHS; Beck et al., 1974) and the Cognitive Negative Errors Questionnaire (CNEQ; Leitenberg, Yost, & Carroll-Wilson, 1986), both administered to the patient. Family environment is assessed by use of the Family Assessment Device (FAD; Epstein, Baldwin, & Bishop, 1983), the Conflict Behavior Questionnaire (CBQ; Robin & Foster, 1989), the Area of Change Questionnaire (ACQ; Jacob & Seilhamer, 1985), and the Family Global Interaction Coding Scale (FGICS;

Hetherington, Hagan, & Eisenberg, 1990); all are administered to both the patient and the parents.

Additional psychiatric services usage by the patient and families were documented using the Longitudinal Interview for Follow-up Evaluations (LIFE; Keller et al., 1987). Parents were assessed at intake with the SADS-L (Endicott & Spitzer, 1978) to render *DSM-III-R* diagnoses. Parental assessments were performed blind to assessments of patients. Moreover, patient follow-up assessments were performed blind to treatment condition.

TREATMENT

Family Psychoeducation

Patients and their families in all three cells received family psychoeducation (e.g., education about affective illness, how the family can help, etc.). This intervention was initially developed because of our clinical experience with patients who were depressed and suicidal; parents often did not regard their adolescents' difficulties as serious, but rather as manipulative. Although the low dropout rate (about 10%) in this study may be attributable to many factors, it is likely that family psychoeducation played some role, as initial studies in open treatment documented parental satisfaction with the intervention (Brent, Poling, et al., 1993). This intervention is distinct from SBFT, insofar as family psychoeducation is designed to be prescriptive and didactic, as distinguished from the more complex and interactive family interventions utilized by therapists in the SBFT cell.

Cognitive–Behavioral Therapy (CBT)

CBT is an adaptation of Beck's approach to depressed adults (Beck et al., 1979). Like Beck's approach, CBT emphasizes collaborative empiricism; the importance of socializing the patient to the cognitive therapy model; and the monitoring and modification of automatic thoughts, assumptions, and basic beliefs. To adapt CBT for adolescents, we have found it important to anchor all explanations and discussions to concrete examples, to spend more time on socialization to treatment, to deal explicitly with issues of autonomy and trust, to emphasize acquisition of social skills, and to attend to issues of impulsivity that are particularly problematic in adolescence and often related to concomitant problems associated with depression (i.e., suicide attempts, substance use, unprotected sex). Therefore, for issues related to impulsivity, we use a problem-solving approach that has been applied successfully by others (Kazdin et al., 1987). Additionally, because difficulty with affect regulation can interfere with the ability to effectively solve problems, there is an explicit focus on regulating affect through the use of a "feeling thermometer," as is described in the treatment manuals of Rotheram-Borus' and our group (Rotheram-Borus et al., 1994; Brent, Poling, et al., 1993). Importance of family involvement in the treatment of suicidal and depressed adolescents is well recognized (Wilkes & Rush, 1988). However, because of our need to keep the treatment cells relatively distinct, for the purposes of this trial, family involvement in this treatment modality consists of education and feedback to the family about the progress of the adolescent in treatment.

CBT is thought to be effective for adolescent depression because cognitive distortions are associated with the onset and recurrence of depression. Moreover, hopelessness is associated with suicide and suicidal behavior. Impulsivity and affect regulation, two of the targets of CBT, are likely to be associated with suicidal behavior and risk-taking, both common problems in depressed youth.

In the following vignette, the patient quickly became socialized to CBT, grasped the principles of cognitive therapy, and generalized them to other areas of her life.

K. L. is a 12-year-old African–American girl who was referred for an evaluation by her mother because of concern about depressive symptoms beginning 6 months previously. K. L. reported decreased contact with her biological father associated with the onset of the depression. The patient noted that since feeling depressed, she had started to avoid people and endorsed marked self-consciousness.

K. L. was seen weekly for 14 sessions and was followed-up monthly for 4 booster sessions. The first part of treatment emphasized the importance of K. L. acknowledging her own feelings as important. She learned to use cognitive techniques to identify automatic thoughts, label cognitive distortions, and challenge her distorted thinking so that she could begin to view herself more objectively and fairly. Another important part of treatment included teaching K. L. problem-solving skills. K. L. had difficulty organizing her homework and chores; using these problem-solving strategies helped K. L. to structure her time and complete necessary tasks.

K. L. became socialized to the cognitive model. Moreover, the relationship between therapist and client was collaborative, and K. L. experienced the therapeutic relationship as empathic. This was especially important as K. L. identified the relationship with her mother as "difficult" because the mother's parenting style was often authoritarian, and K. L.'s response tended to be passive and accommodating, further contributing to feelings of depression. Through communication training and conjoint parent–child sessions, K. L. was able to "find" her own voice, which further enhanced her feelings of competence and self-respect.

Systemic-Behavioral Family Therapy (SBFT)

SBFT, as practiced in this treatment study, is a combination of two treatment approaches that have been utilized effectively for dysfunctional families of adolescents. The first phase of treatment is drawn from Functional Family Therapy (FFT; Alexander & Parsons, 1973) in which the therapist joins with the family through a series of reframing maneuvers to obtain maximal engagement and commitment from each family member without alienating any other family member. After engagement and clarification of the problems and goals that the family wants to achieve through therapy, the treatment moves to the behavioral component, as developed by Robin and Foster (1989). Robin and coworkers have conceptualized the etiology of family conflict involving adolescents as related to deficient communication and problem-solving skills, and structural difficulties (e.g., inappropriate alliances). In the initial phase of treatment, these difficulties are elicited through family tasks and assessments, problem areas are identified, and strategies for improvement are developed and implemented (Robin & Foster, 1989). This phase of treatment involves intensive emphasis on socialization to this treatment model, positive practice both in session and at home, and a commitment on the part of all family members to self-monitoring and positive practice. As one moves to later phases of SBFT, the emphasis is increasingly on generalization. The rationale presented to the family for SBFT is that family conflict and communication difficulties can be related to depression in a given family member, and that if these problems can be ameliorated, then the patient will be less likely to have difficulties with depression in the future.

The following vignette illustrates a successful application of SBFT. Marital conflict was identified and defused, and the parents were transformed into cotherapists to facilitate the patient's growth.

A. B. is a 13.5-year-old White girl who was initially referred by her school psychologist following disclosure of suicidal ideation. Prior to evaluation, the patient had made a suicide gesture in which she took pills out of a bottle, lined them up on the table, but did not ingest them. The patient and family identified peer conflict at school as well as marital conflict between mother and stepfather as current stressors.

A. B. resided with her biological mother and her stepfather, who had lived in the home for the past 10 years. A. B. had one older sister who was currently away at her first year of college. In addition, her stepfather had a daughter who was 2 years older than A. B. and who had resided in the home for approximately 5 years, but had left the home abruptly following family conflict approximately 2 years earlier. In addition, her maternal grandfather also resided in the household. Both biological mother and stepfather worked full time out of the home.

The family was seen for 14 weekly sessions and 3 booster sessions following active treatment. Initially, A. B. was seen with her biological mother and stepfamily to begin to assess family interaction and problem-solving patterns. It was apparent that the intensity of marital conflict often triangulated A. B. and served as a major impediment to any attempts at problem solving. The family pattern was that the marital conflict would escalate, mother often would align with her daughter, and vent and complain to daughter about the conflict with stepfather. The parents were seen alone for 4 sessions to assess and treat the marital conflict. The parents were helped to understand that they needed to work on developing the ability to contain the marital conflict within their own dyad, because A. B. was a "vulnerable child who was extremely sensitive to marital conflict and often found herself in the middle." This frame rallied the parents to work together to protect their daughter. Sessions were then conducted with the parents and their daughter in which the parents modeled problem solving and communication, thus becoming a resource for the patient. This was a very successful intervention. Parents were able to come into the family sessions with a united front and began to use the problem-solving/communication model within their own relationship and to assist A. B. to develop these skills as well.

Treatment then focused on the difficulties that A. B. was encountering with peer interactions, managing her own depression, and adolescent relationship issues. A. B.'s older sister joined the family sessions at the end of the college semester and also reinforced A. B.'s staying out of the marital conflict. The family was seen as "laboratory" for A. B. to practice improved communication and problem-solving skills so that she could then translate these abilities into her peer world and improve relationships outside the family. A. B. reported back to the family sessions a number of success stories.

Several sessions focused on tensions between A. B. and her stepfather, resulting from conflict with stepfather's biological daughter who had left the family abruptly. A. B. and this stepsister had been very close and this cut-off was difficult. A. B. was able to talk to her stepfather about these issues and the family was able to put some closure on an upsetting event that had occurred 2 years earlier.

The family was seen for booster sessions, and parents continued to contain their marital conflict within their marriage. A. B. was working very hard at keeping herself out of the middle and had developed specific signals and techniques to help in that effort. She was doing well in school. At the end of treatment, A. B. was reporting an absence of all depressive symptoms and had reinvolved herself with peers. The family's efforts to restructure so that A. B. did not get triangulated into the marital conflict had eased the tensions in the family and enabled them to improve communication and problem-solving skills. All of these gains affected A. B. positively, and her depression remitted.

Non-directive Support Treatment (NST)

NST is a treatment designed to control for the nonspecific aspects of treatment—the passage of time, the amount of contact with a therapist, and the support of an empathic and concerned skilled professional. Although these elements of treatment are generally acknowledged to be necessary for a successful outcome, it is unclear whether they are sufficient for the treatment of this population. In NST, the therapist encourages the patient to monitor his or her feelings, to learn to identify them and get in touch with them, and to share them with the therapist. The therapist refrains from giving advice or making interpretations, but instead resorts to reflective listening, exhortations and statements of support, clarification, and provision of accurate empathy. The rationale presented to the patient and family for this type of treatment is that depression often is the result of a sense of loneliness and isolation, particularly alienation from adult figures. By providing a sympathetic and empathetic ear to the adolescent, and allowing him or her to explore his or her feelings in a secure environment, he or she may begin to feel less depressed. The adolescent and family are socialized to the importance of self-discovery and of making one's own judgments, rather than expecting advice and direction from the therapist.

This particular method of treatment is well suited to adolescents because of its nondirective and nonthreatening nature, and its use of empathic feedback. There may be some benefit to having access to an understanding adult in a nondirective context wherein teenagers may dictate the course and content of treatment. With this treatment approach, one may be able to help teens identify and understand affective reactions to circumstances, to acknowledge the validity of their personal experiences, and ultimately to use these experiences as a way of counteracting the effects of future distressing experiences. It should be noted that similar models of treatment have been used with no untoward effects in other clinical trials (Gibbons et al., 1978; Hawton et al., 1987; Lerner & Clum, 1990; Rush et al., 1982).

The following vignette illustrates a successful use of NST, in which the adolescent patient derived support and solidity from the therapist in the face of a serious family crisis.

F. G. is a 15-year-old White girl living with her biological mother, older brother, and older sister. F. G. entered treatment for symptoms of depression

F. G. used the therapy sessions to ventilate feelings of sadness and guilt over her parent's divorce and her father's chronic alcoholism. She portrayed herself as lonely and isolated in the family, often forgotten about or criticized. She was able to begin to see her role as "victim" in both family and peer conflicts.

By the 10th session, F. G.'s mood had significantly improved. She was more involved in positive peer relationships and had begun to accept the reality that her parents were not going to reconcile. She was more able to place boundaries between her sadness at her father's alcoholic loneliness and his own role in leading to the disintegration of the marriage. Although still receiving little emotional support from her mother, F. G. was reporting a greater ability to avoid conflict in the home. By the end of treatment, F. G. no longer had any significant symptoms of major depression.

Maintenance of Treatment Integrity

Maintenance of treatment integrity is a critical element of a clinical trial. Therapeutic success across different treatments has been related to adherence to a specific treatment model (Luborsky et al., 1985). More precisely, maintenance of treatment integrity means that the treatment delivered is standard, thereby guarding against variability that could erase a potentially significant effect. Finally, maintenance of treatment integrity preserves distinctness among treatment cells. Treatment integrity is monitored through the following steps: (a) therapists' training and using a treatment manual; (b) monitoring therapists by rating videotaped therapy sessions; (c) monitoring therapists by frequent supervision; and (d) rating of tapes by an external consultant. Adherence to CBT, SBFT, and NST have been monitored by use of the Cognitive Therapy Scale (CTS; Vallis, Shaw, & Dobson, 1986), the modified Family Therapist Rating Scale (Piercy, Liard, & Mohammed, 1983), and eight items from the Vanderbilt Psychotherapy Process Scale (Strupp & Binder, 1984; Suh, Strupp, & O'Malley, 1986), respectively. Thus far, more than 80% of all sessions in all three cells have been rated as acceptable by external and internal raters.

Treatment Distinctness and Flexibility

There may be times when clinical indications require that a therapist in the CBT or NST cell meet with the family. For example, the parent may request feedback from or wish to discuss an issue such as the child's school performance with the clinician. To preserve distinctness of the three models, these sessions may be no more than a total of 4 hours out of the total 12–16 hours allotted for treatment. The clinician is to provide for the parent whatever information is deemed to be clinically useful, but to avoid giving advice, serving as an intermediary, or otherwise falling into the role of a "family therapist." These sessions are reviewed in group supervision, with the investigators present to ensure against therapeutic drift.

Also, such sessions are monitored by the external consultants as noted earlier. An alternative problem, that the family therapist may need to meet individually with a family member to engage them in treatment, presents a similar dilemma. The therapist can explore the concerns of the family member and emphasize the importance of his or her participation, but should avoid either a supportive or cognitive approach. Again, these sessions are reviewed in group supervision and by the external consultants. In all cases, adequate discriminant validity has been preserved, that is, expert raters can distinguish supplemental family sessions from family therapy, and supplemental individual sessions from either CBT or NST.

Patients Who Are Symptomatic at Termination

At 12–16 weeks (termination), subjects undergo a reassessment to determine if they still meet criteria for *DSM-III-R* major depression according to the K-SADS-E. If they still fulfill criteria, then they are offered open treatment. If they do not meet criteria for major depression, then they are followed in the protocol as described.

Removal from the Study

It is necessary in any clinical trial to have clear criteria for removal from the trial, to protect the patient and to ensure that the patient does not incur undue risk. Criteria for removal from treatment would include development of any of the initial exclusionary criteria, such as substance abuse or bipolar disorder, functional impairment due to a comorbid condition such as conduct disorder or suicide attempts, or continued or increased depression. All patients whose depression continues unabated are evaluated by one of the study psychiatrists at 6 weeks to determine whether they are stable enough to continue in the study. This decision is based on severity of symptomatology, functional impairment, severity of suicidal ideation, and a discussion with patient and family as to their wishes (whether to go into open treatment or continue). At the end of treatment, if a patient is still depressed, then the patient and family are offered open treatment and do not continue in booster sessions.

Booster Sessions

All patients who have achieved remission receive up to 4 booster sessions. These 4 sessions are administered over the first 4 months after the end of active treatment. The staggering of booster sessions is designed to minimize the tendency of partially symptomatic patients and their families to fully relapse and to seek treatment elsewhere involving different modalities. Booster sessions consist of a review and reinforcement of what has been learned in treatment. The patient and family are encouraged to survey potential difficulties and rehearse potential coping strategies to meet these potential problems.

Treatment of Parents

As has been reported in family studies of early-onset depression, the rate of parental depression is quite high in youthful depressives (Puig-Antich et al., 1989). Very little attention has been paid in the treatment literature on child and adolescent depression to the recognition and treatment of parental depression. We found, particularly in the SBFT cell, that unless parental depression was treated, it was very difficult to mobilize the family for treatment. Even in the individual cells, failure to identify and treat parental depression meant difficulties in transportation for the patient, and a therapeutic focus on coping with parental depression when it could be dealt with directly. Because we were assessing parents as part of our intake protocol, and therefore knew what their diagnoses were, we felt obligated to disclose this information to them. Once parents sought treatment, they could receive a wide range of therapies, including some psychological therapies that could potentially contaminate this clinical trial. Therefore, because of all of the above considerations, we elected to treat all parental affective disorders within our clinic with pharmacotherapy only. Thus far, approximately one fifth of all patients have had a parent in treatment in our program. The integration of treatment of parents into clinical trials with children or adolescents is an important issue that deserves future consideration.

CURRENT IMPRESSIONS

It is difficult to draw firm conclusions about an ongoing clinical trial. However, it may be helpful to offer certain impressions on the basis of our experience thus far.

All three treatments can be delivered reliably, with fidelity to the manuals. Discriminant validity for all three therapies is very solid. All three treatments are acceptable to families, and the dropout rate for all three cells has been quite low. However, about one in five who received family therapy wished there had been some individual component, and a comparable proportion of those in individual therapy expressed a desire for some family sessions. This suggests a need for a more flexible treatment approach, integrating individual and family models.

Across all three treatments, approximately two thirds achieved a remission of depression within the period of treatment. Those who were less likely to remit included those with comorbid anxiety. This suggests that future treatment development target comorbid anxiety symptoms, because these symptoms appear to render depressed youth relatively resistant to psychosocial treatment. Those patients who *do* respond to psychosocial intervention often do so very rapidly, raising the question of the necessity, in many cases, of more than 6–8 sessions.

It is well known that depressed youth often experience recurrences of depression, and this sample proves no exceptions. During the follow-up period, approximately one third of the subjects experienced a recurrence of their depression, on average about 20 months after treatment termination. Predictors of recurrence included parent–child discord, lack of perceived support, maternal psychopathology, subsyndromal depression, and cognitive distortion. These provide the basis for the development of a maintenance treatment, an important component to the treatment of individuals with a chronic and recurrent condition such as depression.

In summary, the current study is a work in progress. Treatment can be delivered reliably and is acceptable to almost all family members. As our study progresses, we hope to inform the field about the efficacy of these three psychosocial treatments, predictors of treatment response, and indications for the use of pharmacotherapy. Both our data and our experience suggest the need to integrate family and individual models of treatment, to provide treatment for parents who need it, and to develop a maintenance model for those who have successfully remitted.

REFERENCES

Achenbach, T. M., & Edelbrock, C.S. (1983). *Manual for the Child Behavior Checklist and Revised Child Behavior Profile.* Burlington: University of Vermont, Department of Psychiatry.

Alexander, J. F., & Parsons, B. V. (1973). Short-term behavioral intervention with deliquent families: Impact on family process and recidivism. *Journal of Abnormal Psychology, 81,* 219–225.

American Psychiatric Association. (1987). *Diagnostic and statistical manual of mental disorders* (3rd ed., rev.). Washington, DC: Author.

Asarnow, J. R., Goldstein, M. J., Tompson, M., & Guthrie, D. (1993). One-year outcomes of depressive disorders in child psychiatric in-patients: Evaluation of the prognostic power of a brief measure of expressed emotion [Abstract]. *Journal of Child Psychology and Psychiatry, 34,* 129–137.

Asarnow, J. R., Tompson, M., Hamilton, E. B., Goldstein, M. J., & Guthrie, D. (1994). Family-expressed emotion, childhood-onset schizophrenia spectrum disorders: Is expressed emotion a nonspecific correlate of child psychopatholgy or a specific risk factor for depression? *Journal of Abnormal Child Psychology, 22,* 129–146.

Beardslee, W. R., Salt, P., Porterfield, K., Rothberg, P. C., van der Velde, P., Swathing, S., Hoke, L., Moilanen, D. L., & Wheelock, I. (1993). Comparison of preventive interventions for families with parental affective disorder. *Journal of the American Academy of Child and Adolescent Psychiatry, 32*, 254–263.

Beck, A. T., Rush, A. J., Shaw, B. F., & Emerg, G. (1979). *Cognitive techniques: Cognitive therapy of depression*. New York: Guilford Press.

Beck, A. T., Ward, C. H., Mendelson, M., Mock, J., & Erbaugh, J. (1961). An inventory for measuring depression. *Archives of General Psychiatry, 4*, 53–63.

Beck, A. T., Weissman, A., Lester, D., & Trexler, L. (1974). The measurement of pessimism: The Hopelessness Scale. *Journal of Consulting and Clinical Psychology, 42*, 861–865.

Brent, D. A., Perper, J. A., Moritz, G., Allman, C., Roth, C. M., Schweers, J. A., Balach, L., & Baugher, M. A. (1993). Psychiatric risk factors of adolescent suicide: A case control study. *Journal of the American Academy of Child and Adolescent Psychiatry, 32*, 521–529.

Brent, D. A., Poling, K., McKain, B., & Baugher, M. A. (1993). A psychoeducational program for families of affectively ill children and adolescents. *Journal of the American Academy of Child and Adolescent Psychiatry, 32*, 770–774.

Chambers, W. J., Puig-Antich, J., Hirsch, M., Paez, P., Ambrosini, P. J., Tabrinzi, M. A., & Davies, M. (1985). The assessment of affective disorders in children and adolescents by semistructured interview: Test-retest reliability of the schedule for affective disorders and schizophrenia for school-age children, present episode version. *Archives of General Psychiatry, 42*, 696–702.

Clarke, G. N., Hawkins, W., Murphy, M., Sheeber, L. B., Lewinsohn, P. M., & Seeley, J. R. (1995). Targeted prevention of unipolar depressive disorder in an at-risk sample of high school adolescents: A randomized trial of a group cognitive intervention. *Journal of the American Academy of Child and Adolescent Psychiatry, 34*, 312–321.

Emslie, G. J., Weinberg, W. A., Kowatch, R. A., Hughes, C. W., Carmody, T. J., & Rush, A. J. (1995). *Fluoxetine treatment of depression children and adolescents*. Unpublished manuscript.

Endicott, J., & Spitzer, R. L. (1978). A diagnostic interview: The Schedule for Affective Disorders and Schizophrenia. *Archives of General Psychiatry, 5*, 837–844.

Epstein, N., Baldwin, L., & Bishop, D. S. (1983). The McMaster family assessment device. *Journal of Marital and Family Therapy, 9*, 171–180.

Feighner, J. P., Robins, E., & Guze, S. B. (1972). Diagnostic criteria for use in psychiatric research. *Archives of General Psychiatry, 26*, 57–63.

Fendrich, M., Warner, V., & Weissman, M. M. (1990). Family risk factors, parental depression, and psychopathology in offspring. *Developmental Psychology, 26*, 40–50.

Fleming, J. E., & Offord, D. R. (1990). Epidemiology of childhood depressive disorders: A critical review. *Journal of the American Academy of Child and Adolescent Psychiatry, 29*, 571–580.

Garber, J., & Hilsman, R. (1992). Cognitions, stress, and depression in children and adolescents. *Mood Disorders*, *1*, 129–167.

Garrison, C. Z., Jackson, K. L., Addy, C. L., McKeown, R. E., & Waller, J. L. (1991). Suicidal behaviors in young adolescents. *American Journal of Epidemiology*, *133*, 1005–1014.

Geller, B., Cooper, T. B., Graham, D. L., & Marsteller, F. A. (1990). Double-blind placebo-controlled study of nortriptyline in depressed adolescents using a "fixed plasma level" design. *Psychopharmacology Bulletin*, *26*, 85–90.

Gibbons, J. S., Butler, J., Urwin, P., & Gibbons, J. L. (1978). Evaluation of a social work service for self-poisoning patients. *British Journal of Psychiatry*, *133*, 111–118.

Harrington, R., Fudge, H., Rutter, M., Pickles, A., & Hill, J. (1990). Adult outcomes of childhood and adolescent depression: Part 1. Psychiatric status. *Archives of General Psychiatry*, *47*, 465–473.

Hawton, K., McKeown, S., Day, A., Martin, P., O'Connor, M., & Tule, J. (1987). Evaluation of out-patient counselling compared with general practitioner care following overdoses. *Psychological Medicine*, *17*, 751–761.

Hetherington, E. M., Hagan, M. S., & Eisenberg, N. (1990). *Coping with marital transitions* (Monographs of the Society for Research in Child Development). Chicago: University of Chicago Press.

Jacob, T., & Seilhamer, R. A. (1985). Adaption of the areas of change questionnaire for parent–child relationship assessment. *American Journal of Family Therapy*, *13*, 28–38.

Kahn, J. S., Kehle, T. J., Jenson, W. R., & Clark, E. (1990). Comparison of cognitive–behavioral relaxation and self-modeling interventions for depression among middle-school students. *School Psychology Review*, *19*(2), 196–211.

Kandel, D. B., & Davies, M. (1986). Adult sequelae of adolescent depressive symptoms. *Archives of General Psychiatry*, *43*, 255–262.

Kazdin, A. E., Esveldt-Dawson, K., French, N. H., & Unis, A. S. (1987). Problem-solving skills training and relationship therapy in the treatment of antisocial child behavior. *Journal of Consulting and Clinical Psychology*, *55*, 76–85.

Keller, M. B., Beardslee, W. R., Dorer, D. J., Lavori, D. W., Samuelson, H., & Klerman, G. H. (1986). Impact of severity and chronicity of parental affective illness on adaptive functioning and psychopathology in children. *Archives of General Psychiatry*, *43*, 930–937.

Keller, M. B., Lavori, P. W., Friedman, B., Nielsen, E., Endicott, J., McDonald-Scott, P., & Andreasen, N. C. (1987). The longitudinal interval follow-up evaluation: A comprehensive method for assessing outcome in prospective longitudinal studies. *Archives of General Psychiatry*, *44*, 540–548.

Kovacs, M., Akiskal, H. S., Gatsonis, C., & Parrone, P. L. (1994). Childhood-onset dysthymic disorder. *Archives of General Psychiatry*, *51*, 365–374.

Kovacs, M., Feinberg, T. L., Crouse-Novak, M. A., Paulauskas, S. L., & Finklestein, R. (1984a). Depressive disorders in childhood: Part 1. A longitudinal study of characteristics and recovery. *Archives of General Psychiatry*, *41*, 229–237.

Kovacs, M., Feinberg, T. L., Crouse-Novak, M. A., Paulauskas, S. L., Pollock, M., & Finklestein, R. (1984b). Depressive disorders in childhood: Part 2. A longitudinal study of the risk for a subsequent major depression. *Archives of General Psychiatry, 41,* 643–649.

Kovacs, M., Gatsonis, C., Paulauskas, S. L., & Richards, C. (1989). Depressive disorders in childhood: Part 4. A longitudinal study of comorbidity with and risk for anxiety disorders. *Archives of General Psychiatry, 46,* 776–782.

Kovacs, M., Goldston, D., & Gatsonis, C. (1993). Suicidal behaviors and childhood-onset depressive disorders: A longitudinal investigation. *Journal of the American Academy of Child and Adolescent Psychiatry, 32*(1), 8–20.

Kramer, A. D., & Feiguine, R. J. (1981). Clinical effects of amitriptyline in adolescent depression: A pilot study. *Journal of the American Academy of Child and Adolescent Psychiatry, 20,* 636–644.

Kutcher, S., Boulos, C., Ward, B., Marton, P., Simeon, J., Ferguson, H. B., Stalai, J. Katic, M., Roberts, N., Dubois, C., & Feed, K. (1994). Response to desipramine treatment in adolescent depression: A fixed-dose placebo-controlled trial. *Journal of the American Academy of Child and Adolescent Psychiatry, 33,* 686–694.

Kye, C., Waterman, M. D., Ryan, N., Birmaner, B., Williamson, D., Iyengar, S., & Dachille, S. (in press). A randomized controlled trial of amitriptyline in acute treatment of adolescent major depression. *Journal of the American Academy of Child and Adolescent Psychiatry.*

Leitenberg, H., Yost, L. W., & Carroll-Wilson, M. (1986). Negative cognitive errors in children: Questionnaire development, normative data, and comparisons between children with and without self-reported symptoms of depression, low self-esteem, and evaluation anxiety. *Journal of Consulting and Clinical Psychology, 54*(4), 528–536.

Lerner, M. S., & Clum, G. A. (1990). Treatment of suicide ideators: A problem-solving approach. *Behavior Therapy, 21,* 403–411.

Lewinsohn, P. M., & Clarke, G. N. (1990). Cognitive–behavioral treatment for depressed adolescents. *Behavior Therapy, 21,* 385–401.

Lewinsohn, P. M., & Hops, H. (1993). Adolescent psychopathology: I. Prevalence and incidence of depression and other *DSM-III-R* disorders in high school students. *Journal of Abnormal Psychology, 102,* 133–144.

Lewinsohn, P. M., Rohde, P., & Seeley, J. R. (1994). Psychosocial risk factors for future adolescent suicide attempts. *Journal of Consulting and Clinical Psychology, 62,* 297–305.

Luborsky, L., McLellan, A. T., Woody, G. E., O'Brien, C. P., & Auerbach, A. (1985). Therapist success and its determinants. *Archives of General Psychiatry, 42,* 602–611.

Mufson, L., Moreau, D., Weissman, M. M., Wickramaratne, P., Martin, J., & Samoilov, A. (1994). Modification of interpersonal psychotherapy with depressed adolescents (IPT-A): Phase I and II studies. *Journal of the American Academy of Child and Adolescent Psychiatry, 33,* 695–705.

Nolen-Hoeksema, S., Seligman, M. E. P., & Girgus, J. S. (1992). Predictors and consequences of childhood depressive symptoms: A 5-year longitudinal study. *Journal of Abnormal Psychology, 101,* 405–422.

Orvaschel, H. (1990). Early onset psychiatric disorder in high-risk children and increased familial morbidity. *Journal of the American Academy of Child and Adolescent Psychiatry, 29,* 184–188.

Orvaschel, H., Puig-Antich, J., Chambers, W., Tabrizi, M. A., & Johnson, R. (1982). Retrospective assessment of prepubertal major depression with the Kiddie-SADS-E. *Journal of the American Academy of Child and Adolescent Psychiatry, 21*(4), 392–397.

Orvaschel, H., Walsh-Allis, G., & Ye, W. (1988). Psychopathology in children of parents with recurrent depression. *Journal of Abnormal Child Psychology, 16,* 17–28.

Piercy, F. P., Liard, R. A., & Mohammed, Z. (1983). A family therapist rating scale. *Journal of Marital and Family Therapy, 9,* 49–59.

Puig-Antich, J., Goetz, D., Davies, M., Kaplan, T., Davies, S., Ostrow, L., Asnis, L., Twomey, J., Iyengar, S., & Ryan, N. D. (1989). A controlled family history study of prepubertal major depressive disorder. *Archives of General Psychiatry, 46,* 406–418.

Rao, U., Ryan, N. D., Birmaher, B., Dana, R., Williamson, D. E., Kaufman, J., Rao, R., & Nelson, B. (1995). Unipolar depression in adolescents: Clinical outcome in adulthood. *Journal of the American Academy of Child and Adolescent Psychiatry, 34,* 566–578.

Reinherz, H. Z., Giaconia, R. M., Pakiz, B., Silverman, A. B., Frost, A. K., & Lefkowitz, E. S. (1993). Psychosocial risks for major depression in late adolescence: A logitudinal community study. *Journal of the American Academy of Child and Adolescent Psychiatry, 32,* 1155–1163.

Reynolds, W. M., & Coates, K. I. (1986). A comparison of cognitive–behavioral therapy and relaxation training for the treatment of depression in adolescents. *Journal of Consulting and Clinical Psychology, 54,* 653–660.

Robin, A. L., & Foster, S. L. (1989). *Negotiating parent–adolescent conflict: A behavioral–family systems approach.* New York: Guilford Press.

Rotheram-Borus, M. J., Piacentini, J., Miller, S., Sutherland, M., Graae, F., & Castro-Blanco, D. (1994). Brief cognitive–behavioral treatment for adolescent suicide attempters and their families. *Journal of the American Academy of Child and Adolescent Psychiatry, 33,* 508–517.

Rush, A. J., Beck, A. T., Kovacs, M., Weissenberger, J., & Hollon, S. (1982). Comparison of the effects of cognitive therapy and pharmacotherapy on hopelessness and self-concept. *American Journal of Psychiatry, 139,* 862–866.

Rutter, M., & Quinton, D. (1984). Parental psychiatric disorder: Effects on children. *Psychological Medicine, 14,* 853–880.

Shaffer, D., Garland, A., Gould, M., Fisher, P., & Trautman, P. (1988). Preventing teenage suicide: A critical review. *Journal of the American Academy of Child and Adolescent Psychiatry, 27,* 675–687.

Shafii, M., Steltz-Lenarsky, J., Derrick, A. M., Beckner, C., & Whittinghill, J. R. (1988). Comorbidity of mental disorder in the post-mortem diagnosis of completed suicide in children and adolescents. *Journal of Affective Disorders, 15,* 227–233.

Strupp, H. H., & Binder, J. L. (1984). *Psychotherapy in a new key: A guide to time-limited dynamic psychotherapy.* New York: Basic Books.

Suh, C. S., Strupp, H. H., & O'Malley, S. S. (1986). The Vanderbilt process measures: The Psychotherapy Process Scale (VPPS) and the Negative Indications Scale (NIS). In L. S. Greenberg & W. M. Pinsof (Eds.), *The psychotherapeutic process: A research handbook* (pp. 285–323). New York: Guilford Press.

Vallis, T. M., Shaw, B. F., & Dobson, K. S. (1986). The cognitive therapy scale: Psychometric properties. *Journal of Consulting and Clinical Psychology, 54,* 381–385.

Warner, V., Weissman, M. M., Fendrich, M., Wickramaratne, P., & Moreau, D. (1992). The course of major depression in the offspring of depressed parents: Incidence, recurrence, and recovery. *Archives of General Psychiatry, 49,* 795–801.

Weissman, M. M., Gammon, D., John, K., Merikangas, K. R., Warner, V., Prusoff, B. A., & Sholomskas, D. (1987). Children of depressed parents: Increased psychopathology and early onset of major depression. *Archives of General Psychiatry, 44,* 847–853.

Weissman, M. M., Warner, V., Wickramaratne, P., & Prusoff, B. A. (1988). Early-onset major depression in parents and their children. *Journal of Affective Disorders, 15,* 269–277.

Wilkes, T. C. R., & Rush, A. J. (1988). Adaptations of cognitive therapy for depressed adolescents. *Journal of the American Academy of Child and Adolescent Psychiatry, 27,* 381–386.

11

TARGETING THE CHILD AND THE FAMILY: A HOLISTIC APPROACH TO TREATING CHILD AND ADOLESCENT DEPRESSIVE DISORDERS

KEVIN D. STARK, SUSAN SWEARER, CYNTHIA KUROWSKI, DAWN SOMMER, and BLAIR BOWEN

OVERVIEW

This chapter proposes a comprehensive cognitive–behavioral treatment program for depressed youths. The proposed intervention program evolved out of our early treatment outcome research (Stark, 1990; Stark, Reynolds, & Kaslow, 1987) and a program of basic research on childhood depressive disorders. Recognizing the limits of the interventions used in our initial treatment outcome studies, a program of research was initiated into the nature of the cognitive, behavioral, and family disturbances associated with depressive disorders among children. Results of this series of studies guided the expansion of the empirically evaluated treatment program. As a disturbance in emotional, cognitive, behavioral, and familial functioning was identified, an intervention strategy was either retained, or modified, or developed to remediate it. Thus, the proposed treatment model represents an attempt to describe a potentially more effective treatment program than the ones that have been evaluated empirically.

Prior to describing the proposed treatment program, some of the conclusions that were drawn from the program of basic research will be high-

Correspondence regarding this chapter should be directed to Dr. Kevin D. Stark, Department of Educational Psychology, University of Texas, 504 Education Blvd., Austin, TX 78712-1296.

lighted briefly. This is followed by a discussion of implementation issues. After describing the proposed treatment program, research evaluating the efficacy of the initial versions of the proposed intervention and related research is reviewed. Limitations of the proposed intervention are discussed as is its generalizability.

TREATMENT IMPLICATIONS OF BASIC RESEARCH

The intervention should be multifaceted in terms of locus and type of intervention. Treatment should involve the child, parents, and family (Stark, Humphrey, Laurent, Livingston, & Christopher, 1993). The child-focused therapy should address cognitive, behavioral, and affective disturbances while recognizing the contribution of the family context (Stark, Humphrey, Crook, & Lewis, 1990; Stark, Schmidt, & Joiner, in press). At the child-cognitive level, results suggest that depression in children is associated with a distortion in self-evaluation rather than with a deficiency in active information processing (Kendall, Stark, & Adam, 1990). This suggests that an efficacious intervention would be one that teaches depressed children to identify their maladaptive cognitions and to modify them or replace them with more adaptive ones (e.g., Stark, 1990). A central target would be the youngster's self schemata and the processing errors that maintain the negative sense of self (Kaslow, Stark, Printz, Livingston, & Tsai, 1992).

Depressed children may benefit from social skills training (Stark, Linn, MacGuire, & Kaslow, in press). However, this training should not involve simply the teaching and rehearsal of basic social skills. Rather, it should also address the cognitive disturbances and aversive physical arousal that appear to impede successful enactment of social behaviors (Stark, Linn, et al., in press). The content of the social skills training should be directed toward teaching the youngsters to behave in a less bossy, stubborn, complaining, angry, and jealous fashion. Cognitive restructuring interventions should be integrated with the skills training to increase engagement in social interactions; reduce negative expectations, negative self-evaluations, and other negative cognitions; and increase coping self-statements. In addition, because depressed children think that others are "picking on them", they may need to be taught to monitor, perceive, and evaluate more accurately the behaviors and intentions of others. The children note that they are quick to anger, feel jealous, become angry when someone else is successful, and feel lonely (Stark, Linn, et al., in press), suggesting that cognitive interventions and affective education (Stark, 1990) are needed to intervene with the associated affective disturbance. Furthermore, these interventions may need to teach children how to monitor their own expression of anger and irritability, as well as encourage the youngsters to engage in more appropriate behavior. Relaxation training could be incorporated into the treatment to help the youngsters cope with and minimize aversive physical arousal.

The results also have implications for parent training. Our results (Stark, Schmidt, et al. in press) argue for the inclusion of a component that teaches parents to be aware of the messages that they are communicating to their children. Basic training modules could include teaching parents how to communicate positive and realistic messages to their children about the children themselves, the world, and the future. We also would hypothesize that the program should emphasize teaching the parents positive-behavior management skills because such an approach would send the child positive messages about the self, whereas a punitive approach communicates to the child that he or she is a "bad person". Furthermore, guilt-inducing parental behaviors would lead to a sense of self as worthless, bad, and unlovable. Thus, a common theme throughout the parent training would be to teach the parents to ask themselves, "What is the message that I am sending to my child about himself or herself through my actions and verbal exchanges?"

Similarly, the family intervention includes the identification of verbal and behavioral interactions that send maladaptive, schema-consistent messages to the depressed child. In other words, the therapeutic question becomes, what are family members communicating to the child verbally and through their interactions that could lead to the development and maintenance of the child's negative view of the self, world, future, and other maladaptive schemata. Similarly, the therapist can put him- or herself into the child's shoes within the family and try to deduce, from the messages that the child is receiving, the schemata that the child is likely to have guiding his or her information processing. Once the maladaptive interactions are identified, the therapist would work with the family to change them. From a cognitive–behavioral perspective, this may involve cognitive restructuring procedures to change the beliefs that underlie the participants' behavior and teaching family members new ways of interacting through education, modeling, rehearsal, coaching, and feedback. Subsequently, a parent would be assigned the homework task of self-monitoring the occurrence of the maladaptive interactions as well as engagement in more adaptive interactions.

When working with the family, it is important to determine whether conflict exists (Stark et al., 1990) and, if so, its source would be identified and plans would be developed for reducing it. Such plans may include marital counseling. Because a reduced rate of involvement in recreational activities was reported (Stark et al., 1990), it may be useful to include the scheduling of pleasant activities into the family therapy. Caution would have to be taken when doing this because it could create more opportunities for conflicts. The reduction in conflict and engagement in more pleasant activities as a family could enhance the family's sense of cohesion. The results also suggest that it is important to promote the inclusion of the children in some important decisions being made by the family. A balance needs to be struck between encouraging the children to participate in the decision making process and maintaining a sense of the parents functioning as the executive pair in charge.

BRIEF DESCRIPTION OF AN INTERVENTION FOR DEPRESSED YOUTHS

Overview

The intervention program described in the following sections has been implemented and empirically evaluated in school settings with mildly to moderately depressed youngsters (see the section on Treatment Outcomes below). Research is underway to evaluate its effectiveness with clinical populations. The program, delineated in a manual (Stark & Kendall, 1996; Stark, Kendall, McCarthy, Stafford, Baron, & Thomeer, 1996), is designed to reflect a holistic approach to treatment. Consequently, the child is not the sole target of intervention. The youngster's primary environments and significant others also are targets through parent training and family therapy. Intervention with the parents and family appears to support the individual work, to facilitate the child's use of the coping skills in the extra-therapy environment, and to change the environmental events that may be contributing to the development and maintenance of the disturbances.

Experience in implementing the program has led to modifications in the delivery format. Initially, the intervention was delivered solely through a group format. Currently, a combination of individual and group therapy is used to teach the youngsters the cognitive, behavioral, and affective coping skills. In this pilot work, the dual delivery format appears to be more efficacious for a number of reasons. Depressed youngsters, because of the very nature of their disturbance, are especially difficult to engage in therapy. The relationship that develops between the youngster and therapist during individual sessions can serve as leverage to get the child engaged in treatment and to comply with the treatment regimen, including therapeutic homework. By contrast, groups tend to take a longer time to develop a sense of cohesion and a demand characteristic that pushes for treatment compliance. Thus, the relationship that the youngster develops with an individual can serve as a motivational bridge until the group begins to develop an identity and motivational properties. If the treatment program is going to be delivered in the most efficacious fashion, which we believe means that core cognitive structures are identified and systematically changed through carefully planned corrective learning experiences (cognitive restructuring), then the therapist must have an empathic understanding of the child's sense of self and the rules (cognitive structures) that guide his or her behavior and processing of information. This depth of understanding may only arise from the intimacy of individual therapy as well as from the opportunity to combine what is learned during individual sessions with information that arises during group therapy and within the family. Mistrust, especially of peers in a school setting, is a major hurdle to the discussion of personal, potentially embarrassing information within the group. They may divulge such information during individual meetings. Children and most adolescents do not have the introspective abilities of adults and cannot identify themes and rules in their constructions of daily experiences. Thus, the burden for doing this lies with the therapist. Individual therapy typically provides the therapist with more data with which to address this therapeutic objective.

On the other hand, the group therapy format is useful for a number of reasons. By its very nature, the group provides the therapist with a window into each youngster's social skills and interpersonal relationships. The group therapist remains ever vigilant to, and continually assesses, the interpersonal process that is occurring and its implications for the interpersonal functioning of each participant. Once a maladaptive pattern of behavior is recognized, the therapist and, in the best of circumstances, other group members confront the child with the maladaptive behavior and help the youngster identify his or her related thoughts. The group helps the youngster develop a plan for preventing the maladaptive behavior from reoccurring and for replacing it with a behavior that is more adaptive and yet serves the same function (assuming that the function is a healthy one). The group also provides the therapist with an interpersonal context in which to assess the youngster's social perceptions. This information can be used to provide the youngster with corrective learning experiences within both group and individual therapy. Oftentimes, this information is used to develop social skill building exercises, which are taught and processed in individual therapy and, then, practiced within the group. Depressed youngsters have negative expectancies and maladaptive thoughts during interpersonal exchanges that inhibit social interactions as well as the implementation of appropriate social behaviors. These thoughts can be restructured during individual therapy and the new thoughts can be tested during group sessions. In a properly running group, the depressed child experiences safety, acceptance, support, and positive feedback that in and of itself leads to some restructuring of negative beliefs about social situations and about the self in a social context. With adolescents and preadolescents, it is often helpful for them to hear from a peer the same thing that the therapist (an adult) has been saying.

It is difficult with depressed youth to establish and maintain a productive therapeutic process during group therapy. Thus, the group meetings tend to be more content-focused. In other words, focused on skill building rather than relying on the group process to provide therapeutic grist and the medium for change. The content of the groups parallels that in individual therapy (affective education, problem solving, social skills training, and cognitive restructuring).

The description of the intervention that follows is organized by type of disturbance (i.e., affective, cognitive, behavioral, parenting, family). It has been written this way for clarity of presentation and to emphasize the parallelism between the disturbances and the interventions developed for them. In other words, for each empirically identified disturbance, there is a parallel intervention strategy (Table 1). Another reason for this mode of presentation is to assist the reader in the development of interventions that are appropriate for the specific disturbances exhibited by each depressed child-patient. Although the core features of depressive disorders are similar among youngsters with such a diagnosis, the expression of the disorder varies widely. Thus, some intervention strategies are unnecessary for some children because they may not be experiencing that particular disturbance. The composition of the treatment program also is going to vary depending on the presence, number, and type of cooccurring disorders. Additional modifications are necessary to address parental psychopathology, a history of abuse, substance abuse, presence of a learning disability, limited intellectual functioning, marital discord, neglect or abandonment, and the presence of symptoms of a developing personality disorder. With all of this said, it also is evident that this presentation may lead the reader to wonder what is the logical order of presentation of the various treatment components and how do they fit together. Consequently, a prototypic outline of the sequence and integration of the treatment components is provided in Table 2.

Children

Affective Disturbance

During the first few treatment sessions, emphasis is on helping the youngsters gain a better understanding of their emotional experiences; on teaching them the link among thoughts, feelings, and behaviors; and on developing a supportive treatment group. Moreover, recognition of emotions and an understanding of the relationship among thoughts, feelings, and behaviors is the cornerstone on which other coping skills are built. To accomplish these, as well as additional therapeutic objectives, affective education activities are used throughout the first 8 treatment meetings. This process is described below.

TABLE 1
Child, Parent, and Family Disturbances Identified Through Research and Corresponding Treatments

Disturbances	Interventions
Child mood	
Dysphoria	Affective education
Anger	Reducing excessive anger
Anhedonia	Activity scheduling
Excessive worry	Interventions for excessive anxiety
	Pleasant events scheduling
Child behavioral	
Social Skills Disturbances	Social Skills Training
Child cognitive	
Maladaptive schemata	Cognitive restructuring procedures
Distorted information processing	Behavioral experiments
Depressogenic automatic thoughts	What is the evidence?
Negative expectations	Alternative interpretations
Negative self-evaluations	What if?
	Self-evaluation training
	Problem-solving training
	Self-monitoring
Parent cognitive and behavioral	
Punitive behavior management style	Positive behavior management
	Noncoercive discipline
Impulsive anger	Anger management
Unrealistic and perfectionistic expectations	Self-esteem enhancement
Dysfunctional schemata	Cognitive restructuring
Communication disturbances	Empathic listening
Low rates of recreational and social activities	Recreation
Family behavioral	
Low rates of positive reinforcement	Positive parenting
Low rates of social and recreational behavior	Recreational planning
Family decision making	Negotiation skills
Family communication deficits	Communication skills
Family cognitive	
Problem-solving deficits	Problem-solving training
Conflict management deficits	Conflict resolution skills
Communication of negative messages	Positive communications
	Change schema-consistent interactions

TABLE 2
Outline of Treatment Program

Session	Procedure
1	Introductions
	Establishing appropriate expectations
2	Affective education
	Identify and label emotions
	Establishing a within-group incentive system
	Self-monitoring of pleasant emotions
3	Affective education
	Identifying emotions, linking emotions to thoughts and behavior
	Introduction to active coping orientation
	Self-monitoring of pleasant emotions
4	Affective education
	Internal and external cues of emotions, coping with unpleasant emotions, linking emotions to thoughts and behavior
	Extend coping orientation
	Pleasant events scheduling
	Self-monitoring of pleasant emotions
5	Affective education
	Internal and external cues of emotions, coping with unpleasant emotions, link emotions to thoughts and behavior
	Introduction to problem solving
	Self-monitoring pleasant emotions
6	Affective education
	Internal and external cues of emotions, coping with unpleasant emotions, link emotions to thoughts and behavior
	Pleasant events scheduling and self-monitoring pleasant emotions
	Problem solving game
7	Affective education
	Internal and external cues of emotions, coping with unpleasant emotions, link emotions to thoughts and behavior
	Pleasant events scheduling
	Problem-solving game
8	Affective education
	Internal and external cues of emotions, coping with unpleasant emotions, link emotions to thoughts and behavior
	Application of problem solving to mood disturbance
9	Application of problem solving to mood disturbance
	Missing solution activity
10	Introduction to relaxation
	Exercise and mood
11	Problem solving applied to interpersonal problems
	Pleasant events scheduling
	Relaxation as a coping strategy
12	Problem solving applied to interpersonal situations
	Focus on self-evaluation of solution implementation
	Relaxation as a coping strategy
13	Spontaneous use of problem solving
	Relaxation and problem solving
14	Introduction to cognitive restructuring
	Identification of depressogenic thoughts
15	Practice catching negative thoughts
	Cognitive restructuring

(Continued)

TABLE 2 *(Continued)*

Session	Procedure
16	Improve understanding of cognitive restructuring
	Practice catching negative thoughts
	What is the evidence
	What to do when a negative thought is true
17	Alternative interpretation
18	Alternative interpretation
	Identifying negative expectations
	Introduce What if?
19	What if?
20	Review of cognitive restructuring procedures
	Introduction to assertiveness training
	Generate and rehearse coping statements
21	Positive assertiveness
	Generation of coping statements
22	Assertiveness training
	Generation of coping statements
23	Identify personal standards
	Introduction to self-evaluation training
	Identification of areas in need of personal improvement
24	Establish goals and subgoals for self-improvement
25–28	Self-evaluation training/Working toward self-improvement
29–30	Termination issues
	Programming for generalization

Depressed youths experience either dysphoria, anger, anhedonia, or a mix of mood disturbances. Some intervention strategies are specifically designed to impact these disturbances. However, it is important to note that, ultimately, all the intervention components have, as their goal, an improvement in mood. Thus, it is believed that the mood disturbance will be modified progressively as the youth begins to cope with the other symptoms of depression and perceives him- or herself, life in general, and the future in a more positive and realistic fashion.

On the basis of a coping skills model of treatment, a primary goal of affective education is to teach the youngsters to use their mood as a cue to engage in coping activities. The first step to this process involves teaching the youngsters a vocabulary for describing their affective experiences. Depressed youths typically do not have an adequate set of labels for the range of their affective experiences (everything is referred to as "bad" or "sad"), or they mislabel emotions. In addition, they tend to see themselves as either happy or depressed with nothing in between. Thus, the children assess the continuum of emotions that they might experience. Emphasis is placed on the fact that (a) they actually experience a variety of emotions, and (b) each emotion is experienced along a continuum of intensity.

A series of games, including Emotional Vocabulary, Emotional Vocabulary II, Emotion Charades, Emotion Password, Emotion Statues, Emotion Pictionary, and Emotion Expression, is used in the affective education groups to help the youngsters achieve the therapy goals (cf. Stark, 1990). Through participation in these games, the youngsters learn the names of various pleasant and unpleasant emotions and that emotions vary in intensity. In addition, they become able to recognize when they are experiencing particular emotions and to identify them in others. The relationship among emotions, thoughts, and behavior is illustrated, and strategies for coping with unpleasant emotions are identified.

One of the primary tools for altering dysphoric mood is activity scheduling, which is the purposeful scheduling of enjoyable and goal-directed activities into the child's day. Enactment of these activities helps the youngster obtain reinforcement and combat the withdrawal, passivity, and sedentary life style associated with an episode of depression. They also provide the child with a distraction from a preoccupation with negative thinking and lead to cognitive restructuring as the child sees that life can be enjoyable. During individual therapy, the therapist and child literally schedule pleasant activities for the child on a calendar and solicit parental approval and support for the plan. Within a group, the children self-monitor their engagement in pleasant activities (Figure 1), provide each other with encouragement and support for their attempts to become more active, and provide each other with additional ideas about fun things to do. The youths contract for an increase in activity level (Figure 2).

It also is important to include in the schedule some mastery activities, that is, activities that have an instrumental value. Completion of these tasks provides the child with a sense of accomplishment or mastery. For example, completion of a major school project, more homework assignments, a household project, or a hobby kit would lead to a sense of mastery. Within individual and group therapy, the child and therapist work to combat the child's pessimism and inertia through breaking the project down into manageable steps, creating a schedule for completing the steps, and developing coping statements that can be used when the youngster begins to stall or get stuck in negative thinking. Within the group, this process is illustrated through completion of a group project. The sole parameter for choosing an appropriate project is that it be fun and consist of a number of steps that are to be completed over an extended period of time.

Excessive anger is a common problem for depressed youths. Teaching children to cope with anger begins with helping them to recognize the sensations that define anger (emotional, cognitive, physical). It is especially important to help the children recognize the initial physical and cognitive cues that they are becoming angry or else the child becomes overwhelmed with anger too quickly to be able to manage it. Anger is considered to be a cue that a problem needs to be solved. Either the child has to take action

M	T	W	TH	F	S	S	Things I like to do

Figure 1. Workbook form for self-monitoring of engagement in pleasant events.

to change the anger-provoking situation, or the child has to develop and implement plans for coping. Some effective coping strategies include (a) leaving the situation; (b) going to do something enjoyable; (c) using words rather than actions to express anger; (d) doing something physically demanding, like riding an exercise bike; and (e) expressing anger through drawing or writing. Another useful strategy is to leave a provocative situation as soon as anger is evident and to then listen to a progressive muscle relaxation tape as a means of calming down. Once the child is very skilled

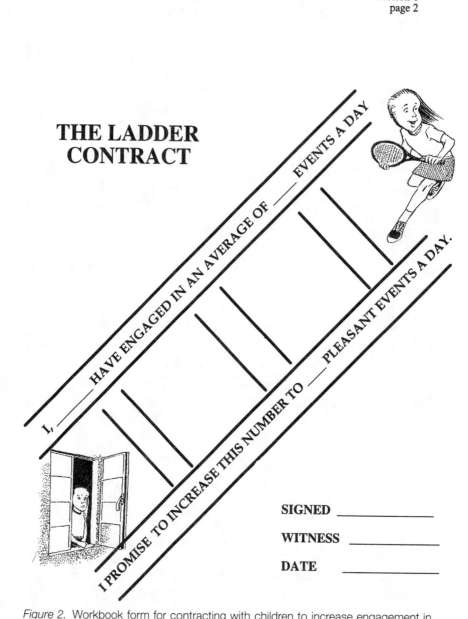

THE LADDER CONTRACT

I, _____ HAVE ENGAGED IN AN AVERAGE OF _____ EVENTS A DAY

I PROMISE TO INCREASE THIS NUMBER TO _____ PLEASANT EVENTS A DAY.

SIGNED _____

WITNESS _____

DATE _____

Figure 2. Workbook form for contracting with children to increase engagement in pleasant events.

at using relaxation, he or she is taught to leave the situation and to direct his or her attention to the muscle tension that is associated with the anger and to focus on relaxing it away. We have found that it is necessary to augment the relaxation training with some self-instructional training and cognitive restructuring, which are described in a later section. The cognitive interventions are used to change or counter the youngster's inflammatory thinking.

It is very difficult for a child to follow through and enact one of these strategies for managing anger. Consequently, parents are taught to encourage their child to cope by establishing an incentive program. In some instances, it is possible for a parent to help cue the child when he or she is becoming angry. This is a sensitive endeavor because telling an angry person that he is angry can often escalate the problem. Consequently, a great deal of preplanning and rehearsal are necessary.

Problem Solving Set

As youngsters appear to acquire a better understanding of their emotions, can accurately identify them, recognize their impact on behavior and thinking, and understand that they can take action to moderate the intensity and impact of their emotions, we begin to teach them to adopt a problem-solving set toward life. In other words, they are taught that problems and disappointments are a natural part of life, and that when a problem is identified, it is best to solve it actively. In addition, they are taught that their manifestations of depression represent problems to be solved and that the procedures described in this chapter represent possible solutions. For example, feeling angry is a cue that a problem exists and that the youngster needs to develop a plan for eliminating the stressor or for coping with the feelings. Problem solving also has an impact on the disturbance in the child's thinking. It counteracts rigidity and hopelessness as the child sees that there often are solutions to problems. The children also gain a sense of self-efficacy as they experience some success and mastery over their environment.

The problem-solving procedure that we have used is a modification of the one described by Kendall and Braswell (1993). Children are taught to break problem solving down into six component steps through education, modeling, coaching, rehearsal, and feedback. Board games, such as checkers, Othello, and jenga, are used as an engaging medium for teaching the steps. Games are a fun, concrete method for teaching the process that provides the youngsters with almost immediate feedback in the form of a game-related consequence (e.g., their checker gets jumped) for not following the steps. In addition, the children readily see the advantages of following the process. As they begin to understand each of the steps and can apply them readily to the games that the group plays, the therapist begins to shift away from game playing to teaching the youngsters to apply the process to hypothetical problems, to interpersonal problems, and then to problems in daily life.

The first step in the process is problem identification and definition. This may be the most difficult step for children in general to learn. Depressed children often view the existence of a problem as a threat to their self-esteem: If a problem exists, then it means that there is something wrong with them or the problem represents an impending loss. In addition, they feel overwhelmed by problems, as if they cannot solve them, and are sure others are going to come up. Thus, their sense of hopelessness has to be combated over time through concrete evidence in their life experiences that demonstrates that they can, in fact, overcome problems. Early in the treatment, when games are being used, each turn or move represents a problem to be defined and solved. Thus, the children get plenty of practice at identifying and defining problems. As treatment progresses, the game format is faded out and children begin to identify their own real life problems and the problems of other group members.

The second step, which represents the modification of Kendall's procedure, is the use of self-talk to counter pessimism and foster motivation. The youngsters identify, record in their workbooks, and rehearse motivational statements. As a group, the youngsters generate a list of self-statements that help them "psyche-up" for facing and solving a problem. Each child records and uses the statements that he or she finds especially motivating. Generally, the statements are of a normalizing ("It's okay, everyone has problems."), coping ("Stay chilled, I can handle it."), and motivational nature ("I'm going to kick its butt!").

The third step in the process is the generation of alternative solutions. Children are taught to brainstorm as many possible solutions as they can without evaluating them. This is very difficult for the depressed youngsters because they can typically come-up with more reasons for why a plan will not work than for why it will work. Even when they cannot identify specific reasons for it not working, they base their prediction on a feeling (emotional reasoning). When beginning to teach the children to generate solutions, often they are very limited in the range and number of possibilities that they can generate. Consequently, they have to be taught additional possibilities. It is important to teach them not to evaluate the alternatives as they are trying to generate them because the youngster might short circuit the process and generate a minimum of possible solutions. Once again, while playing the games, the children are taught to consider many possible moves each time their turn comes around. Initially, as they are learning the steps, they are asked to state aloud each possible solution. In this manner, the therapist and other group members can help to generalize solutions. As treatment progresses and the problems are drawn from real life situations, emphasis is placed on developing solutions that are reasonable, realistic for the context of the adolescent's world, and not merely socially acceptable within an adult's world.

The fourth step, consequential thinking, involves predicting the likely outcomes for each possible solution. Within the context of the games, this involves predicting the outcome of each possible move. As the group progresses into real-life problems, the therapist often has to help the children recognize potential positive outcomes as well as the limitations and self-defeating consequences of other possibilities. Once again, it is necessary, at this step, to combat the youngster's pessimism.

The fifth step involves reviewing the possible solutions, choosing the one that is most consistent with the child's goals, and enacting the plan. The final step is evaluating progress toward solving the problem and the overall outcome. If the outcome is a desirable one, the child self-reinforces. If the outcome is undesirable, the youngster becomes psyched-up, reconsiders the possible solutions, chooses an alternative one, and enacts it.

Maladaptive Behavior

As mentioned earlier in the discussion of the implications of the basic research for the treatment of depressed youths, it is necessary to intervene at multiple levels when trying to remediate the disturbance in the depressed youth's interpersonal behavior. To accomplish this most effectively, we also treat this disturbance with a combination of group and individual therapy. Group therapy is used both as a means of ongoing assessment and as the primary vehicle for teaching the youngsters social skills. Skills are taught through education, modeling, rehearsal, coaching, and corrective feedback. The children are given weekly homework assignments to try to use their new skills. As social disturbances become evident during the natural exchanges among group members, those disturbances are addressed directly through feedback from the group and by teaching the youngster more adaptive behavior. The cognitive disturbances associated with the maladaptive behavior are dealt with during individual therapy, and the new more adaptive ways of thinking are tested out during group therapy.

Maladaptive Cognitions

As is evident in Table 2, children are taught strategies for identifying and altering their maladaptive cognitions. With one exception, these treatment components typically appear late in therapy because they require the youngster to become more self-focused, which actually exacerbates depressive symptoms. In fact, the one exception, altering faulty information processing, is included early in the treatment because it is designed to redirect the youngster's attention from negative thoughts and feelings to more pleasant emotions and positive thoughts, which appears to produce an elevation in mood and energy. An example of such a self-monitoring form can be found in Figure 3. In addition, a goal is to provide the youngsters with a base of potential coping skills that they can use to moderate the severity of symptoms prior to directing them to tune into and try to counter or change maladaptive cognitions. It also appears as though the improvement in mood and symptoms, in general, that results from the other components of the intervention program, provides the youngsters with some personal distance from their maladaptive thoughts and beliefs, which seems to open them to change.

A treatment program for depressed children should address the disturbances in the children's schemata, processing errors, negative self-evaluations, and hopelessness. A number of techniques can be used to intervene directly with disturbances in cognition. Most of the therapeutic work that is designed to change the youngster's maladaptive cognitions is completed during individual sessions. This is not to imply that it is the sole place for using these procedures; many opportunities arise during group meetings. However, the intensity and intimacy of the individual sessions is better suited to the identification and restructuring of maladaptive thoughts.

Methods for Altering Faulty Information Processing. Depressed children tend to focus on the negative things that are occurring in their lives to the exclusion of positive information. This disturbance may stem from a variety of errors in information processing. To counter this, children can be taught to self-monitor (the purposeful and conscious act of observing oneself) positive events and pleasant emotions. This serves as a method for directing the child's attention to more positive things, thus breaking the cycle of negative attention. It helps the children see that there are some positive things going on in their lives. Individualized self-monitoring assignments may be given to the children to fit their specific disturbances. A youngster may be taught to observe certain behaviors, thoughts, feelings, or physical reactions and make a judgment about their occurrence or nonoccurrence. In addition, a youngster may be instructed to monitor what is happening when he or she has a specific thought or emotion.

The first step to teaching children to self-monitor is to define collaboratively the phenomena to be observed and to identify examples and nonexamples of it. It is useful to begin the training with a behavior that is likely to occur during the session, which gives the therapist an opportunity to help the children tune into the occurrence of the behavior, check for accuracy of self-monitoring, model the procedure, if necessary, and provide rewards for successful and accurate self-monitoring. After identifying and defining the target for self-monitoring, which targets pleasant emotions early in the treatment, the children and therapist devise a method for recording their occurrence or nonoccurrence, how to record, when to record, and how often to record. It is important to devise a system that allows the children to record the occurrence of the target immediately after it

Day: _____

Day: _____

Figure 3. Workbook form for self-monitoring mood.

occurs. We have created and used an emotions diary (Figure 4) for this purpose.

Altering Automatic Thoughts. The consciousness of depressed children is dominated by negative automatic thoughts. Especially prevalent are negative self-evaluative thoughts. As these thoughts are identified, the cognitive restructuring procedures discussed below along with cognitive modeling and self-instructional training can be used to alter them directly. These automatic thoughts are commonly the target of the therapist throughout treatment, and the youngsters learn how to identify and modify them on their own as treatment progresses.

The first step for using either procedure is to make the child aware of the tendency to think negatively. This is accomplished through education, thinking aloud while playing games that encourage self-verbalizations (e.g., puzzle building, completing mazes), and helping the child catch them as they occur during the in-session games and other activities. It is especially important to watch for signs that the child's mood has changed within the session and, then, to ask the child to state what he or she is was thinking. After catching a negative thought, the youngster is taught to counter it (Figure 5). Similarly, the group members can help each other to generate positive coping counters.

Another method for accomplishing this is for the therapists to model more adaptive thoughts. Cognitive modeling involves the therapists' verbalizing their own thoughts or verbalizing more adaptive thoughts that the children might use to replace existing thoughts or ones that might occur the next time in which a particular situation arises. Typically, the procedure involves modeling more adaptive thoughts and asking the children to put them into their own words and, then, rehearsing them. In addition to using cognitive modeling when specific thoughts are being targeted, the therapists think aloud whenever they confront a problem or some other situation that enables them to model adaptive thoughts for the children. This is done throughout the treatment as a means of planting seeds of more adaptive thinking.

When a depressed child is having an especially difficult time replacing thoughts, self-instructional training (Meichenbaum, 1977) may be used. Any content of thoughts can be taught. It is especially useful with children who are experiencing a deficit in their verbal mediational skills, such as with a depressed child with attention deficit hyperactivity disorder (ADHD) or a child who blows-up and exerts no control over his or her emotions.

Changing Dysfunctional Schemata. One of the ultimate goals of the treatment program is changing the dysfunctional schemata that are hypothesized to give rise to the errors in information processing, depressogenic automatic thoughts, dysfunctional emotions, and behaviors associated with depressive disorders in children. Cognitive restructuring procedures

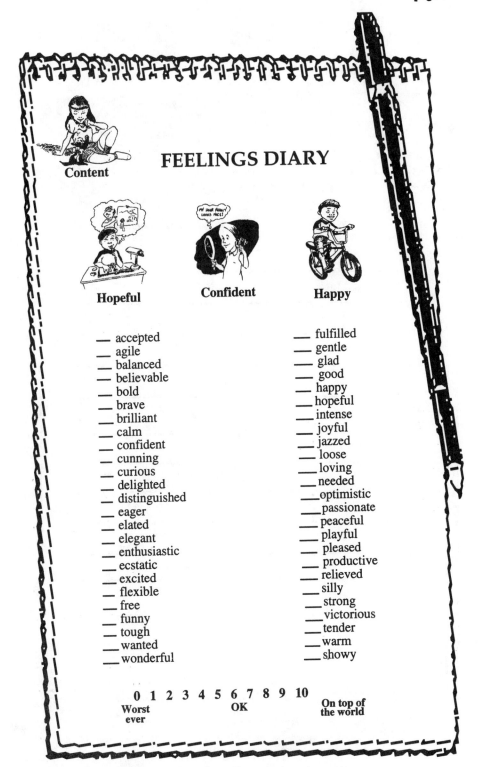

FEELINGS DIARY

Content

Hopeful   Confident   Happy

__ accepted
__ agile
__ balanced
__ believable
__ bold
__ brave
__ brilliant
__ calm
__ confident
__ cunning
__ curious
__ delighted
__ distinguished
__ eager
__ elated
__ elegant
__ enthusiastic
__ ecstatic
__ excited
__ flexible
__ free
__ funny
__ tough
__ wanted
__ wonderful

__ fulfilled
__ gentle
__ glad
__ good
__ happy
__ hopeful
__ intense
__ joyful
__ jazzed
__ loose
__ loving
__ needed
__ optimistic
__ passionate
__ peaceful
__ playful
__ pleased
__ productive
__ relieved
__ silly
__ strong
__ victorious
__ tender
__ warm
__ showy

0 1 2 3 4 5 6 7 8 9 10
Worst   OK   On top of
ever   the world

Figure 4. Another workbook form for self-monitoring of mood.

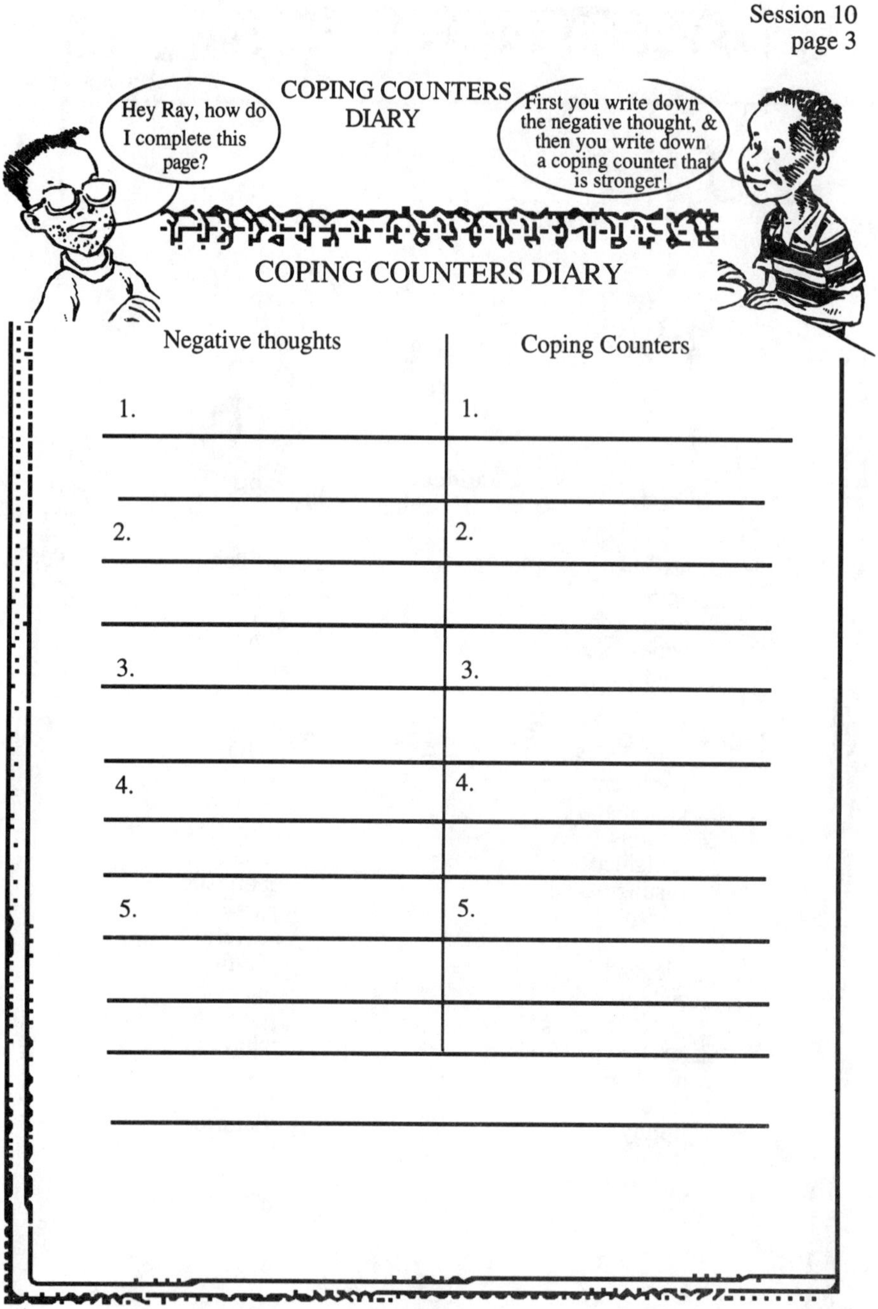

Session 10
page 3

COPING COUNTERS DIARY

Hey Ray, how do I complete this page?

First you write down the negative thought, & then you write down a coping counter that is stronger!

COPING COUNTERS DIARY

Negative thoughts	Coping Counters
1.	1.
2.	2.
3.	3.
4.	4.
5.	5.

Figure 5. Coping counters diary form from the children's workbook.

are designed to modify the client's thinking and the premises, assumptions, and attitudes underlying the client's thoughts (Meichenbaum, 1977). The program includes a number of the cognitive restructuring procedures developed by Beck, Rush, Shaw, and Emery (1979) such as (a) what is the evidence, (b) alternative interpretations, (c) what if, and (d) behavioral experiments. Children are taught to be thought detectives who identify maladaptive thoughts and (a) evaluate the evidence for the thought, (b) consider alternative interpretations, or (c) think about what really would happen if the undesirable event occurred. These procedures are used throughout treatment by the therapist, although the goal is for the children to learn how to restructure their negative thoughts independently. This is accomplished through therapist modeling and the techniques are taught to the youngsters directly (see Table 2).

What is the evidence. *What is the evidence* is a useful technique that most children readily understand. It involves asking a child to work with the therapist to find evidence that supports or refutes the youngster's automatic thoughts and the schemata underlying them. The first step of the procedure involves defining the premise that encompasses the child's maladaptive thoughts. Once this has been defined, the therapist works with the child to establish the evidence necessary to support or disconfirm the underlying premise. After agreeing on the necessary and sufficient evidence, the therapist and the child evaluate the existing evidence and establish a procedure for collecting additional evidence. Subsequently, the therapist and the child review all the available evidence and process the outcome. Finally, the child is given a homework assignment to collect evidence that supports the revised, more adaptive premise.

Alternative interpretations. *Alternative interpretations* is a cognitive restructuring procedure that can be used to counter negative thoughts or to broaden negative thoughts and apply them to the child's thinking. In this case, the manner in which the child interprets events is altered as the therapist and the child work together to generate a number of plausible, more adaptive, and *realistic* interpretations for the child's perceptions of something that has happened or for a particular belief. Next, they collaboratively evaluate the evidence for the alternative interpretations and choose the most plausible. Once again, the goal is to teach the child to do this on his or her own. This is accomplished through the therapist modeling the use of the procedure and through teaching the children how to use it. In addition, we ask the children to teach their parents and teachers how to use it. The parents and teachers can help the child use it when it is appropriate to do so.

What if? Depressed children often exaggerate the significance of a situation and predict unrealistically dire outcomes. *What if* can be used to help them obtain a more realistic understanding of the meaning of the situation and to see that the probable outcome is not going to be as bad as predicted.

When using "What if," the therapist acknowledges the child's distressing situation, but helps the child recognize exaggerated interpretations of the significance of the event. These exaggerations are then countered with evidence for a more realistic outcome; or the youngster might be helped to see that even if the worst outcome occurred, it would not be as bad as the child has predicted.

Behavioral experiments. Perhaps the most efficient way to change a child's thinking is to alter, strategically, behaviors that serve as the base of evidence for the child's thoughts. The alteration in behavior and the resultant change in outcomes provide the child with immediate, direct, and concrete contradictory evidence for a maladaptive schema or supportive evidence for a more adaptive schema. This process of assigning personal experiments requires creativity as the therapist has to be able, first, to identify a maladaptive thought or schema, bring it to the child's recognition, work with the child to establish the necessary evidence to support or refute the thought or schema; and then, devise a behavioral assignment that tests the validity of it directly. Furthermore, steps have to be taken to ensure that the experiment is actually conducted as planned. In some instances, role playing ahead of time, imaginably walking through the assignment, or writing a contract may be used to promote compliance. After the experiment has been completed, the therapist works with the child to process the results. This is an important step because the child may distort the results without the therapist's objective input.

Negative Self-Evaluations. The last portion of the treatment is focused on changing the depressed youngster's negative self-evaluations. This occurs last because all the other self-control and coping skills are brought to bear on the process of working toward and recognizing self-improvement and changing the negative sense of self. Depressed children evaluate their performances, possessions, and personal qualities more negatively than nondepressed youths and their self-evaluations tend to be distorted negatively (Kendall et al., 1990). In other words, they tend to be unrealistically and unreasonably negative in their self-evaluations. Children can be taught to evaluate themselves more reasonably and positively when it is realistic to do so. During this process, they learn to recognize their positive attributes, outcomes, and possessions. The first step of the procedure is to identify the existence and nature of the disturbance. This can be accomplished with the My Standards Questionnaire—Revised (Stark, 1990). This measure allows the therapist to determine whether the child is setting unrealistically stringent standards for his or her performance. If so, when the child evaluates his or her performance relative to these standards, the outcome is inadequacy. When this is the case, cognitive restructuring procedures are used to help the child accept more reasonable standards. When the child sets realistic standards, but evaluates him- or herself negatively, "What is the evidence" and cognitive modeling may be used, and self-monitoring would be used as a means of solidifying the new self-evaluations as the child is instructed to self-monitor the evidence that supports it.

In some instances, the child can benefit from change. In such instances, the goal of self-evaluation training becomes the goal of helping the child translate personal standards into realistic goals and, then, to develop and carry out a plan for attaining these goals. Following the translation process, a plan is formulated for producing improvement in an area in which success is probable. The long-term goal is broken down into subgoals and problem solving is used to develop a plan that will lead to subgoal and, eventually, goal attainment. Prior to enacting the plan, the children try to identify possible impediments to carrying out the plan. Once again, problem solving is used to develop contingency plans for overcoming the impediments. Once the plan, including contingency plans, has been developed, the children self-monitor progress toward change and alterations in the plan are made along the way.

Parents

The parent-training component is designed to (a) educate the parents about depressive disorders, (b) teach the parents how to establish home incentive programs that encourage use of the coping skills, and (c) teach the parents positive behaviors management procedures. In general, the parent training program is designed to foster a more positive family environment. Parents are taught how to use positive behavior management techniques and management skills, how to increase the child's role in the family decision-making process, and methods for improving their child's self-esteem.

One of the central components of the parent training program is teaching them to use primarily positive behavior-management procedures. To accomplish this objective, procedures have been borrowed from Barkley (1987). Initially, the parents are taught to recognize and attend to positive affect and behavior through a series of role-play activities. When they can clearly recognize positive behavior as it occurs, can use verbal praise to encourage it, and understand the notion of extinguishing undesirable behavior through non attention, the parents are assigned the task of spending 15–20 minutes each day playing with their child. They are instructed to make it an enjoyable activity in which they strive to pay attention to their child's positive actions. These positive behaviors are socially reinforced and recorded in a diary by the parent throughout the week.

During the next few meetings, parents are taught how to use reinforcement techniques and about the impact reinforcement has on their child's self-esteem. Once again, role-play activities are used to facilitate acquisition of these skills. Parents work collaboratively with the therapist to identify targets for change and to develop plans to produce the desired change.

In addition to reinforcement techniques, parents are taught the value of praise. Specifically, praise helps children feel good, boosts self-esteem, and can increase the occurrence of desirable behaviors. Thus, parents are instructed to praise their child a minimum of four to six times per day. Moreover, they are taught to be concrete, genuine, and specific when giving praise. They also are cautioned against using hyperbole and left-handed compliments. During this time, when parents are increasing the use of praise, they are also asked to note how often they criticize their depressed child. The goal of this activity is to eventually reduce the number of criticisms by one each day until they are eliminated.

Parents are then taught how to avoid getting caught in a coercive system. They are taught to give clear and effective directives, the time-out procedure, and the use of natural consequences. Following this training, parents are given homework assignments to monitor their effectiveness in implementing the new disciplinary procedures and to record any problematic situations for consideration at the next meeting.

Observations of some families with depressed children have revealed an especially hostile and angry environment in which parents frequently express their anger in a destructive manner. Such personal verbal attacks on the child shatter self-esteem. Although this tendency to lash out at the child is reduced as a result of the skills taught previously, additional steps are taken to teach the parents to control their own anger. In particular, parents receive instruction in the identification of the triggers of their anger and their underlying thoughts. They are taught to use their anger as a cue to leave the situation, cool off, and then take action. Adaptive coping statements and relaxation techniques are used to combat their angry outbursts. The parents are then asked to apply these skills and to gauge their impact on the family as additional homework.

Some of the difficulties in the relationship between depressed youths and their parents stem from the parent's inability to listen empathically. Through education, parents can learn how to express empathy. A four-step model is used to accomplish this. The first step, *active listening*, includes avoiding interruptions during the child's communication and providing the child with nonverbal cues that convey undivided attention. The second step, *reflection techniques* are taught to parents. These techniques serve the dual purpose of forcing parents to listen to their child and of assuring the child that he or she has been heard correctly. Although some parents tend to editorialize during reflection, avoidance of such remarks is stressed during role plays. The third step in the model consists of helping parents to *gain an understanding* of their child's feelings. The culmination of the training model, step four, involves assisting parents in the *use of their new skills* when interacting with their child. Again, homework is assigned to encourage skill acquisition.

Our previously cited research indicates that families of depressed children often fail to engage in recreational activities. Thus, it is important to teach these families to have fun. Parents are asked to identify various low-cost or no-cost activities in which the family can participate. Problem solving is then used to facilitate the scheduling of such activities during the week. In addition to engaging in pleasant activities, parents are instructed to self-monitor the impact of these events on the family.

Family

Research has associated disturbances in family functioning with depressive disorders in childhood. The therapeutic question becomes, what are the family interaction patterns, verbal and nonverbal communications, and family rules that lead to and maintain the child's skills deficits and cognitive disturbances? Common procedures for altering maladaptive family interactions include education, modeling, rehearsal, communication training, coaching, and feedback. Problem-solving and negotiation skills also are used to reduce family conflict.

TREATMENT EFFECTIVENESS AND OUTCOMES

Support for the effectiveness of various components of the proposed treatment program may be found in a handful of case studies (Frame, Matson, Sonis, Fialkov, & Kazdin, 1982; Petti, Bornstein, Delamater, & Conners, 1980) and control group investigations with children (Butler, Miezitis, Friedman, & Cole, 1980) and adolescents (Kahn, Kehle, Jenson, & Clark, 1990; Lewinsohn, Clarke, Hops, & Andrews, 1990; Lewinsohn, Hoberman, & Clarke, 1989; Reynolds & Coates, 1986). Portions of the child component also have proven useful in two investigations conducted by the primary author (Stark et al., 1987; Stark, 1990). Results of these studies will be briefly reviewed in the following paragraphs. It is important to emphasize that the current program was developed to address the limitations of these interventions. In particular, the format has been modified; components have been added, including problem-solving and cognitive restructuring procedures; and parent training and family therapy components have been added.

In our initial study, Stark et al. (1987) evaluated the relative effectiveness of a self-control intervention, a behavioral problem-solving intervention, and a waiting-list control condition for depressed youths. Children in grades 4 to 6 from a public school were assessed for depression using a multiple-gate assessment procedure. A battery of measures, including instruments for assessing related constructs, were completed at pretreatment, posttreatment, and at an eight-week follow-up. Children ($N = 29$) were randomly assigned to one of the three treatment conditions. In each condition, children were divided into small groups of four or five. Each intervention program was conducted at the children's school and consisted of twelve 45- to 50-minute meetings over a five-week period.

The self-control treatment was designed to teach the children skills for self-monitoring, self-evaluation, attributing causation of various outcomes, and self-consequating. The skills were taught through didactic presentations and in-therapy activities, as well as outside homework assignments. During the first 4 sessions, the children were taught self-monitoring skills. These skills were subsequently applied to the children's lives via pleasant-event schedules, which were completed daily throughout the treatment program. To increase the likelihood that the children would complete their assignments, contingency contracts were used that provided the children with tangible rewards on an intermittent schedule. During Sessions 5 and 6, the focus of the self-monitoring shifted to long-term consequences of depressive behavior. The latter portion of Session 6 and all of Session 7 emphasized attribution retraining through education and role playing. During Sessions 8 and 9, a series of educational exercises was used to teach the children more adaptive means of self-evaluation. At this point in treatment, the children were able to use their new repertoire of skills to work toward goal attainment. During the final three sessions, children were taught various forms of self-reinforcement to assist them in achieving their goals.

The behavioral problem-solving therapy consisted of education about feelings and interpersonal behavior. Additional training was provided in problem-solving skills, self-monitoring of pleasant events, activity scheduling, and social skills. These skills were taught using techniques analogous to those used in the self-control conditions (presentations, homework, contracting, etc.).

The waiting-list control condition consisted of children who did not receive treatment until after the posttreatment assessments had been completed. However, it is important to note that these children were not excluded from any services that they would have received through the special education referral process in their school. In fact, two of the students in this condition participated in weekly counseling with the school psychologist.

Results of the study revealed that the children in both active treatment conditions indicated a significant decrease in depressive symptoms at posttreatment assessment and reported significantly less depressive symptomatology than children in the waiting-list condition. On further analysis, it was revealed that 78% of the children in the self-control treatment condition and 60% of the children in the behavioral problem-solving treatment condition scored in the nondepressed range on the Children's Depression Inventory (Kovacs, 1981) at posttreatment. Moreover, all of the children scored in the nondepressed range on a semi-structured clinical interview. In addition, children in both treatment groups reported a significant decrease in anxiety. However, only the children in the self-control condition reported a significant increase in self-esteem. The improvements were maintained or extended during a five-week, follow-up assessment.

The second study (Stark, 1990) was an extension of the first, and it was designed to evaluate the relative efficacy of a cognitive–behavioral treatment and a nonspecific psychotherapy control condition. Once again, children were identified through a multiple-gate screening procedure. Participants were from grades 4 to 7. In addition, they completed measures of depressive cognitions, self-esteem, and hopelessness. Twenty-four children, who exhibited elevated levels of depressive symptomatology as assessed with the Schedule for Affective Disorders and Schizophrenia for School-Aged Children (K-SADS; Puig-Antich & Ryan, 1986), participated in the treatment program. Each child was randomly assigned to either the cognitive–behavioral treatment or the traditional counseling condition that controlled for the nonspecifics of psychotherapy. In the school setting, both treatments consisted of 24 to 26, 45- to 50-minute group sessions, which were conducted over a 3½ month period. Monthly home meetings were also held with the depressed child and his or her family.

The cognitive–behavioral treatment condition incorporated training in self-control skills, social skills, and cognitive restructuring. Specifically, self-control training involved teaching the children self-consequation, self-monitoring, and self-evaluation. This treatment also included assertiveness training (three sessions), which focused on the child's interactions with significant others. Social-skills training (three sessions) featured initiation and maintenance of interactions as well as conflict management. In addition, children were taught cognitive restructuring techniques during three sessions. These interventions were supplemented with problem-solving strategies, relaxation training, and imagery techniques. During meetings with parents, they were encouraged to assist the child in skill development and to engage in more pleasant activities as a family.

The traditional-counseling control condition was designed to control for the nonspecifics of psychotherapy, including meetings and discussions with a group of peers who have similar problems, meetings and discussions with empathic adults, being provided with reasons for depression and strategies for reducing symptoms, being given the expectation of improvement, and completion of therapeutic exercises. The therapists worked in a nondirective fashion and were specifically instructed not to use any cognitive or behavioral procedures knowingly. Family sessions were similar to those in the cognitive–behavioral condition.

Results indicated that subjects in both treatment conditions reported a significant reduction in severity of depressive symptoms, as well as fewer depressive cognitions at posttesting. A seven-month, follow-up indicated that these improvements were sustained. A between-groups comparison revealed that the children in the cognitive–behavioral treatment reported significantly less depression on the K-SADS interview and significantly fewer depressive cognitions on the measure of depressive cognitions. Overall, the results suggest that the cognitive–behavioral program may be an effective treatment for childhood depression. They also point out the need for future research concerning the specific components involved in therapeutic change.

LIMITATIONS

Although results of existing research point to the promise of the intervention program, the entire treatment package should be evaluated empirically. Furthermore, the bulk of existing research has been conducted with nonclinical populations. The efficacy of such interventions with more seriously impaired youths remains essentially unknown. If the intervention program is effective, the next step would be to determine the necessary and sufficient components to produce change. Another unanswered question related to our empirical understanding of the treatment of depressed youths is the interaction effect that antidepressant medication would have with this intervention program. Although antidepressants are commonly prescribed in clinical practice, a paucity of research has been conducted with children, and no one has systematically evaluated the relative efficacy of antidepressants, of comprehensive psychosocial treatment programs, or the effectiveness of interventions that combine psychosocial and pharmacological interventions.

The family and parent training components are crucial parts of the treatment program. From our experience, it is difficult to obtain the desired level of parental and family involvement in the youngster's treatment. In fact, when we were conducting the school-based research, we were fortunate to have the parents in for treatment meetings once a month. They often were too busy working at multiple jobs or with other responsibilities to participate. In a related vein, the mental health of the parents and other family members can limit the impact of the intervention. In some instances, the parents were so seriously disturbed that they required simultaneous intense treatment. In other cases, parental substance abuse would be discovered late in the treatment and the parent would deny having a problem or refuse treatment, which undermined the overall effectiveness of the intervention. Another confounding factor is the stability and health of the marital relationship. A strained or disintegrating marriage creates additional difficulties for the successful treatment of the child.

Recently, we have been working within low-income, high-mobility urban schools. In a number of cases, the children were exposed to so much chaos, poverty, and stress related to survival that it became impossible to intervene at the level of the parents and family. In such cases, an entirely different approach had to be taken. Much work had to be completed by the school social worker or by the individual functioning in this capacity.

GENERALIZABILITY

As noted throughout this chapter, it is believed that the treatment program can be applied to a broad spectrum of children who exhibit depressive disorders. Furthermore, it is believed that the program is applicable to outpatient and school (including special education classroom) settings. However, it is important to note that the existing empirical evidence supports only the efficacy of a less robust version of the intervention program with depressed school children. Unfortunately, there has not been any outcome research completed with clinical populations.

Another issue is the generalizability of the program to children of different ages. Existing outcome research has been completed with children as young as 10 years of age and adolescents of high school age. It is believed that the program, which was initially designed for youngsters between the ages of 9 and 12 years, is suitable for older adolescents. It has been our experience that a minimum of modifications have to be made for adolescents, and most of the modifications that are made are designed to make the activities more age appropriate. The program is less suitable for younger children because of the heavy reliance on cognitive intervention procedures. With some creative work, including the development of illustrated workbooks,[1] the program has been extended to children as young as 8 years of age. It is not deemed to be appropriate for children below this age.

Because of the flexibility and comprehensive nature of the program, it appears to be useful for depressed youngsters who are experiencing a variety of cooccurring disorders. In pilot work, it appears to be especially effective with youngsters who exhibit a combination of depression and oppositional defiant disorder, or depression and ADHD. Clinical experience suggests that it is limited in its effectiveness when parental pathology is present, when there is a history of child maltreatment, and when the parents are in the midst of a divorce or experiencing serious marital discord.

---

[1]For a copy of this workbook, contact author Dr. Kevin D. Stark at the University of Texas in Austin.

DISCUSSION AND RECOMMENDATIONS

The treatment model outlined in this chapter has grown out of treatment-outcome research, as well as a program of research into variables that have relevance to the design of an intervention program. Results of this research have led the authors to develop an intervention program that targets the depressed child, his or her parents, and family. When intervening with the child, it appears to be important to target disturbances in affect, behavior, and cognition, and to do so in a way that recognizes the reciprocal interplay among these different variables. In addition, the youngster's family milieu should become a target of intervention. Parenting skills should be assessed and modified so as to create an encouraging, positive, solution-oriented family environment. The family therapy should be directed toward reducing conflict, increasing cohesion, socializing, and engagement in recreational activities. In addition, the family should be taught how to engage the children in some of the family decisions.

It is acutely apparent that much additional research into the treatment of depressed youths is needed. In addition to completing basic research into the efficacy of such a comprehensive treatment program, it appears to be important to evaluate the process of change. Is change produced as a result of change in cognitive variables, behavior, parenting behaviors, and the family system? Currently, the intervention is delivered via a combined individual and group therapy model. Given the expense of individual therapy, is this necessary or is a group therapy format as effective as the combined format? What is the duration of treatment that leads to the maximum amount of therapeutic change? In other words, is the maximum therapeutic improvement achieved within 12 meetings, 20 meetings, 25 meetings, etc.? Some investigators have suggested that different subtypes of depressive disorders exist. Is the treatment program differentially effective for certain types of depressive disorders? Is it equally effective with early onset and late onset depressives? Does a certain combination of disorders predict treatment outcome? Is parental or family involvement necessary for the success of the treatment program? The underlying point is that we are at a very basic level of understanding of the treatment of depressed youths.

Something that is rarely discussed in the literature on the treatment of children is the importance of the therapeutic relationship. There appears to be both an art and a science to treating youngsters with any disorder. The science is covered within this chapter in the description of the treatment procedures. The art to using this intervention successfully is not as easy to describe. The cornerstone of the intervention is the ability of the therapist to establish a solid relationship with the child clients. This relationship is necessary for the successful implementation of the program. What abilities and skills are necessary for establishing a solid relationship?

This question is yet to be answered. However, in our research, we tend to select therapists who are warm, calm, nonevaluative, creative, optimistic, have a good sense of humor, and enjoy working with children. Another crucial aspect to the art of implementing this intervention program successfully is delivering the content of the program in an engaging and fun fashion. In general, children find cognitive behavioral interventions to be dry and boring. It takes a thorough understanding of the treatment program and of the theory that underlies it, as well as a degree of creativity to engage children in the treatment procedure.

REFERENCES

Barkley, R. A. (1987). *Defiant children: A clinician's manual for parent training.* New York: Guilford Press.

Beck, A. T., Rush, A. J., Shaw, B. F., & Emery, G. (1979). *Cognitive therapy of depression.* New York: Guilford Press.

Butler, L., Miezitis, S., Friedman, R., & Cole, E. (1980). The effect of two school-based intervention programs on depressed symptoms in preadolescents. *American Educational Research Journal, 17,* 111–119.

Kahn, J. S., Kehle, T. J., Jenson, W. R., & Clark, E. (1990). Comparison of cognitive–behavioral, relaxation, and self-modeling interventions for depression among middle-school students. *School Psychology Review, 19,* 196–208.

Kaslow, N. J., Stark, K. D., Printz, B., Livingston, R., & Tsai, S. (1992). Cognitive Triad Inventory for Children: Development and relationship to depression and anxiety. *Journal of Clinical Child Psychology, 21,* 339–347.

Kendall, P. C., & Braswell, L. (1993). *Cognitive behavior therapy for impulsive children* (2nd. ed.). New York: Guilford Press.

Kendall, P. C., Stark, K. D., & Adam, T. (1990). Cognitive deficit or cognitive distortion in childhood depression. *Journal of Abnormal Child Psychology, 18,* 255–270.

Kovacs, M. (1981). Rating scales to assess depression in school aged children. *Acta Paedopsychiatrica, 46,* 305–315.

Meichenbaum, D. (1977). *Cognitive behavior modification.* New York: Plenum Press.

Petti, T. A., Bornstein, M., Delamater, A. M., & Conners, C. K. (1980). Evaluation and multimodality treatment of a depressed prepubertal girl. *Journal of the American Academy of Child Psychiatry, 19,* 690–702.

Puig-Antich, J. H., & Ryan, N. (1986). *Schedule for Affective Disorders and Schizophrenia for School-Age Children.* Pittsburgh, PA: Western Psychiatric Institute and Clinic.

Reynolds, W. M., & Coats, K. I. (1986). A comparison of cognitive–behavioral therapy and relaxation training for the treatment of depression in adolescents. *Journal of Consulting and Clinical Psychology, 54,* 653–660.

Stark, K. D. (1990). *Childhood depression: School-based intervention.* New York: Guilford Press.

Stark, K. D., Humphrey, L. L., Crook, K., & Lewis, K. (1990). Perceived family environments of depressed and anxious children: Child's and maternal figure's perspectives. *Journal of Abnormal Child Psychology, 18,* 527–547.

Stark, K. D., Humphrey, L. L., Laurent, J. L., Livingston, R., & Christopher, J. C. (1993). Cognitive, behavioral, and family factors in the differentiation of depressive and anxiety disorders during childhood. *Journal of Consulting and Clinical Psychology, 61,* 878–886.

Stark, K. D., & Kendall, P. C. (1996). *Treating depressed children: Therapist manual for "ACTION."* Ardmore, PA: Workbook Publishing.

Stark, K. D., Kendall, P. C., McCarthy, M., Stafford, M., Barron, R., & Thomeer, M. (1996). *ACTION: A workbook for overcoming depression.* Ardmore, PA: Workbook Publishing.

Stark, K. D., Linn, J. D., MacGuire, M., & Kaslow, N. J. (in press). The social functioning of depressed and anxious children: Social skills, social knowledge, automatic thoughts, and physical arousal. *Journal of Clinical Child Psychology.*

Stark, K. D., Reynolds, W. M., & Kaslow, N. J. (1987). A comparison of the relative efficacy of self-control therapy and a behavioral problem-solving therapy for depression in children. *Journal of Abnormal Child Psychology, 15,* 91–113.

Stark, K. D., Schmidt, K., & Joiner, T. E. (in press). *Depressive cognitive triad: Relationship to severity of depressive symptoms in children, parents' cognitive triad, and perceived parental messages about the child him or herself, the world, and the future.* Manuscript submitted for publication.

12

THERAPY FOR ADOLESCENT ANOREXIA NERVOSA: ADDRESSING COGNITIONS, FEELINGS, AND THE FAMILY'S ROLE

ARTHUR L. ROBIN, MARQUITA BEDWAY, PATRICIA T. SIEGEL, and MARCIA GILROY

Behavioral family systems therapy (BFST) is an approach to child, adolescent, and family problems that blends behavior modification, cognitive therapy, and family systems therapy. It is a short-term, action-oriented therapy that conceptualizes clinical presenting problems within a family systems context, takes into account contemporary knowledge about child and adolescent development, and relies on empirically tested behavioral and cognitive techniques to produce change. It is based on the premise that we will fail clinically a certain percentage of times unless we not only change behavior and address cognitions and feelings but do so by taking into account the hierarchy within the family and the child's developmental level. It also embraces a strong commitment to empiricism, specificity, and teachability; not only must interventions pass the test of rigorous clinical outcome trials, but they also must be suitable for teaching to other professionals and for replicating through written manuals, videotapes, and professional development workshops.

BFST was developed in the 1970s and 1980s out of work in the areas of parent training, delinquency, and parent–adolescent conflict (Alexander & Parsons, 1973; Patterson, 1982; Robin & Foster, 1989). Most of the

Correspondence concerning this chapter should be directed to Arthur L. Robin, Child Psychiatry and Psychology Department, Children's Hospital of Michigan, 3901 Beaubien Blvd., Detroit, MI 48201.

clinical applications and research evaluations have concentrated on issues such as parenting, noncompliance, aggression, truancy, status offenses, attention deficit disorders, and parent–adolescent conflict. More recently, BFST has been applied to other clinical problems. The purpose of this chapter is to describe the application of BFST to anorexia nervosa in adolescence, which has been the focus of clinical, research, and professional development education activities at Children's Hospital of Michigan and Wayne State University School of Medicine for the past five years.

GOALS AND ISSUES

Anorexia nervosa is a life-threatening disease affecting primarily adolescent girls; involving at least a 15% weight loss or failure to grow as expected; and resulting in being at least 15% underweight, fear of fatness, body image distortions, loss of menstruation, and refusal to eat sufficiently to maintain a normal body weight. There is no single known etiological factor in anorexia nervosa. Generally, it is considered to be a multidetermined disorder, resulting from a combination of biological, cultural, personality, and family factors (Hsu, 1990; Lask & Bryant-Waugh, 1993).

Effective treatment of anorexia nervosa involves a number of targets and components. First, health must be restored by refeeding the adolescent until she reaches an appropriate body weight for her height and age. Depending on the extent of the starvation, the adolescent may need to be hospitalized to sustain life until she reaches a level of nutrition that is safe for resuming her life in the community. Second, eating habits and attitudes must be changed. Girls with anorexia nervosa typically restrict their food intake to selected low-fat, low-calorie foods and develop unusual eating habits, such as dawdling endlessly and cutting their food into very small pieces. Third, bodily distortions and fears of getting fat must be addressed: These are the cognitive underpinnings that contribute to the maintenance of anorexia nervosa. Fourth, generally poor self-images, feelings of personal ineffectiveness, depressed affect, anxiety, and perfectionistic and obsessional personality styles must also be modified. Fifth, maladaptive family interaction patterns often associated with clinical anorexia nervosa must be targeted. These include conflict avoidance, overprotectiveness, and enmeshment; these interactions may impede appropriate achievement of the developmental goal of adolescent individuation.

It is challenging for any therapy to accomplish these goals because of the denial involved in anorexia nervosa. The girls themselves typically deny that they have a problem and do not wish to be treated. Families also often deny or minimize the extent of the adolescent's illness and are easily convinced by the adolescent that she can recover without outside help. The adolescents and their families typically deny or avoid open conflict, claiming they get along very well, and expressing astonishment that their daughter could be starving herself. To make matters worse, adolescents in starvation do not think clearly and are unable to reason effectively, failing to benefit from insight-oriented approaches; typically, they will not restart eating on the basis of the logic of their situation. The physiological effects of starvation further rigidify their thinking, creating a downward spiral. The deeper their starvation, the stronger their fears, and the more intense their denial and resistance to change.

From the viewpoint of family structure, the appropriate hierarchy of parent-in-charge-of-child is reversed in the area of food and eating when these families present for treatment. The adolescent is eating or not eating as she wishes, and her parents have very little influence over her eating behavior; in fact, feeling helpless, many parents make extraordinary efforts to appease their adolescents in the hopes of getting them to eat, going to extreme lengths, such as obtaining unusual foods. Clearly, an effective therapy must restore the appropriate parent–child hierarchy. Traditional family systems therapy has concentrated mostly on building a strong parental coalition to help parents get back in charge of out-of-control, starving adolescents (Minuchin, Rosman, & Baker, 1978). Although such approaches may work well in the hands of highly skilled clinicians, Minuchin and coauthors failed to specify, in sufficient detail, the skills necessary for therapists to teach parents how to take charge of the patient's eating habits and produce reliable change. Such approaches also fail to address the cognitive distortions central to anorexia nervosa. BFST adds behavioral skill and cognitive restructuring components to the structural family therapy component, addressing all aspects of anorexia nervosa.

THE TREATMENT PLAN

BFST for anorexia nervosa may be divided into four phases: (a) assessment; (b) control rationale; (c) weight gain; and (d) weight maintenance (Siegel & Robin, 1987). A fifth phase, inpatient refeeding, usually comes after the first assessment session, but may be necessary at a later time as well, for those patients in severe starvation.

Treatment sessions last typically 60 to 75 minutes and are held weekly until the adolescent has reached target weight; then, sessions are held twice per month. In our clinical research study, treatment lasted 10 to 24 months, with a mean of 16 months. The identified patients and their parents attend jointly, with siblings sometimes invited.

It should be noted that the treatment described in this chapter is designed for the adolescent with restricting anorexia nervosa, without concomitant bulimia nervosa. Although similar interventions can be used with adolescents who have either bulimia nervosa alone or a combination of

TABLE 1
Phases of BFST with Anorexia Nervosa

Assessment
Engage the family in treatment and check weight weekly
Take history of weight, menstruation, eating habits, exercise, mood, medical changes, development, school, peer relations, and family interactions
Coordinate with other members of the team
    Physician: need for hospitalization, target weight
    Dietician: balanced food plan

Control rationale
Therapist puts parents in charge of teen's eating
Therapist deals with family's reaction to control rationale
Therapist coaches parents to develop and implement a behavioral weight gain program

Weight gain
Therapist fine tunes behavioral weight gain program
Therapist begins to address nonfood-related issues
    Distorted thinking: cognitive restructuring
    Family structure: strategic interventions

Weight maintenance
Control over food is gradually returned to the teenager
Teenager learns healthy ways to maintain weight
Therapist works further on family interaction issues
Therapist fosters adolescent individuation

---

bulimia nervosa and anorexia nervosa. Discussion of interventions for such patients is beyond the scope of this chapter.

Assessment

The goals of the assessment phase are to establish rapport with the family and explain the BFST to them; to collect information concerning weight, eating, and individual and family problems; and to determine the adolescent's medical condition and decide whether an inpatient refeeding hospitalization is necessary.

The assessment process typically takes three sessions. Whenever possible, throughout these three sessions, the therapist tries to reframe individual problems within a family context, avoid taking a blaming accusatory tone, and point out the many ways in which the adolescent is out of control and the parents are not working as a team. Although the therapist attempts to establish an alliance with both the parents and the adolescent, if resistance from the adolescent is encountered, the therapist treads lightly, explaining the resistance as a consequence of starvation. As instances of absolutistic thinking and distorted cognitions arise, the therapist also points these out but does not yet attempt to modify them.

In the first session the therapist engages the family, establishes a routine for weekly weigh-ins, and informs the family that no specific interventions will be suggested for several weeks until the therapist understands the problems fully, acknowledging their anxiety about needing to do something now, but assuring them that premature suggestions would not be productive.

During the session, a careful history is taken regarding weight, eating habits and dieting, exercise, medical and physical changes, school functioning, and peer relationships. Each family member is given the opportunity to discuss each of these areas to obtain sufficient details to facilitate making a decision about the need for immediate inpatient hospitalization. As the family members provide their perspective, the therapist attempts to facilitate interchange among the family members to obtain a sample of interaction patterns and communication skills, providing initial material to formulate hypotheses about the family system. The session ends with the therapist introducing the idea that there will be specific assignments between sessions aimed at collecting information or producing change. The first assignment consists of two components: (a) complete the battery of self-report questionnaires used for research (detailed later in this chapter); and (b) keep a daily record of everything that the adolescent eats, on designated food monitoring sheets. The parents are asked to complete this task primarily on the basis of their own observations, rather than on that of retrospective adolescent reports. This request often provokes some controversy because the parents are accustomed to appeasing their daughter around food and may not wish to risk her disapproval by even taking charge of recording her food. The therapist assures the parents that an accurate record is needed for medical and dietary purposes, that their daughter's starvation distorts her thinking; and that, through no fault of her own, she may inaccurately report her food intake; therefore, they need to take this responsibility. In essence, this task introduces, at a relatively nonthreatening level, the notion of parental control, which is discussed later.

The patient is scheduled for a thorough pediatric medical examination as soon as possible after the first session; in cases of severe starvation, requiring immediate attention, the therapist contacts the pediatrician immediately and escorts the family to the emergency room for immediate examination and hospitalization. The therapist provides the pediatrician with a summary of the first session and, after the medical evaluation, decides together with the pediatrician whether the patient needs to be hospitalized for refeeding. Hospitalization is generally considered if: 1) the patient is severely emaciated (less than 75% of ideal weight) and in acute medical danger; has significant cardiac, neurological, or other systemic medical problems; is losing weight rapidly and previous outpatient therapy has failed to reverse the situation; or is actively suicidal. All our adolescent patients are hospitalized in an adolescent medicine unit. The nursing staff implements a structured refeeding program based on a written contract consisting of regularly scheduled meals, dietary counseling, and medical management (Anderson, Morse, & Santmyer, 1985). Patients receive BFST in addition to the refeeding program; therapy sessions focus on preparing the parents for the adolescent's return home. Patients are discharged when they are 80% or more of the target weight, do not have any other acute medical distress, and are eating their meals on a regular basis.

The pediatrician sets a target weight for the patient on the basis of standard growth charts, sets a weight below which hospitalization would be necessary, communicates these weights to the therapist and the dietician, and establishes a routine of regular outpatient medical follow-up visits. The pediatrician also recommends a weight gain of one pound per week and indicates that the dietician will establish how much the patient needs to consume to accomplish this goal. The therapist and pediatrician stay in touch regularly.

In the second and third assessment sessions, we obtain a detailed history of individual and family patterns and problems through questioning and direct observation. At the beginning of the second session, the therapist reviews the homework assignment, collecting the self-report measures and examining the food records, not only for information about eating but, more importantly, to learn about family interactions on the basis of how the family reacted to the task. Did the parents work as a team? What difficulties arose? How resistant was the teenager? Did she try to engage one parent in a coalition to sabotage the task? What other problems arose in family structure, such as triangulation or other coalitional patterns? If the task was partially done or not done at all, how does the family explain this action? Who protects whom? How is conflict handled? As these questions arise, the therapist uses the review of the homework as a springboard to broaden the frame of reference to other situations involving family interaction regarding eating and noneating issues, beginning to build a mental picture of the family process.

Discussion of family interaction blends into a standard developmental history regarding the adolescent, with particular emphasis on temperament, perfectionism, obsessive–compulsive tendencies, depression and suicide, anxiety, rebelliousness, and degree of individuation. The developmental history usually provides an opening to assess siblings, the history of the marriage, and the family in general, in a nonthreatening manner.

The therapist reassigns the task of recording all of the adolescent's eating after the second and third assessment sessions. The family is also scheduled to meet with the dietician at this time. The dietician reviews the food records and the target weight, taking a full dietary recall history.

The dietician outlines a balanced diet on the basis of the diabetic exchange model, starting with a relatively low number of calories (typically 1,200–1,500). The dietitian indicates that the calories will gradually be increased, in coordination with the therapist, to permit a one-pound per-week weight gain. The family is given a detailed handout explaining how to follow the diet, along with sample menus. The food plan is presented in an informational format, and the adolescent's expected distraught reaction to the suggestion that she eat a variety of foods is handled with empathy, referring the family back to the therapist to discuss how to implement the diet.

Control Rationale

In the fourth session, the therapist presents the control rationale to the family. The weekly food record and weight chart are reviewed, pointing out how little the adolescent is eating and how her weight has decreased or remained the same (rarely has she gained weight at this point). The manner in which starvation rigidifies thoughts is reviewed with the family, as well as how the stomach shrinks as one eats less, leading to feeling full faster, which is misinterpreted as "getting fat," thus activating additional fears and less eating, creating a downward spiral. The therapist carefully points out that this downward spiral is not the adolescent's nor the parents' fault; it is the inevitable consequence of anorexia nervosa. The therapist then points out that, in essence, the adolescent's eating and weight loss are beyond her own control; she cannot reverse the downward spiral by herself. The only "medicine" that can help this "disease" is food, yet the fears that drive the disease prevent the patient from taking her medicine. Under other circumstances, when a child does not take her medicine, her parents, who love and care for her, get her to take the medicine. Similarly, in these circumstances, her parents must get her to take the food, which is her medicine.

The parents are asked to assume complete responsibility and control of their daughter's eating, temporarily, until their daughter reaches target weight, and the effects of starvation are reversed; then, control over eating will gradually be returned to her. The parents are asked to see to it that their daughter eats all of the daily food intake prescribed by the dietician. The therapist emphasizes that the couple needs to work as a team in taking charge of their daughter's eating, and that the therapist will help the parents decide how to proceed to work as a team. The therapist defines the parental responsibility to include (a) planning the daily menu; (b) purchasing the necessary groceries; (c) measuring, weighing, and preparing the food for each meal; (d) sitting at the table with their daughter and making sure that she actually eats all of the designated food; (e) recording on the food sheets what was consumed; and (f) staying with their daughter for 45 minutes after each meal to make sure she does not attempt to vomit or exercise.

Throughout the remainder of the fourth session and the next four to eight sessions, the therapist basically does two things: (a) elicits the family members' reactions to the control rationale, responding strategically to their resistance to it; and (b) coaches the parents in working as a team to develop and implement a behavioral weight-gain program at home (Halmi, 1985). The reaction to the control rationale is usually immediate, intense, and negative. The teenager angrily objects to parental controls, claiming that she does not need them, will not follow them, can do it on her own, must deal with her feelings and achieve insight first, etc. Sometimes, previously compliant adolescents throw objects at the therapist or, in one case, the adolescent bolted out of the room and locked herself in the restroom. Parents express skepticism, despair, helplessness, and sometimes open defiance to carrying it out, and may challenge the therapist's competence; they often misperceive and distort the control rationale, thinking they are being asked to be dictators or force feed their daughters. Family members attempt to form coalitions against the therapist.

The therapist must stand firm and must not become defensive. Angry adolescent objections are empathetically acknowledged but not debated; the therapist reinforces the temporary nature of the parental controls as well as the previously mentioned impression of how the adolescent's current and past behavior clearly indicate her inability to control her own eating, and adds that it is not her fault but that, regrettably, these steps need to be taken to prevent her from killing herself from starvation. Parental objections are met nondefensively and openly with understanding, information, paradoxical restraint, and requests for further clarification of the parents' position; we go with the resistance, not against it, as a strategy for overcoming it (Anderson & Stewart, 1983). The therapist never debates the parents or puts down their position; such tactics inevitably backfire.

To the father who feels that he is being asked to "act like Hitler," for example, the therapist might inquire as to what exactly does he mean, whereupon the therapist clarifies that he is not being asked to shove food down his daughter's throat, but rather to establish a set of incentives that will motivate eating behavior. To the mother who suggests that other eating disorder therapists work on feelings first, then on eating, and how will this therapy address the "real, underlying problems," the therapist might reply that (a) there are different approaches, all of which are valid; (b) starvation impedes concentration on feelings, and it is necessary first to get her daughter out of severe starvation before focusing on feelings; and (c) perhaps she might wish to consult with another therapist, if she feels that strongly about this issue. When the adolescent interrupts to enlist a parent in a coalition against the therapist, the therapist blocks the interruption, making comments such as, "Your parents need to discuss this matter with each other now."

Establishing a behavioral weight gain program involves discussing exhaustively, with the family, the following issues: (a) when will the specific meals be planned; (b) how will responsibility for preparing, monitoring, and recording the meals be divided between the mother and father; (c) how will lunch at school be handled; (d) what will be the positive incentives for completing eating each meal, and how will they be scheduled; (e) what longer term contracts can be written for gaining 25, 50, 75%, etc., of the required weight; (f) what will be the consequences for failing to complete a meal; (g) how will calories be preserved (e.g., limited activity) if meals are not consumed; (h) how will they interact with their daughter during mealtime; and (i) what will be the rules governing exercise, athletics, dance, or other activities that involve high expenditures of calories. As a coach, the therapist raises these issues for the couple to consider but does not tell the family exactly how to handle them. The couple is guided to generate solutions to each problem creatively, with the therapist helping in suggesting how other families have dealt with the issues, but trying to take a Socratic approach. It is important for the parents to feel that they developed the specific plan, and that it is tailored to their idiosyncratic situation; this increases their commitment to implementing it more effectively.

In the face of their daughter's resistance, denial, and anger, not to mention their own helplessness and typically past poor track record of working as a couple, the task of working as a team to develop and implement an effective behavioral weight gain program is indeed overwhelming for most couples. The therapist must continually acknowledge the difficulties involved, help the couple break the task into small units, tackling one bit at a time, and unwaivingly back the couple's efforts, blocking adolescent sabotage. After several sessions of explanations, resistance, strategic maneuvering, and behavioral programming, most families begin to achieve success in implementing a behavioral weight gain program. The couple begins to set and enforce effectively limits, rules, and consequences for eating and not eating; the adolescent begins to comply. We call this point the *pivot*, and it signals the start of the next phase of BFST.

Weight Gain

During the weight gain phase of BFST, the parents have effectively taken charge of the patient's eating, and the patient is beginning to follow the dietician's prescribed food plan and, consequently, gain weight regularly. There are two primary goals of this phase of treatment: (a) "fine tune" the behavioral weight gain program, closing off any loopholes and continuing the program until the adolescent reaches her target weight; and (b) begin to explore other issues, including cognitive distortions and family structure problems.

The format of the early sessions of this phase consists of weigh-in and review of the updated weight graph; review of the daily food record sheets, which the parents continue to maintain; and discussion of any problems with selecting, preparing, eating, or monitoring meals, as well as applying agreed-upon short- and long-term consequences. Early in the session, the therapist usually gives the adolescent an opportunity to ventilate any feelings, concerns, or reactions that she may have with regard to the ongoing program. These are responded to in an empathetic manner, reminding her of the temporary nature of parental controls, and when possible, taking her opinions and preferences into account when fine-tuning the behavioral weight gain program. We have found that such a ventilation period is important for maintaining rapport with the adolescent as well as reassuring the parents, who are susceptible to attempts by the adolescent to enlist them in a coalition against the therapist, that the therapist really is interested in the adolescent's opinions and feelings, even though these opinions cannot be permitted to alter the parental control routines.

If the adolescent has gained weight during a given week, then the therapist assumes that the program is going well at home. In addressing the teenager, the therapist praises her and asks what it was like to gain weight, acknowledging how upsetting it can be, and reassuring the teen that she will not be permitted to gain too much weight too fast. If the teenager has accepted the weight gain, her ability to be flexible in her thinking about weight fluctuations is praised. If she has any distorted cognitions about the weight gain, the therapist helps the teenager challenge them, suggesting a more reasonable way to view the weight gain. For example, some adolescents believe that eating one cookie will put on five pounds, or that all fats are unhealthy. The therapist may provide corrective nutritional information or engage in a Socratic discussion challenging the logic of such distortions, helping the adolescent to develop more accurate cognitions about the impacts of specific foods. If the adolescent believes that eating all of her food will cause her stomach to look like a watermelon, she can be asked to measure her stomach with a ruler before and after eating, measure a watermelon, and compare the two sets of measurements. In addressing the parents, the therapist praises their efforts, stresses the positive impact of working as a team, anticipates difficulties that may arise during the next week, and helps them plan to overcome these difficulties.

If the adolescent has stayed the same or has lost weight, the therapist looks for the loopholes by asking the following types of questions:

1. Has the adolescent eaten all of the required food and are the written records accurate;
2. Is the adolescent dumping or hiding food;

3. Is the adolescent failing to eat lunch at school;
4. Is the adolescent doing exercise that the parents are not aware of;
5. Is parental teamwork breaking down;
6. Has the adolescent convinced one parent to "back off" but not admit it;
7. Do one or both parents believe that the program is too strict or harsh;
8. Are the parents failing to enforce the consequences of not eating;
9. Have the incentives lost their value;
10. Is there interference from parental marital or individual psychopathological problems; or
11. What purpose does it serve the family for the adolescent to fail to improve at this point in time?

If none of these factors explains the lack of weight gain sufficiently, then the therapist consults with the dietician about increasing daily caloric intake, usually in increments of 200 calories. If one or more of these factors is operative, the remainder of the session is devoted to discussing and planning to overcome the identified loophole.

Later in the weight gain phase, when the adolescent is regularly gaining the required one pound per week, the sessions begin the change focus to non-food-related issues. The therapist begins to target goals in the areas of positive family communication and problem solving, adolescent independence seeking, changing rigid beliefs about family life, generally perfectionistic expectations for achievement at home and at school, inappropriate adolescent involvement in marital affairs, and sibling and peer relationships. Often, at this phase of the therapy, family members have become comfortable enough with the therapist to "inadvertently let slip" important family secrets, which then set the agenda for particular sessions and usually turn out to be germane to the function of the anorexia in the family system. For example, in one family, the mother's alcoholism became known, and it turned out that by not eating, the adolescent was, in part, trying to tell her mother to stop drinking; in another family, the father's extramarital affair became known, and it turned out that the adolescent's anorexia, in part, was used to distract the couple from their conflict over the extramarital affair. The therapist relies heavily on problem-solving communication techniques (Robin & Foster, 1989) during this phase of the therapy.

Weight Maintenance

When the teenager reaches her target weight, the therapist shifts into the weight maintenance phase of BFST, which has six general goals:

1. gradual return of control over eating and weight from the parents to the adolescent;
2. teaching the adolescent healthy strategies to maintain her weight;
3. further reducing remaining distorted thoughts and misperceptions;
4. teaching the family to identify problems and resolve conflicts without either avoidance or intense upheaval;
5. fostering adolescent autonomy, individuation, socialization, and positive self-esteem; and
6. strengthening the marital dyad, removing the adolescent from any marital conflicts, and helping the couple adjust to their life with a more independent adolescent.

Therapy sessions are scheduled every other week instead of weekly. The dietician is consulted to suggest a reduction in the number of calories appropriate for maintaining weight instead of gaining weight. The stage is set for returning control over eating to the adolescent when the therapist praises the teen for attaining target weight, comments on the teen's regained health, notes any comments or behaviors by the teen that reflect maturity and good judgement, and suggests that as a consequences, the teen has demonstrated that she can be trusted about eating. The therapist asks the parents to develop a plan for gradual return of control over eating to the teenager, assuring them that they can be as cautious as they feel is necessary. Such a plan usually includes one or more of the following elements:

1. giving the adolescent responsibility for one meal at a time;
2. permitting the adolescent to measure or record food or to eat without supervision;
3. permitting the adolescent to be weighed independently;
4. permitting the adolescent to go on all-day outings without any food restrictions; and
5. giving the adolescent more freedom to exercise as she wishes.

The parents often express "ruinous" beliefs about the negative impact of too much freedom too soon, which the therapist must help them to evaluate critically. The therapist suggests that the plan be implemented on an experimental basis for several weeks, with the resulting impact on the adolescent's weight as the ultimate criterion for success. As the plan is found to be working, it is extended, until the teenager is taking appropriate responsibility for her eating. Whenever relapses occur, the family is helped to react appropriately, restoring parental control in stages, not overreacting in an absolutistic manner.

The adolescent is helped to change her cognitions to foster healthy methods of weight maintenance. The therapist inquires about the adolescent's perceptions of her foods and her appearance now that she has reached target weight. Any distortions that are identified are challenged through logical discussion or specific tasks. For example, reluctance to eat forbidden foods may be dealt with by asking the teen to experiment with eating a small amount of the forbidden food and to evaluate her feelings and weight afterward. Exercise is used as a method for maintaining weight, and the adolescent is asked to "guess" how many calories she may need to add to her food plan to maintain weight while exercising as much as she desires. During a general discussion of eating habits, the adolescent is encouraged "to eat the way your friends do."

The therapist spurs adolescent individuation and parental adjustment to these developmental changes by assigning an increasingly broad set of tasks to be completed between sessions. In some cases of highly enmeshed families, for example, the therapist may first have to normalize adolescent rebellious behavior, which may be perceived as ruinous by parents. Then, the adolescent may be asked to do something rebellious secretly during the following week, which the parents are supposed to guess, but that adolescent will not tell anyone until the next therapy session. One girl came up with changing channels on the remote control for the television without her father's permission as the most rebellious act she could imagine; later in therapy, she stayed out past curfew and came home smelling of beer. The increase in her rebelliousness was a clear sign of individuation.

Just as adolescents may need to be assigned tasks to propel them toward autonomy, the couple may need to be assigned tasks to do without their daughter. For example, the therapist might discuss the adolescent's spending a weekend at a friend's house, while the couple goes away for the weekend. Such tasks are designed to help the couple adjust to the changed adolescent and to draw clear boundaries around the marital subsystem in the family. It is at this stage of treatment that marital conflicts may become openly recognized and discussed. Some couples ask to have several sessions without the adolescent present to discuss their marriage; this is viewed as a significant sign of progress. It is also common for the therapist to spend several individual sessions with the adolescent at this time, dealing with peer or other issues.

Problem-solving communication training techniques (Robin & Foster, 1989) are used to teach families to negotiate contracts regarding rules, regulations, and freedoms. Cognitive restructuring is used to help parents deal with ruinous fears of too much adolescent freedom and adolescent fears of parental disapproval. Siblings are invited to selected sessions during this phase of therapy to deal with issues such as sibling conflict, jealousy, chores, etc.

When the adolescent has maintained her weight, controlling her own eating for approximately four to six months, the therapist moves toward termination and follow-up. The interval between sessions is lengthened to four and then six weeks, the family is prepared to deal with relapses, and the family is left with an open invitation to return if it should need help in the future. In our clinical research study, the therapists hold a follow-up session at 12, 30, and 48 months after the termination of treatment.

TREATMENT EFFECTIVENESS AND OUTCOMES

Ideally, the empirical evaluation of a treatment such as BFST should proceed through a number of outcome studies beginning with comparisons of the treatment with no-treatment and attention-placebo control groups, followed by component analyses and comparative psychotherapy outcome studies. Such an approach permits the investigator to control for history, maturation, attention, and expectation effects.

In the real world of clinical outcome research on BFST, there were several constraints that rendered such a sequence of studies impractical: (a) clinical anorexia nervosa is a life-threatening disease, and the investigator considered it unethical to expose such patients to either a no-treatment or an attention-placebo control group; and (b) funding agencies were not overly enthusiastic about such an approach. Instead, we chose to conduct a comparative psychotherapy outcome study contrasting BFST to a maximally different type of treatment (Robin, Siegel, Koepke, Moye, & Tice, 1994; Robin, Siegel, & Moye, 1995). We recognize that the results of such a study leave unanswered some of the basic questions about attention and expectation effects. Perhaps future studies using subclinical eating disordered adolescents in whom the risk of delayed treatment or exposure to placebo conditions is not as high can compare BFST to attention-placebo and no-treatment controls.

We chose as an alternative treatment for our study the ego oriented individual therapy (EOIT). In this approach, the therapist specifically asks the parents not to put any external controls on the adolescent's eating, but to leave the issue of eating to the therapists. It is assumed that only through insight and understanding into the dynamics contributing to the eating disorder will the patient be able to choose to become healthy. The EOIT therapist conducts weekly individual therapy sessions with the adolescent, and twice per month collateral sessions with the parents. Individual sessions focus primarily on the adolescent's ego strength; coping skills; individuation from the nuclear family; confusion about her identity; and other interpersonal issues regarding physical, social, and emotional growth; and the relationship of these issues to eating, weight expectations, and body image. The therapist communicates a nurturant–authoritative stance (e.g., the therapist is strong and available to help a weak adolescent); the therapist respects the adolescent's autonomy and understands her struggle to individuate from a highly dysfunctional family; and the therapist will not coerce the adolescent to gain weight or change her attitudes, but will help her understand how she can choose to be healthy, coping with her dysfunctional family and inner fears without self-starvation. As the adolescent overcomes initial defensiveness, the therapist serves as a tension regulator helping the adolescent identify problems in daily living, understand their link to eating and cognitions about body image–thinness, and collaborate on constructive solutions that promote physical and emotional health.

Through interpretation, support, reflection, and the power of transference, the therapist sets the conditions for the adolescent to realize that she can accept herself as the therapist accepts her; with self-acceptance and a stronger ego, the sense of ineffectiveness, interpersonal distrust, and poor identity formation, which made the pursuit of thinness an appealing alternative to the pursuit of individuation, dissipates, permitting a resumption of normal eating and appropriate weight gain.

In the collateral sessions, the therapist educates the parents about normal adolescent development; provides support while asking them to refrain from direct involvement in their daughter's eating; and prepares them emotionally to cope with a more assertive, demanding, and angrier adolescent.

The design consisted of randomly assigning 40 adolescents meeting the *Diagnostic and Statistical Manual of Mental Disorders* (3rd ed., rev.; [DSM-III-R]; American Psychiatric Association, 1987) criteria for anorexia nervosa to either BFST or EOIT, and to one of five senior female therapists nested within treatment conditions. Four were doctoral-level psychologists; one was a master's-level social worker. The adolescents ranged in age from 11 to 19 years, with the mean ages being 14.7 years for BFST and 13.9 years for EOIT (no significant difference). Thirty eight resided in two-parent families; two resided in single-parent families. Following the intake and random assignment, each adolescent and her parents attended a six-hour, preassessment session conducted by a research assistant. Therapy began shortly after the preassessment, and continued for an average of 16 months. The range of permissible therapy time is 10–18 months. We first planned to limit therapy to 12 months in all cases, but a flexible approach proved necessary to meet clinical needs. The research assistant monitored completion of all of the questionnaire measures to ensure that family members give independent answers. Another six-hour postassessment was completed following termination of therapy. Follow-up assessments were conducted at one, two and one-half, and four years after the completion of therapy.

To standardize treatments, the therapists followed written manuals. In addition, to confirm that the therapists faithfully followed the manuals, all the sessions were audiotaped, and 40 sessions, sampled representatively from the beginning, middle, and end of BFST and EOIT, were rated by a doctoral-level psychologist using a checklist consisting of 27 presence–absence items, 18 covering BFST activities and 9 covering EOIT activities. The number of items endorsed as present comprised the BFST and EOIT scores for each session. The BFST therapists exhibited significantly higher BFST scores and significantly lower EOIT scores than the EOIT therapists (Robin et al., 1994), suggesting adherence to the manuals.

The dependent measures include

1. body mass index;
2. eating attitudes (Eating Attitudes Test completed by the adolescents and by the parents rating the adolescents);
3. ego functioning (the Interoceptive Awareness, Ineffectiveness, and Interpersonal Distrust scales of the Eating Disorder Inventory);
4. depression and internalizing behavior problems (the Beck Depression Inventory and the Internalizing Behavior Disorders scores of the Child Behavior Checklist [adolescent, mother, and father versions]); and
5. family conflict (general conflict and eating-related conflict) assessed through self-report with the Parent Adolescent Relationship Questionnaire and through videotaped interactions coded with the Interaction Behavior Coding System.

It was hypothesized that BFST might be associated with better outcomes than EOIT on the variables that it targeted most closely, such as body mass index, eating attitudes, and family interactions; while EOIT might be associated with better outcomes than BFST on the variables it targeted most closely, such as interoceptive awareness, interpersonal distrust, ineffectiveness, depression, and internalizing behavior problems. Table 2 indicates the number of participants who completed the postassessment and various follow-up assessments.

Repeated measures analyses of variance with treatment condition as a grouping factor, followed by post-hoc contrasts, were conducted. Analyses

TABLE 2
Number of Families Completing Assessments to Date

| | Assessment | | | | |
	Pre-	Post-	12-month	30-month	48-month
BFST[a]	20	13	11	10	9
EOIT[b]	20	11	8	8	3

Note. [a]BFST = Behavioral family system therapy; [b]EOIT = Ego oriented individual therapy.

revealed that from pre- to postassessment, both the BFST and EOIT groups improved on body mass index, but that there was greater improvement on the mean scores for BFST than EOIT; by the 12-month follow-up, the EOIT group had caught up to the BFST group, and the gains were maintained in the reduced sample collected to date up to 48 months following the completion of treatment. The clinical significance of these changes was examined by tabulating the percentage of girls, in each group, who reached the target weights established by the pediatrician or were menstruating after treatment. At postassessment, 64% of the BFST and 64% of the EOIT patients reached target weight; 90% the BFST and 73% of the EOIT patients were menstruating by post-assessment; and 55% of the BFST and 46% of the EOIT patients met the dual criteria of achieving target weight and menstruation. At 12-month follow-up, 82% of the BFST and 50% of the EOIT were at or above target weight; 100% of the girls in both groups were menstruating; and 82% of the BFST and 50% of EOIT patients met the dual criteria of target weight and menstruation. The differences between groups in percentages were not significant, using a Chi-Square test. Clinical significance has not yet been examined beyond 12-month follow-up because of the small sample sizes of girls who reached these points.

BFST and EOIT also both improved from pre- to postassessment on eating attitudes, ineffectiveness, interoceptive awareness, depression, and internalizing behavior problems, with maintenance of change to the 48-month follow-up. For those variables for which parents and adolescents provided data (e.g., eating attitudes and internalizing behavior problems), the positive outcomes were similar whether the adolescent, mother, or father was the respondent.

With regard to family conflict, an interesting discrepancy emerged between self-reported and observed parent–adolescent interaction, and between general conflict and eating-related conflict. Very little general conflict was reported before or after treatment on the Parent Adolescent Relationship Questionnaire, but a great deal of eating-related conflict was reported at preassessment. BFST and EOIT were associated with equally large decreases in self-reported eating-related conflict over the course of treatment; these improvements were maintained through the 30-month follow-up. A great deal of negative parent–adolescent communication was coded based on the videotaped interactions; such interactions were equally negative in a discussion of a noneating related issue and a discussion of the eating and weight problems. BFST and EOIT were generally associated with comparable improvements from pre- to postassessment in negative communication; in several cases, BFST was associated with significantly greater changes in negative communication than EOIT. No follow-up data were collected on videotaped family interactions.

These results should be regarded as preliminary because the study is still in progress, but they certainly strongly suggest that BFST and EOIT are associated with many positive changes. Not only did both treatment groups return to health, but they also manifested pervasive changes in eating attitudes, affect, selected aspects of ego functioning, and family relations. Interestingly, the differential treatment predictions were only partially confirmed, such as the only significant difference between groups was on mean body mass index; however, the power to detect treatment differences will not be adequate until the entire sample has been analyzed, so we should not make any definitive interpretations of these effects at the present time.

Two other studies have evaluated the effectiveness of a family intervention very similar to BFST. Russell, Szmukler, Dare, and Eisler (1987) conducted a random-assignment, controlled comparison of family therapy versus individual therapy following inpatient weight restoration for eighty eating disordered patients with varying degrees of severity. Family therapy produced more improvement than individual therapy on weight, menstrual functioning, and global psychosocial adjustment ratings for a subgroup of adolescents with restricting anorexia nervosa, whose illness began before 19 years of age and was of less than 3-years' duration. In a follow-up study, LeGrange, Eisler, Dare, and Russell (1992) compared joint family therapy (FT), in which the entire family was seen together, with family counseling (FC), in which the parents were seen separately from the adolescent and given advice for managing the adolescent's eating problem, as treatments for teenagers with anorexia nervosa. Both treatments produced comparable changes on weight, eating attitudes, self-esteem, and global adjustment ratings. Family interaction was assessed through self-report on the Family Adaptability and Cohesion Scales III (FACES III) and through observation by coding videotapes of structured family interviews for expressed emotion. There were no systematic effects of either treatment on the FACES III mean adaptability or cohesion scores, but a nonsignificant tendency for more FT than FC families to have higher FACES III dissatisfaction scores after treatment. There was also a nonsignificant trend for parental critical comments, one component of expressed emotion, to increase following FT, but to decrease following FC. Finally, higher rates of preassessment maternal critical comments and FACES III dissatisfaction scores were associated with poorer adolescent weight and menstrual functioning outcomes following either treatment.

Taken together, our preliminary results and Russell's outcomes strongly suggest that BFST and related interventions are associated with significant improvements in health, eating attitudes, affect, and family interaction for young adolescents with restricting anorexia nervosa. These interventions resulted in statistically and clinically meaningful changes on a variety of measurement domains, including weight, eating attitudes, ego functioning, affectual variables, and selected family interaction outcomes.

LIMITATIONS AND GENERALIZABILITY

There are four primary limitations of BFST as an intervention for adolescents with anorexia nervosa:

1. Most of the families in our treatment study had two parents residing at home; assuming parental control over an adolescent's eating has sometimes proven burdensome for a single parent without any backup. In such cases, we have asked the single parent to enlist the assistance of significant others, relatives, friends, etc.

2. Age may be a limiting factor. Eleven to seventeen-year-old adolescents do well in a treatment that demands constant family involvement, but by ages 18 and 19 years, especially when the girls leave home and live at college, it is sometimes difficult to establish the necessary parental involvement necessary for BFST to work. In fact, Russell et. al (1987) found that for young adults with anorexia nervosa, individual therapy was marginally superior to family therapy.

3. BFST does not directly address issues of ego functioning, self-esteem, and emotional functioning. Such topics may be better discussed with adolescents in the absence of parents. In cases in which parents have physically or sexually abused their daughters and such information is uncovered during therapy, it may be dangerous to rely primarily on a family therapy approach.

4. Severe parental dysfunction may make it difficult for parents to take and maintain control of their daughter's eating. A depressed, alcoholic, or schizophrenic parent may not have the emotional capacity to follow through on the necessary interventions. Couples in severe marital distress may not be able to work as a team sufficiently to establish an effective behavioral weight gain program.

In summary, these limitations really represent one factor: BFST requires a major commitment of parental team and effort, and anything that precludes the necessary commitment is a limiting factor.

SUMMARY

The positive clinical and research outcomes obtained with BFST, as applied to anorexia nervosa, illustrate the applicability of a therapy based on a model developed originally for use with oppositional behavior disorders to a novel psychopathological domain; the limitations of this therapeutic approach, to date, point to the need for clinical flexibility in applying any model to real-world cases. Elements of BFST, which were particularly salient in its application to anorexia nervosa, included

1. a highly structured, manualized approach;
2. emphasis on problem-solving and communication training to change family interactions;
3. use of cognitive restructuring to address distorted beliefs and perceptions;
4. integration of strategic–structural interventions with behavioral interventions; and
5. tailoring treatments to the developmental tasks of adolescence.

The BFST model shows great promise for treating a variety of adolescent problems. Hopefully, the efforts described here will spur additional, innovative applications with other behavior disorders.

REFERENCES

Alexander, J. F., & Parsons, B. V. (1973). Short-term behavioral intervention with delinquent families: Impact on family process and recidivism. *Journal of Abnormal Psychology, 81,* 219–225.

American Psychiatric Association. (1987). *Diagnostic and statistical manual of mental disorders* (3rd. ed., rev.). Washington, DC: Author.

Anderson, A. E., Morse, C., & Santmeyer, K. (1985). Inpatient treatment for anorexia nervosa. In D. M. Garner & P. E. Garfinkel (Eds.), *Handbook of psychotherapy for anorexia nervosa and bulimia* (pp. 311–343). New York: Guilford Press.

Anderson, C. M., & Stewart, S. (1983). *Mastering resistance: A practical guide to family therapy.* New York: Guilford Press.

Halmi, K. A. (1985). Behavioral management for anorexia nervosa. In D. M. Garner & P. E. Garfinkel (Eds.), *Handbook of psychotherapy for anorexia nervosa and bulimia* (pp. 147–159). New York: Guilford Press.

Hsu, G. (1990). *Eating disorders.* New York: Guilford Press.

Lask, B., & Bryant-Waugh, R. (1993). *Childhood onset anorexia nervosa and related eating disorders.* Hillsdale, NJ: Erlbaum.

LeGrange, D., Eisler, I., Dare, C., & Russell, G. F. M. (1992). Evaluation of family treatments in adolescent anorexia nervosa: A pilot study. *The International Journal of Eating Disorders, 12,* 347–357.

Minuchin, S., Rosman, B. L., & Baker, L. (1978). *Psychosomatic families: Anorexia nervosa in context.* Cambridge, MA: Harvard University Press.

Patterson, G. R. (1982). *Coercive family process.* Eugene, OR: Castalia Press.

Robin, A. L., & Foster, S. L. (1989). *Negotiating parent–adolescent conflict: A behavioral family systems approach.* New York: Guilford Press.

Robin, A. L., Siegel, P. T., Koepke, T., Moye, A., & Tice, S. (1994). Family therapy versus individual therapy for adolescent females with anorexia nervosa. *Journal of Developmental and Behavioral Pediatrics, 15,* 111–116.

Robin, A. L., Siegel, P. T., & Moye, A. (1995). Family versus individual therapy for anorexia: impact on family interation. *The International Journal of Eating Disorders, 17,* 313–322.

Russell, G. F. M., Szmukler, G. I., Dare, C., & Eisler, B. I. (1987). An evaluation of family therapy in anorexia nervosa and bulimia nervosa. *Archives of General Psychiatry, 44,* 1047–1056.

Siegel, P. T., & Robin, A. L. (1987). *Outpatient therapy manual: Behavioral family systems therapy with anorexia nervosa.* Unpublished manuscript, Wayne State University, Detroit, MI.

IV

ATTENTION DEFICIT
HYPERACTIVITY DISORDER

INTRODUCTION

Attention deficit hyperactivity disorder (ADHD) may be the most common of childhood Axis 1 mental disorders. Prevalence estimates vary widely as a function of diagnostic criteria used, but reasonable estimates suggest that 3–5% of children, nationwide, are affected. Because ADHD accounts for a large proportion of all referrals for child mental health services and comprises a large share of the economic cost and human suffering caused by childhood mental disorders, the development of effective treatments across the childhood and adolescent years is essential. In this section, four chapters present treatment modalities for children with ADHD.

Arthur D. Anastopoulos and his colleagues describe an impressive range of psychosocial treatment studies using parent training (PT), problem-solving communication training (PSCT), and structural family therapy (SFT). These approaches show evidence of significant benefits to children, adolescents, and their parents after 3 months following the end of treatment. The authors note the limitations of some of their earlier studies (lack of direct behavioral observations of children, need for control or comparison groups, etc.). To address some of these concerns, they have developed two new study programs designed to test exactly which psychosocial treatments, alone and in combination, are most effective in treating children with ADHD.

Steven P. Hinshaw has developed cognitive–behavioral treatments (CBT) for children with ADHD to foster self-management of interpersonal behaviors. In his research program, children are reinforced for self-monitoring, demonstrating appropriate responses during anger management exercises, and matching their own self-ratings with those of an objective adult observer. Preliminary evidence suggests that some children do best on a combination of self-monitoring and medication treatments. This work is highly promising, intuitively appealing, and emphasizes the need to shift ADHD treatment approaches to group-based formats in which children can learn and monitor appropriate interpersonal skills.

William E. Pelham and Betsy Hoza have developed an intensive 8-week summer treatment program (STP) that is coupled with the more traditional treatment programs implemented during the child's school year. The STP incorporates operant approaches, CBT, and pharmacological interventions. Great emphasis is placed on teaching and reinforcing a range of social, academic, and recreational skills, all within the context of environments analogous to those that children traditionally experience during the school year. Impressive gains are noted at the end of the STP program. However, as the authors note, without continuing treatments during the school year, these gains may not be sustainable. The authors plan future research (a) to address differential effectiveness of the STP treatments compared with other treatment techniques and controls; (b) to develop strategies to enhance the maintenance of effects; and (c) to determine which components of the STP carry the effects of the intervention.

Howard Abikoff and Lily Hechtman have developed and implemented a state-of-the-art, two-site multimodal treatment (MMT) program that entails the use of optimally titrated stimulant medication, academic study skills training, remedial tutoring as needed, individual psychotherapy, social skills training, parent management training, and strategies to provide home-based reinforcements for school behaviors and performance. In their research program, children receiving this impressive battery of treatments are compared with a conventional stimulant treatment group (CTG) and an attention control group (ACG). It is hoped that this study will clarify the additive effects of specific behavioral and psychosocial treatments, over and above the effects of attention (ACG) or medication alone (CTG). Although the final results of this study are not as yet available, nonetheless, many of the procedures developed in this program have been used in an ongoing, six-site study of multimodal treatments (see later) supported by the National Institute of Mental Health (NIMH).

As noted by each of the chapters' authors, there is abundant evidence of short-term effects of various psychosocial treatments (especially BT and PT) and of medications. However, there are insufficient data concerning which of these treatments, alone or in combination, are effective for which children and in which functioning domains. Furthermore, the effects of longer term treatments on the developmental outcomes of these children are essentially unknown, and there has been great concern among experts about whether treatments make much difference in the long run. The few available long-term outcome studies have not demonstrated long-term effects of treatment, lacked adequate controls, and failed to apply research-based, state-of-the-art treatment methods.

THE NIMH MULTIMODAL TREATMENT FOR ADHD

In response to these urgent public health needs, NIMH began the development of a study of the multimodal treatment of ADHD (MTA) to answer critical questions about the relative long-term effectiveness of the state-of-the-art treatments (medication therapies and behavioral treatment), alone and in combination, comparing them to each other and to standard community treatments. The major questions addressed by the study are which treatments (medication, behavioral treatments, or both) work best for which children (boys vs. girls, with or without other comorbid conditions, etc.), for which areas of functioning (home, school, or peer settings), and for what length of time; and whether these systematically delivered, state-of-the-art, intensive and comprehensive research treatments are more effective than standard community care. Given the estimated 2% of children, nationwide, who take stimulant medications for this condition in a given year, this landmark six-site study will be of great benefit to them.

Using a parallel-groups design, 96 children with ADHD at each of the six sites are randomly assigned to one of four groups:

1. medication alone (closely monitored after an initial double-blind titration to establish the best dose and whether the child is a responder);
2. psychosocial treatment alone (consisting of parent training, school consultation, the intensive 8-week Pittsburgh STP, and 12 weeks of assistance from a paraprofessional classroom aide);
3. both (1) and (2) treatments in combination; or
4. community treatments of participants' and their families' own choosing.

The first 3 groups are given state-of-the-art treatment of the assigned type for 14 months, and all groups are assessed systematically over 5 time points, concluding at 24 months posttreatment initiation.

Given its obvious public health implications, the MTA study is cosponsored by the U.S. Department of Education. Because the study tests the competing comprehensive clinical treatment strategies, it is poised to answer "real world" questions of practical clinical import for children, which are encountered in actual clinical practice. Such children may have various coexisting conditions that, in the past, have been screened out of research samples. For this reason, the MTA accepts a more representative sample recruited not only from mental health settings but also from primary care settings, schools, advertisements, and self-help groups.

Studies of ADHD treatments have progressed rapidly in the last decade. Although many important questions must be addressed in future studies (i.e., determining which specific psychosocial treatments components are differentially effective and necessary for which children), important progress has been made and the next 5 years should provide definitive answers to many pressing questions. The multisite studies in the ADHD field should help lay the foundation for similar efforts for other childhood disorders, including the most common disorders of anxiety and depression and the rarer conditions of autism and childhood schizophrenia.

13

FAMILY-BASED TREATMENT: PSYCHOSOCIAL INTERVENTION FOR CHILDREN AND ADOLESCENTS WITH ATTENTION DEFICIT HYPERACTIVITY DISORDER

ARTHUR D. ANASTOPOULOS, RUSSELL A. BARKLEY,
and TERRI L. SHELTON

Attention deficit hyperactivity disorder (ADHD; American Psychiatric Association, 1987) is a chronic and pervasive condition characterized by developmentally inappropriate levels of inattention, impulsivity, or hyperactivity. Affecting as many as 3 to 5% of the general population, ADHD can have a very serious and harmful impact on a child's or adolescent's psychosocial functioning. A child or adolescent with ADHD is far more likely to exhibit decreased academic productivity, academic underachievement, peer relationship problems, and diminished self-esteem (Barkley, 1990). Such individuals are also at greater risk for experiencing family conflict, especially with their parents, who themselves may be predisposed to higher levels of parenting stress, psychopathology, and marital discord (Barkley, 1990).

The completed parent training project was supported in part by grant S07RR05712-19, awarded to A. Anastopoulos by the Biomedical Research Support Program, Division of Research Resources, National Institutes of Health. The completed family-based adolescent treatment study was supported by grant 41583, awarded to R. Barkley by the National Institute of Mental Health. The ongoing parent training study is supported by grant 46515, awarded to A. Anastopoulos by the National Institute of Mental Health. The ongoing multimodal treatment project is being supported by grant 45714 awarded to R. Barkley by the National Institute of Mental Health. Correspondence concerning this chapter should be addressed to Dr. Arthur D. Anastopoulos, Department of Psychiatry, University of North Carolina at Greensboro, Greensboro, NC 27412.

Since its inception in 1985, the ADHD Clinic at the University of Massachusetts Medical Center has provided a wide range of treatments for children and adolescents with ADHD that has included the use of stimulant medication regimens and other forms of pharmacotherapy. Recognizing that such medical treatments are by no means a panacea for all of the child, family, and peer relationship problems that might result from ADHD, the ADHD Clinic has also routinely included psychosocial treatments in its clinical management of children and adolescents with this condition.

In keeping with its scientist–practitioner philosophy, the ADHD Clinic has been the site of several ADHD psychosocial treatment research projects, two of which remain in progress. This chapter reviews the major goals and findings of two of the Clinic's completed family-based treatment outcome studies and describes the ongoing investigations that are based on this prior research. It concludes with a discussion of the broader impact of this collection of studies for clinicians, researchers, and others involved in the delivery of psychosocial treatment services to children and adolescents with ADHD.

PARENT TRAINING PROGRAM FOR SCHOOL-AGED CHILDREN

Rationale and Treatment Goals

Stimulant medication therapy is by far the most frequently used treatment in the clinical management of children with ADHD (Barkley, 1990). Although stimulants can lead to significant behavioral improvements in a large percentage of children with ADHD (Taylor, 1986), there is a substantial number of children with ADHD for whom stimulant medication therapy is either not viable because of undesirable side effects, or insufficient by itself for meeting the full range of the individual clinical needs, such as during the late afternoon and early evening hours at home. Not uncommonly, therefore, there may be times when health care professionals must consider using alternative or adjunctive treatments in the clinical management of children with ADHD. One such option is behavioral parent training (PT).

Additional justification for using PT stems in part from a consideration of the fact that children with ADHD impose increased caretaking demands on their parents throughout childhood (Cunningham & Barkley, 1979). Although a direct causal link has yet to be established, there is ample correlational evidence to suggest that this disruption in the normal parenting process may adversely affect child and parent functioning in many ways. For example, children with ADHD are at increased risk for developing secondary behavioral complications, such as oppositional–

defiant disorder (ODD) or conduct disorder, which respond well to behavioral interventions (McMahon & Wells, 1989). Above and beyond this potential impact on the child, recent studies have also shown that parents of children with ADHD commonly experience considerable stress in their parenting roles (Anastopoulos, Guevremont, Shelton, & DuPaul, 1992; Fischer, 1990). Moreover, they often view themselves as less skilled—and less knowledgeable—as parents, and derive less value and comfort from their parenting efforts (Mash & Johnston, 1983). They are also at increased risk for depression and other types of personal distress, and for marital discord as well (Cunningham, Benness, & Siegel, 1988). To the extent that such difficulties are a direct consequence of ADHD, it provides a basis for understanding why PT might indeed improve many facets of home functioning. More specifically, as parents use recommended PT strategies, they may gain greater control over their child's home behavior, especially at times when the effects of medication or other treatments are diminishing or absent. Presumably, this may provide children with opportunities for acquiring greater self-control over their own behavior. This in turn may serve to alleviate parental distress, as well as marital discord arising primarily from disagreements over parenting issues.

Although there is a growing body of research attesting to the clinical efficacy of PT within ADHD populations (Dubey, O'Leary, & Kaufman, 1983; Gittelman-Klein et al., 1980; Horn, Ialongo, Popovich, & Peradotto, 1987; Pelham et al., 1988; Pollard, Ward, & Barkley, 1983), most of this research has defined successful treatment outcome in terms of improved child functioning. Apart from one study that found increased parenting self-esteem and reduced parenting stress following PT (Pisterman, McGrath, Firestone, & Goodman, 1989), relatively little is known about the indirect therapeutic impact that PT might have on parent and family functioning. In an effort to gain a better understanding of this situation, we conducted our initial PT investigation using school-aged, clinic-referred children with ADHD (Anastopoulos, Shelton, DuPaul, & Guevremont, 1993). A brief summary of this research is given.

Description of Study and Treatment Program

Over a 2-year period, a total of 36 clinic-referred children and their mothers met the study's eligibility requirements and served as subjects. All of the children met the criteria of the *Diagnostic and Statistical Manual of Mental Disorders*, third edition, revised (*DSM-III-R*; American Psychiatric Association, 1987) for an ADHD diagnosis (American Psychiatric Association, 1987); 16 also had secondary diagnoses, including 14 with ODD, 1 with overanxious disorder, and 1 with functional enuresis. Seven children were on stimulant medication regimens at the start of treatment. Two families dropped out of the project before completing treatment, leaving a final sample of 34 subjects, which included 25 boys and 9 girls, ranging in age from 75 to 123 months (M 97.7, SD 12.7). The overall socioeconomic composition of this sample was predominantly Caucasian and middle class.

Prior to receiving treatment, all subjects were apprised of the possibility of being assigned to a 2-month waiting list because of the great number of cases referred to the clinic's PT program. Thereafter, subjects were assigned randomly either to PT ($n = 19$) or to the waiting list control condition ($n = 15$), depending on clinic caseload limitations at the time in which they entered the project. For ethical reasons, wait list subjects were given information about alternative ADHD treatments and advised to seek them out as needed, without fear of being removed from the research project.

A number of parent-completed rating scales was administered to assess changes in child, parent, and family functioning. For the PT group, all outcome measures were collected prior to treatment, within 1 week following the active portion of treatment, and again approximately 2 months later as a follow-up assessment. For the waiting-list group, these same measures were collected twice: once prior to treatment and again approximately 2 months after the initial assessment, corresponding roughly to the amount of time spent in treatment by PT participants. For ethical reasons, the waiting list participants did not complete a third assessment. Rather, they were placed into PT as soon as possible after the second testing.

A modified version (Anastopoulos & Barkley, 1990) of the 10-step PT program developed by Barkley (1987) was used because of the availability of a detailed treatment manual, the program's inclusion of a parent counseling component, and the fact that its behavioral procedures target not only child noncompliance but also primary ADHD symptomatology. Three licensed PhD-level psychologists, with extensive ADHD and PT experience, implemented the treatment program. Treatment sessions occurred generally on a consecutive weekly basis. Thus, most PT participants completed the program within 2 to 3 months. Mothers and fathers were encouraged to attend PT, but for practical reasons, this was not always possible. To remain eligible for the project, mothers had to attend all treatment sessions.

A summary of the nine-session program that was used appears in Table 1. In Session 1, parents received an overview of ADHD. In Session 2, there was additional discussion of ADHD as needed, as well as a review of a four-factor model for understanding child behavior problems (i.e., child characteristics, parent characteristics, family stress, situational consequences) and a discussion of general behavior management principles. Beginning with Session 2, between-session homework was assigned to parents at the end of each session and reviewed at the start of the next. Sessions 3, 4, and 5 focused on teaching parents specialized, positive reinforcement

TABLE 1
Summary of Parent Training Program for Children with Attention Deficit Hyperactivity Disorder

Session number	Therapeutic content
1	Overview of attention deficit hyperactivity disorder
2	Discussion of 4-factor model of parent–child conflict; review of behavior management principles
3	Using positive attending and ignoring skills during special play time
4	Using positive attending and ignoring skills to promote appropriate independent play and compliance with simple requests; discussion of how to give commands more effectively
5	Setting up a comprehensive, reward-oriented home token/point system
6	Using response cost for minor noncompliance and rule violations
7	Using time out from reinforcement for more serious rule violations
8	How to handle child behavior problems in public
9	Handling future problems; working cooperatively with school personnel (e.g., setting up daily report card systems)

skills, including the use of positive attending and ignoring skills during "special time" play; attending positively to appropriate independent play or compliance with simple requests; and using a comprehensive, reward-oriented home token or point system. Sessions 6 and 7 dealt with the use of punishment strategies, beginning with the addition of a response cost component for minor noncompliance and rule violations, followed by instruction in using time out from reinforcement for more serious rule violations. Having developed some expertise in using such strategies at home, parents next received instruction (Session 8) in how to modify these strategies for use in public places (e.g., stores). In Session 9, the final session, parents received suggestions for handling future problems and for working cooperatively with school personnel, including advice about setting up daily report card systems.

Treatment Outcome: Benefits and Limitations

Relative to those in the wait list condition, individuals receiving PT displayed significant changes in several areas of psychosocial functioning immediately following treatment. PT parents reported, for example, improvements in the overall severity of their child's ADHD symptomatology. These reported changes in child behavior were accompanied by improvements in parent functioning, including reduced parenting stress and enhanced parenting self-esteem. Although there were no significant post-treatment group differences in parent-reported levels of personal distress and marital satisfaction, the observed differences among these measures were in the predicted direction. All such changes remained stable over a two-month follow-up period in which no therapeutic contact was provided. Moreover, none of these observed changes appeared to be due to extraneous factors, such as the child's medication status or stressful life events.

When viewed in the context of their clinical significance, that is, at an individual level (Jacobson & Truax, 1991), the data obtained revealed once again that PT was superior to the waiting list condition at posttreatment. As many as 26 to 64% of the PT participants displayed significant improvements in terms of less severe child ADHD symptoms, reduced parenting stress, or enhanced parenting self-esteem. Only 0 to 27% of the waiting list participants showed this same level of improvement. Of additional clinical significance are the differences that emerged at the other end of the treatment outcome continuum, that is, with regard to the percentages of participants showing no change or deterioration. Depending on the posttreatment measure under consideration, from 47 to 67% of the waiting list participants deteriorated. Hence, even if PT participants did not improve significantly immediately following treatment, their participation in PT may have prevented an intensification of their referral concerns.

Of course, these findings must, be tempered by a consideration of the limitations inherent in this study. For example, one potential confound in the study was the use of a waiting list control group, which leaves open the possibility that the observed group differences resulted from ongoing contact with a therapist, rather than from PT per se. Although this cannot be ruled out definitively, one argument against this possibility is the fact that many of the PT participants, generally, maintained their improved functioning after a 2-month period in which there was no contact with therapists. Additional limitations exist with regard to the narrow range of outcome measures used. For example, all outcome measures were based on maternal report in the absence of any cross-validation, such as reports from fathers, from the children themselves, or from direct observations of parent–child interactions. Moreover, the study did not include any input from teachers, whose perspective would shed light on whether or not PT had any indirect impact on school functioning. Although providing support for the temporal stability of PT over a 2-month follow-up period, questions still remain regarding its longer term impact.

Discussion and Recommendations

Bearing these limitations in mind, the results of this study nevertheless lend support to the contention that PT can have therapeutic benefits not only for targeted school-aged children with ADHD, but also for their parents.

The mechanisms for these reported improvements in child and parent functioning are not entirely clear. Because this study did not include direct observations of parent–child interactions, one cannot ascertain whether there were meaningful changes in child behavior or in parenting style as a result of PT. To the extent that ADHD is indeed a chronic disability (Barkley, 1990), it is unlikely that any of the child's ADHD symptoms were actually eliminated. A more likely explanation for the reported changes in child ADHD symptomatology is that parents learned to manage these symptoms more successfully and, therefore, perceived them as less severe, which in turn was reflected in their child ratings.

The intuitive appeal of this rationale notwithstanding, clinicians and researchers would be well advised to include direct observations of parent–child interactions among their outcome measures to help sort out such matters. The availability of such data would also shed light on the underlying mechanisms of the changes observed in parent functioning. Although it remains possible that PT-induced improvements in child behavior set the stage for this to occur, such changes may well be independent of any real improvements in child behavior. Assuming this to be valid, it is reasonable to consider rather that they may stem from increased parental understanding and acceptance of their child's ADHD and from their increased ability to cope with their child's difficult home behavior, both of which are major therapeutic goals of this particular PT program. Regardless of the exact etiology of these changes, what remains important is that parents themselves felt better after receiving PT. Thus, in addition to serving as co-therapists on behalf of their child, many of the parents who participated in PT were also beneficiaries of this form of treatment.

Although the percentages of participants reporting clinically significant improvements are comparable with those reported in other ADHD treatment studies (Barkley, Guevremont, Anastopoulos, & Fletcher, 1992), the fact that some parents did not benefit from PT attests, nevertheless, to limitations inherent in this form of treatment, especially when used alone. In view of these findings, one issue that needs to be clarified is whether or not there are certain child or parent characteristics that predict who might be best suited for PT. Additional consideration needs to be given to whether or not the overall effectiveness of PT can be enhanced by combining it with other forms of treatment, both for children identified as having ADHD (e.g., receiving stimulant medication therapy) and for their parents (e.g., receiving marital counseling). Given that there seems to be an emerging consensus within the field that no one treatment by itself is sufficient for addressing all the clinical management needs of children with ADHD (Barkley, 1990), perhaps the best way to view the potential therapeutic value of PT is in the context of the role that it might play in multimodal interventions.

FAMILY-BASED TREATMENTS FOR ADOLESCENTS

Rationale and Treatment Goals

Most clinicians and researchers agree that ADHD is a chronic condition that has a significant and serious impact on the psychosocial functioning of adolescents (Weiss & Hechtman, 1986). Although there certainly are some differences in its adolescent presentation, by and large, ADHD in adolescents presents many of the same behavioral, emotional, social, and academic impairments seen among children with this condition (Barkley, Fischer, Edelbrock, & Smallish, 1991; Barkley, Anastopoulos, Guevremont, & Fletcher, 1991). Like their younger counterparts, most adolescents with ADHD respond positively to stimulant medication therapy (Klorman, Coons, & Borgstedt, 1987). Some, however, either do not respond well and display undesirable side effects, or require more therapeutic assistance than that provided by stimulant medication therapy alone. Therefore, alternative or adjunctive treatments, such as psychosocial interventions, must often be included in the clinical management.

Aside from these medication issues, there are other reasons for using psychosocial treatments with adolescents who have ADHD. Adolescents with ADHD, for example, often interact with their parents in ways that are characterized by more frequent instances of conflict, more anger during conflict discussions, and more negative communication patterns (Barkley, Anastopoulos, Guevremont, & Fletcher, 1992). Such family interaction difficulties are even more pronounced when certain comorbid conditions, such as ODD, are present. Of additional clinical significance is that parents of adolescents with ADHD themselves are more likely to experience depression and other types of personal distress, as well as marital discord (Barkley, Anastopoulos, et al., 1992).

Prior research has suggested that chronic parent–adolescent conflicts are predictive of whether or not adolescents with ADHD will display social maladjustment and antisocial behavior on reaching young adulthood (Hechtman, Weiss, Perlman, & Amsel, 1984). Although not yet substantiated empirically, these same conflicts may also contribute, at least in part, to the elevated parental distress and marital discord so often observed within the families of adolescent ADHD populations. Such circumstances highlight the need for incorporating interventions that specifically target parent–adolescent conflict. It was with this purpose in mind that we conducted our initial investigation of the usefulness of three family-based psychosocial treatments for clinic-referred adolescents with ADHD (Barkley,

Guevremont, et al., 1992). The following is a brief summary of this research.

Description of Study and Treatment Program

Over a 3-year period, 64 adolescents and their mothers and fathers met the study's eligibility requirements and served as subjects. All of the teens met *DSM-III-R* criteria for an ADHD diagnosis (American Psychiatric Association, 1987). Three families dropped out of the project before completing treatment, leaving a final sample of 61 subjects, including 56 boys and 5 girls, ranging in age from 12 to 17 years. All the participants were from Caucasian, predominantly middle class families.

Shortly after completing their intake evaluations, the participants were assigned randomly to one of three family-based psychosocial treatments. These were problem-solving communication training (PSCT; Robin & Foster, 1989); a developmentally more appropriate version of the PT program discussed earlier (Barkley, 1987), referred to here as behavior management training (BMT); and structural family therapy (SFT; Minuchin, 1974). Although none of these treatments had been tested previously with a clinic-referred adolescent ADHD population, there was ample evidence, from prior research using similar populations, to suggest that all three held much promise for reducing parent–adolescent conflict in the current investigation.

To assess changes in adolescent, parent, and family functioning, teenagers and their parents completed a number of rating scales and participated in videotaped conflict discussions immediately prior to treatment, within one week following treatment, and once again approximately 3 months later. Two licensed PhD-level psychologists with extensive ADHD and family-based treatment experience implemented each of the three therapy programs. Each therapy program included 8-to-10 treatment sessions, with each session occurring generally on a consecutive weekly basis. For two-parent families, mothers and fathers were encouraged to attend all treatment sessions. To remain eligible for the project, mothers had to attend all sessions. An additional requirement was that identified adolescents had to attend all the PSCT and SFT sessions; none, however, was involved in any of the BMT sessions. A summary of the PSCT treatment program appears in Table 2.

At the start of PSCT, the adolescents and their parents learned a five-step behavioral approach to problem solving, which they practiced both under therapist supervision and on their own between sessions. This phase of training included an emphasis on maintaining neutral affect and on generating multiple solutions to commonly encountered parent–adolescent conflict situations. Next, families learned to communicate with one another in ways that were direct, to the point, and less likely to incite in-

TABLE 2
Summary of Problem Solving Communication Training Program for
Adolescents with Attention Deficit Hyperactivity Disorder

Treatment component	Therapeutic content
Five-step behavioral problem solving	Defining problems, generating solutions to problems, evaluating solutions, choosing a solution, implementing a solution
Communication training	Identifying and remediating maladaptive family communication patterns
Cognitive restructuring	Identifying and reframing irrational family beliefs

terpersonal conflict. On the basis of this foundation, adolescents and their parents also learned how to identify and to reframe irrational beliefs about one another (e.g., if he doesn't make the honor roll in school, he'll *never* get into college), thereby reducing the potential for family conflict. Although the original version of PSCT uses elements of structural family therapy, these were not included in this application of the program.

In principle, the BMT program was essentially the same as the PT program discussed earlier. However, in its application it included procedural modifications to make it more developmentally appropriate for use with adolescents. For example, all families used point systems that emphasized access to weekend and long-range privileges, more than daily goals. Another important difference was that parents learned to use grounding procedures, instead of time out, for handling misbehavior and other household rule infractions.

In contrast with the PSCT and BMT programs, the SFT program, unfolded in a somewhat less rigid, step-by-step fashion. For example, therapists initially determined which conflict issues were of primary concern to the family and how the family had previously attempted to resolve such conflicts. On the basis of such discussions, the therapists subsequently made suggestions that were designed to alter boundaries, alignments, and other aspects of the family structure, believed to be responsible for fostering family conflict. A summary of this treatment approach appears in Table 3.

Treatment Outcome: Benefits and Limitations

When analyzed at a group level, the data from this study suggested that all three treatment conditions produced improvements in several areas of family functioning. For example, adolescents and their parents displayed significantly fewer conflicts, less anger intensity during conflict discussions,

TABLE 3
Components of Structural Family Therapy Used in Treatment of Adolescents with Attention Deficit Hyperactivity Disorder

Treatment components
Identifying conflict issues of primary concern
Reviewing prior family attempts to resolve conflict
Creating transactions, joining transactions, restructuring transactions
Altering boundaries, alignments, power, and other aspects of family structure responsible for maintaining family conflict

and more effective communication immediately following treatment. Such changes were accompanied by significantly less adolescent internalizing symptomatology and lower levels of maternal depression. Of additional clinical interest is the fact that all such improvements were maintained three months after treatment.

When these same data were viewed within the context of their clinical significance, that is, at an individual level (Jacobson & Truax, 1991), a somewhat less promising picture emerged. Only 5% to 30% of the families showed clinical improvements on any of the outcome measures obtained during the posttreatment or follow-up assessments. As was the case for the group analyzed data, there were no statistically significant differences across the three treatment groups. However, more of the PSCT and BMT participants displayed clinically significant improvements after treatment than did subjects those who had received SFT.

Discussion and Recommendations

Given the dearth of research in this area, one of the most important findings to emerge from this study is that psychosocial interventions can be of therapeutic value in the clinical management of adolescents with ADHD. For those families who responded positively to treatment, there were significant improvements in the quality of their parent–adolescent interactions, which were accompanied by significant reductions in both parent- and teen-reported levels of depression and other types of internalizing symptomatology. Whether these affective changes resulted directly from the improvements in the parent–adolescent relationships is not entirely clear. Such changes may also have stemmed from increased adolescent and parental understanding and acceptance of the impact of ADHD on their individual and family functioning.

An equally important and sobering finding is the large percentage of families who did not benefit from any of the three psychosocial treatments.

Although there would seem to be many possible explanations for this un-expected result, one that is worthy of additional consideration is that, after so many years of failure and frustration—at home, in school, and among peers—many adolescents with ADHD may require more intensive inter-vention than that afforded by short-term, psychologically based, single-treatment approaches. If so, then one would predict better outcomes from psychosocial interventions that go beyond 8 to 10 sessions in length, or perhaps from psychosocial interventions that combine elements from dif-ferent treatment modalities (e.g., a combination of PSCT and BMT). Given that a high percentage of adolescents responds positively to stimu-lant medication therapy, another possible mechanism for enhancing treat-ment outcome would be to use psychosocial interventions along with pharmacotherapy.

As one of the first investigations of its kind, the above study shed important new light on the clinical efficacy of family-based, psychosocial interventions for adolescents with ADHD. Left unanswered, however, were many important clinical questions. For example, because fathers were not required to attend all sessions, it was not possible to determine the impact of their attendance on treatment outcome. Although posttreatment im-provements in psychosocial functioning were maintained up to three months following treatment, uncertainty remains as to whether or not these therapeutic changes would remain intact over longer periods of time. These and many other clinical issues need to be addressed in future research.

COMORBIDITY AND PARENT TRAINING OUTCOME RATIONALE AND DESCRIPTION OF STUDY AND TREATMENT PROGRAM

One of the most important findings to emerge from our earlier study (Anastopoulos et al., 1993) was that a substantial percentage of parents and children did not benefit from receiving this form of treatment. This served as the impetus for conducting a research project, nearing comple-tion, dealing with the impact of comorbidity on parent training outcome within a clinic-referred ADHD population. Under the supervision of au-thors Anastopoulos and Barkley, this project focuses on whether or not certain child or parent characteristics, either alone or in combination, al-low for predicting for whom might PT be suited best. The main child dimension of interest is the presence or absence of a secondary oppositional–defiant disorder (ODD) diagnosis. The two-parent variables under consideration are (a) high versus low levels of personal distress or psychopathology, and (b) the presence or absence of adult ADHD symptomatology.

A secondary purpose of our ongoing project is to conduct a preliminary examination of the two major components of the PT program. As noted earlier, one of this program's main treatment goals is to counsel and to educate parents about ADHD as a disorder; its other major objective is to assist parents in their acquisition of specialized contingency management techniques. This raises an important question: When significant posttreatment improvements do occur, do they stem primarily from the contingency management portion of the PT program, which is commonly assumed, or from its ADHD counseling component?

As a first step in clarifying the impact that each of these treatment components may have on outcome, the study in progress compares groups receiving the standard, 10-session PT program (Anastopoulos & Barkley, 1990; Barkley, 1987) versus those receiving didactic ADHD counseling alone.

Building on our earlier study, the present research also assesses treatment outcome from multiple perspectives to capture the broad impact that PT presumably has on the child and the family. For example, whenever possible, fathers are included in both the assessment and treatment processes. Direct observations of parent–child interactions are being used to assess changes in parenting style or child behavior. Mothers and fathers complete rating scales about their child's behavior and emotional functioning. They also fill out self-report questionnaires pertaining to their parenting style and to their levels of parenting stress, parenting self-esteem, personal distress, parenting alliance, and marital satisfaction. The children complete ratings about their own self-esteem and levels of anxiety or depression, as well as about their perceptions of their parents' parenting style. In addition, teachers provide child behavior ratings to assess the indirect impact that PT may have on school functioning. All such measures are collected immediately prior to and following the active portion of treatment. In an extension of our earlier research, the temporal stability of any posttreatment improvements is assessed 6 months after treatment.

When completed, the results from this investigation will shed much light on which therapeutic goals PT can accomplish and which it cannot, when used alone with clinic-referred, school-aged children with ADHD. Its results should also make it easier for clinicians to identify those children and their families for whom PT is an appropriate treatment option, and those for whom it is not. Together, such information may then be used to explore new ways of delivering PT, either alone in some modified form or in combination with other ADHD interventions (e.g., pharmacotherapy) as part of a multimodal treatment package.

PREVENTION-TREATMENT PROGRAM FOR KINDERGARTEN CHILDREN

Rationale and Description of Study and Treatment Program

At some point in their lives, most school-aged children and adolescents with ADHD are likely to experience psychosocial complications (Barkley, 1990). These may include classroom behavior and academic performance difficulties, secondary behavioral problems, less than satisfactory peer and family relations, diminished self-esteem, and other types of emotional distress. More often than not, these sorts of problems develop slowly over time, as secondary manifestations of having ADHD. To the extent that they are indeed absent early on, this suggests that early intervention efforts may serve to reduce the risk for such complications to arise. It was with this objective in mind that we began our ongoing investigation of the impact of early intervention on very young children at risk for ADHD.

Under the supervision of Drs. Barkley and Shelton, the current study screens such children during the kindergarten registration process. Children identified as being at risk and eligible for the project are those for whom parent-completed, child-behavior questionnaires place them above the 93rd percentile on dimensions of impulsivity–hyperactivity and oppositional-conduct problems. Consenting children and their families are then randomly assigned to one of four conditions: (a) a control group receiving the regular kindergarten program available to all children in the community; (b) a group receiving the regular kindergarten program in combination with behavioral PT, similar to that discussed in this chapter; (c) a group receiving an enriched kindergarten program, in which specially trained teachers routinely use contingency management techniques and provide ongoing social skills training with a problem-solving focus; and (d) a group receiving the enriched kindergarten program and the ongoing PT. In addition to this targeted group, a small number of "normal" children, who were not identified as being at risk at the time of screening, was also included in the study as a second control group for developmental comparison purposes.

Children in the enriched kindergarten program later go on to attend first grade classrooms within the regular school system, as do all other children in the project. To facilitate their transition from an enriched program to a regular one, their teachers take formal steps at the end of the kindergarten year to phase out their reliance on the enriched program. This includes, for example, systematic attempts to reduce their exposure to contingency management strategies and to increase their participation in large group instruction, in anticipation of the demands of first grade.

All participating children and their families undergo comprehensive multi-method assessments on several occasions: prior to entering kindergarten, at the end of kindergarten, and at the end of first and second grades. These annual assessments include structured diagnostic interviews with parents, parent and teacher-completed child behavior questionnaires, various parent self-report questionnaires, observations of classroom behavior, observations of parent-child interactions, and psychoeducational testing of the child.

When completed, this project will provide answers to many important questions about the outcome of very young children at risk for ADHD. For example, we should have a much better understanding of the behavioral markers in early childhood that predict later manifestations of ADHD and its associated comorbid conditions. In a similar vein, we should also have a clearer picture of the early developmental course of ADHD. Of additional interest is that the results from this project will go a long way toward clarifying how effective early psychosocial intervention can be in reducing the risk for later negative outcome—at home, in school, and in peer relations. Such information will also allow us to examine the impact that early psychosocial intervention has on subsequent use of special education and child mental health services.

GENERALIZABILITY OF PSYCHOSOCIAL TREATMENTS FOR ADHD

On the basis of the studies that we have completed to date, it seems that the therapeutic impact of our psychosocial treatment programs for ADHD is much broader than previously realized. For example, the tested interventions for children and adolescents produced improvements in psychosocial functioning that were maintained up to three months after treatment. Of additional clinical significance are the treatment-induced changes that extended beyond the behavior of the identified child or adolescent. These include enhanced parenting self-esteem, decreased parenting stress, reduced maternal depression, and mother-reported reductions in adolescent internalizing symptomatology.

Our clinical experience also provides a basis for believing that there may be many other psychosocial areas in which generalization may occur. After completing the parent training program, for example, many parents spontaneously remark that their child's teacher noticed improvements in school functioning, or that they have applied similar parenting strategies to siblings in the family. Anecdotal evidence further suggests that psychosocial treatment effects do indeed persist for periods of time that go well beyond those assessed in our studies. Although these and other generalizability matters cannot be addressed at present, it is our expectation that our ongoing research will shed much light on these issues in the very near future.

CONCLUSIONS AND FUTURE DIRECTIONS

What should be readily apparent from the preceding discussion is that psychosocial interventions do have a place in the overall clinical management of children and adolescents with ADHD. One of the major advantages to using these interventions, as well as other forms of psychosocial treatment, is that they can be used to target not only the child's or adolescent's primary ADHD symptomatology, but also many of their comorbid features, such as their oppositional–defiant behavior and conduct problems. Moreover, because these interventions often use parents as co-therapists, many parents themselves derive indirect therapeutic benefits from their involvement in treatment. Although the long-term impact of psychosocial interventions remains to be seen, preliminary evidence suggests that treatment-induced improvements in psychosocial functioning can be maintained in the absence of ongoing therapist contact, at least in the short run.

As is evident from our earlier discussion, much of our research to date has focused on the clinical efficacy of psychosocial interventions when used alone. One benefit of pursuing this type of research is that it permits a greater understanding of the unique impact that these treatments can have on outcome within an ADHD population. Examination of these treatments by themselves has provided important insight as to their therapeutic limitations. Although some individuals might view these limitations as contraindications for using such treatments, we do not agree with this point of view. Instead, we would interpret such limitations as a clinical reality that applies to all other ADHD treatments, including pharmacotherapy to an extent. Therefore, we would first recommend using this information to guide the development of new methods of implementing these forms of treatment. In keeping with our belief that there is no one treatment that can meet all the clinical management needs of children and adolescents with ADHD, we would also recommend using this information to guide efforts to put complementary treatments together into multimodal intervention packages, with each treatment targeting different facets of the child's or adolescent's psychosocial functioning.

REFERENCES

American Psychiatric Association. (1987). *Diagnostic and Statistical Manual of Mental Disorders* (3rd ed., rev.). Washington, DC: Author.

Anastopoulos, A. D., & Barkley, R. A. (1990). Counseling and training parents. In R. A. Barkley, *Attention Deficit Hyperactivity Disorder: A Handbook for Diagnosis and Treatment* (pp. 397–431). New York: Guilford Press.

Anastopoulos, A. D., Guevremont, D. C., Shelton, T. L., & DuPaul, G. J. (1992). Parenting stress among families of children with Attention Deficit Hyperactivity Disorder. *Journal of Abnormal Child Psychology, 20,* 503–520.

Anastopoulos, A. D., Shelton, T. L., DuPaul, G. J., & Guevremont, D. C. (1993). Parent training for Attention Deficit Hyperactivity Disorder: Its impact on parent functioning. *Journal of Abnormal Child Psychology, 21,* 581–596.

Barkley, R. A. (1987). *Defiant children: A clinician's manual for parent training.* New York: Guilford.

Barkley, R. A. (1990). *Attention Deficit Hyperactivity Disorder: A handbook for diagnosis and treatment.* New York: Guilford.

Barkley, R. A., Anastopoulos, A. D., Guevremont, D. C., & Fletcher, K. E. (1991). Adolescents with Attention Deficit Hyperactivity Disorder: Patterns of behavioral adjustment, academic functioning, and treatment utilization. *Journal of the American Academy of Child and Adolescent Psychiatry, 30,* 752–761.

Barkley, R. A., Anastopoulos, A. D., Guevremont, D. C., & Fletcher, K. E. (1992). Adolescents with Attention Deficit Hyperactivity Disorder: Mother–adolescent interactions, family beliefs and conflicts, and maternal psychopathology. *Journal of Abnormal Child Psychology, 20,* 263–288.

Barkley, R. A., Fischer, M., Edelbrock, C. S., & Smallish, L. (1991). The adolescent outcome of hyperactive children diagnosed by research criteria: Part 3. Mother–child interactions, family conflicts, and maternal psychopathology. *Journal of Child Psychology and Psychiatry, 32,* 233–235.

Barkley, R. A., Guevremont, D. C., Anastopoulos, A. D., & Fletcher, K. E. (1992). A comparison of three family therapy programs for treating family conflicts in adolescents with ADHD. *Journal of Consulting and Clinical Psychology, 60,* 450–462.

Cunningham, C. E., & Barkley, R. A. (1979). The interactions of hyperactive and normal children with their mothers during free play and structured task. *Child Development, 50,* 217–224.

Cunningham, C. E., Benness, B. B., & Siegel, L. S. (1988). Family functioning, time allocation, and parental depression in the families of normal and ADDH children. *Journal of Clinical Child Psychology, 17,* 169–177.

Dubey, D. R., O'Leary, S. G., & Kaufman, K. F. (1983). Training parents of hyperactive children in child management: A comparative outcome study. *Journal of Abnormal Child Psychology, 11,* 229–246.

Fischer, M. (1990). Parenting stress and the child with Attention Deficit Hyperactivity Disorder. *Journal of Clinical Child Psychology, 19,* 337–346.

Gittelman-Klein, R., Abikoff, H., Pollack, E., Klein, D., Katz, S., & Mattes, J. (1980). A controlled trial of behavior modification and methylphenidate in hyperactive children. In C. Whalen & B. Henker (Eds.), *Hyperactive children: The social ecology of identification and treatment* (pp. 221–246). New York: Academic Press.

Hechtman, L., Weiss, G., Perlman, R., & Amsel, R. (1984). Hyperactives as young adults: Initial predictors of outcome. *Journal of the American Academy of Child Psychiatry, 23*, 250–260.

Horn, W. F., Ialongo, N., Popovich, S., & Peradotto, D. (1987). Behavioral parent training and cognitive–behavioral self-control therapy with ADD-H Children: Comparative and combined effects. *Journal of Clinical Child Psychology, 16*, 57–68.

Jacobson, N. S., & Truax, P. (1991). Clinical significance: A statistical approach to defining meaningful change in psychotherapy research. *Journal of Consulting and Clinical Psychology, 59*, 12–19.

Klorman, R., Coons, H. W., & Borgstedt, A. D. (1987). Effects of methylphenidate on adolescents with a childhood history of attention deficit disorder: Clinical findings. *Journal of the American Academy of Child and Adolescent Psychiatry, 26*, 363–367.

Mash, E. J., & Johnston, C. (1983). Parental perceptions of child behavior problems, parenting self-esteem, and mothers' reported stress in younger and older hyperactive and normal children. *Journal of Consulting and Clinical Psychology, 51*, 68–99.

McMahon, R. J., & Wells, K. C. (1989). Conduct disorders. In E. J. Mash & R. A. Barkley (Eds.), *Treatment of childhood disorders* (pp. 73–134). New York: Guilford Press.

Minuchin, S. (1974). *Families and family therapy.* Cambridge, MA: Harvard University Press.

Pelham, W. W., Schnedler, R. W., Bender, M. E., Nilsson, D. E., Miller, J., Budrow, M. S., Ronnel, M., Paluchowski, C., & Marks, D. A. (1988). The combination of behavior therapy and methylphenidate in the treatment of ADD: A therapy outcome study. In L. Bloomingdale (Ed.), *Attention Deficit Disorders* (Vol. 3, pp. 29–48). New York: Spectrum.

Pisterman, S., McGrath, P., Firestone, P., & Goodman, J. T. (1989). Outcome of parent-mediated treatment of preschoolers with Attention Deficit Disorder with Hyperactivity. *Journal of Consulting and Clinical Psychology, 57*, 636–643.

Pollard, S., Ward, E. M., & Barkley, R. A. (1983). The effects of parent training and Ritalin on the parent–child interactions of hyperactive boys. *Child and Family Behavior Therapy, 5*, 51–69.

Robin, A. L., & Foster, S. (1989). *Negotiating parent–adolescent conflict.* New York: Guilford Press.

Taylor, E. A. (1986). Childhood hyperactivity. *British Journal of Psychiatry, 149*, 562–573.

Weiss, G., & Hechtman, L. (1986). *Hyperactive children grown up.* New York: Guilford.

14

ENHANCING SOCIAL COMPETENCE: INTEGRATING SELF-MANAGEMENT STRATEGIES WITH BEHAVIORAL PROCEDURES FOR CHILDREN WITH ADHD

STEPHEN P. HINSHAW

To the casual observer or to the student who is just gaining familiarity with the constellation of symptoms known as attention deficit hyperactivity disorder (ADHD), the core behavior problems of inattentiveness, impulsivity, and overactivity (American Psychiatric Association, 1994) may seem to reflect simple variations of normal development, falling short of major clinical importance. After all, what child is not inattentive at some times? Is impulsivity not linked to creativity and spontaneity? Might it not be more adaptive for a child to be overly active rather than sluggish? Furthermore, do not children grow out of these behaviors?

There is increasing recognition that such assumptions are far from true for the relatively rare group of youngsters who display such behaviors (a) at extreme levels, (b) from an early age, and (c) in multiple settings. Indeed, children with clinical levels of ADHD typically present with clear impairment in academic, behavioral, emotional, and interpersonal functioning. Such youngsters are at risk for such diverse and troublesome problems as school failure, extreme peer rejection, and serious accidents related to impulsive behavior (see Hinshaw, 1994; Szatmari, Offord, & Boyle,

Work on this chapter was supported, in part, by National Institute of Mental Health Grants MH45064 and MH50461. Correspondence concerning this chapter should be addressed to Dr. Stephen P. Hinshaw, Department of Psychology, Tolman Hall, University of California, Berkeley, CA 94720-1650.

285

1989). Furthermore, they are likely to persist with core symptomatology and associated deficits throughout adolescence and even adulthood (Klein & Mannuzza, 1991). The need for coordinated, systematic intervention efforts is real.

For the past 15 years, since the time of graduate training in clinical psychology at the University of California, Los Angeles (UCLA) and extending to current work at the University of California, Berkeley, the author has pursued a program of research related to the integration of behavioral and cognitive–behavioral interventions with pharmacologic treatments and the peer-related problems of children with ADHD. Although this chapter focuses on psychosocial intervention for child disorders, any consideration of psychotherapy or behavior therapy for ADHD must necessarily include discussion of stimulant medication, given the widespread usage and clearly established short-term efficacy of pharmacologic intervention for children with this disorder (Gadow, 1992; Swanson, McBurnett, Christian, & Wigal, 1995). Indeed, at least in the short term, medication treatments for ADHD comprise a standard against which other interventions must be judged (Pelham & Hinshaw, 1992). Yet, several key limitations of medications, to be discussed below, have necessitated the development of alternative or adjunctive psychological therapies for ADHD, particularly for interpersonal difficulties. Thus, comparisons between and combinations of stimulant treatments and behavioral self-management treatments are explicitly discussed throughout this chapter.

At the outset, it must be noted that self-management strategies for ADHD, even when fully integrated with validated behavioral interventions, are typically insufficient for the many facets of this complex disorder. Also, self instructional treatments for attentional deficits have proven to be clinically ineffective (Abikoff, 1991; Hinshaw & Erhardt, 1991). To tackle the extremely poor long-term course of ADHD, the field must (a) integrate diverse psychosocial treatments targeted at multiple domains over long time periods and (b) consider optimal means of coordinating these treatments with medication.

ISSUES AND GOALS

Issues Pertaining to ADHD

As has been extensively documented elsewhere (Barkley, 1990; Hinshaw, 1994; Schachar, 1986), the disorder known today as ADHD has a long history, marked by shifting conceptualizations and changing terminology over the past century. Whatever the label, the symptom constellation when extreme in degree and when present from an early age, is quite frequently accompanied by associated problems in key domains related to developmental competence. The most salient and clinically problematic of these are academic underachievement (Hinshaw, 1992a), family stress and dysfunction (Barkley, 1990), aggressive behavior (Hinshaw, 1987), and difficulties in social and peer relationships (Pelham & Bender, 1982; Whalen & Henker, 1992). Furthermore, as noted earlier and despite contentions to the contrary, ADHD portends a negative course (Klein & Mannuzza, 1991).

The interpersonal domain is particularly salient for those interested in treating children with ADHD. These youngsters are quite likely to be actively disliked by their peers, with such rejection occurring after extremely brief periods of exposure (Bickett & Milich, 1990; Erhardt & Hinshaw, 1994; Pelham & Bender, 1982). Furthermore, disapproval by agemates during childhood has been strongly associated with risk for poor prognosis, including such maladaptive outcomes as school dropout, delinquency, and general risk for psychopathology (Parker & Asher, 1987). Whether social disapprobation is secondary to the underlying psychopathology of ADHD, whether peer rejection constitutes a causal factor for later maladjustment in its own right, or whether both contentions have merit, intervention researchers have become increasingly concerned with the development of treatment strategies that directly target children's interpersonal problems (Asher & Coie, 1990).

During the 1970s, as the current research program was getting underway, another in the long line of shifts in the field about the nature of the disorder was taking place. A number of studies—particularly the systematic research of Douglas (1983) and colleagues—ascribed the underlying mechanism to deficits in abilities to modulate arousal and sustain attention over protracted time periods (Douglas, 1983). Indeed, with the advent of the third edition of the *Diagnostic and Statistical Manual of Mental Disorders* (*DSM-III*; American Psychiatric Association, 1980) the name of the syndrome changed from hyperactivity to attention deficit disorder (ADD). It should be pointed out that such deficits in attention and arousal modulation were held to relate to fundamental difficulties in general self-regulation (Douglas, 1983; Meichenbaum, 1977). Such ideas prompted interest in the development and testing of treatment procedures that could directly address deficits in self-control and self-management.

Behavioral and Cognitive–Behavioral Intervention Strategies

For many years, the predominant modality for treating children's problems of attention regulation and hyperactivity—as well as nearly all other forms of child psychopathology—was individual, insight-oriented play therapy or verbal psychotherapy. Such expressive psychotherapies, however, produced few, if any, gains for either the core symptoms or the aggressive, school-related, or interpersonal features that typically accompany ADHD. By the 1960s, behavior therapists had begun systematic research on the application of operant and social learning principles to emotional and behavioral problems of children (e.g., Patterson, 1965). In the 1970s, tested behavioral procedures for shaping more appropriate academic and social behaviors and for reducing defiant, aggressive behaviors were being evaluated for children with externalizing behavior problems (see O'Leary, Pelham, Rosenbaum, & Price, 1976).

Behavior management programs for children with externalizing behavior problems fall roughly into two major categories (Pelham & Hinshaw, 1992): (a) systematic programs of contingency management, in which reward and response cost procedures are implemented in specialized classroom settings; and (b) clinical behavior therapy strategies, wherein the therapist teaches behavior management procedures to parents and teachers, who implement targeted strategies in the child's natural environment. Despite the important gains yielded from both categories of behavioral programming, effect sizes are typically smaller than those from medications (see Pelham et al., 1993) and issues of generalization and behavior change maintenance have continued to serve as key limitations (Pelham & Hinshaw, 1992). Partly in response to the challenge of providing lasting behavior change and partly related to the growing recognition of the importance of cognition in behavior change processes, a third class of behavioral intervention—cognitive–behavioral strategies—received wide attention in the 1970s and early 1980s.

The origins of cognitively oriented therapies are complex and varied. Of particular note are the key influence of Beck (1976) with regard to adult applications of directive cognitive therapies for problems of anxiety and mood and the influential writings of Bandura (1977), Kanter (1972), and Meichenbaum (1977) regarding a cognitive reconceptualization of traditional operant behavioral strategies. With cognitive–behavioral procedures, the locus of interventions shifts from programing the environment to coaching the client to solve problems via mediational techniques. Through use of such "portable coping strategies" (Meichenbaum, 1977), the hope is that gains will generalize and persist.

Regarding children, the developmental and linguistic theories of Luria (see Luria & Yudovich, 1972) and Vygotsky (1988) were quite influential in moving the field from a strict behavioral perspective to a model in which the child's alleged deficits in self-guiding, internalized speech were held to be central. Self-instructional (SI) therapies soared in popularity in the 1970s and 1980s for children with hyperactivity or ADD (see, particularly, Douglas, Parry, Marton, & Garson, 1976). In the typical SI procedure, the therapist initially guides the child's actions with verbal commands and then fades such control (first to the child's overt speech, then to whispered speech, and finally to internalized verbalizations) as the child performs academic or social tasks. The enthusiastic espousal of such cognitive–

behavioral procedures 15 years ago was another impetus for the launching of the research program under consideration.

Stimulant Medication for Children with ADHD

Stimulant treatments have been employed for child behavior disorders for over half a century (Bradley, 1937). During the past several decades, literally hundreds of well-controlled investigations have documented the impressive improvements in attention deployment, regulation of impulse, and control of extraneous motor movement that pertain to psychostimulant treatment for children with ADHD (Swanson, McBurnett, Christian, & Wigal, 1995). Importantly, such secondary features as aggression are decreased to normal ranges with pharmacologic intervention (Hinshaw, 1991). Most diagnosed children show a favorable response to medication; by many accounts, stimulants comprise the treatment of choice for the disorder.

Yet medication treatments are not without problems. First, evidence regarding improved school performance is decidedly mixed (Pelham, 1986; Swanson et al., 1992). Second, the time course of stimulant actions is quite short, and gains that are made while the medication is active tend not to persist once the medication has worn off (Hinshaw, 1994). Third, only in rare cases are the gains that accrue to stimulant treatment sufficient to yield full clinical improvement (Pelham & Hinshaw, 1992). Fourth, the potential for side effects typically limits stimulant usage to school hours (or, at most, late afternoon time periods); key interactions with family members or with peers may occur when the child is not actively medicated (Hinshaw, 1994). Fifth, despite the short-term gains that typically accrue to medication treatments, no evidence exists to support the long-term benefits of pharmacologic intervention in later life (e.g., Weiss & Hechtman, 1993). Whereas controlled trials of long duration would help to answer the question of persisting benefits with more validity, pharmacologic treatment alone does not appear to be a viable intervention for altering the course of the disorder. As with other domains of psychopathology, investigators are showing increased interest in combining pharmacologic with psychosocial intervention strategies to extend the limited benefits of each single treatment modality (Pelham & Murphy, 1986).

Updated Information Regarding ADHD and Its Treatment

In the previous discussion, three trends that shaped the initiation of the current research program were noted: (a) reconceptualization of hyperactivity/ADHD as an attentional, self-regulatory disorder; (b) increased focus on cognitive–behavioral therapies for self-management; and (c) heightened awareness of the promise as well as the problems of stimulant treatments. Additional findings and advances in the past 15 years also bear mention.

The enthusiastic push toward cognitive therapies for children with ADHD has *not* met with continued support in the 1980s and 1990s. Indeed, despite the clear successes of cognitive and cognitive–behavioral therapies with adult disorders (e.g., depression) and child disorders (e.g., aggression unaccompanied by ADHD), cognitive approaches for children—particularly those relying on SI procedures—have a rather dismal track record for children specifically diagnosed with attention deficits and hyperactivity (Abikoff & Gittelman, 1985; see reviews of Abikoff, 1991; Hinshaw & Erhardt, 1991). In fact, despite some intriguing research underscoring the importance of private speech internalization delays in youngsters with ADHD (Berk & Potts, 1991), there is a paucity of evidence in favor of the contention that SI procedures actually promote behavior change in hyperactive children. Such findings have prompted a renewed emphasis on blending validated mediational procedures with established behavioral strategies as opposed to emphasizing weak SI methods.[1]

Paralleling these findings has been another reconceptualization of the nature of ADHD: In recent research, deficits in sustained attention do not appear specific to the disorder; these appear to accompany many aspects of child psychopathology (Halperin, Matier, Bedi, Sharma, & Newcorn, 1992). Instead, disinhibition, delayed responding, and motoric hyperactivity are increasingly invoked as specific underlying mechanisms (Barkley, 1994; see review in Hinshaw, 1994). Such a conception renders questionable several of the premises of SI-based intervention (e.g., its use to extend attention span or simply to slow fast responses) and places a premium on interventions that can foster controls on disinhibitory processes and behaviors.

A third line of research in recent years has amplified some of the limitations of medication treatments for the social difficulties of youngsters with ADHD. Specifically, even though stimulant treatments have been shown to normalize such socially disruptive behavior patterns as physical and verbal aggression in classroom and playground settings (Gadow, Nolan, Sverd, Sprafkin, & Paolicelli, 1990; Hinshaw, 1991; Hinshaw, Henker, Whalen, Erhardt, & Dunnington, 1989), these pharmacologic agents do not appear to produce comparably powerful effects on social reputations themselves (Hinshaw & McHale, 1991). That is, although peer sociometric

---

[1]Another type of intervention that gained momentum in the 1970s was so-called social skills training, in which children with a wide variety of problem behaviors or social withdrawal were coached and prompted in basic components of social skills (e.g., Oden & Asher, 1977). Yet research since that time has demonstrated that (a) the interpersonal difficulties of youngsters with ADHD are not readily explainable on the basis of social skills deficits per se (Whalen & Henker, 1992), and (b) treatments simply targeting the coaching of social skills are not clinically sufficient for the difficult interpersonal problems of ADHD (Hinshaw & Erhardt, 1991).

assessments show improvement when children with ADHD receive stimulant medication as opposed to a placebo, the gains fall short of clinical significance (e.g., Whalen et al., 1989). Peers may well be the "toughest audience" for detection of treatment-related gains. Interventions that serve chiefly to reduce problem behavior are not likely to be sufficient to promote full social competence; adjunctive psychosocial treatment strategies are necessary to produce clinically sufficient interventions for the crucial domain of interpersonal interactions (Hinshaw, 1992c).

Goals

The goals and aims for the research program follow directly from the background information presented above and the additional findings from recent years. First, because both traditional behavioral procedures and medication fail to provide lasting benefits for children with ADHD, the extension of behavioral treatments through mediational procedures designed to promote and extend the effects of contingency management strategies continues to be an important goal. Thus, an initial objective has been to understand whether specific mediational components (e.g., training in self-evaluation) can extend the benefits of operant behavioral procedures. Conversely, another goal has been to discover whether interventions that are behavioral in nature (e.g., graduated rehearsal of social skills) can enhance purely cognitive, mediational procedures for such important targets as anger control. In short, the overriding aim is to develop integrated cognitive–behavioral treatments that foster self-management for interpersonal targets.

A second goal has been to contrast the effectiveness of such cognitive–behavioral procedures with the gains in social relationships that accrue to medication interventions. Although investigations that attempt to compare psychosocial and pharmacologic treatments are fraught with conceptual and methodologic difficulties (Whalen & Henker, 1991), ascertaining the domains in which one type of treatment outperforms another can have practical as well as theoretical benefits.

Third, in keeping with the zeitgeist toward integration of medication treatment with psychosocial therapies (e.g., Pelham & Murphy, 1986), an additional goal has been to ascertain the combined efficacy of medication and self-management-based cognitive–behavioral intervention strategies. Indeed, given increasing evidence for the tenacity and persistence of ADHD-related symptomatology and accompanying impairment, and given evidence for the clinical insufficiencies of either modality alone, attempts to integrate validated psychosocial procedures with pharmacologic treatments are crucial endeavors.

HISTORY OF THE RESEARCH PROGRAM

As a graduate student, the author was fortunate to have, as a home for research and as a guide for subsequent work, the influential research team headed by Barbara Henker of the University of California (Los Angeles) and Carol K. Whalen of the University of California (Irvine). Among many other contributions, their work has emphasized (a) the social ecological nature of the problems encountered by children with ADHD (e.g., Whalen & Henker, 1980), and (b) the critical importance of understanding the interpersonal difficulties of hyperactive children (e.g., Whalen & Henker, 1992). Their mentoring also fostered an appreciation for the need to comprehend underlying mechanisms of psychopathology, work still under active consideration (e.g., Hinshaw, 1987, 1992b). On the heels of a treatment study contrasting traditional behavioral interventions with cognitive–behavioral self-instructional treatments (Bugental, Whalen, & Henker, 1977), the team encouraged efforts to develop and implement self-management–oriented treatments for hyperactive children.

The first investigations occurred during an after-school, clinic-based treatment program that spanned 1½ years. A treatment manual (Hinshaw, Alkus, Whalen, & Henker, 1979) resulted from this work; it incorporated elements of self-instructional training, problem solving therapy, exercises to enhance self-evaluation abilities, and the explicit teaching of anger management skills. From this early work came an appreciation of the critical need to perform self-management therapy in a group format; attempting to teach crucial self-management techniques to children "one-on-one" does not allow either the appropriate level of affect or the opportunity for practice of social skills afforded by a peer group. In addition, exposure to difficult group interactions fostered a deeper interest in aggressive behavior and the clinically compelling processes involved in peer rejection.[2]

Several components of this intervention showed particular promise, and the next stage of the research program emphasized systematic evaluation of specific facets of training for self-evaluation and for anger management. Work with the resulting manual (Hinshaw, Henker, & Whalen, 1981) yielded several empirical reports in which (a) the relative efficacy of behavioral versus cognitive components of self-management training

---

[2]Pilot work in self-management training provided a sobering lesson as to the importance of therapeutic work with children displaying impulse-control problems. In testing a cognitive–behavioral protocol, the author served as a therapist for a group of 3 boys from an elementary school, one of whom had been identified by school personnel as "impulsive." Some months later, in a chance encounter, the author saw this youngster in the community, with his hand severely bandaged. Despite warnings to the contrary, he had been playing with dangerous equipment in the family garage and had literally blown off several fingers of one hand. As noted earlier, children with attention deficits and impulsivity are at risk for accidents and poisonings (Szatmari et al., 1989); self-regulation skills are clearly of major clinical importance.

were evaluated, and (b) combinations of the psychosocial treatments with stimulant medication were performed.

As part of research funded by the National Institute of Mental Health (NIMH), a clinical trial was performed next with independent replications during the school years following summer research programs. This trial has continued as part of current work at U.C. Berkeley. In this investigation, the effects of medication with and without systematic clinic-based therapy (involving both parent management training plus child group treatment in self-management) are evaluated. Yet even this type of therapeutic intervention has been limited to periods of months, rather than years; given the chronic nature of the interpersonal and psychological problems that pertain to most children with ADHD, far longer and more intensive intervention periods appear necessary (Kazdin, 1987; Pelham & Hinshaw, 1992).

Thus, in the most recent extension of the research program, the author was selected to join with five other sites across the United States in a collaborative project—the Multimodal Treatment Study for Children with ADHD (MTA)—to contrast and combine systematic psychosocial intervention with stimulant medication over lengthy treatment periods (Richters et al., 1995). The psychosocial intervention includes both (a) direct contingency management in intensive summer treatment programs (Pelham & Hoza, chapter 16, this volume) with classroom aides (Swanson, 1992), and (b) clinical behavior therapy with parent training and teacher consultation (Barkley, 1987). The specific self-management programs for self-evaluation and anger management discussed herein are incorporated in the summer treatment program of Pelham and Hoza (chapter 16, this volume). Although specific treatment components will not be compared in this protocol, the entire package will be delivered for a longer time period than has ever been put to a controlled empirical test for children with ADHD, with the goal of assessing whether intensive, long-term treatments, either alone or in combination with medication interventions, can alter the course of ADHD.

Participants

For all of the projects described herein, children were selected on the basis of contemporaneous criteria for hyperactivity, ADD, or ADHD. That is, the samples comprised children of grade-school age (roughly 6–12 years old) with normal intelligence who met inclusionary and exclusionary criteria for the disorder. (For the recently begun MTA study, the age range is 7–9.9 years.) Thus, children with overt neurological handicaps, pervasive developmental disorders, psychosis, or severe emotional disturbance were excluded. To be included, a persistent pattern (extending for at least 6 months, with onset before 7 years of age) of inattention, impulsivity, and overactivity in home and school settings must be present.

In addition, for most of the investigations discussed herein (but not for the MTA study), children were receiving stimulant medication in the community for at least 4 months prior to our work with them. The rationale is that our projects do not replace the family's own medical care; thus, initiating a child's medication treatment in the absence of providing protracted follow-up would be ethically questionable. Because of the previously medicated nature of the various samples, the children under investigation were quite likely to respond positively to stimulant medication. Thus, any effects of psychosocial intervention, either alone or in combination with medication treatment, have been found in samples that are displaying a positive response to stimulants.

It should be noted that approximately half of the samples under consideration have met criteria for comorbid externalizing disorders such as oppositional–defiant disorder (ODD) or, more rarely, conduct disorder (CD). This comorbidity is quite important, given that many of the therapeutic interventions are targeted toward such interpersonal difficulties as anger control and overt aggression. The peer relations, family histories, and prognoses of children with overlapping ADHD and aggression are universally poor (Hinshaw, 1987); evaluating intervention strategies for this severely impaired subgroup is a major priority for the field (Hinshaw & Erhardt, 1991).

A limitation of the samples investigated to date is their exclusively male composition (the MTA investigation does, however, include girls). Certainly, boys far outnumber girls among clinical referrals for ADHD; it is quite difficult, for logistic and ethical reasons, to include a small number of girls in summer research programs or group-oriented treatment projects for children with ADHD. Deliberate oversampling of girls would be an important strategy in subsequent research programs.

Procedures

The types of self-management therapy under discussion have all been performed in group therapy contexts. Small groups of 4 to 5 boys with ADHD meet, on a regular basis, with two leaders. The various curricula have focused on a number of common goals, including the creation of a safe atmosphere for open disclosure and discussion of problems, the promotion of talk about the nature of ADHD and of medication treatments, and the regular rehearsal and practice of cooperative social skills. The key components that were put to empirical test—self-monitoring and self-evaluation skills, and anger management exercises—were introduced only after a significant number of hours of initial trust building and relationship enhancement. Particularly for the anger management assessments and training, in which children actively provoke and taunt one another toward the end of fostering mutual self-control, group leaders must be sure that the exercises are performed after clear levels of trust and support have developed. It is important to note, on the other side of the coin, that the training will become a rather empty exercise (with no hope of generalization) unless realistic levels of affect are produced. In other words, group leaders must maintain respect and safety while fostering realistic provocations from peers—a balance that is not always easy to maintain.

The training in self-management is fully integrated with established behavioral procedures. That is, the participants receive regular systems of reinforcement during the therapy sessions, with contingencies in effect. Indeed, the work in self-evaluation explicitly integrates typical reinforcement programs with training in the child's ability to monitor his own behavior. Mediational procedures without the backup of established behavioral procedures are extremely unlikely to yield benefit in samples that comprise children with ADHD.

Many of the investigations described herein have occurred during summer research programs, settings in which relatively large numbers of ADHD and comparison boys interact together in class, playground, and small-group settings. A major advantage is that procedures learned during therapy groups can be evaluated via rigorous observational methodology in naturalistic settings that place a premium on social interchange. Indeed, given the short-term nature of most of the therapeutic interventions evaluated to date, perhaps the most important contributions from the overall research program emanate from the various assessment measures that have been created to capture important peer interactions as well as the display of aggressive and antisocial behavior.

TREATMENT PLAN

Intervention Components

Because of space limitations, the focus herein is on the two most validated components of the self-management protocols: (a) training in self-monitoring and self-evaluation, and (b) anger management therapy.

Self-Evaluation Skills

Borrowing heavily from the careful work at Stony Brook of Drabman, Spitalnik, and O'Leary (1973) and Turkewitz, O'Leary, and Ironsmith (1975), the author adapted exercises for the explicit teaching of self-monitoring and self-evaluation skills. Children with ADHD are notorious for the inaccuracy of self-reports of their own behavior: The intercorrelation between self-reported aggression and objectively observed aggression in the author's laboratory is $r = .44$ for comparison boys and nearly zero ($r = .04$) for ADHD youngsters (Garcia, Hinshaw, & Zupan, 1996). The hypothesis is that fostering accurate self-evaluation may help to promote more appropriate social behavior in class, play, and home settings.

The group begins by discussing a certain behavioral criterion (e.g., cooperation; paying attention) for the next period of activity. Specific examples, both positive and negative, are discussed and modeled; an operational definition of the criterion behavior is written out. As noted above, children receive reinforcement points at regular intervals for appropriate actions during the groups, so that the newly defined behaviors can be specifically consequated. Next, self-monitoring and self-evaluation are taught via the "Match Game." Specifically, when it is time for the group leaders to give points at the end of a given interval, each child completes a self-evaluation form that lists the behavioral criterion of interest and a 5-point scale ranging from 1 (pretty bad) to 5 (great). As the adults privately complete their ratings of each child's performance in relation to the criterion, each child simultaneously rates himself, attempting to appraise and match the adult rating. The essential part of the training occurs during the ensuing discussion: Following each child's revealing of his reasons for the self-rating, the leaders present *their* ratings and rationale. The objective here is to foster the children's enhanced awareness of the specific behaviors they have just performed.

To reinforce accuracy of self-evaluation, extra points in the reinforcement system are given initially for the child's accurate matching, regardless of the value of the rating. Eventually, the extra reinforcement requires both a "match" *and* a rating above a certain, preannounced threshold. Without this added criterion, some children may learn to intentionally misbehave but still earn full rewards for presenting a self-rating of "1."

The Match Game can accompany nearly any academic, social, or solitary task of the child; it is intended to be repeated—initially with high frequency and then faded to a less frequent schedule—throughout the group therapy. Eventually, Match Game procedures can be utilized by parents and teachers to extend the benefits of reinforcement procedures to home and school. For example, once a Daily Report Card system is enacted in clinical behavior therapy, whereby reinforcers at home are dispensed for progress toward individualized behaviors at school, the child may be able to self-evaluate with respect to the teacher's daily ratings.

Anger Management Training

Because of the severe peer-related difficulties encountered by most children with ADHD—particularly the repeated cycles of taunting from peers and retaliatory aggression from the ADHD child—the author developed and subsequently modified a curriculum to deal specifically with the enhancement of anger control. The curriculum was strongly influenced by the theoretical and empirical work of Novaco (1979) on anger management training for adults; as such, it employs affective, cognitive, and behavioral components designed to foster (a) recognition of internal and external cues that signal incipient anger, (b) deployment of cognitive and behavioral strategies to counteract the anger and ensuing aggressive responses, and (c) graduated rehearsal of the chosen plans under increasingly realistic provocations from peers (see Hinshaw et al., 1981).

The curriculum begins with each child's revealing of names and phrases that bother him. Clearly, a safe atmosphere must be created to foster meaningful disclosure along these lines. Group leaders must point out that, with the child's permission, such phrases will later be used by the rest of the group to help the child practice self-control (see the section on outcome measures, below). Indeed, concepts of self-control are discussed by the group prior to the specific training exercises.

In these specific strategies, recognition of one's own signs of impending anger is the first skill taught. This exercise is particularly difficult for younger children, but preadolescents can be taught to recognize emotional, verbal, or behavioral cues. Next, each child selects, with guidance from the leaders, a particular cognitive or behavioral strategy to employ when he is provoked or teased. The goal here is not necessarily to prevent fighting back, if retaliation is warranted; rather, because of the impulsive tendencies of children with ADHD, the mediational strategies and alternative responses are taught to foster the child's ability to choose a desired response, in the hope of decreasing escalating cycles of impulsive fighting and resultant peer rejection. Third, and critically, the chosen strategy is rehearsed under increasingly realistic provocations from other members of the group. It is important to note that reinforcement from the adult leaders—and self-monitoring and self-evaluation of the child's new attempts at self-control—are important therapeutic features of the curriculum. Furthermore, developmental issues are quite salient in anger management training. Younger children are likely to select overt behavioral strategies to counteract provocation, whereas children approaching adolescence often select self-talk or other mediational approaches to aid with their self-control.

Outcome Measures

Because the aims of the self-management therapies just described are to enhance social competence through the reduction of negative and aggressive behaviors and the promotion of alternatives to retaliation, it is critically important to utilize outcome measures that directly tap both externalizing behaviors and more prosocial alternatives. Thus, the emphasis has been on the development of observational methodologies that can tap specific behavioral responses. Although broader measures of social competence, including sociometric appraisals, are necessary for the evaluation of longer-term comprehensive therapy packages, the focus herein is on naturalistic, clinic-based, and laboratory observational methodologies.

Live Observations of Social Behavior

Improved social behavior with peers and adults beyond the therapy group (i.e., in classroom and playground situations) is a key goal for self-evaluation training. Yet, appraising behavior change in relatively large social settings is fraught with difficulty, particularly because of the logistic difficulties inherent in making discrete, objective behavior counts across wide areas and in obtaining sufficient density of observations for each child. Indeed, videotape coding is typically precluded when one is observing groups of more than 20 children in open spaces.

Live observational procedures in this program of research began with the scan-sampled observation system of Hinshaw, Henker, and Whalen (1984a), in which teams of observers made extremely brief, sequential observations of children in repeated cycles throughout a class or play period. Because of the brief periods of observation—long enough only to code a behavior before moving on to the next child—the number of categories was limited to broad classes of appropriate social behavior, negative social behavior, and nonsocial behavior. The system was subsequently modified to incorporate expansion of the number of codes; importantly, negative social behavior was subdivided into categories of physical and verbal aggression as well as noncompliance. These systems proved quite responsive to effects of both psychosocial and pharmacologic interventions (Hinshaw et al., 1984a; Hinshaw, Henker, et al., 1989); however, the unpaced nature of the observations placed limits on code reliability.

More recently, the observation system has reconfigured into a brief time-sampling procedure, in which observers (paced by headphones) have 5 seconds to find the child on their rosters, 3 seconds to observe, and 5 additional seconds to record the social behavior of interest (Hinshaw, 1995). By such means, observers are yoked to the precise pacing schedule. Chance-corrected interobserver agreement figures are respectable with this system, with kappas for the crucial categories of noncompliance (.65) and aggression (.73) in the acceptable range, particularly in light of the relatively low base rates of these key behaviors. Furthermore, the codes have served as important measures in nonintervention studies as well: In Erhardt and Hinshaw (1994), aggression and prosocial behavior were important predictors of ADHD children's initial peer status, and noncompliance was predicted by negative maternal behavior displayed during parent–child interactions (Anderson, Hinshaw, & Simmel, 1994).

Verbal Provocation Assessments of Anger Control

As a first-stage appraisal of the effects of the anger management therapy procedures described earlier, the author devised verbal provocation assessments within the therapy groups in which training is performed. Specifically, using the disclosed names from each participant that were discussed above, the remainder of the group prepares to taunt the "target" child, who leaves the room during the group's preparations. Upon his return, he sits in the middle of the group, attempting to withstand their taunts for a period of 1 or 2 minutes. Each successive session is videotaped, allowing subsequent coding of anger, aggressive retaliation, and the use of alternative coping strategies for self-control (see Hinshaw, Henker, & Whalen, 1984b; Hinshaw, Buhrmester, & Heller, 1989), as well as more global codes reflecting overall self-management.

In enforcing the rules of no touching or physical aggression, the leaders must forge a balance between overexuberant provocation, on the one hand, and sterile, emotionless taunting on the other. Indeed, unless some real affect is generated in the assessments and in the rehearsal-based portions of the therapy, the procedures will have little likelihood of transcending mere cognitive exercises. A key goal for future research is to devise more naturalistic appraisals of provocation response.

Laboratory Assessment of Covert Antisocial Behavior

Although it is not yet tied to outcomes of psychosocial therapy research, a recent assessment procedure for appraising stealing, property destruction, and cheating was developed as part of NIMH-funded research that also supported summer research programs and therapy outcome studies. Investigators of antisocial behavior are increasingly concerned with the distinction between overt (e.g., aggressive, defiant) and covert or clandestine (e.g., stealing, firesetting, lying) manifestations (Loeber & Schmaling, 1985). In fact, covert antisocial behavior is a key predictor of later delinquency (Hinshaw & Anderson, 1996). Yet, such behavior occurs with a low base rate, and by their very nature covert actions are difficult to observe. Furthermore, global ratings of this domain are likely to be insensitive to longitudinal or therapeutic change. To redress the paucity of empirical data on covert behaviors, the author devised an individual lab assessment where children perform, in solitary fashion, worksheets geared to their developmental level.

In the room, toys and small amounts of money are left in view, and the experimenter "accidentally" leaves the answer key (see Hinshaw, Heller, & McHale, 1992, for details). The amounts taken, the extent of property damage (destroying materials, writing on tables or walls), and cheating can be coded from products left in the room (in early studies, surreptitious videotaping enhanced coding). Measures of stealing and property destruction show concurrent validity with parent and teacher ratings of covert–delinquent actions and with global staff appraisals; they form an empirical factor that is distinct from overt aggression and is far more likely to be shown by ADHD as opposed to nondiagnosed children (Hinshaw, Simmel, & Heller, 1995). Furthermore, stealing and property destruction have been shown to be significantly reduced with stimulant medication; indeed, normalization of these behaviors occurs on medication (Hinshaw et al., 1992). Interestingly, however, cheating *increased* with medication treatment, possibly attributable to the participants' enhanced achievement motivation. Also, the stealing variable was predicted from maternal negativity during parent–child interactions that occurred prior to the summer program (Anderson et al., 1994). In all, this brief laboratory assessment is a promising tool for needed multisource perspectives on covert antisocial behaviors (Hinshaw et al., 1995).

TREATMENT EFFECTIVENESS

Self-Evaluation, Reinforcement, and Stimulant Medication

Hinshaw et al. (1984a) assessed the effects of adding the Match Game self-evaluation procedure to typical token reinforcement for boys with *DSM-III* ADD with hyperactivity. Also, to ascertain the additive effects of medication with the cognitive–behavioral self-evaluation procedure, methylphenidate versus placebo status of the children was also manipulated. Results were assessed in the classroom and playground settings of a summer research program, using the scan-sampled observational system described above.

Following approximately 20 hours of group therapy, in which Match Game procedures were taught and extensively practiced, boys with ADD were assigned to medication (low doses of methylphenidate) or placebo conditions for a 2-day evaluation period of naturalistic observations. Boys alternated, across the days, between token reinforcement only and token reinforcement plus the addition of the Match Game; in both conditions, reinforcement was contingent on cooperative social behavior. In the Match Game condition, full reward value could be obtained only through accurate self-evaluation during each interval. No effects of the cognitive–behavioral procedure appeared in the classroom setting. On the playground, however, (a) medication was associated with fewer negative interactions than was placebo; (b) reinforced self-evaluation (Match Game plus points) yielded fewer negative interaction than did points alone; and (c) the combination of medication plus reinforced self-evaluation led to optimal levels of social behavior (although not significantly better than medication plus reinforcement only or placebo plus reinforced self-evaluation). Thus, during the brief evaluation period, adding a cognitive mediational component enhanced social behavior relative to reinforcement alone, and at least in terms of rank ordering, the combination of pharmacologic and cognitive–behavioral treatments produced the greatest benefit. Only this latter combination, in fact, brought levels of negative social behavior below those of comparison boys.

These results suggest strongly that the effects of behavioral reinforcement procedures can be extended through use of mediational strategies that aim to promote more active self-awareness. A valuable goal for subsequent research would be to ascertain the extent to which more extensive use of self-evaluation training—along with other cognitive–behavioral strategies—could extend the benefits of traditional reinforcement programs. In other words, the goal is not to replace validated behavioral procedures with exclusively cognitive techniques, but to integrate promising mediational therapeutic practices with reinforcement, toward the end of maintaining behavioral and interpersonal gains.

Anger Management Training

The initial test of the anger management curriculum took place in the afterschool treatment program described earlier. In this uncontrolled evaluation, hyperactive children displayed reductions in retaliation and increases in self-control following intervention (Hinshaw et al., 1984b, Study 1). Based on these results, a controlled trial was next performed during a summer research program. Children with ADD were randomly assigned to receive (a) the cognitive–behavioral anger management curriculum versus (b) a control condition comprising cognitive procedures (discussions of empathy and perspective-taking) but not including active rehearsal of coping responses. Furthermore, this therapy manipulation was crossed with stimulant medication versus placebo status, during both the treatment and evaluation procedures. Whereas low dosages of methylphenidate failed to produce any change in the posttreatment provocation assessments, the rehearsal-based cognitive–behavioral training proved superior to the cognitive-only intervention with respect to coping responses, reduction of retaliation, and global self-control (Hinshaw et al., 1984b, Study 2). Within the limits of an immediate posttreatment assessment that took place in the same groups in which the training had occurred, integrated mediational/behavioral intervention procedures proved superior to methylphenidate regarding outcome domains linked to anger control.

In a partial replication, Hinshaw, Buhrmester, and Heller (1989) provided the cognitive–behavioral anger management training to a new sample. At posttreatment verbal provocation assessments, the boys were assigned randomly to placebo versus moderate (0.6 mg/kg) dosages of methylphenidate. In this instance, medication facilitated the enhanced display of self-control and aggression reduction relative to placebo. A viable interpretation is that stimulant medication may enable children with ADHD to utilize previously learned cognitive–behavioral skills to display self-management. Note that, for the domain of anger control, moderate dosage levels of the pharmacologic intervention may be necessary (see discussion in Hinshaw, 1991). The suggestion is that combinations of psychosocial and pharmacologic treatments may yield optimal performance of critical social skills.

Multimodal Treatment Packages

Although promising, the results presented thus far have been limited to rather short-term evaluations of cognitive–behavioral self-management components. To promote lasting changes in social competence, multimodal treatments spanning far longer intervention periods are undoubtedly necessary. In preliminary analyses, the clinic-based trial of weekly parent management training plus child self-management groups has yielded benefits with respect to parent reports of externalizing behavior patterns; the addition of the psychosocial therapy to medication appears to provide greater benefit than medication alone. Evaluation of longer-term multimodal treatments will require close attention to several methodologic issues. For one thing, parents and teachers cannot provide blind evaluations of interventions in which they are central participants; for another, the number of treatment cells necessary to isolate each component of a complex protocol is prohibitive for most studies. Thus, large-scale evaluation efforts require careful attention to methodology as well as sufficient sample sizes to test key hypotheses with sufficient power.

Along this line, the self-evaluation and anger management curricula have been integrated, in recent years, with the comprehensive summer treatment program model of Pelham and Hoza (chapter 16, this volume) at the University of Pittsburgh. In addition, the extensive kindergarten intervention of Barkley at the University of Massachusetts Medical Center includes a modified version of the anger management program. Thus, integrated treatment protocols have found use for the validated procedures from the current research program. Furthermore, the above-noted NIMH MTA investigation will evaluate the most comprehensive and intensive package of psychosocial interventions ever assembled for children with ADHD; notably, the self-evaluation procedures and the anger management curriculum are included in the family, peer, and school-based treatment protocol that is being devised. The aim is to alter the course of ADHD through integrated treatment strategies, leaving for subsequent research the thorny issues of dismantling the active components that contribute to gains in various domains.

Limitations and Generalizability

As has been highlighted throughout this chapter, cognitive interventions for children with ADHD that are not explicitly linked to validated behavioral procedures are doomed to clinical failure. Self-instructional strategies should therefore *not* be utilized as primary treatment strategies for this population, and there should be no expectation that interventions based on social problem-solving or perspective-taking training will provide meaningful clinical benefit. Children with ADHD—particularly those with co-occurring aggression—are particularly refractory to all but the most powerful treatment strategies (Hinshaw & Erhardt, 1991); self-management treatments may be optimal for extending the benefits that can accrue to solid behavioral intervention.

In short, no clinically sufficient treatment strategies have yet been developed or validated for children with the difficult constellation of problems that constitute ADHD. Thus, whereas self-management interventions share the same clinical limitations as other treatments, the hope is that they can be intentionally tied to reinforcement procedures and family treatments to enhance socially competent behavior.

Can therapists in clinical practice provide meaningful treatment for children with attention deficits and hyperactivity? The answer is a qualified "Yes": So long as practitioners are willing to expand on traditional notions of both assessment (i.e., by moving beyond the usual clinic-based evaluations) and intervention (i.e., by working to shape home and school environments and to actively promote self-management), academic and social competence can be forged. The typical forms of one-on-one therapy will require supplementation with group-based treatments, as emphasized earlier; the child will need to become actively involved in collaborative treatment efforts with the parents and teacher. Self-management treatments certainly can be used by community practitioners, but their effective use by clinicians will require flexibility and a willingness to make active outreach into home, school, and peer settings.

FUTURE DIRECTIONS

Recent conceptions of the social difficulties of children with ADHD emphasize that such youngsters do not typically display deficits in knowledge of social situations or even in fundamental social skills. Rather, their chief difficulties appear to relate to social performance in natural interpersonal contexts (Hinshaw, 1992c; Whalen & Henker, 1992). Furthermore, it appears that children with ADHD—particularly those with aggression—have differing social agendas and goals than those of their peers (Melnick & Hinshaw, 1996). Recall, as well, that recent conceptions of ADHD emphasize disinhibitory psychopathology and poor delay of gratification rather than the attentional deficits themselves (Barkley, 1994). The result is that treatments focusing simply on the teaching of social skills will, in all likelihood, fail to produce meaningful change for this population. Interventions must therefore facilitate (a) reductions of the externalizing behaviors that quickly shape negative reputations (Erhardt & Hinshaw, 1994), (b) contextualized performance of skilled interpersonal behavior, (c) enhancement of inhibitory strategies (e.g., anger management), and (d) reformulation of the goals that children with ADHD have for social interchange. In short, traditional notions of social skills intervention and self-instructional treatments require radical change if the dismal social prognoses of children with ADHD are to be altered.

What can practitioners in the community learn from this research? One key implication is that much of the individual focus on therapy with children displaying attention deficits and hyperactivity should shift to consideration of group-based treatments. It is nearly impossible to teach important social skills to a child individually; only in a peer group can needed skills be meaningfully rehearsed. Also, the peer group can provide a safe sounding board for fears, anxieties, and goals. To be sure, performing therapy in groups requires explicit training for generalization and maintenance, just as is the case for individual therapy; the persistent social difficulties of children with ADHD mandate thorough, consistent programing involving the support and training of the important persons in the child's everyday environment. The personal and social devastation incurred by the deficits and excesses associated with ADHD demands nothing less.

REFERENCES

Abikoff, H. (1991). Cognitive training in ADHD children: Less to it than meets the eye. *Journal of Learning Disabilities, 24*, 205–209.

Abikoff, H., & Gittelman, R. (1985). Hyperactive children treated with stimulants: Is cognitive therapy a useful adjunct? *Archives of General Psychiatry, 42,* 953–961.

American Psychiatric Association. (1980). *Diagnostic and statistical manual of mental disorders* (3rd ed.). Washington, DC: Author.

American Psychiatric Association. (1994). *Diagnostic and statistical manual of mental disorders.* (4th ed.). Washington, DC: Author.

Anderson, C. A., Hinshaw, S. P., & Simmel, C. (1994). Mother–child interactions in ADHD and comparison boys: Relationships to overt and covert externalizing behavior. *Journal of Abnormal Child Psychology, 22*, 247–265.

Asher, S. R., & Coie, J. D. (1990). *Peer rejection in childhood.* New York: Cambridge University Press.

Bandura, A. (1977). *Social learning therapy*. Englewood Cliffs, NJ: Prentice Hall.

Barkley, R. A. (1987). *Defiant children: Activities manual for parent training*. New York: Guilford Press.

Barkley, R. A. (1990). *Attention deficit hyperactivity disorder: A handbook for diagnosis and treatment*. New York: Guilford Press.

Barkley, R. A. (1994). Impaired delayed responding: A unified theory of attention-deficit hyperactivity disorder. In D. K. Routh (Ed.), *Disruptive behavior disorders in childhood: Essays honoring Herbert C. Quay* (pp. 11–57). New York: Plenum Press.

Beck, A. T. (1976). *Cognitive therapy and the emotional disorders*. New York: International Universities Press.

Berk, L. E., & Potts, M. (1991). Development and functional significance of private speech among attention-deficit hyperactivity disordered and normal boys. *Journal of Abnormal Child Psychology, 19,* 357–377.

Bickett, L., & Milich, R. (1990). First impressions formed of boys with attention deficit disorder. *Journal of Learning Disabilities, 23,* 253–259.

Bradley, C. (1937). The behavior of children receiving benzedrine. *American Journal of Psychiatry, 94,* 577–585.

Bugental, D. B., Whalen, C. K., & Henker, B. (1977). Causal attributions of hyperactive children and motivational assumptions of two behavior change approaches: Evidence for an interactionist position. *Child Development, 48,* 874–884.

Douglas, V. I. (1983). Attention and cognitive problems. In M. Rutter (Ed.), *Developmental neuropsychiatry* (pp. 280–329). New York: Guilford Press.

Douglas, V. I., Parry, P., Marton, P., & Garson, C. (1976). Assessment of a cognitive training program for hyperactive children. *Journal of Abnormal Child Psychology, 4,* 389–410.

Drabman, R., Spitalnik, R., & O'Leary, K. D. (1973). Teaching self-control to disruptive children. *Journal of Abnormal Psychology, 82,* 10–16.

Erhardt, D., & Hinshaw, S. P. (1994). Initial sociometric impressions of ADHD and comparison boys: Predictions from social behaviors and from nonbehavioral variables. *Journal of Consulting and Clinical Psychology, 62,* 833–842.

Gadow, K. D. (1992). Pediatric psychopharmacology: A review of recent research. *Journal of Child Psychology and Psychiatry, 33,* 153–195.

Gadow, K. D., Nolan, E. E., Sverd, J., Sprafkin, J., & Paolicelli, L. L. (1990). Methylphenidate in aggresive-hyperactive boys: I. Effects on peer aggression in public school settings. *Journal of the American Academy of Child and Adolescent Psychiatry, 29,* 710–718.

Garcia, J., Hinshaw, S. P., & Zupan, B. A. (1996). *Predictive validity of measures of aggression in ADHD and comparison boys*. Poster presented at the meeting of the Western Psychological Association, Los Angeles.

Halperin, J. M., Matier, K., Bedi, G., Sharma, V., & Newcorn, J. H. (1992). Specificity of inattention, impulsivity, and hyperactivity to the diagnosis of attention-deficit hyperactivity disorder. *Journal of the American Academy of Child and Adolescent Psychiatry, 31,* 190–196.

Hinshaw, S. P. (1987). On the distinction between attentional deficits/hyperactivity and conduct problems/aggression in child psychopathology. *Psychological Bulletin, 101,* 443–463.

Hinshaw, S. P. (1991). Stimulant medication and the treatment of aggression in children with attentional deficits. *Journal of Clinical Child Psychology, 20,* 301–312.

Hinshaw, S. P. (1992a). Academic underachievement, attentional deficits, and aggression: Comorbidity and implications for intervention. *Journal of Consulting and Clinical Psychology, 60,* 893–903.

Hinshaw, S. P. (1992b). Externalizing behavior problems and academic underachievement in childhood and adolescence: Causal relationships and underlying mechanisms. *Psychological Bulletin, 111,* 127–155.

Hinshaw, S. P. (1992c). Intervention for social skill and social competence. *Child and Adolescent Psychiatric Clinics of North America, 1,* 539–552.

Hinshaw, S. P. (1994). *Attention deficits and hyperactivity in children.* Thousand Oaks, CA: Sage.

Hinshaw, S. P. (1995). *Behavior observation coding manual for classroom and playground interactions.* Unpublished manuscript, Department of Psychology, University of California, Berkeley.

Hinshaw, S. P., Alkus, S. P., Whalen, C. K., & Henker, B. (1979). *STAR Program training manual.* Unpublished manuscript, University of California, Los Angeles.

Hinshaw, S. P., & Anderson, C. A. (1996). *Oppositional defiant and conduct disorders.* In E. J. Mash & R. A. Barkley (Eds.), *Child psychopathology* (pp. 108–149). New York: Guilford Press.

Hinshaw, S. P., Buhrmester, D., & Heller, T. (1989). Anger control in response to verbal provocation: Effects of stimulant medication for boys with ADHD. *Journal of Abnormal Child Psychology, 17,* 393–407.

Hinshaw, S. P., & Erhardt, D. (1991). Attention-deficit hyperactivity disorder. In P. C. Kendall (Ed.), *Child and adolescent therapy: Cognitive–behavioral procedures* (pp. 98–128). New York: Guilford Press.

Hinshaw, S. P., Heller, T., & McHale, J. P. (1992). Covert antisocial behavior in boys with attention-deficit hyperactivity disorder: External validation and effects of methylphenidate. *Journal of Consulting and Clinical Psychology, 60,* 274–281.

Hinshaw, S. P., Henker, B., & Whalen, C. K. (1981). *A cognitive–behavioral curriculum for group training of hyperactive boys.* Unpublished manuscript, University of California, Los Angeles.

Hinshaw, S. P., Henker, B., & Whalen, C. K. (1984a). Cognitive–behavioral and pharmacologic interventions for hyperactive boys: Comparative and combined effects. *Journal of Consulting and Clinical Psychology, 52,* 739–749.

Hinshaw, S. P., Henker, B., & Whalen, C. K. (1984b). Self-control in hyperactive boys in anger-inducing situations: Effects of cognitive–behavioral training and of methylphenidate. *Journal of Abnormal Child Psychology, 12,* 55–77.

Hinshaw, S. P., Henker, B., Whalen, C. K., Erhardt, D., & Dunnington, R. E. (1989). Aggressive, prosocial, and nonsocial behavior in hyperactive boys: Dose effects of methylphenidate in naturalistic settings. *Journal of Consulting and Clinical Psychology, 57,* 636–643.

Hinshaw, S. P., & McHale, J. P. (1991). Stimulant medication and the social interactions of hyperactive children: Effects and implications. In D. G. Gilbert & J. J. Connolly (Eds.), *Personality, social skills, and psychopathology: An individual differences approach* (pp. 229–253). New York: Plenum Press.

Hinshaw, S. P., Simmel, C., & Heller, T. (1995). Multimethod assessment of covert antisocial behavior in children: Laboratory observations, adult ratings, and child self-report. *Psychological Assessment, 7,* 209–219.

Kanter, F. H. (1972). A behaviorist's excursion into the lion's den. *Behavior Therapy, 3,* 384–416.

Kazdin, A. E. (1987). Treatment of antisocial behavior in children: Current status and future directions. *Psychological Bulletin, 102,* 187–203.

Klein, R. G., & Mannuzza, S. (1991). Long-term outcome of hyperactive children: A review. *Journal of the American Academy of Child and Adolescent Psychiatry, 30,* 383–387.

Loeber, R., & Schmaling, K. B. (1985). Empirical evidence for overt and covert patterns of antisocial conduct problems: A meta-analysis. *Journal of Abnormal Child Psychology, 13,* 337–352.

Luria, A. R., & Yudovich, F. J. (1972). *Speech and the developmental mental processes in the child.* Baltimore: Penguin.

Meichenbaum, D. H. (1977). *Cognitive–behavior modification: An integrative approach.* New York: Plenum Press.

Melnick, S., & Hinshaw, S. P. (1996). What they want and what they get: Social goals and peer acceptance in ADHD and comparison boys. *Journal of Abnormal Child Psychology, 24,* 169–185.

Novaco, R. W. (1979). The cognitive regulation of anger and stress. In P. C. Kendall & S. D. Hollon (Eds.), *Cognitive–behavioral interventions: Theory, research, and procedures* (pp. 241–285). New York: Academic Press.

Oden, S., & Asher, A. R. (1977). Coaching children for social skills for friendship making. *Child Development, 48,* 495–506.

O'Leary, K. D., Pelham, W. E., Rosenbaum, A., & Price, G. H. (1976). Behavioral treatment of hyperkinetic children: An experimental evaluation of its usefulness. *Clinical Pediatrics, 15,* 510–515.

Parker, J. G., & Asher, S. R. (1987). Peer relations and later personal adjustment: Are low-accepted children at risk? *Psychological Bulletin, 102,* 357–389.

Patterson, G. R. (1965). An application of conditioning techniques to the control of a hyperactive child. In O. P. Ullman & L. Krasner (Eds.), *Case studies in behavior modification* (pp. 370–375). New York: Holt, Rinehart, & Winston.

Pelham, W. E. (1986). The effects of stimulant drugs on learning and achievement in hyperactive and learning-disabled children. In J. K. Torgesen & B. Wong (Eds.), *Psychological and educational perspectives on learning disabilities* (pp. 259–295). San Diego, CA: Academic Press.

Pelham, W. E., & Bender, M. E. (1982). Peer relationships in hyperactive children: Description and treatment. In K. Gadow & I. Bialer (Eds.), *Advances in learning and behavioral disabilities* (Vol. 1, pp. 365–436). Greenwich, CT: JAI Press.

Pelham, W. E., Carlson, C., Sams, S. E., Vallano, G., Dixon, M. J., & Hoza, B. (1993). Separate and combined effects of methylphenidate and behavior modification on boys with attention deficit hyperactivity disorder in the classroom. *Journal of Consulting and Clinical Psychology, 61,* 506–515.

Pelham, W. E., & Hinshaw, S. P. (1992). Behavioral intervention for ADHD. In S. M. Turner, K. S. Calhoun, & H. E. Adams (Eds.), *Handbook of clinical behavior therapy* (2nd ed., pp. 259–283). New York: Wiley.

Pelham, W. E., & Murphy, H. A. (1986). Behavioral and pharmacological treatment of attention deficit and conduct disorders. In M. Hersen (Ed.), *Pharmacological and behavioral treatment: An integrative approach* (pp. 108–148). New York: Wiley.

Richters, J. E., Jensen, P. S., Arnold, L. E., Abikoff, H., Conners, C. K., Greenhill, L. L., Hechtman, L. T., Hinshaw, S. P., Pelham, W. E., & Swanson, J. M. (1995). The National Institute of Mental Health Collaborative Multisite Multimodal Treatment Study of Children with Attention Deficit/Hyperactivity Disorder (MTA): Part 1. Background and rationale. *Journal of the American Academy of Child and Adolescent Psychiatry, 34,* 987–1000.

Schachar, R. (1986). Hyperkinetic syndrome: Historical development of the concept. In E. A. Taylor (Ed.), *The overactive child* (pp. 19–40). London: MacKeith.

Swanson, J. M. (1992). *School-based assessments and interventions for ADD students.* Irvine, CA: K. C. Publishing.

Swanson, J. M., Cantwell, D., Lerner, M., McBurnett, K., Pfiffner, L., & Kotkin, R. (1992). Treatment of ADHD: Beyond medication. *Beyond Behavior, 4,* 13–22.

Swanson, J. M., McBurnett, K., Christian, D. L., & Wigal, T. (1995). Stimulant medications and the treatment of children with ADHD. In T. H. Ollendick & R. J. Prinz (Eds.), *Advances in clinical child psychology* (Vol. 17, pp. 265–322). New York: Plenum Press.

Szatmari, P., Offord, D. R., & Boyle, M. H. (1989). Ontario Child Health Study: Prevalence of attention deficit disorder with hyperactivity. *Journal of Child Psychology and Psychiatry, 30,* 219–230.

Turkewitz, H., O'Leary, K. D., & Ironsmith, M. (1975). Generalization and maintenance of appropriate behavior through self-control. *Journal of Consulting and Clinical Psychology, 43,* 577–583.

Vygotsky, L. (1988). On inner speech. In M. B. Franklin & S. S. Barton (Eds.), *Child language: A reader* (pp. 181–187). New York: Oxford University Press.

Weiss, G., & Hechtman, L. T. (1993). *Hyperactive children grown up* (2nd ed.). New York: Guilford Press.

Whalen, C. K., & Henker, B. (1980). *Hyperactive children: The social ecology of identification and treatment.* San Diego, CA: Academic Press.

Whalen, C. K., & Henker, B. (1985). The social worlds of hyperactive (ADDH) children. *Clinical Psychology Review, 5,* 447–478.

Whalen, C. K., & Henker, B. (1991). Therapies for hyperactive children: Comparisons, combinations, and compromises. *Journal of Consulting and Clinical Psychology, 59,* 126–137.

Whalen, C. K., Henker, B., Buhrmester, D., Hinshaw, S. P., Huber, A., & Laski, K. (1989). Does stimulant medication improve the peer status of hyperactive children? *Journal of Consulting and Clinical Psychology, 57,* 545–549.

15

INTENSIVE TREATMENT: A SUMMER TREATMENT PROGRAM FOR CHILDREN WITH ADHD

WILLIAM E. PELHAM, JR. and BETSY HOZA

Attention deficit hyperactivity disorder (ADHD) is one of the major mental health disorders of childhood. Children with ADHD have difficulties in attention, impulse control, and activity level modulation that lead to serious impairment in daily life functioning, including classroom functioning, peer relationships, and family relationships. In addition, children with ADHD are at risk for a variety of problems as adolescents and adults (e.g., Barkley, Fischer, Edelbrock, & Smallish, 1990; Mannuzza, Gittelman-Klein, Konig, & Giampino, 1989). The high societal cost of juvenile delinquency, adult incarceration, alcohol and drug abuse, and mental health services underscores the need for an effective childhood intervention for ADHD that could prevent onset of these difficulties. To date, however, no singularly effective, comprehensive treatment for ADHD has been discovered.

The most common form of treatment for ADHD is medication with central nervous system (CNS) stimulants. Although they often result in dramatic short-term improvements, these medications have a number of limitations (Pelham, 1993; Pelham & Murphy, 1986) and do not result in improved long-term outcome when used as the sole form of intervention

---

Correspondence concerning this chapter should be addressed to Dr. William E. Pelham, Jr., WPIC, 3811 O'Hara Street, Pittsburgh, PA 15213.

(e.g., Weiss & Hechtman, 1986). The second most common treatment for ADHD is behavior modification in the form of parent training and school interventions. Like medication, behavior modification is a helpful short-term treatment (Carlson & Lahey, 1988), but it has similar limitations (Pelham & Hinshaw, 1992).

Recent research has suggested that *combining* medication and behavioral treatments offers significant incremental benefit beyond either treatment alone, and this is becoming the treatment of choice for ADHD (Pelham, 1989; Pelham & Murphy, 1986). However, there is not yet evidence that such multimodal interventions will result in long-term normalization of ADHD children's functioning (cf. Pelham, Schnedler, et al., 1988). There is an emerging belief that more intensive psychosocial treatment programs are necessary to produce substantive changes in long-term outcome (Hoza, Pelham, Sams, & Carlson, 1992; Pelham & Hinshaw, 1992). Notably, a similar conclusion has been reached with regard to childhood conduct disorders (Kazdin, 1987), which is not surprising given the high degree of overlap between the disruptive behavior disorders.

Foremost among the problems of children with ADHD for which standard treatments have not proven efficacious are peer relationship difficulties (Pelham & Bender, 1982). Peer relations may mediate the long-term outcome of children with ADHD (Pelham & Milich, 1984). However, peer relations are very resistant to change and little success has been documented in this area (Krehbiel & Milich, 1986). One reason for this failure is that it is difficult to work on peer relationships in the office or in the classroom, the two locations in which standard outpatient treatments are implemented.

For the past 17 years, we have been developing a comprehensive approach to the treatment of ADHD that is designed to overcome the limitations of existing interventions. We believe that an effective intervention for ADHD must include treatments that focus on the child, the school, and the parents. Comprehensive treatments often will include both psychosocial and pharmacological approaches, intensively implemented over long periods. Our procedures for working in school settings and training parents (e.g., Pelham, Schnedler, et al., 1988; Pelham, in press) are similar to those that have been used for decades (e.g., O'Leary & O'Leary, 1977; Patterson, 1974). What is unique about our approach is its emphasis on intensive work with the child during the summer.

Although children are more readily available for mental health services during summer months than they are during the school year, most mental health centers and professionals reduce or eliminate their therapeutic contacts with families of children with ADHD during the summers, and school-based services are suspended. If treatment is interrupted during the summer, gains made during the school year may be lost as the children and parents regress to old patterns of behavior. Children with ADHD are likely to experience failure in traditional summer camps, or continued impairment and social dysfunction if they simply hang around the neighborhood. The importance of intervening in school settings with children with ADHD is now well recognized (see Davilla, Williams, & MacDonald, 1991); it is important to note that children spend as many hours interacting with peers, siblings, and parents during the summer as they spend in school during the rest of the year.

Therefore, we have been treating children with ADHD in a camp-like setting in which they engage in a variety of activities with age-matched peers. We provide 360 hours of intensive treatment in 8 weeks—more contact than a child with ADHD would receive in 7 years of typical outpatient treatment. We focus on evaluating and treating the children's difficulties in peer relationships in a relatively natural setting. Daily classroom periods enable both intensive academic work during the summer *and* assessment of the children's difficulties and responses to treatment in a classroom setting. In addition, by conducting carefully controlled medication evaluations, we include the pharmacological approach that is necessary for some children with ADHD.

Our summer treatment program (STP) was offered from 1980 to 1986 in the psychology department at the Florida State University and has been conducted, since 1987, at the Western Psychiatric Institute and Clinic, University of Pittsburgh Medical Center. The STP is based on the premise that combining an intensive summer day treatment program with school year, outpatient follow-up is more likely to provide a maximally effective intervention for ADHD than are traditional outpatient treatments. This chapter describes the STP treatment components and presents some preliminary data regarding the efficacy, social validity, and practicality of the STP.

SUMMER TREATMENT PROGRAM OVERVIEW

The STP is an 8-week program for children and adolescents aged 5 to 15 years, who attend from 8:00 A.M. until 5:00 P.M. on weekdays. Children are placed in age-matched groups of 12, and treatments are implemented by teams of five clinical staff members (student interns) for each group. Groups stay together throughout the summer so that the children receive intensive experience in functioning as a group, in making friends, and in interacting appropriately with adults. Each group spends 3 hours daily in classroom sessions conducted by special education teachers and aides who implement behavior modification programs in a classroom context. The remainder of each day consists of recreationally based group activities, during which the treatment strategies described below are implemented. In addition, if the standard STP interventions do not produce the desired behavior change for a child, a functional analysis of the child's problematic behavior is conducted and individualized programs are developed. A typical day's schedule is depicted in Table 1.

Goals of Treatment

In the STP, we use a combination of interventions from the child psychopathology and developmental literatures that have demonstrated short-term efficacy for ADHD. Our goals are to improve the children's peer relationships, interactions with adults, academic performance, and self-efficacy, while concurrently training their parents in behavior management and conducting pharmacological assessments when indicated. Using a social learning approach, we employ treatment components spanning the range from operant and cognitive behavioral treatments to pharmacological interventions. We have modified the interventions so that they are age-appropriate and so that they can be tailored to the needs of each child. A treatment manual that is revised annually describes the program in detail (e.g., Pelham, 1994).

Point System

Using a systematic reward–response cost program, the children continuously earn points (the youngest children earn tokens) for appropriate

TABLE 1
Typical Daily Schedule for the Summer Treatment Program

Time	Activity
7:30–8:00	Arrivals
8:00–8:15	Social skills training
8:15–9:00	Soccer skills training
9:00–9:15	Transition
9:15–10:15	Soccer game
10:15–10:30	Transition
10:30–11:30	Academic learning center
11:30–11:45	Transition
11:45–12:00	Lunch
12:00–12:15	Recess
12:15–1:15	Softball game
1:15–1:30	Transition
1:30–2:15	Art learning center
2:15–2:30	Cooperative task
2:30–2:45	Transition
2:45–3:45	Swimming
3:45–4:00	Transition
4:00–5:00	Computer learning center
5:00–5:30	Departures

behavior and lose points (or tokens) for inappropriate behavior as they engage in activities throughout the day. Such programs have an extensive history in behavior modification and have large, acute effects on children's behavior (e.g., Kazdin & Bootzin, 1972; O'Leary, 1978). The behaviors included in the STP point system are those that are commonly targeted for development (e.g., following rules, paying attention) and elimination (e.g., teasing, noncompliance) in children with ADHD, oppositional-defiant disorder (ODD), or conduct disorder (CD). The points that the children earn are exchanged for privileges (e.g., weekly field trips), social honors, and daily home-based rewards.

Counselors record points awarded to and taken from each child throughout the day. The staff members are trained intensively to enable them to administer and record points reliably, thus eliminating the need for costly, independent observers to provide data for clinical research. Frequent checks are conducted to ensure that the records of points given and taken are accurate reflections of the children's behavior and to ensure the clinical integrity of the program.

Positive Reinforcement and Appropriate Commands

Implicit in the implementation of all behavior management systems is the use of positive reinforcement to shape behavior (Martin & Pear, 1992). The forms of positive reinforcement employed in the STP include the point system, parental rewards, and social reinforcement. In particular, social reinforcement in the form of praise and public recognition (buttons, stickers, and posted charts) is ubiquitously employed to provide a positive, supportive atmosphere for the children. In addition to the liberal use of social reinforcement, the staff members attempt to shape appropriate behavior by issuing commands with characteristics (e.g., brevity, specificity) that minimize noncompliance (Forehand & McMahon, 1981; Walker & Walker, 1991).

Peer Interventions

Treatment also includes training in social skills that are thought to be necessary for effective peer group functioning. Social skills training is provided in brief (10 min), daily group sessions. Sessions include instruction, modeling, role-playing, and practice in key social concepts such as communication (Oden & Asher, 1977), as well as more specific skills (Hinshaw, Henker, & Whalen, 1984; Michelsen, Sugai, Wood, & Kazdin, 1983). In addition to these sessions, the children engage in a daily cooperative group task that is designed to promote cooperation and contribute to cohesive peer relationships (Furman & Gavin, 1989).

The children's implementation of the social skills training programs is prompted and reinforced throughout the day using the point system. The combination of a reward/cost program and social skills training has been shown to be necessary to effect the development of social skills in children with externalizing disorders (Bierman, Miller, & Stabb, 1987; Pelham & Bender, 1982). Blending these peer-focused components may be critical to enhancing change and generalization to the natural environment (Bierman, 1989; Walker, Hops, & Greenwood, 1993).

Although this focus on development of peer group skills is consistent with the social skills literature, we have found that normalization of children with ADHD's peer relationships rarely occurs as a result of even this package of interventions. Hence, a primary focus of our recent work has been on the development of intervention efforts focusing on the *dyad* in addition to the child as a member of a peer *group*. The purpose of our Buddy System is to help children develop individual friendships that may "buffer" them from the possible negative effects of being unpopular (e.g., Furman & Robbins, 1985). This is accomplished by assigning each child a buddy with whom their goal is to form a close friendship. The children engage in a variety of activities with their buddies and meet regularly with adult "buddy coaches" who assist them in working out relationship problems.

The children also have sessions in which they learn group problem-solving skills using a procedure that involves problem identification, brainstorming, writing contracts, and evaluating their contracts. The problem-solving approach was developed by Spivak and colleagues (Spivak, Platt, & Shure, 1976), has been applied in other camp-like settings (Rickard & Dinoff, 1965), and is also the basis for individual social problem solving that has been applied in work with aggressive boys (e.g., Lochman & Curry, 1986).

Daily Report Cards

Daily report cards (DRCs) to parents are among the most ubiquitous interventions that have been employed with children with ADHD (Pelham, in press), and numerous studies have documented their effectiveness (e.g., O'Leary, Pelham, Rosenbaum, & Price, 1976). In the STP, DRCs include individualized target behaviors from the classroom and from the group settings. Target behaviors and criteria for meeting daily goals are revised in an ongoing manner. The parents are taught to provide positive consequences to reward the children for reaching DRC goals.

Sports Skills Training

The children receive intensive coaching and practice in sports skills. Children with ADHD typically do not follow the rules of games and have poor motor skills (Pelham, McBurnett, et al., 1990), deficits that contribute to their social rejection and low self-esteem (Pelham & Bender, 1982). Involvement in sports is thought to enhance self-esteem and self-efficacy, which in turn are thought to play a role in behavior change (Smoll, Smith, Barnett, & Everett, 1993; Weiss, 1987). For children with ADHD who are at risk for low self-esteem, such skills training in a positive environment would appear to be particularly important. Thus, three hours per day are devoted to training in small-group skills and play in age-appropriate sports and games. Techniques that are designed to optimize skill training for young children are employed (e.g., American Coaching Effectiveness Program, 1991; Smoll & Smith, 1987). Because of the intensive practice and time that is necessary to effect changes in sports skills, such training cannot be readily conducted in a weekly visit treatment model. Instead, sports skills training is best conducted during the summer or at an after-school program, thus highlighting the value of the STP setting for this program component.

Time Out

The children are disciplined for certain prohibited behaviors (i.e., intentional aggression, intentional destruction of property, repeated non-compliance), with discipline taking the form of loss of privileges (e.g., swim time, computer time) or time out from ongoing activities. Time out from positive reinforcement is a technique that has been used for many years as an alternative to physical punishment (Martin & Pear, 1992; Ross, 1981). Although it might appear preferable to use only positive approaches to working with children with ADHD, recent research by S. O'Leary and colleagues has made it clear that "prudent punishment" (e.g., appropriate verbal reprimands, privilege loss, time out) is necessary for effective intervention (see Pfiffner & O'Leary, 1993, for a review). The time-out program used in the STP differs from others in current use (cf. Barkley, 1990, Patterson, 1975) in that the initial time assigned is relatively long (e.g., 20 mins), but a child may immediately earn a 50% reduction in time for "good behavior." This puts the child in an earning situation even when he or she is being punished; that is, if the child controls his or her behavior, the punishment is reduced.

Classrooms

The children spend one hour daily in a classroom modeled after an academic special education classroom; they spend a second hour in a computer-assisted instructional classroom and a third hour in an art class. Behavior in the classrooms is managed using a relatively simple point system that includes both reward (earning points for work completion and accuracy) and response-cost (losing points for violating classroom rules) components (Carlson, Pelham, Milich, & Dixon, 1992; Pelham, Carlson, et al., 1993). Public recognition and praise are given for assignment completion and for work accuracy, and the time-out system described above is used in the classrooms.

The children receive a variety of assignments during the academic class, individualized according to each child's needs. In the computer-assisted classroom, the children work on a variety of individualized academic skills, using computer-based instruction on Apple computers. In the art class, the children work on a variety of projects. Given that many children with ADHD have behavioral difficulties in special areas in school (e.g., art, music), this class affords a unique opportunity to work on the children's problems in a setting that closely approximates a natural school setting.

Parent Involvement

A lengthy treatment consent form that details all aspects of treatment is used to inform the parents fully about the STP. The parents have almost daily contact with staff members and with each other when they pick up their children at the end of each day. To facilitate transfer of the gains the children make in the STP to the home setting, their parents participate in weekly group training sessions in how to implement behavior modification programs at home. The general procedures that the parents learn in these sessions are the same as those employed in the STP, with modifications to make them practical for the parents to implement. The parent training packages that we employ have been validated as effective with children with externalizing disorders (e.g., Barkley, 1990; Cunningham, Davis, Bremner, Dunn, & Rzasa, 1993; Forehand & McMahon, 1981; Forgatch & Patterson, 1989; Patterson & Forgatch, 1987). At times, the children and their parents work jointly with the parent group leaders. Parental attendance at parent training sessions is routinely nearly 100%.

Medication Assessment

The CNS stimulants ubiquitously prescribed to children with ADHD are generally inadequately assessed and monitored (Gadow, 1986; Pelham, 1993). Many practitioners have subscribed to the procedure of using medication as the primary treatment with the addition of behavioral treatments as necessary; however, this approach is not currently recommended either by the manufacturers of the CNS stimulants (see pp. 513, 866, and 2095, Physicians Desk Reference, 1990) or by most professionals in the field. In the STP, the children for whom medication is appropriate undergo an extensive, double-blind, placebo-controlled evaluation of the effects of stimulant medication—typically methylphenidate (see Pelham, Greenslade, et al., 1990; Pelham & Hoza, 1987; and Pelham & Milich, 1991, for descriptions of procedures). Data gathered routinely in the STP (e.g., point system records) are evaluated to determine whether the medication was helpful. A beneficial effect of medication is one that is substantial beyond the effects of concurrent behavioral interventions. If medication benefited a child on the symptoms that are most important for him or her, without adverse effects, then medication may be recommended as an adjunct to an ongoing behavioral intervention (see Pelham and Milich, 1991; and Pelham, 1993, for further discussion).

Of 258 boys with ADHD treated in the STPs from 1987 through 1992 (see below for definition of this group of 258), 88% participated in STP medication assessments. Continued treatment with psychostimulants was recommended for 68% of those children. For another 13%, medication was recommended if behavioral interventions alone were insufficient in the natural environment.

Monitoring Treatment Response and Treatment Fidelity

Information is gathered daily from the point systems; academic assignments; counselor, teacher, and parent ratings; and direct observational measures and is entered daily into a customized database in Microsoft Excel®. The information is immediately available to staff members and supervisors to monitor each child's response to treatment and the integrity of the treatment program. An extensive set of documented procedures is implemented daily by staff members and supervisors to monitor and ensure treatment fidelity. The staff members meet daily to receive feedback from supervisors, evaluate the children's responses, and to modify treatment strategies if necessary. In addition, at the end of the STP, the staff members and parents rate each child's improvement on standardized measures in multiple domains of functioning, and direct measures of each child's response are gathered. All of these measures are used to evaluate the children's improvement, as well as to ensure the integrity of the treatment program.

Training

Training is an important goal of the STP. Approximately 100 staff members work in each STP. The majority of these are undergraduate and graduate student interns from the United States and Canada, who are supervised by a small permanent staff. Participating students receive experience and small stipends, and some receive academic credit for the STP clinical experience. The staff receive extensive supervision and feedback that shape their clinical and interpersonal skills. Most staff members attend a weekly seminar on clinical research in child psychopathology. Through the summer of 1992, more than 450 students from more than 85 different colleges and universities have worked in the STP. Most of these students have gone on to graduate or medical school, faculty positions, or mental health or educational positions. Many students say that the experience was the best of their training careers, and they virtually unanimously recommend it to others. In our current Western Psychiatric Institute and Clinic (WPIC) setting, training extends to clinical psychology interns, postdoctoral fellows, and psychiatric residents and fellows.

RESEARCH-BASED CLINICAL TREATMENT: AN EVOLUTIONARY APPROACH

In addition to providing treatment and training, the design of the STP facilitates clinical research. Clinical records double as dependent measures in studies. Clinical observations generate research ideas, and results of empirical studies are used to modify subsequent treatment protocols (e.g., Carlson et al., 1992). The treatments employed in the STP are therefore constantly evolving. Through the summer of 1992, more than 60 empirical studies had been conducted in the STP; many of them dissertations or grant-funded projects. These studies addressed a wide variety of questions regarding the nature and treatment of ADHD.

For example, the medication assessment procedure developed in the STP has been used to study the effects of many pharmacological agents and environmental variables. These have included the efficacy of standard (e.g., Pelham, Bender, Caddell, Booth, & Moorer, 1985; Pelham, McBurnett, et al., 1990; Pelham, Murphy, et al., 1992; Pelham, Vodde-Hamilton, Murphy, Greenstein, & Vallano, 1991; Pelham, Walker, Sturges, & Hoza, 1989) and long-acting preparations (Pelham, Greenslade, et al., 1990; Pelham, Sturges, et al., 1987) of CNS stimulants on social and classroom behavior and cognition; the interaction between behavioral and pharmacologic treatment (Carlson et al., 1992; Hoza et al., 1992; Pelham, Bender, et al., 1985; Pelham, Carlson, et al., 1993); the effects of sugar and aspartame on behavior (Milich & Pelham, 1986); and the effects of medication on distractibility in classroom settings (Pelham, Hoza, et al., 1994). Several of these studies have required the development of dependent measures that we have subsequently integrated into our treatment programs, such as the game awareness questions from our study of methylphenidate effects on baseball skills (Pelham, McBurnett, et al., 1990), which are now the attention questions used with all children in the STP. Indeed, the medication assessment procedure that was initially developed to conduct a study (Pelham, Bender, et al., 1985) quickly evolved into our standard clinical practice (Pelham & Hoza, 1987; Pelham & Milich, 1991).

Similarly, the observation that very little lasting change was achieved in the STP as a function of the group-based peer relations interventions employed led to the development of the STP buddy system described above. We are currently in the process of revising the buddy system based on pilot work in recent STPs. Finally, we have been conducting ongoing investigations of treatments for adolescents with ADHD. The format and structure of the STP have been modified based on pilot work conducted in past STPs with children in the 13-to-16-year age range (e.g., Evans & Pelham, 1991; Evans, Pelham, & Grudberg, 1995), and we are in the process of continuing program development and completing further research in this area (e.g., Smith et al., 1995).

FOLLOW-UP TREATMENT

Of course, not even intensive treatment such as the STP would be expected to have lasting effects without appropriate follow-up. The need for continued intervention to ensure generalization or to maintain treatment gains has long been known (Stokes & Baer, 1977), and this is particularly true for children with externalizing disorders. We view the STP as an intensive beginning to a long-term intervention for ADHD, and beginning with the treatment consent form we make it very clear to parents that without continued treatment, the gains their children make in the STP will be short-lived. The follow-up treatment that we offer consists of a Saturday Treatment Program (SatTP), school interventions in the classrooms to which children return after the STP, and parent booster training.

The SatTP is a biweekly program that runs from September through May. The format and goals are similar to that of the STP, with an emphasis on maintenance and generalization. The point system is not employed, with the counselors instead relying on specific feedback, time out, social reinforcement, natural consequences, and DRCs to modify behavior. Continued emphasis is placed on peer relationships and recreational and academic competencies. Parent booster training (cf. Patterson, 1974) consists of individual sessions that are scheduled biweekly or monthly to continue working on the home-based programs that the parents established during the STP. Much of this continued contact focuses on teaching the parents how to interface with schools.

School interventions are established by therapists working directly with teachers. Using procedures that have a long history in the behavioral literature (e.g., O'Leary & O'Leary, 1977; Walker & Walker, 1991) and that have been validated with children with ADHD (O'Leary et al., 1976; O'Leary & Pelham, 1978; Pelham, Schnedler, Bender, et al., 1988; Pelham, Schnedler, Bologna, & Contreras, 1980; Rapport, Murphy, & Bailey, 1982), classroom management programs are developed that include changes in teacher attention, assignment structure, classroom structure, DRCs, and response cost/reward programs. These typically involve 8–12 direct contacts and numerous telephone contacts during the school year.

PRELIMINARY DATA REGARDING EFFICACY

Our strategy during development of the STP has been to document the effectiveness of the individual components rather than of the STP as a treatment package. However, we are now beginning to study the effectiveness of the STP package as a treatment strategy. We present data below that suggest that the STP is a very promising treatment. The data on pre- and posttreatment measures and ratings of improvement are systematically gathered. Because of their pre–post, uncontrolled nature, the data are preliminary and heuristic rather than conclusive.

Sample

A total of 495 children with ADHD attended the STP between 1987 and 1992. The patients were typically referred for treatment by schools, physicians, mental health workers, or parents. Of these, 258 were good diagnostic ADHD cases, all boys of normal intelligence, between the ages of 5 and 12 years and first-time STP participants (data for girls are not presented because they make up a very small percentage of the STP population). We present the data for only these 258 boys, although their results are characteristic of the entire group. The sample is 86% White and 14% nonwhite, closely reflecting the racial distribution of Allegheny County, Pennsylvania, in which Pittsburgh is located. Sixty-seven percent of the children's parents were married; 26% were separated or divorced; and the remainder were widowed or had never married. Family incomes spanned a wide range: 17% earned less than $10,000, 19% earned $10,000–$20,000, 18% earned $20,000–$30,000, 14% earned $30,000–$40,000, and 10% of the sample earned $40,000–$50,000; the remaining 21% earned more than $50,000 annually. Characteristics of the sample on several demographic and diagnostic measures are shown in Table 2. As Table 2 illustrates, the levels of ADHD and other externalizing behaviors shown by the sample were extreme and comparable to other clinical samples from the ADHD treatment literature. The prevalences of comorbid ODD and CD in the sample are comparable to what has been reported in the literature (Hinshaw, 1987).

Overview of Measures

Several measures have been used to address STP efficacy: (a) anonymous consumer satisfaction ratings completed by parents; (b) domain-

TABLE 2
Means and Standard Deviations of Subject Characteristics at Pretreatment for the Entire Sample and for the Aggressive and Nonaggressive Subgroups

Item	Overall M	Overall (SD)	Non-aggressive M	Non-aggressive (SD)	Aggressive M	Aggressive (SD)
Age in months	109.1	22.5	108.8	22.4	109.3	22.7
Full scale IQ[a]	106.4	13.6	106.8	13.3	106.2	13.8
Woodcock–Johnson reading[b]	99.6	14.2	99.6	14.3	99.6	14.3
Woodcock–Johnson arithmetic[b]	101.6	15.6	102.9	16.3	100.8	15.1
Woodcock–Johnson written language[b]	97.5	14.0	96.6	14.8	98.1	13.5
DSM-III-R items endorsed in a parent structured interview						
ADHD	11.3	2.5	10.9	2.5	11.5	2.4
ODD[f]	5.2	2.6	4.3	2.5	5.8	2.4
CD[f]	1.4	1.7	0.7	1.1	1.9	1.9
Abbreviated Conners Rating Scale—Parent[c,f]	19.9	5.4	19.0	5.7	20.6	5.1
Abbreviated Conners Rating Scale—Teacher[f]	18.2	6.2	16.6	5.9	19.4	6.1
IOWA Conners Teacher Rating Scale[d]						
I/O	10.8	3.0	10.7	3.1	10.9	2.9
O/D[f]	6.4	4.7	4.8	4.1	7.5	4.7
Parent Disruptive Behavior Disorders Rating Scale[e]						
ADHD[f]	1.8	0.5	1.8	0.5	1.9	0.5
ODD[f]	1.5	0.7	1.3	0.7	1.7	0.6
CD[f]	0.4	0.3	0.2	0.2	0.4	0.3
Teacher Disruptive Behavior Disorders Rating Scale[e]						
ADHD	1.8	0.6	1.7	0.7	1.8	0.6
ODD[f]	1.2	0.8	0.8	0.7	1.5	0.8
CD[f]	0.3	0.3	0.2	0.2	0.4	0.3

[a]WISC-R. [b]Achievement cluster standard scores for the Woodcock–Johnson Psychoeducational Battery. [c]Goyette, Conners, & Ulrich, 1978. [d]Pelham, Milich, Murphy, & Murphy, 1989. [e]Pelham, Gnagy, Greenslade, & Milich, 1992. [f]Aggressiveness subgroups differed significantly ($p < .05$) on these measures.

specific parent, counselor, and teacher improvement ratings; (c) pre- and posttest child self-perception ratings; (d) pre- and posttest parent ratings on a standardized rating scale and on a problem severity index; and (e) counselor and teacher ratings of "normalcy" as indices of the social validity of treatment effects. Data have been gathered documenting improvement on many other measures, including parental efficacy beliefs, academic productivity, and peer sociometric ratings, but a report of outcome on those measures is beyond the scope of this chapter. Finally, we report data regarding treatment completion rates and cost information—two important factors to consider for any treatment program.

In addition, we investigated individual differences to determine whether the efficacy data characterized our entire sample or primarily the milder of our treatment cases. We examined two variables that are known to be related to severity and outcome among children with ADHD: (a) concurrent child aggression and (b) parental marital status. We also examined treatment effectiveness as a function of age. Finally, to rule out improvement attributable to medication, we analyzed the measures listed above as a function of children's medication response.

Anonymous Parent Ratings of Benefit

At the end of each STP, parents were asked to rate *anonymously* how much the program benefited their child, how much the program benefited them, and how much their child liked the program (90% of the 258 questionnaires were returned). Parents had overwhelmingly positive responses to the program. More than 80% viewed the treatment as very beneficial both for their children and for themselves, and nearly 100% viewed the STP as at least somewhat beneficial. More than 95% of the parents also reported that their children liked the program. These numbers are impressive compared with other outpatient psychosocial and pharmacological treatments for ADHD, which are generally viewed as effective by only 50% to 70% of the patients (cf. Gittelman et al., 1980; Pelham, Schnedler, et al., 1980; 1988). Moreover, the fact that the ratings were anonymous means that a bias to describe positive changes was minimized.

Parent, Counselor, and Teacher Improvement Ratings

At the end of the 1990 through 1992 STPs, counselors, parents, and STP teachers completed improvement ratings for each child across a number of domains. Table 3 presents the results of the parent ratings. As Table 3 illustrates, parents rated an overwhelming majority of the children as improved. Counselor and teacher ratings followed the same pattern (e.g., counselors rated 91% of the children as at least somewhat improved overall). These percentages are considerably better than what is typically obtained in outpatient treatment studies, which report overall improvement rates of 50% to 70% (cf. Gittelman et al., 1980; Pelham, Schnedler, et al., 1988). Furthermore, STP-related improvements occurred not only in traditional target domains (e.g., rule-following, classroom productivity), but also in other domains that we believe are critical to long-term success (e.g., self-esteem, sports skills). It is notable that improvement was reported in all these domains and by multiple informants. Because the parents did not see the children during the STP treatment days, their reports also suggest that there may have been generalization across settings.

TABLE 3
Percentages of Children Rated as Improved by Parents in the 1990, 1991, and 1992 Summer Treatment Programs

Variable	No problem	Very much worse	Much worse	Somewhat worse	Unchanged	Somewhat improved	Much improved	Very much improved
Teasing/aggression	12	0	0	3	6	50	25	4
Sports skills	14	0	0	0	5	30	36	15
Adult-directed defiance/noncompliance	2	1	0	0	3	50	35	10
Following home rules	1	0	0	0	4	53	34	8
Self-esteem	6	0	1	2	7	43	33	9
Happiness	25	0	1	3	13	28	21	9
Responsibility	2	0	0	0	10	49	31	9
Social skills	5	0	0	3	9	54	24	6
Cooperativeness	2	0	0	1	5	50	36	6
Overall improvement	2	1	0	1	1	36	51	9

Note. Percentages are computed from the 114 parents who responded to the questionnaire; the total sample was $N = 132$. Percentages may not total 100 because of rounding error.

The improvement ratings also suggest treatment areas that need further development. For example, sibling/peer relationships, defiance, and following home rules all need further work, according to parents. This is not surprising, as the STP parent training consists of only seven group sessions. Follow-up parent training across a longer period of time is essential. Given that ADHD is a chronic disorder, we have recently argued that treatment models for ADHD need to be developed that last for years rather than weeks and must focus not only on skill acquisition but also on booster training and *relapse prevention* (Pelham, in press). Similarly, counselors rated many children's teasing/aggression as unchanged or only somewhat improved. Given the well-known refractoriness of aggressive behavior, these ratings are not surprising. However, they highlight the fact that we need to continue our efforts to develop more effective interventions for aggressive peer interactions (Bierman, 1989; Krehbiel & Milich, 1986; Pelham & Bender, 1982).

Child Self-Perception and Global Self-worth Ratings

Fifty-six children who participated in the summers of 1991 and 1992 completed the Self-Perception Profile for Children (Harter, 1985) at the beginning and at the end of the STP. The children rated themselves on a 4-point scale in five domains, as well as on global self-worth (higher scores indicate greater competence). The children's self perceptions reflected improvement in all domains. For example, ratings of global self-worth increased from a pretreatment mean of 3.24 (SD = 0.51) to 3.55 (SD = 0.28), $t(55)$ = −3.30, p < .001. It is noteworthy that for behavioral conduct and global self-worth ratings, the effect sizes (post-M–pre-M/pre-SD) were large—.78 and .61, respectively. In comparison, the only study that has examined changes in self-liking and happiness in response to *medication* (Pelham, Murphy, et al., 1992) showed effect sizes ranging from .18 to .47 (M = .33). Thus, the effect of the STP on global self esteem was twice as great as that of MPH.

Relatively few psychosocial treatment studies of children with externalizing disorders have used measures of self-esteem, and when used, less intensive interventions have yielded null or weak effects (e.g., Bierman & Furman, 1984; Lochman, Burch, Curry, & Lampron, 1984; Lochman & Curry, 1986). Of note is that the STP-related changes occurred in every domain of self-perception of competence. Changes in areas such as self-esteem, happiness, and social skills were of particular interest, as these areas may be important mediators of long-term outcome (Harter, 1981, 1983; Weiss, 1987). Interestingly, these areas also reflect what the parents reported about their children's success in and liking of the program; many tell us that the STP was their child's first positive experience in an organized setting with other children or adults. Indeed, in systematic interviews, nearly 100% of the children respond that they would like to return to the STP—not surprising, given the tremendous self-efficacy experience that the STP gives them.

Parent Ratings on a Standardized Rating Scale

Following the 1991 and 1992 STPs, parents completed a DBD Rating Scale (Pelham, Gnagy, et al., 1992). The Disruptive Behavior Disorders Rating Scale lists the *DSM-III-R* (American Psychiatric Association, 1987) symptoms of ADHD, ODD, and CD and uses the response format and scoring weights of the well-known Conners scales (Goyette, Conners, & Ulrich, 1978). A total of 74 parents completed the scales, which were compared to ratings gathered at intake. A MANOVA showed a significant treatment effect, $F(3, 71) = 17.32$, $p < .0001$. Scores on the ADHD scale showed a 24% decrease, from an average pretreatment score of 1.9 to a posttreatment score of 1.45; ODD scores showed a 28% decrease (1.56 to 1.13); and CD scores showed a 35% decrease (0.3 to 0.2). These ratings provide further indication that the STP is an effective intervention. Although such large changes are not unusual with pharmacological treatments, psychosocial interventions typically yield somewhat weaker results. For example, in a recent study of aggressive children (Kazdin, Siegel, & Bass, 1992), parent Child Behavior Checklist (CBCL) total problem ratings showed 10%, 8%, and 13.5% improvements after 6 months of social problem solving, parent training, and their combination, respectively. Clearly, the STP compares favorably to more traditional outpatient interventions in this respect.

In addition to the DBD ratings, the parents completed a narrative description of their child's impairment before and after treatment. The description included a 7-point scale on which the parents rated the degree to which they thought their child overall had "an extreme problem" (6) or "no problem" (0). Scores changed from a mean pretreatment severity rating of 5.4 ($SD = 1.6$) to a mean posttreatment score of 4.4 ($SD = 2.2$), $t(69) = 5.07$, $p<.0001$. Thirty-five boys were rated as having extreme problems at pretreatment, compared to zero boys rated as having no problem. At posttreatment, these numbers changed to 16 and 10, respectively. These are impressive individual changes.

Individual Differences

Concurrent Aggression

It has long been argued that aggressive boys with ADHD respond more poorly to psychosocial treatment than nonaggressive boys. To investigate the effects of comorbid aggression, we grouped the subjects by concurrent aggressiveness and repeated the above analyses. As others have discussed (Hinshaw, 1987), there are numerous ways to define concurrent aggressiveness. As expected in a sample of elementary-aged children, the number of CD diagnoses in our sample was low (cf. Pelham, Murphy, et al., 1992). Therefore, given the demonstrated predictive value of peer-directed aggression, we defined aggressiveness using specific symptoms reflecting peer-directed aggressiveness from a structured parent interview and teacher DBD. We defined a child as being *aggressive* if teachers or parents endorsed either "initiates physical fights" or "is physically cruel to people" at a level of at least "pretty much" (on the DBD) or "moderate problem" (in the structured interview). Using this definition, 150 boys (58%) were defined as being aggressive, and 108 were defined as being nonaggressive (see Table 2 for differences between groups).

On the anonymous parent ratings of benefit, more parents of aggressive children responded that the STP benefited themselves (90% responded "much" or "very much") than parents of nonaggressive children (80% responded "much" or "very much"), $\chi^2 = 10.9$, $p < .05$. When counselor, teacher, and parent ratings of improvement were reanalyzed, there were no effects of aggressive subgroup with the exception of parent-rated improvement in the area of cooperativeness [$F(1, 64) = 4.29$, $p < .05$], in which aggressive children were rated as more improved (M = 5.5) than nonaggressive children (M = 5.1). The aggressive subgroup did not affect child self-perception ratings, parent DBD ratings, or parents' problem severity ratings. Aggressive and nonaggressive boys showed equivalent improvement over pretreatment ratings. Thus, despite the fact that concurrent aggressiveness is associated with a wide range of adverse factors and negative outcomes (Hinshaw, 1987), the effects of the STP are *the same as or more positive* for children with concurrent aggressiveness than for nonaggressive children with ADHD.

Age

To examine whether treatment efficacy varied as a function of the age of the treated children, the above analyses were also repeated using a median age split (median = 9.0 years). The only measures that differed as a function of age were counselor improvement ratings, where the older children were rated as improving more than the younger children [MANOVA $F(15, 92) = 1.93$, $p < .05$], and global parent ratings of problem severity, $F(1, 68) = 4.37$, $p < .05$, where younger children showed greater improvement than older children. There were no other age differences on the measures described above, and age did not interact with aggressiveness grouping.

Family Characteristics

Considerable data have shown that treatment for children with disruptive behavior problems is generally less successful with single-parent households (Dumas & Wahler, 1985), and it might thus be expected that children of single parents would show less improvement in the STP than children of intact families. Thus, the above analyses were repeated comparing married parents with single parents (separated, widowed, divorced, or never married). On all measures, children from single-parent households improved as much as children from intact families. In addition, single-parent families were as likely as married couples and their children to remain in treatment in the STP. These findings are unique in the field of child psychotherapy and suggest that something about the STP that other treatments lack has a positive effect on single-parent families. It is likely that the supportive "community" environment of the STP, daily interaction with staff, and the parental stress relief provided by an 8-week daily treatment program contribute to this effect.

Medication Response

As noted above, 88% of these 258 boys underwent a double-blind, placebo-controlled clinical medication assessment as part of their STP treatment. To ensure that the changes reported were not a function of medication, we reanalyzed the data comparing children who were medicated and who were positive responders with children who were medicated but who were not positive responders, or who did not participate in medication assessments. There were no differences between these groups on any of the measures. In other words, the positive changes interpreted as resulting from the STP are not due to a subset of children who were responding positively to medication during STP assessments.

Social Validity Ratings of Treatment Impact

These improvement rates and rating scale changes are commendable, but consideration of the STP as an intervention must include an evaluation of the social validity of treatment effects (McMahon & Forehand, 1983). Noteworthy as an index of social validity is that almost without exception, the parents of the 258 boys reported on the anonymous rating forms that they would send their children again if given the opportunity (82% would definitely; 13% would probably) and that they would definitely recommend the program to other parents (93%; another 6% would probably recommend the program). Furthermore, the children liked the treatment and virtually unanimously expressed a desire to return in subsequent summers. Although there have been many studies in which treatment satisfaction has been measured (see McMahon & Forehand, 1983, for a review), we do not know of other studies that have asked clients whether they would repeat the treatment or recommend it to others. These criteria appear to us to be the gold standard of social validity, and, as the data show, the

STP fares well in that respect. Regarding individual differences, the parents of aggressive children were more likely to say that they would definitely send their children again (89% of the respondents) than were the parents of nonaggressive children (74%), $\chi^2 = 13.4$, $p < .01$. The parents' responses to the other items did not differ, and responses did not differ as a function of marital status or child age.

At the same time, the ratings of "normalcy" that the counselors and teachers completed warrant mention. Our goal, after all, is to make the children indistinguishable from their nondeviant peers. The counselors and teachers rated the children's behavior toward adults and toward peers on a scale from 1 ("Not at all like a normal child") to 7 ("Like a normal child"). The counselors rated fewer than 15% of the children in the two highest categories, and the teachers rated fewer than 50% of the children in those two categories. Thus, despite the fact that the counselors and teachers rated the children as *improved*, they nonetheless viewed the majority of the children as remaining some distance away from completely normal child behavior. The ratings did not differ as a function of child age, aggressiveness, or family characteristics. These data are consistent with what others have reported for outpatient behavioral interventions, and when viewed in the context of the intensity of the STP intervention, they are sobering findings. They clearly demonstrate the need for long-term, comprehensive treatments for ADHD, including intensive follow-up.

We have shown in a recent study conducted in the STP classroom (Pelham, Carlson, et al., 1993) that these ratings of "normalcy" are dramatically improved for children in a combined pharmacological–behavioral treatment compared to a behavioral treatment alone (see also Gittelman et al., 1980; and Pelham, Schnedler, et al., 1988). This may be particularly true for the peer relationship domain, in which our behavioral treatments have had relatively less impact but on which the acute effects of medication are dramatic (Whalen & Henker, 1991). This highlights the potential advantage of long-term combined treatments. Indeed, our recommendation of medication combined with behavioral follow-ups for 81% of our STP cases reflects our confidence in this approach (see Pelham, 1989; Pelham & Hinshaw, 1992; and Pelham & Murphy, 1986, for reviews of combined treatment).

Treatment Completion Rate

Finally, it should be noted that a major difference between the STP and other treatment programs is that our dropout rate is extremely low. Of the 495 children with ADHD who attended the STPs from 1987 through 1992, only 13 dropped out or were terminated before the summer ended, yielding a completion rate of 97.4%. Most outpatient treatment programs for children with disruptive behavior disorders have treatment completion rates far below this level, with dropout approaching 50% in many studies (Kazdin et al., 1992; Miller & Prinz, 1990). Furthermore, dropout is the major problem with single mothers' response to parent training (Dumas & Wahler, 1985). The remarkably low STP dropout rate (across family marital status and income level) is one of the most salient characteristics of the STP. A prerequisite to a successful long-term intervention is successful completion of the initial stage of treatment, and the STP virtually ensures that outcome.

COSTS AND BENEFITS

We believe that these preliminary data go a long way toward suggesting that summer treatment programs are a useful, intensive approach to treating ADHD. However, among the primary considerations of the utility of such intensive treatment is whether it provides sufficient incremental effectiveness (beyond, for example, traditional outpatient treatment) to justify the cost of its use. We do not have data regarding this point, but are pursuing that question in our current research. An 8-week STP in the United States can be provided for approximately $3,000 (in 1993 U.S. dollars) per child ($75.00 per day). Innovative staffing arrangements (e.g., course credit rather than salary for some staff) and collaborative arrangements with local school districts (e.g., to loan space or computers) can often reduce this figure to as low as $2,000. STP staffing arrangements depend heavily on college students working for credit and low salaries under the supervision of a small number of permanent staff members. Although it might be argued that this is a limitation of the program because of a perceived small supply of student employees, we do not believe this to be the case. Given that there are more than 2,000 colleges and universities in the United States, virtually all of which have psychology and education programs, it is not difficult to find interested students to staff a summer program. Indeed, the thousands of regular summer camps across the United States are staffed by high school and college students working under similar arrangements. Many students are interested in completing a summer internship in a unique setting such as the STP; our site regularly receives 5–10 applications for every position, and students are willing to work for small stipends or course credit to receive such intensive clinical training.

Comprehensive follow-up to an STP can cost an additional $2,000 per case for 9 months. The cost of follow-up treatment is relatively more expensive on a per-hour basis than the STP due to the fact that more of the treatment delivery is shifted from the paraprofessional-based STP treatment in a group setting to individual, therapist-based treatment for follow-up. For example, follow-up parent training is often conducted individually due to the difficulty of coordinating parents' schedules for groups during the school year. We are currently working to develop procedures to reduce the follow-up costs. For example, BA-level clinicians with an educational background are as effective as PhDs in working with teachers to implement classroom interventions with disruptive children (Kent & O'Leary, 1977), so we are attempting to lower our follow-up costs by utilizing BA-level clinicians, who cost considerably less than PhDs. We anticipate that with greater use of students and BA-level paraprofessionals, we will be able to reduce the cost of follow-up treatment to $1,500. Thus, using the most cost effective model, for $3,500 per child we can provide an intensive and comprehensive treatment for ADHD that consists of an 8-week STP; a medication assessment; 12 to 15 sessions of parent training; a 25-week Saturday program; and a year-long, consultant-assisted, teacher implemented classroom intervention.

Although this might seem a large sum for 1 year of treatment, $5,000 is roughly the cost of weekly sessions of individual therapy for 1 year. We would willingly contrast our treatment to individual therapy in a cost–benefit analysis. If it can be documented that participation in intensive treatment that includes an STP decreases the probability that a child with ADHD will need special education services or have later contact with the juvenile justice system, then the utility and cost effectiveness of STP treatments will be clear. For example, 5 to 7 years of such intensive treatment could be provided for what it typically costs for 1 year of residential treatment or incarceration for an adolescent. A cost utility analysis of this intensive treatment approach is warranted.

REPLICABILITY

Finally, an important question regarding such a comprehensive and complex intervention as the STP is whether it can be replicated. Internally, of course, we have replicated the STP many times. In this chapter, we report on seven consecutive cohorts consisting of different children treated using common methods by seven different staffs. These replications should increase confidence in the internal validity of our admittedly uncontrolled results. Beyond internal replication, however, unless the STP can be replicated in other academic and nonacademic settings, its usefulness is limited.

Although we have operated in both in a psychology department and a medical school, it should be noted that the STP cannot be run out of the physical space of a hospital; a school or camp-like setting is required. At WPIC, we rent a local school for the summer (as do the other sites noted below) and have found that arrangement to be quite satisfactory.

The most basic requirement of programmatic replication is that the procedures are completely documented in detail, and we have done that for the STP. The treatment procedures are detailed in a 400-page manual that is updated annually. All of the forms that are necessary to track a child's progress from intake through final report writing have been developed. A comprehensive set of procedures for ensuring treatment integrity exists, and a customized computer data base that tracks all information on each child on a daily basis has been established. In other words, the program development has been completed, and the STP is ready for clinical settings that do not have the intensive resources that are required for development. With the kind of staff that we use at WPIC (a mix of summer student interns and permanent supervisors), these materials can be easily used to duplicate the STP at other sites.

In recent years, three sites have replicated the STP—a private psychiatric hospital in Houston, Texas, and the medical schools of Emory University (Psychiatry) and Vanderbilt University (Pediatrics). We have typically provided consultation and training in the first year to supplement the program manual and materials; in subsequent years, other sites have taken over complete responsibility for the STP. Using the same staffing pattern and the extensive STP programming materials that we have developed, all three sites have reported very high levels of parent and professional satisfaction with the program. Although the only nonacademic site is the Texas program, plans to establish STPs are currently underway in a wide variety of nonacademic settings, and further information on replicability in nonacademic settings should be forthcoming. It is our belief that the STP can be adapted to almost any setting concerned with treating children with ADHD where appropriate resources for follow-up are available, including mental health centers, school districts, group private practices, and hospitals.

Perhaps reflecting our confidence in its efficacy and potential, in 1993 the STP was selected in a national competition as 1 of 20 model programs for service delivery for child and family mental health by the section on Clinical Child Psychology (Section 1, Division 12) and Division of Child, Youth, and Family Services of the American Psychological Association. In addition, our STP has been integrated as one of the three components of the psychosocial treatments of the National Institute of Mental Health, U.S. Office of Education multimodal treatment study of children with attention deficit hyperactivity disorder. During that study, with consultation from our staff at the University of Pittsburgh, the STP is to be replicated in 1994, 1995, and 1996 at the other five sites of the study (the universities of California at Berkeley and at Irvine, Columbia University, Duke University, Long Island Jewish Medical Center, and Montreal Children's Hospital) in combination with intensive parent training and school interventions.

SUMMARY AND FUTURE DIRECTIONS

Effective treatment for ADHD needs to be comprehensive, effective across domains of functioning, long term, and intensive. As we have outlined above, intensive summer treatment programs offer the potential for unique combinations of intensive treatment components that focus on self, peer, academic, and home domains. Although uncontrolled and therefore admittedly preliminary, we have presented data regarding the STP's short-term effectiveness in each of these critical domains. The STP packs 360 hours of treatment (equivalent to *seven years* of weekly social skills training sessions) into an 8-week period. We believe that such massively intensive regimens are needed to change the trajectory of most children with ADHD. We believe that intensive summer programs in combination with outpatient home- and school-based follow-up will result in more comprehensive treatments with greater impact and more lasting effects than treatments in current use for ADHD. Of course, whether this is true is an empirical question, and additional research is clearly warranted. Future research should emphasize five areas: (a) demonstrating differential effectiveness of this treatment, (b) investigating maintenance of initial treatment gains, (c) analyzing the effective components of this intervention, (d) determining why the treatment appears to be effective with single-parent families and aggressive children, and (e) evaluating the cost–usefulness of the approach. We hope that this chapter has served to stimulate an interest in this approach to intensive treatment for ADHD.

REFERENCES

American Coaching Effectiveness Program. (1991). *Rookie Coaches Basketball Guide*. Champaign, IL: Leisure Press.

American Psychiatric Association. (1987). *Diagnostic and statistical manual of mental disorders* (3rd ed., rev.). Washington, DC: Author.

Barkley, R. A. (1990). *Attention deficit hyperactivity disorder: A handbook for diagnosis and treatment*. New York: Guilford Press.

Barkley, R. A., Fischer, M., Edelbrock, C. S., & Smallish, L. (1990). The adolescent outcome of hyperactive children diagnosed by research criteria: I. An 8-year prospective follow-up study. *Journal of the American Academy of Child and Adolescent Psychiatry, 29*, 546–557.

Bierman, K. L. (1989). Improving the peer relationships of rejected children. In B. B. Lahey & A. E. Kazdin (Eds.), *Advances in clinical child psychology* (pp. 53–84). New York: Plenum Press.

Bierman, K. L., & Furman, W. (1984). The effects of social skills training and peer involvement on the social adjustment of preadolescents. *Child Development, 55*, 151–162.

Bierman, K. L., Miller, C. L., & Stabb, S. D. (1987). Improving the social behavior and peer acceptance of rejected boys: Effects of social skill training with instructions and prohibitions. *Journal of Consulting and Clinical Psychology, 55,* 194–200.

Carlson, C. L., & Lahey, B. B. (1988). Behavior classroom interventions with children exhibiting conduct disorders or attention deficit disorders with hyperactivity. In J. C. Witt, S. M. Elliott, & F. M. Gresham (Eds.), *The handbook of behavior therapy in education* (pp. 653–677). New York: Plenum Press.

Carlson, C. L., Pelham, W. E., Milich, R., & Dixon, M. J. (1992). Single and combined effects of methylphenidate and behavior therapy on the classroom behavior, academic performance and self-evaluations of children with attention deficit–hyperactivity disorder. *Journal of Abnormal Child Psychology, 20,* 213–232.

Cunningham, C. E., Davis, J. R., Bremner, R., Dunn, K. W., & Rzasa, T. (1993). Coping modeling problem solving versus mastery modeling: Effects on adherence, in-session process, and skill acquisition in a residential parent training program. *Journal of Consulting and Clinical Psychology, 61,* 871–877.

Davilla, R. R., Williams, M. L., & MacDonald, J. T. (1991). *Clarification of policy to address the needs of children with attention deficit disorders within general and/ or special education.* Memo from the United States Department of Education, Washington, DC.

Dumas, J. E., & Wahler, R. G. (1985). Indiscriminate mothering as a contextual factor in aggressive–oppositional child behavior: "Damned if you do and damned if you don't." *Journal of Abnormal Child Psychology, 13,* 1–17.

Evans, S. W., & Pelham, W. E. (1991). Psychostimulant effects on academic and behavioral measures for junior high school students in a lecture format classroom. *Journal of Abnormal Child Psychology, 19,* 537–552.

Evans, S. W., Pelham, W. E., & Grudberg, M. V. (1995). The efficacy of notetaking to improve behavior and comprehension with ADHD adolescents. *Exceptionality, 5,* 1–17.

Forehand, R. E., & McMahon, R. J. (1981). *Helping the noncompliant child. A clinician's guide to parent training.* New York: Guilford Press.

Forgatch, M. S., & Patterson, G. R. (1989). *Parents and adolescents living together: Part 2. Family problem solving.* Eugene, OR: Castalia.

Furman, W., & Gavin, L. A. (1989). Peers' influence on adjustment and development: A view from the intervention literature. In T. J. Berndt & G. W. Ladd (Eds.), *Peer relationships in child development* (pp. 319–340). New York: Wiley.

Furman, W., & Robbins, P. (1985). What's the point? Issues in the selection of treatment objectives. In B. H. Schneider, K. H. Rubin, & J. E. Ledingham (Eds.), *Children's peer relations: Issues in assessment and intervention* (pp. 41–54). New York: Springer-Verlag.

Gadow, K. D. (1986). *Children on medication: Hyperactivity, learning disabilities, and mental retardation: Volume 1.* San Diego, CA: College Hill Press.

Goyette, C. H., Conners, C. K., & Ulrich, R. F. (1978). Normative data on revised Conners Parent and Teacher Rating Scales. *Journal of Abnormal Child Psychology*, 6, 221–236.

Gittelman, R., Abikoff, H., Pollack, E., Klein, D. F., Katz, S., & Mattes, J. (1980). A controlled trial of behavior modification and methylphenidate in hyperactive children. In C. K. Whalen and B. Henker (Eds.), *Hyperactive children: The social ecology of identification and treatment* (pp. 221–243). San Diego, CA: Academic Press.

Harter, S. (1981). A model of intrinsic mastery motivation in children: Individual differences and developmental change. In W. A. Collins (Ed.), *Minnesota symposium on child psychology* (Vol. 14, pp. 215–255). Hillsdale, NJ: Erlbaum.

Harter, S. (1983). The development of the self-system. In M. Hetherington (Ed.), *Handbook of child psychology: Social and personality development* (Vol. 4, pp. 275–385). New York: Wiley.

Harter, S. (1985). Self-perception profile for children. Unpublished manuscript, University of Denver, CO.

Hinshaw, S. P. (1987). On the distinction between attentional deficits/hyperactivity and conduct problems/aggression in child psychopathology. *Psychological Bulletin*, 101, 443–463.

Hinshaw, S. P., Henker, B., & Whalen, C. K. (1984). Self-control in hyperactive boys in anger-inducing situations: Effects of cognitive–behavioral training and of methylphenidate. *Journal of Abnormal Child Psychology*, 12, 55–77.

Hoza, B., Pelham, W. E., Sams, S. E., & Carlson, C. L. (1992). An examination of the "dosage" effects of both behavior therapy and methylphenidate on the classroom performance of two children with ADHD. *Behavior Modification*, 16, 164–192.

Kazdin, A. E. (1987). Treatment of antisocial behavior in children: Current status and future directions. *Psychological Bulletin*, 102, 187–203.

Kazdin, A. E., & Bootzin, R. R. (1972). The token economy: An evaluative review. *Journal of Applied Behavior Analysis*, 3, 343–372.

Kazdin, A. E., Siegel, T. C., & Bass, D. (1992). Cognitive problem-solving skills training and parent management training in the treatment of antisocial behavior in children. *Journal of Consulting and Clinical Psychology*, 60, 733–747.

Kent, R. N., & O'Leary, D. (1977). Treatment of conduct problem children: BA and/or Ph.D. therapists. *Behavior Therapy*, 8, 653–658.

Krehbiel, G., & Milich, R. (1986). Issues in the assessment and treatment of socially rejected children. In R. Prinz (Ed.), *Advances in behavioral assessment of children and families* (Vol. 2, pp. 249–270). Greenwich, CT: JAI Press.

Lochman, J. E., Burch, P. R., Curry, J. F., & Lampron, L. B. (1984). Treatment and generalization effects of cognitive–behavioral and goal-setting interventions with aggressive boys. *Journal of Consulting and Clinical Psychology*, 52, 915–916.

Lochman, J. E., & Curry, J. F. (1986). Effects of social problem-solving training and self-instruction training with aggressive boys. *Journal of Clinical Child Psychology, 15,* 159–164.

Mannuzza, S., Gittelman-Klein, R., Konig, P. H., & Giampino, T. L. (1989). Hyperactive boys almost grown up: Part 4. Criminality and its relationship to psychiatric status. *Archives of General Psychiatry, 46,* 1073–1079.

Martin, G., & Pear, J. (1992). *Behavior modification: What it is and how to do it.* Englewood Cliffs, NJ: Prentice Hall.

McMahon, R. J., & Forehand, R. L. (1983). Consumer satisfaction in behavioral treatment of children: Types, issues, and recommendations. *Behavior Therapy, 14,* 209–225.

Michelsen, L., Sugai, D., Wood, R., & Kazdin, A. E. (1983). *Social skills assessment and training with children and adolescents.* New York: Plenum Press.

Milich, R., & Pelham, W. E. (1986). A naturalistic investigation of the effects of sugar ingestion on the behavior of attention deficit disordered boys. *Journal of Consulting and Clinical Psychology, 54,* 714–718.

Miller, G. E., & Prinz, R. J. (1990). Enhancement of social learning family interventions for childhood conduct disorder. *Psychological Bulletin, 108,* 291–307.

Oden, S., & Asher, S. R. (1977). Coaching children in social skills for friendship making. *Child Development, 48,* 495–506.

O'Leary, K. D. (1978). The operant and social psychology of token systems. In A. C. Catania & T. A. Brigham (Eds.), *Handbook of applied behavior analysis: Social and instructional processes* (pp. 179–207). New York: Irvington.

O'Leary, K. D., & O'Leary, S. G. (1977). *Classroom management: The successful use of behavior modification* (2nd ed.). Elmsford, NY: Pergamon Press.

O'Leary, K. D., Pelham, W. E., Rosenbaum, A., & Price, G. (1976). Behavioral treatment of hyperkinetic children: An experimental evaluation of its usefulness. *Clinical Pediatrics, 15,* 510–515.

O'Leary, S. G., & Pelham, W. E. (1978). Behavior therapy and withdrawal of stimulant medication with hyperactive children. *Pediatrics, 61,* 211–217.

Patterson, G. R. (1974). Interventions for boys with conduct problems: Multiple settings, treatments, and criteria. *Journal of Consulting and Clinical Psychology, 42,* 471–481.

Patterson, G. R. (1975). *Families: Application of social learning to family life.* Champaign, IL: Research Press.

Patterson, G. R., & Forgatch, M. S. (1987). *Parents and adolescents living together: Part 1. The basics.* Eugene, OR: Castalia.

Pelham, W. E. (1989). Behavior therapy, behavioral assessment, and psychostimulant medication in treatment of attention deficit disorders: An interactive approach. In J. Swanson & L. Bloomingdale (Eds.), *Attention deficit disorders: Part 4. Current concepts and emerging trends in attentional and behavioral disorders of childhood* (pp. 169–195). Elmsford, NY: Pergamon Press.

Pelham, W. E. (1993). Pharmacotherapy for children with attention-deficit hyperactivity disorder. *School Psychology Review, 22*, 199–227.

Pelham, W. E. (1994). *Children's summer day treatment program 1994 program manual.* Unpublished manuscript, Western Psychiatric Institute and Clinic, University of Pittsburgh Medical Center, Pittsburgh, PA.

Pelham, W. E. (in press). *Attention deficit/hyperactivity disorder: A practitioner's guide to comprehensive diagnosis, assessment, and treatment.* New York: Plenum Press.

Pelham, W. E., & Bender, M. E. (1982). Peer relationships in hyperactive children: Description and treatment. In K. Gadow & I. Bialer (Eds.), *Advances in learning and behavioral disabilities* (Vol. 1, pp. 365–436). Greenwich, CT: JAI Press.

Pelham, W. E., Bender, M. E., Caddell, J., Booth, S., & Moorer, S. (1985). The dose-response effects of methylphenidate on classroom academic and social behavior in children with attention deficit disorder. *Archives of General Psychiatry, 42*, 948–952.

Pelham, W. E., Carlson, C., Sams, S. E., Vallano, G., Dixon, M. J., & Hoza, B. (1993). Separate and combined effects of methylphenidate and behavior modification on the classroom behavior and academic performance of ADHD boys: Group effects and individual differences. *Journal of Consulting and Clinical Psychology, 61*, 506–515.

Pelham, W. E., Gnagy, E. M., Greenslade, K. E., & Milich, R. (1992). Teacher ratings of *DSM-III-R* symptoms for the disruptive behavior disorders. *Journal of the American Academy of Child and Adolescent Psychiatry, 31*, 210–218.

Pelham, W. E., Greenslade, K. E., Vodde-Hamilton, M. A., Murphy, D. A., Greenstein, J. J., Gnagy, E. M., Guthrie, K. J., Hoover, M.D., & Dahl, R. E. (1990). Relative efficacy of long-acting CNS stimulants on children with attention deficit–hyperactivity disorder: A comparison of standard methylphenidate, sustained-release methylphenidate, sustained-release dextroamphetamine, and pemoline. *Pediatrics, 86*, 226–237.

Pelham, W. E., & Hinshaw, S. (1992). Behavioral intervention for attention deficit disorder. In S. M. Turner, K. S. Calhoun, & H. E. Adams (Eds.), *Handbook of Clinical Behavior Therapy* (Vol. 2, pp. 259–283). New York: Wiley.

Pelham, W. E., & Hoza, J. (1987). Behavioral assessment of psychostimulant effects on ADD children in a Summer Day Treatment Program. In R. Prinz (Ed.), *Advances in behavioral assessment of children and families* (Vol. 3, pp. 3–33). Greenwich, CT: JAI Press.

Pelham, W. E., Hoza, B., Sams, S. E., Gnagy, E. M., Greiner, A., Waschbusch, D. A., & Vallano, G. (1994, June). *Rock music and video movies as distractors for ADHD boys in the classroom: Comparison with controls, individual differences, and medication effects.* Poster session presented at the annual meeting of the Society for Research in Child and Adolescent Psychopathology, London.

Pelham, W. E., McBurnett, K., Harper, G., Milich, R., Clinton, J., Thiele, C., & Murphy, D. A. (1990). Methylphenidate and baseball playing in ADD children: Who's on first? *Journal of Consulting and Clinical Psychology, 58*, 130–133.

Pelham, W. E., & Milich, R. (1984). Peer relationships in hyperactive children. *Journal of Learning Disabilities, 17,* 560–567.

Pelham, W. E., & Milich, R. (1991). Individual differences in response to Ritalin in classwork and social behavior. In L. Greenhill & B. P. Osman (Eds.), *Ritalin: Theory and patient management* (pp. 203–221). New York: MaryAnn Liebert, Inc.

Pelham, W. E., & Murphy, D. A. (1986). Attention deficit and conduct disorders. In M. Hersen (Ed.), *Pharmacological and behavioral treatment: An integrative approach* (pp. 108–148). New York: Wiley.

Pelham, W. E., Milich, R., Murphy, D. A., & Murphy, H. A. (1989). Normative data on the IOWA Conners teacher rating scale. *Journal of Clinical Child Psychology, 18,* 259–262.

Pelham, W. E., Murphy, D. A., Vannatta, K., Milich, R., Licht, B. G., Gnagy, E. M., Greenslade, K. E., Greiner, A. R., & Vodde-Hamilton, M. (1992). Methylphenidate and attributions in boys with attention deficit–hyperactivity disorder. *Journal of Consulting and Clinical Psychology, 60,* 282–292.

Pelham, W. E., Schnedler, R. W., Bender, M. E., Miller, J., Nilsson, D., Budrow, M., Ronnei, M., Paluchowski, C., & Marks, D. (1988). The combination of behavior therapy and methylphenidate in the treatment of hyperactivity: A therapy outcome study. In L. Bloomingdale (Ed.), *Attention deficit disorders* (Vol. 3, pp. 29–48). Elmsford, NY: Pergamon Press.

Pelham, W. E., Schnedler, R. W., Bologna, N., & Contreras, A. (1980). Behavioral and stimulant treatment of hyperactive children: A therapy study with methylphenidate probes in a within-subject design. *Journal of Applied Behavior Analysis, 13,* 221–236.

Pelham, W. E., Sturges, J., Hoza, J., Schmidt, C., Bijlsma, J., Milich, R., & Moorer, S. (1987). Sustained release and standard methylphenidate effects on cognitive and social behavior in children with attention deficit disorder. *Pediatrics, 80,* 491–501.

Pelham, W. E., Vodde-Hamilton, M., Murphy, D. A., Greenstein, J., & Vallano, G. (1991). The effects of methylphenidate on ADHD adolescents in recreational, peer group, and classroom settings. *Journal of Clinical Child Psychology, 20,* 293–300.

Pelham, W. E., Walker, J. L., Sturges, J., & Hoza, J. (1989). The comparative effects of methylphenidate on ADD girls and boys. *Journal of the American Academy of Child and Adolescent Psychiatry, 28,* 773–776.

Pfiffner, L. J., & O'Leary, S. G. (1993). Psychological treatments: School-based. In J. L. Matson (Ed.), *Hyperactivity in children: A handbook.* Elmsford, NY: Pergamon Press.

Physician's desk reference. (1990). Oradell, NJ: Medical Economics.

Rapport, M. D., Murphy, H. A., & Bailey, J. S. (1982). Ritalin vs. response cost in the control of hyperactive children: A within-subject comparison. *Journal of Applied Behavior Analysis, 15,* 205–216.

Rickard, H. C., & Dinoff, M. (1965). Shaping adaptive behavior in a therapeutic summer camp. In L. P. Ullman & L. Krasner (Eds.), *Case studies in behavior modification* (pp. 325–328). New York: Holt, Rinehart & Winston.

Ross, A. O. (1981). *Child behavior therapy: Principles, procedures, and empirical basis.* New York: Wiley.

Smith, B. H., Pelham, W. E., Evans, S. E., Molina, B. M., Eggers, S. E., Willoughby, M. T., Owens, S. E., Paul, D., Bukstein, O., Vallano, G., & Presnell, M. (1995, April). *Assessing the effects of methylphenidate on adolescents diagnosed with Attention-Deficit Hyperactivity Disorder.* Paper presented at the Fifth Florida Conference on Child Health Psychology, Gainesville, FL.

Smoll, F. L., & Smith, R. E. (1987). *Sports Psychology for Youth Coaches.* Washington, DC: National Federation for Catholic Ministry.

Smoll, F. L., Smith, R. E., Barnett, N. P., & Everett, J. J. (1993). Enhancement of children's self-esteem through social support training for youth sport coaches. *Journal of Applied Psychology, 78,* 602–610.

Spivak, G., Platt, J. J., & Shure, M. B. (1976). *The problem solving approach to adjustment.* San Francisco: Jossey-Bass.

Stokes, T. F., & Baer, D. M. (1977). An implicit technology of generalization. *Journal of Applied Behavior Analysis, 10,* 349.

Walker, H. M., Hops, H., & Greenwood, C. R. (1993). *RECESS: Reprogramming environmental contingencies for effective social skills.* Seattle, WA: Educational Achievement Systems.

Walker, H. M., & Walker, J. E. (1991). *Coping with noncompliance in the classroom: A positive approach for teachers.* Austin, TX: Pro-Ed.

Weiss, G., & Hechtman, L. (1986). *Hyperactive Children Grown Up.* New York: Guilford Press.

Weiss, M. R. (1987). Self-esteem and achievement in children's sport and physical activity. In D. Gould & M. R. Weiss (Eds.), *Advances in pediatric sport sciences: Part 2. Behavioral issues* (pp. 87–119).

Whalen, C. K., & Henker, B. (1991). The social impact of stimulant treatment for hyperactive children. *Journal of Learning Disabilities, 24,* 193–256.

16

MULTIMODAL THERAPY AND STIMULANTS IN THE TREATMENT OF CHILDREN WITH ATTENTION DEFICIT HYPERACTIVITY DISORDER

HOWARD B. ABIKOFF and LILY HECHTMAN

Most children with attention deficit hyperactivity disorder (ADHD) come to the attention of mental health professionals because of multiple difficulties in school, home, or both settings. For example, in spite of normal intelligence, ADHD youngsters often underachieve in school. This occurs because the primary symptoms of the disorder—excessive motor activity, poor sustained attention, and impulsivity—coupled with the children's distractibility, difficulty in following instructions, and disorganization, all contribute to academic difficulties. In addition, because children with ADHD frequently have poor social skills (Whalen & Henker, 1985), significant interpersonal problems with family, peers, and teachers are also common. Not surprisingly, these difficulties may give rise to poor self-esteem (Weiss, Hechtman, Perlman, Hopkins, & Wener, 1975). These problems are often compounded and amplified by significant comorbidity such as oppositional defiant disorder, conduct disorder, and mood, anxiety, and learning disorders (Abikoff & Klein, 1992; August & Garfinkel, 1989; Biederman, Newcorn, & Sprich, 1991; Bird, Camino, Rubio-Stipic, et al., 1988).

Support for this study was provided by grant MH44848 to H. Abikoff and grant 3RO1 MH44842.0551 to L. Hechtman from the National Institute of Mental Health. Correspondence concerning this chapter should be addressed to Dr. Howard B. Abikoff, Division of Child and Adolescent Psychiatry, Schnider Children's Hospital, Long Island Jewish Medical Center, New Hyde Park, NY 11042.

The most commonly used and best studied treatments for ADHD include stimulant medication, behavior therapy, and cognitive–behavior therapy. The following sections provide a brief overview of these standard treatments.

STIMULANT TREATMENT

The multiple impairments in children with ADHD suggest the need for diverse interventions. Yet, both in current clinical practice and early studies, most children have received only stimulant medication. Although stimulant treatment has limitations, the most important of which are described later, it should be emphasized that the merits of stimulant medication have long been recognized. For example, the short-term clinical effectiveness of stimulants has been studied extensively (see review by Klein, 1987), and a recent report (Elia, Borcherding, Rapoport, & Kayser, 1991) concluded that more than 90% of ADHD children respond favorably to either Ritalin or Dexedrine. With medication, most ADHD youths become more attentive, less impulsive and disruptive, and less overactive in situations in which they need to regulate their activity (Abikoff & Gittelman, 1985c). Additionally, the productivity and accuracy of their academic work improves (Carlson, Pelham, Milich, & Dixon, 1992; Douglas, Barr, O'Neill, & Britton, 1986), and teachers and parents interact more positively with stimulant treated ADHD children (Barkley & Cunningham, 1979; Whalen, Henker, & Dotemoto, 1980; see review by Whalen & Henker, 1991). In some cases, the improvements with medication are so dramatic that the youngsters are able to be maintained in regular classes and do not require special class placement.

The substantial benefits of stimulants notwithstanding, these are not a complete remedy for the disorder. Medication alone does not enhance unmastered social and academic skills, nor does it appear to improve academic achievement. Furthermore, because the most frequently used stimulants are short-acting and are typically given twice-a-day, their effects invariably have worn off by the time the child arrives home from school; consequently, parents often have to deal with child management problems at home. Finally, and perhaps the most important treatment concern, pertains to the lack of sustained and long-term effects of stimulants. Specifically, the positive changes associated with treatment are frequently not maintained when medication is discontinued (Abikoff & Gittelman, 1985b; Gittelman-Klein, Klein, Katz, Saraf, & Pollack, 1976), and there is little evidence that children who receive long-term stimulant treatment have a substantially different outcome from children with ADHD who do not receive such treatment. Follow-up studies of children treated with stimulants indicate that most of these youths continue to have significant academic, social, and emotional problems in adolescence (Charles & Schain, 1981; Weiss et al., 1975) and in young adulthood (Gittelman, Mannuzza, Shenkar, & Bonagura, 1985; Hechtman, Weiss, & Perlman, 1984; Mannuzza, Klein, Bonagura, Malloy, Giampino, & Addalli, 1991).

BEHAVIORAL AND COGNITIVE–BEHAVIORAL TREATMENT

The realization that ADHD children's multiple deficits are often not adequately managed by stimulant treatment alone has led to the use of other interventions, separately or combined with medication. In both clinical research and practice, the most common treatment approaches have been behavioral and cognitive–behavioral interventions.

A number of reviews has been published on the effectiveness of these approaches (e.g., Abikoff, 1987; Hinshaw & Erhardt, 1991; Pelham & Murphy, 1986; Sprague, 1983; Whalen, Henker, & Hinshaw, 1985). Therefore, only an overview of the major conclusions is presented here.

There are some reports that behavioral interventions alone, including parent management training (e.g., Dubey, O'Leary, & Kaufman, 1983) and comprehensive behavior modification classrooms (e.g., Carlson et al., 1992), are helpful in managing the behavior of ADHD children. However, the findings are not always positive, and there are studies that do not report significant gains with behavioral treatment (Abikoff & Gittelman, 1984; Gittelman, Abikoff, Pollack, Klein, Katz, & Mattes, 1980; Pelham, Bender, Caddell, Booth, & Moorar, 1985). Moreover, even if treatment is helpful, the improvements rarely transfer outside the specific treatment setting and, invariably, are not maintained when behavioral treatment is discontinued. Furthermore, comprehensive behavior modification in the classroom is the exception rather than the rule, and regular classroom teachers are not trained or are often unwilling to carry out the procedures necessary for the successful implementation of this approach.

There is some support for the efficacy of behavior therapy in conjunction with methylphenidate. The combination is more useful than either treatment alone in normalizing ADHD children's classroom behavior (Gittelman et al., 1980). Also, ADHD children in behavior modification classrooms may need less medication to improve their behavior compared to their counterparts in regular classrooms (Carlson et al., 1992). However, the overall clinical usefulness of this treatment combination is limited because of the absence of maintenance effects following treatment termination, and because it fails to address all the academic, social, and emotional difficulties common to the disorder.

Cognitive–behavioral therapy (CBT) has an inherent appeal to those working with ADHD children. The approach focuses on teaching youths reflective problem-solving skills as a means of self-regulation, with the expectation that they will attain more self-control over their impulsive response style.

At face value, CBT appears to be a sensible and obvious treatment strategy. However, controlled studies offer little, if any, evidence for the clinical usefulness of this treatment approach. Although it is conceivable that some exceptional ADHD children benefit from CBT, to date, the only suggestions we have with regards to individual differences are that young children and those with poor language skills are least likely to benefit from this approach.

Studies have evaluated the usefulness of combining CBT with medication. Here too, the results have been disappointing. The augmentation of stimulant treatment with CBT has not produced any additional improvements in cognitive functioning, academic performance, or behavior (see reviews by Abikoff, 1987; Hinshaw & Erhardt, 1991).

As this brief overview has indicated, no single or dual treatment approach has yielded a satisfactory, broad therapeutic impact with ADHD children. Related to these disheartening results is the fact that most intervention studies have been short, with treatment rarely provided for more than three or four months. Therefore, other treatment strategies are warranted that are broader both in scope and time.

MULTIMODAL THERAPY

Support for the usefulness of broad-based interventions comes from the reports of James Satterfield and his colleagues regarding the clinical efficacy of multimodal therapy with hyperactive children (Satterfield, Cantwell, & Satterfield, 1979; Satterfield, Satterfield, & Cantwell, 1980, 1981). These investigators, working with 6- to 12-year-old hyperactive children, evaluated a treatment program that consisted of methylphenidate, individual psychotherapy, group therapy, educational therapy, individual parent counseling, group counseling for parents, and family therapy. Children and their families received combinations of these treatments, depending on the needs and disabilities of the youths and their parents. In comparing these findings with other outcome studies, the investigators reported that the outcome of this comprehensively treated group was unusually good; the children showed improvement in home and school behavior and in academic achievement, and reductions in antisocial behavior as well. Moreover, improvements in the latter two areas were reportedly related to the length of treatment; children and their families who received three years of treatment showed better outcomes than those with less than one year of treatment.

OVERALL AIMS

The findings from the Satterfield et al. studies provide the most promising reports yet of a meaningful clinical intervention with ADHD youths. However, the report of treatment efficacy needs to be tempered because the multimodal therapy received by these children was not provided within the context of a controlled, random assignment treatment study. The current authors, supported by a grant from the National Institute of Mental Health, have been conducting such a treatment study for the past several years at Schneider Children's Hospital in New York and at Montreal Children's Hospital. Because this study was completed only recently, the final results are not yet available; however, we are able to present a description of the study protocol and of the treatment program as well as of clinical observations made over the course of the study.

The purpose of the study was to determine whether the provision of multimodal treatment (MMT) to ADHD children receiving methylphenidate results in better social, behavioral, emotional, and academic functioning than that associated with methylphenidate alone, and whether exposure to MMT enables ADHD children to continue to function adequately when medication is discontinued. Children participating in the study received their optimal dose of medication and were randomly assigned to either multimodal treatment or to one of two control groups: a conventional stimulant treatment group (CTG) or an attention control group (ACG) that controls for time and attention with professional staff.

METHOD

Subjects and Selection: Inclusion Criteria

The study includes boys and girls aged 7 to 9 years who meet criteria for ADHD. These include a mean score of at least 1.5, obtained on two separate occasions, on the Hyperactivity factor of the Conners Teachers Rating Scale (CTRS; Goyette, Conners, & Ulrich, 1978) and the ascertainment of a diagnosis of ADHD, on the basis of the *Diagnostic and Statistical Manual of Mental Disorders*, third edition, revised (*DSM-III-R*; American Psychiatric Association, 1987), established via the parent version of the Diagnostic Interview Schedule for Children (DISC-P). Other inclusion criteria include an IQ of at least 85 on the Wechsler Intelligence Scale for Children—Revised (WISC-R), living at home with at least one parent, and able to travel to the clinic on a regular basis. In addition, to participate in the study, children must be designated as stimulant responders.

Determination of Children's Response to Methylphenidate

Systematic procedures are used for establishing optimal clinical dosage and for determining responsivity to stimulants.

Optimal Dosage

A specific titration (three times per day) schedule was used. During titration, which on average requires four to five weeks, children are seen weekly at the clinic and dosage is increased gradually up to a maximum of 50 mg/d, based on weekly assessments. Each week, the teachers complete the 10-item Abbreviated Conners Teacher Rating Scale (ACTRS) and a semi-structured telephone interview to generate clinical information about aspects of the child's functioning on that dose. The teachers, parents, and psychiatrist also complete a weekly Global Improvement Scale (GIS; Gittelman et al., 1980).

The optimal dosage for each child is based on the following rules:

1. Dosage is increased (to a maximum of 50 mg/d) until there is no report of increased improvement with the higher dosage, at which point the child is returned to the previous dosage. Improvement is determined with a rating of "improved" by two of the three raters on the GIS compared with the child's functioning during the previous week, and when the score on the ACTRS is within 1 SD of the mean for the child's age.
2. If a child receives a GIS rating of "completely well" by two raters, and the ACTRS score is within 1 SD of the mean for age, then no further dosage increase occurs.
3. Teacher or parent reports of adverse side effects, determined from specific side effects questionnaires completed weekly, result in a return to a lower dosage.

Methylphenidate Responsivity

The determination of methylphenidate responsivity is based on two factors: positive clinical effects, confirmed by relapse on placebo, and the absence of negative cognitive effects.

Positive clinical response requires that a child show a reduction of at least 25% on the ACTRS score and be rated as improved by two of the three raters on the GIS, and that the child's parents indicate gratification of the child's response to treatment and the desire that the child remain on medication. (This criterion, parent attitude toward treatment, has a great deal of clinical validity).

Placebo confirmation of responsivity requires that children who show a positive clinical response also show clinical deterioration during a placebo trial (blinded for child, parent, and teacher). In setting the criteria for relapse on placebo, we have tried to select standards that are clinically meaningful, while providing objective criteria. These criteria are

1. compared to functioning while on active medication, the child must receive a rating of at least "worse" by two of three raters (teacher, parent, or psychiatrist) on the GIS, which ranges from "completely well" to "very much worse";
2. the child must meet *DSM-III-R* criteria for ADHD, based on a *DSM-III-R* Symptom Checklist completed with the parent; and
3. the child must receive a Hyperactivity factor score, on the CTRS, that is at least 25% higher than the score obtained on his or her optimal dosage.

Children who do not fulfill criteria for a positive clinical response and the criteria for placebo confirmation of responsivity do not participate in the study.

Absence of negative cognitive effects has no agreed upon standards for stimulant induced cognitive impairment. To ascertain that cognitive functioning was not compromised at the child's optimal clinical dosage of methylphenidate, we initially administered an arithmetic test (odd/even test developed by Schachar and Tannock to assess overfocusing dose/response effects of methylphendiate [Tannock, personal communication, July 1989]) at baseline and regularly during titration during the first 2 years of study. Deleterious change in arithmetic performance was defined as a decrement of at least 20% in performance on two separate testings, relative to baseline. If such a change occurs, the most clinically effective dosage not associated with cognitive impairment would be reinstituted. No such instances have occurred. Children regularly showed higher accuracy with increasing dosage, confirming the findings regarding linear dose-response effects with methylphenidate (e.g., Douglas, Barr, O'Neill, & Britton, 1988; Pelham, 1986). Consequently, the study has eliminated the formal cognitive testing procedure during titration. Instead, during a telephone interview, teachers are now asked each week about the child's academic and cognitive performance at given doses of medication to flag decrements.

Exclusion Criteria

The overall goal of the exclusionary criteria is to reduce diagnostic heterogeneity to permit clear generalizability of results. Children are excluded if they have (a) neurological disorders (i.e., cerebral palsy or seizures); (b) psychosis; (c) a current or recent history of physical abuse; (d) tic disorder or Tourette's disorder; (e) a significant learning disability (defined as a standard score, in reading or mathematics on the Kaufmann Test of Educational Achievement [KTEA] of 85 or less [i.e., at least one *SD* below the population mean] and a KTEA score that is at least 15 points [1 *SD*] below their full scale IQ [Halperin, Gittelman, Klein, & Rudel, 1984]); these children are not included in the study because it is unreasonable, and possibly unethical, to withhold academic remediation for as much as two years from children assigned to the two control treatments); and (f) a *DSM-III-R* diagnosis of conduct disorder because these youths probably require targeting of different symptoms and different treatment strategies.

It is important to note that ADHD children with conduct problems are *not* excluded. Children comorbid with oppositional defiant disorder (ODD), as well as ADHD youngsters who would have met *DSM-III* criteria for conduct disorder (CD; one or two conduct problems rather than the more severe *DSM-III-R* criteria for CD [3 conduct problems]) enter the study. The inclusion of these conduct problem children is intended not only to parallel the sample of hyperactive children who participated in Satterfield et al.'s (1979) multimodal study but also to reflect the large percentage of schoolaged ADHD children who are comorbid for these other disruptive behavior disorders (Hinshaw, 1987). In so doing, the results of this treatment study can be generalized to a childhood population that is representative of the ADHD spectrum.

Sequence of Entry Into Study

The specific sequence of procedures for entry into the study is as follows:

1. initial referral and telephone screening;
2. teacher CTRS ratings;
3. diagnostic assessment;
4. IQ and academic assessments;
5. collection of baseline measures (detailed in Table 1 at the end of this chapter);
6. determination of children's response to methylphenidate; and
7. treatment assignment.

Treatment Assignment

Participants who complete all the above assessments are randomly assigned to one of the three treatment groups with group balancing for race, gender, IQ, and rate of oppositional disorders. Assignment is done in blocks of four children at a time to allow for those treatment components that require a group format.

DESCRIPTION OF STUDY TREATMENTS

Multimodal Interventions

The MMT interventions in the study are intended to address the major deficits associated with ADHD. Thus, the treatment program consists of medication, academic study skills training, individualized remedial tutoring, and individual psychotherapy. Social skills training, parent-management training and counseling, and a home-based reinforcement program for school behavior are also provided and integrated into a behavioral systems approach as part of the multimodal treatment regimen. These treatment components are described later.

Stimulant Treatment

As noted previously, methylphenidate is adjusted to the most effective clinical dosage, to a maximum of 50 mg/day. Medication is prescribed three times a day, with the smallest dosage (usually 5 or 10 mg) given at approximately 3:30 p.m. This regimen is designed to maximize attention and cooperation during the after-school treatment sessions. In general, this dosing procedure has not resulted in significant difficulties with sleep onset. The children are maintained on their clinically effective dosage throughout their participation in the study, although the development of side effects or drug tolerance result in dosage adjustment. To facilitate the appropriate management of each child's maintenance stimulant treatment, monthly feedback from parents, teachers, and the child, including behavioral ratings, descriptions of the child's functioning, and assessments of side effects, are obtained.

Generally, when side effects develop, a 4-step procedure is followed. The first step is to see whether the side effects decrease or accomodation occurs within several days. If this does not happen, the second step is to decrease the medication to see whether the side effects decrease with dose reduction. If this does not occur, the medication is discontinued. If side effects disappear with the discontinuation of the medication, and if the child has been very responsive to the medication, a second trial of medication is initiated at a lower dose with a more gradually increasing dose schedule. Frequently, with this approach, the side effects do not reoccur. However, if they do reoccur, the medication is discontinued, and the child is referred for treatment elsewhere, where other medications and approaches may be used.

Social Skills Training

It is common for parents and teachers to complain that the ADHD child does not get along well with his peers. School observations indicate that children with ADHD are similar to other children with regards to the occurrence of neutral and positive peer interactions (Abikoff & Gittelman, 1982). What distinguishes students with ADHD from their peers is the higher frequency of negative social behaviors, such as bossiness, intrusiveness, and aggressiveness. Their awkward interpersonal exchanges with peers stem from a seeming lack of sensitivity to social cues, nuances, and demands; this behavior suggests the presence of social learning disability (Whalen & Henker, 1991).

The social skills training focuses on the development and enhancement of age appropriate interpersonal skills. Embedded within the year-long training are components of two programs that have shown promise in improving children's social competency: Jackson, Jackson, and Monroe's (1983) *Getting Along with Others: Teaching Social Effectiveness to Children* program, and the *Walker Social Skills Curriculum: The ACCEPTS Program* (Walker, H. M., McConnell, Holmes, Todis, Walker, J. L., & Golden, 1983). These programs focus on social skills excesses and deficits and attempt to modify behavior using a variety of techniques, including direct instruction, modelling, behavioral rehearsal, feedback, reactions of others, and social reinforcement. We have used elements of these established training programs, have modified them when necessary to increase their relevance to children with ADHD, and have added training features meant to enhance generalization.

The year-long curriculum addresses different social skills each week (e.g., joining a conversation, giving and receiving positive feedback, waiting for one's turn in games, cooperating in a group activity, etc.). For example, one child had particular difficulty making and keeping friends. She tended to talk continuously and the other children would then ignore and exclude her. One of the ways in which the social skills program addressed her needs was to focus on her conversational, cooperative, and listening skills. Specifically, she was taught to wait her turn, give good eye and ear contact, join a conversation appropriately, and give positive and negative feedback to others. After a short time in the program, both her teachers and her parents reported that she got along well with her peers and was often asked to join in their activities. In the group context, there was considerable improvement in terms of her sensitivity to the other children and her interactions with them.

In-session training components include the use of modeling, role playing, and viewing previously videotaped training sessions. Homework assignments are given to increase skills mastery and to aid in generalization outside the treatment setting.

Throughout the social skills training, a behavior modification system is implemented that initially uses concrete rewards to reinforce appropriate behavior in the session. Subsequently, the children self-evaluate their social behavior during the session (see Hinshaw, Henker, & Whalen, 1984;

Turkewitz, O'Leary, & Ironsmith, 1975), and the corresponding points earned or lost by the children are incorporated into the parent management program at home (described later).

Parent Training and Family Counseling

Children with ADHD have problems adhering to adult rules and to limits setting. These difficulties are often characterized by noncompliant and oppositional behavior, frequently at levels severe enough to warrant a comorbid diagnosis of oppositional defiant disorder (ODD). The resulting child management problems faced by parents (and teachers) are a common reason for which these children are referred to mental health professionals. When child noncompliance and defiance are part of the symptoms, treatment directed at these behaviors seems indicated, especially because the presence of ODD in these children heightens their risk for the development of conduct disorder (Farrington, Loeber, & van Kammen, 1990). Accordingly, parent training, with an emphasis on behavior management strategies and a focus on dealing with the child's oppositional behavior (see Forehand & McMahon, 1981), is included in the multimodal treatment program.

During the first year, the parents participate in a group format for the first 4 months and, then, in weekly individual sessions. The group sessions are based, in part, on Russell Barkley's (1987) behavior management training program for parents of defiant and hyperactive children. The parents are taught how to use contingent praise and attention, and time out and response cost, and how to set up and implement a token economy system at home. The latter consists of a comprehensive point system, whereby daily privileges (e.g., TV, Nintendo games) and special activities and rewards are made contingent on points earned by the child in the social skills sessions in the clinic, at school (based on the use of a daily report-card format described later), and at home. Included in the behaviors targeted for increase at home are doing daily chores and compliance with parental requests. Points are earned or lost on the basis of whether or not the child engages in these positive behaviors. Similarly, there is a list of negative behaviors, individualized for each child, that are targeted for decrease (e.g., noncompliance, tantrums, fighting). A loss of points and, in some instances, time out result when these inappropriate behaviors occur, whereas points are earned when the child does *not* display these negative behaviors at home.

For example, in the parent training group, after parents are taught how to attend positively to their children by spending special time with them and rewarding independent play, a point system is set up to address specific problems like getting ready for school and homework time. In such cases, the child's morning routine might be broken up by making the bed, taking the laundry off the floor, and brushing one's teeth before coming to the table. Similarly, parents might review their child's homework assignment and set goals with him or her regarding the amount of work to be completed in set time periods. This combination of goal and limit setting (often accomplished through a series of small steps), followed up by recording of points and praising performance immediately, frequently results in improvements in the target behaviors. As improvements are maintained, other behaviors are addressed.

Following the group sessions, the parents participate individually for 8 months of once-weekly sessions, of which every 4th one includes the child. During the 2nd year, treatment consists of once-monthly sessions. The individual work with the parents serves to reinforce, support, and clarify parental efforts to apply the behavior management techniques taught in the parent groups. The sessions also focus on any marital discord related to rearing and managing an ADHD child, and counseling regarding these conflicts is provided, if necessary. Although there are as yet no studies that have evaluated the effectiveness of such counseling in parents of ADHD children, studies with parents of oppositional and conduct disordered children suggest that efforts to resolve marital conflict can produce positive behavior changes in both the children and the parents (Dadds, Schwartz, & Sanders, 1987). During the family sessions, efforts are made to enhance communication among family members and to address such issues as parent–child alliances and scapegoating.

Daily School Report Card

The report card system is a cost-effective procedure that is used to monitor, reinforce, set goals, and modify the child's school behavior, while not singling out or stigmatizing the ADHD child in the classroom and minimizing the amount of direct teacher and therapist involvement (see Atkeson & Forehand, 1979; Barkley, 1981; Lahey, Gendrich, Gendrich, Schnelle, Gant, & McNees, 1977). Each child's report card contains a list of several behaviors that the teacher deems important for that individual (e.g., bringing completed homework to class, not interrupting). The teacher rates the child on each behavior and initials the card. The children are required to bring the card home every day from school. The daily ratings are associated with a number of points earned or lost. The point totals are incorporated into the home-based reinforcement program managed by the parents and result in the gain or loss of privileges, activities, or other reinforcers at home. The target behaviors change over time, reflecting changes in the child's comportment.

Academic Skills Training and Remediation

The academic problems of children with ADHD are characterized typically by low or failing grades, grade retention, lower-than-expected achievement test scores, and resource room or special class placement. These negative outcomes are the consequence of the interaction of a variety of possible factors, including specific academic skills deficits, a concurrent learning disability, inattention during classroom lessons, and poor organizational and study skills.

The goal of the first 12 weeks of the academic treatment component is to improve organizational skills and strategies relevant to successful academic performance. To this end, within a group format, the children are exposed to a variety of tasks and activities, most of them academic in nature, that focus on following written and oral instructions, getting ready to work, organizing materials, efficient use of time, reviewing one's work, and so on.

For example, when J. B. was referred to the program, teachers reported that written projects or written assignments were generally incomplete or late. It soon became apparent that J. B. lacked the necessary skills to research the project theme, to take notes, to preplan his presentation, to prepare a draft, to edit, and to review. J. B. also demonstrated that he had considerable difficulty in planning a schedule that would provide the structure necessary to complete the project within the time allotted. Therefore, during the 12 weeks devoted to developing organizational strategies, J. B. received help in the following areas:

1. Making a check list of the necessary tasks and ticking off each task after completion.
2. Preparing a time schedule and leaving at least one full day for the unexpected.
3. Learning how to use the resources in the school and community library.
4. Learning how to take accurate notes and to identify key words.
5. Organizing the notes and ideas into a logical sequential order.
6. Preparing an outline.
7. Writing a draft.
8. Organizing the project (i.e., illustrations, and so on).
9. Editing.
10. Reviewing.

J. B. was also encouraged to assess his work schedule at the end of every 2 days to make adjustments if necessary and to confer with his teacher at least twice during the course of the project to ensure that he was on track (this was negotiated with the teachers of the research project and the teacher responsible for the written project). Providing J. B. with this structure resulted in increased efficiency, particularly in the organization of content and in meeting time requirements.

During the subsequent 9 months, the participants receive weekly re-medial tutoring that targets their specific skill deficits in reading, mathematics, and language. These prescriptive tutoring sessions, conducted by special education teachers, are individualized on the basis of diagnostic evaluations of each child.

Some children are at grade level and do not require remediation. Training with these students focuses on academic skills mastery and continues to emphasize the organizational and study skills described previously. The emphasis during these sessions is on the children's own schoolwork, although supplementary training materials and tasks for specific subskills are available as needed.

Psychotherapy

Given their multiple difficulties, it is not surprising that children with ADHD frequently suffer from low self-esteem. The common experience of being shunned by other children, yelled at by parents and teachers, poor scholastic performance, and a lack of success in dealing with these problems on their own, lead to feelings of demoralization, low self-worth, and a poor self-image. Often, there is also a great deal of underlying frustration, anger, and depression. To address these issues, the multimodal treatment program includes an individual psychotherapy component that attempts to facilitate the child's self-esteem, promote a better understanding of the disorder, change the child's perception of the experienced rejection, and enhance self-effectiveness.

A specific psychotherapy manual outlining interventions in these areas was produced. For example, Robbie came to the clinic with a history of inattention in school, distractibility, and impulsivity. His self-esteem was generally poor; he lacked friends and showed a susceptibility to tears at the least provocation. As an example, his mother complained that it took him hours to get anything done, such as getting dressed in the morning or doing homework, because he was not able to keep his mind on the task at hand. When chastised for this, he would dissolve into tears and say that he never did anything right and that no one liked him. Robbie was put on stimulant medication, which significantly decreased his distractibility, impulsivity, and inattention, making it easier for him to complete tasks. In individual psychotherapy, his impulsive tendencies were the focus of cognitive–behavior therapy interventions, such as teaching him to tell himself to "hold his horses" and "give his brain time to think" before rushing to answer a question. Psychoeducational techniques were used to help him understand some of his difficulties and what medication did for him. He was also helped to identify and express his feelings adaptively, using supportive techniques, reflection, clarification, and interpretation. Gradually, as therapy progressed, Robbie developed a greater sense of competence and improved self-esteem. He began to make overtures to some classmates and crying episodes became less and less frequent. Throughout Robbie's individual psychotherapy, parent counseling helped the parents to develop skills for managing his behavior more constructively and to support the progress that he was making in his individual therapy.

Procedures to Enhance Generalization

As noted earlier, treatment studies of children with ADHD indicate that clinical gains rarely transfer outside of the treatment setting. The achievement of treatment generalization is a daunting challenge, and there are no empirically established methods for achieving this goal. Nevertheless, the multimodal program has incorporated procedures that are intended to increase generalization. For instance, the academic training sessions focus not only on materials and exercises deemed important by the clinical staff but also periodically include the student's actual classwork and homework assignments as well. In this manner, the child has the opportunity to practice organizational and academic skills on tasks that are directly linked to school demands.

As described previously, the children are given social skills homework assignments in-between clinic sessions and are rewarded for following these assignments outside of the treatment setting. In addition, social skills difficulties shown by a child in the clinic, if reported by the child's parents or teacher, are incorporated into the home and school-based programs as well. For example, if a child was found to frequently interrupt when someone is speaking, the child would self-monitor and self-reinforce him or herself for not interrupting when in the social skills group. Not interrupting would be monitored and rewarded by the parent at home and also included on the child's daily school report card. In this manner, the child is encouraged and rewarded for demonstrating specific social skills, not only in the clinic but at school and at home as well.

Treatment Delivery

During the first year of treatment, the various MMT and ACG treatment sessions (described later) are conducted during two afternoons per week after school at the clinic; whereas in the second year, the treatment components are provided once a month, in the form of booster sessions. The treatment arrangement is characteristic of treatment typically delivered within the context of a partial-day treatment program, wherein professional staff provide all the necessary interventions at one site and can readily share relevant treatment issues with each other.

CONTROL TREATMENTS

Attention Control

The attention control interventions, while omitting the putative active treatment ingredients of the MMT interventions, are intended to control for the nonspecific treatment effects of the multimodal interventions that might be related to professional time and attention. The specific attention-control components are described briefly below; and a comparison of the multimodal, attention-control, and conventional stimulant treatment group components may be found in Table 1.

1. *Projects.* The children concentrate on nonacademic projects (e.g., musical instruments, drawings of holiday plans), without formal instruction in organizational and study skills.
2. *Homework.* The children are provided with general assistance with homework assignments. No emphasis is placed on academic skills deficits or on organizational or study skills, and remediation is not given.
3. *Peer Activities.* The children are given opportunities to work together on tasks and activities and to play with appropriate structure and limit setting. No social skills training is provided. The approach is similar to that of a community based afterschool activity program.
4. *Parent Psychoeducational and Support Group.* Parents are given psychoeducational information about ADHD (e.g., etiology, assessment, developmental issues). The parents also participate in a support group format led by a therapist. Formal instruction in behavior management is not provided
5. *Individual Parent Support.* A therapist helps to maintain a supportive, nondirective relationship with the parent and continues to serve as a resource for the provision of psychoeducational information and advice regarding ADHD. General parenting principles (e.g., need for consistency, structure and clarity, avoidance of parental disagreements in front of child) are also dealt with.
6. *Individual Child Support.* Supportive, nondirective sessions focus on the child's unstructured discussion of life events and problems, providing an opportunity for the child to feel understood and accepted. Play and play-related activities are used to foster discussion. Play therapy or other psychotherapeutic interventions are specifically not used.

TABLE 1
Components of Study Treatment Groups

Treatment group

Multimodal	Attention control	Conventional stimulant
Medication ▪ methylphenidate ▪ individually titrated to optimal dose ▪ 3 times per day ▪ 7 days per week	Medication ▪ methylphenidate ▪ individually titrated to optimal dose ▪ 3 times per day ▪ 7 days per week	Medication ▪ methylphenidate ▪ individually titrated to optimal dose ▪ 3 times per day ▪ 7 days per week ▪ monthly medication visit, provided medication monitoring, and family support
Social skills training group* (weekly for 1 yr)**	Peer activity group* (weekly for 1 yr)**	
Daily school report card		
Academic organizational skills group* (weekly for 3 months)**	Working on projects (weekly for 3 months)**	
Academic remediation (dyads, weekly for remaining 8 months)**	Help with homework (dyads, weekly for remaining 8 months)**	
Parent training group* (weekly for 4 months)**	Parent support group* (weekly for 4 months)**	
Parent counseling (individual, weekly for remaining 8 months)**	Parental support (individual, weekly for remaining 8 months)**	
Individual psychotherapy of the child (weekly for 1 year)**	Individual supportive time with adult (weekly for 1 year)**	
Crisis intervention***	Crisis intervention***	Crisis intervention***

*Groups consisted of 4–5 children or families.
**All weekly interventions have monthly booster sessions in the second year.
***A total of eight crisis sessions were available, as needed (e.g., school consultation, intervention with parents or child).

Conventional Stimulant Treatment Group

The children in this control group receive maintenance treatment with methylphenidate throughout their two years in the study. The individual monthly meetings last for approximately 45 minutes and involve medication monitoring, nonspecific clinical management, and crisis intervention, if needed (to a maximum of eight sessions).

MEDICATION WITHDRAWAL FEASIBILITY

As noted earlier, the positive effects of stimulant treatment are often not maintained when medication is discontinued, resulting in remediation for most children. Even when stimulants are combined with other interventions, such as cognitive training, more than 85% of ADHD children resume medication within 1 month of cessation of stimulant treatment (Abikoff & Gittelman, 1985b). A major purpose of the current study is to determine whether exposure to long-term multimodal treatment enables youths with ADHD to be maintained off medication. To this end, blind placebo challenges are implemented after the first and second years of multimodal treatment. Of special interest during the placebo challenges, are comparisons between the multimodal and control groups with regard to the percentage of children who can be maintained off medication, and, for the children who need to be remediated, the length of time before reinstitution of methylphenidate and the dose levels required. Clinical deterioration during these year-end trials is defined using the same criteria as those in the baseline placebo challenge.

CLINICAL OBSERVATIONS AND CONSIDERATIONS

Because the study was only just completed, the effectiveness of this multimodal program is still being evaluated. However, there is one issue worth noting regarding the implementation of such a complex, time-intensive, treatment regimen. We have observed that parents differ widely in their ability to implement and integrate the program's behavioral systems approach. Differences in organizational skills, comprehension, marital discord, and emotional problems, all contribute to treatment implementation. These issues need to be addressed when they interfere with the delivery of treatment. In some cases, the parent counseling sessions can focus directly on these difficulties. There are other instances, however, in which parents need supplemental interventions not available in our treatment program. In these situations, appropriate treatment referrals (e.g., intensive marital therapy, psychotherapy, pharmacotherapy) may be made for the parents.

In all clinical trials, inclusion and exclusion criteria delimit the scope of the study's generalizability. The current study is no exception. The results should be considered most relevant to children whose parents agree to medication treatment (approximately 75% of referrals to the study) and to those who respond to methylphenidate (approximately 90% of the children considered for our study were found to respond to methylphenidate). Likewise, the study's findings may not be applicable to children with ADHD with severe learning disabilities or with conduct disorder (diagnosed with *DSM-III-R* criteria) because these individuals were excluded from the trial. It is important to reiterate, however, that the study included children with ADHD who were comorbid for ODD, as well as those with less severe conduct disorders and learning disabilities and those with anxiety and mood disorders. Given the overall representativeness of this sample, the study findings should be generalizable to a large segment of the elementary-school-aged population of children with ADHD.

The breadth of this multimodal clinical trial notwithstanding, there is a number of issues that still need to be addressed in future studies. Treatment in the current study was provided within the context of an after-school program. It will be important to determine whether the delivery of treatment in nonclinical settings, especially when concentrated in school, can maximize clinical efficacy. Another central question is whether intensive long-term psychosocial treatment alone can demonstrate clinical efficacy. Also pivotal are studies with sample sizes large enough to examine the interaction of treatment and patient characteristics. Studies of this kind are needed to generate essential information regarding which type of treatment is best for which type of patient. Especially pertinent are outcome data that address the implications of comorbidity on treatment planning in children with ADHD. Answers to these questions should be forthcoming at the conclusion of the NIMH Collaborative Multisite Multimodal Treatment Study of Children with ADHD (the MTA Study) recently begun at six centers in the United States and Canada (Richters et al., 1995).

Systematic evaluations regarding the impact of the timing of treatment components on outcome are also needed. Children assigned to the combination of psychosocial and medication treatments in the United States–Canada and MTA multimodal studies begin the two treatments simultaneously in the latter and start with medication in the former. Multimodal designs that evaluate the efficacy of introducing psychosocial treatment prior to pharmacotherapy are warranted. Finally, these two studies use manualized, multipush treatment programs. It is not known whether multimodal treatment regimens that are tailored specifically to the clinical needs of the children and their parents result in better outcomes than with nontailored approaches. The reader is referred to Conners et al. (1994) for a discussion of other issues in multimodality treatment research in children with ADHD.

TABLE 2
Domains Assessed and Study Outcome Measures

Domain	Instrument	What it measures	Type of measure	Informant
Child measures				
Social behavior	Social Skills Rating System (Gresham & Elliott, 1989)	Cooperation, assertion, responsibility, self-control, and total score	Rating scale, norms available	Parents
	Social Skills Rating System (Gresham & Elliott, 1989)	Cooperation, assertion, empathy, self-control, and total score	Self-rating scale, norms available	Child
	Taxonomy of Problem Situations (Dodge, McClaskey, & Feldman, 1985)	Six aspects of social competence in school, total score	Rating scale	Teacher
	Social Interaction Code (revised) (Abikoff, Martin, & Klein, 1989)	Child's social behavior toward peers and teacher and their response, peers' and teacher's social behavior toward child and child's response	Observation system	Observers (blinded)
ADHD behavior	Home Situations Questionnaire (Barkley, 1987)	Situations in which child shows problematic behaviors associated with ADHD	Rating scale, norms available	Parents
	Conners Parent Rating Scale—Revised (Goyette et al., 1978)	Impulsive–hyperactive factor, hyperkinesis index	Rating scale, norms available	Parents
	DSM-III-R Symptom Checklist	*DSM-III-R* ADHD symptoms	Interview questionnaire	Parents

	Conners Teacher Rating Scale (Goyette et al., 1978)	Hyperactivity factor, hyperkinesis index	Rating scale, norms available	Teacher
	School Situations Questionnaire (Barkley, 1987)	Situations in school in which child shows problematic behaviors associated with ADHD	Rating scale, norms available	Teacher
	Classroom Observation Code (Abikoff & Gittelman, 1985a)	12 classroom behaviors during structured work time	Observation system	Observers (blinded)
	Hillside Behavior Rating Scale (Gittelman-Klein et al., 1976)	13 ADHD related behaviors	Rating scale	Observers (blinded)
	Conners Rating Scale	Hyperkinesis index, inattentive/overactive factors from IOWA Conners Rating Scale	Rating scale	Observers (blinded)
Academic performance	Homework Problem Checklist (Anesko & O'Leary, 1982)	26 homework related behaviors, total problem score	Rating scale	Parents
	Stanford Achievement Test (1989 edition)	Mathematics, reading, spelling, listening skills	Standardized achievement test	Child
	Arithmetic Test (Douglas et al., 1986)	Arithmetic productivity, accuracy, time spent, efficiency	Timed performance test (alternate forms)	Child

(continued)

TABLE 2 *(Continued)*

Domain	Instrument	What it measures	Type of measure	Informant
Emotional indices	Piers–Harris Children's Self-Concept Scale (Piers, 1984)	6 aspects of self-concept and total score	Self-rating scale	Child
	Children's Depression Inventory (Kovacs & Beck, 1977)	Total score indicating level of self-reported depression	Self-rating scale	Child
Global indices	Global Improvement Scale (Gittelman et al., 1980)	Global improvement in child functioning	8-point rating scale	Parents, teacher, physician
	Children's Global Assessment Scale (Shaffer et al., 1985)	Overall level of child's functioning	Rating scale	
Parent measures				
Emotional indices	Structured Clinical Interview for the *DSM-III-R* (Spitzer et al., 1988)	Parental psychopathology	Clinical interview	Mother, father

Category	Measure	Construct	Type	Source
Parenting indices	Being A Parent Scale (Johnston & Mash, 1989)	Parenting satisfaction and efficacy	Rating scale	Parents
	Knowledge of Behavioral Principles (O'Dell et al., 1979)	Parents' knowledge of behavioral principles as applied to children	Multiple choice test	Parents
	Parenting Practices Scale (Strayhorn & Weidman, 1988)	Parenting behaviors and parent–child interaction patterns	Self-rating scale	Parents
	Parenting Practices Scale (child report)	Child's report of mother's and father's parenting behaviors	Rating scale	Child
Cognitive measures	Memory Scan Test (Swanson et al., 1991)	Perceptual encoding and motor response times	Information-load processing task	Child
Other measures	Parent Satisfaction	Parental satisfaction with parenting groups	Rating scale	Parents
	Additional Therapeutic Contacts in Study	Number and type of crisis sessions provided by staff to child and parent	Log records	Staff

ASSESSMENT OF TREATMENT OUTCOME

Multimodal studies require multiple assessment procedures and measures to evaluate treatment efficacy. In our ongoing study, information regarding functioning in various domains is collected prior to treatment assignment, when the child is on and off medication, and subsequently at 6-month intervals, from parents, teachers, and children.

The children's school behavior is evaluated using standardized teacher rating scales and observation procedures. At home, the children's behavior is assessed using parent rating scales. Changes in perceptions of parental self-efficacy, child management strategies, and knowledge of behavioral principles are assessed as well. Rating scales are also completed by the children and serve as change measures of self-concept, social skills, and depression. Finally, testing procedures are used to assess changes in academic achievement and performance and in information processing skills. Table 2 lists the specific outcome measures used in the study.

In this chapter, we have attempted to describe the background rationale and implementation of our multimodal treatment study for children with ADHD. The final results from this study are not yet available; however, we have demonstrated that such a controlled study, though challenging and demanding, is feasible with compliance from patients, parents, and teachers. The study has also paved the way for the larger six-site MTA study, which is underway. Our hope is that these studies will result in significant positive, current, and long-term outcomes for children with ADHD and will facilitiate the use and refinement of systematic, comprehensive multimodal treatment strategies for children with ADHD.

REFERENCES

Abikoff, H. (1987). An evaluation of cognitive behavior therapy for hyperactive children. In B. B. Lahey & A. E. Kazdin (Eds.), *Advances in Clinical Child Psychology* (Vol. 10, pp. 171–216).

Abikoff, H., & Gittelman, R. (1982). *The social interactions of hyperactive and normal boys in unstructured school settings*. Unpublished manuscript.

Abikoff, H., & Gittleman, R. (1984). Does behavior therapy normalize the classroom behavior of hyperactive children? *Archives of General Psychiatry, 41,* 449–454.

Abikoff, H., & Gittelman, R. (1985a). Classroom observation code: A modification of the Stony Brook code. *Psychopharmacology Bulletin, 21,* 901–909.

Abikoff, H., & Gittelman, R. (1985b). Hyperactive children maintained on stimulants: Is cognitive training a useful adjunct? *Archives of General Psychiatry, 42,* 953–961.

Abikoff, H., & Gittelman, R. (1985c). The normalizing effects of methylphenidate on the classroom behavior of hyperactive children. *Journal of Abnormal Child Psychology, 13,* 33–44.

Abikoff, H., & Klein, R. G. (1992). Attention deficit hyperactivity and conduct disorder: Comorbidity and implications for treatment. *Journal of Consulting and Clinical Psychology, 60,* 881–892.

Abikoff, H., Martin D., & Klein, R. G. (1989). *Social interaction observation code* (Rev.). Unpublished manuscript.

American Psychiatric Association. (1987). *Diagnostic and statistical manual of mental disorders* (3rd ed., rev.). Washington, DC: Author.

Anesko, K. M., & O'Leary, S. G. (1982). The effectiveness of brief parent training for the management of children's homework problems. *Child and Family Behavior Therapy, 4,* 113–126.

Atkeson, B. M., & Forehand, R. (1979). Home-based reinforcement programs to modify classroom behavior: A review and methodological evaluation. *Psychological Bulletin, 86,* 1298–1308.

August, G., & Garfinkel, B. D. (1989). Behavioral and cognitive subtypes of ADHD. *Journal of the American Academy of Child and Adolescent Psychiatry, 28,* 739–748.

Barkley, R. A. (1981). *Hyperactive children: A handbook for diagnosis and treatment.* New York: Guilford Press.

Barkley, R. A. (1987). *Defiant children: A clinician's manual for parent training.* New York: Guilford Press.

Barkley, R. A., & Cunningham, C. E. (1979). The effects of Ritalin on the mother–child interactions of hyperactive children. *Archives of General Psychiatry, 36,* 201–208.

Biederman, J., Newcorn, J., & Sprich, S. E. (1991). Comorbidity of attention deficit hyperactive disorder with conduct, depressive, anxiety, and other disorders. *American Journal of Psychiatry, 148,* 564–577.

Bird, H. R., Camino, G., Rubio-Stipic, M., Gould, M. S., Ribera, J., Sesman, M., Woodbury, M., Huertas-Goldman, A., Pagan, A., Sanchez-Lacay, A., & Moscosco, M. (1988). Estimates of the prevalence of childhood maladjustment in a community survey in Puerto Rico. *Archives of General Psychiatry, 45,* 1120–1126.

Carlson, C. L., Pelham, W. E., Milich, R., & Dixon, J. (1992). Single and combined effects of methylphenidate and behavior therapy on the classroom performance of children with attention deficit hyperactivity disorder. *Journal of Abnormal Child Psychology, 20,* 213–232.

Charles, L., & Schain, R. (1981). A four year follow up study of the effects of methylphenidate on behavior and academic achievement of hyperactive children. *Journal of Abnormal Child Psychology, 9,* 495–505.

Conners, C. K., Wells, K. C., Erhardt, D., March, J. S., Schulte, A., Osborne, S., Fiore, C., & Butcher, A. T. (1994). Multimodality therapies: Methodological issues in research and practice. *Child and Adolescent Psychiatric Clinics of North America, 3,* 361–377.

Dadds, M. R., Schwartz, S., & Sanders, M. R. (1987). Marital discord and treatment outcome in behavioral treatment of child conduct disorders. *Journal of Consulting and Clinical Psychology, 55,* 396–403.

Dodge, K. A., McClaskey, C. L., & Feldman, E. (1985). A situational approach to the assessment of social competence in children. *Journal of Consulting and Clinical Psychology, 53,* 344–353.

Douglas, V. I., Barr, R. G., O'Neill, M. E., & Britton, B. G. (1986). Short term effects of methylphenidate on the cognitive, learning and academic performance of children with attention deficit disorder in the laboratory and classroom. *Journal of Child Psychology and Psychiatry, 27,* 191–211.

Douglas, V. I., Barr, R. G., O'Neill, M. E., & Britton, B. G. (1988). Dosage effects and individual responsivity to methylphenidate in attention deficit disorder. *Journal of Child Psychology and Psychiatry, 29,* 453–475.

Dubey, D. R., O'Leary, S. G., & Kaufman, K. F. (1983). Training parents of hyperactive children in child management: A comparative outcome study. *Journal of Abnormal Child Psychology, 11,* 229–246.

Elia, J., Borcherding, B. G., Rapoport, J. L., & Kayser, C. S. (1991). Methylphenidate and dextroamphetamine treatment of hyperactives: Are there true nonresponders. *Psychiatry Research, 36,* 141–155.

Farrington, D. P., Loeber, R., & van Kammen, W. B. (1990). Long-term criminal outcomes of hyperactivity–impulsivity–attention deficit and conduct problems in childhood. In L. N. Robins & M. Rutter (Eds.), *Straight and devious pathways to adulthood* (pp. 62–81). New York: Cambridge University Press.

Forehand, R. L., & McMahon, R. J. (1981). *Helping the noncompliant child: A clinician's guide to parent training.* New York: Guilford Press.

Gittelman, R., Abikoff, H., Pollack, E., Klein, D. F., Katz, S., & Mattes, J. (1980). A controlled trial of behavior modification and methylphenidate in hyperactive children. In C. Whalen & B. Henker (Eds.), *Hyperactive children: The social ecology of identification and treatment.* New York: Academic Press.

Gittleman-Klein, R., Klein, D. F., Katz, S., Saraf, K., & Pollack, E. (1976). Comparative effects of methylphenidate and thioridazine in hyperkinetic children: I. Clinical results. *Archives of General Psychiatry, 33,* 1217–1231.

Gittleman, R., Mannuzza, S., Shenkar, R., & Bonagura, N. (1985). Hyperactive boys almost grown up: I. Psychiatric status. *Archives of General Psychiatry, 42,* 937–947.

Goyette, C. H., Conners, C. K., & Ulrich, R. F. (1978). Normative data on revised Conners' Parent and Teacher Rating Scales. *Journal of Abnormal Child Psychology, 6,* 221–236.

Gresham, F. M., & Elliott, S. N. (1989). *Social skills rating system* (Parent and student forms). Circle Pines, MN: American Guidance Service.

Halperin, J. M., Gittelman, R., Klein, D. F., & Rudel, R. G. (1984). Reading-disabled hyperactive children: A distinct subgroup of attention deficit disorder with hyperactivity? *Journal of Abnormal Child Psychology, 12,* 1–14.

Hechtman, L., Weiss, G., & Perlman, T. (1984). Young adult outcome of hyperactive children who received long-term stimulant treatment. *Journal of the American Academy of Child Psychiatry, 23,* 261–269.

Hinshaw, S. P. (1987). On the distinction between attentional deficits/hyperactivity and conduct problems/aggression in child psychopathology. *Psychological Bulletin, 101,* 443–463.

Hinshaw, S. P., & Erhardt, D. (1991). Attention deficit hyperactivity disorder. In P. C. Kendall (Ed.), *Child and Adolescent Therapy: Cognitive–behavioral procedures* (pp. 98–130). New York: Guilford Press.

Hinshaw, S. P., Henker, B., & Whalen, C. K. (1984). Cognitive–behavioral and pharmacologic interventions for hyperactive boys: Comparative and combined effects. *Journal of Consulting and Clinical Psychology, 52,* 739–749.

Jackson, N. F., Jackson, D. A., & Monroe, C. (1983). *Getting along with others: Teaching social effectiveness to children.* Champaign, IL: Research Press.

Johnston, C., & Mash, E. J. (1989). A measure of parenting satisfaction and efficacy. *Journal of Clinical Child Psychology, 18,* 167–175.

Klein, R. G. (1987). Pharmacotherapy of childhood hyperactivity: an update. In H. Y. Meltzer et al. (Ed.), *Psychopharmacology: The third generation of progress* (pp. 1215–1224). New York: Raven Press.

Kovacs, M., & Beck, A. T. (1977). An empirical–clinical approach toward a definition of childhood depression. In J. G. Schulterbrandt & A. Raskin (Eds.), *Depression in childhood: Diagnosis, treatment, and conceptual models* (pp. 1–25). New York: Raven Press.

Lahey, B. B., Gendrich, J. G., Gendrich, S. I., Schnelle, J. F., Gant, D. S., & McNees, M. P. (1977). An evaluation of daily report cards with minimal teacher and parent contacts as an efficient method of classroom intervention. *Behavior Modification, 1,* 381–394.

Mannuzza, S., Klein, R. G., Bonagura, N., Malloy, P., Giampino, T. L., & Addalli, K. A. (1991). Hyperactive boys almost grown up: V. Replication of psychiatric status. *Archives of General Psychiatry, 48,* 77–83.

O'Dell, S. L., Tarler-Benlolol, L., & Flynn, J. M. (1979). An instrument to measure knowledge of behavioral principles as applied to children. *Journal of Behavioral Therapy and Experimental Psychiatry, 10,* 29–34.

Pelham, W. E. (1986). The effects of psychostimulant drugs on learning and academic achievement in children with attention deficit disorders and learning disabilities. In J. K. Torgensen & B. Y. L. Wong (Eds.), *Psychological and educational perspectives in learning disabilities* (pp. 259–295). New York: Academic Press.

Pelham, W. E., Bender, M. E., Caddell, J., Booth, S., & Moorar, S. (1985). The dose-response effects of methylphenidate on classroom academic and social behavior in children with attention deficit disorder. *Archives of General Psychiatry, 42,* 948–952.

Pelham, W. E., & Murphy, H. A. (1986). Attention deficit and conduct disorders. In M. Hersen (Ed.) *Pharmacological and Behavioral Treatment: An Integrative Approach* (pp. 108–148). New York: John Wiley & Sons.

Piers, E. V. (1984). *Piers–Harris children's self-concept scale* (rev. manual). Los Angeles: Western Psychological Services.

Richters, J. E., Arnold, L. E., Jensen, P. S., Abikoff, H., Conners, C. K., Greenhill, L. L., Hechtman, L., Hinshaw, S. P., Pelham, W. E., & Swanson, J. M. (1995). National Institute of Mental Health collaborative multisite, multimodal treatment study of children with attention deficit hyperactivity disorder (MTA): Part 1. Background and rationale. *Journal of the American Academy of Child and Adolescent Psychiatry, 34,* 987–1000.

Satterfield, J. H., Cantwell, D. P., & Satterfield, B. T. (1979). Multimodality treatment: A one year follow-up of 84 hyperactive boys. *Archives of General Psychiatry, 36,* 965–974.

Satterfield, J. H., Satterfield, B. T., & Cantwell, D. P. (1980). Multimodality treatment: A two year evaluation of 61 hyperactive boys. *Archives of General Psychiatry, 37,* 915–919.

Satterfield, J. H., Satterfield, B. T., & Cantwell, D. P. (1981). Three-year multimodality treatment study of 100 hyperactive boys. *Journal of Pediatrics, 98,* 650–655.

Shaffer, D., Gould, M. S., Brasic, J., Ambrosini, P., Fisher, P., Bird, H., & Aluwahlia, S. (1985). CGAS (Children's Global Assessment Scale). *Psychopharmacology Bulletin, 21,* 747–748.

Spitzer, R. L., Williams, J. B. W., Gibbon, M., & First, M. B. (1988). *Instruction manual for the structured clinical interview for DSM III-R (SCID).* New York: Biometrics Research.

Sprague, R. L. (1983). Behavior modification and educational techniques. In M. Rutter (Ed.), *Developmental neuropsychiatry* (pp. 404–421). New York: Guilford Press.

Strayhorn, J. M., & Weidman, C. S. (1988). A parent practices scale and its relation to parent and child mental health. *Journal of the American Academy of Child and Adolescent Psychiatry, 27,* 613–618.

Swanson, J. M., Cantwell, D. P., Lerner, M., McBurnett, K., & Hanna, G. (1991). Effects of stimulant medication on learning in children with ADHD. *Journal of Learning Disabilities, 24,* 219–230.

Turkewitz, H., O'Leary, K. D., & Ironsmith, M. (1975). Generalization and maintenance of appropriate behavior through self-control. *Journal of Consulting and Clinical Psychology, 43,* 577–583.

Walker, H. M., McConnell, S., Holmes, D., Todis, B., Walker, J. L., & Golden, N. (1983). *A curriculum for children's effective peer and teacher skills (ACCEPTS).* Austin, TX: Pro-Ed Publishers.

Weiss, G., Hechtman, L., Perlman, T., Hopkins, J., & Wener, A. (1975). Hyperactive children as young adults: A controlled prospective ten-year follow-up of 75 children. *Archives of General Psychiatry, 36,* 675–681.

Whalen, C. K., & Henker, B. (1985). The social worlds of hyperactive children. *Clinical Psychology Review, 5,* 1–32.

Whalen, C. K., & Henker, B. (1991). The social impact of stimulant treatment for hyperactive children. *Journal of Learning Disabilities, 24,* 231–241.

Whalen, C. K., Henker, B., & Dotemoto, S. (1980). Methylphenidate and hyperactivity: Effects on teacher behaviors. *Science, 208,* 1280–1282.

Whalen, C. K., Henker, B., & Hinshaw, S. P. (1985). Cognitive–behavioral therapies for hyperactive children: Premises, problems, and prospects. *Journal of Abnormal Child Psychology, 13,* 391–410.

V

SOCIALLY DISRUPTIVE BEHAVIOR AND CONDUCT DISORDERS

INTRODUCTION

Disruptive behavior disorders (DBD) in childhood often progress to aggressive, delinquent, criminal, and violent behaviors in adolescence and young adulthood. As a result, these conditions cause significant impairment in many areas, including academic, career, and social functioning in the individual's life. The prevalence rate estimates for conduct disorder range widely, from 6 to 16% for boys under 18 years of age and from 2 to 9% for girls. Earlier onset appears to be associated with a worse prognosis, and conduct disorders seem to have both genetic and familial or environmental contributing factors. Therefore, intervening early in children's lives is likely to be the most parsimonious and cost-effective manner to reverse this devastating developmental course. Although the disruptive behavior disorders constitute a very important public health problem, there is little empirical research to guide health care providers as to which treatments are effective for which forms of DBD. In this section, five chapters propose various treatment strategies for the reduction of antisocial behaviors in children.

Alan E. Kazdin is studying the effect of cognitive problem-solving skills training (PSST) and parent management training (PMT) for the treatment of aggressive and antisocial children. In his treatment studies of inpatient and outpatient children using PSST, PMT, combined PSST + PMT, and various modifications of these techniques, significant treatment gains were achieved, both at posttreatment and at later follow-up assessments. Not only did externalizing behaviors decrease, but prosocial behaviors increased. He discusses the limitations of his studies, the directions for future research with antisocial children, and the implications of his findings for clinical practice.

David J. Kolko describes his work on the treatment of childhood fire-setting using intervention approaches, such as firehouse orientation, training in fire safety skills, and psychological treatment. The latter includes contingency management, negative practice, prosocial skills training, family therapy, and other techniques. The assessment measures are outlined in the chapter. The results, although preliminary, indicated that the intervention effects a significant reduction in fire-related behaviors. The author discusses the limitations of the study as well as offers ideas for future research directions.

Carolyn Webster-Stratton presents her studies of an interactive intervention program for families of young children with oppositional defiant disorder, the BASIC program, which involves parental self-management and conflict-resolution techniques. In addition, a family training intervention component promotes parental self-control, communication skills, problem-solving skills, self-care, and mastery in finding social supports. The treatment programmatic component makes extensive use of videotape vignettes to teach and model parental skills. Posttreatment and follow-up assessments indicated that this intervention is effective in significantly improving parental attitudes and parent–child interactions, reducing coercive or harsh disciplinary approaches by parents, and decreasing child conduct problems. The author discusses the limitations of the study.

Patricia Chamberlain used the Oregon Social Learning Center's Treatment Foster Care (TFC) program, a community-based, family-oriented treatment model, for out-of-home care of adolescents with conduct disorders and delinquency. The components of the model include developing the placement setting, preservice training and ongoing consultation for TFC parents, individual treatment for adolescents, family therapy for both biological and foster parents, consultations with schools and parole and probation officers, and after-care services and support for all involved. The posttreatment and follow-up assessments indicated that the intervention resulted in decreased recidivism, fewer hospitalizations, and less delinquency in the adolescents. The author presents a clinical vignette and discusses the limitations of the study and its generalizability.

Samuel Vuchinich and his coauthors have tested a new treatment approach that integrates child-focused cognitive training, parent training, and family problem-solving training for preadolescents with conduct problems. The authors describe their treatment plan in detail and cite concrete examples of treatment sessions. The investigators have conducted several studies to assess the feasibility of this treatment and preliminary results are positive. Nonetheless, the treatment's applicability may be limited if parents cannot sustain long-term participation, and results are likely to depend on the quality of parents' participation.

This section considers several treatment modalities and combinations of techniques for diverse antisocial behaviors and distinct ages and environments. The results, though mostly preliminary, are promising. It is to be noted that all the studies in this section included girls and minority children. Parents were also an integral part of the treatment because family discord and harsh parental disciplinary methods were found to exacerbate the condition. The authors also recommend that future research needs to focus more on parent and family issues, within the context of the treatment environment, to understand, conceptualize, fully diagnose, and adequately treat the condition. Because DBD is a chronic condition, interventions will need to incorporate multimodal interventions of longer duration and greater intensity and to begin earlier in life than has been the case heretofore.

17

PROBLEM SOLVING AND PARENT MANAGEMENT IN TREATING AGGRESSIVE AND ANTISOCIAL BEHAVIOR

ALAN E. KAZDIN

For the past several years, our group has been treating aggressive and antisocial children and their families. The overall goal of our program is to identify and to develop effective interventions for youth referred for conduct disorder.[1] Developing effective treatments will require a deeper understanding of the clinical dysfunction and the contexts in which it is embedded. Consequently, our program examines diverse facets of children, parents, and families to acquire knowledge that can be integrated into the context of treatment trials.

This chapter discusses the treatment program for youth referred to our clinic. The chapter begins with an overview of the clinical problem as a background to treatment. Next, we examine the treatments in use at our clinic, evidence related to their impact, and limitations of our findings. We also address questions regarding the focus of treatment and the model of delivering services for severely impaired individuals.

Research on this chapter was supported in part by Research Scientist Award MN00353 and grant MH35408 from the National Institute of Mental Health. Correspondence concerning this chapter should be directed to Dr. Alan E. Kazdin, Department of Psychology, Yale University, P.O. Box 208205, New Haven, CT 06520-8205.
[1]In this chapter, conduct disorder refers generally to clinically severe antisocial behavior including aggression, lying, stealing, truancy, running away, and other behaviors. The term is used generically to refer to a constellation of symptoms rather than specifically to the diagnostic category, as in the *Diagnostic and Statistical Manual of Mental Disorders*, fourth edition (*DSM-IV*; American Psychiatric Association, 1994).

CONDUCT DISORDER: OVERVIEW OF THE PROBLEM

Scope of Dysfunction

Conduct disorder refers to a broad pattern of functioning that includes diverse behaviors, such as aggressive acts, theft, vandalism, firesetting, lying, truancy, and running away. The behaviors come in various combinations and vary markedly in severity, chronicity, and frequency. The development of effective treatments for conduct disorder is critically important in light of the scope of the problem and its multiple consequences. To begin, there is the suffering of youth who evince the dysfunction. This is not a small group; the prevalence rate of conduct disorder is between 2%–6% (Institute of Medicine, 1989). In the United States, this translates to approximately 1.3 million to 3.8 million cases. Related, aggressive, disruptive, and antisocial behavior constitute the most frequent basis for clinical referrals for outpatient treatment (Kazdin, Siegel, & Bass, 1990).

The consequences of conduct disorder for individuals, others, and society at large are significant as well. For the individuals themselves, conduct disorder in childhood portends long-term dysfunction. Although fewer than half of these youth are likely to continue the pattern of conduct disorder, the majority suffer significant psychiatric and social impairment into adulthood (Robins, 1966, 1978).

Conduct disorder often has severe consequences for others including siblings, peers, parents, and teachers, as well as strangers who are targets of antisocial and aggressive acts. As antisocial behavior continues into adulthood, there are many victims of acts of murder, rape, robbery, arson, drunk driving, and spouse and child abuse, which are carried out to a greater extent by persons with a history of antisocial behavior than by other persons (see Kazdin, 1995b). Finally, the monetary costs of treatment and of the consequences of the dysfunction make conduct disorder one of the most costly mental health problems (Robins, 1981). Conduct problem youth generate life-long costs as they traverse special education, mental health, juvenile justice, and social services.

Central Features

The overriding feature of conduct disorder is a persistent pattern of behavior in which the rights of others and age-appropriate social norms are violated. Several characteristic behaviors (e.g., fighting, temper tantrums, destroying property, stealing, and firesetting) are likely to appear together as a constellation or syndrome. These behaviors have been studied extensively using varied populations (e.g., clinic and delinquent samples) and defining criteria. As a formal psychiatric disorder, the diagnosis of Conduct Disorder (CD) requires the presence of at least 3 of 15 symptoms within the past 12 months (American Psychiatric Association, 1994). The symptoms include bullying others, initiating fights, using a weapon, cruelty to others, cruelty to animals, stealing while confronting a victim, firesetting, destruction of property, lying, truancy, running away, theft of valuable items, staying out late. It is difficult to draw the line in terms of how long the pattern must be evident and how many symptoms must be present before there is a clinical problem. Also, diagnosis depends on other criteria (e.g., impairment in daily functioning). In clinical work, youth referred for aggressive and antisocial behavior usually surpass the minimal diagnostic criteria in scope and duration of symptoms and impaired functioning in everyday life.

Associated Features

Child Characteristics

Children who meet criteria for CD are likely to meet criteria for other disorders as well. The co-existence of more than one disorder is referred to as comorbidity. In general, diagnoses involving disruptive or externalizing behaviors (CD, oppositional defiant disorder [ODD], and attention deficit hyperactivity disorder [ADHD]) often go together. In studies of community and clinic samples, a large percentage of youth with CD or ADHD (e.g., 45%–70%) also meet criteria for the other disorder (e.g., Fergusson, Horwood, & Lloyd, 1991; Offord, Boyle, & Racine, 1991). The cooccurrence of CD and ODD is common as well. Among clinic-referred youth who meet criteria for CD, 84%–96% also meet concurrent diagnostic criteria for ODD (see Hinshaw, Lahey, & Hart, 1993). CD is sometimes comorbid with anxiety disorders and depression (Hinshaw et al., 1993; Walker et al., 1991).

Several other associated features of CD are relevant to treatment. For example, children with CD also are likely to show academic deficiencies, as reflected in achievement level, grades, being left behind in school, early termination from school, and deficiencies in specific skill areas such as reading. Youth with the disorder are likely to evince poor interpersonal relations, as reflected in diminished social skills in relation to peers and adults and higher levels of peer rejection. Youth with CD also are likely to show a variety of cognitive and attributional processes. Deficits and distortions in cognitive problem-solving skills, attributions of hostile intent to others, and resentment and suspiciousness, illustrate a few cognitive features associated with CD.

Parent and Family Characteristics

Several parent and family characteristics associated with CD (see Kazdin, 1995b; Robins, 1991; Rutter & Giller, 1983) include parental criminal behavior and alcoholism (two of the stronger and more consistently dem-onstrated parental characteristics); poor disciplinary practices and attitudes (especially harsh, lax, erratic, and inconsistent discipline practices); dys-functional relations (reflected in less acceptance of; less warmth, affection, and emotional support for; and less attachment to their children, compared with parents of nonreferred youth); family difficulties (less supportive and more defensive communications among family members, less participation in activities as a family, and more clear dominance of one family member); poor parental relations (unhappy marital relations, interpersonal conflict, and aggression); and poor parental supervision and monitoring of the child and knowledge of the child's whereabouts.

Contextual Conditions

CD is associated with a variety of untoward living conditions such as large family size, overcrowding, poor housing, and disadvantaged school settings (see Kazdin, 1995b). Many of the untoward conditions in which families live place stress on the parents or diminish their threshold for coping with everyday stressors. The net effect can be evident in parent–child interaction in which parents inadvertently engage in patterns that sustain or accelerate antisocial and aggressive interactions (e.g., Dumas & Wahler, 1985; Patterson, Capaldi, & Bank, 1991).

Frequently a child's dysfunction is embedded is a larger context that cannot be neglected in conceptual views about the development, mainte-nance, and course of CD nor in the actual delivery of treatment. For ex-ample, at our clinic, it is likely that a family referred for treatment will experience a subset of these characteristics: financial hardship (unemploy-ment, significant debt, bankruptcy), untoward living conditions (dangerous neighborhood, small living quarters), transportation obstacles (no car or car in frequent disrepair, state-provided taxi service), psychiatric impair-ment of one of the parents, stress related to significant others (former spouses, boyfriends, or girlfriends), and adversarial contact with an outside agency (schools, youth services, courts). CD is conceived as a dysfunction of children and adolescents. The accumulated evidence regarding the symptom constellation, risk factors, and course over childhood, adoles-cence, and adulthood attests to the heuristic value of focusing on individual children. At the same time, there is a child–parent–family context gestalt that includes multiple and reciprocal influences that affect each participant (child and parent) and the systems in which they operate (family, school; Kazdin, 1993c).

IDENTIFYING AND DEVELOPING EFFECTIVE TREATMENTS

A variety of forms of therapy-, medication-, home-, school-, and com-munity-based programs; residential and hospital treatment; and social services have been evaluated for CD (for reviews see Brandt & Zlotnick, 1988; Dumas, 1989; Kazdin, 1985, 1987; Pepler & Rubin, 1991; U.S. Congress, 1991). Although none has been shown to controvert the course of CD, there are several promising leads. We elected to investigate two of them, namely, cognitive problem-solving skills training (PSST) and parent management training (PMT). Treatment selection was based on criteria we adopted to sort through the myriad of available options. These criteria entail a conceptual model of the clinical dysfunction and its development, research that supports the model, preliminary outcome research, and evidence that processes proposed to lead to change in fact relate to outcome (see Kazdin, 1993c). PSST and PMT fare well on these criteria for treating CD.

Problem-Solving Skills Training

Overview

Cognitive processes (perceptions, self-statements, attributions, and problem-solving skills) are frequently accorded a major role in conduct problems (Shirk, 1988). As a case in point, aggression is not triggered merely by environmental events, but rather through the way in which these events are perceived and processed. The processing refers to the child's appraisals of the situation, anticipated reactions of others, and self-statements in response to particular events. For example, attribution of intent to others represents a salient cognitive disposition critically important to understanding aggressive behavior. Aggressive youth show a predisposition to attribute hostile intent to others, especially in social situations where the cues of actual intent are ambiguous (e.g., Dodge, Price, Bachorowski, & Newman, 1990; Dodge & Somberg, 1987). Understandably, when situations are initially perceived as hostile, youths are more likely to react aggressively.

Other cognitive processes and predispositions are relevant as well. For example, several interpersonal cognitive problem-solving processes (e.g., generating alternative solutions, means–end thinking, consequential thinking) are related to social behavior (Spivack & Shure, 1982). Deficits and distortion among these processes relate to teacher ratings of disruptive behavior, peer evaluations, and overt behavior (see Rubin, Bream, & Rose-Krasnor, 1991). Fundamental questions that remain to be resolved regarding the specificity of cognitive deficits, distortions, and predispositions in relation to different patterns of deviant behavior and dysfunction are widely recognized among researchers. Nevertheless, research on cognitive processes among aggressive children has served as a heuristic base for conceptualizing treatment and for developing specific treatment strategies.

PSST consists of developing interpersonal cognitive problem-solving skills and prosocial behavior. Many variations of PSST have been applied to conduct problem children, although several common characteristics can be identified. First, the emphasis is on how the children approach situations. Although it is obviously important that the children ultimately select appropriate means of behaving in everyday life, the primary focus is on the thought processes that guide behavior. Second, the children are taught to engage in a step-by-step approach to solve interpersonal problems. They make statements to themselves that direct attention to certain aspects of the problem or tasks that lead to effective solutions. Third, treatment utilizes structured tasks involving games, academic activities, and stories. Over the course of treatment, the cognitive problem-solving skills are increasingly applied to real-life situations. Fourth, therapists play an active role in treatment. They model the cognitive processes, apply verbal self-statements to diverse problems, and deliver prompts, feedback, and praise to develop correct use of the skills. Finally, treatment usually combines several different procedures including modeling and practice, role-playing, and reinforcement and mild punishment (loss of points or tokens).

Outcome studies have indicated that cognitively based treatment can reduce aggressive and antisocial behavior in children and adolescents (see Baer & Nietzel, 1991; Durlak, Furhman, & Lampman, 1991). A number of fundamental questions about treatment remain. To begin, the basis for therapeutic changes in cognitively based treatments is not clear. Measures of cognitive processes to which gains are attributed often show little or no relation to therapeutic change. Second and related, few studies have elaborated the factors that contribute to treatment outcome. Evidence has suggested that treatment is more effective with older rather than younger children (Durlak et al., 1991), although the reason for age differences is not clear. Third, reliable changes have been achieved with treatment but many youth remain outside of the range of normative. Notwithstanding significant caveats and provisos, cognitively based treatments have achieved gains in several studies with clinically referred youth.

Characteristics of Training

In our program, PSST consists of 20 weekly therapy sessions with the child, each lasting 40–50 minutes. The core treatment may be supplemented with optional sessions, if the child requires additional assistance in grasping the problem-solving steps (early in treatment) or their application in every day situations (later in treatment). Central to treatment is developing the use of five problem-solving steps, which are verbal self-statements (see Table 1) designed to break down interpersonal situations into units that permit identification and use of prosocial responses. The steps serve as verbal prompts the children deliver to themselves to engage in thoughts and actions that guide behavior. Each self-prompt or self-statement represents one step in solving a problem.

TABLE 1
The Problem-Solving Steps and Self-Statements

1. **What am I supposed to do?**
   This step requires that the child identify and define the problem.
2. **I have to look at all my possibilities.**
   This step asks the child to delineate or specify alternative solutions to the problem.
3. **I had better concentrate and focus in.**
   This step instructs the child to concentrate and evaluate the solutions that he or she has generated.
4. **I need to make a choice.**
   During this step, the child chooses the answer that he or she thinks is correct.
5. **I did a good job or Oh, I made a mistake.**
   This final step entails checking to verify the solution: whether it was the best among those available, whether the problem-solving process was followed correctly, or whether a mistake or less than desirable solution was selected (in which case the process should begin anew).

Note. These steps are used by the child to develop an approach toward responding to interpersonal situations. The steps, as presented here, provide the initial set of statements. Over the course of treatment, use of the steps changes in separate ways, for example, steps two and three merge to form a separate question ("What could I do and what would happen?"), which is then answered as the child generates multiple ways of responding and the likely consequences of each. Also, the steps move from overt (aloud) to covert (silent, internal) statements.

To assist the children in the acquisition and generalization of the problem-solving skills, several tasks are taught sequentially. The early sessions use simple tasks and games (e.g., "What comes next," Connect Four) to teach the problem-solving steps, to help to deter impulsive responding, and to introduce the reward system and response cost contingencies, noted below. The majority of treatment focuses on the child's use of the problem-solving steps to generate and to enact prosocial solutions to a range of interpersonal problems or situations. The interpersonal problems are presented in a variety of ways using various approaches, materials, and tasks to encourage the child to think about different nonaggressive ways to handle problems with others. Role playing is used extensively to give the child the opportunity to enact what he or she would do in a situation, thus making these interactions similar to real-life exchanges. Sessions concentrate on situations the child actually encounters (i.e., with peers, parents, siblings, teachers, and others) across multiple stimulus characteristics and conditions in an effort to promote generalization and maintenance (see Kazdin, 1994a).

In a typical session, interpersonal problems (e.g., in relation to school) are addressed. The therapist models application of the steps to one situation, identifies alternative solutions, and selects one of them. The child and therapist enact (role play) that solution. Throughout, the therapist prompts the child verbally and nonverbally to guide performance, provides a rich schedule of contingent social reinforcement, delivers concrete feedback for performance, and models improved ways of performing. Direct reinforcement of behavior is critical and sessions draw heavily on the contingent and immediate delivery of social reinforcement (e.g., smiles, praise, "high fives," applause, and so on).

The children begin each session with tokens (small plastic chips) that can be exchanged for small prizes at a "store" after each session. During the session, the children can lose chips (response cost) for misusing or failing to use the steps. In fact, very few chips are provided or taken away in most of the sessions. Social reinforcement and extinction are relied on more than token reinforcement to alter child behavior. The chips present opportunities to address special issues or problems with the child such as encouraging a particular type of prosocial solution that the child might find difficult.

Critical to treatment is use of the problem-solving approach outside of treatment. In vivo practice, referred to as *supersolvers*, consists of systematically programmed assignments designed to extend the child's use and application of problem-solving skills to everyday situations. The parents are trained to help the child use the problem-solving steps. The parents are brought into sessions over the course of treatment to learn the problem-solving steps and to practice joint supersolver assignments with the child at home. Prompting, shaping, and praise are used by the therapist to develop the parents' behavior. Over time, the child and parent supersolvers increase in complexity and eventually relate to those problem domains that led to the child's referral to treatment.

Parent Management Training

Overview

PMT refers to procedures in which the parents are trained to alter their child's behavior in the home. The parents meet with a therapist or trainer who teaches them to use specific procedures to alter interactions with their child, to promote prosocial behavior, and to decrease deviant behavior. Several specific child-rearing practices within a family have been shown to relate to child dysfunction (see Kazdin, 1985; Patterson, 1982). Coercive interchanges between parent and child have been shown to operate in such a way as to reinforce the increasingly aggressive behavior of the child. Also, parents tend to use punitive practices (e.g., corporal punishment) and many commands in ways that escalate problem behavior and tend to ignore prosocial behavior. Of course, this is not to say that all aggression and antisocial behavior is caused by mismanaged contingencies. Broader conceptual models have been suggested that integrate diverse facets related to parent and family functioning (e.g., parental stress, marital conflict) and their role in the unfolding of antisocial behavior (e.g., Dumas

& Wahler, 1985; Patterson, Reid, & Dishion, 1992). Parent–child interaction sequences remain pivotal in the models and have served as the basis for treatment of antisocial youth.

Although many variations of PMT exist, several common characteristics are shared. First, treatment is conducted primarily with the parent(s), who directly implement several procedures at home. Usually there is no direct intervention of the therapist with the child. Second, the parents are trained to identify, define, and observe problem behaviors in new ways. Careful specification of the problem is essential for the delivery of reinforcing or punishing consequences and for evaluating progress. Third, the treatment sessions cover social learning principles and the procedures that follow from them including positive reinforcement (e.g., the use of social praise and tokens or points for prosocial behavior), prompting and shaping, mild punishment (e.g., use of time out from reinforcement, loss of privileges), negotiation, and contingency contracting. Fourth, the sessions provide opportunities for the parents to see how the techniques are implemented, to practice using the techniques, and to review the behavior-change programs in the home.

The effectiveness of PMT has been evaluated extensively with conduct problem children varying in age and degree of severity of dysfunction (see Kazdin, 1987; McMahon & Wells, 1989; Miller & Prinz, 1990). Several controlled studies have demonstrated improvements in child behavior at home and at school. PMT has brought the problematic behaviors of treated children within normative levels of their peers who are functioning adequately. Improvements often remain evident 1 year after treatment; the continued benefits of treatment have been reported up to 10–14 years later (Forehand & Long, 1988; Long, Forehand, Wierson, & Morgan, 1994). In addition to reductions in deviant behavior of the target child, PMT has led to reduced deviant behavior of siblings and reduced stress and depression in the parents (see Kazdin, 1985).

Several characteristics of treatment administration contribute to outcome including the duration of treatment, providing parents with in-depth knowledge of social-learning principles, and utilizing time out from reinforcement in the home (see Kazdin, 1987). Parent and family characteristics also relate to treatment. Families characterized by multiple risk factors associated with childhood dysfunction (e.g., marital discord, parent psychopathology, social isolation, and socioeconomic disadvantage) are less likely to remain in treatment, show fewer gains even when they complete treatment, and are less likely to maintain therapeutic gains (e.g., Dumas & Wahler, 1983; Kazdin, Mazurick, & Bass, 1993; Webster-Stratton, 1985). Thus, variables that moderate treatment outcome have begun to be elaborated.

Many issues remain to be addressed. First, the requirement of active participation on the part of a parent makes the treatment inapplicable to some cases where parent dysfunction and unwillingness cannot be surmounted. Second, further follow-up data are needed. Given the recalcitrance of severe conduct problems, evidence is needed to assess the long-term impact. Third, PMT usually is applied to parents of preadolescent youth (e.g., up to age 12). Preadolescents may be more amenable to change through parenting techniques because parents can control many more contingencies of reinforcement of their children and because youth may be in the home in greater contact with the parent during this period. Some evidence suggests that PMT is effective with adolescents (Bank, Marlowe, Reid, Patterson, & Weinrott, 1991), but only a few studies are available. Overall, PMT is one of the more well developed and researched techniques for CD.

Characteristics of Training

In our program, the core treatment consists of 16 sessions (approximately one hour each) conducted weekly. As with the child, optional sessions are interspersed as needed to convey the approach, to develop or to ensure that the procedures are being implemented at home and at school, and to alter specific behavior-change programs. Meetings with the parents consist of developing behavior change skills in the parents and programs that can be implemented at home and at school. The program begins with relatively simple tasks for the parents. These build over the course of treatment to develop increasingly complex proficiencies in the parents' child-rearing repertoire and practices in everyday life.

A number of content and skill areas focus on treatment, as mentioned previously. The general format of the individual sessions is to convey content, to teach specific skills, and to develop use of the skill in the home in relation to child behavior. Thus, the session usually begins by discussing the general concept (e.g., positive reinforcement) and how it is to be implemented. Typically, a specific program is designed for implementation at home. The programs take into account special features of the family situation (others in the home, schedules), target behaviors of the child (e.g., noncompliance, fighting), available incentives, and parameters that are required for effective implementation (e.g., rich reinforcement schedule, shaping, immediacy, and contingency of consequences). The bulk of the treatment session is devoted to modeling by the therapist and role-playing and rehearsal of the parents for such tasks as presenting the program to the child, providing prompts, and delivering consequences. As part of this rehearsal, the therapist and parents may alternate roles of parent and child to develop proficiency of the parents. For example, delivery of reinforcement (e.g., praise) by the parent is likely to be infrequent, flat, delayed, and connected to parental nagging. Shaping begins with the initial parent repertoire and moves progressively to obtain more consistent, enthusiastic, and immediate praise, reduced nagging, clearer prompts, and so on.

A token reinforcement system is implemented in the home to provide the parents with a structured way of implementing the reinforcement contingencies. The tokens vary from stars, marks, points, coins, and other materials based on the child's age, ease of delivery for the parent, and other practical issues. The tokens, paired with praise, are contingent on specific child behaviors. Among the many advantages of token reinforcement is the prompting function they serve for the parents to reinforce consistently. Also, tokens facilitate tracking of reinforcement exchanges between parents and child (earning and spending the tokens). The token reinforcement programs reflect an effort to shape both child (e.g., prosocial behaviors) and parent behavior (e.g., child-rearing practices). At the beginning of each treatment session, the therapist reviews precisely what occurred in the previous week or since the previous phone contact and in many cases re-enacts what the parents actually did in relation to the child.

PMT also focuses on the child's performance at school. The child's teachers are contacted to discuss individual problem areas including deportment, grades, and homework completion. A home-based reinforcement system is devised in which the child's performance at school is monitored with consequences provided at home by the parents. Programs in the classroom also may be implemented by the teachers. Monitoring of the school program is maintained through telephone contact with the school as well as by parent discussions during the treatment sessions.

Over the course of treatment, the child is brought into the PMT sessions to ensure that he or she understands the program and that the program is implemented as reported by the parent, and to negotiate behavioral contracts between parent and child. The review of the program focuses on concrete examples of what was done, by and to whom, and with what consequences. An effort is made to identify how parent and child behavior can be improved (shaping), to practice and to provide feedback to the parent, and to refine or alter programs as needed. Modeling, rehearsal, and role play are used here as well.

Treatment Implementation

Common Treatment Characteristics

PSST and PMT are the core treatments at our clinic. Two therapists are involved with each case, so that the child and parents can be seen during the same visit. Although PSST and PMT differ in their conceptualization of CD, they are conceptually compatible. Each addresses different processes shown to relate to antisocial behavior, yet, the emphasis in both techniques is on changing how individuals perform (i.e., what they do in everyday life). In the case of PSST, treatment is directed specifically at changing how the child responds in interpersonal situations at home, at school, and in the community and in interactions with teachers, parents, peers, siblings, and others. In the case of PMT, treatment focuses on altering a number of specific parent–child interaction practices in relation to developing behavior, and responding to inappropriate behavior. Both treatments emphasize the development of behavior and generality of that behavior across situations.

PSST and PMT draw heavily on learning theories and research findings. This has been useful because learning research provides vast and diverse literatures from which to draw, much of which focus specifically on how to develop, alter, and eliminate behavior and the conditions necessary for change. Within PSST and PMT, several procedures, drawn from basic as well as applied learning research, are used to develop behaviors of the child and parents. For example, within each treatment session, whether for child or parent, there is extensive use of modeling, prompting and fading, shaping, positive reinforcement, practice and repeated rehearsal, extinction, and mild punishment (e.g., time out from reinforcement, response cost) (see Kazdin, 1994a).

Another feature of treatment pertains to monitoring of patient progress. As the child and parents are trained, one can readily assess how well each person is doing in everyday life. The child and parents use of the skills and their efforts are monitored in the session to see if a program is being implemented, is having the desired effects, has obstacles, and so on. If there is little or no progress, the obstacles usually can be attended to immediately within the treatment sessions. The programs are revised, requirements are reduced or altered, and changes are made to improve implementation and to move toward the goals. Feedback from external sources (e.g., teachers, principles) is also obtained during treatment. Monitoring of progress also comes from telephone contact with the children and parents during the week.

Finally, both PSST and PMT are fixed and flexible. The fixed feature refers to the fact that each treatment has a core set of treatment sessions (20 in PSST, 16 in PMT) provided to each parent and child. The core sessions convey central content areas, themes, and skills; yet, treatment is flexible and individualized in many ways. First, within the core sessions, child, parents, and family circumstances including problem areas, domains of dysfunction, special conditions of the family (e.g., living conditions, job schedules, custody issues, presence of extended family members) are accommodated. Also, flexibility is achieved by providing optional sessions (usually 1–5) for the child or family to address specific problems or to work on a theme that was not sufficiently well conveyed in the core session. Thus, a session is not merely delivered; rather, the content and programs from that session are critically important to achieve change in the child and parent.

Underpinnings of Treatment

Several features underlie treatment delivery that receive little attention in research reports and are often overlooked in efforts to extend treatment to clinical practice. To begin, therapist training is especially noteworthy. Full-time therapists (masters' degree training in one of the mental health professions) provide treatment. They undergo an additional period of training of approximately 18 months. Repeated practice, viewing of sessions of others, and simulated treatment is completed before a therapist is assigned a patient. Supervision of the initial treatment case consists of viewing live sessions (through a video system) and discussing concretely all facets of the session. Modeling, role-playing, practice, shaping, and reinforcement are used individually and in group format to train therapists.

Second, treatments are codified in manual form. The manuals provide the content and focus of individual sessions as well as the presentation, dialogue, and specific procedures to be used. Manuals facilitate therapist training. Also, the manuals are revised based on therapist experience and research findings to better accomplish particular goals with children or parents.

Third, therapist supervision, training, and feedback are ongoing. All sessions are videotaped, and routine as well as difficult sessions are reviewed. In addition, all treatment can be observed live from video monitor stations in the clinic. Review of tapes and live observation of treatment improve the quality of treatment because the entire treatment team can assist in deciding the focus of the next session or how to improve upon what has been accomplished.

Fourth, much of the treatment is conducted outside of the session in programs at home and at school. The therapists contact the parents between sessions to monitor the programs at home and at school, to handle crises, and to refine procedures. This ensures that programs in the home are more likely to succeed and that problems do not wait for one week (until the next session) to be addressed.

TREATMENT EFFECTIVENESS: CLINICAL TRIALS AND MAJOR FINDINGS

Objectives

The goal of the research is to identify and to develop effective psychotherapeutic interventions for aggressive and antisocial children. Our studies embrace several characteristics. First, we are interested in evaluating treatment with clinically referred cases. Our research is integrated in an outpatient clinical service. Second, we have adopted a constructive evaluation strategy (Kazdin, 1992b) to build an effective treatment package to address child and family dysfunction. Third, to evaluate treatment outcome, we assess diverse domains of functioning (e.g., antisocial behavior and delinquency, psychiatric symptoms, prosocial functioning), in different contexts (e.g., home, school, community), and with different informants (children, parents, teachers, therapists). Fourth, we evaluate outcome in relation to developmentally based normative functioning of nonreferred peers to examine the clinical significance of change and the outcome status of treated cases. Finally, we evaluate follow-up functioning up to at least 1 year after treatment is terminated. Although our focus is on developing an effective treatment package, the long-term objectives can be augmented by understanding children and families better and integrating this information into outcome research. Thus, the project assesses child, parent, and family factors that may significantly influence treatment outcome.

Methods

Setting and Participants

Children (13 years of age and under) referred for aggressive and antisocial behavior are seen at our clinic, the Yale Child Conduct Clinic, a treatment service affiliated with the Yale Child Study Center. Children usually meet criteria for a primary diagnosis (using DSM criteria) of CD or ODD. Approximately 70% of the youth meet criteria for more than one disorder. Most youth fall within the normal range of intelligence, although a broad range is represented (e.g., full scale from about 60–135 on the Wechsler Intelligence Scale for Children—Revised). The racial breakdown of our cases are primarily White, African American, or Hispanic American (approximately 60%, 30%, and 5%, respectively), with mixed or Asian American forming the remainder. Approximately 60% of our cases come from two-parent families. Most cases are from lower and lower middle socioeconomic classes. Approximately 20%–30% of families receive social assistance.[2]

---

[2]Over the course of this project, the Child Conduct Clinic has relocated from Pennsylvania (University of Pittsburgh School of Medicine) to Connecticut (Yale University). In each setting, the clinic has been part of child psychiatry services in which cases are referred to a general triage center and then referred to separate services. Although screening criteria for the clinic have not changed appreciably over time, the demographic characteristics have changed to match the change in geographical locale. Consequently, the statistics describing the sample are approximate and are based on the overall characteristics of all cases. More precise descriptions of samples of individual studies may be obtained from the primary references.

Assessment and Intervention

The goals of treatment are to reduce antisocial behavior and to improve the children's functioning at home, at school, and in the community; to reduce parental stress and dysfunction; and to improve family functioning. Several measures are administered immediately before and after treatment and at follow-up. Table 2 presents the primary measures related to our outcome studies.

TABLE 2
Primary Measures Related to Treatment Evaluation

Measures	Domains assessed
Intake measures	
General Information Sheet	Subject and demographic characteristics
Research Diagnostic Interview	Child DSM diagnosis, number of conduct disorder symptoms, total number of symptoms
Risk Factor Interview	Child school functioning, history of delinquency, contact with delinquent peers, parental history of antisocial behavior, adverse child-rearing practices, poor living accommodations
Child functioning	
Interview for Antisocial Behavior	Child aggressive and antisocial behavior
Self-Report Delinquency Checklist	Child delinquent acts
Children's Action Tendency Scale	Child aggressiveness, assertiveness, submissiveness
Parent Daily Report	Parent evaluation of problems at home
Child Behavior Checklist (Parent)	Diverse behavior problems and social competence
Child Behavior Checklist-TRF (Teacher)	Diverse behavior problems and adaptive functioning
Peer Involvement Inventory	How child relates to peers in school
Parent and family functioning	
Dyadic Adjustment Scale	Perceived quality of marital relation
Family Environment Scale	Domains of family functioning
Parenting Stress Index	Perceived parental stress and life events
Beck Depression Inventory	Parent depression
Hopkins Symptom Checklist	Overall parent impairment
Quality of Life Inventory	Parent evaluation of quality of life
Evaluation of treatment	
Child, parent, and therapist evaluation inventory	Acceptablility of and progress in treatment

Note. The assessment procedures and details of and references for individual measures are described elsewhere (see Kazdin et al., 1992, 1993).

Cases who participate in our clinic are assigned randomly to alternative treatment conditions. Our initial studies examined alternative treatment and control conditions. In our current work, each condition represents a viable treatment alternative. A given treatment outcome study requires a minimum of 4–5 years to complete. The duration pertains both to the special demands of treatment and to assessment. In most cases, two therapists are involved with a given family (one for the child, the other for the parents). In addition, treatment is somewhat protracted. Although treatment can be completed within a period of 8 months, recruitment of cases and delays (e.g., not showing up for treatment, seasonal holidays, vacation breaks during the summer) conspire to extend the duration of the treatment to 10–12 months. After treatment, annual follow-up assessments are conducted, currently, up to 3 years.

Treatment Effectiveness

In our initial work, we evaluated treatment with inpatient children admitted for acute crises. Treatment began when the children were inpatients and continued on an outpatient basis. In the first study, we evaluated the effects of PSST and nondirective relationship therapy (RT) for the treatment of antisocial child behavior (Kazdin, Esveldt-Dawson, French, & Unis, 1987a). Children ($N = 56$, ages 7–13) were assigned randomly to either PSST, RT, or to a treatment-contact control condition (in which the children met individually with a therapist but did not engage in specific activities designed to alter antisocial behavior). PSST led to significantly greater decreases in externalizing behaviors and overall behavioral problems at home and at school (after discharge) and increases in prosocial behaviors and overall adjustment than the RT and contact-control conditions, both at posttreatment and at a 1-year follow-up. The RT and control conditions did not produce consistent improvements. A significantly higher proportion of PSST children, compared with those in other conditions, fell within the normative range for prosocial behavior at posttreatment and follow-up. Even so, the majority of PSST children and almost all of those in the RT and control groups remained outside the normative range of deviant behavior.

In a second study with inpatient cases ($N = 40$, ages 7–12), children and their parents were assigned randomly to one of two conditions: PMT + PSST combined or a contact-control condition (Kazdin, Esveldt-Dawson, French, & Unis, 1987b). In the combined treatment, the parents received PMT and the children received PSST. In the control condition, the parents received contact meetings in which the child's treatment was discussed; the children met with a therapist in individual sessions where they discussed activities on the ward. At posttreatment and 1-year follow-up, the children in the PMT + PSST condition showed significantly less aggression and externalizing behavior at home and at school and greater prosocial behavior and overall adjustment than the contact-control children. A higher proportion of the PMT + PSST children than control children fell within the normative range of behavioral problems and prosocial behaviors at posttreatment and follow-up.

In a third study, we altered PSST on the basis of prior experience including the elaboration of in vivo practice (Kazdin, Bass, Siegel, & Thomas, 1989). Inpatient and outpatient cases (N = 112, ages 7–13) participated and were randomly assigned to one of three treatments: PSST, PSST with in vivo practice (PSST-P), which included therapeutically planned activities to extend training to settings outside of treatment; or client-centered relationship therapy (RT). The PSST and PSST-P children showed significantly greater reductions in antisocial behavior and overall behavior problems and greater increases in prosocial behavior than the RT children at posttreatment and 1-year follow-up on measures of child performance at home and at school. The PSST-P children showed greater changes than the PSST children on measures of functioning at school at posttreatment, but these differences were no longer evident at follow-up. The children in both PSST conditions showed significant reductions in deviant behavior and improvements in prosocial behavior from pretreatment to follow-up, whereas the RT children tended to remain at their pretreatment level of functioning.

In a fourth study, we evaluated the separate and combined effects of PSST and PMT in the treatment of outpatient children (N = 97, ages 7–13) (Kazdin, Siegel, & Bass, 1992). Children and their families were assigned randomly to PSST, PMT, or PSST + PMT combined. Each treatment improved child functioning (reduced overall deviance, aggressive, antisocial, and delinquent behavior, and increased prosocial competence). PSST + PMT combined led to more marked changes in child and parent functioning (parental stress, depression, and overall symptoms) at posttreatment and follow-up and placed a greater proportion of youth within the range of nonclinic (normative) levels of functioning at home and at school.

Our focus on outcome studies reflects an interest in developing treatment in an iterative fashion. The treatments have evolved based on clinical experience and research findings. An advantage of programmatic research is the opportunity to codify these changes and to develop better methods of implementation as well. In addition to direct tests of various treatments, we are interested in identifying child, parent, family, and contextual characteristics that contribute to outcome. We know that some children and families respond well to treatment. It is important to be able to identify the predictors of responsiveness to understand how treatment operates and also to direct cases better to treatments for which they are likely to be suited. For example, in a recent study we found that severity and breadth of child impairment, parental stress and psychopathology, and family dysfunction predicted treatment outcome (Kazdin, 1995a). More severe dysfunction in any of these domains predicted less responsiveness to treatment. This work is only a beginning; our goal is to identify predictors that may be associated with responsiveness to specific treatments (e.g., problem-solving skills training) as well as those predictors that may influence responsiveness more generally (i.e., across a range of treatments).

Overall, our major findings indicate that:

- PSST, alone and in combination with PMT, produces reliable and significant reductions in antisocial behavior and increases in prosocial behavior among children (ages 7–13).
- Improvements are not plausibly explained by the passage of time, repeated contact with a therapist, or nonspecific (common) treatment factors associated with participation in treatment.
- The effects of treatment are evident in performance at home, at school, and in the community both immediately after treatment and up to a 1-year follow-up assessment.
- Treatment effects have been obtained with both inpatient and outpatient cases.
- Improvements are evident in child behavior as well as parent stress, depression, and overall symptom scores.
- Responsiveness to treatment is influenced by impairment and dysfunction prior to treatment in the child, the parents, and the family.

Related Findings: Briefly Noted

Other work from our program has helped us understand antisocial children and families and their treatment. We have devised measures to assess a broad range of overt and covert antisocial behaviors (Kazdin & Esveldt-Dawson, 1986) and aggression and hostility (Kazdin, Rodgers, Colbus, & Siegel, 1987). Children who vary in overt and covert antisocial behavior have other characteristics that might be helpful in selecting treatment (see Kazdin, 1992a). Also, critical to our program is the evaluation of the extent to which parents and children view treatment as acceptable and hence measures have been developed toward that end as well (Kazdin, Siegel, & Bass, 1992). Finally, we also have devised measures to operationalize several areas of risk (e.g., parent child-rearing practices, family characteristics, parent history of antisocial behavior) that may moderate response to treatment (Kazdin, 1989; Kazdin et al., 1993).

We also have begun to evaluate patient attrition in large part because parents and families of antisocial children are known to experience significant dysfunction, stress, and socioeconomic disadvantage, all variables likely to influence premature termination from treatment (Armbruster & Kazdin, 1994). Our work has shown that premature termination from treatment is greater for younger mothers, single parents, and minority group families; for families with socioeconomic disadvantage, high stress and life events, adverse family child-rearing practices; and for children with greater severity of antisocial behavior (Kazdin et al., 1993; Kazdin, Mazurick, & Siegel, 1994; Kazdin, Stolar, & Marciano, 1995). Interestingly, children and families who drop out early in treatment are quite different from those who drop out later (Kazdin & Mazurick, 1994). The study of patient attrition is directly related to the development of our treatment. The goal is to help identify families at risk for dropping out, to devise interventions to retain cases in treatment, and to help identify factors that may relate to outcome. Characteristics of children, parents, and family that relate to dropping out of treatment overlap with those factors that predict less responsiveness to treatment among those who remain in treatment (e.g., Kazdin, 1995a; Kazdin et al., 1995).

ISSUES AND LIMITATIONS

Magnitude of Therapeutic Change

Our studies have shown that statistically significant improvements are made with treatment and that these effects are maintained over time. Yet, do the gains make a difference to the youth or to others in everyday life? *Clinical significance* refers to the practical value or importance of the effect of an intervention, that is, whether it makes any "real" difference to the clients or to others, and can be measured in many ways (see Kazdin, 1992b). We have examined the extent to which treatment returns individuals to normative levels of functioning. For example, in a study mentioned previously, we compared the effectiveness of PSST, PMT, and PSST + PMT combined (Kazdin et al., 1992). Among the outcome measures were standardized scales (Child Behavior Checklist) completed by parents and teachers. The scales reflect a broad range of emotional and behavioral problems. Development of the scales indicated that the 90th percentile is the cutoff point that best delineates clinic from community (nonreferred) samples (Achenbach & Edelbrock, 1983). We consider change as clinically significant if children's scores at the end of treatment fall below this cutoff.

Figure 1 shows the means at pre- and posttreatment, and at a 1-year follow-up, for antisocial children. Both parent (upper panel) and teacher evaluations (lower panel) are presented and show mean levels in relation to the normative range. In addition to the means, we are of course very interested in how many individuals fall within the normative range. In the parent-based measure, 33%, 39%, and 64% of youth from PSST, PMT, and

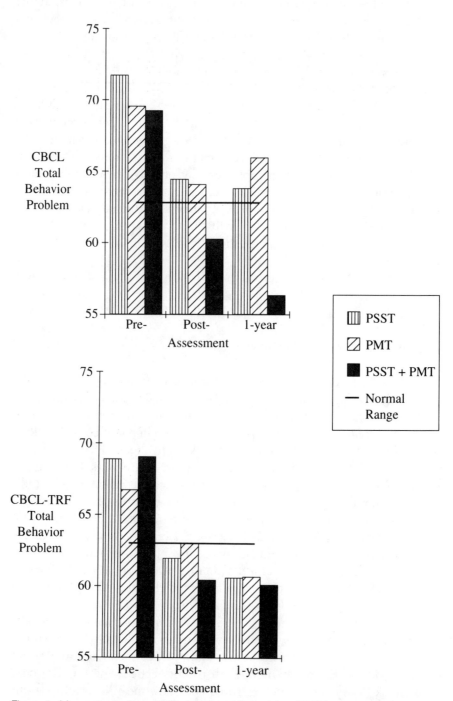

Figure 1. Mean scores for problem-solving skills training (PSST), parent management training (PMT), and PSST + PMT combined for the total behavior problem scales of the parent-completed Child Behavior Checklist (CBCL, upper panel) and teacher-completed CBCL (lower panel). The horizontal line reflects the upper limit of the nonclinical (normal) range of children of the same age and sex. The scores below this line fall within the normal range. (From Kazdin et al. [1992] with permission.)

combined treatment, respectively, fell within the normal range at posttreatment. The results convey the limits of the outcomes. Reliable changes have been found with treatment but the magnitude of change leaves considerable room for improvement.

Maintenance of Change

The above comments focus on the magnitude of change. No less significant is whether treatment effects are maintained. In child and adolescent psychotherapy research, most (59%) studies do not report follow-up data. Among studies that do include follow-up, assessment takes place 5–6 months after treatment ends (Kazdin, Bass, Ayers, & Rodgers, 1990; Weisz, Weiss, Alicke, & Klotz, 1987). Obviously, follow-up assessment is critically important because developmental change is a strong competitor with treatment for many problems. Also, outcome results and the relative effectiveness of alternative treatments occasionally vary at posttreatment and follow-up (Kazdin, 1988). Consequently, the conclusions about treatment may be very different depending on the point of outcome assessment.

Follow-up assessment in our program has focused primarily on evaluation of child functioning 1 year after completing the program. Measures of home functioning are completed by the parents, who are well aware of the child's treatment history. However, measures of school functioning are completed by teachers who, at the time of follow-up, do not know the child's treatment history. Data from both informants typically show that reductions in symptoms as well as increases in prosocial behavior are maintained at home and at school. A limitation of this work has been the restriction to 1-year follow-up.

Outcome Criteria

There is a range of outcomes in which one might be interested in relation to the child. Symptom reduction alone is not likely to ensure the child's adjustment. Prosocial functioning and academic functioning are two domains that also relate to current as well as to long-term adjustment. These latter domains are infrequently assessed and very rarely focused on in treatment (Kazdin, Bass, et al., 1990). In our work, we have been interested in symptom reduction and prosocial functioning as treatment outcomes. Prosocial functioning can include a variety of components such as positive interactions with others, social interaction, and participation in activities. As might be expected, symptom scores and prosocial functioning are negatively correlated and tend to change together (see Kazdin, 1993a). Yet, the magnitude of the correlations is only moderate (e.g., .3–.5), indicating relatively little overlap even when the rater is the same (i.e., both prosocial and symptom measures completed by the parent). From the standpoint of treatment evaluation, those cases who show significant improvement in one domain may not show a gain in another domain. Related, we also are interested in evaluating performance across separate settings given that youth with CD often show dysfunction at home, at school, and in the community. Here too, the severity of symptoms at home and at school and the change in these measures over the course of treatment are not highly correlated (Kazdin, 1993a). The same can be said for changes in prosocial functioning across settings.

In general, the conclusions reached about the impact of treatment can vary by domain, setting, and informant. There continues to be a thirst for simple verdicts about treatment (i.e., what "works" and what "works better"). Investigators are not being oppositional when they note that the answer "depends." The pattern of findings can vary by different measures; sometimes treatments are different on one set of measures but not others (e.g., Kazdin et al., 1989; Szapocznik et al., 1989). This pattern can result from a variety of methodological influences (e.g., restricted range or weak reliability of the measure), as well as the likelihood that treatments affect different domains differently.

Expansion of Outcome Criteria

Symptom reduction and prosocial functioning improvement of the conduct disordered youth present a sufficient challenge for treatment research. Yet, our daily contact with families has led us to take a broader view of treatment outcome. Although the children are clearly impaired, a focus on measures of child functioning alone ignores a great deal of clinically relevant information. Specifically, parents and family members usually experience considerable stress associated with the child's dysfunction. For example, stress from school is ongoing for many families. Parents are frequently called about their children and children are constantly dismissed, detained, or expelled. The net effect is to create a number of other problems (e.g., day care for the child at home, search for an alternate school). Clearly the quality of life is affected by the impact the child can have on the family as a system. In addition, parents often experience psychiatric impairment and sources of stress (e.g., marital conflict, poverty) not directly resulting from the child. Yet, these facets of parent and family life may contribute to and be exacerbated by the child's dysfunction.

Our research has focused primarily on child functioning in diverse settings, clearly the central thrust of our treatment program. At the same time, we have begun to see this as a limited conceptual view of outcome. In our work, we have shown that parent stress and depression decrease with treatment of the child (Kazdin et al., 1992). Additional work assessing the outcomes of family members and the interrelations of these outcomes with maintenance of change will be important.

IMPROVING TREATMENT OUTCOMES: DIRECTIONS FOR RESEARCH

Several research directions have been proposed to advance child psychotherapy research, including an expansion in the range of techniques that are studied, the study of treatment processes and mechanisms, and the integration critical moderators (e.g., child sex, developmental level, ethnicity) into treatment (see Kazdin, 1994b). In relation to the development of effective treatment of CD, additional directions are especially relevant.

Extended Care in the Delivery of Treatment

The model for psychotherapy research usually consists of a brief, time-limited intervention. In the majority of studies with children and adolescents, treatment lasts 8–10 weeks with 1-hour weekly sessions. In clinical work, the duration is likely to be much longer for youth with CD (Silver & Silver, 1983). CD is a pervasive and enduring type of impairment, and one wonders whether weekly versions of treatment are likely to have impact. More extended and enduring treatment in some form may be needed to achieve clinically important effects with the greatest number of youths. Two ways of delivering extended treatment illustrate the point.

The first variation might be referred to as a *chronic-care model*. The model of treatment delivery that may be needed can be likened to the model used in the treatment of diabetes mellitus. With this disorder, ongoing treatment (insulin) is needed to ensure that the benefits of treatment are sustained. The benefits of treatment would end with discontinuation of treatment, à la the conventional model of psychotherapy. In the context of conduct disorder, a variation of ongoing treatment (chronic care) may be needed. Perhaps after the child is referred, treatment is provided to address the current crises and to have impact on functioning at home, at school, and in the community. After improvement is achieved, treatment is altered rather than terminated. At that point, the child could enter into maintenance therapy (i.e., continued treatment perhaps in varying schedules ["doses"]). Treatment would continue but perhaps on a more intermittent basis. Continued treatment in this fashion has been effective as a model for treating recurrent depression in adults (see Kupfer et al., 1992).

The second variation might be referred to as a *dental-care model*. After initial treatment and demonstrated improvement in functioning in everyday life, treatment is suspended. At this point, the child's functioning begins to be monitored systematically (with standardized measures) and regularly (e.g., every 3 months). Treatment could be provided as needed (*pro re nata* [PRN]) based on the assessment data or emergent issues raised by the family, teachers, or others. The approach might be likened to the more familiar model of dental care in the United States in which "check-ups" are recommended every 6 months; an intervention is provided if, and as, needed based on these periodic checks.

The main difficulty in treating CD has not been in the development of interventions per se. Rather, our conceptualizations of CD and of clinical trials greatly limit the clinical effectiveness we can achieve. There is a great deal that can be accomplished if we do not consider CD as merely a confined set of symptoms of the child and do not conceive of treatment as a brief, time-limited regimen of care. A number of cognitive-, behavioral-, family-, and community-based interventions have shown that they can effect change (see Kazdin, 1985). Intermittent continuation of treatment would be reasonable until more abbreviated treatments with long-term impact were identified.

Matching Children and Families to Treatment

Child and psychotherapy research, unlike research with adults, has rarely made efforts to identify child, parent, and family factors that moderate treatment effects for a given technique (Kazdin, Bass, et al., 1990). In the case of CD, there are many viable leads that consist of ways of conceptualizing and identifying subgroups. For example, many different ways of subtyping CD have been suggested based on youth whose primary symptoms are aggression versus stealing (Patterson, 1982); whose aggression is reactive (in response to others) rather than proactive (as an initial way of goal attainment) (Dodge, 1991); whose antisocial behavior is primarily overt (fighting) rather than covert (lying, truancy) (Loeber & Schmalling, 1985); and whose symptoms have an onset in childhood rather than adolescence (Moffitt, 1993; Patterson, DeBaryshe, & Ramsey, 1989).

There are many other leads to delineating among youth with CD. Child, parent, and family loading of risk factors might be one. Perhaps those whose risk loading is very high are the more difficult to treat and the ones for whom current treatments produce nugatory effects. Other, more parsimonious, leads might derive from looking at severity, chronicity, and breadth of child symptoms. Also, age, sex, and ethnicity might well influence treatment outcome and serve as a basis of matching youth to treatment, because each of these variables can play a significant role in the pattern, onset, and risk factors related to antisocial behavior.

An important research direction will be to identify youth who respond to currently available treatments, to replicate these effects, and then to screen and direct such youth to the demonstrably effective treatments. At the same time, of course, further work can continue to identify treatments for other antisocial youth and to continue to seek ways of increasing the proportion of youth who can be effectively treated. As noted earlier, it may be that some segment of antisocial youth require life-long monitoring and treatment. Yet, much remains to be completed to identify youth who vary in their amenability to treatment.

Intervening to Treat Parental Stress and Dysfunction

Parents and families of youth with CD often experience multiple factors that can play a role in child dysfunction as well as treatment. Specifically, socioeconomic disadvantage, marital conflict, parent psychopathology, stress, and social isolation are among the many characteristics in the families of children with CD. Families who show adversity in one or more of these domains are more likely to drop out of treatment prematurely, to show fewer gains in treatment (among those who remain), and are less likely to maintain therapeutic gains (e.g., Dadds & McHugh, 1992; Dumas & Wahler, 1983; Kazdin, 1995a; Kazdin et al., 1993; Webster-Stratton, 1985). The precise mechanism(s) through which family adversity operates has not been isolated, in part because many of the factors (e.g., socioeconomic disadvantage, marital conflict, social isolation) often come together as a "package." Occasionally, stress has been evaluated as a key construct to mediate the impact of the many factors that impinge on the family. Stress has been found to disrupt discipline practices of the parent in ways that promote deviant child behavior (see Dumas & Wahler, 1985; Patterson et al., 1992). Yet, many factors may mediate this effect (e.g., maternal depression, single-parent status).

It is likely that much greater attention will be required to address parent and family issues in the context of treatment of children with CD. Few studies can be brought to bear on the matter. As an illustration, in one study for youth with CD, a parent training program was used to alter child functioning (Dadds, Schwartz, & Sanders, 1987). Parents were classified as experiencing marital discord or not experiencing discord at the beginning of treatment. All families received parent training; families were randomly assigned to receive additional treatment component (partner support) designed to address marital conflict, communication, and problem-solving. The addition of a parent component did not yield differences in therapeutic change among the children at posttreatment assessment. However, at a 6-month follow-up, families with marital discord who had received partner support maintained the gains in treatment to a greater extent than those who did not receive partner support. Thus, addressing parent and family issues had an impact on the therapeutic change of the child. In general, the importance of parent and family influences are widely acknowledged in clinical applications of treatment for children and adolescents (Kazdin, Siegel, & Bass, 1990). However, the impact of interventions that address these influences is infrequently studied.

IMPLICATIONS FOR CLINICAL PRACTICE

The implications of our research for clinical work with CD can be discussed in different ways. First and most obvious is that cognitively based treatment and parent management training for clinically referred children are reasonable interventions to apply in clinical work. There also are a number of treatment manuals that encompass these techniques or variations and are readily available (see Kazdin, 1994b). Few of the techniques used in clinical practice with children and adolescents have any empirical evidence in their behalf (Kazdin, 1988). In the case of CD, a number of treatments (e.g., PSST, PMT, functional family therapy, multisystemic family therapy) have evidence in their behalf and are prime candidates for clinical use.

A second implication of our work is somewhat less obvious, but arguably as critical for clinical practice. Several features of the research are designed to augment treatment implementation and therapeutic effects. To begin, therapist training in the techniques is extensive. There is no doubt a great deal of skill and art in the delivery of treatment; yet, there also is a great deal of skill and performance of the therapist to the criteria in that what is said, how it is said, when it is said, and what is not said can be explicitly rehearsed and trained under a variety of conditions. In our own program, and other programs as well, therapists can be trained to a level of mastery and supervised in an ongoing basis to sustain and improve that level. Such practices greatly depart from the level of training and mastery of treatment in many clinical settings. The manner of training therapists, rehearsing treatment practices and skills, and providing ongoing feedback helps to ensure treatment integrity.

In addition, treatment supervision also aids clinical care. In our own program, and many other programs as well, all treatment is videotaped and also can be viewed live to provide immediate feedback to a therapist and to problem solve with the therapist regarding how to redress a problem. This kind of supervision not only maintains the integrity of treatment but also enhances quality of the treatment for the individual case.

Procedures to train and to supervise therapists, to monitor treatment integrity, and to manage patient care are features of research that may have critically important implications for clinical practice. The results of treatments in research may rely on the quality of training, supervision, monitoring, and patient management that are often routine. Many of these practices could be implemented in clinical settings.

Overall, the techniques emphasized in treatment research receive the major attention. Specifically, one looks to research to evaluate techniques with the idea that once identified, these can be disseminated to clinical practice. Perhaps this goal is attainable. However, from our experience (admittedly limited to only one program, primarily one disorder, and within a restricted age range), the effectiveness of treatment is not separate from the quality of therapist training, monitoring of treatment, and feedback to therapists. More broadly, a number of practices of research can be adapted for clinical use to improve the quality of individual patient care (see Kazdin, 1993b).

FINAL COMMENTS

Our program is devoted to the treatment of children with CD and their families. We have focused on combined cognitive–behavioral procedures to focus on the interpersonal cognitive processes of the child (problem-solving skills training) and the parent–child interactions (parent management training). The treatments are conceptually and procedurally compatible by at once focusing on facets within the individual (e.g., cognitive and behavioral repertoires, predisposition to respond to potentially problematic situations), as well as external and interactional events (e.g., antecedents and consequences from others) to promote prosocial behavior. With both of the treatments, emphasis is placed on altering performance outside of the treatment setting, specifically at home, at school, and in the community. Although formal treatment sessions form the basis of the intervention, much of the treatment is conducted outside of the sessions. The child, parents, and teachers have separate but interrelated roles guided by the therapist. Treatment outcome studies, our own and those of others, have indicated that clinically referred patients improve with PSST and PMT and that effects are maintained at least to 1-year follow-up assessment.

CD represents a special challenge, given the multiple domains of functioning that are affected. Although one might like to restrict the focus of treatment to the symptoms of the child, broader influences (parent, family, peer) often must be considered because of their demonstrated relation to antisocial behavior or because of the opportunities they provide for producing change. A tenet in child psychopathology is that improved treatment will result from improved diagnosis. Unfortunately, the notion of diagnosis has been restricted to the focus on symptoms and symptoms constellations of the child. Yet, in the case of CD, multiple domains of the child, parent, family, and context may be relevant to understand child functioning and adjustment and for treatment selection and evaluation of outcome. In relation to the child, for example, symptoms, and prosocial and academic functioning are quite relevant for long-term adjustment. In relation to the parents and family, stress, conflict, and untoward child-rearing practices (e.g., harsh punishment, neglect, poor supervision) are significant as well. Finally, environments are critically important to understand, conceptualize, and "diagnose." In this context, diagnosis does not mean to pathologize but rather to consider in systematic ways so as to relate to child functioning and treatment outcome.

Advances in treatment for children emerge from focusing on treatments and dysfunctions. Yet, in the case of CD, there is consistent evidence that problems emerge in an interpersonal and social context and that factors not only within the individual, but also within the family and society, can contribute. This does not mean that every source of influence has to be integrated into treatment. At the same time, the broad range of influences and the absence of clearly effective treatments for CD mean that it might be profitable to reconsider treatment models and options. In this broader context, the present research has focused on developing PSST and PMT and integrating them in a way to encompass child functioning across diverse settings and domains of functioning. We have only begun to explore some of the family issues that may warrant intervention as well, other than those directly involved in child rearing.

REFERENCES

Achenbach, T. M., & Edelbrock, C. S. (1983). *Manual for the Child Behavior Checklist and Revised Child Behavior Profile*. Burlington, VT: University Associates in Psychiatry.

American Psychiatric Association. (1994). *Diagnostic and statistical manual of mental disorders* (4th ed.). Washington, DC: Author.

Armbruster, P., & Kazdin, A. E. (1994). Attrition in child psychotherapy. In T. H. Ollendick & R. J. Prinz (Eds.), *Advances in clinical child psychology* (Vol. 16, pp. 81–108). New York: Plenum.

Baer, R. A., & Nietzel, M. T. (1991). Cognitive and behavioral treatment of impulsivity in children: A meta-analytic review of the outcome literature. *Journal of Clinical Child Psychology, 20*, 400–412.

Bank, L., Marlowe, J. H., Reid, J. B., Patterson, G. R., & Weinrott, M. R. (1991). A comparative evaluation of parent-training interventions for families of chronic delinquents. *Journal of Abnormal Child Psychology, 19*, 15–33.

Brandt, D. E., & Zlotnick, S. J. (1988). *The psychology and treatment of the youthful offender*. Springfield, IL: Charles C. Thomas.

Dadds, M. R., & McHugh, T. A. (1992). Social support and treatment outcome in behavioral family therapy for child conduct problems. *Journal of Consulting and Clinical Psychology, 60*, 252–259.

Dadds, M. R., Schwartz, S., & Sanders, M. R. (1987). Marital discord and treatment outcome in behavioral treatment of child conduct disorders. *Journal of Consulting and Clinical Psychology, 55*, 396–403.

Dodge, K. A. (1991). The structure and function of reactive and proactive aggression. In D. J. Pepler & K. H. Rubin (Eds.), *The development and treatment of childhood aggression* (pp. 201–218). Hillsdale, NJ: Erlbaum.

Dodge, K. A., Price, J. M., Bachorowski, J., & Newman, J. P. (1990). Hostile attributional biases in severely aggressive adolescents. *Journal of Abnormal Psychology, 99*, 385–392.

Dodge, K. A., & Somberg, D. R. (1987). Hostile attributional biases among aggressive boys are exacerbated under conditions of threats to the self. *Child Development, 58*, 213–224.

Dumas, J. E. (1989). Treating antisocial behavior in children: Child and family approaches. *Clinical Psychology Review, 9*, 197–222.

Dumas, J. E., & Wahler, R. G. (1983). Predictors of treatment outcome in parent training: Mother insularity and socioeconomic disadvantage. *Behavioral Assessment, 5*, 301–313.

Dumas, J. E., & Wahler, R. G. (1985). Indiscriminate mothering as a contextual factor in aggressive oppositional child behavior: "Damned if you do and damned if you don't." *Journal of Applied Behavior Analysis, 13*, 1–17.

Durlak, J. A., Fuhrman, T., & Lampman, C. (1991). Effectiveness of cognitive–behavioral therapy for maladapting children: A meta-analysis. *Psychological Bulletin, 110*, 204–214.

Fergusson, D. M., Horwood, L. J., & Lloyd, M. (1991). Confirmatory factor models of attention deficit and conduct disorder. *Journal of Child Psychology and Psychiatry, 32*, 257–274.

Forehand, R., & Long, N. (1988). Outpatient treatment of the acting out child: Procedures, long-term follow-up data, and clinical problems. *Advances in Behaviour Research and Therapy, 10*, 129–177.

Hinshaw, S. P., Lahey, B. B., & Hart, E. L. (1993). Issues of taxonomy and comorbidity in the development of conduct disorder. *Development and Psychopathology, 5*, 31–49.

Institute of Medicine. (1989). *Research on children and adolescents with mental, behavioral, and developmental disorders.* Washington, DC: National Academy Press.

Kazdin, A. E. (1985). *Treatment of antisocial behavior in children and adolescents.* Homewood, IL: Dorsey Press.

Kazdin, A. E. (1987). Treatment of antisocial behavior in children: Current status and future directions. *Psychological Bulletin, 102*, 187–203.

Kazdin, A. E. (1988). *Child psychotherapy: Developing and identifying effective treatments.* Elmsford, NY: Pergamon.

Kazdin, A. E. (1989). Hospitalization of antisocial children: Clinical course, follow-up status, and predictors of outcome. *Advances in Behaviour Research and Therapy, 11*, 1–67.

Kazdin, A. E. (1992a). Overt and covert antisocial behavior: Child and family characteristics among psychiatric inpatient children. *Journal of Child and Family Studies, 1*, 3–20.

Kazdin, A. E. (1992b). *Research design in clinical psychology* (2nd ed.). Needham Heights, MA: Allyn & Bacon.

Kazdin, A. E. (1993a). Changes in behavioral problems and prosocial functioning in child treatment. *Journal of Child and Family Studies, 2*, 5–22.

Kazdin, A. E. (1993b). Evaluation in clinical practice: Clinically sensitive and systematic methods of treatment delivery. *Behavior Therapy, 24*, 11–45.

Kazdin, A. E. (1993c). Treatment of conduct disorder: Progress and directions in psychotherapy research. *Development and Psychopathology, 5*, 277–310.

Kazdin, A. E. (1994a). *Behavior modification in applied settings* (5th ed.). Pacific Grove, CA: Brooks/Cole.

Kazdin, A. E. (1994b). Psychotherapy for children and adolescents. In A. E. Bergin & S. L. Garfield (Eds.), *Handbook of psychotherapy and behavior change: An empirical analysis* (4th ed., pp. 543–594). New York: Wiley.

Kazdin, A. E. (1995a). Child, parent, and family dysfunction as predictors of outcome in cognitive–behavioral treatment of antisocial children. *Behaviour Research and Therapy, 33*, 271–281.

Kazdin, A. E. (1995b). *Conduct disorder in childhood and adolescence* (2nd ed.). Thousand Oaks, CA: Sage.

Kazdin, A. E., Bass, D., Ayers, W. A., & Rodgers, A. (1990). Empirical and clinical focus of child and adolescent psychotherapy research. *Journal of Consulting and Clinical Psychology, 58*, 729–740.

Kazdin, A. E., Bass, D., Siegel, T., & Thomas, C. (1989). Cognitive–behavioral treatment and relationship therapy in the treatment of children referred for antisocial behavior. *Journal of Consulting and Clinical Psychology, 57*, 522–535.

Kazdin, A. E., & Esveldt-Dawson, K. (1986). The Interview for Antisocial Behavior: Psychometric characteristics and concurrent validity with child psychiatric inpatients. *Journal of Psychopathology and Behavioral Assessment, 8*, 289–303.

Kazdin, A. E., Esveldt-Dawson, K., French, N. H., & Unis, A. S. (1987a). Problem-solving skills training and relationship therapy in the treatment of antisocial child behavior. *Journal of Consulting and Clinical Psychology, 55*, 76–85.

Kazdin, A. E., Esveldt-Dawson, K., French, N. H., & Unis, A. S. (1987b). The effects of parent management training and problem-solving skills training combined in the treatment of antisocial child behavior. *Journal of the American Academy of Child and Adolescent Psychiatry, 26*, 416–424.

Kazdin, A. E., & Mazurick, J. L. (1994). Dropping out of child psychotherapy: Distinguishing early and late dropouts over the course of treatment. *Journal of Consulting and Clinical Psychology, 62*, 1069–1074.

Kazdin, A. E., Mazurick, J. L., & Bass, D. (1993). Risk for attrition in treatment of antisocial children and families. *Journal of Clinical Child Psychology, 22*, 2–16.

Kazdin, A. E., Mazurick, J. L., & Siegel, T. C. (1994). Treatment outcome among children with externalizing disorder who terminate prematurely versus those who complete psychotherapy. *Journal of the American Academy of Child and Adolescent Psychiatry, 33*, 549–557.

Kazdin, A. E., Rodgers, A., Colbus, D., & Siegel, T. (1987). Children's Hostility Inventory: Measurement of aggression and hostility in psychiatric inpatient children. *Journal of Clinical Child Psychology, 16*, 320–328.

Kazdin, A. E., Siegel, T. C., & Bass, D. (1990). Drawing upon clinical practice to inform research on child and adolescent psychotherapy: A survey of practitioners. *Professional Psychology: Research and Practice, 21*, 189–198.

Kazdin, A. E., Siegel, T., & Bass, D. (1992). Cognitive problem-solving skills training and parent management training in the treatment of antisocial behavior in children. *Journal of Consulting and Clinical Psychology, 60*, 733–747.

Kazdin, A. E., Stolar, M. J., & Marciano, P. L. (1995). Risk factors for dropping out of treatment among White and Black families. *Journal of Family Psychology, 9*, 402–417.

Kupfer, D. J., Frank, E., Perel, J. M., Cornes, C., Mallinger, A. G., Thase, M. E., McEachran, A. B., & Grochocinski, V. J. (1992). Five-year outcome for maintenance therapies in recurrent depression. *Archives of General Psychiatry, 49*, 769–773.

Loeber, R., & Schmalling, K. B. (1985). Empirical evidence for overt and covert patterns of antisocial conduct problems: A meta-analysis. *Journal of Abnormal Child Psychology, 13*, 337–352.

Long, P., Forehand, R., Wierson, M., & Morgan, A. (1994). Does parent training with young noncompliant children have long-term effects? *Behaviour Research and Therapy, 32*, 101–107.

McMahon, R. J., & Wells, K. C. (1989). Conduct disorders. In E. J. Mash & R. A. Barkley (Eds.), *Treatment of childhood disorders* (pp. 73–132). New York: Guilford Press.

Miller, G. E., & Prinz, R. J. (1990). Enhancement of social learning family interventions for child conduct disorder. *Psychological Bulletin, 108*, 291–307.

Moffitt, T. E. (1993). Adolescence-limited and life-course-persistent antisocial behavior: A developmental taxonomy. *Psychological Review, 100*, 674–701.

Offord, D. R., Boyle, M. H., & Racine, Y. A. (1991). The epidemiology of antisocial behavior. In D. J. Pepler & K. H. Rubin (Eds.), *The development and treatment of childhood aggression* (pp. 31–54). Hillsdale, NJ: Erlbaum.

Patterson, G. R. (1982). *Coercive family process.* Eugene, OR: Castalia.

Patterson, G. R. (1986). Performance models for antisocial boys. *American Psychologist, 41*, 432–444.

Patterson, G. R., Capaldi, D., & Bank, L. (1991). An early starter model for predicting delinquency. In D. J. Pepler & K. H. Rubin (Eds.), *The development and treatment of childhood aggression* (pp. 139–168). Hillsdale, NJ: Erlbaum.

Patterson, G. R., DeBaryshe, B. D., & Ramsey, E. (1989). A developmental perspective on antisocial behavior. *American Psychologist, 44*, 329–335.

Patterson, G. R., Reid, J. B., & Dishion, T. J. (1992). *Antisocial boys.* Eugene, OR: Castalia.

Pepler, D. J., & Rubin, K. H. (Eds.). (1991). *The development and treatment of childhood aggression*. Hillsdale, NJ: Erlbaum.

Robins, L. N. (1966). *Deviant children grown up*. Baltimore, MD: Williams & Wilkins.

Robins, L. N. (1978). Sturdy childhood predictors of adult antisocial behavior: Replications from longitudinal studies. *Psychological Medicine, 8*, 611–622.

Robins, L. N. (1981). Epidemiological approaches to natural history research: Antisocial disorders in children. *Journal of the American Academy of Child Psychiatry, 20*, 566–580.

Robins, L. N. (1991). Conduct disorder. *Journal of Child Psychology and Psychiatry, 32*, 193–212.

Rubin, K. H., Bream, L. A., & Rose-Krasnor, L. (1991). Social problem solving and aggression in childhood. In D. J. Pepler & K. H. Rubin (Eds.), *The development and treatment of childhood aggression* (pp. 219–248). Hillsdale, NJ: Erlbaum.

Rutter, M., & Giller, H. (1983). *Juvenile delinquency: Trends and perspectives*. New York: Penguin Books.

Shirk, S. R. (Ed.). (1988). *Cognitive development and child psychotherapy*. New York: Plenum.

Silver, L. B., & Silver, B. J. (1983). Clinical practice of child psychiatry: A survey. *Journal of the American Academy of Child Psychiatry, 22*, 573–579.

Spivack, G., & Shure, M. B. (1982). The cognition of social adjustment: Interpersonal cognitive problem solving thinking. In B. B. Lahey & A. E. Kazdin (Eds.), *Advances in clinical child psychology* (Vol. 5, pp. 323–372). New York: Plenum.

Szapocznik, J., Rio, A., Murray, E., Cohen, R., Scopetta, M., Rivas-Vasquez, A., Hervis, O., Posada, V., & Kurtines, W. (1989). Structural family versus psychodynamic child therapy for problematic Hispanic boys. *Journal of Consulting and Clinical Psychology, 57*, 571–578.

United States Congress, Office of Technology Assessment. (1991). *Adolescent health* (OTA-H-468). Washington, DC: U.S. Government Printing Office.

Walker, J. L., Lahey, B. B., Russo, M. F., Christ, M. A. G., McBurnett, K., Loeber, R., Stouthamer-Loeber, M., & Green, S. M. (1991). Anxiety, inhibition, and conduct disorder in children: I. Relation to social impairment. *Journal of the American Academy of Child and Adolescent Psychiatry, 30*, 187–191.

Webster-Stratton, C. (1985). Predictors of treatment outcome in parent training for conduct disordered children. *Behavior Therapy, 16*, 223–243.

Weisz, J. R., Weiss, B., Alicke, M. D., & Klotz, M. L. (1987). Effectiveness of psychotherapy with children and adolescents: Meta-analytic findings for clinicians. *Journal of Consulting and Clinical Psychology, 55*, 542–549.

18

EDUCATION AND COUNSELING FOR CHILD FIRESETTERS: A COMPARISON OF SKILLS TRAINING PROGRAMS WITH STANDARD PRACTICE

DAVID J. KOLKO

Childhood firesetting is a prevalent and costly problem in communities (Grolnick, Cole, Laurenitis, & Schwartzman, 1990; Kafry, 1980) and among psychiatric patients (Kolko, 1989; Kolko & Kazdin, 1988b). In 1985, juveniles committed approximately 57,000 arson fires at a cost of $631 million (Cook, Hersch, Gaynor, & Roehl, 1989). In 1986, approximately 40–70% of those arrested for arson were juveniles (U.S. Federal Bureau of Investigation, 1987) who accounted for a significant proportion of the nation's 1.828 billion dollars in property losses from incendiary fires, and for approximately 300 deaths and 4,000 injuries, most of which involved children (National Fire Protection Association [NFPA], 1987; Wooden & Berkey, 1984). Pediatric burn trauma, the most likely medical consequence of firesetting requiring hospitalization, may result in the formation of stress response symptoms, such as posttraumatic stress and depression (Cella, Perry, Kulchycky, & Goodwin, 1988). Such complications are even more likely to occur given the moderate rates of recurrent fire-

Preparation of this chapter was supported, in part, by a renewal of grant MH-39976 from the National Institute of Mental Health. Many of the background studies reviewed herein were conducted in collaboration with Alan E. Kazdin, PhD. Correspondence concerning this chapter should be directed to Dr. David J. Kolko, Director, Child and Parent Behavior Clinic, Western Psychiatric Institute and Clinic, University of Pittsburgh Medical Center, 3811 O'Hara St., Pittsburgh PA 15213.

setting found among children referred to community fire departments (65%; Parrish et al., 1985) or to psychiatric centers (23–58%; Kolko & Kazdin, 1988b; Stewart & Culver, 1982).

Although there is growing consensus regarding the clinical and social impact of childhood firesetting, studies and clinical reports differ widely in their description and definition of childhood firesetting or firestarting (see Gaynor & Hatcher, 1987; Kolko, 1989). Cases described in the literature differ in the ages of the children, frequency of firesetting, presence of property damages, nature of children's motives, and level of family dysfunction, among other characteristics. Yet, few comparison studies have examined how these characteristics influence the severity of the child's firesetting or other clinical problems. Clearly, some children exhibit serious firesetting characterized by frequent, intentional, concealed, and destructive incidents (Bumpass, Fagelman, & Brix, 1983; Jacobson, 1985b; Kolko & Kazdin, 1986; Stewart & Culver, 1982). Other children, often younger ones, have set a single fire at home, which appeared to be accidental or the result of curiosity or experimentation; these may be among the most common motives for children. Limited social effectiveness and skill, often manifested by emotional (e.g., anger) expressiveness difficulties, also have been implicated in the motives for firesetting (see Kolko, 1989). Accordingly, the use of fire may permit one to achieve interpersonal outcomes that could not have been easily produced through more direct expressive means.

Although motives and antecedent characterisics are important to understand, it is plausible that certain children may start additional fires because of the absence of any swift parental consequence or referral for services, or because unsanctioned fireplay has gotten out of control (Kafry, 1980); however, these explanations have not been well examined empirically (Kolko, 1988). In our research, children who acknowledge or whose parents acknowledge an unsanctioned use of fire that produces at least some damage to property have been classified as firesetters. Some evidence, described in a later section, has suggested that children who simply play with matches are more similar to firesetters than nonfiresetters. The absence of prospective, empirical studies makes it difficult to determine which children have clinically significant problems with fire and are likely to set additional ones, and what interventions they should receive. Other aspects of these cases make them challenging to the practitioner, such as the difficulty in predicting who is likely to set another fire and under what circumstances, in knowing whether psychological problems or more benign environmental factors underlie firesetting behavior and should be targeted during intervention, what individual and family characteristics should be targeted during treatment, and what to look for in terms of clinical response or improvement.

This chapter describes the application of several assessment and intervention findings, obtained from prior empirical studies of childhood firesetters, to the development and evaluation of an intervention outcome study for child firesetters. In this clinical trial, firesetters (aged 5–13 years) are assigned to intervention conditions that reflect contemporary methods used by both fire service officials (community: fire safety education) and mental health practitioners (clinic: psychological counseling). Some children were assigned to a standard practice condition. Accordingly, intervention is designed to be short-term, executed by trained specialists using program manuals, monitored to ensure therapeutic integrity, and evaluated using multiple measures from multiple sources. Pre–post comparisons will be supplemented with 1-year follow-up data. By way of introduction, evidence to suggest the need for such a study is reviewed.

CHARACTERISTICS AND CORRELATES OF CHILD FIRESETTING

Background Research Studies

Much of the evidence presented herein was based on a grant awarded to David J. Kolko and Alan E. Kazdin that compared and followed firesetting children and their nonfiresetting peers.[1] The scientific goals of that application were to (a) describe empirically the clinical profiles of firesetting children; (b) examine the antecedents, characteristics, and consequences of firesetting incidents; and (c) develop predictors of both the continuation and cessation of firesetting. As an overview to the present treatment study, the results of several studies designed to address these aims are reported briefly in this section.

Prevalence, Continuity, and Parent-Child Correspondence

Evidence from an initial study documented high prevalence rates for firesetting and matchplay among outpatients (19.4%, 24.4%) and inpatients (34.6%, 52.0%), and high rates of firesetting recidivism among inpatients (Kolko & Kazdin, 1988b). A related study found moderate-to-high parent–child agreement (κs = .58–.86) in rating these behaviors and other firesetting characteristics from a firesetting history interview that serves as the basis for classification of many of the samples to be reported in subsequent studies (Kolko & Kazdin, 1988a).

Measurement of Risk Factors for Firesetting

Separate interview measures of risk factors for firesetting were then operationalized for parents (the Firesetting Risk Inventory or FRI; Kolko

---

[1]Grant 39976 from the National Institute of Mental Health.

& Kazdin, 1989a) and children (Children's Firesetting Inventory or CFI; Kolko & Kazdin, 1989b). Parents of firesetters acknowledged significantly higher scores on measures of firesetting contact (e.g., curiosity about fire, involvement in fire-related acts, exposure to peers or to family fire models) and general child–parent behavior (e.g., negative behavior) or family environment (e.g., use of harsh punishment, less effective mild punishment). On the CFI, firesetters acknowledged more attraction to fire, past fireplay, family interest in fire, exposure to friends or family who smoke, and, somewhat surprisingly, knowledge of things that burn, but they tended to show less fire competence (skill) on role plays than nonfiresetters.

Description and Parameters of Children's Firesetting Incidents

Details of children's firesetting incidents were reported in two studies. In one study, parents completed the Fire Incident Analysis (FIA) to document parameters of their children's most serious incidents (Kolko & Kazdin, 1991c). Firesetters were classified as high and low on each of two primary motives (curiosity, anger). Heightened curiosity was associated with greater psychopathology, firesetting risk, and fire involvement; whereas heightened anger was associated with firesetting risk measures and behavioral problems. A parallel study of 95 firesetters described the Fire Incident Analysis for Children (FIA-C; Kolko & Kazdin, 1993). Access to incendiaries, lack of child remorse and of parental consequences, and motives of curiosity and fun were commonly reported characteristics. Four fire characteristics predicted their overall severity of involvement in fire at follow-up (i.e., fire out of home, acknowledgement of being likely to set another fire, a neutral or positive reaction to the fire, no parental response to the fire).

Child, Parent, and Family Dysfunction

Other evidence has documented a relationship between childhood firesetting and several forms of child dysfunction, such as heightened aggression, psychopathology, and social skills deficits (Kolko, Kazdin, & Meyer, 1985). In an extension of this study (Kolko & Kazdin, 1991b), firesetters were reported to exhibit more covert behavior than both matchplayers and nonfiresetters, and firesetters and matchplayers received more extreme scores than nonfiresetters on measures of aggression, externalizing behaviors, impulsivity, emotionality, and hostility, though they did not differ from one another. In contrast, child report measures revealed only a few differences associated with firesetting (e.g., aggression, unassertion, low self-esteem), relative to nonfiresetters.

Firesetting has also been associated with heightened personal psychiatric distress, marital disagreement, and exposure to stressful life events, and less child acceptance, monitoring, discipline, and involvement in activities that enhance the child's personal development and family relationships (Kazdin & Kolko, 1986). Firesetters have characterized their parent's child rearing practices as involving greater lax discipline, nonenforcement, and anxiety induction, with scores for matchplayers generally falling between firesetters and control children.

Recidivism and Follow-up

A prospective study that followed a sample of 138 children for 1 year showed that 14 of 78 nonfiresetters (18%) later had set a fire, and that 21 of 60 firesetters (35%) had set an additional fire by follow-up (Kolko & Kazdin, 1992). Late starting was associated only with limited family sociability, whereas recidivism was associated with child knowledge about combustibles and involvement in fire-related activities, community complaints about fire contact, child hostility, lax discipline, family conflict and limited parental acceptance, family sociability, and use of rules and of an organized home environment. Some of these variables parallel certain characteristics that have been associated with adult arson (Rice & Harris, 1991).

Summary of Risk Factors and Correlates

When integrated with our initial risk-factor model (Kolko & Kazdin, 1986) and more recent research (Kolko, 1989), the individual factors associated with the onset and continuation of firesetting, on the basis of this work, appear to aggregate into two primary domains (see Table 1). The first domain (involvement with, interest in, and/or awareness of fire) includes experiences or conditions that support fireplay (e.g., exposure to fire models), idiosyncratic causes (e.g., curiosity, motive resolution), and limited fire competence (see Cole et al., 1983, 1986; Kafry, 1980; Kolko & Kazdin, 1989a, 1989b). The second domain (general behavioral and environmental dysfunction or conditions) reflects variables such as the use of indirect forms of aggression, other antisocial behaviors, and parental or family dysfunction (Cole et al., 1986; Gaynor & Hatcher, 1987; Jacobson, 1985a, 1985b; Kolko et al., 1985; Showers & Pickrell, 1987; Stewart & Culver, 1982). Similar characteristics have been found in adult arsonists (see Geller, 1987; Kolko, 1985). Firesetting has been associated with conduct disorder in some studies (see American Psychiatric Association, 1987; Heath, Hardesty, Goldfine, & Walker, 1985; Kelso & Stewart, 1986), but not others (Kolko et al., 1985; Kolko & Kazdin, 1989a, 1989b).

TABLE 1
Factors Associated with Firesetting Behavior

Involvement with, interest in, or awareness of fire

Experiences or conditions that support use of fire
1. Exposure to fire models
   Early exposure to models
   Early experiences with fire/interest
   Exposure to adult and peer models and incendiary/smoking materials
2. Idiosyncratic causes or motives
   Curiosity, fascination with or attraction to fire
   Anger or revenge, interpersonal control
3. Limited fire competence
   Limited fire-safety skill

General behavioral or environmental dysfunction or conditions

Reinforcement of aggression or coercive behavior without direct confrontation
1. Behavioral repertoire of aggressive, antisocial, and delinquent behavior (e.g., conduct disorder)
2. Poor impulse and anger control
3. Social competence and skills deficits

Parent or family factors that increase child deviant behavior
1. Inconsistent or harsh discipline
2. Limited parental consequences
3. Limited monitoring of child behavior
4. Discordant, dysfunctional, and abusive or neglectful families

Note. Adapted from Kolko & Kazdin (1986) with permission.

INTERVENTION AND TREATMENT

Approaches and Procedures

Intervention methods vary in the degree to which they target fire-specific experiences or more general behavioral and environmental characteristics (Gaynor & Hatcher, 1987; Kolko, 1985, 1988; Wooden & Berkey, 1984). To place this literature in historical perspective, what is regarded as standard practice in the fire service is described briefly.

Standard Practice in the Fire Service

Existing practice in the fire service has consisted primarily of a firehouse orientation or tour for the typical "young and curious" firesetter and is designed to heighten the child's awareness of the dangers of fire, with an occasional follow-up visit or call to the family (Gaynor, McLaughlin, & Hatcher, 1984; Kevin Mellott, personal communication, January 9, 1989). Because such brief and informal contact with a firefighter may be insufficient, training in fire safety skills or treatment designed to alter the child's cognitive–behavioral practices may be a more effective intervention.

Fire Safety Education

Instruction in fire safety skills and practices (e.g., stop/drop/roll) is commonly provided by community programs (Cook, Hersch, Gaynor, & Roehl, 1989). The materials include risk interviews and technical materials for intervention (e.g., Interviewing and Counseling Juvenile Firesetter Program [ICJF]; Federal Emergency Management Agency [FEMA], 1979, 1983). Among didactic presentations (e.g., Dennis, 1979), the Learn Not To Burn (LNTB) program (NFPA, 1979) emphasizes protection (e.g., fire drills), prevention (e.g., using matches safely), and persuasion (e.g., practicing safe smoking), and may be the only program that has demonstrated its impact on firesafety knowledge, relative to control children (NFPA, 1978). Other approaches provide training in fire evacuation and assistance skills (Jones, Kazdin, & Haney, 1981; Jones, Ollendick, & Shinske, 1989).

Psychological Treatment

Among case reports and empirical studies, four general approaches have been used:

1. contingency management procedures that discourage involvement with fire and reinforce contact with nonfire materials (Adler, Nunn, Northam, Lebnan, & Ross, 1994; Stawar, 1976);
2. negative practice (repeatedly lighting matches) to satiate and then extinguish a child's interest in fire (Holland, 1969; Kolko, 1983; McGrath, Marshall, & Prior, 1979);
3. prosocial skills training in the expression of anger and emotional arousal to address the motives for setting fires (Kolko & Ammerman, 1988; McGrath et al., 1979), or in other cognitive–behavioral skills (DeSalvatore & Hornstein, 1991); and
4. family therapy (Eisler, 1974; Madanes, 1981; Minuchin, 1974).

Certain applications offer related services, such as graphs that depict personal and environmental correlates of a fire (Bumpass, Fagelman, & Brix, 1983) and individual or family psychotherapy or both (Bumpass, Brix, & Preston, 1985). Most interventions have incorporated several procedures (e.g., contingencies or behavioral training skills) and reported reduced firesetting at follow-up, although few controlled data have been noted. These reports highlight the need to consider the behavioral and functional context of firesetting and its relationship to the child's interpersonal practices, and the use of punishment and reinforcement procedures.

Pilot and Background Studies of Intervention and Treatment

In an effort to understand the relevance of these findings to the intervention process (Gaynor & Hatcher, 1987; Kolko, 1985, 1988; Wooden & Berkey, 1984), the author examined the content and operations of various intervention or treatment programs using survey and experimental studies. These studies are reviewed briefly.

Description and Comparison of National Intervention Programs

A national survey of 16 FEMA-sponsored ICJF and 13 Firehawks affiliates determined the characteristics, functions, and service delivery issues associated with community treatment (Kolko, 1988). These findings suggested the importance of teaching fire safety skills and making psychosocial intervention available, assessing child and family variables associated with firesetting, basing interventions on conceptual models and empirically supported procedures, and conducting a formal follow-up to assess outcome and evaluate its predictors.

Evaluation of Fire Safety and Education Skills with Psychiatrically Disturbed Children

Another study documented the benefit of intervention with hospitalized firesetters who were randomly assigned to Group Fire Safety/Prevention Skills Training (FSST) or Individual Fire Awareness/Discussion (FAD) (Kolko, Watson, & Faust, 1991). FSST was associated with a reduction of contact with fire-related toys and matches in an analogue task, and an increase in fire safety knowledge, relative to FAD children. Parent-report measures, at 6-month follow-up, showed that FSST children were less frequently engaged in all four forms of involvement with fire than PSD children (16.7% vs. 58.3%). Although this study offered preliminary empirical findings to support FSST, relative to a standard practice condition, additional expansion and evaluation of this educational approach is clearly needed.

Application of Selected Behavioral and Psychological Procedures

Applications of specialized cognitive–behavioral and contingency management procedures by the author have been conducted with referred children, including home-based reinforcement and response-cost contingencies (Kolko, 1983), graphing of prior incidents and psychological skills training (Kolko & Ammerman, 1988), and fire safety assessment and skills training and parent management training (Cox-Jones, Lubetsky, Fultz, &

Kolko, 1990). These interventions were associated with reduced firesetting behavior and suggest the need to target child behavior or environmental contingencies.

Summary of Intervention Procedures

The anecdotal, clinical, and limited empirical evidence mentioned earlier highlights the role of two primary domains associated with firesetting: (a) experience with, exposure to, and interest in fire (fire-specific involvement), and (b) individual and family conditions that influence child behavior (behavioral and environmental control). Accordingly, fire safety education targets the former, whereas psychosocial intervention targets the latter, such that each approach addresses specific characteristics associated with increased firesetting risk (Cook et al., 1989; Gaynor, 1985). There exists only anecdotal or limited empirical support for the usefulness of these approaches. A comparative evaluation of both interventions would advance the treatment of childhood firesetters. This population is suited to the proposed treatments because of the sizable population of firesetters that may set multiple fires and exhibit psychosocial maladjustment, firesetters are referred to fire service and mental health systems for intervention, and factors in the two-risk factor domains may be translated effectively into procedures applied to reduce firesetting behavior.

TREATMENT OUTCOME STUDY: DESIGN AND METHODS

Objectives

On the basis of a review of the fire service and mental health literature, the current outcome study may represent the first controlled comparison study of intervention for child firesetters. Firesetting children, aged 5–12 years, were assigned randomly to either fire safety education (FSE) or psychosocial treatment (PT) groups. Because of logistic considerations and referral patterns, cases that could not be randomized or would not consent to randomization were assigned to a brief and routine condition that was designed to reflect contemporary educational practices in the fire service, namely, a home visit from a firefighter (FHV). Thus, the two intensive programs were first compared with one another and, then, with a third, minimal-content condition without the use of a notreatment or waitlist control group. These approaches were selected to parallel the methods used by both fire service programs in the community and by practitioners in mental health clinics. It is important to recognize that only the FHV condition included cases that were not randomized to intervention conditions.

The primary aim was to evaluate and compare the impact of the three interventions on the frequency of involvement with fire and related activities and on the specific psychosocial correlates or firesetting risk factors, such as interpersonal practices, antisocial behavior, and parent–family stress. This comparison will determine whether brief exposure to a firefighter, as is commonly practiced, is as effective as active participation in more intensive skills training procedures derived from firesetting research findings. It was hypothesized that FSE and PT will result in a significant reduction in child involvement with fire and severity of firesetting at the two follow-up periods, relative to FHV. Additionally, it is expected that PT will be superior to FSE or FHV in reducing the psychosocial correlates of firesetting, and that FSE will be superior to PT or FHV in improving fire safety knowledge and skill.

The second aim was to derive the predictors of treatment outcome (e.g., firesetting recidivism or severity) and moderating variables to document client intervention interactions using background, posttreatment, and 3-month follow-up variables. Whether differential response to FSE or PT can be predicted using specific correlates of firesetting identified during the research for the previous grant (e.g., fire safety knowledge and skill, curiosity about fire, antisocial behavior) will be examined. It is expected that FSE will be more effective for children high in curiosity and low in knowledge about fire, whereas PT will be more effective with children high in antisocial behavior. By documenting the breadth and stability of change, and cost effectiveness of intervention, the findings should permit subsequent programs to match clients to treatments more effectively.

Participants

Boys were referred by the Young Firesetters Program (YFP) sponsored by the City of Pittsburgh Bureau of Fire (e.g., arson investigator), by direct parental solicitation, or by another professional (e.g., mental health practitioner, burn unit). By conducting this project with the cooperation of the city of Pittsburgh, a network of arson investigators, educators, referral agencies, and other resources was used. The initial sample consisted of 19 PT cases, 15 FSE cases, and 18 HFV cases.

The boys had to meet the following criteria: age, 5–13 years; current residence with at least one parent or legal guardian; documentation of child firesetting within the previous 2 months in which property was burned and damaged; normal intelligence level (> 70 on two WISC-R subtests); and parent consent and child assent for participation. The boys were excluded for an acute or chronic medical condition that would complicate participation; participation in a related treatment program; identification of a major stressor or crisis that could precipitate family instability (disruption), complicate involvement in treatment, or entail highly burdensome case management requirements (e.g., recent physical or sexual abuse, living in a shelter); and current psychosis, suicidality, or a diagnosis of an affective disorder (e.g., major depression) based on a semistructured clinical interview.

Intake, Screening, and Recruitment

There had to be clear documentation of the child's involvement in a fire that resulted in property damages followed by a formal investigation of the cause and origins of the fire by a city arson investigator or, in the absence of an investigation, confirmation of an incident by the child or parent. Parents whose children met preliminary background inclusion criteria were informed of the purpose, procedures, and benefits of the project. An initial telephone screening was made to obtain additional details of the fire (e.g., characteristics, consequences) and of the family structure and status, to select appropriate candidates. A clinical interview later evaluated intelligence (WISC-R subtests) and the presence of a psychiatric disorder. Upon determining eligibility and documenting motivation, children and parents were familiarized with all study procedures and asked to provide written consent for participation before being assigned to an intervention condition. When appropriate, referral for treatment of child or parent dysfunction was discussed.

Settings and Staff

As per fire department protocol, the initial fire investigation (cause and origin report) were conducted in the child's home. Intake and screening and all subsequent assessments were conducted at the Western Psychiatric Institute and Clinic (WPIC). Program interventions (FSE and PT) were conducted in the outpatient clinic at WPIC or in the child's home (FHV).

The firefighter educators and therapists were responsible for implementation of the intervention conditions. Firefighters were identified by the fire chief on the basis of several criteria (e.g., equivalence of four-year baccalaureate degree, at least two years of experience as a firefighter, potential as educator, no history of child maltreatment, excellent attendance and work record) and later interviewed by the author to determine final eligibility. Three of the six firefighters had already served in a similar capacity through the YFP and two were selected for this role. The mental health therapists had BA, MA, or MSW degrees, clinical experience with children exhibiting externalizing behavior disorders, prior training in contingency management and cognitive–behavioral procedures, and experience in teaching child management techniques to parents. There was a balance in terms of staff gender and ethnicity across intervention conditions.

In light of the selection of staff with specialized expertise, time limitations, financial constraints, and obstacles in crossing all staff across all conditions, staff members were assigned to one condition only (i.e., nested). This assignment strategy eliminated the potential confounding of intervention conditions and capitalized on the respective expertise of the staff selected from the fire service and mental health systems that, by paralleling existing practices, would facilitate the administration of treatment in the most representative manner possible. Accordingly, each fire service condition (FSE, FHV) was staffed by three firefighters; the PT condition was staffed by three therapists. This decision was intended to maximize treatment distinctiveness, overall efficacy, and the generalizability of outcomes.

Characteristics and Administration of Intervention

Children were assigned randomly to FSE or PT in an effort to compose groups that were comparable in developmental or family background status. To ensure comparability on certain key variables relating to firesetting behavior, risk for recidivism, or response to treatment (Cole et al., 1986; Kolko, 1989; Kolko & Kazdin, 1989a; Wooden & Berkey, 1984), Efron's (1980) biased coin toss was used to balance the groups on age (7–9 years vs. 10–12 years), low socioeconomic status ($\leq$ II; based on Hollingshead & Redlich, 1958), and number of parents in household (one vs. two).

Treatment commenced approximately 1 week after completion of a pretreatment assessment interview. Participants in all conditions met individually with a trained staff member in semistructured sessions using material in manual form. Staff members in the FSE and PT conditions used instructions, modeling, role playing or behavioral rehearsal, feedback, and social reinforcement that were supplemented with supervision sessions for discussion of case issues. All conditions required parent and child involvement. The FSE and PT interventions were designed to be comparable in session length (1 hour/session) and treatment duration (8 weekly sessions). To parallel this time period, the FHV condition consisted of an initial 1-hour session and follow-up call that were spaced 6-to-8 weeks apart. With this interval, the duration of involvement in (but not dose of) treatment was expected to be comparable across the three interventions. For the first 30 children, an average of 7.6 ($SD = 3.0$) and 5.1 ($SD = 2.1$) sessions were conducted in the PT and FSE conditions, respectively. Children in these two conditions participated for 6.5 ($SD = 3.6$) and 5.6 ($SD = 2.1$) hours, and parents for 4.2 ($SD = 2.9$) and 5.6 ($SD = 2.1$)

hours. The number of weeks in treatment was 8.4 ($SD = 3.4$) and 8.7 ($SD = 6.2$) for the PT and FSE conditions, respectively.

Intervention Conditions

Fire Safety Education

Fire Safety Education (FSE) incorporates procedures based on the descriptive differences between firesetters and nonfiresetters identified from our previous firesetting grant (e.g., knowledge of combustibles, role plays of emergency responses) and the content of the initial FSST intervention. Other procedures to promote fire safety prevention and evacuation were adapted from the LNTB curriculum and related programs (e.g., Adler et al., 1988; Cole et al., 1986; Dennis, 1979; FEMA, 1979; Gaynor et al., 1984; Jones & Haney, 1985; NFPA, 1979, 1982). In general, FSE provides instruction in fire safety skills that may provide abilities that are incompatible with continued involvement in firesetting fireplay activities. The children and parents meet together or, at other times, separately with a firefighter educator throughout the intervention condition. Session content is outlined in Table 2.

Briefly, early sessions involve a review, with the child, of selected details of the fire (e.g., motive, format, role of peers) and a discussion, with parents, of the causes of firesetting. A few sessions involve child training in fire safety education principles and tasks that teach fire safety concepts (Adler et al., 1994; Gaynor et al., 1984), fire protection and evacuation strategies (e.g., stop-drop-roll, emergency phone calls, exiting a burning house to contact a neighbor; Dennis, 1979; FEMA, 1979; Gaynor et al., 1984; Jones & Haney, 1985); and methods to identify, report, and control a fire (NFPA, 1979). The content is designed to facilitate an understanding of the effects of fire and various preventive strategies (e.g., special placement of flammable liquids or matches, uses and abuses of fire); whereas the latter phase is designed to teach specific responses and practices (e.g., giving matches to an adult, declining an invitation to engage in matchplay). Parents receive a similar overview of fire prevention and additional details in the form of home fire safety information and guidelines to provide a context for the child's short-term fire safety project (FEMA, 1979). A review of the fire safety project is conducted to demonstrate a commitment to its underlying principles. To enhance generalization, role plays are used to enhance retention of all material (Jones et al., 1989). Children then receive a certificate of achievement.

Psychosocial Treatment

Psychosocial treatment (PT) involves the application of cognitive–behavioral procedures designed to modify the characteristics and correlates

TABLE 2
Outlines of Content for Each Primary Intervention Manual

Session number

Psychosocial treatment condition (PT)
1 C: Child interests and problems and review of fire incident
  P: Family characteristics and stress management
2 P: Monitoring, attending, ignoring, positive reinforcement
3 C: Feelings, automatic and balanced thoughts
     Introduction to problem solving (define, goal, think)
4 C: Generating alternatives, considering consequences, and choosing the best solution
5 P: Logical consequences, removing privileges or fines, home contingencies, allowances, point systems
6 C: Applications to problems, leisure activities, and fire activities
7 C+P: Home contingency program, family contract
8 C: Assertion, complaints, requests, and review of home program

Fire safety and education (FSE)
1 C+P: Fire facts, causes of fires, review details of fire
  C+P: Overview of session and intervention
2 C+P: How fires start, impact of fire, children's motives, film, worksheet
3 C: Matches are tools, helpers and hazards, fire fighters and equipment
4 C: Fire evacuation and reporting
5 C: Home fire escape plan, injury prevention, first aid
6 P: Home fire prevention, safety, match safety
     Smoke detectors, fire extinguishers, other fire risks
7 C: Fire safety concepts
  C+P: Fire safety project
8 C+P: Discussion of fire safety project
     Fire safety achievement certificate

Note. C = Child; P = Parent.

of firesetting noted in the mental health literature (see Adler et al., 1994; FEMA, 1979, 1983; Gaynor & Hatcher, 1987; Kolko, 1983, 1985; Kolko & Ammerman, 1988; Wooden & Berkey, 1984). By teaching aspects of generalized self-control and establishing environmental conditions that encourage behaviors other than firesetting, these procedures seek to alter the psychological significance of firesetting, the child's social–cognitive skills, and the functional context in which they occur. As in FSE, children and parents in PT participated both separately and together in different sessions with a mental health therapist (see Table 2 for outline of content).

Children are first exposed to the graphing technique (for examples, see Bumpass et al., 1983, 1985; Kolko & Ammerman, 1988) to help them understand how their motives for the fire were related to specific events or affective states. Three sessions are devoted to teaching general problem-solving skills and self-instructions (see Kazdin, Esveldt-Dawson, French, & Unis, 1987) in different steps (e.g., problem identification, generation of alternative solutions) geared toward critically evaluating the risks and benefits of involvement in negative or undesirable behaviors, including fire. Children learn how to apply the skills to personally relevant situations (e.g., loneliness, boredom) associated with firesetting based on findings from our prior work. Children also receive training in assertion skills and are encouraged to use specific prosocial responses to interpersonal conflicts that are likely to be reinforced.

Parents are taught about the environmental context of firesetting (e.g., motives) and the need to monitor child behavior and promote their children's involvement in prosocial activities. Training is provided in basic child management principles, such as attending, ignoring, and praise. Content emphasizes the establishment of contingent positive consequences for engaging in behaviors or activities other than fireplay (Adler et al., 1988; Holland, 1969; Kolko, 1983) and forfeiture of privileges or other reinforcing objects contingent upon involvement or contact with fire-related activities (Holland, 1969; Kolko, 1983). A home-based contingency is developed jointly (e.g., duration criterion, types of reinforcers, types of alternative activities—athletics, recreation) along with the criteria to be used to withdraw the contingency gradually.

Firefighter Home Visit

This brief, two-contact condition represents an enhanced version of some of the routine practices found in most fire departments. The content was derived from field surveys of juvenile counseling program directors and local firefighters, and the author's national survey. The specific content of the first contact included telling children about the danger of fires (e.g., to themselves, family, pets) and functions of firefighters, asking children to promise not to get involved again with unsanctioned fireplay (nofire contract), and distributing program materials to serve as a reminder to avoid using fire (e.g., coloring book on fire safety, a plastic fire helmet). The child's parent was encouraged to participate in the session and received a home fire-safety handout (e.g., secure all incendiary materials). In the second contact, the firefigher contacted the child and parent to review specific concepts (e.g., the dangers and functions of fire) and to elaborate on prior topics (e.g., play with matches or lighters begins as a simple activity). In contrast with the other two conditions, FHV children were not randomized to this condition.

Credibility and Integrity of Intervention

Information regarding both participants' expectations of the credibility and usefulness of each treatment condition were solicited prior to their randomization to treatment. Four questions that reflected key aspects of the PT (e.g., wanting to learn how to change one's behavior), FSE (e.g., wanting to learn fire safety skills), and HFV (e.g., wanting to learn about firefighters) conditions were rated on 5-point Likert scales of content importance and usefulness. The initial results indicate that children and parents in each condition perceived all three conditions as generally credible and of potential benefit in reducing involvement in firesetting. Specifically, ratings of the content of each condition assigned by children in the three groups were as follows: PT items (Ms = 14.3–18.5), FSE items (16.1–18.0), and HFV items (Ms = 14.2–16.5). Ratings of the content of each condition assigned by parents were also comparable across the three conditions, as follows: PT items (Ms = 17.1–17.8), FSE items (17.6–19.3), and HFV items (Ms = 15.6–16.3).

Several procedures were designed to uphold the integrity of each distinct intervention. Staff received extensive training in all procedures and materials developed for their respective condition, administered intervention with at least two training cases, and review videotapes with the supervisor and receive feedback. Formal intervention commenced for each staff member on meeting at least 80% of expectations for treatment administration on the basis of role plays. Throughout intervention, the author maintained regular contact with all staff and reviewed their audio- or videotapes of case materials, selected at random, to identify issues or obstacles, assure compliance, and maintain treatment integrity and adherence. To facilitate treatment integrity assessment, the material to be delivered each session per condition was written as individual objectives and tasks. A trained independent observer viewed tapes of a random sample of 30% of the sessions per condition and rated each session item on a 3-point scale of correctness and completeness (1 = content not covered during the session; 2 = content was covered only minimally, or partially, or was somewhat unclear, confusing, or disorganized; 3 = most or all of the content was covered as stated and in a clear manner), and ratings were used to compute the percentage of correctly administered items per session. The mean and range for these correctness ratings were generally high for both the PT (overall mean = .97; SD = .06; range: .93–.99) and FSE conditions (overall mean = .91; SD = .10; range: .84–.98).

In addition, the treatment process and adherence were monitored by therapists or firefighter educators who completed individual session summary ratings (1 = not at all; 5 = very much) to document important aspects of the administration of intervention. The mean ratings of each individual item for patients in the PT and FSE conditions, respectively, were as follows:

1. on-task/attentiveness (4.2, 3.9);
2. interest in material (4.0, 3.9);
3. level of participation or involvement (4.4, 4.1);
4. level of compliance (4.5, 4.1);

5. level of understanding of material (4.3, 4.2);
6. amount of material covered (4.3, 4.2);
7. overall therapist rating of participant progress (4.2, 4.1); and
8. overall participant rating of participant progress (4.2, 4.1).

In general, participants were appropriately engaged in and responsive to their respective interventions.

Assessment Measures

The children and their parents or guardians were administered several self-report instruments and brief interviews by trained research associates in a separate office from those used for any of the intervention conditions. Measures also were obtained from juvenile court and social service records. The measures were administered at pretreatment (intake), posttreatment, and follow-up. Table 3 lists representative measures in each domain and the schedule of administration of these measures. Selected measures in each domain are described briefly.

Fire Involvement, Interest, and Awareness

Measures in this domain evaluated the child's history of firesetting or involvement in fire-related activities in the home or the community (FHS; FHS-C), details of firesetting incidents (FIA-C; Kolko & Kazdin, 1993), the child's general knowledge of fire safety concepts included in the LNTB program (FKT; NFPA, 1979), and involvement in fire safety and prevention activities (PQ; NFPA, 1979).

Firesetting Risk

This domain examined risk factors for firesetting based on child (CFI; Kolko & Kazdin, 1989b) and parent reports (FRI; Kolko & Kazdin, 1989b), and items related to children's desire for contact with fire (FAIS; Kolko & Kazdin, 1992).

Behavioral and Environmental Measures

In this domain, there are several measures of child psychopathology (YSR; Achenbach & Edelbrock, 1989) and psychiatric diagnoses (Kiddie-SADS; Chambers et al., 1985), social competence (CATS; Deluty, 1979), social problem-solving (SPS; Coie & Dodge, 1987), and sensation seeking (SSS-R; Russo et al. 1993). Related measures completed by parents examined child psychopathology (CBCL; Achenbach & Edelbrock, 1983), and antisocial behavior and hostility (IAB; Kazdin & Esveldt-Dawson, 1986; CHI, Kazdin, Rodgers, Colbus, & Siegel, 1987). Other parent-completed measures evaluated parent and family stress (CLEI; Chandler,

TABLE 3
Representative Assessment Measures Per Domain and Schedule of Administration

Measure	Source	Assessment Period		
		Pre	Post	FU
Fire Involvement, interest, awareness				
Fire History Screen	C	X	X	X
Home Fire History or Involvement (screen)	P	X	X	X
Fire Incident Analysis	C/P	X	X[1]	X[1]
Fire Knowledge Test	C	X	X	X
Parent Questionnaire	P	X	X	X
Firesetting risk				
Children's Firesetting Interview	C	X	X	X
Firesetting Risk Interview	P	X	X	X
Firesetting Attraction and Interest Scale	C/P	X	X	X
Behavior and environment				
Kiddie-SADS Interview	C/P	X		X
Youth Self-Report	C	X		X
Child Behavior Checklist	P	X		X
Interview for Antisocial Behavior	P	X		X
Children's Hostility Interview	C/P	X		X
Children's Manifest Anxiety Scale-R	C	X		X
Children's Action Tendency Scale	C	X		X
Social Problem-Solving Interview	C	X		X
Sensation-Seeking Scale-R	C	X		X
Brief Symptom Inventory	P	X		X
Parenting Stress Inventory	P	X		X
Child Rearing Interview	P	X		X
Family Environment Scale	C/P	X		X
Children's Life Events Inventory	P	X		X
Archival records				
Children/Youth Service Records	CO			X[2]
Juvenile Court Records	CO			X[2]
Treatment evaluation				
Children's Evaluation Inventory	C		X	
Therapist Evaluation Inventory	T		X	
Parent Consumer Satisfaction	P		X	

Note. C = child; P = parent; CO = community adults, T = therapist.
[1]Administered only if child has set a fire since the previous period.
[2]Follow-up assessment will cover all prior assessment periods.

1984; PSI; Abidin, 1983); parental psychopathology (BSI; Derogatis, Rickels, & Rock, 1976); child rearing practices, such as discipline and monitoring (CRPI; Stouthamer-Loeber & Loeber, 1985); and various dimensions of family environment and interpersonal relationships, such as cohesion and conflict (FES; Moos, Insel, & Humphrey, 1974).

Records of Social Service and Juvenile Court Involvement

Measures of contact with county child and youth services and juvenile courts are being collected at the conclusion of follow-up to determine the presence of child abuse or neglect, child protective services involvement, and involvement in fire-related delinquent activities.

Treatment Evaluation

To assess treatment satisfaction overall, three measures were included in this domain to evaluate the children's perspectives of the credibility and helpfulness of their respective treatment conditions (CEI; Kazdin et al., 1987), parent's satisfaction with services, and therapist's perceptions of the benefit of intervention for the child (TEI; Kazdin et al., 1987).

Attrition of Participants

Although preliminary figures based on the prior studies and reports suggest good compliance with treatment, dropout may be a more salient concern in the present study than in the prior applications in which treatment was very brief or delivered during inpatient hospitalization. Certain procedures were instituted to minimize dropout:

1. treatment commenced within one-two weeks of screening;
2. sessions were scheduled at the family's convenience;
3. families received an orientation to assure understanding of treatment and likely impact;
4. families that missed a session were contacted immediately to reschedule;
5. children and parents received monetary compensation for attendance and completion of the measures; and
6. children were given a certificate on completion of the treatment.

Analyses of Clinical Outcome and Impact

Initial analyses have examined the preliminary impact of the three interventions on frequency of fire involvement or contact (e.g., presence and severity of firesetting) and other psychosocial correlates or risk factors (e.g., curiosity about fire, involvement in fire-related behaviors). For example, weekly child and parent reports documenting the child's progress during PT or FSE found that most children reported no involvement with (64%) or exposure to (57%) fire, and noted no child or family problems (61%). Initial t-tests revealed significant reductions in child reports of fire involvement in PT versus FSE children, and reductions in parent-reported fire involvement for both groups ($p < .05–.01$).

Other analyses will examine variables associated with the continuation of firesetting (e.g., limited fire safety knowledge, curiosity about and interest in fire, covert antisocial behavior, physical or sexual abuse or neglect, parental stress or dysfunction). Group comparisons also will determine whether performance on measures at posttreatment and follow-up was in accord with the actual content of each condition. The analysis will evaluate, for example, whether children who received FSE made the greatest gains in fire safety knowledge and showed a greater reduction in curiosity about fire, and whether children who received PT showed the most improvement in interpersonal abilities, antisocial behavior, and parent functioning.

Summary and Future Directions

The intervention conditions used in this study were based on the findings of prior empirical assessment and follow-up studies and of existing fire safety programs. Two skills-based interventions representing mental health (psychosocial treatment or PT) and fire service (fire safety education or FSE) approaches were compared to a third, standard-practice condition (firefighter home visit or FHV). The study may provide initial data on the feasibility and effectiveness of alternative interventions by examining changes in children's contact with and use of fire and their recent level of behavioral dysfunction. From a practitioner's perspective, findings may be helpful in identifying useful methods to evaluate firesetting history and other important psychosocial characteristics. The findings would also bear implications for the packaging and implementation of effective interventions with which practitioners may need to become more familiar. If training in fire safety skills is more effective for curious children, and if psychosocial treatment is more useful for behaviorally disturbed children, the findings would offer clear directions for initiating an intervention program. Finally, it may be helpful to practitioners to use risk assessments based on the background characteristics and treatment experiences associated with recidivism. It is important to reiterate that these findings are limited by the fact that children were randomized only to the PT and FSE conditions.

Additional studies are still needed to evaluate other features of these treatments and their therapeutic effectiveness. Specifically, it would be important to investigate the following topics to enhance the scope and impact of intervention: (a) the relative benefits of comprehensive (multimodal) interventions that combine various approaches, such as fire safety and psychological counseling; (b) the benefit of interventions that are longer in duration or more intensive; (c) the use of other paraprofessional groups to conduct assessment and intervention procedures; (d) the application of specialized audiovisual materials (e.g., films) as cost-effective alternatives to treatment; and (e) the development of treatment procedures for very young children or for children with a significant attraction to fire. Certainly, greater information is needed to understand better the etiology of firesetting and the methods that are most likely to modify the expression of this troublesome behavior.

REFERENCES

Abidin, R. R. (1983, August). *Parenting Stress Index: Research update*. Poster presented at the conference of the American Psychological Association.

Achenbach, T. M., & Edelbrock, C. (1983). *Manual for the Child Behavior Checklist and Revised Child Behavior Profile*. Vermont: Queen City Publishers.

Achenbach, T. M., & Edelbrock, C. (1989). *Manual for the Youth Self Report*. Vermont: Queen City Publishers.

Adler, R. J., Nunn, R. J., Laverick, J., & Ross, R. (1988, October). *Royal Children's Hospital/Metropolitain Fire Brigade Juvenile Fire Awareness and Intervention Program: Research and Intervention Protocol*. Unpublished paper.

Adler, R. J., Nunn, R. J., Northam, E., Lebnan, V., & Ross, R. (1994). Secondary prevention of childhood firesetting. *Journal of the American Academy of Child and Adolescent Psychiatry, 33,* 1194–1202.

American Psychiatric Association. (1987). *Diagnostic and statistical manual of mental disorders—revised* (3rd ed., rev.). Washington, DC: Author.

Bumpass, E. R., Brix, R. J., & Preston, D. (1985). A community-based program for juvenile firesetters. *Hospital and Community Psychiatry, 36,* 529–533.

Bumpass, E. R., Fagelman, F. D., & Brix, R. J. (1983). Intervention with children who set fires. *American Journal of Psychotherapy, 37,* 328–345.

Cella, D. F., Perry, S. W., Kulchycky, S., & Goodwin, C. (1988). Stress and coping in relatives of burn patients: A longitudinal study. *Hospital and Community Psychiatry, 39,* 159–166.

Chambers, W. J., Puig-Antich, J., Hirsch, M., Paez, P., Ambrosini, P. J., Tabrizi, M. A., & Davies, M. (1985). The assessment of affective disorders in children and adolescents by semistructured interview: Test–retest reliability of the K-SADS-P. *Archives of General Psychiatry, 42,* 696–702.

Chandler, L. A. (1984). *The Children's Life Events Inventory: Its use in clinical assessment*. Unpublished manuscript, University of Pittsburgh, Pittsburgh, PA.

Coie, J. D., & Dodge, K. A. (1987). Social-information processing factors in reactive and proactive aggression in children's peer groups. *Journal of Personality and Social Psychology, 53,* 1146–1158.

Cole, R. E., Grolnick, W. S., McAndrews, M. M., Matkoski, K. M., & Schwartzman, P. I. (1986). *Rochester Fire Related Youth Project: Progress report* (Vol. 2). Rochester, NY: Office of Fire Prevention and Control, New York Department of State.

Cole, R. E., Laurenitis, L. R., McCandrews, M. M., McKeever, J. M., & Schwartzman, P. (1983). *Final report of the 1983 fire-related youth program development project.* Rochester, NY: State Office of Fire Prevention and Control.

Cook, R., Hersch, R., Gaynor, J., & Roehl, J. (1989, April). *The national juvenile firesetter/arson control and prevention program: Assessment report, executive summary.* Washington, DC: Institute for Social Analysis.

Cox-Jones, C., Lubetsky, M., Fultz, S. A., & Kolko, D. J. (1990). Inpatient treatment of a young recidivist firesetter. *Journal of the American Academy of Child Psychiatry, 29,* 936–941.

Deluty, R. H. (1979). Children's Action Tendency Scale: A self-report measure of aggressiveness, assertiveness, and submissiveness in children. *Journal of Consulting and Clinical Psychology, 47,* 1061–1071.

Dennis, N. (1979). *Young children: A new target for public fire education.* Washington, DC: Federal Emergency Management Agency, U.S. Fire Administration, Office of Planning and Education.

Derogatis, L., Rickels, K., & Rock, A. F. (1976). The SCL–90 and the MMPI: A step in validation of a new self-report scale. *British Journal of Psychiatry, 128,* 280–289.

DeSalvatore, G., & Hornstein, R. (1991). Juvenile firesetting: Assessment and treatment in psychiatric hospitalization and residential placement. *Child and Youth Care Forum, 20,* 103–114.

Efron, B. (1980). *Biostatistics casebook.* Stanford: Stanford University Press.

Eisler, R. M. (1974). Crisis intervention in the family of a firesetter. *Psychotherapy: Theory, Research and Practice, 9.*

Federal Emergency Management Agency. (1979). *Interviewing and Counseling Juvenile Firesetters.* Washington, DC: U.S. Goverment Printing Office.

Federal Emergency Management Agency (1983). *Juvenile firesetter handbook: Dealing with children ages 7 to 14.* Washington, DC: U.S. Goverment Printing Office.

Gaynor, J. (1985). Child and adolescent fire setting: Detection and intervention. *Feelings and Their Medical Significance, 27,* 1–10.

Gaynor, J., & Hatcher, C. (1987). *The psychology of child firesetting: Detection and intervention.* New York: Brunner/Mazel.

Gaynor, J., McLaughlin, P. M., & Hatcher, C. (1984). *The Firehawk Children's Program: A Working Manual.* San Francisco: National Firehawk Foundation.

Geller, J. L. (1987). Firesetting in the adult psychiatric population. *Hospital and Community Psychiatry, 38,* 501–510.

Grolnick, W. S., Cole, R. E., Laurenitis, L., & Schwartzman, P. I. (1990). Playing with fire: A developmental assessment of children's fire understanding and experience. *Journal of Clinical Child Psychology, 19,* 128–135.

Heath, G. A., Hardesty, V. A., Goldfine, P. E., & Walker, A. M. (1985). Diagnosis and childhood firesetting. *Journal of Clinical Psychology, 41,* 571–575.

Holland, C. J. (1969). Elimination by the parents of firesetting behaviour in a 7-year old boy. *Behaviour Research and Therapy, 7*, 135–137.

Hollingshead, A., & Redlich, F. (1958). *Social class and mental illness: A community study.* New York: Wiley.

Jacobson, R. R. (1985a). Child firesetters: A clinical investigation. *Journal of Child Psychology and Psychiatry, 26*, 759–768.

Jacobson, R. R. (1985b). The subclassification of child firesetters. *Journal of Child Psychology and Psychiatry, 26*, 769–775.

Jones, R. T., & Haney, J. L. (1985). Behavior therapy and fire emergencies: Conceptualization, assessment, and intervention. M. Hersen, R. Eisler, & P. Miller (Eds.), *Progress in Behavior Modification* (Vol. 19, pp. 177–216). New York: Academic Press.

Jones, R. T., Kazdin, A. E., & Haney, J. I. (1981). Social validation and training of emergency fire safety skills for potential injury prevention and life saving. *Journal of Applied Behavior Analysis, 14*, 249–260.

Jones, R. T., Ollendick, T. H., & Shinske, F. K. (1989). The role of behavioral versus cognitive variables in skill acquisition. *Behavior Therapy, 20*, 293–302.

Kafry, D. (1980). Playing with matches: Children and fire. In D. Canter (Ed.), *Fires and human behaviour* (pp. 41–60). Chichester, England: Wiley.

Kazdin, A. E., & Esveldt-Dawson, K. (1986). The Interview for Antisocial Behavior: Psychometric characteristics and concurrent validity with child psychiatric inpatients. *Journal of Psychopathology and Behavioral Assessment, 8*, 289–303.

Kazdin, A. E., Esveldt-Dawson, K., French, N., & Unis, A. (1987). Problem-solving skills training and relationship therapy in the treatment of antisocial child behavior. *Journal of Consulting and Clinical Psychology, 55*, 76–85.

Kazdin, A. E., & Kolko, D. J. (1986). Parent psychopathology and family functioning among childhood firesetters. *Journal of Abnormal Child Psychology, 14*, 315–329.

Kazdin, A. E., Rodgers, A., Colbus, D., & Siegel, T. (1987). Children's Hostility Inventory: Measurement of aggression and hostility in psychiatric inpatient children. *Journal of Clinical Child Psychology, 16*, 320–328.

Kelso, J., & Stewart, M. A. (1986). Factors which predict the persistence of aggressive conduct disorder. *Journal of Child Psychology and Psychiatry, 27*, 77–86.

Kolko, D. J. (1983). Multicomponent parental treatment of firesetting in a developmentally disabled boy. *Journal of Behavior Therapy and Experimental Psychiatry, 14*, 349–353.

Kolko, D. J. (1985). Juvenile firesetting: A review and critique. *Clinical Psychology Review, 5*, 345–376.

Kolko, D. J. (1988). Community interventions for childhood firesetters: A comparison of two national programs. *Hospital and Community Psychiatry, 39*, 973–979.

Kolko, D. J. (1989). Fire setting and pyromania. In C. Last & M. Hersen (Eds.) *Handbook of Child Psychiatric Diagnosis* (pp. 443–459). New York: Wiley.

Kolko, D. J., & Ammerman, R. T. (1988). Firesetting. In M. Hersen & C. Last (Eds.), *Child Behavior Therapy Casebook* (pp. 243–262). New York: Plenum.

Kolko, D. J., & Kazdin, A. E. (1986). A conceptualization of firesetting in children and adolescents. *Journal of Abnormal Child Psychology, 14,* 49–62.

Kolko, D. J., & Kazdin, A. E. (1988a). Parent–child correspondence in identification of firesetting among child psychiatric patients. *Journal of Child Psychology and Psychiatry, 29,* 175–184.

Kolko, D. J., & Kazdin, A. E. (1988b). Prevalence of firesetting and related behaviors in child psychiatric inpatients. *Journal of Consulting and Clinical Psychology, 56,* 628–630.

Kolko, D. J., & Kazdin, A. E. (1989a). Assessment of dimensions of childhood firesetting among child psychiatric patients and nonpatients. *Journal of Abnormal Child Psychology, 17,* 157–176.

Kolko, D. J., & Kazdin, A. E. (1989b). The Children's Firesetting Interview with psychiatrically referred and nonreferred children. *Journal of Abnormal Child Psychology, 17,* 609–624.

Kolko, D. J., & Kazdin, A. E. (1991a). Matchplaying and firesetting in children: Relationship to parent, marital, and family dysfunction. *Journal of Clinical Child Psychology, 19,* 229–238.

Kolko, D. J., & Kazdin, A. E. (1991b). Aggression and psychopathology in matchplaying and firesetting children: A replication and extension. *Journal of Clinical Child Psychology, 20,* 191–201.

Kolko, D. J., & Kazdin, A. E. (1991c). Motives of childhood firesetters: Firesetting characteristics and psychological correlates. *Journal of Child Psychology and Psychiatry, 32,* 535–550.

Kolko, D. J., & Kazdin, A. E. (1992). The emergence and recurrence of child firesetting: A one-year prospective study. *Journal of Abnormal Child Psychology, 20,* 17–37.

Kolko, D. J., & Kazdin, A. E. (1993). Children's descriptions of their firesetting incidents: Characteristics and relationship to recidivism. *Journal of the American Academy of Child Psychiatry, 33,* 114–122.

Kolko, D. J., Kazdin, A. E., & Meyer, E. C. (1985). Aggression and psychopathology in childhood firesetters: Parent and child reports. *Journal of Consulting and Clinical Psychology, 53,* 377–385.

Kolko, D. J., Watson, S., & Faust, J. (1991). Fire safety/prevention skills training to reduce involvement with fire in young psychiatric inpatients: Preliminary findings. *Behavior Therapy, 22,* 269–284.

Madanes, C. (1981). *Strategic family therapy.* San Fransisco: Jossey-Bass.

McGrath, P., Marshall, P. T., & Prior, K. (1979). A comprehensive treatment program for a firesetting child. *Journal of Behavior Therapy and Experimental Psychiatry, 10,* 69–72.

Minuchin, S. (1974). *Families and family therapy*. San Fransisco: Jossey-Bass.

Moos, R. H., Insel, P. M., & Humphrey, B. (1974). *Family work and group environment scales*. Palo Alto, CA: Consulting Psychologists Press.

National Fire Protection Association. (1978). *Executive summary report of the Learn Not to Burn Curriculum*. Quincy, MA: Author.

National Fire Protection Association. (1979). *Learn Not to Burn Curriculum*. Quincy, MA: Author.

National Fire Protection Association. (1982). *Sparky's coloring book*. Quincy, MA: Author.

National Fire Protection Association. (1987). *United States Arson Trends and Patterns*. Quincy, MA: Author.

Parrish, J. M., Capriotti, R. M., Warzak, W. J., Handen, B. L., Wells, T. J., Phillipson, S. J., & Porter, C. A. (1985, November). *Multivariate analysis of juvenile firesetting*. Paper presented at the annual meeting of the Association for the Advancement of Behavior Therapy, Houston, TX.

Rice, M. E., & Harris, G. T. (1991). Firesetters admitted to a maximum security psychiatric institution: Offenders and offenses. *Journal of Interpersonal Violence, 6*, 461–475.

Russo, M. F., Stokes, G. S., Lahey, B. B., Christ, M. A. G., McBurnett, K., Loeber, R., Stouthamer-Loeber, M., & Green, S. M. (1993). A sensation seeking scale for children: Further refinement and psychometric development. *Journal of Psychopathology and Behavioral Assessment, 15*, 69–86.

Showers, J., & Pickrell, E. P. (1987). Child firesetters: A study of three populations. *Hospital and Community Psychiatry, 38*, 495–501.

Stawar, T. L. (1976). Fable mod: Operantly structured fantasies as an adjunct in the modification of firesetting behavior. *Journal of Behavior Therapy and Experimental Psychiatry, 7*, 285–287.

Stewart, M. A. & Culver, K. W. (1982). Children who set fires: The clinical picture and a follow-up. *British Journal of Psychiatry, 140*, 357–363.

Stouthamer-Loeber, M., & Loeber, R. (1985). *Child Rearing Practices: Pilot version*. Unpublished instrument, Pittsburgh Youth Study, Western Psychiatric Institute and Clinic, University of Pittsburgh, PA.

U.S. Federal Bureau of Investigation. (1987). *Uniform Crime Reports*. Washington, DC: Author.

Wooden, W., & Berkey, M. L. (1984). *Children and arson: America's middle class nightmare*. New York: Plenum.

19

EARLY INTERVENTION WITH VIDEOTAPE MODELING: PROGRAMS FOR FAMILIES OF CHILDREN WITH OPPOSITIONAL DEFIANT DISORDER OR CONDUCT DISORDER

CAROLYN H. WEBSTER-STRATTON

OVERALL GOALS

The ultimate purpose of the Parenting Clinic's program of research is to develop, evaluate, and improve cost-effective, widely applicable, and theory-based early intervention programs of treatment for families with young children who suffer from oppositional–defiant disorder (ODD) or conduct disorder (CD). Children with these disorders typically exhibit a broad range of antisocial behaviors (i.e., lying, cheating, stealing, fighting, oppositional behaviors, and noncompliance to parental requests) at higher than normal rates. Our interest in such children was stimulated by research showing the high prevalence rates—rates that are increasing—for these conditions (4–10%); and, even more important, by research indicating that these aggressive children are at increased risk for being rejected by their peers (Coie, 1990) and abused by their parents (Reid, Taplin, & Loeber, 1981), as well as for school dropout, alcoholism, drug abuse, depression, juvenile delinquency, adult crime, antisocial personality, marital disruption,

This research was supported by grants from the National Institutes of Health, Institute of Nursing (5 RO1 NR01075-09) and from the National Institute of Mental Health (Research Scientist Development Award, MH00988-03). Correspondence concerning this chapter should be addressed to Dr. Carolyn H. Webster-Stratton, Department of Parent and Child Nursing, Box 354801, University of Washington, Seattle, WA 98195.

interpersonal problems, and other diagnosable psychiatric disorders (Kazdin, 1985; Loeber, 1991). Conduct disorders are one of the most costly of mental disorders to society because such a large proportion of antisocial children remains involved with mental health agencies or criminal justice systems throughout the course of their lives.

Developmental theorists have suggested that there may be two developmental pathways related to conduct disorder: the early starter versus the late starter models (Kazdin, 1985; Loeber, 1991; Patterson, DeBaryshe, & Ramsey, 1989). The hypothesized early-starter pathway begins formally with the emergence of ODD in early preschool years, progresses to aggressive and nonaggressive (e.g., lying, stealing) symptoms in middle childhood, and then develops into the most serious symptoms by adolescence, including interpersonal violence and property crimes (Lahey, Loeber, Quay, Frick, & Grimm, 1992). In contrast, the late starter pathway begins with a history of normal social and behavioral development during the preschool and early school years and progresses to symptoms of CD during adolescence. The prognosis for late starter adolescents appears to be more favorable than for adolescents who have a history of CD beginning in their preschool years; adolescents who first evidenced ODD symptoms in the preschool years followed by an early onset of CD are most likely to be chronically antisocial. These early-starter CD children also account for a disproportionate share of delinquent acts in adolescence. Thus, ODD is a sensitive predictor of CD; indeed, the primary developmental pathway for serious conduct disorders in adolescence and adulthood appears to be established during the preschool period (Campbell & Ewing, 1990; Loeber, 1991).

The preceding model showing the progression from ODD to CD suggests that, perhaps, the most strategic point for intervention in the child's development is the preschool and early elementary school years (i.e., ages 4 to 7 years). Our decision to focus our interventions on this age period was based on several considerations. First, there is evidence that ODD and CD children are clearly identifiable at this age. Our prior studies have revealed that even children as young as 4 years of age have already been expelled from two or more preschools and have experienced considerable peer and teacher rejection. Second, there is evidence that the younger the child at the time of intervention, the more positive the child's behavioral adjustment will be at home and at school (Strain, Steele, Ellis, & Timm, 1982). Third, the move to school—from preschool through the first years of elementary school—is a major transition and a period of great stress for many children and their parents. The child's early success or failure in adapting to school sets the stage not only for the child's future behavior at school and relationships with teachers and peers but also for the parents' future attitudes toward their child's schools and their own relationships with teachers and administrators. It is our belief that early intervention, if it occurs strategically during the high-risk child's first major transition point, can counteract those risk factors and reinforce protective factors, thereby helping to prevent a developmental trajectory from early-onset conduct problems (i.e., young children with high rates of symptoms of ODD or CD) to increasingly aggressive and violent behaviors, negative reputations, peer rejection, low self-esteem, conduct disorders, and spiraling academic failure.

TREATMENT PLAN

Parent Skills Training Interventions

Rationale for Parent Training

One of the major intervention strategies for reducing child ODD and CD involves parent training. This approach uses a model in which ineffective parenting skills are the most important risk factor and intervening variable in the development and maintenance of conduct problems. We have been strongly influenced by G. R. Patterson's (1982, 1986) seminal work and theoretical formulations concerning the development of conduct disorder and problem behaviors. His social learning, interactional-based model emphasizes the importance of the family socialization processes. Patterson developed the *coercion hypothesis*, which postulates that children learn to get their own way and escape (or avoid) parental criticism by escalating their negative behaviors; this, in turn, leads to increasingly aversive parent interactions. As this coercive training in a family continues over time, the rate and intensity of aggressive behaviors, on the part of parents and children, increase. Moreover, as the child observes increasingly frequent parental anger and negative discipline, the child is provided with additional modeling (observational learning) of aggression (Patterson, 1982). The pioneering research of Patterson and others has found that parents of children with conduct disorders exhibit fewer positive behaviors, use more violent disciplinary techniques, are more critical, more permissive, less likely to monitor their children's behaviors and more likely to reinforce inappropriate behaviors while ignoring, or even punishing, prosocial behaviors (Patterson, 1982). Accordingly, we felt that if we could intervene with parent training, while these children were still very young and their families' negative styles of interaction still malleable, we could improve the poor long-term prognoses for these children and their families.

Videotape Modeling Methods

We were particularly interested in determining which methods of training parents were most effective, that is, cost-effective, widely applicable, and sustaining. Cost effectiveness is vital because conduct disorders are increasingly widespread, creating a need for service that far exceeds available personnel and resources. For instance, data suggested that less than 10% of children who needed mental health services actually received them (Hobbs, 1982). Most of the early parent training programs relied largely on verbal methods, such as didactic lectures, brochures, and group discussions. Although these methods are cost effective, they have been shown to be ineffective for inducing behavioral changes in parents (Chilman, 1973). In addition, such methods are not optimal for parents whose literacy and educational levels, or general intellectual level is deficient. On the other hand, performance training methods, such as live modeling, role rehearsal, and individual video feedback, had proven effective in producing behavioral changes in parents and children (O'Dell, 1985); however, implementation was time consuming and costly, making them impractical in the face of increasing demand. Videotape modeling, on the other hand, was one method that appeared to be practical and cost effective.

In accordance with Bandura's (1977) modeling theory of learning, we hypothesized that parents could develop their parenting skills by watching (and modeling) videotape examples of parents interacting with their children in ways that promoted prosocial behaviors and decreased inappropriate behaviors. We theorized that videotape would provide a more flexible method of training than didactic instruction or role playing—that is, we could portray a wide variety of models and situations. We hypothesized that this flexible modeling approach would result in better generalization of the training content and, therefore, in better long-term maintenance. Furthermore, it would be a better method of learning for less verbally sophisticated parents. Finally, such a method, if proven effective, would have the advantage not only of low individual training cost when used in groups but also of possible mass dissemination. Thus, in 1979, we initiated our program of research to develop and evaluate videotape modeling parent intervention programs for families of young children with ODD and CD. We were interested both in evaluating the program's efficacy and in testing a theory of change processes. (See Table 1 for an outline of the videotape interventions tested.)

Content and Process of the BASIC Parent Training Videotape Modeling Programs

In 1980, we developed an interactive, videotape-based parent intervention program (BASIC) for parents of children aged 3 to 8 years. Heavily guided by the modeling literature, the BASIC program attempted to promote modeling effects for parents by creating positive feelings about the videotape models. For example, the videotapes show parents of differing ages, cultures, socioeconomic backgrounds, and temperaments, so that par-

TABLE 1
Overview of Videotape Interventions

Interventions	Skills targeted	Person trained	Setting targeted
Parenting skills training (BASIC)	Parenting skills ■ Play, involvement ■ Praise, rewards ■ Limit setting ■ Discipline	Parent	Home
Interpersonal skills training (ADVANCE)	Interpersonal skills ■ Problem solving ■ Anger management ■ Communication ■ Depression control ■ Giving and receiving support	Parent	Home, work, community
Academic skills training (PARTNERS 1)	Academic skills ■ Academic stimulation ■ Learning routine after school ■ Homework support ■ Reading ■ Limit setting ■ Involvement at school ■ Teacher conferences	Parent	Home–school connection

(continued)

TABLE 1 (Continued)

Interventions	Skills targeted	Person trained	Setting targeted
Child skills training (KIDVID)	Social skills ■ Friendship ■ Teamwork ■ Cooperation, helping ■ Communication Problem solving ■ Anger management ■ Steps 1–7 Classroom behavior ■ Quiet hand up ■ Compliance ■ Listening ■ Stop–look–think–check ■ Concentrating	Child	Home and school
Teacher training (PARTNERS 2)	Classroom management skills Promoting parent involvement	Teacher	School

ents will perceive at least some of the models as similar to themselves and their children, and will therefore accept the tapes as relevant. Videotapes show parent models (unrehearsed) in natural situations with their children "doing it right" and "doing it wrong" to demystify the notion there is perfect parenting and to illustrate how one can learn from one's mistakes. This approach also emphasizes our belief in a coping and interactive model of learning (Webster-Stratton, 1981b); that is, parents view a videotape vignette of a parent doing it wrong and then discuss how the parent might have handled the interaction more effectively. This approach serves not only to enhance parents' confidence in their own ideas but also to develop their ability to analyze different situations with their children and select an appropriate parenting strategy. In this regard, our training differs from other parent training programs wherein the therapist provides the analysis and recommends a particular strategy.

The BASIC parent training program takes 26 hours, or 13–14 weekly sessions. It encompasses 10 videotape programs of modeled parenting skills (250 vignettes, each of which is approximately 1–2 minutes long) shown by a therapist to groups of parents (8–12 parents per group). The video-tapes demonstrate behavioral principles and serve as the stimulus for focused discussions, problem solving, and collaborative learning. The program is also designed to help parents understand what are normal variations in children's development, emotional reactions, and temperaments. After each vignette, the therapist works with parents by soliciting their ideas and involving them in the process of problem solving, sharing, and discussing ideas and reactions. We see the therapists' role as one of supporting and empowering parents by teaching, leading, reframing, predicting, and role playing, always within a collaborative context (Webster-Stratton & Herbert, 1993, 1994). The collaborative context is designed to ensure that the intervention is sensitive to individual cultural differences and personal values. The program is tailored to each family's individual needs and goals, as well as to each child's personality and behavior problems.

Our program implies a commitment to parental self-management. We believe that this approach empowers parents by giving back dignity, respect, and self-control to parents who are often seeking help for their children's problems at a vulnerable time of low self-confidence and intense feelings of guilt and self-blame. By using the group process, the program is not only more cost effective but also addresses important risk factors for conduct disorders: the family's isolation and stigmatization. The parent groups provide a parent support group that becomes a model for parent support networks. (For details of therapeutic processes, please see Webster-Stratton & Herbert, 1994.)

The first two segments of the BASIC program focus on teaching parents to play with their children—interactive and reinforcement skills. This material is derived from the early research of Hanf (1970) and Robinson and Eyberg (1981). The third and fourth segments teach parents a specific set of nonviolent discipline techniques including commands, time out, and ignore as described by Patterson (1982) and Forehand and McMahon (1981), as well as logical and natural consequences and monitoring. The fourth segment also shows parents how they can teach their children problem-solving skills (D'Zurilla & Nezu, 1982; Spivak, Platt, & Shure, 1976). Table 2 provides a brief description of the content of each program.

Family Training Interventions

Rationale for Broader-Based Training

In addition to parenting behavior, other aspects of parents' behavior and personal lives constitute risk factors for child conduct problems. Researchers have demonstrated that personal and interpersonal factors, such as parental depression, marital discord, lack of social support, and environmental stressors, disrupt parenting behavior and contribute to relapses after the parent training (e.g., Dumas, 1984; Webster-Stratton, 1990b, 1990c). In our own analysis of the marital status of 218 parents of children with ODD and CD, we found that 36% were single (defined as divorced, separated, and not currently living with a partner for more than 3 months). Of the remaining 140 subjects (67%) who were married or had been living with a partner for more than 3 months, nearly half (49%) reported significant marital distress (scores of less than 100 on the marital adjustment scale or experiences with spouse abuse). Of the maritally distressed group, 31% were second or third marriages. Of the half that reported supportive marriages, 23% were in second or third marriages. In summary, 75% of the sample had been divorced at least once or were currently in stressful marriages. Half of the married couples reported current experiences with spouse abuse. These findings highlight the importance of marital conflict as a potential key factor influencing the development of conduct disorders. This research is corroborated by the earlier work of Rutter, Cox, Tupling, Berger, & Yule (1975), who reported that marriages characterized by tension and hostility were associated more closely with children's behavior disturbances than marriages characterized by apathy and indifference. The role played by the parents' open conflict and expression of negative affect is further emphasized in studies of parents in laboratory situations either requiring interpersonal negotiation or provoking discord (Love & Kaswan, 1974). Studies suggest that factors such as children's exposure to marital conflict (Grych & Fincham, 1990; Porter & O'Leary, 1980), physical aggression between spouses, and disagreements over child rearing (Jouriles, Murphy, & O'Leary, 1989) account for variance beyond that of general marital stress in a control sample.

TABLE 2
Parenting Skills Training Intervention (BASIC)

Content	Objectives	Content	Objectives
Program 1: Play			
Part 1: How to play with a child	▪ Recognizing children's capabilities and needs ▪ Providing positive support for children's play ▪ Helping children develop imaginative and creative play ▪ Building children's self-esteem and self-concept ▪ Handling children's boredom ▪ Avoiding power struggles with children ▪ Understanding the importance of adult attention	Part 2: Helping children to learn	▪ How to talk with children ▪ Ways to foster language development ▪ Building children's confidence in learning ability ▪ How to help children learn to solve problems ▪ Helping children deal with frustration ▪ Avoiding the criticism trap ▪ Making learning enjoyable through play
Program 2: Praise and rewards			
Part 1: The art of effective praising	▪ Understanding ways to praise more effectively ▪ Avoiding praising only perfection ▪ Recognizing common traps ▪ Handling children who reject praise ▪ Providing physical warmth ▪ Recognizing child behaviors that need praise ▪ Understanding the effects of social rewards on children ▪ Doubling the impact of praise ▪ Building children's self-esteem	Part 2: Tangible rewards	▪ Providing unexpected rewards ▪ Understanding the difference between rewards and bribes ▪ Recognizing when to use the "first–then" rule ▪ Providing ways to set up star and chart systems with children ▪ Recognizing ways to carry out point programs ▪ Understanding how to develop programs that are age appropriate

(continued)

TABLE 2 (Continued)

Content	Objectives	Content	Objectives
			- Understanding ways to use tangible rewards for problems such as dawdling, not dressing, noncompliance, not sharing, sibling fighting, picky eating, messy room, not going to bed, and soiled diapers

Program 3: Effective limit setting

Content	Objectives	Content	Objectives
Program 1: How to set limits	- Helping parents identify important household rules - Understanding ways to give more effective commands - Avoiding unnecessary commands - Avoiding unclear, vague, and negative commands - Providing children with positive alternatives - Understanding when to use the "when–then" command - Recognizing the importance of warnings and helpful reminders - Understanding ways to use problem-solving approaches	Part 2: Helping children to learn to accept limits	- Dealing with children who test the limits - Understanding when to divert and distract children - Avoiding arguments and "why games" - Recognizing traps that children set for parents - Ignoring inappropriate responses - Following through with commands effectively - Helping children to be more compliant

Part 3: Dealing with noncompliance

- Understanding how to implement time out for noncompliance
- Understanding ways to explain time out to children
- Avoiding power struggles
- Dealing with the child who refuses to go to time out or refuses to stay in time out
- Ignoring children's inappropriate responses
- Following through effectively and consistently
- Avoiding common mistakes concerning time out

Program 4: Handling misbehavior

Part 1: Avoiding and ignoring misbehavior

- Anticipating and avoiding frustration
- Showing disapproval
- Ignoring and distracting
- Handling noncompliance, screaming, arguing, pleading, and tantrums
- Handling crying, grabbing, not eating, and refusing to go to bed

Part 3: Preventive strategies

- Encouraging sharing and cooperating between children
- Using puppets and story books to teach children social skills
- Effective talking and listening
- Problem solving with children
- Review of points to remember when using time out

Part 2: Time out and other penalties

- Explaining time out to a school-age child
- Using time out for hitting behaviors
- Using the time out chair with a toddler
- Explaining time out to a toddler
- Using a time out room with a toddler
- Using time out to help stop sibling fights
- Following through when a child refuses to go to time out
- Spitting
- Threats
- Logical consequences
- When discipline does not work
- Telephone syndrome
- TV syndrome

This evidence linking parental factors other than parenting behavior (e.g., marital distress, social isolation and lack of support, and poor problem-solving ability) to child conduct problems and treatment relapses led us to expand our theoretical and causal model concerning conduct problems. Parents' personal and interpersonal factors may disrupt parent–child interactions and family systems (Patterson, 1986; Webster-Stratton, 1989a, 1990c; Webster-Stratton & Hammond, 1988; Whipple & Webster-Stratton, 1991). For example, rather than the child's conduct problems being the result of parenting deficits, we hypothesized that the child's conduct in general and poor peer interactions in particular are modeled from the marital interactions. The child learns communication and problem-solving styles directly from observing the parents' interactions. In our revised model, a conflict resolution deficit model, we hypothesized that parents with children who have conduct disorders have more general relational deficits in communication, conflict resolution skills, and affect regulation. We believe that these deficits are manifested in marital and interpersonal difficulties, inability to get support or cope with life stressors, problematic parenting, and difficulty in coping with child misbehaviors. These, in turn, exacerbate their ineffectual parenting and, thereby, contribute to the development of child conduct problems (Dadds, Schwartz, & Sanders, 1987; Griest, Forehand, Rogers, Breiner, Furey, & Williams, 1982).

Content of ADVANCE Parent Training Videotape Modeling Programs

In light of this research and of the results of our long-term follow-ups indicating the potency of marital distress and divorce as predictors of treatment relapse, we developed the ADVANCE treatment program in 1989. We theorized that a broader-based training model (i.e., one involving more than parenting training) would help mediate the negative influences of these personal and interpersonal factors on parenting skills and promote increased maintenance and generalizability of treatment effects. This program has the same theoretical basis as the BASIC parent skills training program, namely, cognitive social learning theory. The therapeutic process and methods are also the same as those of the BASIC program because our prior research had indicated that therapist-led parent group discussions and interactive videotape modeling techniques were highly effective methods of producing behavior change and of promoting interpersonal support. Moreover, it was theorized that the group approach would provide more social support and decrease feelings of isolation for parents. Finally, it would be a cost-effective alternative to the conventional format of individual marital or interpersonal therapy.

The content of this 14-session videotape program (60 vignettes), which is offered following the completion of the BASIC training program, involves four components:

1. *Personal self-control.* Parents are taught to substitute coping and positive self-talk for their depressive, angry, blaming self-talk. This therapy component builds on the well-established research and clinical writings of Beck (1979), Lewinsohn, Antonuccio, Steinmetz, & Teni (1984), and Meichenbaum (1977). In addition, parents are taught specific anger management techniques.
2. *Communication skills.* Parents are taught to identify blocks to communication and to learn the most effective communication skills for dealing with conflict. This component builds on the communication work of Gottman, Notarius, Gonso, and Markman (1976) and the social learning-based marital treatment developed by Jacobson and Margolin (1979).
3. *Problem-solving skills.* In segments 6 and 7 of the videotape, parents are taught effective strategies for coping with conflict, with spouses, employers, extended family members, or children. These segments build on the research by D'Zurilla and Nezu (1982), but are also influenced by the marital programs of Gottman, Notarius, Gonso, and Markman (1976) and Jacobson and Margolin (1979).
4. *Strengthening social support and self-care.* This concept is woven throughout the group sessions by encouraging the group members to ask for support when necessary and to give support to others (see Table 3).

Academic Skills Training Intervention for Parents

Rationale for Academic Skills Training

In follow-up interviews with parents who had completed our parent training programs, 58% requested guidance on how to encourage their children to do their homework, how to handle resistance; how to communicate with teachers concerning their children's behavior problems at school; and how to promote their children's reading, academic, and social skills. These data suggested a need for teaching parents how to access schools, collaborate with teachers, and supervise children's peer relationships. In addition, 40% of teachers reported problems with children's compliance and aggression in the classroom and requested advice on how to manage these problems. Clearly, integrating interventions across settings (home and school) and agents (teachers and parents) to target school and family risk factors

TABLE 3
Interpersonal Skills Training Intervention (ADVANCE)[a]

Program 5: How to communicate effectively

Content	Objectives	Content	Objectives
Part 1: Active listening and speaking up	• Understanding the importance of active listening skills • Learning how to speak up effectively about problems • Recognizing how to validate another's feelings • Knowing how and when to express one's own feelings • Avoid communication "blocks" such as not listening, storing up grievances, and angry explosions	Part 2: Communicating more positively to oneself and to others	• Understanding the importance of recognizing self-talk • Understanding how angry and depressive emotions and thoughts can affect behaviors with others • Learning coping strategies to stop negative self-talk • Learning coping strategies to increase positive self-talk • Increasing more positive and polite communication with others • Avoiding communication "blocks" such as put-downs, blaming, and denials • Understanding the importance of seeing a problem from the other person's point of view
Part 3: Giving and receiving support	• Understanding the importance of support for a family or an individual • Recognizing communication styles or beliefs that block support • Fostering self-care and positive self-reinforcement strategies in adults and children • Avoiding communication "blocks" such as defensiveness, denials, cross complaints, inconsistent or mixed messages		

- Knowing how to get feedback from others
- Understanding how to turn a complaint into a positive recommendation
- Promoting consistent verbal and nonverbal messages
- Knowing how to make positive requests of adults as well as children
- Understanding why compliance to another's requests is essential in any relationship
- Learning how to be more supportive to others

Program 6: Problem solving for parents

Part 1: Adult problem solving

- Recognizing when to use spontaneous problem-solving skills
- Understanding the six important steps to solve problems
- Learning how and when to collaborate effectively
- Avoiding "blocks" to effective problem solving such as blaming, attacks, anger, side-tracking, lengthy problem definition, missed steps, and criticizing solutions
- Recognizing how to use problem-solving strategies to get more support
- Learning how to express feelings about a problem without blaming

Part 2: Family problem solving

- Understanding how to use the six problem-solving steps with school-aged children
- Recognizing the importance of evaluating plans during each problem-solving session
- Understanding the importance of rotating the leader for each family meeting
- Learning how to help children express their feelings about an issue
- Reinforcing the problem-solving process

(continued)

TABLE 3 (Continued)

Content	Objectives	Content	Objectives
	Program 7: Problem solving with children		
Part 1: Teaching children to solve problems through stories and games	■ Understanding a variety of games and stories that can be used to help children begin to learn problem-solving skills ■ Appreciating the developmental nature and process of problem solving and learning how to enhance these skills in children ■ Strengthening a child's beginning empathy skills or ability to understand a problem from another person's viewpoint ■ Recognizing why both aggressive and shy children need to learn these skills ■ Learning how to help children think about the feeling and behavioral consequences to solutions proposed	Part 2: Teaching children to solve problems in the midst of conflict	■ Understanding the importance of adults not imposing solutions on children but fostering a thinking process about conflict ■ Recognizing how and when to use guided solutions for very young children or for children who have no positive solutions in their repertoire ■ Discovering the value of first obtaining the child's feelings and view of the problem before attempting to solve the problem ■ Learning how to foster children's empathy skills and ability to perceive another's point of view

- Knowing how to help older children evaluate their proposed solutions
- Understanding the importance of validating children's feelings
- Avoiding "blocks" to effective problem solving with children such as lectures, quick solutions, judgments, criticisms, too many questions, and exclusive focus on proper solutions
- Learning how to help children make more positive attributions about another person's intentions
- Recognizing the value of adults modeling their own problem solving for children to observe

- Recognizing when children may be ready to solve problems on their own
- Avoiding "blocks" to effective problem solving with children such as lectures, negative or quick judgments, exclusive focus on the right response and failure to validate a child's feelings

[a]BASIC and ADVANCE have been incorporated into our current version of training called FAMILY training.

fosters greater between-environment consistency and offers the best possibility for long-term reduction of antisocial behavior.

Content of PARTNERS Academic Skills Training

Over the past 2 years, we have developed an interactive videotape modeling, academic skills training intervention (PARTNERS 1) as an adjunct to our parent skills and family intervention. This intervention consists of 6–8 additional sessions beyond the BASIC and ADVANCE programs. It focuses on collaboration with teachers and fostering children's academic readiness and school success through parental involvement in school activities, homework, and peer monitoring. This program's methods are consistent with the BASIC and ADVANCE interventions: videotape modeling, role playing, homework, and therapist-led group discussion. We have recently been funded to examine the added effectiveness of combining this new, academic skills, parent training program with our parent training interventions.

This six-session program involves six components (see Table 4 for summary):

1. *Promoting children's self-confidence.* Parents are taught to lay the foundation for their children's success in school by helping their children feel confident in their own ideas and in their ability to learn. Specifically, we teach parents how to prepare their children for reading; how to foster language development and problem solving; and how to promote children's reading, writing, and story-telling skills.
2. *Fostering good learning habits.* Parents are taught to establish a predictable homework routine, set limits concerning television and computer games, and follow through with consequences for children who test these limits.
3. *Dealing with children's discouragement.* Parents are taught how to set realistic goals for their child and how to increase gradually the difficulty of the learning task as the child acquires mastery, using praise, tangible rewards, and attention to motivate and reinforce progress.
4. *Participating in homework.* Parents are taught ways in which to play a positive and supportive role in their children's homework.
5. *Using teacher–parent conferences to advocate for your child.* This segment shows parents how to collaborate with their children's teachers to develop jointly plans to address their children's difficulties, such as inattentiveness, tardiness, and aggression in school.

TABLE 4
Academic Skills Training Intervention for Parents (PARTNERS 1)

Program 8: How to support your child's education

Content	Objectives	Content	Objectives
Part 1: Promoting your children's self-confidence	■ Recognizing the capabilities of young children ■ Providing positive support for children's play ■ Helping children develop imaginative and creative play ■ Building children's self-esteem and self-confidence in their learning ability ■ Making learning enjoyable through play ■ Teaching children to problem-solve ■ Understanding the importance of adult attention and listening skills for children ■ Fostering children's reading skills and storytelling through interactive dialogues, praise, and open-ended questions	Part 2: Fostering good learning habits	■ How to set up a predictable routine ■ Understanding how television interferes with learning ■ Effective limit-setting regarding homework ■ Understanding how to follow through with limits ■ Understanding the importance of parental monitoring ■ Avoiding the criticism trap
Part 3: Dealing with children's discouragement	■ Helping children to avoid a sense of failure when they cannot do something ■ Recognizing the importance of children learning according to their developmental ability and learning style	Part 4: Participating in homework	■ Understanding the importance of parental attention, praise, and encouragement for children's homework activities ■ Recognizing that every child learns different skills at different rates according to their developmental ability

(continued)

TABLE 4 (Continued)

Content	Objectives	Content	Objectives
			■ Understanding how to build on children's strengths ■ Understanding how to show active interest in children's learning at home and at school
	■ Understanding how to build on children's strengths ■ Knowing how to set up tangible reward programs to help motivate children in a difficult area ■ Understanding how to motivate children through praise and encouragement		
Part 5: Using parent–teacher conferences to advocate for your child	■ Understanding the importance of parental advocacy for their children in school ■ Understanding how to focus on finding solutions to children's school difficulties (not blame) ■ Recognizing effective communication and problem-solving strategies for talking to teachers ■ Knowing ways to support teachers in their teaching efforts ■ Recognizing strategies to motivate children at school ■ Understanding the importance of continuity from home to school		

6. *Discussing a school problem with your child.* In this segment, parents are taught how to talk with their children about academic problems and how to set up a plan with them to maximize their success at school.

TREATMENT EFFECTIVENESS OF BASIC AND ADVANCE PARENT INTERVENTIONS

Short- and Long-term Outcome

Researched in a series of five randomized studies, our videotape modeling group discussion program (BASIC) has been shown to be effective in improving parental attitudes and parent–child interactions, along with reducing parents' reliance on violent disciplinary approaches and reducing child conduct problems, when compared with control groups and other treatment approaches (Webster-Stratton, 1981a, 1982a, 1982b, 1984, 1990a; Webster-Stratton, Hollinsworth, & Kolpacoff, 1989; Webster-Stratton, Kolpacoff, & Hollinsworth, 1988). In the initial study, the BASIC program was shown to be highly effective in improving parent and child behaviors in comparison with a control group. Behavioral observations indicated that treated mothers contradicted, intruded, and corrected less; they were less critical of their children and more positive. Children, in turn, were more independent and less negative and domineering when interacting with their mothers. Nearly identical changes occurred in the delayed treatment control group after completing the program. In the second randomized study with low-income single mothers of highly conduct-disordered children, the therapist-led BASIC program was shown to be as effective as the individualized one-to-one parent training with a therapist using "bug-in-the-ear" feedback (a procedure wherein the parent wears a small cordless microphone in the ear so that the therapist may coach the parent through a one-way mirror as the parent interacts with the child) and individual coaching (Webster-Stratton, 1984). However, the BASIC program was five times more cost-effective, using 48 hours of therapist time versus 251 hours in the one-to-one program.

Our third study was conducted to ascertain which element of the overall BASIC program (group support and discussion, therapist leadership, or videotape modeling) contributed most to its effectiveness. It was crucial to understand the independent role of each of these elements. Results indicated that all three treatment conditions resulted in significant improvements in comparison to the control group; when there were differences, the combined BASIC treatment was favored consistently (Webster-Stratton, 1989b; Webster-Stratton, Kolpacoff, & Hollinsworth, 1988). However, the completely self-administered (individually) intervention

(IVM), that is, without therapist feedback or group support, was also shown to be modestly effective (Webster-Stratton, 1990a, 1992). One year later, 93.1% of families were assessed on the basis of teacher and parent reports and home observations. Results indicated that all the significant improvements reported immediately post-treatment were maintained. Moreover, two-thirds of the entire sample showed "clinically significant" improvements (Webster-Stratton, Hollinsworth, & Kolpacoff, 1989).

Three years after treatment, by which time all the children were enrolled in school, we assessed 82.1% of the families again to determine the presence of long-term differences among treatment groups in terms of numbers of relapses and children's functioning at school and at home. Follow-up reports from parents and teachers indicated overall improvements in child behavior when compared to baseline behavior reports. However, only the combined videotape modeling group–discussion treatment (BASIC) achieved stable improvements; the other two treatment groups showed significant relapses. These data suggest the importance of therapist leadership and parent group support used in conjunction with videotape modeling in producing the most effective results. In sum, these studies have indicated that videotape modeling, plus parent group discussion (BASIC), is not only an effective therapeutic method in terms of producing significant behavior change, which generalizes from home to school and over time, but is also highly cost effective, with good consumer satisfaction regardless of the parents' educational or socioeconomic background (Webster-Stratton, 1990b).

Evaluation of the clinical significance of the treatment programs indicated that, after 3 years, 25% to 46% of parents were concerned about school-related problems, such as peer relationships, aggression, noncompliance, and academic underachievement. Data from parents pointed to a need to help parents to become more effective in supporting their child's education and to collaborate with their child's teacher in addressing their child's social and academic difficulties. Data from teachers revealed a need to expand the intervention to include training for teachers in ways to manage classroom behavior problems and in ways to collaborate with parents (Webster-Stratton & Hammond, 1990; Webster-Stratton, Kolpacoff, & Hollinsworth, 1988). These data led us to develop the parent, academic skills training intervention described earlier and, more recently, to develop a teacher training component (PARTNERS 2), which is currently under evaluation.

Of particular interest were the findings in the third study regarding the totally self-administered treatment. In contrast with the control families, the IVM treatment resulted in significant improvements in child conduct difficulties (as reported by parents) and in parent–child interactions (according to independent observers). These findings are remarkable in light of the fact that these multiproblem families had no direct therapist contact or group support throughout the entire training series and suggest that parents who are motivated can learn to change their own and their children's behaviors by means of a self-administered program. Clearly, this program has major implications for treatment and prevention.

Nonetheless, although the IVM treatment was extremely cost effective, it was not as potent as the BASIC treatment in terms of consumer satisfaction and long-term effects. Consequently, we sought to determine how to enhance the effectiveness of IVM treatment while maintaining its cost effectiveness. Because IVM families saw the lack of personal contact with a therapist as a limitation of the program, we added brief therapist consultation to the IVM program. Comparing IVM, IVM plus therapist consultation (IVMC), and a waiting-list control group at pretreatment, posttreatment, and 1 year later, our fourth study found that both treatment groups of mothers reported significantly fewer child behavior problems, reduced stress levels, and less use of spanking than those in the control group. Home-visit data indicated that both treatment groups exhibited significant behavioral changes, which were maintained 1 year later. There were relatively few differences between the two treatment conditions on the outcome measures. However, the IVMC children were significantly less deviant than the IVM children, suggesting that therapist consultation improves this treatment approach (Webster-Stratton, 1990a, 1990b, 1992). These findings have implications for reaching many more families in cost-effective treatment or prevention programs to help prevent behavior difficulties from escalating in the first place.

In a fifth study, we examined the effects of adding the ADVANCE intervention component to the BASIC intervention. Parents of 78 families with children with ODD and CD received the initial BASIC parent training and, then, were randomly assigned to either ADVANCE training or no additional contact. Families were assessed at baseline, and at 1 month, 1 year, and 2 years posttreatment by parent and teacher reports of child adjustment and parent distress (i.e., depression, anger, and stress), as well as by direct observations of parent–child interactions and marital interactions (discussing a problem). For both treatment groups, there were significant improvements in child adjustment and in parent–child interactions and a decrease in parent distress and child behavior difficulties. These changes were maintained at follow-up. ADVANCE children showed significant increases in the total number of solutions generated during problem solving, most notably in prosocial solutions (as compared with aggressive solutions) in comparison with their counterparts. Observations of parents' marital interactions indicated significant improvements in ADVANCE parents' communication, problem-solving, and collaboration skills when compared with parents who did not receive ADVANCE. Only one family dropped out of the ADVANCE program, which attests to its perceived usefulness by families. All the families attended more than two-thirds of the sessions with the majority attending more than 90% of sessions. ADVANCE parents reported significantly greater consumer satisfaction than did parents who did not receive ADVANCE, with parents reporting the problem-solving skills to be the most useful and anger management the most difficult.

Next, we looked at how clinically significant improvements (30%) in parents' communication and problem-solving skills were related to improvements in their parenting skills. We found that, in the case of fathers, improvement in marital communication skills was related to a significant reduction in the number of criticisms in their interactions with their children; fathers' improved marital communication was also related to improvements in the child's prosocial skills. These results indicate the importance of fathers' marital satisfaction as a determining factor in their parenting skills. Overall, these results suggest that focusing on helping families to manage personal distress and interpersonal issues through a videotape modeling group discussion treatment (ADVANCE) is highly promising, in terms of (a) improvements in marital communication, problem-solving, and coping skills; (b) improvements in parenting skills; (c) improvements in children's prosocial skills; and (d) consumer satisfaction, that is, being highly acceptable and perceived as useful by families (Webster-Stratton, 1994).

Parent Training Treatment Limitations

As reported earlier, we have followed families longitudinally (1, 2, and 3 years posttreatment) and have assessed not only the statistical significance of treatment effects but also their clinical significance. In assessing the clinical significance, three criteria were used: (a) the extent to which parent and teacher reports indicated that the children were within the normal or (b) within the nonclinical range of functioning (Jacobson, Follette, & Revenstorf, 1984); and (c) whether families requested additional therapy for their children's behavior problems at the follow-up assessments. These outcome criteria were chosen to avoid reliance on a single informant or criterion measure, thereby providing greater validity for the findings. In our 3-year follow-up of 83 treated families, we found that 25–46% of parents and 26% of teachers still reported clinically significant child behavior difficulties (Webster-Stratton, 1990b). These findings are similar to other long-term treatment outcome studies that suggest that 30–50% of families relapse or fail to show continuous long-term benefits from treatment (e.g., Jacobson, Schmaling, & Holtzworth-Monroe, 1987; McMahon & Forehand, 1984; Wahler & Dumas, 1984).

We also found that the families, whose children had continuing externalizing problems (according to teacher and parent reports) at our 3-year follow-up assessments, were characterized by maritally distressed or single-parent status; increased maternal depression; lower social class; high levels of negative life stressors; and family histories of alcoholism, drug abuse, and spouse abuse (Webster-Stratton, 1990a, 1990b, 1990c; Webster-Stratton & Hammond, 1990). These predictors of poor outcome emerged regardless of whether the intervention was the combined BASIC program or the IVM condition. These prediction studies were limited, however, in that they examined only one predictor at a time and relied largely on predictors related to mothers' psychological status or perceptions (not fathers'). Most recently, we attempted to determine whether some of these predictors are more powerful than others and the extent of amplification among predictors. The best predictor of the amount of child deviance for home observations was single-parent status or marital adjustment. For families who had a father present, the degree of negative life stress experienced by the father in the year after treatment was the best predictor of child deviance. Marital status was the best predictor of teacher reports of child adjustment (Webster-Stratton & Hammond, 1990). Thus, divorce, marital distress, and negative life stress were the key predictors in determining the child's long-term treatment outcome. Thus, we hypothesize that, by strengthening families' coping skills and marital communication in the ADVANCE program, we may be able to improve the long-term results.

Summary and Significance

In focusing on parenting training, we were targeting the most proximal links in the development of conduct disorders. We hypothesized that, because parents are the most powerful—and potentially malleable—influence on young children's social development, intervening with parents would be the most strategic first step. Indeed, our studies have shown that videotape modeling parent training is highly promising as an effective therapeutic method for producing significant behavior change. It has received good consumer satisfaction reports, regardless of parents' educational or socioeconomic background (Webster-Stratton, 1989b). Approximately 65% of families achieved sustained improvements in their children's conduct disorders. Moreover, our effects were further enhanced when we targeted other parental risk factors, such as marital distress, anger management, and maternal depression. These interventions strengthened parental coping skills and helped buffer the disruptive effects of these personal and interpersonal stressors on parenting and on children's social development. Nonetheless, when we looked at predictors of relapse and the failure of improvements in child behaviors to generalize beyond home to school and peer relationships, our long-term data suggested that our model, concerning the development of conduct problems, was incomplete.

Child Social Skills Training Intervention

Rationale for Child Training Intervention

One reason for which the improvements in child behavior resulting from parenting training did not generalize from home to school might be the exclusive focus on parent skills as the locus of change, that is, the lack of attention to the role that child factors play in the development of conduct problems. Indeed, research has indicated that children with ODD and CD have some neurological, physiological, and temperament difficulties that contribute to their difficulties with peers and to the parenting difficulties of their parents. Studies have suggested that children with conduct disorders are more hyperactive and impulsive (Lillenfield & Waldman, 1990), are more likely to have difficulty solving social problems (Rubin & Krasnor, 1986), and respond with more agonistic and incompetent strategies to hypothetical conflict situations (Milich & Dodge, 1984; Richard & Dodge, 1982). Aggressive children also search for fewer cues or facts when determining another person's intentions (Dodge & Newman, 1981), focus more on aggressive cues (Goutz, 1981), are more likely to misattribute hostile intentions to others (Dodge, 1985), and are less empathic than their nonaggressive peers (Ellis, 1982). This line of research suggests that children with conduct disorders lack the critical cognitive, social, and behavioral skills needed for positive interactions; it has spawned what has been termed the *child-deficit hypothesis* by Asher and Renshaw (1981).

Those who subscribe to this child-deficit model have developed cognitive–behavioral interventions to train children directly in social and problem-solving skills (Dodge, Price, Bachorowski, & Newman, 1990; Kendall, 1985; Rubin & Krasnor, 1986; Spivak, Platt, & Shure, 1976). A review of this research is encouraging (Kendall & Braswell, 1985), especially for improving older children's social skills at school. However, such improvements have not been shown to generalize to other settings (e.g., the home). Also, a large proportion of children appears to be relatively unaffected by treatment, particularly the younger, the cognitively less mature, and the more aggressive children (Asher & Coie, 1990).

We hypothesized that there were several reasons why existing social skills programs had not been able to help younger children with conduct problems. First, many of these programs were originally developed for older adolescents and subsequently applied to younger age groups; as a consequence, these programs were not developmentally appropriate for young preschool children (who are preoperational in their thinking). Second, existing programs did not focus specifically on the child's aggression and noncompliance, nor did they address these children's specific academic difficulties. Third, some child social skills programs did not involve a parent or family training component, a limitation that would seem to make generalizing to other settings less likely. We hypothesized that a comprehensive intervention, combining a parent training component with a child training component specifically designed for young, aggressive children, would be more effective than either component alone.

Content and Process of the KIDVID Child Social Skills and Problem-Solving Training Intervention (Dinosaur Curriculum)

In 1990, we developed a new videotape modeling child training program (KIDVID) for conduct-problem children (ages 3–8 years). Our efforts to create a developmentally appropriate, theory-based intervention for aggressive preschool and early-school-aged children were guided both by the available literature and by our own observations comparing oppositional–defiant and conduct-disordered children with behaviorally normal children. Traditional social skills training programs typically did not have content that was directly relevant to conduct disorder and aggression. Our program targets selected child risk factors (problem-solving and social skills deficits, peer rejection, loneliness, and negative attributions) and uses the child directly as an agent of change. The intervention is designed to enhance children's school behaviors, promote social competence and positive peer interactions, as well as nonaggressive conflict management strategies. In addition, the program teaches children how to integrate themselves successfully into the classroom and how to develop friendships.

This 22-week program consists of a series of nine videotape segments (more than 100 vignettes) that teach children problem-solving and social skills. Organized so as to dovetail with the content of the parent training program, the program consists of seven main components:

1. introduction and rules (1–2 sessions);
2. empathy training (2–3 sessions);
3. problem-solving training (3–4 sessions);
4. anger control (2–3 sessions);
5. friendship skills (3–4 sessions);
6. communication skills (2–3 sessions); and
7. school training.

The children come to our clinic once a week to meet in small groups of six children for 2 hours. In this curriculum, we use videotape modeling examples in every session to foster discussion, problem solving, and modeling of prosocial behaviors. To enhance generalization, the scenes selected for each of the units involve real-life conflict situations at home and at school (playground and classroom), such as teasing, lying, stealing, and destructive behavior. For example, the videotapes show children of differing ages, sexes, and cultures interacting with adults (parents or teachers) or with other children "doing it right" or "doing it wrong." Then, the tapes are paused so that the children can discuss feelings and generate ideas for more effective responses and role-play alternative scenarios. In addition to interactive videotape modeling teaching, the therapists use life-size puppets to model appropriate behavior and thinking processes for the children. The use of puppets appeals to children on the fantasy level, so predominant in this preoperational age group. Because young children are more vulnerable to distraction, are less able to organize their thoughts, and have poorer memories, we use a number of strategies for reviewing and organizing the material to be remembered

1. playing Copy Cat to review skills learned;
2. videotape examples of the same concept in different situations and settings;
3. cartoon pictures and specially designed stickers used as cues to remind children of key concepts;
4. role playing with puppets and other children to provide not only practice opportunities but also experience with different perspectives;
5. reenacting videotape scenes;
6. visual story examples of key ideas;
7. play, art, and game activities to rehearse skills;
8. homework to practice key skills; and
9. letters to parents and teachers explaining the key concepts that the children are learning and asking them to reinforce these behaviors whenever they see them occurring throughout the week.

For example, if the concept being taught is teamwork, teachers and parents will be asked to reinforce examples that they see of children sharing, helping, and cooperating during the week and to give the child a note about these behaviors, which is to be brought to the next session (special Dinosaur notes are given to teachers and parents, which they may use with the children). See Table 5 for a summary of the content of the KIDVID program.

CHILD TRAINING TREATMENT EFFECTIVENESS

Families of 97 children with early-onset conduct problems, aged 4–8 years, were randomly assigned to one of four conditions: a treatment group that received the FAMILY intervention (including BASIC parenting skills training as well as ADVANCE interpersonal training), a treatment group that received the child training program (KIDVID), a treatment group that received both the parent and child training programs, or a waiting-list control group (CON). We hypothesized that families who received the

TABLE 5
Child Social Skills and Problem-Solving Training (KIDVID)

Content	Objectives	Content	Objectives
	Program 1: Wally introduces Dinosaur School		
Making new friends and learning school rules	▪ Helping children understand the importance of rules ▪ Helping children participate in the process of rule making ▪ Understanding what will happen if rules are broken ▪ Learning how to earn rewards for good behaviors ▪ Promoting children's friendships		
	Program 2: Understanding and detecting feelings		
Wally teaches clues for detecting and understanding feelings	▪ Learning words for different feelings ▪ Learning how to tell how someone is feeling from verbal and nonverbal expressions ▪ Increasing awareness of nonverbal facial communication used to portray feelings ▪ Learning different ways to relax ▪ Helping children understand why different feelings occur ▪ Helping children understand feelings from different perspectives ▪ Practicing talking about feelings		

(continued)

TABLE 5 (Continued)

Program 3: Detective Wally teaches problem-solving steps

Content	Objectives	Content	Objectives
Parts 1, 2, and 3: Detective Wally teaches problem-solving steps	▪ Learning how to identify a problem ▪ Thinking of solutions to hypothetical problems ▪ Learning verbal assertive skills ▪ Learning how to inhibit impulsive reactions ▪ Understanding what apology means ▪ Thinking of alternative solutions to problem situations, such as being teased and hit ▪ Learning to understand that solutions have different consequences ▪ Learning how to evaluate solutions critically, one's own and others'	Parts 4 and 5: Detective Wally teaches how to control anger	▪ Recognizing that anger can interfere with good problem solving ▪ Understanding Tiny Turtle's story about managing anger and getting help ▪ Understanding when apologies are helpful ▪ Helping children recognize anger in themselves and others ▪ Helping children to understand that anger is okay to feel inside but not to act out by hitting or hurting someone else ▪ Learning how to control anger reactions ▪ Helping children understand that things that happen to them are not necessarily hostile or deliberate attempts to hurt them ▪ Practicing alternative responses to being teased, bullied, or yelled at by an angry adult ▪ Learning skills to cope with another person's anger

Part 1: Helping
Part 2: Sharing

Program 4: Molly Manners teaches how to be friendly

Part 3: Teamwork at school
Part 4: Teamwork at home

- Learning what friendship means and how to be friendly
- Understanding ways to help others
- Learning the concept of sharing and the relationship between sharing and helping

- Learning what teamwork means
- Understanding the benefits of sharing, helping, and teamwork
- Practicing friendship skills

Program 5: Molly Manners explains how to talk with friends

- Learning how to ask questions and tell something to a friend
- Learning how to listen carefully to what a friend is saying
- Understanding why it is important to speak up about something that is bothering you
- Understanding how and when to give an apology or compliment
- Learning how to enter into a group of children who are already playing
- Learning how to make a suggestion rather than give commands
- Practicing friendship skills

Program 6: Dina Dinosaur teaches how to do your best in school

Part 1: Listening, waiting, quiet hands up

Part 2: Concentrating, checking, and cooperating

- Learning how to listen, wait, avoid interruptions, and put up a quiet hand to ask questions in class
- Learning how to handle other children who poke and interfere with a child's ability to work at school

- Learning how to stop, think, and check work first
- Learning the importance of cooperation with the teacher and other children
- Practicing concentrating and good classroom skills

combined child and parent training programs would show greater improvement and more sustained results. Baseline, posttreatment, and 1-year follow-up assessments included parent and teacher reports, observations of parent–child interactions, observations of peer interactions during competitive play situations, and child social skills and problem-solving testing.

Posttreatment assessments indicated that all three treatment conditions result in significant improvements in comparison with control participants, as measured by mother and father reports, daily observations of targeted behaviors at home, and laboratory observations of interactions with a best friend. Comparisons of the three treatment conditions indicated that children who participated in KIDVID (with or without parient training) showed significant improvements in problem solving as well as in conflict management skills, as measured by independent observations of their interactions with a best friend; differences among treatment conditions on these measures consistently favored the KIDVID condition over the FAMILY condition. As for parent and child behavior at home, families who participated in one of the two conditions that involved parent training had significantly more positive parent–child interactions in comparison with families who participated only in the KIDVID training, as measured by independent observations.

One-year follow-up assessments indicated that all the significant changes noted immediately posttreatment were maintained over time in both the clinical and home settings. Moreover, child conduct problems at home had lessened significantly over time. Analyses of the clinical significance of the results suggested that the combined child and parent training intervention (FAMILY + KIDVID) produced the most significant improvements in child behavior at 1-year follow-up. However, children from all three treatment conditions showed increases in behavior problems at school 1 year later, as measured by teacher reports. (For more details about this study, see Webster-Stratton, 1995a).

RECOMMENDATIONS AND FUTURE DIRECTIONS

It could also be argued that, for some families, the lack of long-term effectiveness of family programs and the failure of child behavior improvements to generalize, beyond the home, to school and to peer relationships may be attributable to the fact that the school environment and teachers themselves play a role in the development and maintenance of conduct disorders. Perhaps, an exclusive focus on parent and child skills is still too narrow to be effective as treatment or prevention.

Academic performance has been implicated in child conduct disorder. Children with conduct problems often manifest low academic achievement during the elementary grades and on through high school (Kazdin, 1987). Reading disabilities, in particular, are associated with conduct disorder (Sturge, 1982). The overlap of underachievement in reading and aggressive behaviors occurs at rates well above chance levels (Rutter, Tizard, & Whitmore, 1970). One study indicated that the reading ability of children with conduct disorders lags 28 months behind that of normal children (Rutter, Tizard, Yule, Graham, & Whitmore, 1976). Furthermore, this relationship between poor academic performance and conduct disorder is not merely unidirectional, but may be bidirectional, that is, disruptive behavior problems and academic problems may lead to each other. It is clear that conduct problems and reading deficits place the child at high risk for lower self-esteem, continued academic failure, additional conduct disorders, and school dropout.

The school setting has also been studied as a risk factor contributing to conduct disorders. Rutter and his colleagues (1976) found that characteristics such as the degree of emphasis on academic work and individual responsibility, the amount of teacher time spent on lessons, the extent of the teacher's use of praise, the degree of teacher availability, and the teacher–student ratio were related to delinquency rates and academic performance. In light of the influence of the school environment and of teachers in particular on conduct disorders, it is surprising that training programs for parents of conduct-problem children have not, in general, involved teachers. Typically, teachers are left struggling alone in the classroom with a difficult child who exhibits academic as well as behavior difficulties. Moreover, in spite of the documented links among conduct problems and underachievement, language delays, and reading disabilities, there have been no attempts to increase the effectiveness of parent training programs by adding an academic skills training component for parents. Yet, parents need to know how to help their children not only with their antisocial problems, but also with their academic difficulties (e.g., reading and writing). In addition, parents need to know how to work with school personnel to foster a supportive relationship between home and school settings. Such a coordinated effort between home and school, regarding social and academic goals, might lead to better generalization of child improvements across settings. If intervention occurs when children are preschoolers, if it involves teachers as well as parents and children, and if it includes content related to school issues as well as home issues, the prognosis for preventing and reducing conduct problems would seem to be far more favorable than through more traditional parent training or child training programs. We currently have a study underway in which we are examining the added benefits of combining teacher training (PARTNERS 2, based on videotape modeling) with our parent and child interventions.

SUMMARY

In summary, a review of our own research suggests that comprehensive interactive videotape family training methods are highly promising, especially for parents of young children with conduct difficulties. Even a self-administered videotape training format that did not involve a therapist or group support produced significant improvements in parent–child interactions and a reduction in conduct difficulty. However, treatment outcome was related directly to marital distress. Our most effective interventions involved videotape training not only in parenting skills, but also in marital communication, problem solving, and conflict resolution. These findings have pointed to the need for interventions that help strengthen families' protective factors, specifically, parents' interpersonal skills and coping skills, so that they may be able to cope more effectively with their added stresses. Our research has also suggested that videotape modeling is a highly effective strategy for building young conduct-problem children's social skills and problem-solving strategies. We hypothesize that a videotape-based academic skills enhancement program would further increase the effectiveness of intervention programs for families of children with conduct problems.

Our intervention studies may be viewed as an indirect test of theoretical models regarding the development of conduct disorders. We started with a simple parenting skills deficit model and have evolved to a more complex interactional model. In our current model we hypothesize that the child's eventual outcome will be dependent on the interrelationships among children, parents, teachers, and peers. Therefore, the most effective interventions should be those that involve schools, teachers, and the child's peer group. Such programs hold promise for prevention programs, which should be offered early to high-risk populations, before the disorder develops in the first place. We are currently collaborating with the Johns Hopkins University Prevention Center in a trial to evaluate the usefulness of a family component of our intervention programs as a prevention program in the early grades of a number of inner-city Baltimore schools. We have begun our own preventive research project with Puget Sound Educational Service District Head Start in Seattle to determine whether the development of conduct problems can be prevented through early interventions involving parent and teacher training. To date, 500 Head Start program families have participated in this trial, and initial baseline analysis has indicated that, according to mothers, 40% of the children exhibited aggressive and disruptive behaviors in the clinical range. Head Start centers were assigned randomly to two conditions: (a) an experimental condition in which parents, teachers, and family service workers participated in training (BASIC + PARTNERS 2); or (b) a control condition in which parents, teachers, and family service workers participated in their regular center-based Head Start program. Parents in the experimental schools participated in an abbreviated prevention version of BASIC (8–9 group sessions). Preliminary short-term results are highly promising. Intervention mothers made significantly fewer critical remarks, used less physically negative discipline, and were more positive, appropriate, and consistent in their discipline style when compared with control mothers. Intervention children were observed to exhibit significantly fewer negative behaviors in the home, less noncompliance, more positive affect, and more prosocial behaviors than control children (Webster-Stratton, 1995b). Given the high base rates of ODD in this high risk sample of primarily single mothers on welfare and the continuity of the problem from early childhood, through adolescence, and often into adulthood (with its implication for the intergenerational transmission of deviance), the opportunity of breaking the link in the cycle of disadvantage is a public health matter of the utmost importance.

REFERENCES

Asher, S. R., & Coie, J. D. (1990). *Peer rejection in childhood*. Cambridge, England: Cambridge University Press.

Asher, S. R., & Renshaw, P. D. (1981). Children without friends: Social knowledge and social skill training. In S. R. Asher & J. M. Gottman (Eds.), *Children without friends: Social knowledge and social skill training* (pp. 273–296). Cambridge, England: Cambridge University Press.

Bandura, A. (1977). *Social learning theory*. Englewood Cliffs, NJ: Prentice Hall.

Beck, A. T. (1979). *Cognitive therapy and emotional disorders*. New York: New American Library.

Campbell, S. B., & Ewing, L. J. (1990). Follow-up of hard-to-manage preschoolers: Adjustment at age 9 and predictors of continuing symptoms. *Journal of Child Psychology and Psychiatry, 31,* 871–889.

Chilman, A. (1973). Programs for disadvantaged parents. In B. U. Caldwell & W. N. Ricciuti (Eds.), *Review of child development and research* (Vol. 3). Chicago: University of Chicago.

Coie, J. D. (1990). Toward a theory of peer rejection. In S. R. Asher & J. D. Coie (Eds.), *Peer rejection in childhood* (pp. 365-398). Cambridge, England: Cambridge University Press.

Dadds, M. R., Schwartz, M. R., & Sanders, M. R. (1987). Marital discord and treatment outcome in behavioral treatment of child conduct disorders. *Journal of Consulting and Clinical Psychology, 16,* 192–203.

Dodge, K. A., (1985). Attributional bias in aggressive children. In P. C. Kendall (Ed.), *Advances in cognitive–behavioral research and therapy* (pp. 73–110). San Diego, CA: Academic Press.

Dodge, K. A., & Newman, J. P. (1981). Biased decision-making processes in aggressive boys. *Journal of Abnormal Psychology, 90*, 375–379.

Dodge, K. A., Price, J. M., Bachorowski, J. A., & Newman, J. P. (1990). Hostile attributional biases in severely aggressive adolescents. *Journal of Abnormal Psychology, 99*, 385–392.

Dumas, J. E. (1984). Interactional correlates of treatment outcome in behavioral parent training. *Journal of Consulting and Clinical Psychology, 52*, 946–954.

D'Zurilla, T. J., & Nezu, A. (1982). Social problem-solving in adults. In P. C. Kendall (Ed.), *Advances in cognitive–behavioral research and therapy* (pp. 107–126). New York: Academic Press.

Ellis, P. L. (1982). Empathy: A factor in antisocial behavior. *Journal of Abnormal Child Psychology, 10*, 123–133.

Forehand, R. L., & McMahon, R. J. (1981). *Helping the noncompliant child: A clinician's guide to parent training.* New York: Guilford Press.

Gottman, J. M., & Katz, L. F. (1989). Effects of marital discord on children's peer interactions and health. *Developmental Psychology, 3*, 373–381.

Gottman, J. M., Notarius, C., Gonso, J., & Markman, A. (1976). *A couple's guide to communication.* Champaign, IL: Research Press.

Goutz, K. (1981). Children's initial aggression level and the effectiveness of intervention strategies in moderating television effects on aggression. *Journal of Abnormal Child Psychology, 15*, 181–197.

Griest, D. L., Forehand, R., Rogers, T., Breiner, J., Furey, W., & Williams, C. A. (1982). Effects of parent enhancement therapy on the outcome of treatment and generalization of a parent training program. *Behaviour Research and Therapy, 20*, 429–436.

Grych, J. H., & Fincham, F. D. (1990). Marital conflict and children's adjustment: A cognitive contextual framework. *Psychological Bulletin, 108*, 267–290.

Hanf, C. (1970). *Shaping mothers to shape their children's behavior.* Unpublished manuscript, University of Oregon Medical School, Portland.

Hobbs, N. (1982). *The troubled and troubling child.* San Francisco: Jossey-Bass.

Jacobson, N. S., Follette, W. C., & Revenstorf, D. (1984). Psychotherapy outcome research: Methods for reporting variability and evaluating clinical significance. *Behavior Therapy, 15*, 336–352.

Jacobson, N. S., & Margolin, G. (1979). *Marital therapy: Strategies based on social learning and behavior as exchange principles.* New York: Brunner/Mazel.

Jacobson, N. S., Schmaling, K. B., & Holtzworth-Monroe, A. (1987). Component analyses of behavioral mental therapy: Two-year follow-up and prediction of relapse. *Journal of Marriage and the Family, 13*, 187–195.

Jouriles, E. N., Murphy, C. M., & O'Leary, K. D. (1989). Interspousal aggression, marital discord, and child problems. *Journal of Consulting and Clinical Psychology, 57*, 453–455.

Kazdin, A. E. (1985). *Treatment of antisocial behavior in children and adolescents.* Homewood, IL: Dorsey Press.

Kazdin, A. E. (1987). Treatment of antisocial behavior in children: Current status and future directions. *Psychological Bulletin, 102*, 187–203.

Kendall, P. C. (1985). Toward a cognitive–behavioral model of child psychopathology and a critique of related interventions. *Journal of Abnormal Psychology, 13*, 357–372.

Kendall, P. C., & Braswell, L. (1985). *Cognitive–behavioral therapy for impulsive children*. New York: Guilford Press.

Lahey, B. B., Loeber, R. L., Quay, H. C., Frick, P. J., & Grimm, J. (1992). Oppositional Defiant and Conduct Disorders: Issue to be Resolved for DSM-IV. *Journal of the American Academy of Child and Adolescent Psychiatry, 31*.

Lewinsohn, P. M., Antonuccio, D. O., Steinmetz, S. L., & Teni, L. (1984). *The coping with depression course*. Eugene, OR: Castalia Publishing Co.

Lillenfield, S. O., & Waldman, I. D. (1990). The relation between childhood attention deficit hyperactivity disorders and adult antisocial behavior reexamined: The problem of heterogeneity. *Clinical Psychology Review, 10*, 669–725.

Loeber, R. (1991). Antisocial behavior: More enduring than changeable? *Journal of the American Academy of Child and Adolescent Psychiatry, 30*, 393–397.

Love, L. R., & Kaswan, J. W. (1974). *Troubled children: Their families, schools, and treatments*. New York: Wiley.

McMahon, R. J., & Forehand, R. (1984). Parent training for the noncompliant child: Treatment outcome, generalization, and adjunctive therapy procedures. In R. F. Dangel & R. A. Polster (Eds.). *Parent training: Foundations of research and practice* (pp. 298–328). New York: Guilford Press.

Meichenbaum, D. (1977). *Cognitive behavior modification*. New York: Plenum Press.

Milich, R., & Dodge, K. A. (1984). Social information processing in child psychiatric populations. *Journal of Abnormal Child Psychology, 12*, 471–489.

O'Dell, S. L. (1985). Progress in parent training. *Progress in Behavior Modification, 19*, 57–108.

Patterson, G. R. (1982). *Coercive family process*. Eugene, OR: Castalia Publishing Co.

Patterson, G. R. (1986). Performance models for antisocial boys. *American Psychologist, 41*, 432–444.

Patterson, G. R., DeBaryshe, B. D., & Ramsey, E. (1989). A developmental perspective on antisocial behavior. *American Psychologist, 44*, 329–335.

Porter, B., & O'Leary, K. D. (1980). Marital discord and childhood behavior problems. *Journal of Abnormal Child Psychology, 16*, 97–109.

Reid, J., Taplin, P., & Loeber, R. (1981). A social interactional approach to the treatment of abusive families. In R. Stewart (Ed.), *Violent behavior: Social learning approaches to prediction management and treatment* (pp. 83–101). New York: Brunner/Mazel.

Richard, B. A., & Dodge, K. A. (1982). Social maladjustment and problem solving in school-aged children. *Journal of Abnormal Psychology, 50*, 226–233.

Robinson, E. A., & Eyberg, S. M. (1981). The dyadic parent–child interaction coding system: Standardization and validation. *Journal of Consulting and Clinical Psychology, 49,* 245–250.

Rubin, K. H., & Krasnor, L. R. (1986). Social–cognitive and social behavioral perspectives on problem solving. In M. Perlmuller (Ed.), *Minnesota symposia on child psychology* (pp. 1–8). Hillsdale, NJ: Erlbaum.

Rutter, M., Cox, A., Tupling, C., Berger, M., & Yule, W. (1975). Attainment and adjustment in two geographical areas: Pt. 1. The prevalence of psychiatric disorder. *British Journal of Psychiatry, 126,* 493–509.

Rutter, M., Tizard, J., & Whitmore, K. (1970). *Education, health, and behaviour.* London: Longmans.

Rutter, M., Tizard, J., Yule, W., Graham, P., & Whitmore, K. (1976). Research report: Isle of Wight studies. *Psychological Medicine, 6,* 313–332.

Spivak, G., Platt, J. J., & Shure, M. B. (1976). *The problem solving approach to adjustment.* San Francisco: Jossey-Bass.

Strain, P. S., Steele, P., Ellis, T., & Timm, M. A. (1982). Long-term effects of oppositional child treatment with mothers as therapists and therapist trainers. *Journal of Applied Behavior Analysis, 15,* 1163–1169.

Sturge, C. (1982). Reading retardation and antisocial behavior. *Journal of Child Psychology and Psychiatry, 23,* 21–23.

Wahler, R. G., & Dumas, J. E. (1984). Changing observational coding styles of insular and noninsular mothers: A step toward maintenance of parent training effects. In R. F. Dangel & R. A. Polster (Eds.), *Parent Training: Foundations of research and practice* (pp. 379–416). New York: Guilford Press.

Webster-Stratton, C. (1981a). Modification of mothers' behaviors and attitudes through a videotape modeling group discussion program. *Behavior Therapy, 12,* 634–642.

Webster-Stratton, C. (1981b). Videotape modeling: A method of parent education. *Journal of Clinical Child Psychology, 10,* 93–98.

Webster-Stratton, C. (1982a). The long term effects of a videotape modeling parent training program: Comparison of immediate and one year follow-up results. *Behavior Therapy, 13,* 702–714.

Webster-Stratton, C. (1982b). Teaching mothers through videotape modeling to change their children's behavior. *Journal of Pediatric Psychology, 7,* 279–294.

Webster-Stratton, C. (1984). Randomized trial of two parent training programs for families with conduct disordered children. *Journal of Consulting and Clinical Psychology, 52,* 666–678.

Webster-Stratton, C. (1985a). The effects of father involvement in parent training for conduct problem children. *Journal of Child Psychology and Psychiatry, 26,* 801–810.

Webster-Stratton, C. (1985b). Predictors of treatment outcome in parent training for conduct disordered children. *Behavior Therapy, 16,* 223–243.

Webster-Stratton, C. (1989a). The relationship of marital support, conflict and divorce to parent perceptions, behaviors, and childhood conduct problems. *Journal of Marriage and the Family, 51,* 417–430.

Webster-Stratton, C. (1989b). Systematic comparison of consumer satisfaction of three cost-effective parent training programs for. conduct problem children. *Behavior Therapy, 20,* 103–115.

Webster-Stratton, C. (1990a). Enhancing the effectiveness of self-administered videotape parent training for families with conduct-problem children. *Journal of Abnormal Child Psychology, 18,* 479–492.

Webster-Stratton, C. (1990b). Long-term follow-up of families with young conduct problem children: From preschool to grade school. *Journal of Clinical Child Psychology, 19,* 144–149.

Webster-Stratton, C. (1990c). Stress: A potential disruptor of parent perceptions and family interactions. *Journal of Clinical Child Psychology, 19,* 302–312.

Webster-Stratton, C. (1991). Annotation: Strategies for helping families with conduct-disordered children. *Journal of Child Psychology and Psychiatry, 32,* 1047–1062.

Webster-Stratton, C. (1992). Individually administered videotape parent training: "Who benefits?" *Cognitive Therapy and Research, 16,* 31–35.

Webster-Stratton, C. (1994). Advancing videotape parent training: A comparison study. *Journal of Consulting and Clinical Psychology, 62,* 583–593.

Webster-Stratton, C. (1995a). *Comparison of Parent and Child Training Programs for Children with Early Onset Conduct Problems.* Unpublished manuscript, University of Washington, Seattle.

Webster-Stratton, C. (1995b, April). *Preventing conduct problems in Head Start children: Short-term results of intervention.* Paper presented at the meeting of the Society for Research in Child Development.

Webster-Stratton, C., & Hammond, M. (1988). Maternal depression and its relationship to life stress, perceptions of child behavior problems, parenting behaviors, and child conduct problems. *Journal of Abnormal Child Psychology, 16,* 299–315.

Webster-Stratton, C., & Hammond, M. (1990). Predictors of treatment outcome in parent training for families with conduct problem children. *Behavior Therapy, 21,* 319–337.

Webster-Stratton, C., & Herbert, M. (1993). What really happens in parent training? *Behavior Modification. 17,* 407–456.

Webster-Stratton, C., & Herbert, M. (1994). *Troubled families—Problem children. Working with parents: A collaborative process.* New York: Wiley.

Webster-Stratton, C., Hollinsworth, T., & Kolpacoff, M. (1989). The long-term effectiveness and clinical significance of three cost-effective training programs for families with conduct problem children. *Journal of Consulting and Clinical Psychology, 57,* 550–553.

Webster-Stratton, C., Kolpacoff, M., & Hollinsworth, T. (1988). Self-administered videotape therapy for families with conduct problem children: Comparison with two cost-effective treatments and a control group. *Journal of Consulting and Clinical Psychology, 56,* 558–566.

Whipple, E., & Webster-Stratton, C. (1991). The role of parental stress in physically abusive families. *Child Abuse and Neglect, 15,* 279–291.

20

INTENSIFIED FOSTER CARE: MULTI-LEVEL TREATMENT FOR ADOLESCENTS WITH CONDUCT DISORDERS IN OUT-OF-HOME CARE

PATRICIA CHAMBERLAIN

During the past 10 years, the number of adolescents with severe behavioral and emotional problems who are placed outside of their family homes has been increasing dramatically. For example, more than 617,000 children spent time in out-of-home care during 1990, up 100,000 from only 2 years before (Allen, 1991). In the most severe cases, the families' inability to control these teenagers, coupled with the community's need to protect its citizens from their illegal and sometimes violent acts, creates a need for effective models of out-of-home care. Although, currently, diverse treatment models are used to provide a wide array of services in a variety of placement settings (e.g., hospital inpatient units, residential care centers, state training schools), there are few controlled studies evaluating the effectiveness and limitations of these settings or models of care. In fact, relative to the large and escalating numbers of children and adolescents living in out-of-home care, the paucity of empirical work in this area is startling (see review by Curry, 1991). With a few exceptions, studies as-

This chapter was written with support provided by grant R01 MH 47458 from the Center for Studies of Violent Behavior and Traumatic Stress, National Institute for Mental Health, U.S. Public Health Service; grant 90CW0994 from the Administration for Children, Youth, and Families, Child Welfare Services, Human Development Services, Department of Health and Human Services; and grant H237E20018 from the Office of Special Education Programs, U.S. Department of Education. Correspondence concerning this chapter should be directed to Dr. Patricia Chamberlain, Oregon Social Learning Center, 207 East 5th Avenue, Eugene, OR 97401.

475

sessing the effectiveness of residential treatment models use no comparison or control groups and rely only on examining the participants' pre-to-post treatment changes.

This chapter describes a recently articulated, community-based, family-oriented treatment model for out-of-home care. Like other treatment models developed in the 1980s, which targeted adolescents with severe and chronic problems (e.g., Henggeler, Rodick, Borduin, Hanson, Watson, & Urey, 1986), the treatment foster care (TFC) model described here is characterized by multi-component, multi-level interventions. These interventions target, often simultaneously, all the key settings in which the adolescents interact. Typically, these include the teenager's daily interchanges with parents, peers, and teachers, recognizing that these key relationships are embedded in and influenced by broad social contexts, such as neighborhoods and schools.

In addition to the standard normative social contexts adolescents experience, those youths in out-of-home care are influenced by the ecology of their placement setting (Moore, Osgood, Larzelere, & Chamberlain, 1994). Several reviews (e.g., Small, Kennedy, & Bender, 1991; Wells, 1991) of residential care describe varying characteristics of placement living settings on key dimensions such as level of restrictiveness, amount and type of supervision and discipline, importance of peer relations, and types and frequency of transactions with adults. Although the residential care literature contains several excellent descriptions of the therapeutic milieus (e.g., Redl & Wineman, 1957) along with theoretically grounded hypotheses about the salient change mechanisms, no data exist that connect directly how these factors influence adolescents' adjustment and progress in care, let alone their post-placement outcomes. We will present preliminary findings on the relationship of some characteristics of placement settings to adolescent outcomes.

OVERVIEW OF THE PROGRAM

The Oregon Social Learning Center's Treatment Foster Care (TFC) programs serve two adolescent populations: those with chronic delinquency and conduct problems, and those with severe emotional disturbance. The Monitor program for youths with delinquency or conduct problems is the focus of this chapter. Adolescents (12–18 years of age) are referred from the juvenile courts as an alternative to placement in one of the two state training schools. Foster families are recruited, trained, and supervised to provide daily treatment to the adolescent placed with them.

Daily treatment in the foster home is augmented by six other service elements:

1. individual therapy,
2. family therapy for the adolescent's biological (or adoptive) relatives,
3. regular school consultations, including on-site observations and school-based interventions, as needed,
4. consultation with parole/probation officers,
5. psychiatric consultation, as needed, and
6. case management to coordinate all of the services delivered and to provide ongoing supervision and consultation to the treatment foster parents.

Regular home visits are scheduled throughout the placement in the majority of cases (i.e., 85%), for which the goal is to return the adolescents to their families of origin. Those families and teenagers also participate in a 12-month aftercare program.

The average placement is 6 months. Typically, only one adolescent is placed in a TFC home. TFC parents are paid from $800 to $1,000 per month, which is approximately 2.5 times the rate paid by the State of Oregon for regular foster care. The program is funded through a state contract that pays $72 per day per child. Aftercare and school-based services, as well as research on those components, have been funded separately through federal grants (i.e., Chamberlain, 1990, 1992).

Development and implementation of the TFC program model is usually conducted by private nonprofit or state agencies (Hudson, Nutter, & Galaway, 1992) and is probably beyond the scope of what an individual, private clinician would organize and supervise. However, in the 1980s, TFC programs became increasingly widespread as an alternative to group and institutional care placements. For example, the Foster Family-Based Treatment Association, the national organization representing TFC programs, has over 250 member agencies in 44 states and 4 Canadian provinces. In the 1980s, the TFC model became a key component in the National Institute of Mental Health (NIMH)-sponsored Child and Adolescent Services System for severely emotionally disturbed youngsters (Stroul & Friedman, 1986). Because of the TFC model's popularity with policy makers, its flexibility which allows it to fit individual treatment needs, and its relatively low cost (compared to inpatient or residential care), clinicians working in state and private inpatient and community-based programs are likely to see locally tailored examples of TFC in practice or emerging in their communities in the 1990s. The components of the treatment model, which are described in detail in Chamberlain (1994), are reviewed later.

Developing the Placement Setting: Recruiting, Screening, and Hiring Treatment Foster Parents

One- and two-parent families from diverse social, ethnic, cultural, and economic backgrounds have served as successful Monitor TFC parents. We attempt to select strong families with regard to stability and parenting skills. A four-stage selection and hiring process, consisting of an initial telephone interview, followed by a written application, a home visit, and preservice training, is used. Because of the magnitude of the problems presented by adolescents referred to the program, TFC parents must be willing to work actively as part of a treatment team. This aspect of the program appeals to many experienced foster parents, whereas others who prefer their own ways of conducting foster care are not interested. Foster parents are recruited through word-of-mouth and newspaper advertisement. Current TFC parents are paid a $100 finder's fee for referring families that we eventually train.

Preservice training for treatment foster parents is adapted from the social learning parent training model developed at our center and elsewhere (Miller & Prinz, 1990; Wahler & Sansbury, 1990; Webster-Stratton & Hammond, 1990). The treatment model requires that TFC parents engage in specific activities centered around providing the adolescent with frequent reinforcement and clear and consistent limits. Training focuses on examples of how these processes can be tailored to fit the adolescent's individual needs, as well as the foster family's daily living schedule and priorities. All Monitor parents complete 20 hours of training before a child is placed with them.

Ongoing consultation with TFC parents is the cornerstone of the treatment model. Without ongoing consultation, our experience is that TFC parents are quickly shaped by adolescents to respond in nontherapeutic ways, often relying on punitive or anger-based methods of control. For example, given adolescent rule violations or other misbehaviors, the "natural" adult reaction is anger and irritability. For the children treated in Monitor, these types of reactions seem to increase the probability that their problem behavior will continue. The adult then avoids teaching or relating positively to the teenager. Eventually, problem behaviors escalate until finally, the adolescent is rejected from the home. Preservice training alone is not sufficient to maintain foster parent motivation or performance.

Case managers, who are trained both in the social learning treatment model and developmental psychopathology and who are experienced with adolescents, act as consultants to TFC parents. They provide support and supervision in formal weekly meetings attended by six to eight sets of foster parents. They also have daily telephone contact with TFC parents to collect data on the adolescents' problems and progress during the previous 24 hours using the Parent Daily Report (PDR) Checklist (Chamberlain & Reid, 1987). PDR data are also used in the weekly supervision meeting with TFC parents to review cases and make adjustments in the teenagers' daily treatment plans. During PDR telephone contacts, the case managers also provide support and supervision, as needed, and help TFC parents in troubleshooting anticipated problems.

Case managers consult with TFC parents to develop an individualized Daily Treatment Plan (DTP) for each youth in the program. The DTP includes a point and level system that TFC parents use to provide adolescents with frequent reinforcement for accomplishing normative daily tasks such as self-care and punctuality, and for specifically targeted behaviors indicated in their treatment plans. Points are exchanged for privileges that expand increasingly as the adolescent progresses through the program. Points are lost for minor rule breaking and problem behaviors.

Individual treatment is provided to the adolescents at least weekly. The aim is to help them cope with the stress and anxiety associated with being in out-of-home care, to provide support and advocacy for the youth within the program, and to provide treatment around case-specific issues. These often include issues such as coping with rejection, past abuse, parental abandonment, and problems with individuals in authority. The individual therapist is available to the adolescents by telephone at all times and, in coordination with the case manager, conducts crisis intervention, as needed. The adolescents are encouraged to discuss any difficulties that they may be experiencing in the program, including problems in the foster home, at school, or with the daily program. The individual therapist helps them to negotiate changes in their program and, in the process, works on teaching and modeling good problem-solving skills. Other interventions in individual treatment are coordinated with the treatment occurring in the TFC home and at school. For example, if developing alternatives to punching the wall and swearing is a target behavior in the TFC home, the therapist might use role playing and discuss various options with the teenager and support the practice of these between individual sessions.

Family therapy with the adolescent's biological, adoptive, or other after-program living resource takes place weekly. Treatment content and methods are based on the social learning family treatment model developed by Patterson (1985). Parents are taught to implement the same daily program (i.e., the DTP) that their child is experiencing in the TFC home. During regularly scheduled home visits, parents practice using this system with which they, ideally, become well-versed by the time their adolescent returns home to live upon completion of the program.

Family treatment is undoubtedly the most complicated and difficult aspect of the model. Families often have had negative contacts with social service agencies, are suspicious of organized efforts to address their children's problems, and are hesitant to participate. We see it as part of our mandate to find a way to productively engage families and have developed several strategies to do so. Family therapists are all experienced clinicians who have been trained and supervised in the social learning treatment approach for at least 2 years. Treatment usually consists of a balance between helping parents to implement effective encouragement, supervision, and discipline practices, and to deal with the personal and family system barriers that they face. The family therapist usually conducts a series of initial sessions with the parent(s) alone and then brings in other family members (e.g., siblings, the program adolescent) after they have established a collaborative relationship.

Consultation with schools and parole or probation is conducted regularly by the case manager. The adolescent carries a daily school card that is filled out by each teacher. Attendance, behavior in class, and assignments are tracked on the card, which is returned to the TFC parents each day. The adolescent receives points for carrying the card and for appropriate in-school behavior. When this monitoring system is not enough to meet the adolescent behavioral or academic needs, in-school consultation is conducted. Intensive involvement by the TFC program staff allows the majority of program youths to attend public schools, often in special education settings. Research is currently being conducted on the characteristics and effectiveness of the program's school services delivery component (Chamberlain, 1992).

Case managers have regular telephone contact with parole or probation officers assigned to the cases and send them copies of the adolescents' weekly PDR Checklist data. When serious rule infractions or law violations occur, parole or probation officers are consulted so they can have input into the adolescents' consequences. In these instances, point loss, work chores, overcorrection, and sometimes short-term stays in juvenile detention may be used as consequences.

The case manager is the key staff person who coordinates program components. Case managers handle a maximum caseload of 10 clients. In addition to having the necessary training and experience, they must be able to interact effectively with and keep in perspective the viewpoints of a diverse group of professionals that include the TFC parents, school personnel, individual and family therapists, juvenile judges, consulting psychiatrists, and parole or probation officers. Case managers are responsible for developing and implementing the overall treatment plan, making all decisions on modifications and revisions of the plan, and acting as advocates for the TFC parents, especially as they relate to individual and family therapists. Case managers meet with the program director and individual and family therapists weekly to review and revise each youth's treatment plan.

Aftercare services and support are provided to the adolescents' parents or other adults in their post-program living resource for one year following treatment. These services include weekly parent group meetings, family therapy sessions as needed, and ongoing school consultation. A book describing program components, clinical examples, and efficacy studies (Chamberlain, 1994; see outline in Appendix 1) as well as a foster parent preservice training manual (Chamberlain, Antoine, Moore, & Davis, 1994), and a 40-session curriculum for the aftercare parent group (Antoine & Chamberlain, 1994) are available.

OUTCOMES AND RESEARCH EVIDENCE

The program's effectiveness has been evaluated in three studies. A fourth, larger-scale study (NIHM, Mediators of Male Delinquency, MH47458) is currently underway and some preliminary findings are presented. The first two studies examined the feasibility of using a TFC model for severely delinquent (Chamberlain, 1990) and disturbed youngsters (Chamberlain & Reid, 1991), and the relative outcomes for adolescents placed in TFC compared to those placed in other models of residential care. The third study looked at the applicability of selected elements of TFC to a sample of children and foster parents in regular state foster homes (Chamberlain, Moreland, & Reid, 1992). The study in progress examines several variables thought to play a key role in mediating outcomes in a sample of adolescents with chronic delinquency who have been randomly assigned to TFC or group care.

In the first study, the participants were referred for chronic delinquency and were compared with participants in a matched group who were placed in other models of community-based residential care (e.g., group homes, residential treatment centers). In the second study, the participants were referred from the state mental hospital and assigned randomly either to the TFC or the "treatment as usual" conditions. Both of these clinical populations had a high prevalence of family and child risk factors, with the state hospital youths being probably more stressed, overall.

Does Placement in TFC Reduce Subsequent Institutionalization?

This question was addressed in both studies. In each, institutionalization rates were lower for those in the TFC condition. For the group referred for delinquency, prior to treatment, 75% of the cases had been incarcerated at least once in the state training school. The average number of days spent incarcerated during the year prior to treatment was 29.2 for the TFC cases and 14.9 for the comparison group. One year posttreatment,

38% of the TFC and 88% of the comparison youths had spent some time in the state training school. For those in the TFC group, this was an average of 86 days of incarceration; whereas for those in the comparison group, the average was 160 days. The findings were similar for the second-year follow-up: 43% of the TFC youths spent an average of 44 days incarcerated, whereas 62% of the control youths spent an average of 67 days incarcerated in Year 2. At the estimated (probably low) rate of $75 per day for incarceration costs, the difference between the two groups for such costs was $122,000 (i.e., costs were $150,000 for the TFC youths and $272,000 for the control youths).

In Study 2, hospitalization rates for a group of children and adolescents who had spent most of the year prior to referral in the state mental hospital were compared in TFC and "treatment as usual" placements. The average length of time between referral and placement out of the hospital for the two groups was examined. TFC participants were placed within an average of 81 days (SD = 42); whereas it took an average of 182 days (SD = 136) to place the control participants, and 3 of these were never placed in the community during the 2 years of the study. Excluding the latter 3 and comparing the 7 control individuals who were eventually placed with the 10 TFC individuals who were placed, a reliable difference was evident between the two groups in the time from referral to community placement, favoring those in the TFC condition.

Once the children were placed in the community, the next step was to look at the amount of time that they remained in the placement. During the year following placement, the TFC participants spent an average of 288 days (SD = 138) living in their communities. Three were rehospitalized during the first 6 months of their placements, another one was hospitalized for 10 days and then returned to her TFC home. For the 7 control youths, the average number of days spent living in the community during the year postplacement was 261 (SD = 157). Two were rehospitalized during the first 6 months and another was hospitalized briefly (3 days) and then returned to community living. The difference between the number of days living outside of the hospital for the two groups was not statistically reliable.

Assuming that severely disturbed youths can be maintained in TFC placements, how do they adjust to living in a family setting? Daily data were collected by telephone using the Parent Daily Report (PDR) Checklist at three measurement points: before community placement when they were hospitalized, and at 3 and 7 months post-community-placement. A score was calculated for each child that reflected the average number of problem behaviors reported per day. The average daily rates for both control and experimental groups were elevated at baseline, with over 20 problem behaviors reported per day. This can be compared to an average of 5 problem behaviors reported by parents of nonreferred, normal children (Chamberlain & Reid, 1987). At 3 and 7 months postbaseline, the TFC group showed a reduction of more than 50%, whereas the rate of reported problems for the control group showed no significant decrease. These data indicate that the day-to-day difficulties of these youths were not perceived by their caretakers to escalate or to be more unmanageable outside than inside the hospital setting. Being placed in a TFC setting resulted in faster and more dramatic drops in the rates of problem behaviors than for the control group.

Which Components of the TFC Model Can Be Shown to Be Effective?

There is a great deal of variation in TFC as it is practiced throughout the United States and Canada (Meadowcroft, Thomlison, & Chamberlain, 1994). A central clinical issue is: Which are the salient components of the model and how do these vary with different populations? Research in this area is needed.

In a study testing the effectiveness of the consultation (to foster parents) component of the TFC model, we examined whether enhanced training and support of foster parents would produce measurable changes in their abilities to manage and provide care for the children placed with them (Chamberlain, Moreland, & Reid, 1992). To do this, we randomly assigned 72 children and their foster parents from three Oregon counties to one of three conditions:

1. enhanced training and support (ETS) plus an increased payment of $70 per month to compensate them for costs associated with participation,
2. increased payment of $70 per month only (IPO), and
3. foster care as usual with neither enhanced training or support nor increased payment.

Those in the ETS group participated in weekly foster parent meetings and received daily telephone consultation, including collection of PDR data as described above.

Outcome measures were on the stability of care, which children left care and under what circumstances, and on foster parent reports of child problem behaviors using the PDR Checklist. Results showed that during the study period, 18 children were returned to their family homes. There was no difference in the return rates between the groups. Of the 54 who remained in foster care, those in the ETS group showed significantly more stability in their placements than those in the other two conditions. This meant that they were moved less often to different foster homes because of behavior problems, ran away fewer times, and were placed in residential care, juvenile detention, or other more restrictive settings less frequently. Foster parents in the ETS group also reported more dramatic drops in daily occurrences of problem behaviors than did those in the other two groups.

We were surprised to find that significantly fewer foster parents in the ETS group dropped out of providing foster care during the 2-year period following initiation of the study than did those in the other two groups (9.6% of ETS; 14.3% of IPO; and 25.9% of the control group). This study demonstrated that a component of the TFC model, consultation to the foster parents, can be helpful in increasing their ability to manage child problem behavior, and in increasing foster parent retention rates.

What Are Mediators of Treatment Outcomes?

Longitudinal studies have identified poor parental supervision and discipline as being precursors to conduct problems. Harsh, punitive discipline appears to be associated with aggression, delinquency, and self-destructive behavior (e.g., McCord, 1979; Patterson & Capaldi, 1991; Sears, Maccoby, & Levin, 1957; Yesavage & Widrow, 1985). On the other hand, adult involvement and positive attention are thought to enhance child adjustment in multiple realms.

Models of residential care attempt to expose children to a therapeutic milieu or to corrective experiences that are designed to enhance their ability to function outside of the placement setting. Group models of care use the peer culture to help achieve treatment goals. In TFC, a family-centered, adult-mediated approach is used.

The relationship among key variables (e.g., supervision, discipline, positive involvement) identified by previous research and case outcomes is currently being addressed in the context of a study comparing those in TFC with those in residential group care (RGC; Chamberlain & Reid, 1994). Boys aged 12–18 years, who are at risk for commitment to the state training school, are randomly assigned to the TFC or the RGC condition. Before placement, the TFC and RGC settings are assessed on the types of supervision, discipline, and encouragement strategies that are used typically. At 3 months postplacement, boys and caretakers are assessed to determine how supervision, discipline, and encouragement are actually implemented. In addition, the boys report on their associations with peers, daily activities, and involvement in rule or law-breaking activities.

Preliminary results indicate that there are substantial differences in the way that TFC and RGC placements operate (Chamberlain, Ray, & Moore, 1994). For example, the following differences have been found on the preplacement interview. RGC staff reported that peers have relatively more influence and that adults have relatively less influence on the boys' success in the program than on those in the TFC program. They also reported that in RGC, boys spend significantly more hours outside of adult supervision than do boys in TFC. In TFC, adults (vs. peers) determined the discipline to be used more frequently than they did in RGC settings. As would be expected, in RGC, boys were spending a greater proportion of their day with peers and less time with adults alone than those in TFC.

During-treatment measures also revealed important differences between the TFC and RGC settings. For example, in both the TFC and RGC settings, the care-taking adults reported that boys, on average, engaged in 4 problem behaviors per day. On the other hand, the boys in TFC said that they engaged in 3 problem behaviors per day; whereas the RGC boys said that they engaged in 7 problem behaviors. In terms of the consequences the boys received, those in TFC agreed more with what their caretakers said than those in RGC. TFC boys and caretakers agreed about consequences 41% of the time, whereas RGC boys and caretakers agreed only 19% of the time. Agreement between boys and caretakers was also higher in TFC than in RGC on the amount of supervision that boys actually received as well as on how much time they spent with peers. Initial outcomes for this sample show that, on confidential measures of self-reported delinquency, the boys in TFC report committing significantly fewer offenses at 6 months and 12 months postbaseline than those in RGC. These findings are preliminary, based on only half of the study sample size, but they do indicate that, in terms of supervision and discipline practices and of peer and adult relationships, there are probably meaningful differences between these two residential care models and that these differences appear to relate to delinquency outcomes.

CLINICAL VIGNETTE

Brad was small for his age but big on fighting. For him, this had gone beyond schoolyard bullying. He had four assault charges during the previous six months, including threatening rape and beating up a much younger boy who was mentally challenged. The family was being asked to leave their apartment complex becuse of Brad's aggressive behavior and several stealing incidents. Other official arrests included burglaries and trespassing. Brad had participated in a number of outpatient services, including anger management classes in which he had done well, but obviously he was not applying what he had learned to everyday life. He was referred to the OSLC TFC program by the juvenile court judge.

Prior to placement, Brad had lived with his mother and older brother. Their family life had been characterized by many disruptions, including contact with several abusive father figures and frequent moves. Mrs. B had epilepsy that was not controlled with medication. She experienced several seizures per week. Brad's older brother also had a record with the juvenile authorities, but his offenses were confined to property crimes and the use of alcohol. He had graduated from an inpatient substance abuse program. Brad and his brother had a history of physical fighting. Prior to the boys' births, Mrs. B had had two children removed from her custody by state protective services. Mrs. B was very protective of Brad. She felt that the police and schools had it "in for him" and regularly defended him as having been provoked or blamed falsely. Although she was devastated at having Brad removed from her home, Mrs. B reported that she could no longer deal with Brad's aggression.

Brad responded well to the daily structure of the TFC program. He was placed in a two-parent home with no other children and seemed to thrive on being the center of the foster parents' attention. Family therapy with Mrs. B began slowly with her missing several appointments and being very guarded and withdrawn. Brad's older brother was invited to the sessions as was Mrs. B's boyfriend, who subsequently left the family. The family therapist stressed to Mrs. B that the sessions were not about blaming her or uncovering her past wrongs but rather to plan for Brad's future. Regular home visits were scheduled during which Mrs. B used the DTP point program. She had a problem with covering for Brad when he misbehaved, and there was a great deal of fighting between the boys.

Mrs. B was kept informed of Brad's difficulties in the TFC home and of actions taken by the TFC parents and program staff to provide him with consequences. She was encouraged to express her opinions about the fairness of this aspect of Brad's treatment. Weekly treatment sessions and frequent phone calls with Mrs. B focused on how she could protect her son while at the same time providing him with guidance and teaching him how to become a nonabusive man. Slowly, a trusting relationship between Mrs. B and the family therapist emerged. She allowed him to help her obtain appropriate medication and to place Brad's brother in individual treatment. However, tension remained between Mrs. B and the case manager. Mrs. B disagreed with some of the decisions about giving Brad consequences for small rule infractions. As a result, Mrs. B was still playing the protector role and giving Brad the message that he was being treated unfairly, which we thought contributed to his sense of righteousness regarding aggressive acts. At a clinical staff meeting, it was decided to move toward putting Mrs. B in charge of the consequences that Brad received in the TFC home. The aim was twofold: to provide her with experience in establishing consequences without the difficulties involved in having to follow through (the TFC parents and program would do this for her), and to give Brad a clear message that his mother disapproved of his aggression, and that she and the program were working together to help him find other ways of behaving. A procedure was set up whereby the case manager called Mrs. B when Brad needed a consequence. The case manager would tell her about the incident and offer options for possible consequences. Mrs. B responded well. It became apparent that she had closely tied anger toward Brad with taking action to correct him. He had to do something rather severe to anger her, but when it happened she wanted to react strongly. Mrs. B was often overly harsh in the consequences she recommended. The idea that small consequences could be used to teach Brad about the results of his lower level aggressive acts was new to her. After a time, Mrs. B began to generate appropriate consequences, such as small work chores or privilege removal. Finally she began using these herself during home visits.

In this vignette, only one aspect of the treatment for Brad was discussed. Other interventions occurred with the family, in the TFC home, in school settings, and with Brad's brother. Brad was reunited with his family after 7 months in the program. His mother participates actively in the weekly aftercare group for parents.

DISCUSSION AND LIMITATIONS

It is not known which elements of the TFC model relate to effective treatments for various populations or individuals. It is possible that outcomes would be more powerful if elements were tested in combination rather than singly (e.g., Does the effectiveness of individual therapy increase because it is used as part of a coordinated treatment plan?).

TFC is a multifaceted model and therefore complicated to implement and supervise. It may be tempting to select one salient element of the model to the exclusion of other key services. For example, the State of Oregon Mental Health Division recently implemented a TFC program with a strong financial support component for foster parents ($1,600 per month) and a relatively unstructured, low-intensity, foster parent consultation component. We believe that this is unwise, as case management and consultation appear to be key components of this model because (a) case managers are the link to the foster parents, keeping them motivated and supported because foster parents provide the bulk of the direct treatment to the adolescents in the form of the daily treatment plan; and (b) case managers bring order and direction to the case through the integration of the treatment goals identified by the child and family therapists, courts, and schools. It is not sufficient to have the various treatment agents "network." In cases involving complex clinical issues, decisions need to be made about the timing and content of interventions that consider the entire system rather than only one aspect of it (e.g., goals of family therapy).

Another key aspect that seems to influence clinical outcomes is the relationship between the TFC parents' provision of a supportive living environment and the adolescent's progress in the program. This notion may have theoretical grounding in the matching law (e.g., Herrnstein,

1961, 1970, 1974; McDowell, 1988) that suggests that the probability of the child behaving positively is associated directly with the extent to which the child experiences a supportive, reinforcing environment. This hypothesis has yet to be examined empirically in the context of the TFC model.

A hallmark of the TFC model is the provision of services that are individualized to fit the needs of program participants and their families. Youths may be exposed to different service components or different dosages of various components based on their differing treatment needs. This individualized, flexible service approach, also sometimes referred to as a *wraparound service model of care*, allows TFC programs to be responsive to a wide range of clinical problems and shifting community needs. Unlike residential care in which it is important that the child fit into the therapeutic milieu being offered, in TFC, the child's needs drive the design of the program. In at least two studies (Chamberlain, Moreland, & Reid, 1992; Clark et al., 1993), aspects of the TFC model have been applied to children in regular foster care.

Controlled studies conducted on TFC so far have used small sample sizes. Also, research that has used appropriate control groups is extremely limited. TFC programs are extremely variable in terms of key areas, such as treatment, parent training, and supervision. The generalizability of the TFC model appears to be promising as indicated by it's spread across the United States and Canada over the last decade, but much work remains to be done in examining the applications and limitations of TFC.

REFERENCES

Allen, M. (1991). Crafting a federal legislative framework for child welfare reform. *American Journal of Orthopsychiatry, 61*(3), 610–623.

Antoine, K., & Chamberlain, P. (1994). *Aftercare curriculum.* Manuscript in preparation.

Chamberlain, P. (1990). *Teaching and supporting families: A model for reunification of children with their families.* Grant No. 90CW0994, Administration for Children, Youth, and Families, Child Welfare Services, Human Development Services, Department of Health and Human Services.

Chamberlain, P. (1992). *Family alliances change teens (FACT): A research study.* Grant No. H237E22018, Office of Special Education Programs, U.S. Department of Education.

Chamberlain, P. (1994). *Family connections* (Vol. 5). Eugene, OR: Castalia Publishing.

Chamberlain, P., Antoine, K., Moore, K. J., & Davis, J. P. (1994). *The OSLC Monitor program foster parent training manual.* Available from the Oregon Social Learning Center, 207 East 5th Avenue, Suite 202, Eugene, OR.

Chamberlain, P., Moreland, S., & Reid, K. (1992). Enhanced services and stipends for foster parents: Effects on retention rates and outcomes for children. *Child Welfare, 71*, 387–401.

Chamberlain, P., Ray, J., & Moore, K. J. (1994). *Characteristics of residential care: A comparison of assumptions and practices in two program models.* Manuscript submitted for publication.

Chamberlain, P., & Reid, J. B. (1987). Parent observation and report of child symptoms. *Behavioral Assessment, 9*, 97–109.

Chamberlain, P., & Reid, J. B. (1991). Using a Specialized Foster Care treatment model for children and adolescents leaving the state mental hospital. *Journal of Community Psychology, 19*, 266–276.

Chamberlain, P., & Reid, J. B. (1994). Differences in risk factors and adjustment for male and female delinquents in Treatment Foster Care. *Journal of Child and Family Studies, 3*, 23–39.

Clark, H., Boyd, L., Redditt, C., Foster-Johnson, L., Hardy, D., Kuhns, J., Lee, G., & Stewart, E. (1993). An individualized system of care for foster children with behavioral and emotional disturbances: Preliminary findings. In K. Kutash, C. Liberton, A. Algarin, & R. Friedman (Eds.), *Proceedings of the 5th Annual Research Conference for a System of Care for Children's Mental Health* (pp. 365–370). Tampa, FL: University of South Florida, Florida Mental Health Institute, Research and Training Center for Children's Mental Health.

Curry, J. F. (1991). Outcome research on residential treatment: Implications and suggested directions. *American Journal of Orthopsychiatry, 61*, 348–357.

Henggeler, S. W., Rodick, J. D., Borduin, C. M., Hanson, C. L., Watson, S. M., & Urey, J. R. (1986). Multisystemic treatment of juvenile offenders: Effects on adolescent behavior and family interactions. *Developmental Psychology, 22*, 123–141.

Herrnstein, R. J. (1961). Relative and absolute strength of response as a function of frequency of reinforcement. *Journal of Experimental Analysis of Behavior, 4*, 267–272.

Herrnstein, R. J. (1970). On the law of effect. *Journal of the Experimental Analysis of Behavior, 13*, 243–266.

Herrnstein, R. J. (1974). Formal properties of the matching law. *Journal of the Experimental Analysis of Behavior, 21*, 159–164.

Hudson, J., Nutter, R., & Galaway, B. (1992, June). *A Survey of North American specialist foster family care: Programs and research.* Paper prepared for the Alberta Mental Health Advisory Council, Edmonton, Canada.

McCord, J. (1979). Some child-rearing antecedents of criminal behavior in adult men. *Journal of Personality and Social Psychology, 37*, 1477–1486.

McDowell, J. J. (1988). Matching theory in natural human environments. *The Behavior Analyst, 11*, 95–109.

Meadowcroft, P., Thomlison, B., & Chamberlain, P. (1994). Treatment Foster Care services: A research agenda for child welfare. *Child Welfare, 73*, 565–581.

Miller, G. E., & Prinz, R. J. (1990). Enhancement of social learning family interventions for childhood conduct disorder. *Psychological Bulletin, 108,* 291–307.

Moore, K. J., Osgood, D. W., Larzelere, R. E., & Chamberlain, P. (1994). Use of pooled time-series in the study of naturally occurring clinical events and problem behavior in a foster care setting. *Journal of Consulting and Clinical Psychology, 62,* 718–728.

National Institute of Mental Health. (1991). *Mediators of male delinquency: A clinical trial.* Grant No. RO1 MH 47458, Center for Studies of Violent Behavior and Traumatic Stress, NIMH, U.S. PHS.

Patterson, G. R. (1985). Beyond technology: The next stage in the development of a parent training technology. In L. L'Abate (Ed.), *Handbook of family psychology and therapy* (Vol. 2, pp. 1344–1379). Homewood, IL: The Dorsey Press.

Patterson, G. R., & Capaldi, D. M. (1991). Antisocial parents: Unskilled and vulnerable. In P. A. Cowan & E. M. Hetherington (Eds.), *Advances in family research: Vol II. Family transitions* (pp. 195–218). Hillsdale, NJ: Lawrence Earlbaum.

Redl, F., & Wineman, D. (1957). *The aggressive child.* New York: Free Press.

Sears, R. R., Maccoby, E. E., & Levin, H. (1957). *Patterns of childrearing.* Evanston, IL: Row & Peterson.

Small, R., Kennedy, K., & Bender, B. (1991). Critical issues for practice in residential treatment: The view from within. *American Journal of Orthopsychiatry, 61,* 327–338.

Stroul, B. A., & Friedman, R. M. (1986). *A system of care for severely emotionally disturbed children and youth.* Washington, DC: Georgetown University Press.

Wahler, R. G., & Sansbury, L. E. (1990). The monitoring skills of troubled mothers: Their problems in defining child deviance. *Journal of Abnormal Child Psychology, 18,* 577–589.

Webster-Stratton, C., & Hammond, M. (1990). Predictors of treatment outcome in parent training for families with conduct problem children. *Behavior Therapy, 21,* 319–337.

Wells, K. (1991). Placement of emotionally disturbed children in residential treatment: A review of placement criteria. *American Journal of Orthopsychiatry, 61,* 339–347.

Yesavage, J. A., & Widrow, L. (1985). Early parental discipline and adult self-destructive acts. *The Journal of Nervous and Mental Disease, 173,* 74–77.

APPENDIX

Outline of Family Connections: A Treatment Foster Care Model for Adolescents with Delinquency

I.   Characteristics of Monitor Program participants
    A. Case study: Referral information
        1. Psychological evaluation
        2. School history
        3. Current living situation
        4. Family
    B. From conduct problems to later delinquency: Discussion of variables related to the presence of delinquency
    C. A four-stage developmental model
        1. Training at home
        2. The child goes to school
        3. Making friends with deviant peers
        4. Adult antisocial lifestyles
    D. Characteristics of Monitor Program youths
    E. Monitor Program goals
    F. Summary

II.   Recruitment, screening, and preservice training of treatment foster parents
    A. Characteristics of successful foster parents
    B. Monitor program foster parents
    C. Length of service
    D. Recruitment and screening
    E. Recruiting potential foster parents
    F. A four-step screening process

1. Telephone contact and brief interview
2. Sending application
3. Home visit by recruiter and case manager
4. Referral to children's services division for certification

G. The preservice training course: Overview of sessions
1. Program overview
2. Policies and procedures
3. Nuts and bolts
   a. Level 1
   b. Reward positives
   c. Immediate consequences
   d. Identify specific problem areas

H. The written agreement

I. Guidelines for working with foster parents
1. Open and egalitarian relationship
2. Daily contact through PDR
3. Case manager model
4. Court mandated program
5. Weekly support meetings

III. Preparing the adolescent and foster parents for the placement
A. Preparing the adolescent for placement: Case manager interview
1. Ground rules
   a. Stipulations of parole agreement
   b. Be in custody of foster family
   c. Participate in program
   d. Accountability
   e. Attend school daily
   f. Agreement not to violate law
2. Introduction of level system
3. Brief description of family

B. Getting the foster parents ready for the placement
1. Reading case file
2. Discussion with case manager
3. Placement of child

C. Level system: Underlying rationale
1. Program's therapeutic milieu
2. Restructuring the foster home environment
3. Suppress child's misbehavior and encourage positive behavior
4. Skill building

D. Overview of the three-level system
1. Level 1
   a. Close supervision and immediate reinforcement
   b. Short in duration
   c. Limited privileges

2. Level 2: Expanded privileges
3. Level 3
    a. Daily rating rather than points
    b. Expanded privileges
E. Privileges and rewards
   1. They are well defined
   2. They fit the adolescent's level of maturity and interests
   3. The privileges or rewards are affordable and readily available
   4. The criteria for the reward is realistic; that is, the adolescent can achieve it with a reasonable amount of effort
F. Point fines
G. Level system charts
   1. Level 1
   2. Level 2
   3. Level 3
H. Point system economy: Realistic and balanced
I. Assigning point values
J. Giving and taking points
K. Reviewing the point chart
L. Rewards
M. Case example
   1. A small backfire
   2. Family treatment

IV. Family treatment for the child's biological or adoptive parents
A. Establishing a working relationship
   1. Build a supportive, trusting relationship with the parents
   2. Ask parents to describe past events and current factors that may be related to their child's problems
   3. Assess parents' strengths, their relationship with their children, and the extent of their social support network
   4. Help parents understand the treatment model that will be used to work with their child
B. Research on resistance to family therapy
C. Setting up the placement
D. The preplacement interview
E. Weekly family therapy sessions
F. Using role-playing exercises in treatment
G. Troubleshooting and solving problems
H. Case example
I. Actions and reactions
J. Summary

V. Individual therapy for the child
A. The acceptance meeting
B. The initial phase of treatment

1. Building a support base
2. From advocacy to empowerment
3. Case coordination and targeting behaviors for change
C. The reenactment technique: Case example
D. Teaching social and relational skills
   1. Modeling problem solving skills
   2. Teaching alternatives to problem behavior
   3. Decreasing "zapping" among family members
   4. Using immediate rewards and sanctions
E. Case example
F. Summary
VI. Case management 1: Working with foster parents, biological parents, and their therapists
A. Communication with foster parents
B. Communication with therapists
C. Balancing the agendas of foster parents and therapists
D. Communication with the child's biological or adoptive parents
E. Case example
F. Summary
VII. Case management 2: Coordinating services with other community agencies
A. School liaison: The school card
B. Parole or probation staff liaison
C. Case example
D. Liaison with judges
F. Summary
VIII. Aftercare services for children and families
A. Reducing the risks associated with transitions
B. Teaching and supporting families in aftercare
   1. Parent group meetings
   2. Coaching sessions
C. Case example
D. Respite care
E. Customizing aftercare services
F. Summary
IX. Outcome evaluation of treatment foster care program participants
A. Study 1: Effectiveness of TFC for delinquent youths
B. Study 2: Effectiveness of TFC for emotionally disturbed youths
   1. Hospitalization rates
   2. Occurrence of problem behaviors and symptoms
   3. Social competency and problem solving
C. Summary
X. Methods of case and program evaluation

A. The parent Daily Report Checklist
   1. Studies on reliability and stability
   2. Validity of PDR
B. Clinical Applications of PDR in TFC Programs
C. Do boys and girls respond differently to TFC?
D. Summary

21

COALITIONS AND FAMILY PROBLEM SOLVING IN THE PSYCHOSOCIAL TREATMENT OF PREADOLESCENTS

SAMUEL VUCHINICH, BARBARA WOOD, and JOSEPH ANGELELLI

In recent years, there has been an increasing awareness of the benefits of involving parents in the treatment of the mental health difficulties of children and adolescents. Such involvement ranges from an exclusive focus on the parents during parent training treatments (e.g., Patterson, 1986) to an indirect support role in cognitive interventions (Kendall, 1991) or drug therapy. Despite the increasing participation of parents in these treatments, there is little systematic research in the clinical psychology literature on the implications of active involvement of both parents and children. The family therapy tradition requires such involvement but is based on a separate paradigm of etiological assumptions, treatment techniques, and research methods that complicates application in many areas of clinical psychology. In this chapter, we address key issues associated with the involvement of both parents and children in the treatment of child and adolescent conduct disorders.

To respond to these issues, we describe a new treatment program that integrates individual cognitive training for the child, training for the parents (or parent surrogates), and family problem-solving training that ac-

---

Correspondence concerning this chapter should be directed to Dr. Samuel Vuchinich, Department of Human Development and Family Sciences, Oregon State University, Milan Hall, Corvallis, OR 97331.

tively involves parents and children. Clinical trials have already shown that a combination of the first two of these components is superior to either one individually (Kazdin, Siegel, & Bass, 1992). Thus, our focus is on the feasibility of and prospects for adding a family problem-solving component to that program. We maintain that the addition of this component can increase treatment success and reduce relapse rates.

Family problem-solving treatment components with the active participation of parents and children have been developed for treating parent–adolescent conflict (Forgatch & Patterson, 1989; Robin & Foster, 1989) and ADHD (Braswell & Bloomquist, 1991). These provide a strong basis of conceptualization, technique, and treatment materials for our application to child and adolescent conduct disorder, even though there have been no clinical trials. Before such trials are conducted, it is necessary to consider further the feasibility of and potential problems with the active involvement of children with conduct disorder and their parents in family problem-solving training. This is especially pertinent because of the prevalence of parent–child conflict and of other problematic dynamics in such families. Our current research contributes to the preliminary work by studying how family dynamics influence family problem solving, and how family problem solving is associated with negative adolescent outcomes, such as police arrest. These studies involve samples of families with preadolescents referred for the treatment of antisocial behavior, a sample of families with children at risk for antisocial behavior, and a comparison sample. This chapter describes the proposed treatment program, raises key questions associated with involving both parents and children in the treatment, and describes our research on the questions.

Our research program is concerned with treatments for children who are 7 to 16 years of age and emphasizes work with preadolescents who are 9 to 12 years of age. In this chapter, for convenience, we use the terms *child* and *children* to refer to the 7- to 16-year range, acknowledging that this includes individuals in late childhood, preadolescence, and adolescence. The treatment implications of these developmental phases are addressed where needed. One key feature of parental participation in treatment is that families have many different forms. A child's biological parents may not be part of the current and relevant family context. Other individuals often function as surrogate parents. These include stepparents, foster parents, grandparents, older siblings, aunts, uncles, adoptive parents, and so on. When we refer to "parental" involvement in the child's treatment, we are referring to functional parents. These are typically those who live with the child and have strong emotional ties. The participation of two such parents is usually beneficial, but the proposed treatment can involve the child and one functional parent.

ISSUES AND GOALS

Involving Parents in the Treatment of Children and Adolescents

Involving more than one person in a treatment program immediately makes it more complex for a therapist or a team to manage. Indeed, the involvement of parents in the treatment creates new sources of resistance to and attrition from the treatment. Parents of children with conduct disorders can be as difficult to work with in treatment as the children themselves. Studies of parent-based child treatments for conduct disorder show that it is often difficult to persuade parents to participate (Hawkins et al., 1992); parents of the most seriously affected children are the least likely to participate, and attrition rates are high (Reid, 1993). Such difficulties in treating conduct disorder are not unique to the parent training model, which is generally recognized to have the best verified success rates of about 70% under good treatment conditions (Kazdin, 1987; Reid, 1993).

These difficulties with parental participation in the child's treatment are, however, overshadowed by two major benefits that are derived: generalization of treatment gains to the home, and maintenance of the gains over time. When parents are part of the treatment, the therapist is exposed to a major part of the home environment and can adjust the treatment to fit that environment better. Because most parents will live with the child in the future, they can contribute to the maintenance of treatment gains over time and reduce relapse. These benefits may be critical to the success of parent training treatments when parents complete the program.

Family Dynamics in Child and Adolescent Treatment

Cognitive training for children and training for parents usually occurs within an educational frame of reference that structures how parents and children interact. However, once parents and children are brought together in an active problem-solving context, problematic family dynamics may emerge, and they usually do emerge in families with children with conduct disorders. This is, at the same time, a blessing and a curse for the therapist. It is a curse because it requires more skillful management of more intense family interactions, which may become explosive; but it is a blessing as well because it reveals behavior patterns, beliefs, relationships, and coalitions that need to be addressed if the treatment is to be successful.

Taking Sides During Family Problem Solving

Theory and case studies in family therapy suggest that the structure of coalitions within the family is a primary source of negative emotions and of excessive dysfunctional family conflict (e.g., Madanes, 1981). Such coalitions structure and regulate primary domains of affect and control within the family group. Problems develop when the coalition between parents is too weak, and the parent–child relationship is too close; or when the parental coalition is too strong, and the child is treated as a scapegoat (Gurman & Kniskern, 1981; Haley, 1976; Vuchinich, Emery & Cassidy, 1988). Our research has addressed this variable carefully because dysfunctional coalitions could subvert problem-solving components if not directly addressed by the treatment.

Family dynamics of this nature require special attention in family problem-solving treatment components. This may involve a focus on the parents' negative beliefs about the child or the strengthening the marital relationship. Prior to clinical trials, it is important to demonstrate empirically that such coalitions influence family problem solving. One goal of our research was to determine whether such an influence exists. Details of the family problem-solving treatment are described below.

Goals

The practical goal of the treatment is to enable a family member to raise a serious current family problem and, then, in a family group meeting, make significant progress toward resolving that problem. Active and constructive participation in such family sessions over time fosters appropriate affect regulation, beneficial attributions about the intentions of others, reinforcement for constructive interactions, better interpersonal negotiation skills, respect for the feelings and views of others, and better self-esteem. These elements can help compensate for biological predispositions toward aggressive behavior. Because such benefits should promote better adolescent adjustment, we would predict that children who experience better family problem solving in preadolescence should have a lower risk of antisocial behavior through adolescence.

The age of the child is a consideration in this approach to treatment. Patterson, Dishion, and Chamberlain (1993) found that parent training was effective in 63% of cases when the child was between 3 and 6 1/2 years of age, but effective in only 27% of cases when the child was between 6 1/2 and 12 years of age. This suggests the need for additional treatment components when older children are the focus of treatment. Addition of cognitive training for the children was provided by Kazdin, Siegel, and Bass (1992) who had a 64% success rate with an 8-month treatment program. We suggest that adding a joint, family problem-solving component can improve that success rate even more.

THE TREATMENT PLAN

The proposed treatment integrates three programs that have been applied separately already:

1. individual problem-solving skills training for the child,
2. training for parents, and
3. joint, family problem-solving training involving the child and the parents.

Upon referral of the child, the parents are interviewed to determine their potential for success in the training. This includes determining their motivation level, willingness and ability to attend weekly training sessions, the presence of learning or other disabilities that could require special training methods, perceptions of the child's behavior problems, and assessment of the extent of the disorder. The child is interviewed and tested for the presence of cognitive deficits, anxiety disorders, or physical difficulties. If comorbidity is found to be present, supplements to the treatment may be recommended (e.g., drug therapy) or an alternative treatment may be deemed more appropriate.

Once a family is determined to be suitable for the treatment, it attends an introductory section that explains the problem-solving perspective on treating conduct disorders; avoids blaming the parents or labelling the child; provides motivation for the program (perhaps with videotape examples), including positive expectations for outcomes; and describes the phases of the treatment.

The basic treatment plan consists of a 22-week program divided into two 10-week training phases that use weekly sessions. These two training phases are separated by a 2-week home practice period. During the first 10-week training phase, parents receive management training in small groups (eight parents, maximum) of other parents in the same treatment program. These parent groups provide a support function and avoid stigmatizing individual parents. Sessions with individual parents may be needed in some cases to deal with especially sensitive issues.

The parent-training component is based on social learning principles. Parents are taught to observe the child carefully and to identify good and bad behaviors clearly. The training then focuses on how to reinforce good behavior effectively and to punish mildly (e.g., using procedures such as "time out") the bad behavior. Consistency and reasoning are emphasized and power-assertive coercive parenting is discouraged. Negotiation and behavior contracting round out the parent training. This training has been used for many years, and manuals for parents and therapists are widely available (e.g., Forehand & McMahon, 1981; Patterson & Forgatch, 1987; Patterson & Gullion, 1971; Patterson, Reid, Jones, & Conger, 1975). This program includes behavior charts and home practice exercises. Adaptations are made for the age of the child.

During the first 10-week training phase, while parents receive their training, the children participate in a cognitive, problem-solving skills, training program in a small group setting with other children (4 to 8, maximum) who may or may not have a conduct disorder. This treatment follows well-established programs for changing the way in which children think about themselves, their feelings, and others in social situations (Spivak, Platt, & Shure, 1976). The training is oriented toward such cognitive adjustments as correcting distorted perceptions about the intentions of others, encouraging consideration of alternative actions in social situations, and considering the consequences of actions in a step-by-step process. This training is made engaging by the use of games, stories, and role playing as well as of structured tasks. Therapists are active in modeling the appropriate thought processes, prompting children for responses, and providing feedback and praise for applications of the skills. Homework is given but begins with easy assignments that are likely to meet with success. Over the 10 weeks of training, successively more difficult real-life situations are introduced. Parents are involved in this homework and receive written guidelines for prompting and reinforcing the application of the child's cognitive skills at home (Kazdin, Siegel, & Bass, 1992).

At the end of the first, 10-week training phase, parents and children are instructed to apply their new skills at home for two weeks with no treatment sessions. They are told that, during that time, they will receive a weekly telephone call that will interview each parent and child for an assessment of their progress with applications. At the end of two weeks, parents and children begin the second, 10-week training session, which focuses on family problem solving.

The goals of the family problem-solving component are to (a) consolidate, apply, and adjust (if necessary) the cognitive and parenting skills, learned in the previous treatment components, to the context of focused family interaction; (b) provide new skills needed for more extended, complex negotiations and compromises; (c) address features of family dynamics that impede problem solving; and (d) apply the problem-solving skills to the most difficult parent–child situations that emerge in the course of training or that emerge typically in adolescence.

These goals are pursued by training the families to apply well-established, step-by-step procedures for group family problem solving (Braswell & Bloomquist, 1991; Forgatch & Patterson, 1989; Robin & Foster, 1989). These procedures are

1. define the problem clearly;
2. generate alternative solutions for it;

3. consider advantages and disadvantages of the alternatives and select the best one;
4. act on this solution; and
5. evaluate the success of this solution and make adjustments, if necessary.

The children, and to a lesser extent, the parents have already been exposed to some of these concepts during the first training phase, which supplies a good foundation for applying them within the family group. Defining a problem or generating alternatives as a family is much more complex than doing it as an individual.

This treatment phase is intended to train and motivate families to participate in weekly family meetings or *family forums* (Forgatch & Patterson, 1989) on their own after the termination of treatment. One primary function of such meetings is to create a recurring structured occasion at home when family members can discuss and seek to resolve problems that come up on a week-to-week basis. Although much of this training phase is oriented toward addressing problems effectively, it is important that such meetings do not become associated exclusively with the often difficult work of problem solving. Thus, a second function of the meetings is to provide an occasion for building solidarity within the family through sharing positive events and feelings, showing support and encouragement for each other, planning enjoyable family activities, as well as comforting and consoling each other when needed. Such meetings should be organized to provide time devoted to both solidarity building and problem solving.

Some families may not be expected to have weekly meetings long after treatment terminates; but the skills taught, group experiences provided, and confidence instilled that the family is able to handle tough problems provide the basis for effective and less frequent family meetings as needed. Furthermore, effective training of this nature typically results in the application of the principles in dyadic family interactions outside the context of a formal meeting. Thus, training for problem solving in family meetings is a heuristic for establishing more effective ways for parents and children to deal with problems that come up. The generalization of the benefits of family meetings to other family contexts has been recognized for some time (Dreikurs, 1964) and has been a basis for parent education efforts in diverse populations (Dinkmeyer & McKay, 1989).

The first weekly session of family problem-solving training may occur in a group setting with as many as 20 people, including parents and children. In Session 1, the benefits of improved family problem solving are emphasized, and an outline of the 10-week training is given. The importance of defining clearly what a "problem" is and determining whether others agree that it is a problem is addressed with examples and group exercises.

Sample Exercise on "What Is a Family Problem?"

Exercise goals:

1. to show clients that family members have differing views of what family problems are; and
2. to introduce the idea that these differences are healthy because they provide a starting point for making everyone in the family happier.

Example

Therapist: I'm going to give each of you a piece of paper and a pencil, and I want you to write down what you see as a problem in your family. Now, don't talk to each other while you are doing this. Just write down your own ideas.
(After everyone has finished writing.)
Therapist: Now pass your sheet to the other members of your family. (After a few moments to allow the sheets to be passed.) "Okay, how many families had the same problem written down on each of their sheets? None? (or "Not many?") What does that mean? It means that each person sees the family in a different way. That is important because seeing how everyone views the family is the first step in solving any of the problems."

This session also details how to present a problem and how to receive a problem within a family meeting (Forgatch & Patterson, 1989). The key concepts here are clearly specifying what behaviors are the source of the trouble, avoiding inaccurate negative attributions about others, and expressing negative feelings that might accompany the problem without becoming angry and hostile.

Receiving the problem entails verifying that the perceived problem was accurately communicated while controlling any anger reactions to accusations. One goal of the initial step is to allow negative emotions to be expressed but to do so while retaining a commitment to a rational problem solving procedure.

Example of how not to present a problem

Dad: Billie, you never do anything I tell you to. I try to be nice about it, but you always push me to the edge. If you don't straighten out pretty soon you're going to end up out on the streets!

Example of how not to receive a problem

Billie: But Dad, you always treat me like a slave or a little baby. You're always bossing me around and I get sick of it. Mom doesn't treat me that way. It's not fair.

Example of how to present a problem

Dad: Billie, it really bothers me when you don't take out the trash when I ask you to.

Example of how to receive a problem

Billie: Okay, Dad. I guess I can tell that it bugs you when I don't take out the trash.

Sessions 2 to 10 should involve only one family and one therapist. In Session 2, the therapist solicits the family's perception and evaluation of the treatment up to this point. Special difficulties are considered and may be used to adapt the remaining sessions to reflect the strengths or deficits of the family. After this, the training resumes by reviewing the presenting and receiving of problems. Each family member is asked to present a problem in the family that they are concerned about. The therapist provides guidance as needed. Additional problems may be presented. The therapist also introduces procedures for building family solidarity and for implementing them at the family meetings.

Sessions 3 and 4 are devoted to brainstorming for alternative solutions. General characteristics of good solutions are discussed along with the importance of being specific. The importance of the creative potential of group problem solving is emphasized. Examples are given of how new solutions can be found when an idea from one person triggers a different idea in another, and of how "two or three heads are better than one." Families are given exercises in opening their thoughts to creative alternatives, avoiding criticism of solutions proposed, and keeping a written record of all alternatives. An example of an exercise for stimulating different approaches to solutions is to have parents and children switch roles (i.e., children take a parent role and parents take a child role), or imagine how they would solve the problem if they had $10 million to do it.

Example of brainstorming in a family meeting

(The problem here is how to handle the dinner dishes on a weekly basis.)
Mom: Let's hire a maid.
Dad: Okay, I'll write that down. Yeah, and we'll get a dish-washing robot too.
Billie: Come on, let's just have mom do them all the time.
Mom: Okay, let's have Billie do them all the time.
Susie: How about if we have mom and dad take turns?
Dad: Well, why not have Susie and Billie take turns?

Mom: We could have kids do them one night and the parents do them the next night and alternate like that.

Billie: Or what if we just use paper plates so there are no dishes to do?

Mom: Maybe we should just have TV dinners every night.

In Session 4, the family practices brainstorming on some hypothetical problems first and then on some of the problems that were presented in Session 3.

Sessions 5 and 6 focus on evaluating the alternatives proposed and selecting the best alternative. If brainstorming is sufficiently open, about six concrete alternatives will be proposed and a few of these will be recognized by all as being unrealistic. After eliminating the unrealistic ones, the advantages and disadvantages of each alternative are weighed. New combinations may be suggested. This weighing should ultimately exclude all but one alternative, the one considered most likely to succeed. Ideally, a consensus for this option is achieved. Realistically, it may be necessary to use a voting mechanism. Part of the training encourages compromises at this step and acceptance of the majority decision even if reluctantly.

Example of evaluating solutions and of compromising

Mom: Okay, we're down to two options on how to get the dinner dishes done. Billie and Susie think Mom and Dad should take turns. Dad and I think Billie and Susie should take turns.

Billie: Well, kids really shouldn't have to do parents' work. We're only kids.

Dad: No way, Bill. Mom and I both work hard to support you kids so we shouldn't have to do all the work around the house. You're plenty old enough to do some chores.

Susie: Okay, what if we all take turns and a different person does them each night. That way we would only have to do them about twice a week.

Mom: I guess that makes pretty good sense.

Dad: Sounds fair enough.

Billie: Well, I don't know. I guess we can try it. It might work.

Solutions selected are typically tried on a one- or two-week basis and are reevaluated for their effectiveness at family meetings. This time-limited test of how well a solution works means that decisions at family meetings are binding but are subject to reevaluation, adjustment, or replacement at future family meetings. These sessions involve families collectively in the evaluation of the hypothetical alternatives and, then, of the workable alternatives that are proposed. Families are instructed to try a family meeting at home.

Sessions 7 and 8 provide more detail and practice on implementing and reevaluating solutions over time. Written contracting is described and, depending on the family, may be recommended for all decisions or only for certain circumstances. Contracts specify exactly what each person involved will do, when it will be done, and what consequences or rewards will follow. Contracts are signed by family members and kept for future reference.

During these meetings, criteria are established for determining how well a given solution has succeeded, how this is brought up in family meetings, and what options are available for adjusting or replacing that solution. When solutions work, some rewards or celebration ritual may be beneficial. Families again are instructed to have a family meeting at home.

In Session 9, the therapist prepares the family for treatment termination by reviewing the strengths that it has shown in the treatment exercises and reminding it of any specific areas that it should try to improve in. Detailed strategems from convening family meetings regularly are presented. These include setting a regular meeting time, techniques for assuring attendance, rotation of leadership of specific meetings so that all family members may play the leader role in turn, record keeping, rules on telephone calls and visitors during meetings, and conditions for postponing or ending meetings. The results of the home family meeting are discussed and evaluated. Families again have a home meeting, establish their guidelines for future meetings, and work on solving one specific problem selected by the child.

In Session 10, the therapist reviews the meeting rules that the family has developed and gages the likelihood of their being followed. Suggestions are offered where appropriate. The process and outcome of the last home meeting are reviewed. Based on the family's progress during the training, the therapist devotes much of this session to discussion and interaction regarding specific skills, relationships or difficulties that are most likely to promote better family problem solving. Families are told there will be two follow-up telephone calls 2 and 4 weeks after termination of the training during which progress will be monitored and questions answered. Ideally, families are given a certificate of completion or some other token representing their "graduation" from the training.

A typical pattern in families having a child with conduct disorder is that the parents begin blaming the child for most of the problems in the family. In family meetings, this scapegoating usually takes the form of the parents "ganging up" on the child. Parents will often take turns verbally chiding the child or opposing anything that the child says during segments of a meeting. This relatively common pattern has disastrous consequences for this treatment program, and the therapist must be alert to recognize it and correct it.

Without the child being present, the therapist can point out this pattern to the parents and emphasize how damaging it is to the child and to the treatment. Typically, such parents need to be instructed in how to listen appropriately to the child express feelings and suggestions, while controlling their own negative emotional reactions to what the child says. In addition, such parents often need help in making constructive rather than destructive contributions to the problem-solving process and in implementing the child's views by creating compromise positions. If successful, these instructions can reduce the "ganging up" pattern so that even if one parent verbally attacks a child's comment, the other one can follow up in a more constructive manner, rather than just continue the attack.

Tables 1 and 2 summarize the treatment program. This cognitive and social learning treatment provides a systematic method for correcting negative individual thought distortions and dysfunctional family interaction patterns. It also provides a context within which other specific individual or family problems can become apparent to the therapist. This could include child abuse, substance abuse, and previously undiagnosed psychological disorders. Additional treatment plans would be needed to address such problems.

TREATMENT OUTCOME AND FEASIBILITY STUDIES

Clinical trials have shown that cognitive training and parent training have had moderate success in the treatment of conduct disorder in various settings (Kazdin, 1987; Kendall, 1991), and that a combination of both is more successful than either one separately (Kazdin, Siegel, & Bass, 1992). Family problem-solving training has been shown to be effective in resolving parent–adolescent conflict (Robin & Foster, 1989) but no clinical trials exist for conduct disorder. The combination of cognitive training, parent training, and family problem-solving training has been proposed for ADHD treatment but has not been evaluated yet. The treatment plan described here has no clinical trials.

The clinical trials that have shown success indicate, nevertheless, that about 30% of patients are not helped significantly, that relapse is frequent, and that treatment is less effective with older children (Kazdin, Siegel, & Bass, 1992; Reid, 1993). Thus, the extant outcome studies indicate the need for improvement in success relapse and rates. The treatment proposed here was designed to improve these rates. It is possible that the inclusion of drug therapy in the treatment could further boost success rates when this therapy is understood more fully.

TABLE 1
Outline of the First 10 Weeks of Treatment: Separate Group Training for Parents and Children

Week	Parent training	Child problem-solving skills training
1	Rapport building exercise Statement of objectives	Rapport building exercises
2	Observing and defining children's behavior	What are problems? Why should they be solved?
3	Positive reinforcement for good behavior	Recognizing problems and talking about them
4	Shaping child behavior	Problems, thoughts, and feelings
5	Negotiating and contracting	What are solutions and plans?
6	Following through	What are good solutions and plans?
7	Using time-out methods	Consequential thinking
8	Using reprimands	Anticipating obstacles
9	Stages of problem-solving introduction	Following through on a plan
10	Parenting and family meetings	Finding out whether a plan worked and adjusting

Our research program has completed several studies that assess the feasibility of the proposed treatment. These studies were based on a series of investigations on the nature of family conflict, problem solving, and their consequences for children (Patterson, Crosby, & Vuchinich, 1992; Vuchinich, 1984, 1986, 1987, 1990; Vuchinich, Bank, & Patterson, 1992; Vuchinich, Emery, & Cassidy, 1988; Vuchinich, Hetherington, Vuchinich, & Clingempeel, 1991; Vuchinich & Teachman, 1993; Vuchinich, Teachman, & Crosby, 1991; Vuchinich, Vuchinich, & Coughlin, 1992; Vuchinich, Vuchinich, & Wood, 1993).

Three questions were addressed to determine whether family problem solving was systematically linked to intrafamily coalitions and negative child outcomes:

1. Do families with an antisocial child referred for treatment exhibit less effective problem solving than families with a child at risk for antisocial behavior and than comparison-group families?
2. Do coalitions in the family influence the effectiveness of family problem solving?
3. Does the effectiveness of family problem solving when the child is 10 years old influence the risk of arrest by age 17?

These studies developed valid and reliable observational measures for family problem-solving effectiveness, parental coalitions, parent–child co-

TABLE 2

Outline of the Second 10 Weeks of Treatment: Family Treatment With
Parents and Children Together

Week	Family treatment
11	Defining a problem, presenting a problem, receiving a problem
12	Begin one family per therapist for remainder of treatment
	Evaluate special issues in the family
	Review problem-solving goals
	Practice presenting and receiving problems
13	How to brainstorm
	Opening creative channels for good solutions
	How to hold back immediate criticism of suggestions
14	Using brainstorming as a tool in problem solving
	Writing down six brainstormed solutions
	Practice brainstorming and writing down solutions
15	Evaluating brainstormed solutions
	What makes a good solution
	Encouraging everyone to have a say
	Practice finding pros and cons of solutions
16	Selecting one solution to try out
	Following through on a solution; contracts to try solutions
17	Finding out if a solution is working
	Celebrations for good solutions
	Making adjustments to partial solutions and trying again
	Trying different solutions
18	Review the family's problem solving strengths, areas needing work
	Encourage plans for regular family meetings
	Review family meeting logistics
19	Party and closing ceremony with entire cohort treatment group
	Issue certificates of completion, encouragement materials (bumper stickers, refrigerator magnets, logo note pads)
20	Follow-up telephone calls are made 2 and 4 weeks after treatment termination to answer questions, monitor progress, and encourage family meetings

alitions, and parental warmth based on videotapes of family problem-solving sessions in the home and in clinical setting. These measures apply a *global coding* method in which trained coders observe a 10-minute segment of family videotape and then rate these specific characteristics of the family on 7-point scales. For example, the parental coalition measure requires a coder to rate "the extent to which the mother and father [take] sides with each other against the child" on a 7-point scale ranging from "not at all" = 1, to "all the time" = 7 (Vuchinich, Vuchinich, & Wood, 1993; Vuchinich, Wood, & Vuchinich, 1994). These measures were validated using sequential coding procedures (Vuchinich, Emery, & Cassidy, 1988).

Three samples of families participated in the studies: (a) a sample of 30 families with a child (age range 7–13 years) who was referred for treatment of antisocial behavior; (b) a sample of 206 families with a child (a son 10 years of age) considered to be at-risk for antisocial behavior because of high delinquency rates in the neighborhood (by age 17, 44% of these boys had been arrested at least once); and (c) a comparison sample of 90 families (two biological parents in residence) with at least one child (boy or girl aged 10 years). All the families were assessed using the same video-taped family problem-solving procedure.

Families in all three samples followed the same family problem-solving procedure. The procedure took place in a comfortable room with only the family triad present. A video camera was in view and families were informed that they would be videotaped. To acclimate them to the setting, they were first instructed to plan for 5 minutes a "fun family activity" that they might do in the next 2 weeks. After that, the parents and the child were given a list of 49 parent–child issues that are typically the source of parent–child difficulties in the home (e.g., allowance, bedtime, chores, fighting with brothers or sisters). The parents and, independently, the child were instructed to select one issue that had been a problem for them at home during the previous month. After the selections were recorded, families were asked to take one of the issues and try to resolve it, or make progress toward solving it, for 10 minutes. This procedure has been used in previous studies of family coalitions. Half of the families were instructed to take the child-selected problem first, and half, the parent-selected problem first. After 10 minutes, the families ended discussion of the first problem and then discussed the second problem for 10 minutes. These two 10-minute sessions were videotaped. The at-risk and referred families took part in these problem-solving sessions at the counseling and research center. The comparison families videotaped the sessions at home. In no cases were researchers or therapists present in the room during the discussions. A number of self-report instruments were administered at other times. Trained coders rated the videotapes for family problem-solving effectiveness, coalitions, parental agreement, and other scales (Vuchinich, Vuchinich, & Wood, 1993).

Comparison of the three samples clearly demonstrated that family problem solving was significantly worse in families with an antisocial child than in the others (Vuchinich, Wood, & Vuchinich, 1994). In addition, it was significantly poorer in at-risk families than in the comparison families. Although this is not surprising and does not establish causal direction, it is consistent with expectations and is evidence for the predictive validity of the observational measures. There was also evidence that parental coalitions were stronger in the referred and at-risk samples. Although there are currently no objective criteria for parental coalitions that are excessive, the higher prevalence of such coalitions in these family types is noteworthy. It suggests that scapegoating or some similar family dynamic may often be present in families having children with conduct disorder.

A second study focused on the link between the parental coalition and effective problem solving in the at-risk sample. It found that strong parental coalitions were associated with significantly lower levels of family problem solving (Vuchinich, Vuchinich, & Wood, 1993). This result held even after effects for child externalizing, marital satisfaction, mother–father conflict, and family structure were taken into account. This result was replicated in the referred sample, but not in the comparison sample (Vuchinich, Wood, & Vuchinich, 1994). Parental coalitions seem to impact problem solving negatively only when the family is under stress.

Parental agreement on child issues predicted good family problem solving. Thus, parental agreement was beneficial so long as it was not overtly turned against the child in the form of a parental coalition. These results are consistent with the scapegoating family pattern in which parents place excessive blame on the child. The child may react to this by seeking to undermine any progress in family problem solving. This is not difficult for a child to do because even silent withdrawal from discussion withholds active involvement or at least agreement with proposed solutions. The child may also simply disagree with everything that the parents say. An alternative explanation, not based on scapegoating, is that strong parental coalitions do not allow the child any autonomy, and the child reacts defensively by sabotaging the family problem-solving process.

In either case, the findings indicate that strong parental coalitions are a family dynamic that disrupts problem solving and should be addressed in family problem-solving training. Specifically, parents should be encouraged not to gang up on the child repeatedly. Parents who agree can usually be very influential even if they allow the child some modifications of their ideas, and do not force closure because it is "two against one."

The third study found that, in two-parent families ($n = 130$), effective family problem solving at child age 10 years significantly reduced the risk of arrest by age 17 years even after taking into account the effects of socioeconomic status, the child's level of antisocial behavior, quality of peer relations, and number of parental transitions that the child experienced (Coughlin & Vuchinich, 1994). This is powerful evidence that family problem solving is a key marker variable in preadolescence that predicts serious antisocial behavior through adolescence.

However, in single-parent families ($n = 72$), better problem solving at age 10 years increased the risk of arrest by age 16 years. We believe this is due to the enmeshed relationship that can develop between a single parent and a preadolescent or adolescent child after divorce. This relationship helps parent and child cope with their current situation but has negative long-term consequences for the child as the normal developmental processes are disrupted. In such families, problem solving would appear to be very effective at age 10 years with considerable warmth and concern for the other's needs being salient, but this does not continue and the child is unable to cope with the transition to adolescence and tends to act out.

Taken together, these results suggest that good family problem solving in preadolescence is a protective factor against early arrest in two-parent families. It is thus feasible that training families in problem solving when the child is a preadolescent could prevent continuation or increase in antisocial behavior that leads to arrest. It is also feasible that such training could be effective in treating conduct disorder.

The result for single-parent families suggests that problem solving may function differently in that family structure. Because our studies included no clinical trials, we cannot conclude that single-parent families are a contraindication for family problem-solving therapy with preadolescents. However, the finding does point to the need for additional work on problem solving in single-parent families before clincal trials are conducted with that family type. The present result in single-parent families could be an artifact of the way in which problem solving was measured here, so alternative measurement methods are recommended. Additional studies should also include measures of enmeshment to determine the extent to which enmeshment is associated with problem solving.

Overall, these analyses of more than 200 families were able to predict accurately whether or not 72% of the children would be arrested by age 17 years on the basis of data from age 10 years. Another study found that family problem solving predicted good peer relations (Hadlock, 1994), which is a key correlate of antisocial behavior in adolescence (Dodge, 1993; Reid, 1993).

Our on-going research is investigating other questions related to family problem solving. These include the following:

1. Is family problem solving with a female preadolescent more effective than with a male preadolescent?
2. Does family problem solving with one child differ from problem solving with two children present?
3. Is family problem solving among Native American families different from problem solving among Anglo-American families?
4. Does family problem-solving effectiveness change as a result of behavioral family therapy?

LIMITATIONS

The individual cognitive and the parent training treatments for conduct disorder are based on theories that consider many aspects of family dynamics, such as coalitions, to be of secondary importance. The moderate success of these treatments is evidence that the theories have some validity, but also that they may not tell the entire story. Changing key thought patterns and reinforcement techniques have taken treatments of conduct disorder a long way, but there is an emerging consensus that they may have accomplished all they can and must be supplemented with other techniques if additional progress is to be made. The treatment proposed here supplements these treatments with techniques that allow therapists to address explicitly the developmental issues of autonomy and family dynamics in a format compatible with drug therapy. This proposal also includes a format for expanding gains associated with the cognitive and parent training treatments.

Because the proposed treatment requires a greater involvement of parents in more complex problem-solving training, a potential limiting factor is whether parents having children with conduct disorder are willing or capable of sustained participation over a 6-month period. Kazdin, Siegel, and Bass (1992) observed 22% attrition in their comprehensive 8-month program, which did not include joint, family problem-solving training. This, along with other parent training studies (Reid, 1993), suggests that most parents of children with conduct disorder are willing and able to participate when considerable treatment program effort is extended. Whether the additional complexity of family meetings and extended negotiations would reduce or enhance parent participation in the treatment is an open question.

Another potential limiting factor is the quality of participation by surrogate parents. This is an important issue because by the time many children with conduct disorder become preadolescents, the biological parents are not in the home. How important is the strength of the affective bond between parent and child to the success of this treatments based on family problem solving? Our research indicates that the presence of two parents, even if one is a stepparent, is an important factor in the protective effects of family problem solving. Additional work is needed to clarify this issue in single-parent families.

No ultimate single cause of conduct disorder has yet been isolated. The best current research indicates that there are multiple causes that may include genetic factors, such as temperament, or cognitive deficits, parenting practices, or social disadvantage (e.g., Dodge, 1993). Furthermore, there seem to be several developmental pathways (Cicchetti & Richters, 1993) that lead to conduct disorder. Under such complex etiological conditions, a single "cure" for conduct disorder does not seem likely. Indeed, there have been recent compelling suggestions that the very nature of the disorder, and methods for measuring it, need to be reconsidered (Richters & Cicchetti, 1993). Emerging work on behavioral genetics and drug therapy hold some promise for early identification and treatment supplements in cases in which there is a physical basis. Although it is not currently known in what proportion of cases there is a primarily physical basis, there are indications that it is relatively small (Dodge, 1993).

GENERALIZABILITY

The cognitive child training and parent training treatments described earlier have already been applied in diverse settings showing that success in research samples generalizes to other populations. This would be expected given the straightforward conceptual nature and delivery format of these treatments. Family problem-solving components to treatment have not yet been extensively evaluated outside of research populations. However, such components have been widely and successfully applied in non-clinical parent training efforts (Dreikurs, 1964) for many years in very diverse populations. Because these techniques represent a systematic extension of the widely used cognitive and parent training treatments in terms of both application and theory, the success in research populations should generalize to other groups.

CONCLUSIONS AND RECOMMENDATIONS

Results from research and clinical practice converge with the conclusion that family problem solving is a key marker variable for antisocial behavior in preadolescence and adolescence. Psychosocial treatments that include training in family problem solving show considerable potential for reducing symptoms of conduct disorder and maintain this reduction over time. Secondary beneficial effects may be expected in the areas of better peer relations and school performance. The application of family problem-solving components, however, requires attention to aspects of family dynamics that are frequently not addressed in treatments that train children and parents separately. Therapists need to provide clients with conflict management and proactive problem-solving skills that are effective in the emotion-laden parent–child conflicts during the preadolescence and adolescence of children with conduct disorder. It is also important to caution parents against excessive interparental coalitions against the child, which can inadvertently subvert progress in problem solving. Parental restraint in this regard may require special coaching because "taking sides" with each other is a natural coping strategy for parents of a child with conduct disorder.

Our research indicates that family structure has a moderating effect on the association between family problem solving and child antisocial behavior. In stepfamilies, the protective benefits of good family problem solving are especially strong. However, in single-parent families, such benefits were not present. It is possible that the presence of two parents (or parent surrogates) in the treatment and at home are needed to realize the full benefits of family problem-solving training.

The work reported here leads to a recommendation for clinical trials of a treatment program for conduct disorder that integrates cognitive training for the child, training for the parents, and joint family problem-solving training. The trials should include boys and girls with conduct disorder from age 9 to 12 years in families with two parents (or parent surrogates) in residence. Our research indicates that more background work is needed on the functioning of problem solving in single-parent families before trials are conducted. The key issue that the recommended trials should address is whether the inclusion of joint family problem-solving training adds significantly to the success of treatments that use separate training for children and parents.

REFERENCES

Braswell, L., & Bloomquist, M. L. (1991). *Cognitive–behavioral therapy with ADHD children: Child, family and school interventions.* New York: Guilford Press.

Cicchetti D., & Richters, J. E. (1993). Developmental considerations in the investigation of conduct disorder. *Development and Psychopathology, 5,* 331–344.

Coughlin, C., & Vuchinich, S. (1994). *Family factors in the development of adolescent delinquency.* Unpublished manuscript, Department of Human Development and Family Sciences, Oregon State University, Corvallis.

Dinkmeyer, D., & McKay, G. D. (1989). *The parent's handbook.* Circle Pines, MN: American Guidance Service.

Dodge, K. A. (1993). The future of research on the treatment of conduct disorder. *Development and Psychopathology, 5,* 311–320.

Dreikurs, R. (1964). *Children: The challenge.* New York: Hawthorn Books.

Forehand, R. L., & McMahon, R. J. (1981). *Helping the noncompliant child: A clinician's guide to parent training.* New York: Guilford Press.

Forgatch, M., & Patterson, G. R. (1989). *Parents and adolescents living together: Part 2. Family problem solving.* Eugene, OR: Castalia Press.

Gurman, A. S., & Kniskern, D. P. (1981). *Handbook of family therapy.* New York: Brunner-Mazel.

Hadlock, T. G. (1994). *Parenting styles and child outcomes mediated by family problem solving.* Doctoral dissertation, Department of Human Development and Family Studies, Oregon State University, Corvallis.

Haley, J. (1976). *Problem-solving therapy: New directions for effective family therapy.* San Francisco: Jossey-Bass.

Hawkins, J. D., Catalano, R. F., Morrison, D. M., O'Donnell, J., Abbott, R. D., & Day, L. E. (1992). The Seattle Social Development Project: Effects of the first four years on protective factors and problem behaviors. In J. McCord & R. Tremblay (Eds.), *The prevention of antisocial behavior in children and adolescents* (pp. 139–161). New York: Guilford Press.

Kazdin, A. E. (1987). Treatment of antisocial behavior in children: Current status and future directions. *Psychological Bulletin, 102,* 187–203.

Kazdin, A. E., Siegel, T. C, & Bass, D. (1992). Cognitive problem solving skills training and parent management training in the treatment of antisocial behavior in children. *Journal of Consulting and Clinical Psychology, 60,* 733–747.

Kendall, P. C. (1991). *Child and adolescent therapy: Cognitive–behavioral procedures.* New York: Guilford Press.

Madanes, C. (1981). *Strategic family therapy.* San Francisco: Jossey-Bass.

Patterson, G. R. (1986). Performance models for antisocial boys. *American Psychologist, 41,* 432–444.

Patterson, G. R., Crosby, L., & Vuchinich, S. (1992). Predicting risk for early police arrest. *Journal of Quantitative Criminology, 8,* 335–355.

Patterson, G. R., Dishion, T. J., & Chamberlain, P. (1993). Outcomes and methodological issues relating to treatment of antisocial children. In T. R. Giles (Ed.), *Effective psychotherapy: A handbook of comparative research* (pp. 114–132). New York: Plenum Press.

Patterson, G. R., & Forgatch, M. (1987). *Parents and adolescents living together: Part 1. The basics.* Eugene, OR: Castalia Press.

Patterson, G. R., & Gullion, M. E. (1971). *Living with children: New methods for parents and teachers.* Champagne, IL: Research Press.

Patterson, G. R., Reid, J. B., Jones, R. R., & Conger, R. W. (1975). *A social learning approach to family intervention* (Vol. 1). Eugene, OR: Castalia Press.

Reid, J. B. (1993). Prevention of conduct disorder before and after school entry: Relating interventions to developmental findings. *Development and Psychopathology, 5,* 242–262.

Richters, J. E., & Cicchetti, D. (1993). Mark Twain meets *DSM-III-R:* Conduct disorder, development, and the concept of harmful dysfunction. *Development and Psychopathology, 5,* 5–31.

Robin, A. L., & Foster, S. L. (1989). *Negotiating parent–adolescent conflict: A behavioral–family systems approach.* New York: Guilford Press.

Spivak, G., Platt, J. J., & Shure, M. B. (1976). *The problem solving approach to adjustment.* San Francisco: Jossey-Bass.

Vuchinich, S. (1986). On attenuation in verbal family conflict. *Social Psychology Quarterly, 47,* 281–293.

Vuchinich, S. (1987). Starting and stopping spontaneous family conflict. *Journal of Marriage and the Family, 49,* 591–601.

Vuchinich, S. (1990). The sequential organization of closing in verbal family conflict. In A. D. Grimshaw (Ed.), *Conflict Talk: Sociolinguistic Investigations of Argument* (pp. 118–138). Cambridge, England: Cambridge University Press.

Vuchinich, S., Bank L., & Patterson, G. R. (1992). Parenting, peers, and the stability of antisocial behavior in preadolescent males. *Developmental Psychology, 28*, 510–521.

Vuchinich, S., Emery, R. E., & Cassidy, J. (1988). Family members as third parties in dyadic family conflict: Strategies, alliances, and outcomes. *Child Development, 59*, 1293–1302.

Vuchinich, S., Hetherington, E. M., Vuchinich, R. A., & Clingempeel, W. G. (1991). Parent–child interaction and gender differences in early adolescents' adaptation to stepfamilies. *Developmental Psychology, 27*, 618–626.

Vuchinich, S., & Teachman, J. (1993). Influences on the duration of wars, strikes, riots and family arguments. *Journal of Conflict Resolution, 37*, 544–568.

Vuchinich, S., Teachman, J., & Crosby, L. (1991). Families and hazard rates that change over time: Some methodological issues in the study of transitions. *Journal of Marriage and the Family, 53*, 898–912.

Vuchinich, S., Vuchinich, R. A., & Coughlin, C. (1992). Family talk and parent–child relationships: Toward integrating deductive and inductive paradigms. *Merrill–Palmer Quarterly: A Journal of Developmental Psychology, 38*, 69–94.

Vuchinich, S., Vuchinich, R. A., & Wood, B. (1993). The interparental relationship and family problem solving with preadolescent males. *Child Development, 64*, 1389–1400.

Vuchinich, S., Wood, B., & Vuchinich, R. A. (1994). Coalitions and family problem solving in referred, at-risk and comparison families. *Family Process, 33*, 409–424.

VI
AUTISTIC DISORDER

INTRODUCTION

Autistic disorder is characterized by impairments in communication and social skills, and a marked absence of interest in participating in age-appropriate social activities. In addition, cognitive skills are usually impaired, and comorbid conditions such as aggressiveness, self-injurious behaviors, hyperactivity, and affective variability can be present. The autistic symptoms may be expressed in different forms depending on the age and developmental level of the child. The incidence of autism is 6.6 to 13.6 per 10,000 individuals, and the rates for boys are 4 to 5 times greater than girls. One goal of psychosocial interventions is to reverse these dysfunctional aspects by intervening as early as possible in the course of the child's development, often by building therapeutic strategies into the approaches used by primary caregivers or other individuals available in the child's milieu. This section comprises three chapters that present various intervention strategies.

Laura Schreibman and Robert L. Koegel are investigating the effectiveness of parent training as an avenue for the treatment for autism. In their chapter, they describe how parents are trained to identify and target a few pivotal behaviors for the intervention, with the goal of encouraging the child's increased independence. Analyses indicate that the experimental group is superior to the control group. The authors caution that their intervention may not be helpful for severely handicapped children or for parents who do not volunteer for research protocols. They recommend that self-management procedures be refined further to ensure greater applicability across children, and they call for studies that can identify the various parent and child characteristics that may affect treatment outcomes.

Lynn and Robert Koegel describe their intervention procedures designed to enhance language in children with autism, and they outline their techniques of teaching children to be active communicators. Their manualized treatment program consists of teaching communication skills, functional analysis communication interventions, self-management, and speech intelligibility. Preliminary results indicate the promising nature of this procedure, with some evidence of generalization at home. Evidence indicates that this treatment results in a decrease in disruptive behaviors, self-injury, aggression, and self-stimulation. Lack of response to treatment may relate to a variety of complex issues involving family variables, child characteristics, or the suitability of the intervention to a given target behavior. The authors recommend that greater attention be directed to individualizing treatments to correspond with specific child, family, and target behavior characteristics.

Phillip S. Strain and his collaborators describe their therapeutic strategy, "Learning Experiences . . . an Alternative Program" (LEAP), for preschoolers. This program encompasses parent training (including active parental participation in the treatment) and classroom-based interventions. The LEAP intervention also involves the training of peers to perform as teacher assistants to facilitate the child's communicative and social interaction. The outcomes are encouraging and the peer-mediated intervention technique appears to be effective. However, the generalizability of the treatment is uncertain at this point, and the authors recommend that future research should address the effectiveness of longitudinal and community wide interventions.

All the therapeutic modalities included in this section involve the training of parents to participate actively in the treatment of their children. Although treatment effects appear to be beneficial, many unanswered questions remain. Could these interventions be used with other more at-risk populations (i.e., those with lower socio-economic level and less educated families), with various ethnic groups, with children of various levels of impairment, or with children of various ages and levels of functioning? Could these interventions be beneficial when performed in other than laboratory settings? Because children with developmental disorders can precipitate stress and discord in their families, should parent–family treatment be an integral part of the children's interventions? These studies provide an introduction to the larger amount of work still to be done in this area. Future studies must address not only the above-mentioned issues, but also must embrace more comprehensive approaches to the treatment of autism, such as the use of combinations of therapeutic interventions across modalities and settings.

22

FOSTERING SELF-MANAGEMENT: PARENT-DELIVERED PIVOTAL RESPONSE TRAINING FOR CHILDREN WITH AUTISTIC DISORDER

LAURA SCHREIBMAN and ROBERT L. KOEGEL

This chapter describes a systematic line of clinical research that focuses on the involvement of parents as treatment providers for their children with autism. We begin with a brief description of autism and the impact such children have on their parents. The following section describes the advantage of parent training over a program in which the child is treated exclusively by clinicians in a clinic setting. Then, we discuss the evolution of an optimal form of parent training, Pivotal Response Training. The core of this research begins with a comparison of a parent training program that treats only individual target behaviors with a parent training program that focuses on "pivotal" behaviors in autism (motivation and responsivity to multiple cues). Because of limitations in the generalization of this approach and continued reported high stress in parents, a third pivotal behavior, self-management, was added.

Preparation of this chapter and the research reported herein were supported by U.S. Public Health Service research grants MH 39434 and MH 28210 from the National Institute of Mental Health. Correspondence concerning this chapter should be directed to Dr. Laura Schreibman, Department of Psychology, University of California (San Diego), 9500 Gilman Drive, LaJolla, CA 92093.

AUTISM

Autistic disorder, as defined in the fourth edition of the *Diagnostic and Statistical Manual of Mental Disorders* (DSM-IV; American Psychiatric Association, 1994) is a severe form of psychopathology often apparent from the beginning of life and diagnosable by the age of 3 years. It is characterized primarily by severe and pervasive deficits in social attachment, social behaviors, and communication. It is characterized also by restricted patterns of behavior (e.g., stereotypic rocking, flapping) and restricted interests (compulsive and ritualistic behaviors), attentional deficits, disturbances of affect, and, in approximately 75% of cases, mental retardation. The incidence of strictly defined autistic disorder is typically reported to be approximately 4 per 10,000 children (with autistic-like symptoms occurring in many more children) and it is found in boys versus girls at the ratio of 3 or 4 to 1.

Understandably, rearing a child with such a severe developmental disorder places an extreme burden on parents. Added to this is the historical fact that for many years parents were implicated in the etiology of the disorder (e.g., Bettelheim, 1967). The severity of the disorder and the erroneous conception of autism as a psychogenically based disorder prevented parents from being considered as treatment agents for their children with autism. However, recent research indicating that autism is a neurodevelopmental disorder (e.g., Denckla & James, 1991) and the development of behavioral parent training programs have allowed for the successful use of parents as an important clinical resource.

DESCRIPTION OF THE PROGRAM

The focus of this chapter is on research that explores the effectiveness of parent training as an avenue for the delivery of treatment for autism. In early studies (Koegel, Schreibman, Britten, Burke, & O'Neill, 1982; Lovaas, Koegel, Simmons, & Long, 1973), researchers systematically compared the effectiveness of behavioral treatments delivered by a trained clinician versus the same treatments delivered by a parent trained in the implementation of the treatments. Results consistently showed that parents typically produced as much or greater initial behavioral gains in their children, and far greater generalization and maintenance of treatment gains. Furthermore, this avenue of treatment delivery improved the overall pattern of family interactions, permitting far greater freedom and pursuit of leisure-time family activities than when equivalent treatment was provided by a clinician instead of a parent. Because this approach appears to be more effective for the child, and more economical and satisfying for the family, and because it provides for the feasibility of treatment delivery to children living in areas removed from clinical centers, we have embarked on a large scale research program to identify the most effective forms and most effective content of parent training in order to have a maximum impact on autism per se, as well as on overall family functioning.

In spite of the very positive results, one rather serious limitation to date has been that the children can become extremely dependent on their treatment provider (in this case, their parents) and may continue to exhibit relatively limited autonomous responding even after extensive treatment. Based on the literature and our pilot data, we hypothesize that the most productive parent training avenue is one that involves the children as major contributors to their own treatment. Specifically, we feel that parent training programs, involving content focused on treatment that motivates the children to initiate and maintain social interactions and to self-manage their own behaviors, are critical to the children's long-term development. The types of changes that are required of the children over the years are those that need to be evidenced in an infinite number of environments, including many where their parents are not present. Furthermore, as the children mature, their need for independent functioning becomes greater.

GOALS AND ISSUES

The literature (e.g., Freeman & Ritvo, 1976; Koegel, Glahn, & Nieminen, 1978; Wing, 1972) and the results of our previous research (Koegel et al., 1982; Koegel, Schreibman, Johnson, O'Neill, & Dunlap, 1984; Koegel, Schreibman, O'Neill, & Burke, 1983; Runco & Schreibman, 1983, 1988; Schreibman, Koegel, Mills, & Burke, 1981; Schreibman, Runco, Mills, & Koegel, 1982) suggest that although parent training proved to be superior to clinic treatment on a variety of dependent measures, limitations remained to the effectiveness of parent training. These limitations related strongly to problems in generalization, with treatment gains evident in the presence of the parents, but often not evident in the parents' absence. Also, treatment gains were very specific, showing little or no generalization to nontreated behaviors. Our research into the impediments to generalization implicated deficits in *motivation* and *responsivity* as important variables. Deficits in motivation were noted when a child would learn a behavior, but not perform the behavior spontaneously. Deficits in responsivity were noted when a child's breadth of attention was too narrow to allow observational learning in the home environment. The child usually learned only when the parents directly taught the behavior.

Subsequent advances have shown that treatment delivered in naturalistic conditions that focused on improving *motivation* had a major impact on improving the breadth of treatment gains. Rather than improving only single behaviors at a time, such treatments appeared to influence widespread areas of the children's functioning. Because so many untreated behaviors also were affected, we called this type of treatment Pivotal Response Training.

This new pivotal parent training program involved teaching the parents specific procedures that have been reported in the research literature to enhance motivation and to increase the children's responsivity to cues in the environment (Dunlap, 1984; Koegel, Camarata, & Koegel, in press; Koegel, Dyer, & Bell, 1987; Koegel, O'Dell, & Dunlap, 1988; Koegel, O'Dell, & Koegel, 1987; Koegel & Schreibman, 1977; Koegel & Williams, 1980; Laski, Charlop, & Schreibman, 1988; Schreibman, Charlop, Koegel, 1982). These treatments provided not only widespread response generalization in that many behaviors improved, but the speed of training parents was faster, the rate of acquisition of new behaviors on the part of the children was faster, disruptive behaviors decreased to almost zero without the need for separate intervention, and the affect of the children and their parents was considerably more positive during both treatment and nontreatment interactions. However, in spite of the considerable optimism over these achievements, the significant problem of the children appearing to be dependent on cues from adults, and on continued treatment from adults, remained. The children failed to exhibit the autonomy required to function normally in most social contexts.

Accordingly, we and others have extended this line of Pivotal Response Training to include the pivotal behavior of *self-management* as a major treatment target (Koegel & Koegel, 1988). This type of training is a direct and logical outgrowth of the previous pivotal response training, which was based heavily on naturalistic treatment procedures. Self-management continues to extend this research in several ways. For example, the use of natural reinforcers intrinsic to the child-selected activities provides the opportunity for the child to naturally provide self-reinforcement.

Self-management has several advantages as a means of facilitating generalized and independent responding for children with autism. First, self-management procedures allow a child to take an active role in his or her therapy, reducing the need for constant clinician vigilance (Fowler, 1984). Second, by teaching the child the skill of self-management as a pivotal behavior, an indefinite number of behaviors can be targeted in virtually any environment the child enters. Third, many factors that are included in self-management programs have previously been shown to be successful in promoting generalization. These include the administration of delayed rewards (e.g., Dunlap, Koegel, Johnson, & O'Neill, 1987) and of unpredictable rewards (Koegel & Rincover, 1977). Fourth, the use of the self-management techniques and/or the occurrence or improvement of the target behavior may encourage other individuals in the natural environment to provide reinforcers (Baer, Fowler, & Carden-Smith, 1984), initiating a favorable cycle of a steadily improving environmental interactions. Fifth, the child's use of a recording device (to monitor his or her behavior) may lead to the device acquiring discriminative stimulus properties such that it acquires stimulus control for the occurrence or improvement of the desired target behaviors (Nelson & Hayes, 1981). Other factors discussed by Stokes and Baer (1977) that may contribute to generalization, and that are also included in many self-management programs, are loose training, including multiple exemplars, and training in multiple environments. As mentioned, self-management is a widely researched treatment technique that utilizes the client as an active participant in the treatment process. These procedures have not only been shown to be effective with normal populations (e.g., Drabman, Spitalnik, & O'Leary, 1973; O'Brien, Riner, & Budd, 1983; Sagotsky, Patterson, & Lepper, 1978), but have also been used successfully with persons evidencing mild to moderate mental retardation (Gardner, Cole, Berry, & Nowinski, 1983; Horner & Brigham, 1979; Shapiro & Klein, 1980; Shapiro, McGonigle, & Ollendick, 1980; Sugai & Rowe, 1984). Particularly important, a recent study (Koegel & Koegel, 1990) demonstrated that severely handicapped children with autism can successfully reduce a difficult behavior (self-stimulation) using self-management procedures.

Thus, to address the remaining generalization problems still evident in parent training, we are directing our research toward the comparison of two parent training programs. One consists of a typical parent training approach where the *parents* are taught to manage their child's behavior. The other is an approach where the parents are taught to include their *child* as a central part of the treatment delivery through self-management techniques. We hypothesize that the new parent training approach will remediate the limitations and allow the achievement of generalized gains in the children's behavior and allow them to function more independently in their social environments.

TREATMENT PLAN

As discussed, a main issue in the treatment of children with autism is the generalization of treatment effectiveness. Thus, we seek to develop treatments that will be expressed (a) in a wide variety of stimulus situations, (b) across a range of individual behaviors, and (c) over extended periods of time. Focusing on pivotal behaviors means a greater economy and efficiency in our efforts because we assume a greater overall impact as a function of targeting a few (pivotal) behaviors.

Treatment Content

Because *motivation, responsivity to multiple cues,* and *self-management* have each been shown to affect generalized treatment gains in children with autism, these are the specific targets of training for the parents who participate in our program.

Motivation

Parents are taught to increase their child's motivation by using several individual strategies that each have been demonstrated to increase motivation and to enhance learning (Koegel & Egel, 1979; Koegel, Dyer, et al., 1987; Koegel & Williams, 1980; O'Dell, Dunlap, & Koegel, 1983; O'Dell & Koegel, 1981; Turner, 1978). The strategies include

1. *Clear instructions and questions.* The parents are taught to present instructions only when the child is attending; to present the instructions in a clear, unambiguous manner; and to present instructions that are relevant and appropriate to the task.
2. *Interspersed maintenance tasks.* To enhance motivation by keeping the overall success and reinforcement level high, previously mastered tasks are interspersed frequently among more difficult tasks.
3. *Child choice.* To maximize the child's interest in the learning situation, he or she is given a great deal of input in determining the specific stimuli and the nature of the learning interaction. A variety of materials (e.g., toys, games, snacks) is presented and the child is allowed to select an activity or object about which the learning interaction will take place. The parents are encouraged to be alert to the child's changing interests and to allow the child to change to another preferred activity.
4. *Direct and natural reinforcers.* Direct, rather than indirect, reinforcers are used. Direct reinforcers are consequences that are related directly to the response they follow. A direct reinforcer for the verbal response "car" might be access to a toy car, as opposed to a food or a token reinforcer. Access to a toy car is a direct and natural consequence of saying "car," whereas food is not.
5. *Reinforcement of attempts.* To maximize reinforcement and therefore enhance the child's motivation to respond, we train the parents to reinforce all reasonable attempts to respond made by the child. Thus, reinforcers are contingent on attempts that may not be completely correct, and that may not

be quite as good as previous attempts, but that are within a broader range of correct responses.

Responsivity to Multiple Cues

Prior research has identified an attentional deficit, *stimulus overselectivity*, that characterizes many children with autism. This pattern of attention is characterized by a failure to respond to simultaneous multiple cues such as typically occur in a learning situation (see Schreibman, 1988, for a review of this literature). This deficit has been implicated in a wide range of behavioral deficits including failure to generalize (e.g., Lovaas, Koegel, & Schreibman, 1979; Schreibman, 1988). We also know that for many children with autism, overselectivity may be remediated by training the children on a series of successive *conditional discriminations* (Koegel & Schreibman, 1977; Schreibman Charlop, et al., 1982). A conditional discrimination is one that *requires* response to multiple cues. For example, asking a child to go get her red sweater is a conditional discrimination task because the child undoubtedly has more than one red item of clothing and more than one sweater. Correct responding depends on attention to *both* color and object. In our training, parents are taught to present their children with tasks involving conditional discriminations. We reason that as the children learn to respond on the basis of multiple cues, their attention is more normalized, allowing for more environmental cues to become functional. Because stimulus control of behavior is no longer as restricted, enhanced generalization should result.

Self-Management

The third pivotal behavior that contributes to generalization of treatment effects is self-management. Once a child has learned to use self-management to control his or her own behavior, this skill can be taken into any setting and applied to any behavior. In other words, generalization is systematically programmed. To accomplish this, we teach the parents a series of steps to train their child to use self-management:

1. *Identification of target behavior and reinforcer.* To begin, the parents choose and define a target behavior to be self-managed. Ideally the child would choose the target behavior, but this is often not possible, especially during the initial self-management programs. The parents are encouraged to allow the child to participate as much as possible in choosing behaviors to maximize their quality of life (Turnbull, Bateman, & Turnbull, 1993). Also, the parents allow the child to choose the reinforcer (again maximizing motivation) for appropriate self-management.

2. *Identification of target behavior by the child.* Here, the parents teach their child to identify the target behavior. This is accomplished by presenting to the child appropriate and inappropriate examples of the behavior and reinforcing the child for correct identifications of the behavior. For example, if a parent is trying to teach a child to self-manage appropriate play, the parent models appropriate play and asks the child, "Was that good playing?" On a subsequent trial, the parent may throw the toy across the room and ask, "Was that good playing?" This continues until the child correctly discriminates the behavior on a minimum of 80% of random presentations. Following this, the child is asked to provide examples of appropriate and inappropriate behavior (to ensure the child knows it is his or her own behavior that is to be monitored). The parents are taught to reinforce the child's correct responses on a continuous reinforcement schedule.

3. *Teaching self-monitoring of the target behavior.* Once the child can identify the target behavior correctly, the parents begin implementation of self-management proper. Depending on the target behavior, the child is taught to record instances of the behavior (e.g., responses to social initiations) or the occurrence of the behavior within an interval (e.g., an interval of appropriate play). Specifically, the parents learn to teach their child to record (on a wrist counter or a checksheet) occurrences of the appropriate behavior. For example, a parent may say to the child, "Show me behavior X. Ready, go!" Initially, each time the child engages in the behavior, the parent is taught to prompt the child to conduct the relevant self-management activity. For example, the parent might say at the end of a previously established interval, "It's time! Did you do behavior X?" The child is then verbally or physically prompted to record the behavior. Accurate recording of the behavior is reinforced. Similarly, accurate recording (or withholding of recording) of inappropriate behavior also is reinforced (e.g., "That's right, you did not do behavior X. Let's try again."). The previously selected reinforcer is available to the child after a predetermined interval or number of correct responses. Initially, the intervals or required number of responses are set at a very low level to ensure the child's success.

4. *Increasing self-management independence.* Following successful implementation of these procedures, the parents are taught to increase self-management independence. Thus, parent prompts to self-record are gradually faded, prompts for the

child to exchange recorded points for reinforcers are faded, and the schedule of reinforcement is gradually thinned by increasing the number of recorded points required for a reinforcer and/or by increasing the time interval required for self-managing until the child is able to self-manage his or her behavior for periods of up to several hours. Next, the parents are taught to fade their supervision of the child by fading their presence and, if possible, the presence of the self-management materials (e.g., recording devices). Finally, the parents are taught to validate their child's appropriate use of self-management in the parents' absence, by communicating with significant others in the child's environment. Thus, by the completion of training, the parents have learned to teach their child to evaluate the appropriateness of his or her behavior, to self-record and self-reinforce trial-by-trial responding, and to recruit parental reinforcement following extended periods of correctly self-managed behavior. Each of these steps is detailed in a self-management training manual (Koegel, Koegel, & Parks, 1990).

Treatment Delivery

Our research suggests that 25 hours are adequate for training in the three pivotal behaviors. The initial training session is devoted to assessments of the child's level of naturalistic language use, social interaction, and appropriate responding in a more structured situation. The first session usually entails a 15-minute unstructured interview with the child's parents to determine under what conditions and at what level of sophistication and success the child typically exhibits appropriate spontaneous behavior. The child is present and given access to a wide variety of age-appropriate activities, and may be provided various opportunities for language and social interaction in unstructured situations with unfamiliar persons.

At the end of the first session, the parents are given the *Pivotal Response Training Manual* (Koegel, Schreibman, et al., 1989), which covers the motivation and responsivity pivotal behaviors, and a homework reading assignment to be completed by the next training session. The following sessions are designed to ensure that the parents understand the general principles and can apply them at home. During each session, the trainer reviews the exercises in the manual with the parents and answers questions.

When the parents have completed the *Pivotal Response Training Manual*, they are brought into the training situation with their child. Here they first observe a trained therapist utilizing the pivotal response training components and then they are gradually introduced into the training sessions, with responsibility for implementing the training gradually transferred to them. The transition rate depends on the parents' rate of mastery of the procedures and usually requires several sessions. Parents are given immediate feedback about their use of the training procedures. The training continues until the parents demonstrate a minimum of 80% correct usage of each procedure (e.g., child choice, direct reinforcers) during a 10-minute fidelity of implementation assessment. When the parents have completed this training, they begin training in self-management.

Training in self-management parallels the training of the other two pivotal behaviors. The parents read the self-management manual (Koegel et al., 1990), which goes into detail about the specific procedures outlined earlier (e.g., training in identification of target behavior). As with training on the other pivotal behaviors, the parents read sections of the manual focusing on each procedure and then discuss the procedures during the following training sessions. Once the manual is completed, the parents begin training their child in self-management. The parent trainer models implementation of the specific procedures and the parents begin implementation, with appropriate feedback from the trainer. Training is considered complete when the parents have independently trained two target behaviors via self-management. To ensure that self-management procedures are actually being implemented in the home setting, we conduct three 2-hour home probes at 2 weeks, 6 months, and 12 months posttraining. Again, the criterion is a minimum of 80% correct use of self-management procedures for clinic and in-home fidelity of implementation assessments.

Assessment

As with the development of any effective behavioral treatment plan, accurate, comprehensive, and appropriate assessment is an integral part of the process. We divide our assessments along two lines of dependent measures: (a) assessments designed to evaluate directly the effects of the training on a wide range of relevant *child* variables, and (b) assessments designed to evaluate the impact of the training on *the parents and the family*. We view this second group of assessments as particularly important because ours is a *parent* training program and no matter how effective the treatment is with the children, the parents will be disinclined to use the treatment if they find it too taxing, too disruptive to family life, or ineffective. Assessments are conducted at pre- and posttreatment, and at follow-up intervals.

Child Measures

The measures of the child's behavior are divided into two subareas reflecting stimulus and response generalization: (a) *Social adaptation*, an index of the child's level of functioning relative to his or her social environment, along nonverbal dimensions; and (b) *language development*, along both receptive and expressive dimensions. These subareas were chosen because impairments in the social and language areas encompass the majority of the major symptoms of autism (Kanner, 1943; Rimland, 1964; Rutter, 1971; Schreibman, 1988).

Social Adaptation

We employ both a behavioral measure and a standardized questionnaire to assess social adaptation. The behavioral measure consists of a structured observation wherein the child is observed in a large living room-type environment equipped with several toys, couch, table, etc. The child is observed with a therapist and with an unfamiliar adult, to assess the child's behavior independent of the parents. These sessions are videotaped; later analysis and scoring of multiple responses provide for a quantitative description of the degree to which specified behaviors are present or absent in a free-play setting (e.g., Lovaas et al., 1973). Four behaviors characteristic of autism are scored: (a) self-stimulation, (b) appropriate play, (c) social nonverbal behavior (e.g., responding to request, imitating), and (d) tantrum or crying.

The standardized measure of social adaptation is the Vineland Adaptive Behavior Scales (Sparrow, Balla, & Cicchetti, 1984), which yields scores relating to socialization, communication, daily living skills, an adaptive behavior composite, and level of maladaptive behavior. This generalization measure reflects the child's competence and independence in his or her social environment.

Language Development

We obtain both behavioral measures and standardized test measures in the area of language development. For the behavioral measure, we use the structured livingroom setting procedure (described earlier), scoring several categories of verbal behavior, including appropriate imitation of speech of others, answers to questions presented by others, spontaneous speech, and other appropriate speech. We also score inappropriate speech (e.g., echolalia, neologisms, idiosyncratic language, or a combination).

For our standardized measures of language development, we employ the Assessment of Children's Language Comprehension (Foster, Giddan, & Stark, 1973), which provides a detailed, in-depth analysis of the child's level of generalized language development with respect to population norms, with information regarding the amount of simultaneous language components a child is able to utilize (this also provides a generalization assessment regarding our responsivity to multiple cues pivotal behavior). We also administer the Peabody Picture Vocabulary Test (Dunn & Dunn, 1981) to assess the child's receptive language level.

Parent and Family Measures

Because we are interested in the impact of our treatment conditions on the family system, we obtain data on dependent measures designed to provide information on important family variables. The specific measures we use are those that have been shown to be sensitive to important clinical aspects of the family (e.g., Koegel et al., 1982; Schreibman & Koegel, 1989) and that are likely to show changes as the child shows increasing amounts of independent behavior.

Family Environment and Interaction

We use several indices of the atmosphere of the whole family system and the specific nature of parent–child interactions. To obtain information about how the families budget their time over a day, parents are asked to keep a 24-hour Time–Activity Diary (e.g., Berk & Berk, 1979) for one weekday and for one weekend day. The diary asks the parents to indicate how much time they spent in various activities (e.g., teaching their child, leisure activity, custodial care of child) and who was with them during the activity. It also asks for their perception of the valence of each activity (i.e., "pleasant," "work," etc.). We then systematically review the forms and tabulate the amount of time during which the parents are involved in various types of activities, how the parents rate the particular activity, and other important information. This information provides a clearer picture of the influence of our program on family interactions and structure. We feel that the inclusion of this measure is very important because it has provided extremely interesting results during our research (Koegel et al., 1982), indicating that it is sensitive to changes in how parents change the structure of their time as a function of the parent training.

A video assessment is conducted during the dinner hour. This unstructured home observation allows us to gather information on changes in both the child's and the parents' behaviors as a function of our different training packages (e.g., motivation, responsivity to multiple cues, self-management). We score these videotapes for style of family interactions; specifically, we assess (a) level of happiness of the interaction, (b) level of parental interest in the interaction, (c) level of stress in the interaction, and (d) level of sternness or pleasantness of the interaction.

To obtain generalized effects of the parent training in a more structured setting, we use the structured laboratory observations described earlier in the context of the child measures. During the assessments relating to the parent, the parent is the adult present with the child in the room. The parent is instructed to present specific interactions that enable us to determine the extent to which the child exhibits appropriate and psychopathological spontaneous independent behavior in a free-play setting with the parent. We also can determine the extent to which the child engages in social interactions with the parent and the nature of these interactions.

Parenting a child with autism is a challenging task, and we wish to acquire information relating to the perceived stress of these parents as a function of training. We have chosen an assessment that allows us to compare our results easily with those of other researchers. The Questionnaire on Resources and Stress (QRS, Holroyd, 1974; Holroyd, Brown, Wikler, & Simmons, 1975) is a paper-and-pencil, true–false item questionnaire designed to measure variables pertinent to families with handicapped family members (Holroyd, 1982). The questionnaire (short form) has a total of 66 questions measuring parent stress along 11 subscales:

1. dependency and management,
2. cognitive impairment,
3. limits on family opportunity,
4. life span care,
5. family disharmony,
6. lack of personal reward,
7. terminal illness stress,
8. physical limitations,
9. financial stress,
10. preference for institutionalization, and
11. personal burden.

The QRS is a multidimensional, quantifiable, and simple-to-administer assessment that has been validated against several clinical populations including children with autism (Holroyd et al., 1975; Holroyd & McArthur, 1976; Koegel et al., 1992).

OUTCOMES

Motivation and Responsivity

To best understand the results of this research it is first necessary to present a summary of the outcomes related to the primary underlying framework of our approach, which has been to focus our training on teaching the parents to target pivotal responses likely to improve widespread areas of their children's behavior. Our work in this area began with a focus on the important pivotal responses of motivation and responsivity to multiple cues, a focus that has provided important results in its own right, and that also provided the basic foundation that we use in our later work (see below) on the pivotal behavior of self-management. Thus, the specific aim of our early research was to evaluate the differential effectiveness and impact of two parent training programs. Families were assigned randomly to one of two treatment conditions. In our control condition, parents were trained to teach numerous individual target behaviors (ITB condition). In the experimental condition (pivotal condition), parents were trained to teach their children the pivotal behaviors of motivation and responsivity to multiple cues. Initial assessments were made in the areas of child behavior, family stress, and social validation of the significance of treatment change. Analyses indicated that the pivotal condition was superior in a number of important ways. Some interesting and important residual problem areas also surfaced during the analyses, suggesting an extremely profitable addition to future parent training efforts. First, consider the identified strengths of the pivotal approach to parent training.

Number of Hours Required for Training

The average number of hours required for training the parents in the pivotal group (15 hours) was only half the number required for the ITB group (32 hours). These results are consistent with those of our earlier research in which the ITB condition was our major intervention, and in which it also required approximately this same number of hours (range: 25 to 50 hours). Thus, we believe this result to be a robust estimate of the number of hours required to train parents in the use of behavior modification for the purpose of teaching their child individual target behaviors. The much more rapid training in the pivotal condition suggests not only an improvement in efficiency, but also the likelihood of an easier intervention for the parents to implement. This likelihood also is suggested by the following additional analyses.

Time Activity Diaries

Our preliminary results show that following parent training, the parents in the pivotal condition engaged in *more leisure and recreational* activities than the parents in the ITB condition. Similarly, the parents in the pivotal condition engaged in more naturalistic (everyday, ongoing) teaching activities with their children than did the parents who completed the ITB condition (Moes, Koegel, & Schreibman, 1993). These results may relate to the fact that the pivotal type of teaching, by its nature, lent itself to integration into natural ongoing activities, whereas the ITB type of teaching usually was carried out during a special time that the parents set aside to work with the child. In any case, the parents in the pivotal condition spent more of their day in leisure activities and more of their day in teaching activities than did the parents in the ITB intervention. This is also consistent with our results indicating that the parents in the pivotal condition were happier when implementing the training were the parents in the ITB condition (see below).

Parental Affect

A residual problem noted during our early research was that although our objective measures indicated the superiority of parent training over clinic treatment, parent training was not necessarily associated with parental liking or satisfaction (Schreibman, 1983). We hypothesized that one of the benefits of the pivotal response training would be increased satisfaction from the parents. To assess differential effects of our ITB and pivotal treatments on parental affect (a measure of satisfaction/liking), we had groups of undergraduate students rate parents in both conditions working with their children. The observers were asked to rate, on a Likert-type scale, the degree to which the parents appeared to be interested, enthusiastic, and happy while working with their children. The results showed that parents in the pivotal condition showed more positive affect than did those parents in the ITB condition (Schreibman, Kaneko, & Koegel, 1991).

Child Behavior

In preliminary analyses of our structured laboratory observations (free-play setting), both groups of children showed substantial pretreatment to posttreatment improvement on behavioral measures when with their parents and when with unfamiliar adults. As per our expectations, the pivotal group showed more improvement than did the ITB group when they were assessed with an unfamiliar person, indicating greater generalization of initial treatment effects with training in the pivotal behaviors of motivation and responsivity. However, preliminary analyses at this stage suggest some decrease in gains at follow-up and thus the need to focus on improving the maintenance of the generalization effects. These findings support the need for an intervention such as self-management, wherein facilitation of the treatment gains is accomplished by the child essentially providing the treatment across time and generalization environments.

Preliminary analyses suggest that for most of the subscales of the Vineland Adaptive Behavior Scales, the pivotal condition resulted in larger gains than did the ITB condition. In no case was the ITB condition superior to the pivotal condition. Furthermore, differences between conditions appear to be large for the social and communicative scales, suggesting improvements in areas considered to be the hallmarks of autism, and that have been especially resistant to change in the past.

Consistent with the findings showing especially large gains in areas related to social behavior and communication, the Assessment of Children's Language Comprehension (ACLC) revealed greater gains for the pivotal group than for the ITB group. This was true for the two general indicator subportions of the test (overall vocabulary and overall composite score). More important, the largest differences were on those subtests requiring the children to respond to verbal instructions with multiple components. This result suggests that the multiple-cue training aspect of the pivotal condition was very powerful, and that it generalized to the extent that the gains were evident under standardized language testing conditions.

Residual Problems

Although these results represent the general pattern of findings from this phase of the research (i.e., that the pivotal condition produced more widespread behavior change in a number of important ways), there also were findings that suggest important residual problems to be remedied.

Measures of Family Stress

Although there were some indications of reductions in stress following the pivotal training condition, other measures indicated substantial long-term levels of parental stress that are likely to require special intervention. This is illustrated by the results from the QRS. Our intake assessments on the QRS stress measure indicated extremely high levels of stress. We thus undertook an extensive investigation in this area. First, we assessed stress in parents of autistic children from a variety of cultures to determine the robustness of the measure (Koegel et al., 1992). We obtained data from families living in metropolitan Southern California, families living in rural Appalachia, and families living in metropolitan Munich, Germany. The data showed that all of these cultures exhibited nearly identical patterns of stress related to having an autistic child in their family. Furthermore, the levels of stress on scales 1, 2, 3, and 4 were extremely high and appeared to relate to a general severe concern regarding the well-being of their child after the parents die, which literally every family expressed. Thus, the parents were extremely concerned about the future of their child, the child's level of cognitive impairment (i.e., ability to function independently), and the child's ability to be accepted in the community. As might be expected, this type of stress was not significantly reduced by either of our treatment conditions, as neither condition addressed long-term needs nor the transition from childhood to adulthood. Although the pivotal condition did produce a significant reduction in stress on one scale (related to concern regarding the child's cognitive impairment), none of these other severe types of stress were affected by either condition. As a result, we see the need for a critical new dimension to the parent training intervention to remediate this problem.

Stigmatizing Social Behaviors

Although the children made generally large gains following treatment, they still continued to exhibit certain behaviors that defined them as severely abnormal and socially unacceptable in the community (cf. Koe-gel & Frea, 1993). For example, although some children showed marked improvement in language skills, their self-stimulatory behavior was still severely stigmatizing in social situations. For other children, even those whose gains were extremely large (i.e., they had normal IQs and were in normal classes in school), they still exhibited subtle but severe social and communicative problems that characterized them as severely in need of further treatment (they talked in excessive and inappropriate detail; they exhibited inappropriate facial expressions during social interactions; they did not respond to social cues to switch the conversation off of an unde-sired topic, etc.). These behaviors occurred much more frequently in chil-dren with autism functioning typically than they did in normal children functioning typically. Furthermore, when normal adults were asked to rate these children on a scale of 1 to 9, in which 1 represented severely ab-normal and 9 represented normal, the normally functioning autistic child was rated as severely abnormal (i.e., 2) whereas the normal child was rated 9. Such results fit with our subjective impressions and with societal records (such as public school records), which show that these children are still being severely ostracized by their peers, are still being recommended for exclusion from normal community and educational activities, and are still a source of considerable concern to their parents. Such abnormalities are greatly in need of definition and measurement and must be considered in the implementation of any parent training program.

Improved Responsivity With Adults, But Not With Children

Our preliminary analyses also suggest an emerging problem by which the children show adequate (compared to normal peers) levels of respon-sivity to adults, but, in marked contrast to the normal children, the autistic children almost never respond to other children. We hypothesize that this is because literally all of their treatment intervention was conducted by adults from an adult-oriented perspective. We anticipate that future re-finements in treatment will require either the incorporation of children as treatment coagents (e.g., Pierce & Schreibman, 1995) or the addition of a new treatment focus that expands the generalizability of treatment gains to areas involving specific childhood activities and pivotal skills.

SELF-MANAGEMENT

Building on our earlier work on the pivotal behaviors of motivation and responsivity to multiple cues, we have begun an important extension in the area of self-management. To assess the feasibility of the proposed self-management research, we conducted a series of pilot studies to address major unanswered questions in the literature relating to new aspects of our research. Specifically, we conducted pilot studies addressing the questions of: (a) whether severely handicapped children could learn self-management techniques, (b) whether self-management would have a broad impact on behavior; and (c) whether parents could learn to teach self-management skills to severely handicapped children. Each of these pilot studies is summarized.

The Effectiveness of Self-Management With Severely Handicapped Children

In our first study (Koegel & Koegel, 1990), we asked the question of whether a severely disabled population would be able to learn self-management skills. Stereotypic behavior was selected as a target behavior because it is present typically in the most severely affected autistic children, and because it has been shown to interfere frequently with such children's acquisition of new skills. Thus, we reasoned that if these children could learn to use self-management skills to modify that particular behavior, then we would likely be able to use self-management techniques across a relatively broad population of children and target behaviors. Four autistic children participated in the study. They were selected because they were severely handicapped, and because they exhibited stereotypic behavior that was so severe that it was jeopardizing their placement at home, school, or both. These children had a chronological age between 9 and 14 years and a mental age between 2 and 5 years. The self-management training procedure focused on teaching the children: (a) to discriminate and identify appropriate versus inappropriate behavior, (b) to record the presence versus the absence of stereotypic behavior; (c) to exchange these recordings for reinforcers of their choosing; and (d) to engage in these behaviors in the absence of a treatment provider for periods of up to 1 week at a time. The results revealed that the children were able to use self-management procedures to reduce their stereotypic behavior in clinic, school, and community settings from baseline levels of 80% to 100% down to levels frequently approaching 0%. The results of this initial study showed that even very severely handicapped autistic children are likely to be able to use self-management techniques to modify even severely interfering behaviors.

The Broader Impact of Self-Management

Although the previous study showed that self-management could be used with severely handicapped autistic children, we also were concerned about assessing the likelihood of self-management techniques achieving a broader impact across behaviors, leading to more generalized behavior change. We now have reported numerous case histories and experimental studies in this area, assessing both generalization across settings and across target behaviors. Three articles (Koegel & Frea, 1993; Koegel & Koegel, 1988; Koegel, Koegel, & O'Neill, 1989) present case histories showing that when the self-management procedures described here and in our training manual were employed to treat individual behaviors ranging from disruptive behavior to hygiene skills to voice intonation, a broad degree of response generalization was achieved. By defining the behaviors and stimulus conditions such that they included broad classes of behavior (such as disruptive behavior) and broad classes of stimuli (such as people), it was possible to achieve large increases in general responsivity to the environment (such as increases in responding to social interactions, increases in initiating social interactions, increases in responsivity of complex multiple verbal cues, etc.). Such increased responsivity to the environment then provided additional natural learning opportunities (i.e., incidental learning) and environmental feedback, producing large degrees of behavior change.

In addition to these studies, we also conducted additional experimental analyses in this area using single-subject methodology. The first of these studies assessed three different target behaviors in two different settings. In this study (Stahmer & Schreibman, 1992), we used self-management to target appropriate play because this behavior is considered to be of broad developmental significance, associated with progress and success in school (e.g., Brown, 1960; Russo & Koegel, 1977) and with cognitive development (e.g., Fenson & Ramsay, 1981; Wehman, 1977). Three children participated in the study. They had chronological ages of 8, 12, and 13 years, and IQ scores of 43, 46, and 65. Each of these children was instructed in self-management using the procedures outlined in our self-management manual and used in the pilot study discussed earlier. The children received training in a clinic setting or in the home. Stimulus generalization to other settings and concomitant changes in self-stimulatory and other inappropriate behaviors (e.g., throwing play materials or staring blankly at the floor) were assessed. The results showed broad generalization effects. Specifically, although the children's baseline levels of appropriate play were low, once treatment was implemented at the designated point in the multiple baseline, the target behavior (appropriate play) changed dramatically. Of greater significance with respect to the purpose of this study is the fact that other behaviors (self-stimulation and other inappropriate behavior) also changed in the desired direction and in multiple settings. Thus, these results provide encouragement that broad gains are likely to be achieved by this type of intervention.

In a related pilot study, we targeted a child's responses to questions asked by others, and simultaneously recorded both appropriate (i.e., attempts to answer questions) and inappropriate (i.e., bizarre answers, stereotypic behavior, or running away) behaviors. When asked a question, the child was verbally unresponsive approximately half of the time during the baseline condition and he exhibited high levels of disruptive behavior. Verbal responses to questions were targeted through self-management by teaching the child to evaluate and record whether or not he made a verbal attempt to answer questions asked him by adults. Specifically, if he attempted to answer a question he pressed a wrist counter. If he exhibited a bizarre or inappropriate behavior, he did not press the wrist counter. Treatment was implemented in a clinic setting, and generalization measures on all behaviors were recorded in the clinic and in community settings without the presence of a treatment provider. Generalization occurred in all settings, but was not observed in the community settings until after he was instructed to engage in self-management in those settings. Concomitant changes in stereotypic and running away behaviors were observed without additional intervention.

These pilot studies suggest that broad changes in behavior are likely to occur if the children are taught to target broadly defined target behaviors across broadly defined stimulus conditions. If so, global behavioral changes seem likely with very minimal treatment provider contact.

The Feasibility of Parental Implementation of Self-Management

The studies described, suggest that a wide range of children is likely to show a broad range of behavior change with a self-management intervention. However, it is critical to the proposed research that parents be able to learn to teach this skill to their children. Although parents had participated in some aspects of the case histories and pilot studies described earlier, we wished to obtain data on a parent implementing self-management intervention without any other clinical assistance. Our preliminary data show that similar to the previous study on responsivity, when we targeted responsivity to questions asked by persons in the child's home setting with all of the treatment conducted by a parent without any other treatment provider contact in the home, we obtained similar results. Specifically, the mother was taught the procedures in our clinic, and then instructed to implement the procedures in her home. The data showed that at baseline the child was typically unresponsive to questions in his home, but following the parent's implementation of the self-management procedures, responsivity to questions increased to nearly 100%.

Implications

These data indicate that self-management treatment may be programmed to occur effectively in a broad range of settings in the absence of a treatment provider and likely can be implemented by parents. These results may be discussed with regard to several different practical and theoretical issues. First, the results indicate that a very broad application of the self-management strategy is possible and that this is likely to be a very profitable avenue for research, that is, even very severely handicapped children are quite likely to benefit from at least some aspects of the approach. Although we still do not know the exact lower limits where the approach is likely to fail, it now seems that the lower limits are quite low, and that the majority of autistic children will benefit. Second, given that self-management does work, in those instances the benefits of our Pivotal Response Training should be enhanced considerably. Because, as noted above, one of the major advantages of Pivotal Response Training is to increase motivation, it is important to note that many theorists have suggested that self-control should significantly enhance such effects. Specifically, researchers as varied as Harter (1978), Koegel and Egel (1979), Piaget (1952), Seligman (1972), Watson and Ramey (1972), and White (1959) all have suggested that when individuals bring behaviors and environmental consequences under their own control, there is greater benefit to their future performance than if the environmental consequences are under the control of a source other than themselves. Thus, problems such as learned helplessness should be reduced (Goetz, Schuler, & Sailor, 1983; Koegel & Mentis, 1985) and overall responsivity to the environment (especially to learning activities) should increase (O'Neill, 1987).

Limitations and Generalizability

We know that self-management treatment can be implemented effectively in a broad range of settings in the absence of a treatment provider and likely can be implemented by parents. However, although we may feel confident that even severely handicapped children can benefit from at least some aspects of the approach, we still do not know the exact lower limits where the approach is likely to fail. Our current pilot results suggest that some of the most cognitively and linguistically impaired children are having significant difficulty with the self-management program. Thus, we are attending closely to the specific characteristics of those children with whom the self-management intervention is minimally effective or perhaps ineffective. Although presently this information is useful in terms of treatment selection for these children (i.e., perhaps parent management is the treatment of choice for these most impaired children), in the future this information will lead to the development of refined self-management training techniques that will allow these children to benefit.

Accordingly, in recent work we have begun to modify our self-management technique to allow it to be effective with children for whom our standard technique has proven very difficult, ineffective, or both. We have noted that some of the children have great difficulty learning how to self-monitor and record their behavior. To work around this problem, we investigated the feasibility of using pictures (as opposed to verbal stimuli) in the self-management procedure (Pierce & Schreibman, 1994). Three children with autism were taught daily living skills (e.g., making lunch, dressing, setting the table) using a pictured sequence of the steps involved in completing the behavior. The children first chose a reinforcer and then were presented with a small photo book containing a picture for each step in the sequence. The children were taught to respond to the pictures in sequence so that at the end of the sequence the entire behavior was performed. The children take the book, open it, and perform the behavior indicated in the first picture. Then, they monitor their own behavior by turning to the next picture, until the sequence is completed. At the end of the sequence, a "smiley face" indicates the opportunity to self-reinforce. Using this procedure, the children learned to complete the target behaviors in the absence of a treatment provider and generalized their skills to different settings and target behaviors. This pictorial self-management procedure is one way to extend the generalizability of self-management as a treatment approach.

One important reason that we are optimistic about the generalizability of our self-management program is that it is implemented by parents. As has already been well documented in the behavioral literature, parent training is an important means of achieving generalization because the parents are in many of the children's environments and thus treatment is provided in a variety of settings, across a variety of behaviors, and across times of the day. However, it must be acknowledged that our research, as well as that of most other researchers, involves programs where parents voluntarily commit to participation in a research program, often in a university setting. These parents are thus motivated to enter the parent training program. In addition, most of these parents are literate and can benefit from our written training manuals. However, what we do not yet know is how our treatment may be differentially effective with parents who do not come to us but rather, for example, are randomly picked from schools to participate. We also do not know how effective our program would be if parents were illiterate and were provided the training via vocal instructions. Again, these points speak to the issue of generalizability of our training program.

Another issue, and one that is underrepresented in the parent training literature, is the issue of different ethnicities and cultures. It is certainly not surprising that cultural differences might affect how parents perceive, utilize, and evaluate our training programs. For instance, specific cultures differentially value target behaviors. Thus, a child's independence may be considered a very important treatment goal by one culture whereas another culture may find it of less significance. Parents of different cultures may find certain specific aspects of treatment more or less acceptable or easy to implement. The possibilities for variability here are almost endless and we need to address these issues if we are to maximize the generalization of our treatment applicability.

Recommendations

Given the issues discussed, it is clear what our next research emphases need to be. The issues of refining self-management procedures to affect wider applicability across children is crucial. Furthermore, a more detailed understanding of child and parent variables is essential. Both of these relate to improved generalization of treatment applicability and treatment effects.

On the basis of our research to date, and that of other researchers, we feel our future direction is clear. To provide the most effective and generalized treatment, we will need to identify the interaction of child, treatment, and parent–family variables so that ultimately we may be able to individually prescribe specific treatments for specific cases. Thus, child characteristics such as cognitive and verbal abilities may affect treatment presentation and success. Similarly, parent and family characteristics such as motivation, education level, stress, number of children, culture, social and financial resources, etc., may be expected to affect how the parents learn and implement treatment. We already know that different treatment procedures may have differential success with various child characteristics and parent–family variables. Therefore, what should be available in the future is a means for assessing these variables and how they interact so as to allow us to design and implement a treatment program that is maximally beneficial to the child and to the entire family. Fortunately, the behavioral approach to treatment, by definition, is designed to assess and refine the procedures continually. We anticipate that additional research along the lines dictated by our current efforts will make even greater advances toward improving the lives of these families.

REFERENCES

American Psychiatric Association. (1994). *Diagnostic and statistical manual of mental disorders* (4th ed.). Washington, DC: Author

Baer, M., Fowler, S. A., & Carden-Smith, L. (1984). Using reinforcement and independent-grading to promote and maintain task accuracy in a mainstreamed class. *Analysis and Intervention in Developmental Disabilities, 4,* 157–170.

Berk, R. A., & Berk, S. F. (1979). *Labor and leisure at home: Content and organization of the household day.* Beverly Hills, CA: Sage.

Bettelheim, B. (1967). *The empty fortress.* New York: Free Press.

Brown, J. (1960). Prognosis from presenting symptoms of preschool children with atypical development. *American Journal of Orthopsychiatry, 30,* 382–390.

Denckla, M. B., & James, L. S. (1991). An update on autism: A developmental disorder. *Pediatrics, 87*(May suppl.), 751–796.

Drabman, R. S., Spitalnik, R., & O'Leary, K. D. (1973). Teaching self-control to disruptive children. *Journal of Abnormal Psychology, 82,* 10–16.

Dunlap, G. (1984). The influence of task variation and maintenance tasks on the learning and affect of autistic children. *Journal of Experimental Child Psychology, 37,* 41–64.

Dunlap, G., Koegel, R. L., Johnson, J, & O'Neill, R. E. (1987). Maintaining performance of autistic clients in community settings with delayed contingencies. *Journal of Applied Behavior Analysis, 20,* 185–191.

Dunn, L. M., & Dunn, L. M. (1981). *Peabody Picture Vocabulary Test—Revised.* Circle Pines, MN: American Guidance Service, Inc.

Fenson, L., & Ramsay, R. (1981). Effects of modeling action sequences on the play of twelve-, fifteen-, and nineteen-month-old children. *Child Development, 52,* 1028–1036.

Foster, R., Giddan, J. J., & Stark, J. (1973). *Assessment of Children's Language Comprehension.* Palo Alto, CA: Consulting Psychologists Press.

Fowler, S. (1984). Introductory comments: The pragmatics of self-management for the developmentally disabled. *Analysis and Intervention in Developmental Disabilities, 4,* 85–89.

Freeman, B. J., & Ritvo, E. R. (1976). Parents as paraprofessionals. In E. R. Ritvo (Ed.), *Autism: Diagnosis, current research, and management* (pp. 277–285). New York: Spectrum Publications.

Gardner, W. I., Cole, C. L., Berry, K. L., & Nowinski, J. M. (1983). Reduction of disruptive behaviors in mentally retarded adults. *Behavior Modification, 7,* 76–96.

Goetz, L., Schuler, A., & Sailor, W. (1983). Motivational considerations in teaching language to severely handicapped students. In M. Hersen, V. Van Hasselt, & J. Matson (Eds.), *Behavior therapy for the developmentally physically disabled* (pp. 57–77). San Diego, CA: Academic Press.

Harter, S. (1978). Effectance motivation reconsidered: Toward a developmental model. *Human Development, 21,* 34–64.

Holroyd, J. (1974). Questionnaire on Resources and Stress: An instrument to measure family response to a handicapped family member. *Journal of Community Psychology, 2,* 92–94.

Holroyd, J. (1982). *Questionnaire on Resources and Stress.* Unpublished manuscript.

Holroyd, J., Brown, N., Wikler, L., & Simmons, J. Q. (1975). Stress in families of institionalized and noninstitutionalized autistic children. *Journal of Community Psychology, 3,* 26–31.

Holroyd, J., & McArthur, D. (1976). Mental retardation and stress on the parents: A contrast between Down's syndrome and childhood autism. *American Journal of Mental Deficiency, 80,* 431–436.

Horner, R. H., & Brigham, T. A. (1979, February). The effects of self-management procedures on the study behavior of two retarded children. *Education and Training of the Mentally Retarded, 14*, 18–24.

Kanner, L. (1943). Autistic disturbances of affective contact. *The Nervous Child, 3*, 217–250.

Koegel, R. L., Camarata, S. M., & Koegel, L. K. (in press). Aggression and non-compliance: Behavior modification through naturalistic language remediation. In J. L. Matson (Ed.), *Autism in children and adults: Etiology, assessment, and intervention.* Sycamore, IL: Sycamore Press.

Koegel, R. L., Dyer, K., & Bell, L. K. (1987). The influence of child preferred activities on autistic children's social behavior. *Journal of Applied Behavior Analysis, 20*, 243–252.

Koegel, R. L., & Egel, A. (1979). Motivating autistic children. *Journal of Abnormal Psychology, 88*, 418–426.

Koegel, R. L., & Frea, W. D. (1993). Treatment of social behavior in autism through the modification of pivotal social skills. *Journal of Applied Behavior Analysis, 26*, 369–377.

Koegel, R. L., Glahn, T. J., & Nieminen, G. S. (1978). Generalization of parent training results. *Journal of Applied Behavior Analysis, 11*, 95–109.

Koegel, R. L., & Koegel, L. K. (1988). Generalized responsivity and pivotal behaviors. In R H. Horner, G. Dunlap, & R. L. Koegel (Eds.), *Generalization and maintenance: Life-style changes in applied settings* (pp. 41–66). Baltimore: Paul H. Brookes Publishing Co.

Koegel, R. L., & Koegel, L. K. (1990). Extended reductions in stereotypic behavior through self-management in multiple community settings. *Journal of Applied Behavior Analysis, 23*, 119–127.

Koegel, R. L., & Koegel, L. K., & O'Neill, R. E. (1989). Generalization in the treatment of autism. In L. V. McReynolds, & J. E. Spradlin (Eds.), *Generalization strategies in the treatment of communication disorders* (pp. 116–131). Toronto, Canada: B. C. Decker Inc.

Koegel, R. L., Koegel, L. K., & Parks, D. R. (1990). *How to teach self-management skills to individuals with severe handicaps: A training manual.* University of California: Santa Barbara.

Koegel, R. L., & Mentis, M. (1985). Motivation in childhood autism: Can they or won't they? *Journal of Child Psychology and Psychiatry, 26*, 185–191.

Koegel, R. L., O'Dell, M. C., & Dunlap, G. (1988). Producing speech use in nonverbal autistic children by reinforcing attempts. *Journal of Autism and Developmental Disorders, 18*, 525–538.

Koegel, R. L., O'Dell, M. C., & Koegel, L. K. (1987). A natural language teaching paradigm for nonverbal autistic children. *Journal of Autism and Developmental Disorders, 17*, 187–200.

Koegel, R. L., & Rincover, A. (1977). Some research on the difference between generalization and maintenance in extra-therapy settings. *Journal of Applied Behavior Analysis, 10*, 1–16.

Koegel, R. L., & Schreibman, L. (1977). Teaching autistic children to respond to simultaneous multiple cues. *Journal of Experimental Child Psychology, 24,* 299–311.

Koegel, R. L., Schreibman, L., Britten, K. R., Burke, J. C., & O'Neill, R. E. (1982). A comparison of parent training to direct clinic treatment. In R. L. Koegel, A. Rincover, & A. L. Egel (Eds.), *Educating and understanding autistic children* (pp. 260–279). San Diego, CA: College Hill Press.

Koegel, R. L., Schreibman, L., Good, A., Cerniglia, L., Murphy, C., & Koegel, L. L. (1989). *How to teach pivotal behaviors to children with autism: A training manual.* University of California: Santa Barbara.

Koegel, R. L., Schreibman, L., Johnson, J., O'Neill, R. E., & Dunlap, G. (1984). Collateral effects of parent training on families with autistic children. In R. G. Dangel & R. A. Polster (Eds.), *Parent training: Foundations of research and practice* (pp. 358–378). New York: Guilford Press.

Koegel, R. L., Schreibman, L., Loos, L. M., Dirlich-Wilhelm, H., Dunlap, G., Robbins, F. R., & Plienis, A. J. (1992). Consistent stress profiles in mothers of children with autism. *Journal of Autism and Developmental Disorders, 22,* 205–216.

Koegel, R. L., Schreibman, L., O'Neill, R. E., & Burke, J. C. (1983). The personality and family-interaction characteristics of parents of autistic children. *Journal of Consulting and Clinical Psychology, 51,* 683–692.

Koegel, R. L., & Williams, J. (1980). Direct vs. indirect response–reinforcer relationships in teaching autistic children. *Journal of Abnormal Child Psychology, 4,* 536–547.

Laski, K. E., Charlop, M. H., & Schreibman, L. (1988). Training parents to use the natural language paradigm to increase their autistic children's speech. *Journal of Applied Behavior Analysis, 21,* 391–400.

Lovaas, O. I., Koegel, R. L., & Schreibman, L. (1979). Stimulus overselectivity in autism: A review of research. *Psychological Bulletin, 86,* 1236–1254.

Lovaas, O. I., Koegel, R. L., Simmons, J. Q., & Long, J. S. (1973). Some generalization and follow-up measures on autistic children in behavior therapy. *Journal of Applied Behavior Analysis, 6,* 131–166.

Moes, D., Koegel, R. L., & Schreibman, L. (1993). *Behavior therapy paradigms and parenting stress.* Paper presented at the 1993 Annual Convention of the Association for the Advancement of Behavior Therapy, Atlanta, GA.

Nelson, R. O., & Hayes, S. C. (1981). Theoretical explanations for reactivity in self-monitoring. *Behavior Modification, 5,* 3–14.

O'Brien, T. P., Riner, L. S., & Budd, K. (1983). The effects of a child's self-evaluation program on compliance with parental instructions in the home. *Journal of Applied Behavior Analysis, 16,* 69–79.

O'Dell, M. C., Dunlap, G., & Koegel, R. L. (1983, August). *The importance of reinforcing verbal attempts during speech training with nonverbal children.* Paper presented at the 91st Annual Convention of the American Psychological Association, Anaheim, CA.

O'Dell, M. C., & Koegel, R. L. (1981). *The differential effects of two methods of promoting speech in nonverbal autistic children.* Paper presented at a meeting of the American Speech–Language–Hearing Association, Los Angeles, CA.

O'Neill, R. E. (1987). *Environmental interactions of normal children and children with autism.* Unpublished doctoral dissertation, University of California, Santa Barbara.

Piaget, J. (1952). *The origins of intelligence in children.* Madison, CT: International Universities Press.

Pierce, K., & Schreibman, L. (1994). Teaching children with autism daily living skills in unsupervised settings through pictorial self-management. *Journal of Applied Behavior Analysis, 27,* 471–481.

Pierce, K., & Schreibman, L. (1995). Increasing complex social behaviors in children with autism: Effects of peer-implemented Pivotal Response Training. *Journal of Applied Behavior Analysis, 28,* 285–295.

Rimland, B. (1964). *Infantile autism.* New York: Appleton-Century-Crofts.

Runco, M. A., & Schreibman, L. (1983). Parental judgments of behavior therapy efficacy with autistic children: A social validation. *Journal of Autism and Developmental Disorders, 13,* 237–248.

Runco, M. A., & Schreibman, L. (1988). Children's judgments of autism and social validation of behavior therapy efficacy. *Behavior Therapy, 19,* 565–576.

Russo, D. C., & Koegel, R. L. (1977). A method for integrating an autistic child into a normal public school classroom. *Journal of Applied Behavior Analysis, 10,* 579–590.

Rutter, M. (1971). The description and classification of infantile autism. In D. W. Churchill, G. D. Alpern, & M. K. DeMyer (Eds.), *Infantile autism* (pp. 8–28). Springfield, IL: Charles C Thomas.

Sagotsky, G., Patterson, C. J., & Lepper, M. R. (1978). Training children's self-control: A field experiment in self-monitoring and goal setting in the classroom. *Journal of Experimental Child Psychology, 25,* 242–253.

Schreibman, L. (1983). Are we forgetting the parent in parent-training? *The Behavior Therapist, 6,* 107–109.

Schreibman, L. (1988). *Autism.* Newbury Park, CA: Sage.

Schreibman, L., Charlop, M. H., & Koegel, R. L. (1982). Teaching autistic children to use extra-stimulus prompts. *Journal of Experimental Child Psychology, 33,* 475–491.

Schreibman, L., Kaneko, W. M., & Koegel, R. L. (1991). Positive affect of parents of autistic children: A comparison across two teaching techniques. *Behavior Therapy, 22,* 479–490.

Schreibman, L., & Koegel, R. L. (1989). *Assessment of subareas of high stress in mothers of autistic children: A comparison across three populations.* Paper presented at the 15th Annual Convention of the Association for Behavior Analysis, Milwaukee, WI.

Schreibman, L., Koegel, R. L., Mills, J. I., & Burke, J. C. (1981). The social validation of behavior therapy with autistic children. *Behavior Therapy, 12*, 610–624.

Schreibman, L., Runco, M. A., Mills, J. I., & Koegel, R. L. (1982). Teachers' judgments of improvements in autistic children in behavior therapy: A social validation. In R. L. Koegel, A. Rincover, & A. L. Egel (Eds.), *Educating and understanding autistic children* (pp. 78–87). San Diego, CA: College Hill Press.

Seligman, M. E. P. (1972). Learned helplessness. *Annual Review of Medicine, 23*, 407–412.

Shapiro, E. S., & Klein, R. D. (1980). Self-management of classroom behavior with retarded/disturbed children. *Behavior Modification, 4*, 83–97.

Shapiro, E. S., McGonigle, J. J., & Ollendick, T. H. (1980). An analysis of self-assessment and self-reinforcement in a self-managed token economy with mentally retarded children. *Applied Research in Mental Retardation, 1*, 227–240.

Sparrow, S. S., Balla, D. A., & Cicchetti, D. V. (1984). *Vineland Adaptive Behavior Scales*. Circle Pines, MN: American Guidance Service, Inc.

Stahmer, A. C., & Schreibman, L. (1992). Teaching children with autism appropriate play in unsupervised environments using a self-management treatment package. *Journal of Applied Behavior Analysis, 25*, 447–459.

Stokes, T. F., & Baer, D. M. (1977). An implicit technology of generalization. *Journal of Applied Behavior Analysis, 10*, 347–367.

Sugai, G., & Rowe, D. (1984). The effect of self-recording on out-of-seat behavior of an EMR student. *Education and Training of the Mentally Retarded, 19*, 23–28.

Turnbull, H. R., III, Bateman, D. F., & Turnbull, A. P. (1993). Family empowerment. In P. Wehman (Ed.), *The ADA mandate for social change* (pp. 157–173). Baltimore: Paul H. Brookes.

Turner, B. L. (1978). *The effects of choice of stimulus materials on interest in the remediation process and the generalized use of language training*. Unpublished master's thesis, University of California, Santa Barbara.

Watson, J. S., & Ramey, C. T. (1972). Reactions to response-contingent stimulation in early infancy. *Merrill–Palmer Quarterly, 18*, 219–227.

Wehman, P. (1977). Research on leisure time and the severely developmentally disabled. *Rehabilitation Literature, 38*, 98–105.

White, R. W. (1959). Motivation reconsidered: The concept of competence. *Psychological Review, 66*, 297–333.

Wing, L. (1972). *Autistic children: A guide for parents*. New York: Brunner/Mazel.

23

THE CHILD WITH AUTISM AS AN ACTIVE COMMUNICATIVE PARTNER: CHILD-INITIATED STRATEGIES FOR IMPROVING COMMUNICATION AND REDUCING BEHAVIOR PROBLEMS

LYNN KERN KOEGEL and ROBERT L. KOEGEL

Early communication problems often antedate serious psychosocial problems and are therefore being recognized as a major health problem for young children. Scientific research is beginning to suggest that early intervention that focuses on communication may have the benefit of preventing a wide variety of problems that may directly or indirectly correlate with difficulties in communication. The purpose of this chapter is to discuss techniques that extend presently available language intervention procedures for children with autism that emphasize the adult as the initiator of language, and to focus instead on interventions that teach the child to be an active communicative partner in the dyad. Pilot data are presented on important linguistic structures that show improvement as a result of such language intervention, in addition to concomitant improvements in a number of other disruptive and interfering behaviors. These data suggest that, for children with autism, treatment is vastly enhanced if the children are recruited as active participants in the habilitation process. By providing

Preparation of this manuscript was supported in part by U.S. Public Health Service Research Grant MH28210 from the National Institute of Mental Health; U.S. Department of Education, National Institute on Disability and Rehabilitation Research Cooperative Agreement G0087C0234; and by U.S. Department of Education Research Grant H023C30070. Correspondence concerning this chapter should be directed to Dr. Lynn Kern Koegel, Graduate School of Education, University of California, Santa Barbara, CA 93106-9490.

them with self-initiated procedures to access language learning, the need for extensive adult initiations is greatly reduced, with widespread language improvements and increases in independence and autonomy for the child.

GOALS AND ISSUES

Communication difficulties are pathognomonic to children with autism and have been reported to precipitate many severe behavior problems. Amelioration of communication problems in young children with autism is particularly important, as the literature has clearly demonstrated that children who fail to meet developmental milestones in the area of expressive language skills by the age of 2 are very likely to exhibit a variety of related disabilities, including delayed phonological development (Paul & Jennings, 1992), delayed receptive language skills, and deficits in socialization (Paul, 1991). Perhaps, more alarming is the fact that longitudinal studies suggest that many preschoolers with language disabilities continue to present speech and language delays over extended periods of time (Aram & Nation, 1980) and are at risk for social and academic difficulties. One follow-up study that assessed children diagnosed as having language impairments (without hearing impairment, or neurological or craniofacial abnormalities) during the preschool years found significant academic, social, and behavior problems 10 years later. In fact, 89% of the children received some type of specialized service such as tutoring or special class placement, or required grade retention. Furthermore, the majority of these children were rated as being less socially competent and having more behavioral problems than their peers (Aram, Ekelman, & Nation, 1984).

These statistics have led researchers to assess variables relating to how children learn language. Logically, focus has been on mother–child interactions and maternal input to toddlers. Initially, authors suggested that expressive language difficulties may result from language impoverished environments. Although this certainly may be the case in children who suffer from neglect, there is an accumulating database suggesting that children demonstrating language delays may be providing their mothers with a different set of stimuli to which to respond, which in turn affects the mother's input to the child. For example, Whitehurst et al. (1988) found that even though mothers' linguistic input to their children with language delays was different from age-matched peers, it was similar to that of mothers of children who had the same expressive language age. One specific difference is the number of expansions and extensions that adults provide to their children. Mothers of children with language delays do not provide expansions and extensions as often as mothers of typical language developers. However, if one assesses the proportion of expansions and extensions to child utterances (as opposed to the proportion of maternal utterances containing expansions and extensions), the difference disappears (Paul & Elwood, 1991). That is, when children with language delays give their mothers something to expand, the mothers do so, but this cycle occurs much less frequently than with typical language developers. Therefore, it is becoming increasingly evident that children with language disabilities converse less frequently and provide adults with fewer sophisticated structures to which to respond, thereby limiting their ability to access environmental learning. This reduced conversational interaction and sophistication in the very early years can cause problems for future language and discourse development (cf. Yoder, Davies, Bishop, & Munson, 1994).

As a result of this apparent lack of motivation to communicate, a major change arose in approaching language intervention; one that differed in emphasis from the more traditional, highly imitative, and adult-controlled procedures. This change emphasized the reciprocal interactive nature of communication and, therefore, accentuated the child's role as an active communicative partner in the dyad (Camarata & Nelson, 1992; Hart & Risley, 1968; Kaiser, Yoder, & Keetz, 1992; Koegel, O'Dell, & Koegel, 1987; Yoder, Kaiser, Alpert, & Fischer, 1993). This represented a shift from the previous techniques that failed to consider the child's role while developing goals, selecting stimulus items, etc.

One successful approach incorporating these techniques has been an emphasis on improving the child's motivation to communicate. This is frequently accomplished by arranging the child's environment to increase opportunities to use language, particularly to gain access to desired items or privileges. For example, Yoder et al. (1993) showed that following the child's lead, whereby teaching episodes occurred only when the child had sustained attention to a target object or intentionally communicated about the target object, resulted in considerably greater noun acquisition than when the treatment provider intrusively recruited the child's attention and then taught. The same effect was demonstrated with children with specific language impairment (Camarata & Nelson, 1992). In that study, children were taught structures during play interactions that *they* were involved in as opposed to the activity the clinician had chosen. The results indicated that with the exception of infrequently used target language structures, the children learned new language structures more rapidly during the play activity they were involved in rather than the clinician-chosen condition. Table 1 summarizes the major variables in this approach to treatment (Koegel et al., 1987). The procedures appear to be especially suited to providing treatment for children in the early stages of language learning, particularly for children who do not verbalize frequently and who are learning an initial lexicon. However, there are several linguistic areas that need to be emphasized if communicative competence is to be achieved.

First, a high degree of clinician control, which often involves withholding a desired item until the child requests it, can result in excessive

TABLE 1
Differences Between the Analog and the Natural Language Paradigm
(NLP)

Item	Analog condition	NLP condition
Stimulus items	Chosen by clinician Repeated until criterion is met Phonologically easy to produce, irrespective of functionality in the natural environment	Chosen by child Varied every few trials Age-appropriate items found in child's natural environment
Prompts	Manual (e.g., touch tip of tongue or hold lips together)	Clinician repeats item
Interaction	Clinician holds up stimulus item; stimulus item not functional within interaction	Clinician and child play with stimulus item (i.e., stimulus item is functional within interaction)
Response	Correct responses or successive approximations reinforced	Looser shaping contingency to reinforce attempts to respond verbally (except self-stimulation)
Consequences	Edible reinforcers paired with social reinforcers	Natural reinforcer (e.g., opportunity to play with the item) paired with social reinforcers

and restrictive control of the interaction. This can present several problems. For example, the child may become excessively dependent on the clinician prompt (e.g., withholding the item, or asking the child "What do you want?") before an expressive utterance is emitted. Furthermore, researchers have shown that for children with language disabilities, many of these opportunities for child language use do not occur, or occur infrequently, if treatment providers and other significant individuals in the child's natural environment are not specifically taught to provide or increase opportunities for such language interactions (Peck, 1985; Sigafoos, Roberts, Kerr, Couzens, & Baglioni, 1994). Thus, without specific training, paraprofessionals and even highly competent treatment providers may not provide adequate opportunities necessary for child language gains.

In addition, although some significant increases in language and vocabulary acquisition may be evidenced with adult-driven approaches, the end result is that the child is still language-limited, in that the vocabulary growth under such procedures typically encompasses only highly desired items and the child is not using a wide variety of linguistic forms. This is important when one considers that the utterances of children with autism and other language delays lack both adequate quantitative and qualitative aspects as compared to typical children's language (Paul & Shiffer, 1991; Wetherby & Prutting, 1984; Yoder et al., 1994). Very few studies in the area of autism have focused on the qualitative aspects of language, such as the types of communicative intentions a child uses. The use of child initiations that further linguistic competence, increase spontaneous language use, and further topic continuity are areas where deficits seem to persist for children with autism, and decisively warrant further research.

The specific aim of this chapter is to discuss pilot work that suggests that teaching young children with autism to evoke language learning from their environments may be especially likely to result in rapid language growth. Preliminary research also suggests that when such efforts are made to improve self-initiated communicative strategies, desirable concomitant changes are likely to occur, including reductions in aggression, self-stimulation, self-injury, and tantrums.

TREATMENT PLAN

Communication treatment for individuals with autism needs to be comprehensive, coordinated, and multifaceted. There are four components that we consider pivotal if communicative competence is to be achieved. First, motivating the child to solicit language teaching interactions from the natural environment through self-initiated queries both accelerates language development and reduces the need for adult-driven treatments. For example, spontaneous information-seeking strategies seem to be necessary for language development and provide reciprocal interactions that enhance social skills. Second, providing the child with self-initiated communicative skills to replace disruptive behaviors needs to be an ongoing process; determining the communicative function of disruptive behaviors and replacing them with communicatively equivalent appropriate behaviors improves behavior through communication and reduces the need for punitive procedures. Third, equipping the child with tools, such as self-management, that promote widespread use of newly learned behaviors, fosters generalization of responding. Teaching self-management has the end goal of providing the child with a means of self-initiating and self-evaluating behavior in any given setting in the absence of a treatment provider. Fourth, improving intelligibility so that the child can be understood by adults and peers appears to be important to reduce frustration and increase the likelihood of maintaining reciprocal interactions. Strategies for achieving each of these four integrated goals are described below. Then, following these descriptions, in the Treatment Outcomes section, preliminary data are presented to give an indication of the typical length of time for treatment and the type of results to be expected.

Self-Initiated Queries

One component of our research relates to instating or increasing linguistic structures, such as queries, that will result in access to additional learning. Therefore, in our program a variety of queries such as, "What's that?" "Where is it?" and "Whose is it?" are targeted for child initiations. "What" and "Where" questions emerge within the second year of life and "Whose" appears within the third year of life in most typical language developers. These structures, often used for both social purposes and as a means of accruing additional linguistic information, appear to be important for widespread communication development.

Teaching "What's That?"

One component focuses on teaching "What's that?" to increase expressive vocabularies (noun labels). The initial treatment step focuses on improving the child's motivation to engage in self-initiated queries by incorporating motivational components (see Table 1) proven to be effective in improving responsivity. To do this, we analyze the children's pretreatment videotapes for items that are likely to be highly desired, such as pieces to favorite puzzles, food treats, etc. To encourage the children to use the queries, the items are hidden in a bag and the children are prompted to ask, "What's that?" and then are shown the item. The prompt is faded gradually until the children are frequently emitting the question during the session. Next, before the desired item is shown to the children, they are prompted to repeat the name of the item after the clinician answers them. The prompt to repeat the label is then gradually faded. At this point, the session's dialogue may resemble the following:

Child: "What dat?"
Clinician: "It's an A." (Said while removing a puzzle piece from the bag.)
Child: "A."
Clinician: Shows the child the puzzle piece (the child may take the puzzle piece if he or she desires).

Once the child is asking the question and repeating the noun at a fast rate, new (neutral) items, with unknown labels, are gradually introduced into the sessions. These items, which appear to have no special appeal to the child on the basis of pretreatment analysis and testing, are gradually added until almost all neutral items are presented. In addition, the bag is gradually faded so that unknown items are merely sitting around the room. This is an important step, because it represents the transition between the use of only highly desired items, to the use of a larger variety of items to promote the child's general curiosity about the environment.

Teaching "Where Is It?"

To expand the child's self-initiated questions to later emerging forms, a second procedure focuses on teaching the child to ask "Where" questions to access preposition use from others. To do this, the child's favorite items are selected and hidden in *specific* locations; the child is prompted to ask "Where is it?"; the adult tells the child the location of the item and allows the child to take it from that location. Once this form of question-asking is at a stable rate, the child is prompted to repeat the preposition before access is provided. A typical dialogue follows:

Child: "Where cracker?"
Clinician: "Under the napkin."
Child: "Under."
Clinician: "Right, it's under."
Child: Looks under the napkin and takes the cracker.

As with the first question type, all of the children are taught to use "Where" questions under a variety of conditions to elicit learning of a variety of prepositions (e.g., in, on, under, behind, in front, etc.).

Teaching "Whose Is It?"

A third procedure focuses on teaching "whose is it" to provide the child with a self-initiated tool to learn the expressive use of the possessives, "yours" and "mine." To accomplish this, parents bring in a variety of items that their child clearly associates with a particular member of the family. The child is prompted to ask, "Whose is it?"; the clinician responds and gives the child the item. Eventually, the child is prompted to repeat the possessive form. A sample dialogue resembles the following:

Child: "Whose is it?"
Clinician: "It's Mommy's." (Mother holds up her purse.)
Child: "Mommy's purse."
Clinician: "Right, it's Mommy's." (Gives child the purse.)

Teaching "yours" and "mine" is accomplished in the same manner. Highly desired objects are used (e.g., candies, favorite toys); however, when the clinician says, "It's yours," the child is prompted to say "mine," and then is given the item. This reversal has been noted to be particularly difficult for children with autism to acquire, but using highly desired objects greatly facilitates acquisition.

Functional Assessment and Functional Communication

Preliminary research suggests that self-initiated queries, such as those described above, are extremely successful in expanding linguistic skills;

however, children with autism seem to need additional skills to deal with existing "crisis situations" that have developed and been maintained as a result of their failure to use appropriate communication. Child-initiated verbalizations that occur frequently in typically developing children, such as strategies to seek attention (e.g., "Look mommy!" or "Mommy!"), request actions (e.g., "Help!"), and request clarification (e.g., "What?" or "Huh?"), occur at a much lower frequency in children with language disabilities (Paul & Shiffer, 1991). Instead, children with language disabilities often use inappropriate and disruptive behaviors to meet these needs (Carr & Durand, 1985; Horner & Budd, 1985). The communicative function can be determined for approximately 80% of disruptive behaviors, and then functionally equivalent behaviors can be developed to reduce or eliminate them. The purpose of a functional analysis is to attempt to determine why a disruptive or inappropriate behavior occurs and to replace the undesired behavior with an equivalent appropriate communicative behavior. To analyze a behavior functionally, one must operationally describe the undesirable behavior(s), predict the times and situations in which the behavior(s) will and will not be performed across the range of typical daily routines, and define the function(s) or maintaining variables that the undesirable behavior(s) produce for the individual (Frea, Koegel, & Koegel, 1994; O'Neill, Horner, Albin, Storey, & Sprague, 1989).

Our pilot work suggests that parents can be extremely useful as adjuncts in the functional analysis process. In a preliminary study, parents collected data relating to four areas (see Figure 1). First, they describe the disruptive behavior (e.g., hit, turned off light, threw toy, etc.), the time, and the place in which the particular behavior(s) occur. Second, parents note what happens immediately before the occurrence of the disruptive act (a checklist is provided so that the parents can check a box that contains likely setting events, such as the child being alone or ignored). Third, parents record what occurs after the disruptive behavior (a checklist is provided that contains likely consequences of the child's behavior, such as engaging in actions that provide the child with attention). The final section of the recording sheet contains a checklist with items that attempt to evaluate and understand why the disruptive behavior occurs. This checklist provides common reasons for disruptive behavior including: (a) to get out of something, (b) a transition, (c) to obtain something, (d) for attention, (e) to avoid a person or a place, or (f) another reason not listed that the parent needs to specify. In Figure 1, the function most commonly hypothesized by the parents was that the child was being disruptive to obtain attention.

In such a case, the child might then be taught appropriate replacement communicative behaviors, such as saying "Look!" or "Let's play!," to provide the child with an efficient form of appropriate verbal communication that is likely to be effective in obtaining attention. The goal is to

Date: Sept. 23

BEHAVIORS

	Threw toy	Hit Mom	Had tantrum	Hit child at park	Grabbed phone				
Time	9:00	9:30	10:00	3:00	5:00				
Place	Home Kitchen	Living room	Bedroom	Park	Kitchen				

Before

Told to do nothing			X						
Change in activity									
Moved									
Alone									
Interrupted									
Other _____	X	X		X	X				

After

Given attention									
Given something									
Lost something									
Removed from area				X					
Ignored			X						
Punished	X	X		X					
Other _____									

WHY

Get out of . . .			X						
Transition									
To obtain . . .									
Attention	X	X		X	X				
Avoid (person or place)									
Other _____									

Figure 1. Example of data sheet for functional analysis.

reach the point where the child will self-initiate the appropriate verbal behavior when the need for that particular function (to obtain attention) arises under natural conditions. Parents work to teach the replacement behavior on a daily basis (several times a day) when a disruptive behavior is *not* occurring. The child is also prompted to engage in the appropriate replacement behavior when disruptive behavior is likely to occur.

Self-Management

A third area in which children with autism seem to have reduced communicative abilities is in the area of self-management. Typically, reduced responsivity and failure to maintain the continuity of verbal interactions result in an inability to receive appropriate environmental feedback. Without environmental feedback, speakers are unable to adjust their behavior appropriately according to ongoing interactions.

Some preliminary research (cf. Koegel & Frea, 1993; Koegel, Koegel, Hurley, & Frea, 1992) demonstrated that increases in fluent discourse can be accomplished by teaching self-monitoring skills to children with autism. One way to accomplish this is to provide the child with a wrist counter (e.g., an inexpensive golf counter purchased from a sporting goods store or a department store). The child is taught to record a point on the wrist counter following every appropriate (verbal) response during a communicative interaction. The child earns self-selected rewards for gradually increasing the numbers of responses. Once the child is able to record considerable amounts of behavior independently, he or she is taught to solicit his or her own rewards. Finally, self-management of fluent responsivity during communicative interactions is extended to the home, community, and school settings in the absence of a treatment provider.

Ultimately, the child learns to monitor appropriate socio-linguistic responses with peers at school (e.g., when friends ask, "Are you buying lunch today?"), with parents at home (e.g., when parents ask, "What did you do at school today?"), and with adults in the community (e.g., when the grocer asks, "Do you want a bag?"). The major goal of this portion of the treatment is to teach the child to maintain a fluid involvement in the conversational interaction, so he or she can more effectively initiate contextually relevant verbal contributions. Our preliminary data focusing directly on initiations suggest that even very young children with autism can learn to initiate social communicative interactions successfully, by simply being prompted to self-monitor appropriate initiations (e.g., asking a peer "Wanna play?"). We are also beginning to teach children to use topic continuing questions and reflections through self-management. For example, if a communicative partner is talking about a video game, the child with autism is taught, through self-management, to respond by asking questions that reflect the previous conversation (e.g., "So, you like that game?").

Speech Intelligibility

A final important area that needs to be addressed with many children with autism and other speech delays, particularly while child-initiated strategies are taught, is speech intelligibility. Children with severe language delays typically have much smaller repertoires of consonants than their peers, which leads to a greater degree of unintelligibility in their attempts to communicate. This issue has led us to study procedures to improve the treatment of speech intelligibility, so that attempts to use new or existing structures are not disregarded because of adults' and peers' failure to understand the child. The procedures developed approximate closely the way in which typical language-learners appear to acquire phonological skills from their parents. That is, studies of speech input to typically developing children suggest only that parents speak more slowly and articulate more clearly when speaking to young children (Bernstein-Ratner, 1983; Malsheen, 1980; Stoel-Gammon, 1983). On the basis of these premises, we have begun some pilot studies that suggest that the general naturalistic procedures used in motivating language use (see Table 1) may also produce more efficient learning when applied to the area of speech intelligibility.

These procedures include selecting stimulus items that contain the target speech sound from a pool of items readily available in the child's natural environments, according to the child's preference. Also, instead of presenting individual stimulus items serially until the child reaches criterion on that item, a pool of stimulus items containing the target phonological sound are presented so that items can be varied according to the child's interests. Finally, treatment is conducted within the context of natural play interactions.

For example, if a child's target sound is /f/, we pick a number of different highly desired items containing that target sound. One child liked balls, so we chose a foam ball, a football, a funny ball, etc. He had to request the particular ball he wanted to throw it into a basketball hoop. He was given feedback for clear attempts (the target sound was repeated by the clinician using the correct pronunciation), and the child was rewarded with the opportunity to throw the ball.

TREATMENT OUTCOMES: PRELIMINARY STUDIES

The results of our preliminary research suggest that teaching self-initiated language use can be an extremely effective treatment procedure. We have now collected pilot data on the effectiveness of child-initiated interactions, functional assessment, functional communication, self-management procedures, and speech intelligibility procedures.

Self-Initiated Queries

In a first study (Koegel, 1993), we taught three children with significant language delays and associated severe behavior problems (e.g., self-injury, aggression, etc.) to ask, "What's that?" in response to unfamiliar items with unknown labels. Prior to the start of treatment, the children typically used no queries at all and had extremely limited expressive vocabularies. The purpose of this study was not only to teach the children to use queries but also to assess the effect of this information-seeking strategy on subsequent language skills (in this study, expressive vocabulary development). Results demonstrated that all the children learned to use the query, "What's that?" and all demonstrated significant increases in expressive vocabulary as a result of this self-initiated strategy. The children who participated in this research were able to learn the query in 1 to 2 sessions, and completion of the treatment was typically accomplished after 8 to 15 sessions. By that time, the children were learning an average of 6 words per hour of treatment. Furthermore, upon completion of the clinic sessions, generalization data demonstrated that all of the children continued to use the query appropriately with their mothers at home, and the resulting maternal response (labeling) also resulted in new vocabulary acquisition for the children. In many cases the children were learning as many as eight new vocabulary words per hour at home. This was an especially important outcome, as pretreatment baseline assessments indicated that the children *never* used these queries with their mothers, and evidenced no new vocabulary acquisition at all.

A second preliminary study attempted to teach the children to ask "Where is it?" to access prepositions. The children all acquired the query during the first session and showed generalized use of the query to acquire two to four prepositions after 4 half-hour sessions. Furthermore, cumulative acquisition of other prepositions continued after subsequent sessions. Similarly, the children who participated in a preliminary study learned to ask "Whose is it?" in one to two sessions, and probes after every four sessions (2 hours of treatment) indicated that the children learned the query to acquire possessives in an average of 10 half-hour sessions. We are now assessing the possibility of expanding temporal verb use and diversity of verbs through child-initiated queries.

Finally, it was interesting to note that prior to the implementation of treatment, the children demonstrated high levels of disruptive behavior, such as self-injury, aggression, and self-stimulation. In contrast, following the implementation of treatment, all of the children demonstrated decreased levels of these behavior problems, suggesting that their ability to take control over learning may have decreased the frustration involved in such interactions.

Functional Assesment and Functional Communication

The second area of pilot studies focused on teaching a child-initiated strategy to meet needs that were being communicatively expressed through disruptive behavior. One pilot study focused on using collaborative parent–professional consultation to conduct functional analyses to assess variables related to problem behaviors. On the basis of functional assessments of problem behaviors, parents taught their children self-initiated strategies that they could use in their natural daily environments.

For example, data from assessment sheets, such as those shown in Figure 1, indicated that one child was disruptive (engaging in behaviors such as aggression, throwing objects, and screaming) when he wanted to obtain attention from his grandparents (with whom he lived). The functionally equivalent verbal self-initiation that he learned was to say, "Look, Nana," whenever he wanted attention from his grandmother. Another nonverbal child appeared to be engaging in disruptive behavior whenever he had to transition from one task he was involved in to another. Every time he was told that the activity was going to be changed, he engaged in a tantrum. This child was taught to hold up his hand to indicate that he wanted to wait "just a second," so he could rapidly finish whatever activity he had started before he needed to begin transitioning. Once the children begin to self-initiate such functionally equivalent appropriate communications, the disruptive behavior(s) with the same communicative intent were significantly reduced or eliminated without any direct treatment. For example, one child dumped his plate off the table during every meal. Data indicated that this usually occurred after the child had eaten most of his dinner. The strategy to deal with this disturbing behavior was to teach him to say, "I'm done" when he finished his meal. This functionally equivalent, self-initiated phrase, developed entirely by his parents, eliminated the disruptive behavior problem completely.

Preliminary data collected suggest that some children acquire the replacement behaviors within the first week of treatment and show dramatic decreases in disruptive behavior. Other children show gradual but steady increases in the use of the replacement behavior and gradual decreases in the disruptive behavior.

Self-Management

The third area of pilot data suggests that self-management may be an extremely useful self-initiated strategy for ensuring widespread use of communicative behaviors. For example, in an initial study, four children who were very unresponsive to others (i.e., answered others' questions less than half of the time and appeared to frequently lose track of the conversational topic, thereby interfering with the flow of discourse) were taught to self-manage their responsivity to questions. Following implementation of the self-management procedures, all four children increased their responsivity, generally answering more than 80% of adults' questions, and maintaining a fluid involvement in their conversations. The children also demonstrated the ability to use these self-initiated procedures in natural settings in the absence of a treatment provider. Finally, these children exhibited considerable improvements in untreated disruptive behavior, decreasing their self-stimulation, aggression, and self-injury. This suggests that maintaining a fluent involvement in the conversational topic flow may have reduced the frustration of participating in fragmented, often unrelated pieces of the total conversational interaction.

To date, we have successfully implemented more than 500 self-management programs in schools, homes, and other community settings. Most of the children who have some language skills begin to learn to self-manage their behavior within the first session. Some adaptations, using picture cues, seem to be necessary for lower-functioning children. Within several months, most of the children become quite proficient at monitoring and the device can be faded with maintenance of the clinical gains. However, a subgroup of children, particularly those who are more severely disabled, seem to require the monitoring device to cue self-management. Nevertheless, once the children learn to self-manage their behavior, gains are demonstrated in the absence of a treatment provider, thereby reducing the need for constant adult supervision and vigilance.

Speech Intelligibility

The final area of pilot research relates to speech intelligibility. Again, a history of reduced intelligibility often leads to frustration and subsequent reduced initiations of speech. Our preliminary data suggest that incorporating the naturalistic motivational variables shown to enhance language development (discussed earlier and outlined in Table 1) into the treatment of speech sounds, results in widespread improvements in speech intelligibility in the children's natural settings (i.e., home and school). Our present studies consist of implementing 25 sessions that are 35 minutes in length. Sessions are implemented twice per week. During both types of interventions (i.e., analog drill intervention and motivational naturalistic intervention) the children learn the speech sounds, but only during the motivational procedures is the generalization of intelligibility improved to the point where raters score the children's speech as "mostly intelligible" outside of the clinical interactions. It is also interesting to note that data collected in a series of reversals suggest that the children's behavior was much more appropriate (without severe behavior problems) when the naturalistic procedures were being implemented. Thus, these data continue corroborated in all research areas, suggesting that given constant target behaviors, when teaching procedures known to enhance motivation to initiate and participate in interactions are implemented, the children appear to be much less frustrated, and show significantly reduced levels of disruptive behavior.

Results

Overall, these preliminary studies demonstrate four major points: (a) The children could rapidly (usually within a matter of weeks) learn self-initiated communication strategies that parallel those used by typical language developers; (b) the strategies resulted in the acquisition of large numbers of new vocabulary items, nouns, pronouns, prepositions, etc., as well as increases in fluid conversational interactions; (c) the improvements in language use were almost always accompanied by untreated collateral decreases in problematic disruptive social behaviors; (d) certain (naturalistic) paradigms resulted in decreases in parental stress, while other (analog) paradigms did not.

IMPLICATIONS

These results draw attention to an important question in relation to the early acquisition of language; that is, "Does an understanding of how typical language-developers learn language help in devising communication interventions for autism?" Of importance here is the fact that research shows that for typically developing children, considerable social and communicative competence is gained by child initiations and reciprocal participation in communicative interactions. Strategies such as question-asking, which enhance linguistic competence, are some of the earliest emerging forms of speech emitted by typically developing children. Even in the preschool years, when most children have learned to use complex grammatical structures, they continue to use a large number of questions with both adults and peers (Hart & Risley, 1968). In contrast, the extremely limited style of interacting that children with autism exhibit severely limits the types of interactions to which they are exposed. Because utterances are emitted infrequently, the children are likely to be involved in very few communicative interactions. Furthermore, the communicative functions most frequently used by children with autism (requesting and protesting) are more likely to result only in simply getting their needs met, rather than evoking the social use of language. In contrast, the pilot data suggest that interventions emphasizing self-initiations result in quantitative and qualitative improvements in communication, with widespread concomitant decreases in disruptive behavior and frustration.

LIMITATIONS AND GENERALIZABILITY

Although we have always been able to document substantial and empirically measurable improvements in the communication of children with autism, we also have been able to describe a subgroup of children who have not responded favorably to certain specific interventions. We believe that this difficulty does not necessarily relate to the effectiveness of a particular intervention, but may relate to a complex set of issues involving child characteristics, family variables, and the suitability of the intervention procedures to a given target behavior.

With regard to child characteristics, recent research in the field of autism and our substantial database indicate that considerable variability exists within the population of individuals with the diagnosis of autism. It is now well recognized that the behavioral expression of the symptoms of autism varies significantly across children, and the clinical picture within the children themselves changes throughout development (Waterhouse, Fein, Nath, & Snyder, 1987). Such heterogeneity suggests the importance of shifting attention to the individualization of treatment techniques that correspond with specific child characteristics to maximize the effectiveness of treatment. For example, although communication treatment needs to be multicomponent, incorporating all of the areas discussed earlier, queries appear to be important for a wide range of children with autism who initially have some existing language, although approaches that emphasize areas such as intelligibility may be especially critical for children who are largely nonverbal. Other procedures emphasizing self-management of topic continuation and reflection may be most useful with higher functioning children whose primary deficits are in the area of pragmatics (Koegel & Frea, 1993).

A second issue concerning heterogeneity relates to variability in family characteristics. For example, the literature in the area of parent education suggests that some types of treatment programs may actually increase the stress parents experience (Benson & Turnbull, 1986; Gallagher, Beckman, & Cross, 1983), and that treatment effectiveness may correlate with certain types of parents' stress, educational level, socioeconomic status, and marital status (Clark & Baker, 1983). Data collected in our clinics suggest that certain types of treatment programs (e.g., naturalistic procedures) actually reduce many types of parental stress, while other types of more traditional (analog) procedures do not (Moes, Koegel, & Schreibman, 1994). Yet, although such procedures are likely to decrease parental stress, it also is likely that individual needs will need to be assessed to enhance communication within particular families' idiosyncratic styles of interactions, cultural values, and demographic conditions (Kellegrew, 1994).

Finally, related to the extreme variability in child and family characteristics is the implicit necessity of individualizing the treatment based on the particular goals identified. That is, specific target behaviors seem to have an interactive effect with treatment type. For example, a first lexicon responds significantly better when naturalistic variables known to influence motivation (described earlier) are incorporated (Koegel et al., 1987). In contrast, grammatical structures that occur infrequently (Camarata & Nelson, 1992) appear to be enhanced with at least some components of more structured environmental manipulations to increase opportunities. Such individualization, depending on child characteristics (Yoder, Kaiser, & Alpert, 1991), family variables, and target behaviors are likely to result in the necessity of an individualized prescriptive treatment model, incorporating selected components for specific children, families, and target behaviors.

SUMMARY

Highly specialized intervention strategies have evolved over the last decade to improve the communication of children with autism. Early approaches were highly analog in nature and imitation-based; they typically involved decreasing inappropriate behaviors through punishment, then attempting to teach appropriate behaviors beginning with nonverbal imitation, and gradually focusing on verbal imitation (Lovaas, 1977). Although many general skills improved under such conditions, the children often failed to show generalized use of newly learned language and spontaneous use of language with the highly structured aspects of this treatment (Lovaas, 1977; Schreibman, 1988). As a result, a major change arose in approaching language intervention that differed in emphasis from the more traditional, highly imitative, and adult-driven techniques. This change emphasized the reciprocal interactive nature of the communicative interaction and therefore accentuated the child's role as an active communicative partner in the dyad (Camarata & Nelson, 1992; Hart & Risley, 1968; Kaiser, Yoder, & Keetz, 1992; Koegel, O'Dell, & Koegel, 1987; Yoder, Kaiser, Alpert, & Fischer, 1993) .

These naturalistic and child-initiated procedures have the serendipitous benefit of not only improving communication and decreasing disruptive behaviors, but also of reducing the inordinate number of hours of adult-driven treatment in a formal clinical session. This alleviates the great financial burden for families and other agencies to provide these long-term, costly services, which may be unavailable altogether for families who do not live near a qualified clinician. In contrast, self-initiated learning techniques are both cost and time efficient, as the child continues to exhibit "therapeutic" interactions with the environment both within and outside of the formal therapy sessions. Procedures such as teaching question-asking and self-management, where the child takes an active role in his or her own treatment, not only creates independence on the part of the child, but also parallels procedures that typically developing children use regularly and continuously throughout the day and throughout their development. The results of pilot research suggest that future development of techniques designed to promote self-learning and independence will likely result in more efficient treatments for children with autism, more significant generalization and maintenance of treatment gains, and greater reductions in parental stress.

REFERENCES

Aram, D., Ekelman, B., & Nation, J. (1984). Preschoolers with language disorders: 10 years later. *Journal of Speech and Hearing Research, 27,* 232–244.

Aram, D., & Nation, J. (1980). Preschool language disorders and subsequent language and academic difficulties. *Journal of Communication Disorders, 13,* 159–170.

Benson, H. A., & Turnbull, A. P. (1986). Approaching families from an individualized perspective. In R. H. Horner, L. Meyer, & H. D. Fredericks (Eds.), *Education of learners with severe handicaps: Exemplary service strategies* (pp. 127–157). Baltimore: Paul H. Brookes.

Bernstein-Ratner, N. (1983). *Increased vowel precision in the absence of increased vowel duration.* Paper presented at the annual convention of the American Speech–Language–Hearing Association, Cincinnati, OH.

Camarata, S. M., & Nelson, K. E. (1992). Treatment efficiency as a function of target selection in the remediation of child language disorders. *Clinical Linguistics and Phonetics, 6,* 167–178.

Carr, E. G., & Durand, V. M. (1985). Reducing behavior problems through functional communication training. *Journal of Applied Behavior Analysis, 18,* 111–126.

Clark, D. B., & Baker, B. L. (1983). Predicting outcome in parent training. *Journal of Consulting and Clinical Psychology, 51,* 309–311.

Frea, W. D., Koegel, L. K., & Koegel, R. L. (1994). *Understanding why problem behaviors occur.* Santa Barbara, CA: University of California.

Gallagher, J. J., Beckman, P. J., & Cross, A. H. (1983). Families of handicapped children: Sources of stress and its amelioration. *Exceptional Children, 50,* 10–19.

Hart, B. M., & Risley, T. R. (1968). Establishing the use of descriptive adjectives in the spontaneous speech of disadvantaged preschool children. *Journal of Applied Behavior Analysis, 1,* 109–120.

Horner, R. H., & Budd, C. M. (1985). Acquisition of manual sign use: Collateral reduction of maladaptive behavior, and factors limiting generalization. *Education and Training of the Mentally Retarded, 20,* 39–47.

Kaiser, A. P., Yoder, P. J., & Keetz, A. (1992). Evaluating milieu teaching. In S. F. Warren & J. Reichle (Eds.), *Causes and effects in communication and language intervention* (pp. 9–47). Baltimore, MD: Paul H. Brookes.

Kellegrew, D. H. (1994). *The impact of daily routines and opportunities on the self-care skills of young children with disabilities*. Unpublished doctoral dissertation, University of California, Santa Barbara.

Koegel, L. K. (1993). *Teaching children with autism to use a self-initiated strategy to learn expressive vocabulary*. Unpublished doctoral dissertation, University of California, Santa Barbara.

Koegel, R. L., & Frea, W. D. (1993). Treatment of social behavior in autism through the modification of pivotal social skills. *Journal of Applied Behavior Analysis, 26,* 369–377.

Koegel, L. K., Koegel, R. L., Hurley, C., & Frea, W. D. (1992). Improving social skills and disruptive behavior in children with autism through self-management. *Journal of Applied Behavior Analysis, 25,* 341–353.

Koegel, R. L., O'Dell, M. C., & Koegel, L. K. (1987). A natural language paradigm for teaching non-verbal autistic children. *Journal of Autism and Developmental Disorders, 17,* 187–199.

Lovaas, O. I. (1977). *The autistic child: Language development through behavior modification*. New York: Irvington.

Malsheen, B. (1980). Two hypotheses for phonetic clarification in the speech of mothers to children. In G. Yeni-Komshian & C. Ferguson (Eds.), *Child Phonology* (Vol. 2, pp. 173–184). San Diego, CA: Academic Press.

Moes, D., Koegel, R. L., & Schreibman, L. (1994). *Behavior therapy paradigms and parenting stress*. Paper presented at the 102nd Annual Convention of the American Psychological Association, Los Angeles, CA.

O'Neill, R. E., Horner, R. H., Albin, R. W., Storey, K., & Sprague, J. R. (1989). Functional analysis: A practical assessment guide. Sycamore, IL: Sycamore Press.

Paul, R. (1991). Profile of toddlers with slow expressive language development. *Topics in Language Disorders, 11,* 1–13.

Paul, R., & Elwood, T. (1991). Maternal linguistic input to toddlers with slow expressive language development. *Journal of Speech and Hearing Research, 34,* 982–988.

Paul, R., & Jennings, P. (1992). Phonological behavior in toddlers with slow expressive language development. *Journal of Speech and Hearing Research, 35,* 99–107.

Paul, R., & Shiffer, M. E. (1991). Communicative initiations in normal and late-talking toddlers. *Applied Psycholinguistics, 12,* 419–431.

Peck, C. A. (1985). Increasing opportunities for social control by children with autism and severe handicaps: Effects on student behavior and perceived classroom climate. *Journal of the Association for Persons with Severe Handicaps, 10,* 183–193.

Schreibman, L. (1988). *Autism. Developmental Clinical Psychology and Psychiatry* (Vol. 15). Newbury Park, CA: Sage.

Sigafoos, J., Roberts, D., Kerr, M., Couzens, D., & Baglioni, A. J. (1994). Opportunities for communication in classrooms serving children with developmental disabilities. *Journal of Autism and Developmental Disorders, 24,* 259–279.

Stoel-Gammon, C. (1983). *Variations of style in mother's speech to young children.* Paper presented at the annual convention of the American Speech–Language–Hearing Association, Cincinnati, OH.

Waterhouse, L., Fein, D., Nath, J., & Snyder, D. (1987). Pervasive developmental disorders and schizophrenia occurring in childhood: A review of critical commentary. In Gary L. Tischler (Ed.), *Diagnosis and classification in psychiatry: A critical appraisal of DSM-III* (pp. 335–368). Cambridge, England: Cambridge University Press.

Wetherby, A. M., & Prutting, C. A. (1984). Profiles of communicative and cognitive–social abilities in autistic children. *Journal of the American Speech–Language–Hearing Association, 27,* 364–377.

Whitehurst, G., Fischel, J., Lonigan, C., Valdez-Menchaca, M. C., DeBaryshe, B., & Caulfield, M. (1988). Verbal interaction in families of normal and expressive language-delayed children. *Developmental Psychology, 24,* 690–699.

Yoder, P. J., Davies, B., Bishop, K., & Munson, L. (1994). Effect of adult continuing wh-questions on conversational participation in children with developmental disabilities. *Journal of Speech and Hearing Research, 37,* 193–204.

Yoder, P. J., Kaiser, A. P., & Alpert, C. L. (1991). An exploratory study of the interaction between language teaching methods and characteristics. *Journal of Speech and Hearing Research, 34,* 155–167.

Yoder, P. J., Kaiser, A. P., Alpert, C. L., & Fischer, R. (1993). Following the child's lead when teaching nouns to preschoolers with mental retardation. *Journal of Speech and Hearing Research, 36,* 158–167.

24

LEARNING EXPERIENCES . . . AN ALTERNATIVE PROGRAM: PEER-MEDIATED INTERVENTIONS FOR YOUNG CHILDREN WITH AUTISM

PHILLIP S. STRAIN, FRANK W. KOHLER, and HOWARD GOLDSTEIN

Peer-mediated interventions for young children with autism have, as their theoretical foundation, the notions that: (a) peers can be as or perhaps more effective than direct adult intervention agents; (b) for many skill domains, the contexts created by peer-mediated interventions are closer to the everyday, clinically relevant environments where clients must ultimately be able to function; (c) the abundance of peers in most settings creates natural opportunities for clients to learn from multiple examples (a technique generally recognized to improve generalizations of intervention gains); and (d) the natural variability of peers' adherence to intervention agent roles creates many opportunities for clients to learn under "loose" training conditions (another feature of instruction widely held to facilitate generalized outcomes).

In application, the peer-mediated interventions detailed in this chapter can be traced historically to Harlow's pioneering work with primates reared in isolation. A series of landmark studies (e.g., Novak & Harlow, 1975; Suomi & Harlow, 1972) showed that pairing isolate monkeys with slightly younger but socially normal monkeys largely remediated the pro-

Preparation of this chapter was supported by National Institute of Mental Health grant MH37110-12 to the Early Learning Institute at St. Peter's Child Development Centers. Correspondence concerning this chapter should be directed to Dr. Phillip S. Strain, Center for Collaborative Education and Learning, 1444 Wazee Street, Suite 230, Denver, CO 80202.

found social deficits displayed by the isolate-reared primates. Significantly, pairing with same-age and adult monkeys had no therapeutic effect. Later, Furman, Rahe, and Hartup (1979) showed similar effects by pairing withdrawn preschoolers with socially competent peers.

Another foundational line of clinical research to the current use of peer-mediated interventions began with Wahler's (1967) early study of peers as social reinforcement agents. From Wahler's initial study, a large body of research has emerged on the power of peer reinforcement, either mediated by individuals or by groups (Furman, Rahe, & Hartup, 1979; Greenwood, Todd, Hops, & Walker, 1982; Odom, Hoyson, Jamieson, & Strain, 1985). Although the data are somewhat mixed, it is significant to note that when a direct comparison is made, peer-based group contingencies yield better outcomes than do adult-mediated approaches (Sancilio, 1987).

The programmatic research on peer-mediated interventions described in this chapter was conducted within the context of a comprehensive early intervention program known as Learning Experiences . . . An Alternative Program (LEAP) for preschoolers and parents. In effect, LEAP represents an attempt to test the limits of peer-mediated interventions by applying these tactics for extended periods of time to a wide variety of behavior goals. A brief overview of the LEAP model will be provided prior to describing specific intervention studies.

OVERVIEW OF LEAP

The LEAP research and demonstration program is designed to meet the educational needs of both typical preschool children and those with autism within an integrated classroom setting. LEAP offers parents a cost-free program that operates 5 days per week in a local community early childhood center. A master's level teacher and an assistant provide individualized educational programming to 10 normally developing children and 3 to 4 children with autism. Six classrooms of this composition are in operation. In addition, a full-time speech and language pathologist, supervisory staff, and contracted occupational and physical therapists work directly with the children in their classrooms. Parents of children with autism participate in a parent program designed to teach more effective skills for interacting with their preschoolers in school, home, and community environments. LEAP also arranges consultation services to parents from physicians, child development specialists, and mental health personnel. Moreover, parents of all LEAP children operate their own education and support group.

LEAP comprises four major program components: (a) referral process, (b) classroom instruction, (c) parent involvement and education, and (d) future educational placement planning. Each of these components is briefly described here, followed by a synopsis of overall program outcomes.

Referral Process

Referrals for the preschool originate from a variety of sources. Referrals for typical preschoolers originate primarily from families and friends whose children have previously attended LEAP preschool. Referrals for children with autism originate from (a) local preschools serving children with disabilities, (b) residential treatment programs, (c) local medical and mental health specialists, (d) local educational agencies, and (e) parental contact.

During the initial contact with a family, information is obtained concerning the child's existing medical condition, any general parental concerns, provisions for transportation, and parental availability and interest in involvement. An initial visit is then scheduled for interested parents. During this visit, prospective parents are provided with a detailed description of the program. Specific information relating to the child's current level of functioning and parental concerns are reviewed and discussed.

For families of children with autism, an individual education plan (IEP) meeting is conducted by the local education agency and LEAP staff to determine placement. Children who are considered to be appropriate candidates for LEAP typically display at least three of the following behavioral criteria: (a) significantly delayed social skills, (b) significantly delayed language skills, (c) excessive levels of disruptive or stereotypic behaviors, and (d) minimal level of preacademic competencies. In addition to these behavioral criteria, children in the research protocol meet *Diagnostic and Statistical Manual of Mental Disorders*, fourth edition (*DSM-IV*; American Psychiatric Association, 1994) criteria for autism based on independent evaluations. In effect, then, these criteria serve as our operational definition of autism. Assistance is provided in the selection of an alternative placement for families for whom it is determined that the LEAP preschool is not the most appropriate program.

After placement at LEAP is decided, the child may participate in the classroom and the parent in additional interviews before they begin. This offers parents additional opportunities to meet the staff and allows the child to become comfortable with the setting.

Classroom Instruction

The first four weeks of each child's placement within the LEAP classroom is devoted, in part, to assessing the child's current level of functioning. Standardized preschool assessment instruments used include the Battelle Developmental Inventory (Newborg, Stoek, & Wenck, 1984) and the

McCarthy Scales of Children's Abilities (McCarthy, 1972). In addition to these standardized preschool assessments, observational data are collected on (a) prerequisite learning skills (i.e., engagement in play activities and appropriate verbalizations); (b) independent functioning skills; and (c) social interaction skills. A speech and language consultant evaluates each child who is suspected of or who demonstrates significant delays in language development.

At the end of this assessment period, an IEP update meeting is scheduled. Short-term objectives for each child are developed from target behavior checklists completed by his or her parents. Individualized goal plans are then developed for each child and reviewed weekly by the staff. A formal IEP update occurs every 3 to 4 months.

The Creative Curriculum for Early Childhood (Dodge & Colker, 1988) is used as a guide for instructional planning. The physical environment of each classroom is arranged so that there are clearly defined interest areas (e.g., blocks, house corner, table toys, art, sand and water, library) that support child-initiated, child-directed play. Themes such as dinosaurs, transportation, and families are used to help the children learn about the world around them and to enable them to acquire information and concepts through planned activities that take place in each interest area. The classroom daily schedule is designed to provide a balance of activities that include quiet and active; individual, small group, and large group; child-directed and teacher-directed; large muscle and small muscle; and indoor and outdoor learning activities. Weekly instructional planning focuses on both general skill concepts to be emphasized with all children during both child-directed and teacher-directed learning activities (e.g., recalling a sequence of events, identifying functional use of objects, sharing toys with peers) as well as individual goals for children with autism (e.g., verbally requesting desired food items during snack time).

To meet the needs of children with autism, the early childhood curriculum is supplemented with learning activities and instructional strategies specifically designed to facilitate the development of functional skills, independent play and work skills, social interaction skills, language skills, and adaptive behavior. Functional skills instruction focuses on teaching children with autism skills such as transitioning from one activity to another, selecting play activities, following classroom routines, and participating in group activities.

The early childhood curriculum also is adapted as needed to meet the needs of children who display challenging behaviors. Intervention procedures include the development and implementation of strategies to prevent behavior problems (e.g., effective use of classroom rules, environmental arrangements, scheduling, activities, and materials) as well as the use of positive procedures for conducting functional analyses of behaviors.

Instructional strategies used by the classroom teachers reflect both a developmentally appropriate practice approach to early childhood education as well as a "best practice" approach to early intervention. Teachers facilitate all children's learning by (a) providing opportunities for the children to choose from a variety of activities, materials, and equipment; (b) facilitating their engagement with materials by assisting and guiding children; and (c) extending their learning by asking questions or making suggestions that stimulate their learning.

As needed, teachers modify instructional practices to best meet the needs of children with autism. The following guidelines are used by classroom teachers when making decisions about instructional strategies for young children with autism:

1. Instructional strategies for young children with disabilities should be as normalized as possible (i.e., they should approximate the instructional strategies used with same-age typical peers whenever possible.

2. Instructional strategies should focus on teaching functional skills during naturally occurring routines and events in the classroom.

3. Instructional strategies should incorporate learning objectives into child-selected activities and teach the necessary skills (e.g., choice making, independent work/play skills, etc.) children with disabilities need to participate in activities.

4. Instructional strategies should be individually determined for the child, for the task, and for where the child is in the learning process.

5. Instructional strategies should include multiple methods for enhancing the probability of skill generalization.

6. Instructional strategies should be effective (that is, they should result in children successfully learning desired skills).

Each individual child's progress toward identified goals and objectives is monitored on an ongoing basis. Skill acquisition is evaluated frequently, focusing on how long, how, with what level of assistance (e.g., level of prompts), and under what conditions (e.g., materials, adults, activities, settings, etc.) the child performs desired skills. In addition, the monitoring of maintenance and generalization is conducted as a means of evaluating the effectiveness of instructional strategies.

Social interaction intervention is another important component of the LEAP classroom. Systematic intervention is believed to be a necessary catalyst for the development of positive social interaction between typical children and those with autism. The LEAP program, therefore, utilizes a variety of different intervention strategies to encourage social interaction:

(a) teacher prompting and reinforcement; (b) structuring the environment to facilitate interaction; (c) selecting materials to promote interaction; and, most important, (d) peer-mediated social interaction training (specific peer-mediated strategies and outcome data follow).

Student progress on both engagement and social skill objectives is monitored via direct observational systems. For preschoolers with autism, child progress demonstrated in the classroom environment is compared with skill competencies demonstrated in the home and community. Multiple baseline designs across settings are utilized to evaluate long-term maintenance and generalization of intervention gains.

Family Involvement

Family involvement is considered essential to the success of the LEAP program. All families participate in the program in some capacity. In the classroom, parents may choose to participate in a variety of activities that include: (a) construction of instructional materials, (b) preparation of activity centers, and (c) provision of direct intervention. Parents of children with autism may choose to participate in a parent education program up to 3 times per week in home and community environments. Parents of children who are LEAP "graduates" may provide support and informational services to new parents.

We begin with an assessment of parent and child entry-level skills. Specific parent and child target behaviors are assessed through several initial play observation sessions. Child target behaviors are also determined by having parents select specific child behaviors that they would like to see either increased or decreased.

Although parents may necessarily acquire different skills to meet the educational needs of their children, all parents are provided with a self-instructional core curriculum that addresses such skills as providing clear instructions, prompting and shaping successive approximations, and providing consistent consequences. Initially, parents replicate instructional procedures that project teachers have demonstrated to be most effective with their child. Along with individualized work with families in the home, school, and community, parents may elect to apply their new skills in the classroom setting. The skill performance of parents in both individual and group instructional formats is closely monitored, along with continuous feedback from the parents on their level of satisfaction with the program.

Evaluation of project participation is conducted by assessing the effects of parent participation on both parent and child target behaviors. In addition, the generalization of these skills to other settings is also assessed. Changes in the social functioning of the family are assessed through preintervention and follow-up assessment of stress variables within the family, and extra-family social contacts. These general areas of family functioning were selected because of the high incidence of reported stress and insularity among parents of children with autism (Schreibman, 1988).

Future Education Placement Planning

The LEAP staff and parents work together on planning the future educational placement of LEAP's graduates. During numerous program planning meetings, educational placement options are outlined for each family and staff recommendations are reviewed. Possible future placement sites are visited by a staff–parent team. It is the goal of the LEAP project to work cooperatively with the professionals who will be serving the child once he or she leaves the program. Future teachers of LEAP preschoolers are invited into the classroom to observe the children in their present classroom environment. Technical assistance is offered to future teachers on the intervention strategies that have been identified by the LEAP staff to be most effective for working with a particular child. Follow-up visits can be scheduled with future teachers to monitor maintenance and generalization of child intervention gains.

Overall Program Outcomes

During our first 12 years of inquiry we have shown that

1. Children in the experimental program generally show significant reductions in autistic symptoms after 2 years in treatment.
2. Children make marked developmental progress on intellectual and language measures.
3. On observational measures taken in school and home, children are generally more appropriate, social, and actively engaged after 2 years of intervention.
4. No negative and some positive (e.g., better social skills, fewer disruptive behaviors) outcomes have been noted for normally developing children in the experimental program.
5. Gains for experimentally treated children tend to maintain following program participation, with 24 or 51 children now enrolled in regular education classes (the oldest is now in 10th grade). Many parents enrolled their children in neighborhood kindergartens without any reference to their child's prior treatment history.

Within the context of LEAP, we have pursued two related areas of peer-mediated intervention: communicative and peer social interaction. Each endeavor is described here.

Communicative Interaction

The specific steps to implementing communicative intervention include (a) teaching peers to use facilitative strategies, and then (b) prompting and reinforcing the use of the strategies during play with a classmate with autism.

A teacher and an adult "actor" conduct the training of typical peers. A parent may serve as the "actor." Training can be accomplished with as few as one child and as many as six children at a time. During training, the peers are told that they are learning how to get their friends to talk with them. A training script is available for introducing specific behavioral strategies to the children. The script provides directions to the adults (teacher and actor) for modeling the use of the strategies for getting others to talk, and encouraging the children to practice verbalizing the intent of these strategies.

The selection of strategies was based on peer-mediated interventions focusing on social interaction, developmental literature, and the practices speech pathologists and special educators typically use to evoke conversations in unstructured situations. The strategies taught to peers are (a) establishing eye-contact; (b) describing one's own or other children's play; (c) initiating joint play; (d) repeating, expanding, or requesting clarification of utterances made by the child with autism; (e) establishing joint focus of attention; and (f) prompting requests.

During training, strategies are introduced one at a time using a direct instruction approach. After the required responses are modeled by the adults and verbally rehearsed according to the prepared script, each child practices using the strategies with the adult actor. The actor pretends to be a child with autism and makes it progressively more difficult for the peers to evoke appropriate responses. The actor waits for longer time periods before responding to the peer's initiations. Thus, the peers experience more realistic, difficult situations and learn to be persistent and to modify their use of the strategies.

A set of posters illustrating each of the strategies is employed in training and is used to prompt the use of the strategies. These posters can be available later during daily free-play periods and can be used to prompt the use of the strategies by the peers. The peers practice using the strategies with the adult actor serving as the child with autism until each typical peer demonstrates independent use of the strategies. Mastery can be set at four uses of the strategies in the role-play situation without prompting. The children have to be persistent to use the strategies successfully. Thus, the adult actor becomes a more reticent responder over the course of training to give the peers practice with more challenging situations.

During structured free play, two or three typical peers are paired with a child with autism for 5 to 10 minutes. Before each play period, the peers are reminded that they are to try to get their classmate to talk with them. The teacher lists the strategies that the peers have been taught. For example, the teacher might say, "Remember, you can get your friend to look at you, you can suggest some things to do together, you can talk about what you are doing, and you need to listen to your friend and make sure you understand what he or she said, so you can repeat it."

During free play, the teacher tries not to be an active interactor. When the teacher becomes involved, interaction among the children tends to be inhibited. In addition to prompting the peers to use the strategies, the teacher is responsible for overall monitoring of the activity (e.g., the teacher may redirect the activity to facilitate cooperative play, may have to resolve conflicts, and may have to confiscate disputed materials).

The teacher prompts strategy usage in a nonintrusive manner. The best way to prompt is by pointing to the poster that depicts the desired strategy. An alternative way to prompt, when necessary, is to whisper a suggestion into the ear of a peer.

During free-play sessions, the teacher monitors the number of times the peers use the facilitative strategies effectively by putting little tokens on the posters or checks on a blackboard above the posters. Different areas of the posters can be set aside for different peers. At the end of the free-play period, the teacher counts the number of successful strategy uses. This may be used as a basis for a reinforcement system, whereby the children can earn stickers, small toys, privileges, or treats when they meet criterion performance (e.g., five successful uses of a strategy per child).

Experimental Results

Results of our studies have been quite encouraging. The teaching and prompting of specific strategies to facilitate verbal communication between children with autism and their typical peers appears to be an effective method. The studies on communicative interaction have resulted in a number of findings:

1. Peers' use of several facilitative strategies have resulted in higher rates of communicative interaction in preschoolers with autism, especially in the most relevant, on-topic verbal response category (Goldstein & Wickstrom, 1986).
2. Effects of peer intervention on the initiations of preschoolers with autism have been inconsistent. One possible confound

is the tendency of teachers to prompt the preschoolers with autism prior to the peer intervention. Related experimental analyses have indicated that sharp reductions in teacher prompting of the children with autism were responsible for reductions in initiation rates (Goldstein & Ferrell, 1987).

3. Maintenance and generalization of effects, although not consistently impressive, are encouraging. Peer-mediated interventions to promote social interaction that have not focused on communication have rarely resulted in as much maintenance and generalization (e.g., Day, Powell, Dy-Lin, & Stowitschek, 1982; Odom, Hoyson, Jamieson, & Strain, 1985). This may indicate that the communicative behaviors that we have targeted have greater potential for "naturally" reinforcing, reciprocal interaction. Nevertheless, further research is needed to discover the best methods for increasing and generalizing interactions.

4. Reinforcement of children with autism (in addition to reinforcement for peers' strategy use) resulted in maintenance of improved initiation rates that were initially associated with increased teacher prompting. Teaching more specific facilitative strategies to children with autism is likely to enhance the success of a peer-mediated treatment approach.

5. Peer strategy use was maintained even though a natural (i.e., unprogrammed) decline in teacher prompting was demonstrated as the studies progressed. Furthermore, preschoolers with autism were equally responsive to teacher prompted and unprompted strategy use by their peers. This finding is suggestive of the potential for peers to take on more responsibility in instituting the intervention.

Social Interactions

We have developed and evaluated a protocol for teaching children to engage in high levels of positive reciprocal social interaction and play. Teachers implement their own versions of a programmed training package developed by Kohler, Shearer, and Strain (1990). An entire class of preschoolers, including children with autism and their typical peers, participate in training, which occurs within a range of structured play activities on a daily basis (Kohler & Strain, 1993).

Children participate in ongoing training sessions consisting of at least one child with autism and multiple peers. Five prosocial skills are learned and practiced in these sessions: (a) play organizer suggestions, (b) share offers and requests, (c) assistance offers and requests, (d) compliments, and

(e) affection. These skills are learned in this sequence through three different strategies. First, each skill is used *to initiate and extend/continue* play interactions with another child. For example, children might direct a share offer to a youngster who is playing alone. Second, children learn *to respond positively* by accepting or agreeing with their playmate's overture. Finally, children learn *to be persistent* in their use of initiations and responses. Overtures that are ignored or refused are followed by different or more elaborate offers or requests.

Social skills training occurs throughout the year and entails three stages for teaching each skill. Teachers introduce and model a single skill during Stage 1, which lasts 1 to 2 sessions. During Stage 2 (1 to 2 days), children rehearse that skill with the teacher, who provides ongoing instructions, models, and feedback (correction and praise) to individual children. Children practice the skill with each other independent of close teacher direction during Stage 3. Two criteria are set for terminating the final stage of training for each skill: (a) children with autism and their peers can produce at least four exchanges of the newly taught skill during a 6-minute period; and (b) typical children can exhibit at least 50% of their skills independently of adult prompts. After these two criteria are met, the teacher begins Stage 1 with a new social skill (e.g., training for sharing begins after children have completed all three stages of training for play organizers).

The training protocol is tailored to fit a diverse range of play activities that are rotated on a daily basis. For example, play organizer, sharing, and assistance overtures are suited to dramatic, manipulative, and gross motor activities. The sequence and scope of training are also tailored to meet children's individual needs and abilities. For example, children with spontaneous language skills practice directing play organizer suggestions (e.g., "Let's play trucks") and assistance offers or requests to peers. Conversely, youngsters lacking language skills might learn to exhibit nonverbal share requests or offers and to respond positively to other children's overtures.

During and following training, children participate in daily play activities to exchange and further refine their newly taught overtures. The teacher begins each session by reviewing the various play materials and roles with a group of 3 to 4 youngsters, including one child with autism and 2 to 3 typical peers. Children rehearse a range of designated skills or strategies with the teacher, who provides instructions and models.

Next, the teacher implements some form of peer-mediated intervention to maintain children's prosocial exchanges and play. Typical children assume a primary role in these interventions by directing a variety of positive initiations to their playmates with autism (Strain, 1977). The teacher monitors and facilitates children's interactions with prompts and reinforcement. Like training, the specific reinforcement contingency is always tailored to meet children's individual needs and abilities. Some youngsters with autism receive prompts and reinforcement for directing social initiations to peers, while less capable children are expected initially to only respond positively to peers' social overtures.

Experimental Results

Approximately three dozen studies have been conducted to understand better the conditions that lead to the most robust social outcomes for the social intervention tactic. The following findings were obtained:

1. Typically developing peers as young as 36 months can be readily taught to engage in persistent social approaches toward their socially withdrawn peers (Strain, 1977; Strain, Shores, & Timm, 1977).
2. The peer-mediated intervention most often yields "day-one" effects, suggesting that the poor social abilities characteristic of young children with autism may be attributable, in part, to the socially unresponsive contexts in which they are often educated (Strain, 1977; Strain & Odom, 1986).
3. For many target children, the level of positive peer behavior produced falls within normative limits for age and social context (Strain, 1987).
4. Cross-setting behavior change is achievable with relatively minor alterations in the social responsiveness of generalized settings (Strain, 1985).
5. Typical peers have experienced no negative outcomes from participation as intervention agents. To the contrary, their social relations with other typical children and their general class deportment may improve (Strain, 1987).

DISCUSSION AND FUTURE DIRECTIONS

The field of peer-mediated intervention for preschool-age children with autism is at a crossroads—a crossroads marked on one side by our meager short-term successes and on the other by our lack of success when it comes to reliably and consistently producing truly powerful and long-term effects. What are the hallmarks of our success or lack thereof, and which path might we choose for the future?

If one defines the universe of social contexts, demands, and challenges by our prevailing, single-case experimental paradigm, we do pretty well as social intervention agents. That is, we almost always improve skills to above the pretraining level of performance (e.g., Strain et al., 1977). We almost always find that individuals do more than they are directly taught to do (when this happens we do not see the phenomenon as a problem of experimental control, incidentally; e.g., Goldstein, Wickstrom, Hoyson, Jamieson, & Odom, 1988). Of course, when individuals perform poorly, not as they are taught, we resort to experimental control issues (e.g., lack of fidelity of treatment, specific intervention agent effects) as our explanatory mechanism of choice. On more rare occasions, we show that individuals continue, to some extent, to behave more socially when there are not obvious incentives offered by the experimenters to do so (e.g., Day et al., 1982). Not so surprisingly, we do not tend to interpret this event as an issue of poor experimental control either.

So what are the limitations or problems with these kinds of effects? The problems are not so much a lack of behavioral effect as such; rather, they extend to the context and timeframe within which our interventions most often occur. Stated simply, many social relationship and communicative interventions with preschoolers, for the most part, represent something akin to using a bandage to close a wound from a grenade. Our interventions are often too little and too trivial. Presuming for the moment, however, that our intervention methods and foci for change are correct, let us explore the more simple problem of intensity.

Consider the answers to the following questions:

- In which settings do clients need good communicative and social relations? All settings.
- With whom must clients engage communicatively and socially? Everyone.
- During what times do clients need to engage communicatively and socially? Most of the time.

If, in fact, there is a certain "universality" to communicative and social skillfulness; if, in fact, these skills, to some extent, are needed with everyone, at most times, and in all contexts, then how do our standard intervention practices compare to this challenge? Most experimental demonstrations offer, within school-only contexts, maybe 20 minutes of intervention per day, at most in two settings, maybe involving a couple of preschool social agents. Moreover, if we consider that most experiments last 3 to 5 months, then these interventions have provided about one full day or 24 hours of cumulative intervention time toward altering how a young child will interact with all social agents in all social contexts, across all times of the day. In reality, the cumulative intervention time in most studies could provide *only* one 24-hour example for the individual!

The above commentary in no way dismisses the value of the work done to date. Much has been discovered about functional social skills (Strain, 1984, 1985), about motivational mechanisms to enhance skill display (McConnell, Sisson, Cort, & Strain, 1991), about the influence of socially responsive environments (Fox et al., 1984), and about the myriad ways to assess social relationships (Greenwood, Todd, Hops, & Walker,

1982). The argument here simply is this—the easy experimental demonstrations of effect are now behind us, and we should proceed with designing, implementing, and evaluating the longitudinal, communitywide interventions that are necessary to achieve the magnitude, breadth, and longevity of behavior change that our clients need and the contextually complex social world demands.

REFERENCES

American Psychiatric Association. (1994). *Diagnostic and statistical manual of mental disorders* (4th ed.). Washington, DC: Author.

Day, R., Powell, T., Dy-Lin, E., & Stowitschek, J. (1982). An evaluation of the effects of a social interaction training package on mentally handicapped preschool children. *Education and Training of the Mentally Retarded, 17*, 125–130.

Fox, J. J., Gunter, P., Brady, M. P., Bambara, L., Spiegel-McGill, P., & Shores, R. E. (1984). Using multiple peer exemplars to develop generalized social responding of an autistic girl. In R. Rutherford & C. M. Nelson (Eds.), *Monograph on Severe Behavioral Disorders of Children and Youth, 7*, 17–26.

Furman, W., Rahe, D. F., & Hartup, W. W. (1979). Rehabilitation of socially withdrawn preschool children through mixed-age and same-age socialization. *Child Development, 50*, 915–922.

Goldstein, H., & Ferrell, D. R. (1987). Augmenting communicative interaction between handicapped and nonhandicapped preschoolers. *Journal of Speech and Hearing Disorders, 19*, 200–211.

Goldstein, H., & Wickstrom, S. (1986). Peer intervention effects on communicative interaction among handicapped and nonhandicapped preschoolers. *Journal of Applied Behavior Analysis, 19*, 209–214.

Goldstein, H., Wickstrom, S., Hoyson, M., Jamieson, B., & Odom, S. (1988). Effects of sociodramatic play training on social and communicative interaction. *Education and Treatment of Children, 11*, 97–117.

Greenwood, C. R., Todd, N. M., Hops, H., & Walker, H. M. (1982). Behavior change targets in the assessment and treatment of socially withdrawn preschool children. *Behavioral Assessment, 4*, 273–297.

Kohler, F. W., Shearer, D., & Strain, P. S. (1990). *Peer mediated intervention manual.* Pittsburgh, PA: University of Pittsburgh.

Kohler, F. W., & Strain, P. S. (1993). Teaching preschool children to make friends. *Teaching Exceptional Children, 25*, 41–43.

McCarthy, D. A. (1972). *Manual for the McCarthy Scales of Children's Abilities.* San Antonio: The Psychological Corporation.

McConnell, S. R., Sisson, L. A., Cort, C. A., & Strain, P. S. (1991). Effects of social skills training and contingency management on reciprocal interaction of behaviorally handicapped preschool children. *Journal of Special Education, 24*, 473–495.

Newborg, J., Stock, J. R., & Wenck, L. (1984). *Battelle Developmental Inventory*. Allen, TX: DLM Teaching Resources.

Novak, M. A., & Harlow, H. F. (1975). Social recovery of monkeys isolated for the first year of life: I. Rehabilitation and therapy. *Developmental Psychology, 11,* 453–465.

Odom, S. L., Hoyson, M., Jamieson, B., & Strain, P. S. (1985). Increasing handicapped preschoolers' peer social interactions: Cross-setting and component analysis. *Journal of Applied Behavior Analysis, 18,* 3–16.

Sancilio, M. F. M. (1987). Peer interaction as a method of therapeutic intervention with children. *Clinical Psychology Review, 7,* 475–500.

Schreibman, L. (1988). *Autism.* Thousand Oaks, CA: Sage.

Strain, P. S. (1977). Training and generalization effects of peer social initiations on withdrawn preschool children. *Journal of Abnormal Child Psychology, 5,* 445–455.

Strain, P. S. (1984). Social behavior patterns of nonhandicapped and nonhandicapped–developmentally disabled friend pairs in mainstream preschools. *Analysis and Intervention in Developmental Disabilities, 4,* 15–28.

Strain, P. S. (1985). Social and non-social determinants of acceptability in handicapped preschool children. *Topics in Early Childhood Special Education, 4,* 47–58.

Strain, P. S. (1987). Parent training with young autistic children: A report on the LEAP model. *Zero to Three, 7,* 7–12.

Strain, P. S., & Odom, S. L. (1986). Peer social initiations: An effective intervention for social skills deficits of exceptional children. *Exceptional Children, 52,* 543–551.

Strain, P. S., Shores, R. E., & Timm, M. A. (1977). Effects of peer initiations on the social behavior of withdrawn preschoolers. *Journal of Applied Behavior Analysis, 10,* 289–298.

Suomi, S. J., & Harlow H. F. (1972). Social rehabilitation of isolate-reared monkeys. *Developmental Psychology, 6,* 487–496.

Wahler, R. G. (1967). Child–child interactions in free-field settings: some experimental analyses. *Journal of Experimental Child Psychology, 5,* 278–293.

VII

TREATMENTS NOT SPECIFIC TO A PARTICULAR DISORDER

INTRODUCTION

Sometimes people seek treatment not because they meet *DSM* diagnostic criteria for a major psychiatric disorder but because of life stresses, difficulty in adjusting to a new cultural milieu, low self-esteem not related to depression, or personality traits that seem to be in the way of reaching their full potential in life. This section consists of four chapters, each presenting innovative approaches for the treatment of various types of psychological problems that afflict children and adolescents. These treatments employ theoretically based techniques, blending multiple approaches when required. The development of comprehensive combined techniques may be the future for treatment research and offers the promise of greater approximation of the work done by clinicians.

Fred Frankel and his coauthors discuss a social skills training program for elementary-school aged children who are rejected by their peers. The assessment and outcome measures are delineated in the chapter. The treatment plan consists of didactic presentations and behavioral rehearsal with the children, coached play, child socialization homework, and didactic presentations to parents. The results are promising for children with sufficient cognitive abilities, but less so for those with oppositional defiant disorder. Some evidence suggests that this treatment approach can be used in school settings as well as by other than Caucasian children.

Peter Fonagy and Mary Target present their work on psychodynamic developmental therapy for children (PDTC), which incorporates psychoanalytic concepts and techniques for the treatment of severely disturbed children. This procedure is based on an understanding of psychodynamic and developmental processes and incorporates the knowledge of children's emotional, cognitive, and social development into their treatment. The authors delineate the treatment plan and offer clinical vignettes to provide preliminary evidence that PDTC is a promising treatment for children who do not respond to other interventions. Further studies of effectiveness are needed, and the authors recommend that future research should begin at an early age and be longitudinal. The generalizability of this model remains to be tested.

Giuseppe Costantino and Robert G. Malgady discuss the use of Puerto Rican *cuento* (folktale) and hero–heroine modeling therapies as therapeutic approaches for the treatment of Puerto Rican children and adolescents who present severe behavior problems in school and at home, but who do not meet *DSM* criteria for a specific diagnosis. The folktales and biographies, which convey a message or moral to be emulated, are techniques based on the principles of social learning theory. The authors indicate that self-concept and ethnic identity were enhanced and anxiety symptoms were reduced at posttreatment assessment. They acknowledge, however, that more work must be done in this area. Additional assessment measures need to be developed, and comparisons of cuento therapy with other treatments (e.g., family therapy, cognitive–behavioral therapy), must be carried out. Furthermore, studies are needed to test the cuento therapy's applicability in school settings, to examine its exportability to other cultural groups, and to ascertain whether it can be performed by other than ethnically matched therapists. The authors recommend that future research address these issues, as well as identify the specific cultural elements that influence treatment outcomes.

William M. Kurtines and José Szapocznik describe an innovative, theory-based procedure using structural family therapy (SFT) for Cuban and other culturally diverse families of children with behavior problems and drug abuse. They describe in detail the principles of SFT and the modifications made for its transcultural use. The effectiveness of SFT has been established in a variety of settings and applications with Hispanic families and is now being tested with African American families. However, the authors recommend that with changing times and the changing needs of families, work in the field needs to continue to evolve to meet the multiplicity of problems that families will continue to confront.

The studies described in this section are creative treatment modalities that attempt to combine techniques derived from various theoretically based, yet differing, models. To a small extent, these studies also attempt to consider the developmental level of the children, their emotional and cognitive abilities, and the nuclear and broader milieux. Parents are included in the therapeutic study programs presented in this section. In addition, there is a serious shortage of empirical studies concerning psychosocial treatments with culturally and ethnically diverse youth and their families. Many issues must be addressed in this area. For instance, we need to develop appropriate assessment measures to discern differences in the expression of psychopathology between children from various ethnic and cultural backgrounds, and to develop tailored treatments to address their needs. The National Institutes of Health and the National Institute of Mental Health are aware of the research gaps and are increasing the rigor of requirements for inclusion of minorities and women in funded research projects.

25

HELPING OSTRACIZED CHILDREN: SOCIAL SKILLS TRAINING AND PARENT SUPPORT FOR SOCIALLY REJECTED CHILDREN

FRED FRANKEL, DENNIS P. CANTWELL, and ROBERT MYATT

Socially rejected children rarely admit difficulty with peers and may overstate their popularity. They may name several classmates they consider friends, but cannot recall any recent play dates. When asked whom they play with at home, they may name a parent or sibling. We ask the children entering our program whether they are interested in taking a class that teaches children how to make and keep friends. They are never told that they need the class or given any feedback indicating that they need to learn better skills. Despite the occasional denial that they need such a class, they seem willing to take it and usually look forward to it: of 194 children entering our program to date, only 10 did not wish to stay in treatment.

Peers generally attribute to a child whom they reject as a playmate a combination of some or all of the following traits: intrusiveness, immaturity, insensitivity, or obnoxiousness. They note that the socially rejected child does not follow instructions and rules in the classroom or during team sports. Observational studies (e.g., Bierman, 1989) suggest that peers hold fixed negative stereotypes of the rejected child that may be resistant to change: Peers notice the socially rejected child's negative but not prosocial behaviors.

Correspondence concerning this chapter should be directed to Dr. Fred Frankel, Director, University of California Parent Training and Children Social Skills Programs, 300 UCLA Medical Plaza, Los Angeles, CA 90024-6967.

Parents become aware of their child's social adjustment problems in one of several ways, depending on the parents' sophistication in observing their child's social functioning. Some parents report becoming acutely aware of their child's peer difficulties when they invite the child's acquaintances (e.g., from the child's elementary school class) to the child's birthday party and no one comes. Other parents report that their child does not receive invitations to play, usually does not invite children home, and that children who come over to play once never want to come over again. When asked how their child plays with others, parents typically report that the child is bossy and argumentative. They may also report that their child seems lonely, excessively demanding, or overly reliant on a parent or sibling to serve as their playmate.

Between 10% and 20% of school-aged children are socially rejected by their classmates (Burleson, 1985). Rejected status has been shown to be predictive of a child's later social problems (Hymel, Rubin, Rowden, & LeMare, 1990; Michelson, Foster, & Ritchey, 1977; Tremblay, LeBlanc, & Schwartzman, 1988), delinquency (Roff, Sells, & Golden, 1972), and adult maladjustment (Cowen, Pederson, Babigan, Izzo, & Trost, 1973). Parker and Asher (1987) report that rejected children who are also aggressive are at higher risk for school drop-out and later criminality.

The socially rejected child also may fail to form close, reciprocal, confiding relationships (chumships). Chumships become stable by about the fourth grade (cf. McGuire & Weisz, 1982). Having one or two chums is of great importance to later adjustment, can buffer the impact of stressful events (Miller & Ingham, 1976), and correlates positively with self-esteem and negatively with anxious and depressive symptomatology (Buhrmeister, 1990). Chums may promote the development of social competence: Although conflicts with acquaintances can inhibit future social interaction, conflicts among chums and their resolution are associated with subsequent increases on measures of social problem solving (Nelson & Aboud, 1985).

Our treatment hypothesis was that socially accepted children and their parents follow rules of etiquette, and build and effectively utilize social networks, while socially rejected children and their parents commit faux pas. Goals for treatment included helping socially rejected children and their parents identify and correct these faux pas and helping parents begin to develop social networks that are more functional for their child's peer acceptance.

UNDERSTANDING THE SOCIAL CONTEXT

Formation of the Child's Social Network

An examination of the context of peer relationships proves useful for developing an integrated approach to treatment that may readily generalize to a child's natural environment. Schools provide much of this context. The neighborhood school offers a context that can foster friendships among children by providing them with common experiences, a common place to play after school, and common social networks, and by serving as a springboard for more accessible, intimate peer interaction (Rubin & Sloman, 1984). Today, many parents have abandoned the neighborhood school. Less than half of the children in our sample attended a school within walking distance of their homes. Most children were transported several miles, so that neighborhood social resources are unfamiliar to them and their parents.

Neighborhood streets, formerly alive with the sound of children playing, are quiet. Parent worries about crime lead them to discourage play in front of the house, where children could be more easily accessed by peers (cf. Cochran & Davila, 1992). Furthermore, the typical child views 27 hours of television per week (Bryant & DeMorris, 1992), reducing the time available for play. Reduced accessibility and availability of peers for play has made parent social networks of paramount importance (Ladd, 1992; Rubin & Sloman, 1984). Parents must now devote considerable effort to making friends and acquaintances specifically to stimulate their child's social relationships.

The term *play date* (prearranged play sessions with individual companions) has been introduced into our social vernacular (Ladd, 1992; Parke & Bhavnagri, 1989). Kenniston (1975, reported in Gottman, 1983) reported that between 55% and 90% of children have play dates. A successful play date is characterized by a sustained, mutually pleasurable interchange (perhaps with occasional disagreements; cf. Gottman & Parkhurst, 1980) and reciprocated play date invitations by the guest. Play dates are cornerstones in the development of "chumships."

Many structured community activities have far less direct impact on the child's social development. Research (Ladd & Price, 1987) has shown that involvement in structured activities, such as organized team sports and scouting, are not significantly related to social adjustment. Therefore, the most important social contributions from structured activities occur immediately before and after the meetings (arranging play dates and meeting new acquaintances). Parents must not only maintain the structured activities and associated community networks, but must ensure that their children use them as a springboard to more intimate friendships (Parke & Bhavnagri, 1989).

The Child's Acquisition of Peer Etiquette Rules

Another way to understand social context is by examining social etiquette—rules of behavior enforced by the peer group. Children first learn social rules through specific instruction from parents (Gralinski &

Kopp, 1993; Rubin & Sloman, 1984). As children become more proficient with these rules, they become less tolerant of infractions by others. By the end of first grade, children must master many of these rules in order to be accepted by peers. Children attain a reputation (social rejection) through frequent infractions of these rules.

Subsequent learning of peer etiquette may be more difficult for the socially rejected child because the natural development and transmission of peer etiquette requires generally positive and sustained interaction with peers and learning from chums. Continued isolation makes deficits in the knowledge of peer etiquette more obvious as the child gets older. Thus, an effective intervention must identify key situations and accompanying rules of etiquette and effectively instruct the socially rejected child.

Trends in Social Skills Training

School-based interventions for children's social skills have been used for the past 15 years (e.g., Gresham & Nagle, 1980; Oden & Asher, 1977; Walker et al., 1983). Bierman (1989) has concluded that although these interventions may demonstrate immediate changes in children's social behavior within the treatment situation, few studies have obtained durable changes that generalized to the child's social environment.

These few studies comprised interventions for training in socially valid skills. For example, praising and cooperation with peers characterize accepted but not rejected children. Training in these skills improved peer ratings in the classroom immediately after treatment as well as at follow-up (Gresham & Nagle, 1980; Oden & Asher, 1977). These school-based programs demonstrated that it is possible to improve the rejected child's social network. However, no increases were obtained in the number of friends (Oden & Asher, 1977).

In contrast with the promising results of school-based programs on nonclinical populations, interventions on clinic-referred children have not demonstrated positive effects on classroom ratings of the teacher (Gresham, 1985; Michelson et al., 1983; Michelson & Wood, 1980; Tremblay et al., 1991) or peers (Bierman, 1989; La Greca & Santogrossi, 1980). This may be due to differences in either diagnostic categories or severity of social problems. Several of these studies measured only the changes on the aggressive–disruptive dimension and not on the social competence dimension.

School-based and outpatient clinic programs have not promoted the development of "chums". Parents, the schedulers and monitors of play dates, also have not been involved (Budd, 1986). The next sections of this chapter describe our clinical research program.

THE TREATMENT PLAN

The parent-assisted children's social skills training conformed to social validity criteria as enumerated by Wolf (1978):

1. Previous research determined the social significance of most behaviors and skills to be trained—children were trained to behave more like accepted peers (Budd, 1986), and parents were taught to behave more like the parents of accepted peers.
2. The intervention procedures were administered in a socially acceptable manner—children were seen in a group setting apart from their regular peer milieu (cf. Gresham, 1985); and evaluation instruments were employed that utilized socially significant others (i.e., mothers and teachers) and were previously shown to be related to social adjustment (cf. Ladd & Mize, 1983).

The treatment plan attempted to address the socially rejected child's current relationships with peers in four crucial areas: (a) abating the effects of the child's reputation within the current peer group (cf. Bierman, 1989) by instruction on rules of peer etiquette; (b) diminishing the importance of the rejecting peer group for the child by training skills to expand the social network; (c) instructing parents and children how to work together to promote more successful play dates (it was hypothesized that this would allow the development of chums despite a nonfunctional social network); and (d) avoiding continuing provocation from peers by improving the child's competence at nonaggressive responses to teasing and conflicts with children and adults.

The training program was conducted with boys and girls between the ages of 7 and 12 whose parents requested their participation in the UCLA Children's Social Skills Program. Because our referral rate strongly favored boys (ratio of 5.7 : 1), only data from boys were analyzed in the initial study. In all cases, the parents reported that the patients were having difficulty making and/or keeping friends. Teacher assessments confirmed that almost all the boys were actively rejected by their peers. Twelve treatment groups of between 6 and 9 boys each were administered the treatment in its initial format (Frankel, Myatt, & Cantwell, 1995).

Session Structure

Children and their parents were seen concurrently in separate locations (except for the finalization of the homework assignment). Table 1

TABLE 1
Overall Plan for Parent-Assisted Children's Social Skills Training

Session		
Child	Parent	Homework Assignment[a]
1. Session rules; communication	Goals and limits of the program	Bring outside game
2. Times and places to meet friends; playing detective	Encouragement and discouragement	Play detective [bring outside game]
3. Dos and don'ts of group entry	Parent support of social skills	[Play detective; bring outside game]
4. Slipping in; rejection	Group entry and rejection	[Play detective; bring outside game]
5. Praising others; negotiating game switches	Praise; group entry	Group entry [play detective; bring outside game]
6. Praising others; negotiating game switches	(No handout)	Bring inside game [group entry; play detective]
7. Being a good host	How to have a play date	Play date [bring inside game; play detective]
8. Bag on the bag; being a good host	Bag on the bag	Bag on the bag [play date; bring inside game; play detective]
9. Confrontations with adults; being a good host	Adult confrontations	Bring team game [bag on the bag; play date; play detective]
10. Being a good winner; being a good host	(No handout)	[Bring team game; bag on the bag; play date; play detective]
11. Avoiding physical fights	Consequences for physical fights	[Play date; play detective]
12. Graduation; posttests	Where to go from here	

[a]Brackets denote continuing homework assignments.

outlines the content of the 12 sessions, listed separately for child session, parent session, and homework assignment.

Each child session (except for the first and last) was organized into four segments. First, each child reported on the results of the previously assigned socialization homework. Then, a 15-minute didactic presentation, related behavioral rehearsal, and coaching were implemented. Coached play followed for 25 minutes, either on an outdoor play deck or indoors with toys brought from home. During the last 10 minutes, the group leaders formalized the child's socialization homework assignment with the parents.

Each parent session was subdivided in a manner similar to the child session. First, parents reviewed their own and their child's performance on the homework assignment. Problems of compliance were addressed. Next, an informational handout was presented (except for Sessions 6 and 10) and the content of the concurrent child session was briefly reviewed (except for Sessions 4, 8, and 9, for which the informational handout covered this in greater detail). The homework assignment for the following week was then presented and potential obstacles were discussed. Finally, the parent and child were reunited and contracts for homework compliance were negotiated between them. Parent and child group leaders conferred after each session to assess the validity of child and parent reports of homework completion.

Didactic Presentation and Behavioral Rehearsal With the Children

The order of presentation of skills across the 12 sessions is presented in the left-hand column of Table 1. In Session 1, the children were introduced to the rules of the sessions (raise hand first before talking, be serious when first meeting someone, tokens and stars given for good behavior) and then taught communication techniques, such as voice volume, smile, and physical closeness (Bierman & Furman, 1984). Session 2 introduced good times and places (playgrounds, etc.) and bad times and places (in the class, while teacher is talking) to try to make friends. These rules were enforced throughout the sessions (i.e., no talking during the didactic part of the sessions, but talking was encouraged during the coaching activities). Session 2 also introduced information sharing and query techniques under the rubric of "playing detective" (Gottman, 1983; Gottman, Gonso, & Rasmussen, 1975). Gottman et al. (1975) demonstrated that accepted children are better at these skills than rejected children. The following is an example of how this was presented in sessions:

Leader: We're going to learn how to play detective. Before you get together to play with someone else, you need to know if you both like playing the same things. The easiest way to do this is to ask if someone likes to play a certain game. John, what are things you like to play at home?
John: I like to play chess.
Leader: Good. There are two questions you can ask: "Do you like to play chess?" or, "What's your favorite game?" Which question would you like to ask?
John: What's your favorite game?
Leader: Okay, turn to Charlie sitting next to you, and in a clear voice ask him.
John: (Turns to Charlie, but doesn't say anything. The leader stands behind Charlie and stoops down to Charlie's eye level. He mouths very obviously, "What's your favorite game?" This is enough to get John to say it.) What's your favorite game?
Charlie: I like to play Super Mario (a videogame).

Leader: Excellent. You spoke right to Charlie!

Sessions 3 through 6 were devoted to training the following rules of etiquette for entry into a group of peers at play (cf. Garvey, 1984): Do not ask questions (this bothers the children who are playing); do not disagree, criticize, or make suggestions (it is not your game); be sure you know what the group is playing, the rules, and who is losing; slip into the ongoing activity by waiting for a pause in the action and offering to help them play their game (e.g., ask to play with the side that is losing or that has fewer children).

Session 4 introduced the expectation that approximately one half of entry attempts are rejected by play groups (Corsaro, 1981). Reasons for rejection and what to do after rejection were presented. Praising other children (e.g., "good shot"; Gottman et al., 1975), techniques of persuasion (cf. Gottman, 1983), and negotiating to allow children to shift to new common ground activities (Gottman, 1983; Gottman & Parkhurst, 1980) were added in Sessions 5 and 6. Session 7 was devoted to skills needed during the play date (the rules of a good host). Host etiquette, functional in the context of play dates, comprises the following rules aiding in conflict avoidance:

1. Play dates are supervised by parents best from afar (Ladd & Golter, 1988).
2. The guest gets to pick what he or she wants to play (cf. Lollis & Ross, 1987, cited in Ladd, 1992; a corollary of this rule is that if you do not want the guest to play with certain toys, hide them before the play date).
3. Be loyal to the guest (do not have more than one child at a time to an exclusive play date and do not leave the guest by him- or herself for an extended period of time).
4. Prohibit all noninteractive activities (e.g., television and videogames).

Although more competent children may react to teasing by humor or assertion (Perry, Williard, & Perry, 1990), children with poor conflict management skills may get angry or upset when teased. This type of reaction probably motivates the perpetrator to continue, even if the victim uses physical aggression (cf. Shantz, 1986). Therefore, in Session 8 children were taught to react neutrally or humorously to teasing in the following manner (Coie & Dodge, 1988): Each child produced a tease (bag) someone had used on them and identified the perpetrator. Several "bags on the bag" were modeled, which were intended to tease the perpetrator about their inability to tease well (cf. Perry et al., 1990). Children practiced "bagging on the bag" in response to structured teasing from the class

(Goodwin & Mahoney, 1975). The following is an example of how this is taught:

> *Leader:* A good way to stop teasing is to make fun of the tease, not to tease back. Who's been teased by someone?
>
> *John:* I have.
>
> *Leader:* What's the name of the teaser?
>
> *John:* Brandon. He's always teasing me.
>
> *Leader:* What does he say?
>
> *John:* He says I'm a fat slob.
>
> *Leader:* The answer to that is, "That's so old it's got dust on it" (after a short silence, some children begin to giggle) or "Can't you think of anything else to say?" Can anyone else think of something to say?
>
> *Charles:* "When I first heard that, I fell off my dinosaur!"
>
> *Leader:* (Laughing) That's a good one.
>
> *John:* "You're fat too."
>
> *Leader:* That's not what we mean. That's teasing back. Let's try one. I'll pretend I'm Brandon. "You're a fat slob."
>
> *John:* "So what?"
>
> *Leader:* That's another good one! Now we're going to take turns being the teaser and getting teased.

Session 9 dealt with respectful responses to adults during confrontations (e.g., do not argue or roll your eyes, remain quiet and attentive). Children were warned that they would be unjustly accused during the ensuing coached play activity, but would earn tokens for responding appropriately. Session 10 addressed being a good winner (praise teammates, pretend winning is not important). Session 11 outlined a strategy for avoiding physical fights: Group pressure was used to label physical fighting as undesirable. Techniques to avoid "bullies" were also presented (e.g., stay out of their reach, stay with other children, do not tease or antagonize them). Session 12 consisted of a graduation party and ceremony with the children, and posttreatment evaluation with the parents.

Coached Play

Coached play began in Session 2. Coaches were prohibited from taking part in the children's play activities but watched, dispensed token and verbal reinforcement, and provided prompts and 2-minute time-outs for misbehavior (Ladd & Golter, 1988). Socially rejected children seem to define the purpose of a game as "to win at all costs," without consideration that the interaction with the game partner go smoothly so as to continue the relationship (Ladd & Mize, 1983). Coin-shaped plastic tokens served as rewards, and also effectively divided the children's attention so that they could not concentrate on "winning at all costs."

Beginning with Session 2, toys suitable for outside play were brought from home by the children. It was sometimes necessary to have parents purchase toys (balls, etc.), as children did not have them or did not initially choose to play with them. During Sessions 3 and 4, the children practiced group entry and making relevant comments in the following manner: One or two dyads were chosen to play games. Children not involved in play were coached until they understood the game structure. Then they were coached to join the game in progress by making relevant comments, praising other children (Black & Hazen, 1990), and acting in concert with them. An example of this is as follows:

> *Coach:* (Has John watching, Charles and George playing) What are they playing?
> *John:* I don't know.
> *Coach:* As soon as you know what they're playing, you can try to join them.
> *John:* (After a while) They're playing volley ball.
> *Coach:* That's right! Who's winning?
> *John:* (Pointing) That side.
> *Coach:* (Gives token) That's right! Which side would you join?
> *John:* The side that's losing.
> *Coach:* (Gives another token) That's right! When would you ask to join?
> *John:* After they score the next point.

Sessions 5 and 6 focused on praising others and negotiating switches in games when bored. The focus was turned to play dates in Sessions 7 and 8. The children brought indoor interactive games and took turns being the host and the guest. Highly competitive outdoor games were avoided until their introduction in Session 9 (Tryon & Keane, 1991), and continued until Session 11. Unannounced pseudoconfrontations were posed to children during deck play (a coach wrongly accusing them of cheating, etc.) to practice techniques discussed in the didactic segment of the session. The children were always debriefed immediately after each mock confrontation.

Child Socialization Homework

The right-hand column of Table 1 lists the child socialization homework assignments for each session. Telephone calls were assigned to pairs of group members for all sessions. The assignment given in Session 1 was to set the mechanics of the phone call in place: Parents of a pair of children assigned to call each other were to work out the date and time of the call before leaving the session. After Session 2, the children were to use the call to practice "playing detective." After Session 3, the children were required to make an additional call to a child not in the group. Eventually, the children were required to make this call to a potential guest before a play date was set up (Session 7) in order to establish common ground activities prior to a play date ("What should we play when we get together?").

At the end of Sessions 1 through 5, the parents were to agree with the child on a toy to bring into the next session with which the child could potentially engage other children at playgrounds or other outside locations. If a child had no such toy, the group leader made suggestions to the parent for purchases. Toys with violent themes such as toy guns, provocative toys such as water pistols, and solitary toys such as books and electronic toys were prohibited. Occasionally a child brought in a toy that he seemed too interested in playing and would prefer solitary play when other children did not wish to join in. In these cases, prompts were given to join the group. The parents and children were instructed to avoid this toy for subsequent interaction with peers.

The homework assignments given at the end of Sessions 6 through 11 required play dates inside or directly adjacent to the home (to allow indirect monitoring by a parent). Play dates between intervention group members were prohibited. The child was to bring in toys appropriate to this situation (e.g., board games). The prohibitions introduced for the outside toys continued to be enforced. Homework assignments given in Sessions 9 through 11 consisted of bringing in toys to be used in competitive (team) games.

At the end of Sessions 5 and 6, each parent and child agreed on a place and time that the child would attempt to join in an ongoing play group of children not currently in their social network. The children were encouraged to join a group of younger children if they wanted to maximize the chances of their acceptance (Tryon & Keane, 1991). Parents of younger children (7 to 9 years old) could pretend to read a newspaper on a bench a short distance away. Parents of older children were to set the date when the homework was to be attempted, and to remind the child on that day to do the assignment.

The homework assignment given for Sessions 7 to 11 was the culmination of the training of etiquette and network-building skills. The children were to pick someone they had met during the group entry homework assignment and play detective with them to establish activities of mutual interest for a play date. Each child was then to invite the other child to his or her house. If the invitation was accepted, the parent was to call to arrange the date and time. Immediately before the time of the play date, the parents were to remind the child of the rules of a good host and to exclude noninteractive activities. At the time of the play date, the parents were to monitor the play date from another room (Ladd & Golter, 1988), to enforce good host rules, and to praise the child for compliance. The initial play date was to be no longer than 2 hours (subsequent play dates with the same child could be longer). The parents were also encouraged to get to know the guest child's parents.

After Sessions 8 through 10, the children were to practice "bagging the bag" with a selected child who had teased them and/or role play this with a parent (e.g., the mother was to pretend that she was a peer and say "You mother's ugly," etc.). After Sessions 9 and 10, the children were to practice respectful ways to handle confrontations with adults.

Didactic Presentation to the Parents

The middle column of Table 1 lists the topics of didactic presentations to the parents; each was summarized in a handout given to the parent. The goals of these presentations were to (a) inform the parents of their roles in peer acceptance of their children, (b) ensure that the parents took their assigned roles in the child socialization homework, and (c) ensure that the parents provided supportive feedback for the principles the children were being taught. On the way home from session, the children would often mention rules they learned in the group. The parents were to praise children for accurate recall and make corrections as necessary. In addition to a review of material presented in the child session and discussion of homework assignments, the following additional information was presented to parents.

In Session 1, the goals of treatment, methods to be used, and parent requirements were explicitly stated. The parents were cautioned that development of friendships within the group was not one of these goals: Children and parents were to focus on friendships that could be cultivated after the intervention was completed. Session 2 focused on parent encouragement of the child and his friendships (e.g., select potential playmates *with* the child, do not talk about your child's faults in front of others, and model talking about and acting respectfully to other adults in the presence of the child). Session 3 reviewed the parents' tapped and untapped sources for potential playmates for their children and resources for play dates (private play area in the home, interactive activities, and time availability for play dates). A common impediment to homework assignments within our sample was overscheduling the child in structured community activities ("Sorry, he's too busy with teams to have a play date"). This impediment was addressed at this time. Session 4 reviewed rules of etiquette for group entry. Session 5 focused on parent use of praise. Session 7 reviewed how to prepare for and have a conflict-free play date. Session 8 reviewed the "bag the bag" technique. Session 9 concerned parent options for defusing repeated confrontations between their child and another adult (polite discussion with the other adult, listening to the other side of the confrontations, expressing concern, and availability to work together). Session 11 was devoted to parent support for their child's efforts to avoid physical fights and guidelines for providing decelerative consequences for fighting. Session 12 included a review of the major points of the intervention and further tips for parents on selecting playmates with their children.

Measurement of Outcome

Selection of assessment tools to measure the effects of social skills training in outpatient settings requires the clinician to balance the difficulty of data collection with the established concurrent and/or predictive validity of measures to be used. Table 2 lists the most commonly used types of measures. Because the ultimate goals of social skills training in an outpatient setting are to increase peer acceptance and begin the formation of chumships, measures of demonstrated validity for the assessment of these goals must be selected. In this regard, informal clinical indexes of improvement such as unstructured parent feedback, child behavior changes in session, and the clinician's impressions of change, are easy to collect but the least valid for determining treatment effectiveness: Parents are usually glad for having brought their child to the groups; children nearly always have a good time; and when behavioral techniques are used, the children are usually better behaved in this setting by the end of treatment. However, peer acceptance or development of friendships are not assessed.

TABLE 2
Aspect of Socialization Tapped, Validity, and Convenience of Different Types of Measurement of Peer Relationships for Outpatient Social Skills Training

Type of instrument	Aspect of Socialization Tapped			Validity	Convenience
	Peer network	Chums	Behavior outside of group		
Informal clinical assessment	No	No	No	No	Yes
Self-report	No	No	?	?	Yes
Structured behavioral observation	No	No	Yes	No	No
Peer rankings—school	Yes	No	Yes	Yes	No
Peer rankings—treatment group	No	No	No	No	Yes
Teacher scales	Yes	No	Yes	Yes	Yes
Parent scales	No	Yes	?	Yes	Yes

Self-report indexes that ask what the child would do in hypothetical situations show the least intercorrelation with other assessments, may be susceptible to social desirability response set (Ledingham, Younger, Schwartzman, & Bergeron, 1982), and may not correspond to the child's actual behavior (Damon, 1977). Behavioral ratings by independent naive observers have not been shown to discriminate between the accepted and the socially rejected children (Budd, 1986). For instance, rate (rather than quality) of peer interaction is not related to measures of peer acceptance (Asher, Markell, & Hymel, 1981).

Having peers in the patient's classroom rank the patient (among others in the class) on most-liked and least-liked dimensions may predict long-term adjustment (Cowen et al., 1973), but is not practical to collect for outpatients. Having the children in the intervention group rank each other has not been shown to correlate with classroom rankings, may have negative repercussions on the least-liked children, and may show reactivity on repeated administration (La Greca, 1981).

Teacher scales assessing peer relationships correspond well to peer ranking in the classroom (Glow & Glow, 1980). One of the most commonly used teacher scales is the Pupil Evaluation Inventory (PEI; Pekarik, Prinz, Liebert, Weintraub, & Neil, 1976). It consists of 35 items and takes less than 10 minutes to complete. Withdrawal, Likability, and Aggression scales were derived through factor analysis of peer ratings (Pekarik et al., 1976). Peer–teacher correlations exceeded .54 on all scales (Ledingham et al., 1982). Teacher and peer assessments in first grade have been shown to be equally good predictors of peer acceptance 7 years later (Tremblay et al., 1988).

To tap chumships, teacher reports must be supplemented with standardized assessments using parents. The Social Skills Rating System (SSRS; Gresham & Elliott, 1990) is an example of a parent questionnaire. It consists of 48 items divided into two major scales. The Social Skills scale (30 items) inquires about social situations with peers and parents. The Problem Behavior scale (18 items) concentrates on internalizing, externalizing, and hyperactivity problems. Correlations reported by Gresham and Elliot for the parent version with teacher ($r = .36$) and peer versions ($r = .12$) were low but statistically significant.

Frankel and Myatt (1994) have shown that the PEI Withdrawal and Likability scales and the SSRS Social Skills scale tap a common social competence dimension. In contrast, two SSRS Problem Behavior subscales (externalizing and hyperactivity), and the PEI Aggression scale tap an aggressive–disruptive dimension. Both dimensions should be of concern to clinicians wishing to improve a child's social status in terms of treatment goals and assessment.

TREATMENT EFFECTIVENESS

The initial treatment program (Frankel, Myatt, Cantwell, & Fineberg 1995) consisted of all of the child didactic presentations except Sessions 9 and 11 (see Table 1) and all accompanying socialization homework modules. However, only parent modules for Sessions 1 and 2 were developed at this time. Parents were encouraged, but not required, to wait in the meeting room and socialize with each other until the last 15 minutes of Sessions 3 through 11. During these last 15 minutes, the contents of the child session were reviewed, parents were given a handout covering the socialization homework, and potential obstacles to compliance were discussed.

Our initial study (Frankel et al., 1995) compared 36 boys receiving treatment with 17 wait-list controls. Significantly greater mean improvement for the Social Skills scale score of the SSRS was obtained for boys receiving treatment. Child diagnosis did not affect outcome. This was a surprise, as we thought that boys diagnosed with attention deficit hyperactivity disorder (ADHD) or oppositional–defiant disorder (ODD) might have more difficulty in following the rules of a good host and, therefore, would not show improvement at home.

Changes in school were harder to obtain either because treatment did not generalize as well or because the measures employed were less sensitive to change. Mean improvement on the teacher-reported PEI Withdrawal and Aggression scales was statistically significant only for boys without ODD ($n = 18$ in the treatment group). Again, we were surprised that the presence of ADHD ($n = 40$) did not have a significant impact on outcome. This result has continued to the present time. Fifty-six boys diagnosed with ADHD were administered our treatment program thus far. Within this group, there were no significant differences in outcome on any variable related to whether the boy was maintained on Ritalin or Dexedrine ($n = 28$) or other medication ($n = 7$) versus unmedicated ($n = 21$). However, in a few cases it was necessary to suggest a delay in the later dosage of medication (later dosage of Ritalin might be postponed to 4:00 P.M. as groups were conducted between 6:00 and 8:30 P.M.). This suggests that some children showed benefits of medication. Future research should be designed to assess synergistic effects of stimulants in social skills training on individual rather than groups of children.

We were able to develop models for predicting teacher-reported outcome on the Withdrawal, Likability, and Aggression scales of the PEI (Frankel, Myatt, Cantwell, & Fineberg, 1995). Fifty-two participants were divided into treatment responders and nonresponders using a double median split procedure (eliminating participants improving at the median of each outcome measure). Parent Achenbach Child Behavior Checklist

(CBCL; Achenbach, 1991) ratings and *DSM-III-R* diagnosis for boys completing our original intervention were submitted to multiple logistic regression analysis (cf. Afifi & Clark, 1984; Frankel & Simmons, 1992). Scores on the CBCL Thought Problems factor were significantly related to whether or not a subject was a treatment responder in PEI Aggression, while the absence of the *DSM-III-R* diagnosis of ODD predicted that the subject would be a treatment responder in PEI Withdrawal. A majority of subjects who were predicted to be responders for either Aggression or Withdrawal came from only 2 of the 12 treatment groups (randomization tests, $ps < .05$). Parents in these treatment groups chose not to stay and socialize during the unstructured time, but did attend the last segment of each session as required.

Modifications of the Program

Our initial results prompted augmentation of the structure of the parent meetings. Therefore, the remaining modules and accompanying handouts listed in Table 1 were added. Parent attendance was required for the entire session. It was hoped that the formalized structure for the parents would enhance their roles in the homework assignments and uniformly improve the results across all treatment groups.

Thus far, four treatment groups ($n = 16$ boys and 5 girls) have completed the Enhanced program. The preliminary results were compared with the outcome obtained on the original program with 26 additional treated subjects (total $n = 50$ boys and 12 girls, Original program). A reliability of change score [RC = (pretreatment − posttreatment)/SE_{ds}, where SE_{ds} is the standard error of the difference scores for each measure] was calculated for each subject in the pathological range on each measure at baseline. An RC > 2 was designated as reliable. Results are presented in Table 3. Inspection of the table reveals that significantly more teachers were reporting reliable change in PEI Aggression and Likability after the Enhanced versus Original program. A nonsignificant trend was also apparent

TABLE 3
Proportion of Children Showing Reliable Change After Wait-List, Original, and Enhanced Versions of the Program Social Skills Training

Measure	Treatment Condition			χ^2 (O-E)
	Wait List	Original	Enhanced	
Social Skills (SSRS)	.27	.73	.89	ns
Aggression (PEI)	.27	.50	.79	5.81
Likability (PEI)	.40	.41	.65	2.92
Withdrawal (PEI)	.53	.50	.55	ns

Note. SSRS = Social Skills Rating System. PEI = Pupil Evaluation Inventory.

for proportion of parents reporting reliable change on the SSRS Social Skills scale after the Enhanced program. Proportion of patients in the wait-list (22 boys and 4 girls) showing reliable change is presented for each measure for comparison. Also evident from the table is that RCs after the Enhanced program were substantially above wait-list levels, except for PEI Withdrawal.

LIMITATIONS

The social etiquette of middle-class Caucasian children and the social network practices of their parents served as the basis of our intervention. The participants were primarily (86%) Caucasian children or were trying to fit into this reference group (i.e., Hispanic or African American children within a school with predominantly Caucasian children). In principle, the program can be extended to fit social network constraints in poorer areas, different ethnic subcultures, and rural areas. Significant changes also occur in adolescence that affect the content and delivery of many of these modules so that extensive program modifications would be necessary for the program to be extended to children older than 12 years of age. However, it is first essential to understand the differences in social etiquette and successful parent approaches to social networking, and to modify the program accordingly. The present authors could find no research that would be helpful in making these modifications. Such research needs to be done.

Our program was designed for elementary school children with at least average cognitive functioning and who were not psychotic. The program depended in part on the child's ability to understand and conform to features of social etiquette, once these were taught. It is doubtful that children lacking in sufficient cognitive development to understand these social nuances (e.g., autistic and developmentally delayed children) would be able to benefit from a program aimed at this level of socio-cognitive competence.

GENERALIZABILITY

Teacher reports provided clear evidence that the intervention generalized to the school situation. The skills taught discriminated rejected from accepted children. Our clinical observations suggest that the cognitive training facilitated the children's attention toward key situations in their social world. The children could observe accepted children experiencing success from using the skills taught. We suspect that homework assignments were instrumental in getting children to try the skills at school and at home.

It was possible that some or all of the following elements in the assignment format promoted homework compliance: (a) the date, time, and other party to the assignment was contracted between parent and child at the end of each session; (b) parents were to promote the assignment at the contracted time; (c) the first assignments were easier and later assignments more difficult; (d) children and parents were held accountable for their parts of the homework assignments at the beginning of the following session; (e) peer pressure from the group seemed to set the expectation that the assignments were to be done; and (f) children were required to bring in their own toys, which they would have and use when the group was not in session.

It is also possible that the context of the intervention may have contributed to generalization. The intervention was presented to the children as a class intended to teach them how to make and keep friends. The classroom-like format (6 to 9 children with didactic and homework components) might have aided in generalizing programmatic features to the school situation. The coached play segment was held in a large outside area with a basketball court and swings, similar to a playground. This may have facilitated generalization to recess at school and playgrounds.

Extrapolations to the Private Practice Setting

Most of the features discussed in the previous section of this chapter can be implemented within a private practice setting. The most difficult feature to implement may be the gathering of sufficient numbers of children (at least five) to provide the necessary "critical mass" for group processes and economic viability. A minimum of two professionals are required (one to run the child group and another to conduct the simultaneous parent group). We recommend one assistant for a group of five children and two assistants for a group of nine children to help maintain discipline and provide a sufficient level of coaching and reinforcement.

DISCUSSION AND RECOMMENDATIONS

Outpatient children referred for peer socialization problems were instructed on socially validated skills within classroom- and playground-like settings. The intervention confronted current problems in the children's social environments, such as negative reputation and teasing, and trained parents and children to behave more like socially accepted counterparts. Parents and children were instructed to work together to promote more successful play dates to facilitate the development of chums. Results demonstrated improvement on measures of socialization reported by parents and teachers. In our initial intervention, children with ODD did not do as well on teacher-reported measures as children without this diagnosis. With increased structured parent involvement, children with ODD were able to demonstrate generalization to the school environment.

Similar improvement has not been noted previously in outpatient settings, even when parents have been involved in the treatment. For instance, Tremblay et al. (1991) involved mothers in a multiyear treatment that included social skills training and parent reinforcement of prosocial behaviors. Immediately after treatment, mothers reported that their children were more disruptive and inattentive. The present results may represent a significant departure from these findings. However comparison with the results of Tremblay et al. must be made with caution as many features (e.g., outcome measures and treatment periods) differed from the present study.

Our intervention raised four questions for additional research. First, did social behavior improve at home? Parents were part of treatment and it was possible that the change they reported did not reflect improvement in social behavior with peers at home. Because the use of other observers may have unknown validity, and direct observation of play behaviors has failed to show significant correlations with peer acceptance (Asher et al., 1981; Budd, 1986), future research should "blind" parents to the treatment condition by randomly assigning them to treatment or a condition that mimics treatment. Second, why did children with ODD not do as well in the school setting after treatment as children without this disorder? How did Enhancement of the parent participation increase Likability and decrease Aggression in school? We are currently awaiting replication of results within the Enhanced program. Future research may have to examine how treatment effects break down for these children. Possible areas of breakdown are in decreased homework compliance or greater persistence of reputational effects at school. Third, did children receiving the enhanced program make lasting friends? This was not directly assessed in the present studies. Anecdotal parent reports suggest that play dates took place and were generally successful. Reliable and valid measures that specifically target the acquisition of chums need to be developed for use in an outpatient setting. Fourth, is there a positive impact upon the long-term adjustment of these children? The first step in answering this question is to follow the children into their next school year (new teachers and reshuffling of classmates). Anecdotal information spontaneously offered by teachers suggests durable changes. The techniques discussed in this chapter appear to offer promise in changing peer status and chumships in socially rejected children. The answers to these four questions will help to determine whether the results of these techniques warrant their use in clinical practice.

REFERENCES

Achenbach, T. (1991). Integrative guide for the 1991 CBCL/4–18, CSR, and TR profiles. Burlington: University of Vermont Department of Psychiatry.

Afifi, A., & Clark, V. (1984). *Computer aided multivariate analysis*. Toronto, Canada: Lifetime Learning.

Asher, S. R., Markell, R. A., & Hymel, S. (1981). Identifying children at risk in peer relations: A critique of the rate-of-interaction approach to assessment. *Child Development, 52*, 1239–1245.

Bierman, K. L. (1989). Improving the peer relationships of rejected children. In B. B. Lahey & A. E. Kazdin (Eds.), *Advances in clinical child psychology* (Vol. 12, pp. 53–85). New York: Plenum Press.

Bierman, K. L., & Furman, W. (1984). The effects of social skills training and peer involvement in the social adjustment of preadolescents. *Child Development, 55*, 151–162.

Black, B., & Hazen, N. L. (1990). Social status and patterns of communication in acquainted and unacquainted preschool children. *Developmental Psychology, 26*, 379–387.

Bryant, B. K., & DeMorris, K. A. (1992). Beyond parent–child relationships: Potential links between family environments and peer relations. In R. D. Parke & G. W. Ladd (Eds.), *Family–peer relationships: Modes of linkages* (pp. 159–189). Hillsdale, NJ: Erlbaum.

Budd, K. S. (1986). Parents as mediators in the social skills training of children. In L. L'Abate & M. A. Milan (Eds.), *Handbook of social skills training and research* (pp. 245–262). New York: Wiley.

Buhrmeister, D. (1990). Intimacy of friendship, interpersonal competence, and adjustment during preadolescence and adolescence. *Child Development, 61*, 1101–1111.

Burleson, B. R. (1985). Communication skills and childhood peer relationships: An overview. In M. McLaughlin (Ed.), *Communication yearbook* (vol. 9, pp. 143–180). London: Sage.

Cochran, M., & Davila, V. (1992). Societal influences on children's peer relations. In R. D. Parke & G. W. Ladd (Eds.), *Family–peer relationships: Modes of linkages* (pp. 191–212). Hillsdale, NJ: Erlbaum.

Coie, J. D., & Dodge, K. A. (1988). Multiple sources of data on social behavior and social status. *Child Development, 59*, 815–829.

Corsaro, W. A. (1981). Friendship in the nursery school: Social organization in a peer environment. In S. R. Asher & J. M. Gottman (Eds.), *The development of children's friendships* (pp. 207–241). New York: Cambridge University Press.

Cowen, E. L., Pederson, A., Babigan, H., Izzo, L. D., & Trost, M. A. (1973). Long-term follow-up of early detected vulnerable children. *Journal of Consulting and Clinical Psychology, 41*, 438–446.

Damon, W. (1977). *The social world of the child*. San Francisco: Josey-Bass.

Frankel, F., & Myatt, R. (1994). A dimensional approach to the assessment of the social competence of boys. *Psychological Assessment, 6,* 249–254.

Frankel, F., Myatt, R., & Cantwell, D. P. (1995). Training outpatient boys to conform with the social ecology of popular peers: Effects on parent and teacher ratings. *Journal of Clinical Child Psychology, 24,* 300–310.

Frankel, F., Myatt, R., Cantwell, D. P., & Fineberg, D. T. (1995). *Use of parent ratings and psychiatric diagnosis in predicting outcome of children's social skills training.* Manuscript submitted for publication.

Frankel, F., & Simmons, J. Q. (1992). Parent behavioral training: Why and when some parents drop out. *Journal of Clinical Child Psychology, 21,* 322–330.

Garvey, C. (1984). *Children's talk.* Cambridge, MA: Harvard University Press.

Glow, R. A., & Glow, P. H. (1980). Peer and self-rating: Children's perception of behavior relevant to hyperkinetic impulse disorder. *Journal of Abnormal Child Psychology, 8,* 397–404.

Goodwin, S. E., & Mahoney, M. J. (1975). Modification of aggression through modeling: An experimental probe. *Journal of Behavior Therapy and Experimental Psychiatry, 6,* 200–202.

Gottman, J. M. (1983). How children become friends. *Monographs of the Society for Research in Child Development, 48* (Serial No. 201).

Gottman, J. M., Gonso, J., & Rasmussen, B. (1975). Social interaction, social competence and friendship in children. *Child Development, 46,* 709–718.

Gottman, J. M., & Parkhurst, J. T. (1980). A developmental theory of friendship and acquaintanceship processes. In W. A. Collins (Ed.), *Development of cognition, affect and social relationships: Minnesota symposium on child psychology* (vol. 13, pp. 197–253). Hillsdale, NJ: Erlbaum.

Gralinski, J. H., & Kopp, C. (1993). Everyday rules for behavior: Mother's requests to young children. *Developmental Psychology, 29,* 573–584.

Gresham, F. M. (1985). Utility of cognitive–behavioral procedures for social skills training with children: A critical review. *Journal of Abnormal Child Psychology, 13,* 411–423.

Gresham, F. M., & Elliott, S. N. (1990). *Social skills rating system: Manual.* Circle Pines, MN: American Guidance Service.

Gresham, F. M., & Nagle, R. J. (1980). Social skills training with children: Responsiveness to modeling and coaching as a function of peer orientation. *Journal of Consulting and Clinical Psychology, 48,* 718–729.

Hymel, S., Rubin, K. H., Rowden, L., & LeMare, L. (1990). Children's peer relationships: Longitudinal prediction of internalizing and externalizing problems from middle to late childhood. *Child Development, 61,* 2004–2021.

Ladd, G. W. (1992). Themes and theories: Perspectives on processes in family–peer relationships. In R. D. Parke & G. W. Ladd (Eds.), *Family–peer relationships: Modes of linkages* (pp. 3–34). Hillsdale, NJ: Erlbaum.

Ladd, G. W., & Golter, B. S. (1988). Parents' management of preschoolers peer relations: Is it related to children's social competence? *Developmental Psychology, 24,* 109–117.

Ladd, G. W., & Mize, J. (1983). A cognitive–social learning model of social skill training. *Psychological Bulletin, 90*, 127–157.

Ladd, G. W., & Price, J. M. (1987). Predicting children's social and school adjustment following the transition from preschool to kindergarten. *Child Development, 58*, 1168–1189.

La Greca, A. M. (1981). Peer acceptance: The correspondence between children's sociometric scores and teachers' ratings of peer interactions. *Journal of Abnormal Child Psychology, 9*, 167–178.

La Greca, A. M., & Santogrossi, D. A. (1980). Social skills training with elementary school students: A behavioral group approach. *Journal of Consulting and Clinical Psychology, 48*, 220–227.

Ledingham, J. E., Younger, A., Schwartzman, A., & Bergeron, G. (1982). Agreement among teacher, peer and self-ratings of children's aggression, withdrawal and likability. *Journal of Abnormal Child Psychology, 10*, 363–372.

McGuire, K. D., & Weisz, J. R. (1982). Social cognition and behavior correlates of preadolescent chumship. *Child Development, 53*, 1478–1484.

Michelson, L., Foster, S. L., & Ritchey, W. L. (1977). Social skills assessment of children. In B. Lahey & A. Kazdin (Eds.), *Advances in clinical child psychology* (Vol. 4, pp. 119–165). New York: Plenum.

Michelson, L., Mannarino, A. P., Marchione, K. E., Stern, M., Figeroa, J., & Beck, S. (1983). A comparative outcome study of behavioral social-skills training, interpersonal problem-solving, and non-directive control treatments with child psychiatric outpatients. *Behavior Research and Therapy, 21*, 545–556.

Michelson, L., & Wood, R. (1980). A group assertive training program for elementary schoolchildren. *Child Behavior Therapy, 2*, 1–9.

Miller, P. M., & Ingham, J. G. (1976). Friends, confidants, and symptoms. *Social Psychiatry, 11*, 51–58.

Nelson, J., & Aboud, F. E. (1985). The resolution of social conflict between friends. *Child Development, 56*, 1009–1017.

Oden, S., & Asher, S. R. (1977). Coaching children in social skills for friendship making. *Child Development, 48*, 495–506.

Parke, R. D., & Bhavnagri, N. P. (1989). Parents as managers of children's peer friendships. In D. Belle (Ed.), *Children's social networks and social supports* (pp. 241–259). New York: Wiley.

Parker, J. G., & Asher, S. R. (1987). Peer relations and later personal adjustment: Are low accepted children at risk? *Psychological Bulletin, 102*, 357–389.

Pekarik, E., Prinz, R., Liebert, D., Weintraub, S., & Neil, J. (1976). The Pupil Evaluation Inventory: A sociometric technique for assessing children's social behavior. *Journal of Abnormal Child Psychology, 4*, 83–97.

Perry, D. G., Williard, J. C., & Perry, L. C. (1990). Peer perceptions of the consequences that victimized children provide aggressors. *Child Development, 61*, 1310–1325.

Roff, M., Sells, B., & Golden, M. (1972). *Social adjustment and personality development in children*. Minneapolis: University of Minnesota Press.

Rubin, Z., & Sloman, J. (1984). How parents influence their children's friendships. In M. Lewis (Ed.), *Beyond the Dyad* (pp. 223–250). New York: Plenum Press.

Shantz, D. W. (1986). Conflict, aggression and peer status: An observational study. *Child Development, 57*, 1322–1332.

Tremblay, R. E., LeBlanc, M., & Schwartzman, A. E. (1988). The predictive power of first-grade peer and teacher ratings of behavior: Sex differences in antisocial behavior and personality at adolescence. *Journal of Abnormal Child Psychology, 16*, 571–583.

Tremblay, R. E., McCord, J., Boileau, H., Charlebois, P., Gagnon, C., Le Blanc, M., & Larivee, S. (1991). Can disruptive boys be helped to become competent? *Psychiatry, 54*, 148–161.

Tryon, A. S., & Keane, S. P. (1991). Popular and aggressive boys' initial social interaction patterns in cooperative and competitive settings. *Journal of Abnormal Child Psychology, 19*, 395–406.

Walker, H., McConnell, S., Holmes, D., Todis, B., Walker, J. L., & Golden, N. (1983). *A curriculum for children's effective peer and teacher skills (ACCEPTS)*. Austin, TX: Pro-Ed Publishers.

Wolf, M. M. (1978). Social validity: The case for subjective measurement or how applied behavior analysis is finding its heart. *Journal of Applied Behavior Analysis, 11*, 203–214.

26

A CONTEMPORARY PSYCHOANALYTICAL PERSPECTIVE: PSYCHODYNAMIC DEVELOPMENTAL THERAPY

PETER FONAGY and MARY TARGET

Child psychoanalysis became popular as a treatment in the 1930s and has informed many forms of psychodynamic treatment of children and families. Individual *psychodynamic therapy* is a form of psychosocial treatment frequently used and highly regarded among child psychiatrists and psychologists (Kazdin, Bass, Siegel, & Thomas, 1990). However, it has become apparent that traditional child psychodynamic therapy has severe limitations: It is a relatively uniform method of treatment, leading to the possibly inappropriate application of the technique in certain cases; the technique has not been operationally described and can lack structure and focus, perhaps leading to lengthy treatments that are not cost effective; and evidence for its efficacy is sparse.

Our own chart review of 763 case records of children and adolescents in psychodynamic treatment suggested that psychodynamic treatments were most effective for children with anxiety disorders, but also were surprisingly effective for some children with relatively severe and complex psychosocial problems. Our examination of the records also revealed that, in the latter cases, many of the techniques used were not among those normally included in textbooks of the technique, and critical components

Correspondence concerning this chapter should be directed to Dr. Peter Fonagy, Department of Psychology, University College London, Gower Street, London WC1E 6BT, UK.

of the treatment may not have been the interpretation of unconscious conflict and the attainment of insight.

This chapter describes a psychodynamic developmental therapy for children (PDTC) that overcomes many of the shortcomings of the traditional approach, and that is targeted at a group of pervasively impaired children for whom there appear to be no alternative, proven treatments (Kazdin, 1994), whom our chart review suggests we can help. We have retained general psychodynamic principles: the notion of unconscious ideation and its role in shaping behavior, symptomatology, and personality structure; the central role of the child's emotional reactions in the organization of the child's representational world; the value of a developmental perspective; and the relationship with the therapist as the primary vehicle of therapeutic change.

The group of children for whom PDTC may be appropriate are not treated as a distinct group in the fourth edition of the *Diagnostic and Statistical Manual of Mental Disroders* (*DSM-IV*; American Psychiatric Association, 1994) or the tenth edition of the *International Classification of Diseases* (World Health Organization, 1988). They are closest to the group encompassed by Asperger's Disorder, and resemble descriptions offered by Towbin, Dykens, Pearson, & Cohen (1993) of Multiple Complex Developmental Disorder (MCDD). They manifest disturbances of social and emotional development, including impairment of peer relationships, affect regulation, frustration tolerance, impulse control, self-esteem and self-image, cognitive functioning, and verbal communication. Understanding of words relating to emotions is often especially lacking, so that a child may have great difficulty in putting words to his or her feelings, or understanding what others mean by simple words, such as "worry" or "want." Because we cannot be sure that these children would have met the criteria proposed for MCDD, we refer to them as *showing developmental disturbances*.

GOALS AND ISSUES

The program that we have developed addresses developmental disturbances from the point of view of a deficit in the development of the self, which we believe is at the core of the pathology of most such cases. We believe that, for a variety of possible reasons, including constitutional, psychosocial, and possibly other factors, these children are deprived of the socio-cognitive experiences that normally underlie the development of the self, leaving them relatively vulnerable in all interpersonal situations. We assume the process to be a transactional one, whereby the beginnings of such a deficit deprive the individual of the benefit of subsequent social experiences that might have facilitated further development of self-representation.

In psychodynamic terms, the dialectical theory of self-development assumes that the psychological self (in which the self is seen not as a physical entity but as an intentional being with goals based on thoughts, beliefs, and desires) develops through the perception of oneself, in another person's mind, as thinking and feeling (Davidson, 1983). We speculate that the parent who cannot think about the child's particular experience of himself deprives him[1] of a core self structure that he needs to build a viable sense of himself. These ideas have much in common with formulations of psychological disturbance advanced by attachment theorists such as Bowlby (1969, 1973, 1980), and in fact we consider the roots of developmental disturbances to lie in the failure of early attachment relationships, particularly likely in circumstances that include maltreatment, parental psychiatric illness, or physical illness or disability in the child. These ideas are elaborated much more fully in other publications (Fonagy, 1991; Fonagy, Moran, & Target, 1993; Fonagy & Target, 1995).

We have delineated some "hallmarks" of developmental disturbances that distinguish these children from those with primarily neurotic disturbances. We have formulated these difficulties in terms of inferred deficits in mental processes, which we have suggested elsewhere (Fonagy, Moran, Edgcumbe, Kennedy, & Target, 1993), that are crucial to the etiology of these disorders: Not only are specific mental representations (thoughts, feelings, fantasies, etc.) unusual, but the mental processes assumed to generate representations are shown to be deficient by the absence or distortion of whole categories of representation and mental experience.

PDTC is designed to provide children with developmental disturbances with corrective cognitive experiences that directly address the limitations of self-representation, and that help the children to develop an awareness of the mental states of other people as well as of themselves. This capacity has been called *mentalization* (Morton & Frith, 1995), or *theory of mind* (see Astington, 1994). PDTC then has as its primary aim the facilitation of normal developmental processes through the removal of obstacles and the direct encouragement of more advanced modes of mental functioning. Below, we outline the lines of evidence from experimental studies of the development of social cognition in normal and abnormal children, and from studies of parent–child attachment, which support our belief that a disorder of mentalization is the crucial problem in the clinical group on which we have focussed.

---

[1]For clarity, we sometimes refer to the child as *he*, and to the caregiver or therapist as *she*. This makes the text easier to follow and corresponds to the actual gender in most instances.

EMPIRICAL SUPPORT

There is substantial accumulating evidence indicating that theory of mind mechanisms (ToMM) are dysfunctional in children with autism (Baron-Cohen, 1995; Mayes & Cohen, 1994), some of whose symptoms children with developmental disturbances share to a mild degree. The ToMM deficit in autism seems to be biologically based (see Baron-Cohen, 1995, for review). We maintain, nevertheless, that lesser degrees of ToMM deficit, with a large psychosocial component in its etiology, are prevalent in the group of children with developmental disturbances whom we have considered. This suggestion is consistent with the expectations of developmental psychologists working on the development of ToMM in normal children, who have explored the likely consequences of a child not "discovering the mind" in the normal way (see, for example, Astington, 1994). A number of distinct lines of evidence converge to underline the plausibility of the model that we propose.

Harris (1994), in his review of emotional development, identified the social determinants of the capacity to understand mental states, particularly emotional states. Studies of parent–child attachment have also demonstrated that attachment is predictive of performance on ToMM tasks and the quality of peer relationships (e.g., Main, 1991; Steele, Holder, & Fonagy, 1995). Similarly, studies of maltreated children show that they have disrupted attachment (Cicchetti & Barnett, 1991), and that they have a specific difficulty in acquiring mental state language (Beeghley & Cicchetti, 1994). Studies of young adult psychiatric patients with borderline personality disorder demonstrate that they have histories of severe maltreatment, together with current substantial difficulties in understanding mental states (Fonagy, Leigh, et al., in press).

To clarify the type of causal sequence that we propose, Table 1 gives examples of the types of difficulty that we frequently encountered in children with developmental disturbances, the dysfunctional mental processes we think may underlie such difficulties, and the types of early experience that we suggest might lead to such disturbances.

TREATMENT PLAN

The goal of PDTC is to enhance the child's mentalizing self, and thus to strengthen his capacity to monitor internal states, be these thoughts, feelings, or physiological sensations. An increased capacity to reflect on mental states will improve the child's ability to manage his own behavior. In turn, learning to manage his own behavior will help him to think about his mental states. Therapy also aims to assist the child to think about motivation in others, to understand better their reasons for doing things

TABLE 1
Mental Processes and Environmental Influences in Developmental Disorders

Area of mental functioning	Example	Possible environmental influence
Organization and control of impulses	Mental processes that delay gratification of sexual and aggressive impulses	Over-stimulation (e.g., extensive exposure to parental sexual behavior)
Organization and control of affects	Altering unpleasant ideas and affects to reduce painful feelings	Overwhelming affective experiences that parent does not contain (e.g., a case of parental psychiatric illness or serious, chronic physical illness in child)
Reality-orientation	Curiosity of and taking interest in the external world and in the activities it stimulates	Lack of secure base providing reference point for safety from which child could explore (e.g., blind child cannot readily check parent's attitude)
Relationships with others: external	Mental processes that permit the setting aside of self-interest to meet the emotional and physical needs of another	Parent over-indulges child, as long as child remains dependent, and brutally rejects child when he shows self-determination and self-sufficiency
Relationships with others: internal	Mental processes responsible for the capacity to maintain stable representations of other people	Parent presents a confusing, inconsistent picture of him- or herself to the child
Self-organization	Mental processes that maintain a distinct self-representation, while allowing emotional involvement with others	Parent directly threatens the child, sexually or physically, but offers safety and comfort at other times
Self-monitoring and self-evaluation	Mental processes that form a realistic assessment of one's own achievements and capacities and that differentiate the approval or criticism of others from one's own self-evaluation	Parent is unable to give developmentally appropriate praise or criticism of the child's performance: indiscriminate praise, unwarranted criticism, inconsistency

and to develop the structure of thought necessary to elaborate ways of achieving objectives. The child is helped to develop a metacognitive mode of representing reality, by which he can perceive these representations as neither actual nor unreal, but rather as standing for what is real. The therapist uses a number of techniques to achieve this, some of which we present here.

Enhancing Reflective Processes

The child with a developmental disturbance needs to learn to observe his own emotions; to understand and label his emotional states, including their physiological and affective cues; and to realize and understand the relationship between his behavior and internal states. The child may not be able to accept complex mental states of conflict or ambivalence or changes in mental states across time, but may understand simple states of belief and desire. For this reason, working with current moment-to-moment changes in the child's mental state within the therapy situation is an important facet of PDTC with this group of patients.

One child, a 5-year-old boy with very immature development of social relationships and emotional control, frequently attacked his therapist at the end of sessions. She tried to help him put his feelings into words, linking his attacks to his reluctance to see her go. After a month, he enacted his feelings by lassoing her foot, and was thrilled when she correctly understood what he wanted. Gradually, he became able to verbalize his feelings as well, and after a year he more often responded with "I don't want you to go!" or "Come back! Don't leave me all alone!" accepting that she would go anyway, but also being able to represent what that made him feel.

Therapists generally do not attempt, early in the therapy, to link a child's affect with unconscious thoughts. An individual who does not understand his subjective experience as that of "feeling something" cannot meaningfully relate this to something else. The child may not even know what his affective experience is, as when one 9-year-old boy spent long periods opening and shutting doors, and asked the therapist whether this was good for him, or whether it was one of his worries (Rosenfeld & Sprince, 1965).

In the absence of a mentalizing capacity, the child may experience many of his thoughts and feelings only as bodily states (Sifneos, 1977). The therapist may draw attention, for example, to the child's gestures or flushed face as signs that she can interpret (and that the child can learn to interpret) as indications of feeling angry. Later, the child may need help in thinking about degrees of emotion. A 7-year-old girl suggested constructing an anger thermometer with which she would record her angry feelings with her teacher, her mother, and her therapist. Many children find such solutions in the course of normal development, but therapists of children with developmental disturbances may need to introduce similar procedures that can serve to stimulate deficient internal mechanisms. Children with developmental disturbances may need help to understand which thoughts and ideas make them feel things, and the kinds of things they say to themselves that will aggravate or modulate their emotional experience. There are obvious parallels here with cognitive therapy techniques for children (e.g., Kendall, 1991).

Helping Strengthen Impulse Control

The child with developmental disturbance, at least to begin with, may need considerable help in coping with his or her impulses. A little boy, Pedro, took on the role of an omnipotent but uncontrolled mechanical object. He was the most powerful train engine in the world. He proved his strength by climbing and jumping on a high windowsill, whistling like a train, pulling the curtains down, and threatening to jump out of the window (as it was impossible for such a powerful train to be damaged). His therapist suggested that really powerful vehicles had brakes and part of his strength was being able to start and stop at his own command. Pedro took eagerly to the game of stopping and starting, and the therapist then introduced the idea of a mechanic who was very clever at understanding how the train worked and what could go wrong, so that he could prevent breakdowns and damage. Pedro was able to use this bridge between psychological and physical reality to gain much greater recognition and control of his feelings.

Similarly, the patient may use the therapy as a situation in which he induces the therapist to act out the behavior he himself finds impossible to manage. For example, a 10-year-old boy climbed up onto a third-floor window ledge and threatened to jump out. The therapist acted to protect the child, but felt very anxious while doing so. She said this to the child, then narrated her subjective attempt at coping with the anxiety she was being forced to experience. This may help the child to perceive and internalise this regulatory capacity; in social learning theory terms, the therapist models self-reflective and self-regulatory processes for the child, using the affect that the child finds overwhelming as an example. The emphasis is constantly on the mental experience with which the child is struggling, either in his own mind or in his picture of the therapist's mind.

Becoming Aware of Others

The therapeutic situation helps the child become aware of the mental state of another person. Some children avoid contact with the therapist at the psychological level for long periods, especially at the beginning of therapy. The therapist has to focus the child's attention on her own mental state rather than attempting to comment on the child's thoughts and feelings. It is assumed that many such children find the mental states of adults around them either confusing or frightening because of their earlier experiences with attachment figures. The therapeutic environment provides such children a relatively safe context for getting to know the way they are seen by others, which can then become the core of their own perceptions of themselves. Examples of this type of intervention include statements such as "You seem to feel I am angry with you," or "You behave as though I have forgotten about you today." It is important to note that the therapist is not taking this as an opportunity for self-revelation—the thoughts or feelings she discusses may well in fact not be what she is experiencing—but rather she shares with the child her perception of how the child might be seeing the state of her mind at that moment.

Developing the Capacity to Play

For some children with developmental disturbances, games and pretend role-plays may be too "real." Frequently, their experiences of maltreatment, or the confusing behavior of psychiatrically disordered parents, makes them reluctant to treat any interaction with an adult in the context of pretence or play. We maintain that the capacity to take a playful stance to the psychological world may be critical in the acquisition of metacognitive capacities, because these require holding two realities in mind simultaneously: the pretend and the actual. For such a child, the therapist often needs to create a context where an attitude of pretence is possible, for example, by exaggerating actions to mark for the child the pretend nature of the interaction, or choosing objects that are clearly incapable of adopting any intentional stance (crude toys, parts of the body).

Working in the Transference

Therapists working with children with developmental disturbances do not work in the transference in the classical sense of expecting the children to "transfer" their thoughts and feelings about their primary attachment figures onto the therapists. This is not to say, however, that the child's feelings about the therapist may be ignored. Sometimes the differentiation of the child's feelings about himself and his feelings about the therapist is the only possible way of helping him to develop a mentalizing capacity.

We suggest that the most difficult aspect of such clarifications of emotional state is the complexity of the communication required of the therapist at an emotional level. Clearly, a merely verbal communication is inadequate for such children. The therapists seems to convey in the emotional coloring of her expression both appreciation of the child's affect and a capacity to cope with it. The sensitive therapist, like the sensitive parent, seems to be able to strike a balance between offering too much reflection (empathy only) and too much coping (insensitivity). Obviously, this is technically difficult to achieve, and may evolve with a particular child after the predictable phases of trying to make sense of the child's material, then perhaps finding the experience hard to be attuned to, then finding a way of conveying that the affect can be understood and managed by another person.

Interpreting the Child's Unconscious Mental States

In traditional psychoanalysis, interpretations provide understanding of unconscious meaning by focusing on aspects of the child's thinking of which he is unaware, and yet which are most accessible to the child at that moment. In particular, the therapist focuses on relationship themes; what the child says about himself, others, and the therapist; and the nature of the relationship that these imply between himself and others. Frequently, what the child omits, such as no references to one parent, to school, or to important events in the child's life, is as important as what he does talk about. In cases in which this more traditional form of therapy becomes appropriate, which is by no means for all children with developmental disturbances, the therapist offers explorations and explanations of the child's behavior in terms of unconscious feelings, conflicts, and defenses, usually within the context of a relationship.

Involving Parents

Discussing the child's development and symptoms with the parents enables them to gain greater awareness of their child's difficulties and, usually, insight into possible reasons why these problems have arisen and become established. This may be combined with discussion of more practical aspects of management, which may help the parents discover useful ways of relating to the child and more effective ways of dealing with the child's difficult symptoms in the family. Parents also are helped to make connections, such as between stress and somatic symptoms, for example, between marital strains and emotional symptoms in children. Some stresses can be removed and others cannot, but even here ways of limiting damage may be found.

The therapist aims gradually to enhance the parents' concern with the child's mental state and sensitivity to the child's worries, limitations, and concerns. This may involve work on aspects of the child's environment or family that may impinge on his development, and the exploration of ways to free the child from avoidable stresses and constraints. Sometimes this involves offering parents therapy for themselves, but much more often it is enough to help the parents think more objectively and perceptively about the child, and together to find ways of overcoming obstacles to his development.

Phases of the Therapy

Although PDTC is not formally structured so that specific activities are covered in specific sessions, with length of treatment agreed at the outset, it falls into four fairly discrete phases: (a) getting to know the patient and parents, including their background; and forming an estimate of their capacities, the major areas that need to be worked on, and the pace of change that seems realistic; (b) developing strategies for enhancing reflective processes, strengthening impulse control, enhancing self-regulation, increasing awareness of others, and developing capacities to play; (c) implementing these strategies, the "practice phase"; and (d) using generic psychodynamically interpretive work if and when the child's mentalizing capacity becomes able to support this. Where this does become possible, it allows additional work on the more neurotic symptoms that many children with developmental disturbances also may present.

The duration of PDTC is variable; the average duration at our center is 2 years. Thus, it is a long-term therapy. It should be noted, however, that this applies to less focused applications of PDTC than the form that has been described in this chapter.

Conclusion

In summary, the enhancement of reflective function is achieved through a number of specific techniques, many of which are also appropriate when working with a very young child. The value added by a developmental approach is in making developmental progress not a by-product, but the legitimate primary goal, enabling the therapist to focus in different ways on mentalization in the child's psychic world, which is often a precondition for further therapeutic help. What we are suggesting here does not replace generic psychotherapeutic interventions, but these have been comprehensively described elsewhere (Sandler, Kennedy, & Tyson, 1980; Fonagy, Target, Edgcumbe, Moran, & Miller, in press). We maintain that the careful selection of relevant techniques and the exclusion of irrelevant and counterproductive techniques, on the basis of a clear theoretical model of developmental disturbances not covered by the traditional neurotic model, is bound to increase the effectiveness of psychodynamic therapy for these very impaired children.

TREATMENT OUTCOME

Heinicke and Ramsey-Klee (1986) reported a study of a small sample of children with learning problems linked to psychological disturbances who received psychoanalytic psychotherapy, either one or four sessions per week over 2 years. Greater improvement was found at follow-up in the group that received more frequent therapy. These improvements were not only in the target symptom of reading difficulties, but also in broader areas of personality and adaptation. However, although this study was an impressive attempt to evaluate psychodynamic therapy, in terms relevant to both psychotherapists and other clinicians, it suffered from the defects of most outcome research at that time. The population was poorly characterized, and the therapy was described only as analytically oriented and delineated only in terms of the frequency of contact.

Fonagy and Moran (1990) and Moran, Fonagy, Kurtz, Bolton, and Brook (1991) conducted a series of studies of PDTC with children suffering from so-called brittle diabetes. These young people appear to be incapable of maintaining their blood sugar levels close to normal, and therefore their lives are constantly disrupted by life-threatening episodes of hypoglycemia and ketoacidosis. The outcome of PDTC was assessed using physical measures: average blood glucose levels and growth rate. The first study explored the relationship between metabolic control and the process of PDTC in a single case study of a diabetic adolescent girl, using time-series analysis. The study revealed a close statistical relationship between fluctuations of metabolic control and key themes in the patient's therapeutic material. The second study compared two equivalent groups of 11 children with dangerously uncontrolled diabetes. Patients in the treatment group were offered intensive inpatient treatment that included PDTC three to four times weekly. Treatment lasted 15 weeks on average. Patients in the comparison group were offered only inpatient medical treatment. The children in the treatment group showed considerable improvements in diabetic control, maintained at 1 year follow-up. The comparison group children returned to pretreatment levels within 3 months of discharge. The third study was a series of experimental single-case investigations. This assessed the impact of treatment on growth rate (measured by changes in height and bone age) in three children whose height was consistently below the 5th percentile for age. Changes in three growth indicators were recorded for 6-month periods before, during, and after treatment. For all three children, treatment was associated with an acceleration of growth and a substantial increase in predicted adult height.

Methodological Issues

We have been grappling with the issues of how to measure outcome in the context of dynamic psychotherapy for children, how to specify the treatment, and how to monitor adherence to prescribed techniques.

Measurement of Outcome

In addition to the more usual measures of symptomatology, to assess the effectiveness of PDTC it is necessary to evaluate the child's developmental progress. Sadly, although there are standardized ways of describing change in psychiatric symptoms, there are no adequately validated, easy-to-administer measures of social and developmental changes in children of a kind that could be successfully used to measure change following PDTC (see Rutter, Tuma, & Lann, 1988). We have been working on the validation of an interview-based, developmentally sensitive global measure of social adaptation (Target & Fonagy, 1993). For a comprehensive outcome battery, we also need to draw on recent progress in developmental psychology, adopt measures devised to chart the cognitive and social development of children, and collect normative data on these measures. The relevant fields should include development of the child's so-called theory of mind, appreciation of right and wrong, understanding of emotions, capacity to play, and so on. Equally important is the capacity to form relationships with adults and peers, and the development of the mental representations underlying these relationships (e.g., assessments of the child's internal working models of relationships using behavioral- and narrative-based techniques).

Manualization

Although there is vast literature on technique in adult and child psychoanalytic treatment, this is not written in the explicit "operational" terms that are required to define a treatment approach in studies of efficacy. Nevertheless, Paulina Kernberg and her colleagues have prepared an impressive manual on supportive–expressive psychotherapy for children with conduct disorders (Kernberg & Chazan, 1991), and we have recently prepared and a PDTC manual (Fonagy, Target, et al., in press) which we are validating (Miller, 1993) for use in outcome studies.

Monitoring of Treatment Integrity

We have developed a scale for recording the process of PDTC, to be used with videotaped treatment sessions. The scale was inspired by Enrico Jones' Psychotherapy Q-sort (Jones & Windholz, 1990), which we have extensively adapted for use on child analytic material. The scale has more than 400 operationally defined items and provides a measure of the content and quality of the work with each patient.

Background Data Collection on Predictors of Therapeutic Outcome

The study to be described used retrospective chart review methodology to examine predictors of treatment outcome. 763 cases treated at the Anna Freud Centre in either high- or low-frequency psychodynamic therapy (4–5 or 1–2 sessions per week) were systematically reviewed. In approaching this collection of clinical material, we decided to use standardized behavioral and psychiatric, as well as psychoanalytic, descriptions of the children treated. This allowed much readier comparison between these children and those offered other forms of psychiatric treatment.

Three main studies of this data have been carried out so far. For detailed accounts of the measures used, criteria for clinically significant improvement, and results, readers are referred to published papers (Fonagy & Target, 1994; Target & Fonagy, 1994a, 1994b).

Children With Emotional Disorders

This study examined the effectiveness of PDTC for children and adolescents with *DSM-III-R* diagnoses of anxiety or depressive disorders (Target & Fonagy, 1994b). 352 charts were reviewed for a wide range of demographic, clinical, treatment, and outcome measures. Using the Children's Global Assessment Scale (CGAS; Shaffer et al., 1983) as the main indicator of outcome, the study showed that: (a) 72% of those treated for at least 6 months showed reliable, clinically significant improvement in adaptation, and only 24% had a diagnosable disorder at termination; (b) phobic children were most likely, and depressed children were least likely, to return to normal CGAS levels; (c) children younger than 11 years old were significantly more likely to be well at the end of treatment; (d) although longer treatment was predictably associated with good outcome, more frequent sessions (4–5 times per week) also led to greater improvements independently of the child's age and length of treatment; (e) high-frequency treatment was significantly more helpful for children who presented with more severe disturbance, in terms of multiple diagnoses or CGAS scores below 45.

Children With Disruptive Disorders

In this study, 135 children with disruptive disorders were matched on demographic, clinical, and treatment variables with children presenting with emotional disorders (Fonagy & Target, 1994). Overall improvement rates were significantly lower for disruptive disorders. However, nearly one third of the disruptive children withdrew within 1 year of starting treatment. Early termination was associated with higher age, low frequency treatment, less well-functioning mother (Global Assessment of Functioning score), fewer learning difficulties at school, and lack of concurrent parental guidance. Of those disruptive children who remained in treatment, 69% were no longer diagnosable at termination. The main predictors of improvement included the presence of an anxiety disorder, the absence of other comorbidity (particularly developmental disorders), younger age, and high frequency treatment.

Developmental Considerations

This third report examined the way in which the age of a child or adolescent when treated in psychoanalytic psychotherapy related to the outcome of that treatment (Target & Fonagy, 1994a): 127 children were matched on relevant variables, from each of three age bands (under 6, 6–12, and adolescents). Younger children generally improved to a greater extent. Children under 12 benefited from high-frequency (4–5 times weekly) treatment more than from low-frequency (1–2 times weekly) treatment, but this was not true of adolescents. There were interactions between age and certain diagnostic categories. Division into age groups improved the accuracy of prediction of improvement: Between one third and one half of the variance in outcome could be accounted for using only the variables known at referral.

Inevitably, retrospective studies of this kind suffer serious methodological limitations (see Fonagy & Target, 1994). Among the most important are: (a) nonrandom assignment of patients (e.g., to high- and low-frequency treatment); (b) the lack of untreated controls; (c) restriction to chart-based information; (d) the confounding of length of treatment with the interval between assessments (spontaneous remission); (e) the unrepresentativeness of the sample; and (f) possible bias from early dropouts (although those withdrawing voluntarily did not have significantly worse outcome, for the same length of therapy, than those terminating for external reasons such as moving to another city).

One very important consideration in evaluating these findings of the outcome of ordinary practice in psychodynamic psychotherapy is the issue of attrition rates, and perhaps the influence of hidden attrition, so that for instance an apparent superiority of high-frequency therapy could be attributable to children or families with better prognosis (on clinical or demographic grounds) being transferred to less intensive therapy. We have investigated these possibilities and found that, among the complex set of factors (such as age and diagnostic group) affecting attrition, the single most powerful factor was intensity of treatment. Surprisingly, in view of the burden of attending frequently, we found that children who were seen more often were far less likely to withdraw within the first months: 13.9% versus 30.7% across the full sample. In a detailed comparison of these cases, there was no evidence of differential assignment to more or less intensive therapy according to factors known to be associated with therapy outcome or natural history.

LIMITATIONS AND GENERALIZABILITY

Our model implies that children with developmental disturbances may benefit from PDTC. More empirical work is required before the distinction between neurotic and developmental disorders is unequivocally established. Our retrospective data indicate that PDTC appears to be most effective when applied early, certainly before the onset of puberty and adolescence. For many of these children, high-frequency treatment and early family involvement appear to protect the child, albeit only to some degree, from discontinuing treatment within the first year. If the analyst is successful in maintaining the child beyond the first year, the chances of significant gain are high.

PDTC is a long and costly treatment. At the moment, there is no good evidence to demonstrate that the cost of the treatment is offset by subsequent reduction in service use, even though the rationale of the treatment is the enhancement of the child's long-term adjustment and resilience. All types of service use will be costed in a prospective study, and we are undertaking a major follow-up study to assess long-term impact, but at present these data are unavailable.

The use of developmental techniques brings psychodynamic approaches closer to other treatment approaches, primarily those originating in social learning theory (Bandura, 1986), although PDTC does not stress the contingencies of individual actions. It is an exemplar of a growing body of therapies that aim to integrate diverse theoretical frameworks. Clinicians with a behavioral orientation are placing increasing emphasis on the identification of common therapeutic strategies across orientations (see Goldfried & Davison, 1994). In PDTC, the crucial therapeutic component is seen as the liberation, through practice, of developmental processes that have been stunted by environmental or constitutional factors. Direct suggestions to the child may occur from time to time, but are not central.

PDTC has much in common with cognitive therapy, which similarly focuses on latent, maladaptive cognitive structures; however, PDTC considers a broader range of cognitive processes than is normally tackled in more symptom-oriented approaches. In brief, although PDTC is an active intervention in comparison with other forms of psychodynamic therapy, it is more passive than cognitive or behavioral approaches. It aims to facilitate natural emotional and cognitive development, rather than to correct specific deficits in, for instance, social behavior. This is not to say that cognitive–behavioral therapists would not recognize and perhaps claim some PDTC interventions as their own. More traditional behavioral methodology is still alien to the psychodynamic field, thus reinforcements, diaries, systematic scheduling of techniques, and similar procedures are rarely used. By contrast, many PDTC strategies might equally well have emerged from a framework of cognitive restructuring, or schema therapy. The fundamental difference between cognitive approaches and PDTC is the assumption that the child's symptomatic behavior is a nonconscious adaptation to his understanding of a painful reality. Thus, therapists are primed to expect the child to resist their attempts at intervention, and perhaps from time to time to sabotage the helping process. Also, for most cognitive therapists the formulation of the problem of the child tends to be at the level of distorted mental representations, although in PDTC the conceptual focus is on entire processes of mental functioning, with consequent distortions and even more commonly gaps in the child's representational world.

The important question arises of whether PDTC is necessarily a form of psychodynamic treatment, requiring lengthy psychoanalytic training, or whether the techniques can be practiced by a much wider group of child therapists. We believe that although elements of the approach can be and are practiced by, for instance, play therapists or cognitive–behavioral therapists, there are certain aspects that require additional skills with this very challenging group. The major reasons for this belief are: (a) the therapist needs to be able to understand the nature and origin of the child's anxieties that have led to the drastic defense of stunting the development of mental processes; and (b) the therapist needs to be able to withstand the enormous pressures placed on anyone whose mind is being used as a psychological crutch by another person over a long period of time. The therapist is not simply providing intensive "parenting" for a child who missed out on key experiences in infancy, she is having to do this while experiencing the full force of the child's subsequent distorted emotional development and capacity for relationships. We, therefore, suggest that there may be a legitimate need for the intensive training and framework of psychodynamic therapy, or at least supervision that can support and lend this perspective to work by other professionals.

SUMMARY

We feel that there are children who are so distressed, and whose prognoses are sufficiently bleak, for psychodynamic developmental therapy to be considered a realistic treatment. Increasingly, referrals to centers such as ours show a tendency to use PDTC as a last resort therapy, after cheaper and briefer alternatives have been tried.

The etiology of these developmental process disorders is complex. It is unlikely that children manifest such disturbances to a serious degree without constitutional vulnerabilities or severe environmental deprivations. There is tentative evidence available that, if treated sufficiently early and with sufficient commitment on the part of both the therapist and the family, even children with severe conditions can show a clinically significant change. At least at developmentally early stages, such character disorders may be conceived of as adaptations to excessively stressful environments, in which the child inhibits specific aspects of his or her mental functioning in order to cope with conditions falling outside the expectable range.

The method of treatment combines an insight-oriented and developmental or educational approach, each facilitating and building on the other. For these children, the developmental work is seen as more central, although traditionally, psychodynamic clinicians have tended to emphasize insight-oriented techniques. In the context of PDTC, insight still makes a contribution not just in correcting the child's distorted expectations about himself and others, but in communicating to the child the possibility of human understanding, strengthening the therapeutic bond between patient and clinician, and creating the possibility of healthy development propelled by freeing the child's maturational potential.

REFERENCES

American Psychiatric Association. (1987). *Diagnostic and statistical manual of mental disorders* (3rd ed., rev.). Washington, DC: Author.

American Psychiatric Association. (1994). *Diagnostic and statistical manual of mental disorders* (4th ed.). Washington, DC: Author.

Astington, J. W. (1994). *The child's discovery of the mind.* London: Fontana Press.

Bandura, A. (1986). *Social learning theory.* Englewood Cliffs, NJ: Prentice Hall.

Baron-Cohen, S. (1995). *Mindblindness: An essay on autism and theory of mind.* Cambridge, MA: Bradford, MIT Press.

Beeghley, M., & Cicchetti, D. (1994). Child maltreatment, attachment, and the self system: Emergence of an internal state lexicon in toddlers at high social risk. *Development and Psychopathology, 6,* 5–30.

Bowlby, J. (1969). *Attachment and loss: Vol. 1. Attachment.* New York: Basic Books.

Bowlby, J. (1973). *Attachment and loss: Vol. 2. Separation: Anxiety and Anger.* London: Hogarth Press & Institute of Psycho-Analysis.

Bowlby, J. (1980). *Attachment and loss: Vol. 3. Loss.* New York: Basic Books.

Cicchetti, D., & Barnett, D. (1991). Attachment organisation in preschool aged maltreated children. *Development and Psychopathology, 3,* 397–411.

Davidson, D. (1983). *Inquiries into truth and separation.* London: Oxford University Press.

Fonagy, P. (1991). Thinking about thinking: Some clinical and theoretical considerations in the treatment of a borderline patient. *International Journal of Psychoanalysis, 72,* 639–656.

Fonagy, P., Leigh, T., Steele, M., Steele, H., Kennedy, R., Mattoon, G., Target, M., & Gerber, A. (in press). The relationship of attachment status, psychiatric classification and response to psychotherapy. *Journal of Consulting and Clinical Psychology.*

Fonagy, P., & Moran, G. S. (1990). Studies on the efficacy of child psychoanalysis. *Journal of Consulting and Clinical Psychology, 58,* 684–695.

Fonagy, P., Moran, G. S., Edgcumbe, R., Kennedy, H., & Target, M. (1993). The roles of mental representations and mental processes in therapeutic action. *Psychoanalytic Study of the Child, 48,* 9–48.

Fonagy, P., Moran, G. S., & Target, M. (1993). Aggression and the psychological self. *International Journal of Psycho-Analysis, 74,* 471–485.

Fonagy, P., & Target, M. (1994). The efficacy of psycho-analysis for children with disruptive disorders. *Journal of the American Academy of Child and Adolescent Psychiatry, 33,* 45–55.

Fonagy, P., & Target, M. (1995). Understanding the violent patient: the use of the body and the role of the father. *International Journal of Psycho-Analysis, 76,* 487–501.

Fonagy, P., Target, M., Edgcumbe, R., Moran, G. S., & Miller, J. (in press). *The Hampstead Manual of Intensive and Non-Intensive Dynamic Psychotherapy with Children.* New York: Guilford Press.

Goldfried, M. R., & Davison, G. C. (1994). *Clinical behavior therapy.* New York: Wiley.

Harris, P. L. (1994). The child's understanding of emotion: Developmental change and the family environment. *Journal of Child Psychology and Psychiatry, 35,* 3–28.

Heinicke, C. M., & Ramsey-Klee, D. M. (1986). Outcome of child psychotherapy as a function of frequency of sessions. *Journal of the American Academy of Child Psychiatry, 25,* 247–253.

Jones, E., & Windholz, M. (1990). The psychoanalytic case study: Toward a method for systematic inquiry. *Journal of the American Psychoanalytic Association, 38,* 985–1015.

Kazdin, A. E. (1994). Psychotherapy for children and adolescents. In A. E. Bergin & S. L. Garfield (Eds.), *Handbook of psychotherapy and behavior change* (4th ed., pp. 543–594). New York: Wiley.

Kazdin, A. E., Bass, D., Siegel, T., & Thomas, C. (1990). Cognitive behavioral treatment and relationship therapy in the treatment of children referred for antisocial behavior. *Journal of Consulting and Clinical Psychology, 58*, 76–85.

Kendall, P. C. (Ed.). (1991). *Child and adolescent therapy: Cognitive–behavioral procedures*. New York: Guilford Press.

Kernberg, P., & Chazan, S. E. (1991). *Children with conduct disorders: A psychotherapy manual*. New York: Basic Books.

Main, M. (1991). Metacognitive knowledge, metacognitive monitoring, and singular (coherent) vs. multiple (incoherent) models of attachment: Findings and directions for future research. In P. Harris, J. Stevenson-Hinde, & C. Parkes (Eds.), *Attachment across the lifecycle* (pp. 127–159). London: Routledge & Kegan-Paul.

Mayes, L. C., & Cohen, D. J. (1994). Experiencing self and others: Autism and psychoanalytic social development theory. *Journal of the American Psychoanalytic Association, 42*, 191–218.

Miller, J. M. (1993). *The manualization of child psychoanalysis*. Unpublished doctoral dissertation, University of London.

Moran, G. S., Fonagy, P., Kurtz, A., Bolton, A., & Brook, C. (1991). A controlled study of the psychoanalytic treatment of brittle diabetes. *Journal of the American Academy of Child and Adolescent Psychiatry, 30*, 926–935.

Morton, J., & Frith, U. (1995). Causal modelling: A structural approach to developmental psychopathology. In D. Cicchetti & D. J. Cohen (Eds.), *Developmental Psychopathology: Vol. 1. Theory and Methods*. New York: Wiley.

Rosenfeld, S., & Sprince, M. (1965). Some thoughts on the technical handling of borderline children. *Psychoanalytic Study of the Child, 20*, 505–512.

Rutter, M., Tuma, H. A., & Lann, I. S. (Eds.). (1988). *Assessment and diagnosis in child psychopathology*. London: David Fulton.

Sandler, J., Kennedy, H., & Tyson, R. (1980). *The technique of child analysis: Discussions with Anna Freud*. London: Hogarth Press.

Shaffer, D., Gould, M. S., Brasie, J., Ambrosini, P., Fisher, P., Bird, H., & Aluwahlia, S. (1983). A children's global assessment scale (CGAS). *Archives of General Psychiatry, 40*, 1228–1231.

Sifneos, P. E. (1977). The phenomenon of 'alexithymia'. *Psychotherapy and Psychosomatics, 28*, 47–57.

Steele, H., Holder, J., & Fonagy, P. (1995). *Quality of attachment to mother at 1 year predicts belief-desire reasoning at 5 years*. Paper presented at a meeting of the Society for Research in Child Development, Indianapolis, IN.

Target, M., & Fonagy, P. (1993). *Rater's Manual for the Hampstead Child Adaptation Measure*. Unpublished manuscript.

Target, M., & Fonagy, P. (1994a). The efficacy of psychoanalysis for children: Prediction of outcome in a developmental context. *Journal of the American Academy of Child and Adolescent Psychiatry, 33,* 1134–1144.

Target, M., & Fonagy, P. (1994b). The efficacy of psycho-analysis for children with emotional disorders . *Journal of the American Academy of Child and Adolescent Psychiatry, 33,* 361–371.

Towbin, K. E., Dykens, E. M., Pearson, G. S., & Cohen, D. J. (1993). Conceptualising "borderline syndrome of childhood" and "childhood schizophrenia" as a developmental disorder. *Journal of the American Academy of Child and Adolescent Psychiatry, 32,* 775–782.

World Health Organization. (1988). *International Classification of Diseases* (10th ed.). Geneva, Switzerland: Author.

27

CULTURALLY SENSITIVE TREATMENT: CUENTO AND HERO/HEROINE MODELING THERAPIES FOR HISPANIC CHILDREN AND ADOLESCENTS

GIUSEPPE COSTANTINO and ROBERT G. MALGADY

In 1993, there were nearly 23 million Hispanics/Latinos living in the United States, representing an increase of more than 50% between the 1980 and 1990 censuses (U.S. Bureau of the Census, 1994). This is a growth rate of more than seven times that of any other ethnic population and is attributed to high birth rates, youthful age distribution, and high levels of immigration. These figures do not include an estimated 5% of the Spanish speaking population missed by the 1990 census (U.S. Bureau of the Census, 1991), an estimated 2.5 million undocumented Hispanic/Latino immigrants (Warren, 1994), and the more than 3.5 million population of the Commonwealth of Puerto Rico.

Epidemiological studies of psychiatric prevalence rates and symptomatology have, for the most part, neglected the rapidly growing population of Hispanic children and adolescents. Some early studies found lower self-esteem among Hispanic children than among White children (Anderson & Johnson, 1971; Fisher, 1974), whereas others reported more behavioral problems among Hispanic children and adolescents compared with White

Research reported in this chapter was supported by grants ROI-MH33711 and ROI-MH30569 from the National Institute of Mental Health, Division of Biometry and Applied Sciences, Minority Research Branch; and by grant 83-0868 from the William T. Grant Foundation. Correspondence concerning this chapter should be addressed to Dr. Giuseppe Costantino, Hispanic Research Center, Thebaud Hall, Fordham University, Bronx, New York 10458.

639

children (e.g., Langner, Gersfen, & Eisenberg, 1974). More recently, Canino, Gould, Prupis, and Schafer (1986) found that Hispanic children and adolescents reported more depression and anxiety symptoms than did Black children. However, the literature on depression is equivocal, with some studies reporting more severe depressive symptoms among Hispanic youth relative to other ethnic groups (e.g., Emslie, Weinberg, Rush, Adams, & Rentelmann, 1990), and other studies not (e.g., Garrison, Jackson, Marsteller, McKeon, & Addy, 1990). Roberts (1992) reported that Hispanic adolescents express somatic complaints more prominently, compared with White and Black adolescents.

According to some estimates (Aspira, 1983; Canino, Earley, & Rogler, 1980; New York City Department of City Planning, 1994; New York City Board of Education, 1990), Hispanic youths exhibit the highest high school dropout rate of all ethnic groups and alarming rates of referral for problems, such as social and emotional disorientation, conduct and anxiety disorders, adjustment reactions with anxiety features, and low self-esteem. Estimates of dropout rates in Puerto Rico have ranged as high as 60%, and comparative data indicate that New York City rates are "as bad as or worse" than the national average (National Puerto Rican Forum, 1980). Studying prevalence and risk factors among a multinational group of Hispanic early adolescents, Vega, Zimmerman, Warheit, Apospori, and Gil (1993) found a high prevalence of drug use. One study, with therapeutic implications, indicated that adherence to more traditional Hispanic cultural values was associated with lower risk of drug use among Hispanic youth (Pumariega, Swanson, Holzer, Linskey, & Quintero-Salinas, 1992).

Related to school dropout and substance use, Hispanic youth are the most rapidly increasing incarcerated population in the United States (Martinez, 1987). According to the New York State Office of Mental Health (1994), among the primary *Diagnostic and Statistical Manual of Mental Disorders*, third edition, revised, (*DSM-III-R*; American Psychiatric Association, 1987) diagnoses of nearly 8000 children and adolescents enrolled in community-based services, the rate of disruptive behavior disorders (46.9%) eclipses all others. Furthermore, these disorders are nearly equally distributed between conduct and oppositional defiant disorders.

Rogler, Malgady, and Rodriguez (1989) have indicated that Hispanic families present a profile of demographic characteristics, such as low socioeconomic status (SES), ethnic minority status, and high rate of single-parent households, that are associated with increased risk of mental disorder. The fragmented picture that emerges from the scattered research efforts suggests that such risk factors are associated with lower self-esteem and possibly increased anxiety, depression, and substance use. The undeniable result, however, is an alarmingly high rate of high school dropout and disruptive behavior disorder.

In 1978, the Special Populations Sub-Task Panel on the Mental Health of Hispanic Americans reported to the President's Commission on Mental Health that Hispanic youths were especially at high risk of mental disorder, but that mental health research had contributed little to the resolution of the problem. Today, over a decade and a half later, neglect of the special mental health needs of Hispanic children and adolescents persists, and there remains a need to develop and evaluate effective psychotherapeutic modalities for Hispanic youths (Padilla, Ruiz, & Alvarez, 1975; Rogler et al., 1989). This chapter describes a program of research that has developed and evaluated culturally sensitive narrative interventions for at-risk Puerto Rican youths.

The research reported in this chapter focuses on at-risk Puerto Rican children and adolescents who present severe behavior problems in school and at home. The youngsters did not present *DSM-III-R* mental disorders, but were considered to be at risk because of their behavior problems, high rate of single-parent households, low SES, and cultural marginalization. The interventions were sensitized to Puerto Rican culture according to age-appropriate group therapy narrative modalities. The modality for young children was based on *cuentos* or folktales taken from the Puerto Rican culture, whereas the modality for adolescents was based on biographies of heroic characters in Puerto Rican history. The target of the intervention was the reduction of maladaptive psychosocial functioning, by impacting on such problems as aggressive behavior, anxiety, and low self-esteem.

CULTURALLY SENSITIVE INTERVENTIONS

The goal of culturally sensitive psychotherapy, broadly conceived, is to attenuate cultural distance between the client and the therapeutic situation, thereby promoting more effective treatment outcomes than would be obtained by standard mainstream treatments (Rogler et al., 1989). According to Rogler, Malgady, Costantino, and Blumenthal (1987), cultural sensitivity involves increasing accessibility to treatment (e.g., location, bilingual staff), adapting mainstream services to Hispanic cultural characteristics (e.g., family therapy), or bringing cultural elements directly into treatment (e.g., *cuento* therapy [folktale therapy], folk heroes modeling therapy).

Puerto Ricans in the United States live between two cultures, and the healthy development of their children depends on a balanced integration of the values, beliefs, and behaviors of both the Hispanic and the Anglo-American cultures. Taking both cultures into consideration, the first study used both original stories taken from Puerto Rican culture and adapted stories that reflected the dominant Anglo-American culture. Folktales have survived for untold centuries only because they have constantly changed through the incorporation of new elements while maintaining the content of the tale. Furthermore, it is the folktale's ability to incorporate new elements from the dominant culture that makes it a contemporary instrument to effect change and, at the same time, retain the basic cultural values of the ethnic group. The acculturation of Puerto Rican youths in the dominant American society rests on their ability to bridge the gap between their Hispanic heritage and the prevailing American values. The process of transcultural adaptation can be helped along through appropriate culturally sensitive therapy interventions.

This chapter first presents an overview of the cultural roots of storytelling, leading to the narrative process in psychotherapy. We then present the theoretical framework underlying the two culturally sensitive interventions, followed by a description of how the interventions were implemented and an evaluation of the effectiveness of treatment outcomes. Finally, the chapter concludes with a discussion of limitations, generalizability, and future directions.

THE FUNCTIONS OF STORYTELLING

The use of storytelling is rapidly gaining acceptance as a culturally sensitive therapy modality. Several cognitive psychologists, such as Bruner (1986), Mair (1989), and, in particular, Howard (1991), affirm that the development of human identity occurs as a result of life-story construction: psychopathology as an incoherent story with a wrong ending and psychotherapy as a coherent story with a right ending. Howard describes the technique of storytelling as the most adept process in understanding culturally diverse individuals and in conducting cross-cultural psychotherapy.

For millennia, storytelling—perhaps the oldest form of literature— was the sole method of educating the young. Societal rules and customs, standards of morality, and the achievements of heroes were divulged across generations in folktales, which were told either by a professional storyteller (e.g., Homer) or by the older generations (e.g., Rooth, 1976). For this reason, folktales have come to be perceived as a repository of the cultural heritage of a given ethnic or racial group, and as a vehicle for the transmission of societal values and cultural traditions from one generation to the next (Arbuthnot, 1976) to educate the young (Rooth, 1976). It appears that the metaphorical language of folktales has an intrinsic expressive ability to transform words into readily understood images, with the expressed forms representing imaginal models of pedagogical and therapeutic value. Goethe often wrote that the fairy tales that his mother told him during childhood had been one of the most important factors in contributing to his poetic imagination and his motivation to become a great poet (Bettelheim, 1977). Folktales have also been one of the most instrumental means of keeping intact the identity of an ethnic group under foreign domination or in adverse social conditions (Amor, 1969; Faro, 1939; Madrid, 1953).

Storytelling in Psychotherapy

Despite the ostensible psychological value of folktales, there have been surprisingly few attempts to use folktales as a systematic therapy modality. Nevertheless, some eminent clinicians are beginning to use folktales to ameliorate emotional problems in children. Bettelheim (1977) used fairy tales to treat severe psychological dysfunctions in children and adolescents and reported that this technique made a positive psychological contribution to the child's personality growth. Furthermore, Gardner (1971) indicated that his innovative "mutual story-telling" modality appeared to be effective with neurotic and borderline children. His technique used stories created by the children themselves during the therapy session, which were then retold by the therapist during the same session with changes to reflect more adaptive personalities of the characters. In a similar study, Jilek (1976) described the use of the mutual fairytale technique to gain the trust of Canadian Indian patients and to understand their symptoms within their cultural context.

The clinical usefulness of folktales as a therapeutic modality is also buttressed by two psychiatric case studies. In one, Klosinski (1978) reported the successful treatment of a 12-year-old anorectic girl by the use of "painting and fairy-tale therapy," which ameliorated the obsessional symptoms that had afflicted the girl since the age of 4 years. In another study, Weimer (1978) reported the case of a 22-year-old woman with depression and psychotic symptomatology, who was treated successfully with the use of fairy tales. The fairy tale of Rapunzel was used allegorically to give the patient insight into her excessively dependent relationship on her mother and to point out the role of this symbiosis in the patient's illness.

Notwithstanding the growing clinical interest in folktales as a therapy modality, carefully controlled evaluation of treatment outcomes is scarce. Saltz and Johnson (1973), in their preliminary evaluation of a 4-year follow-up study, indicated that thematic fantasy play (TFP) may be a promising therapeutic modality for culturally disadvantaged children. The children were from the lower socioeconomic classes, and included northern and southern Whites, Blacks, and Chicanos. The treatment involved verbal role-dramatization in a group setting in which the children acted out traditional fairy tales such as "The Three Billy Goats Gruff" and "Cinderella." Saltz and Johnson reported that TFP was found to foster higher incidence of spontaneous sociodramatic play, increased interpersonal skills, and better story memory and storytelling skills on specially constructed tasks. Amato, Evans, and Ziegler (1973), studying the effectiveness of drama and storytelling in a group of primary school children, found that neither modality appeared to have any effect on the children's interest and reading achievement. However, there were indications that storytelling may have had more influence than creative dramatics on self-image and empathy. Westone and Friedlander (1974) explored the effect of live, televised, and audio story narration on primary school children and found that their listening comprehension significantly improved the most when exposed to a videotaped presentation, next when exposed to a live presentation, and the least when exposed to an audio presentation. These data suggest that the storytelling technique may be a promising modality to foster personality growth and cognitive skills. Smilansky (1968) found that storytelling and sociodramatic play fostered social skills and creativity in disadvantaged children.

THEORETICAL FRAMEWORK

Psychological theory provides a rationale for how *cuentos* (folktales) can be used therapeutically to enhance specific personality functions. Because folktales are literary forms that convey a message or a moral to be emulated (or perhaps avoided) by others, cuento therapy is most appropriately framed as a modeling technique, that is, a method of psychotherapy that derives from the principles of social learning theory (Bandura, 1977; Bandura & Walters, 1967).

According to Bandura (1977), social learning and, hence, personality development occur largely through children's observation of salient models in their environment, such as parents, peers, teachers, television or storybook characters, or even heroic figures in a society. Social learning theory suggests that observers acquire symbolic representations of the behaviors displayed by a model and, as the observed behaviors become psychologically internalized, they subsequently become part of the psychological makeup of the observer. This implies that affect, personality structure, and, hence, behavior can be changed through the vicarious experience of a model whose behavior has been tailored to a particular therapeutic goal. For example, in a traditional modeling therapy, a child might be exposed to an attractive model who does not aggress against the protagonist, but rather displays a more adaptive mechanism for coping with stress induced by the provocation. Given repeated exposure to such a model, the socially appropriate coping mechanism becomes infused into the child's behavioral repertoire.

As an interesting illustration of this process in a naturalistic context, Bandura and Walters (1967) recount a scenario from the Cantelense Indian culture of Guatemala:

The young Cantelense girl is provided with a water jar, a broom, and a grinding stone, which are miniature versions of those used by her mother. Through constantly imitating the domestic activities of the mother, who provides little or no tuition, the child readily acquires a repetory of sex-appropriate responses. Similarly, small Cantelense boys accompany their fathers while the latter are engaged in occupational activities and reproduce their fathers' actions with the aid of smaller versions of adult implements (pp. 47–48).

By contrast, in more modern societies, children's social learning occurs much more often through verbal and pictorial modeling; as pictorial models are more prevalent through the viewing of television, for example, parents are becoming less influential as role models (Bandura & Walters, 1967).

One of the most fundamental principles of social learning theory is that mere vicarious experience is ineffectual unless the observer attends to and accurately perceives the salient features of the modeled behavior (Bandura, 1977). Consequently, modeling therapy must be structured in a way that the child is attracted to the model, facilitating identification with the model, and then the therapist can filter out the target behaviors of the model so that the probability of the child's imitation of the appropriate behaviors is increased. For these reasons, favorite characters in popular television programs or movies or even bedtime stories can prove to be clinically useful vehicles in modeling therapy with children. As a child is attracted to a popular character in a story or movie, the child eventually imitates the model's actions. Such imitative behavior is the outcome of the child's internalization of the model's behavior, which is reinforced by the social consequences (reward or punishment) accompanying the child's imitative actions. Thus, Bandura (1977) assumes that "modeling influences operate principally through their informative function and that observers acquire mainly symbolic representations of modeled events rather than specific stimulus-response associations" (p. 16).

Consistent with the idea of using folktales in modeling therapy, Singer (1973) indicated that storytelling fosters imaginative behavior or establishes situations that children are likely to imitate. Therefore, a pure cognitive theory, such as that of Piaget, can be integrated into the social learning theory that has been shown to have powerful impact on child development, as evidenced in the work of Bandura (1977).

Within this theoretical framework, folktale characters can be therapeutically presented as symbolic models of adaptive emotional and behavioral functioning within the Puerto Rican and American cultures in which the children live. The cuentos serve to motivate attentional processes by presenting culturally familiar characters of the same ethnicity as the children; by modeling beliefs, values, and behaviors with which the children can identify; and by modeling a more functional relationship with parents.

In addition to the intrinsic cultural values embodied in the original Puerto Rican cuentos, the adapted cuentos graft themes of adaptive functioning within the American culture into the plots of the stories. In this manner, on the basis of principles of modeling therapy, cuento therapy promotes a new synthesis of bicultural symbols and, thereby, fosters adaptive personality growth in children who are in conflict between two cultures.

CUENTO THERAPY WITH CHILDREN

In the first study of cultural intervention with children, Costantino (1980) and Costantino, Malgady, and Rogler (1985, 1986) developed a storytelling modality using Puerto Rican cuentos organized within the framework of modeling therapy. Because folktales convey a message or moral to be emulated by others, the characters were posed as therapeutic role models of adaptive emotional and behavioral functioning within Puerto Rican and American cultures. The presentation of indigenous Puerto Rican folktale characters serves, first, to motivate children's attention to the models; second, to portray beliefs, values, and behaviors with which children can easily identify; and, third, to reinforce children's imitation of the role models in a therapeutic setting to facilitate social learning of the target behaviors.

Other studies have used storytelling and fantasy play to treat dysfunctional nonminority (Bettelheim, 1977; Gardner, 1971) and minority children (Freyberg, 1973; Smilansky, 1968), and quantitative evaluations have suggested favorable treatment outcomes. The cuento study was designed to evaluate treatment outcomes of cultural intervention compared with play/activity therapy and no therapy. Play/activity therapy is a traditional therapy modality based on a series of tasks, such as relating personal events, playing with family-type puppets, drawing, coloring, playing bingo, assembling puzzles, and playing with various play materials. The purpose of play/activity therapy is to have the child communicate through play. Two versions of cuento therapy were developed: one based on original Puerto Rican folktales, and one also based on original folktales adapted to reflect the life experience of Puerto Rican children in the United States.

Methods

Treatments were conducted in group sessions with 210 Puerto Rican mother–child dyads—boys and girls (grades kindergarten to three; mean age = 7.45 years) and their mothers. More than 500 children were screened for behavior emotional problems in school and at home (by teacher and parental ratings), and selection was limited to those children with the most severe ratings, on the basis of a median split on the Conner's Behavior

Ratings Scale (Conners, 1973). These children were considered to be at risk but were not presenting *DSM-III-R* disorders. The selected children's families were of low socioeconomic status; the father was absent from 68% of the households; and most parents were unemployed (mothers, 88%; fathers in household, 39%) and had not completed high school (mean education = 8.5 years).

A panel of Puerto Rican psychologists and of parents selected 40 cuentos taken from Puerto Rican folklore on the basis of thematic content expressing cultural values. Development of a therapy modality from these original cuentos was consistent with the approach of isomorphic reproduction of culture in treatment (Rogler et al., 1987). A second modality was developed by adapting these 40 cuentos to bridge Puerto Rican and American cultures and to redirect the thematic content of each story to be more adaptive. The cuentos were rewritten to reflect settings common in urban life (e.g., a rural plantation was changed to an inner-city playground; mango trees were changed to apple trees; and small town tricksters were changed into owners of a small circus). The ethnic identity of the main character remained Puerto Rican, but secondary characters were presented as multiethnic (i.e., Hispanic, Black, and White) to reflect inner-city social interactions more naturally. Original themes were altered to stress social judgment, control of anxiety and aggressive impulses, delay of gratification, and parent–child conflict. At each session to balance sex-role modeling, the protagonist of one cuento was a boy and of the other, a girl.

The rationale for adapting the 40 original cuentos lies in the psychohistorical development of folklore in general and of folktales in particular. Earlier, we noted that what made the folktale an effective cultural instrument as a repository and transmitter of human values in Puerto Rican society was its adaptability to Puerto Rican settings, characters, and experiences of life on the island. Hence, the adapted cuentos represent an accelerated psychohistorical process of acculturation aimed at reviving the values of Puerto Rican culture and, at the same time, inculcating personality functions valued in the American culture, thus helping the children to bridge the gap between the two cultures. We took the original cuentos and altered them to make them more congruent with the host society's culture. The adapted cuentos retained their original Puerto Rican "flavor" as the names of the characters and the basic plots were preserved. Otherwise, the adapted cuentos embody changes that are designed to reinforce personality functions, which would help children adapt to American culture values.

In the cultural intervention sessions, the therapists and the mothers with their children read the two cuentos bilingually. The therapists then conducted a group discussion of the character's feelings and behavior and the moral of the story. Once the target behaviors of the session were understood, the opportunity for imitative behavior was provided: A mother–child dyad dramatized the story and resolved the basic conflict. Videotapes of the role-playing exercise were reviewed by the groups and the therapist led a discussion of members' personal experiences with similar conflict, and of which solutions were adaptive and maladaptive in terms of reducing conflict. A control group participated in traditional play/activity therapy sessions conducted by a therapist and a school teacher.

Children were randomly assigned by sex and grade level to treatment groups and 26 weekly 90-minute sessions were led by male and female Puerto Rican therapists. Sessions were held at two public schools within the Hispanic community. Attendance at the sessions was above 80%.

Measurement of Treatment Outcomes

Children were pre- and posttested individually with a battery of measures by bilingual Puerto Rican examiners blinded to treatment group assignments. Tests were administered in a child's preferred language or bilingually. A second follow-up posttest administration was conducted 1 year later with 178 children (85% of the original number; Costantino et al., 1986).

The screening criteria for inclusion in the study and the targets of the therapy intervention were anxiety symptoms, conduct problems (aggressiveness, disruptiveness, inability to delay gratification), poor social judgment, and low self-esteem. Anxiety symptoms were measured by the Trait scale of the State–Trait Anxiety Inventory (Spielberger, Edwards, Lushene, Montuori, & Platzek, 1973); mean item responses are reported here on a 3-point scale denoting the frequency of a given anxiety symptom (2 = often, 1 = sometimes, 0 = hardly ever). Social judgment was measured by the Comprehension subtest of the Wechsler Intelligence Scale for Children—Revised (WISC-R; Wechsler, 1974): This subtest, taken from the WISC-R, consits of 17 questions designed to assess the verbal comprehension of a number of social situations that involve practical judgment in everyday behavior, social acculturation, interpersonal relationships, and moral reasoning. For example, Question 1 asks, "What is the thing to do if a boy (girl) much smaller than yourself starts to fight with you?" Age-appropriate standardized scale scores were derived ($M = 10$, $SD = 3$). Observation data were collected in experimental situations designed to elicit aggression (response to a frustrating task, provocation by a schoolmate), disruptiveness (frequency of disruptions while under instruction to maintain silence during a structured task), delay of gratification (number of days willing to wait for increasingly larger monetary rewards), and self-concept of competence (selection of tasks varying in perceived difficulty from below age level, age-appropriate, to above age level). Five trials in each situation were administered. Aggressiveness and disruptiveness of children's behavior were rated on a 5-point scale (5 = high aggression/disruptiveness, 1 = low aggression/disruptiveness) by independent observers who were previously trained to at least 80% agreement. Delay of gratification (number of days) and self-concept (age level selection) were recorded objectively.

Cuento Therapy Session Format

Cuento therapy with children is considered to be a short-term intervention. This intervention works in tandem with the school year, starting in October and ending in June. There are two variations of cuento therapy; in cases in which mothers are unavailable, therapists use videotapes of cuentos. In this modality, the children see the videotapes of the cuentos and also read the cuentos, with the other elements of the modality remaining the same. Cuento therapy may also be used with multiple family members. In all variations, the group should not exceed 10 members.

The typical session took place in a group therapy room. The participants sat in a circle, with each of the five mother–child pairs sitting next to each other. A group leader and co-leader led each session. Both leaders welcomed the participants. While the group leader took attendance, the co-leader distributed both Spanish and English versions of the cuentos to each mother–child pair. Two cuentos were read in each therapy session, alternately by the therapist and by each mother–child pair. The cuentos were read in both English and Spanish, hence, English and Spanish versions of the cuentos were distributed in accordance with the participants' preferred language. The bilingual narration was accomplished by having each participant read one paragraph in English and then having the same paragraph reread in Spanish. When necessary, the leaders helped the participants to read the stories. To balance the role modeling of the cuento characters in each session, one cuento had a girl as the principal character, while the other cuento had a boy as the principal character. Following the reading, the cuento was discussed for semantic content and ego functions exhibited by the characters. Personal experiences of the participant were shared vis-à-vis the experiences of the characters. Adaptive functions depicted in the cuentos were role-played. The following is a cuento and its protocol as used in a therapy session.

Adapted Cuento

The Little Boy Who Wanted to Become a Big Man

Not too long ago, there was a boy called Juanito who did not want to go to school. One day, he said to his parents, "I'm sick and tired of being treated like a little boy. I am old enough to be on my own and do what I want to do."

His parents became very sad. His mother said, "You can't leave us. You're too little to live by yourself. I would worry about you all the time and I would get sick."

His father added, "Son, wait until you finish school. You're too young. It would be hard for you to find a good job. Don't you know what happened to your grandfather, Juan? He didn't want to go to school and learn; he became so stupid that everybody started to call him Donkey Juan. We are afraid that if you don't go to school, people will call you Juanito el Burrito," said his parents.

"I'm a big boy now. I know a lot. I can work and make money. I can do what I feel like doing. Give me my things. I am going away!" said the little boy. His mother gave him a sack with his clothes and some food. His father gave him a few dollars. The little boy said goodbye to everyone and left.

The little boy was lucky to find a grocery store owner who gave him work; but he paid the boy only with food and a place to sleep. The boy was given so little food that people used to say, "He works like a donkey but eats like a chicken."

After a while, the little boy became tired of that life. He thought, "What a stupid donkey I am! I left my house where I had plenty of food and a good bed to sleep in, where I didn't have to work so hard. At home, I only had to go to school, learn my lessons, and do some chores. I am leaving this store. I want to go home." But the little boy was afraid to go back home.

One day, while he was carrying two large bags of groceries, he met Mr. Fox and Mr. Dog, sitting on a bench and reading a newspaper. "Listen, little boy, your boss makes you work a lot but pays you very little. Leave your job and come with us; we'll give you lots of money," said Mr. Fox and Mr. Dog.

The boy really wanted to return home to his parents, but he did not want to go back without money. So, he delivered the groceries and when he returned to the store he told his boss that he was quitting his job and returning home.

Instead of going straight back home, he went to see Mr. Fox and Mr. Dog. The little boy said, "Tell me all about the job I have to do to get lots of money."

Mr. Fox said, "We've discovered a treasure in an abandoned house. But the bags full of gold are so heavy that we can't carry them."

Mr. Dog added, "So we need a strong boy like you to carry the gold. We'll give you lots of money if you come with us."

"Let's go, I'm ready," said the little boy.

"First, we'll eat a good meal. You have to be very strong. Then we will wait until night, because we don't want to share the money with anyone else," said Mr. Fox and Mr. Dog.

They ate a hearty meal and when night came they went to get the treasure. When they arrived, the boy said, "This is a beautiful home where rich people must live, it's not an abandoned house. I am not going to be part of your plans to steal anything from anyone!"

"Listen, boy," said Mr. Dog and Mr. Fox in a convincing voice, "believe us, there is nobody in the house. If we don't take the money, Mr. Mouse will eat it. Stay here by the window, and we'll go in and take the bags of money."

The little boy believed them. Mr. Fox and Mr. Dog put the bags on the boy's back. As the three were leaving, a neighbor yelled, "Police! Call the police! I see three thieves!"

Mr. Fox and Mr. Dog quickly ran away, but the little boy with the two heavy bags could not run. When the police arrived they caught him and took him to the police station.

"We caught you stealing money from some rich people. We're going to put you in jail!" a police officer said.

The boy began to cry and said, "I didn't know I was stealing. Mr. Dog and Mr. Fox said that we were going to get a treasure in an abandoned house and if we did not get it, Mr. Mouse would eat the money."

"How stupid!" said a police officer. "The house was not abandoned, the owners were away on vacation." When the boy heard the word stupid, he began to cry louder, because he remembered the words of his father: "You should continue going to school. . ." Crying, the boy said, "I want to go home."

"You can't go home until we find out who really stole the money." While they were asking the boy all kinds of questions, a police officer brought in Mr. Fox and Mr. Dog. The two thieves confessed that they had attempted to steal and added, "That boy is so stupid that he doesn't even know he was stealing."

The boy felt insulted and very bad, but he was happy that a Hispanic police officer was taking him home. As he was climbing the stairs, he heard his family having a party and heard his parents say, "What a pity! Today is our boy's birthday. Only God knows where he might be. If he were only here with us. We miss him very much." Hearing that his parents still loved him, the little boy went in. His parents and his brothers and sisters were very happy, and they all celebrated his birthday.

From that day on, the boy went to school, learned his lessons, and listened to his parents. He was on his way to becoming a big and intelligent man.

Adapted Cuento: Ego Functions

Moral of the Story or Basic Meaning

Growing up is a long, painful, but rewarding process. However, at times, children wrongly think that they are old enough to make their own decisions and do what they like, without listening to their parents' advice. Unfortunately, these children end up making bad mistakes and paying the consequences for pretending to be grown-ups and acting in an age-inappropriate manner. So, it pays to grow up naturally, through stages set by nature, our family, and society.

Achievement Motivation

At the beginning, the boy, who in this story is called *El Burrito* because he behaves like a stupid donkey, shows poor school achievement motivation. In fact, he decides to drop out of school. However, he shows some kind of vocational achievement motivation because he wants to work. His achievement motivation is not so functional because he does not have any skills and can do only menial work.

Once he is on his own, he works very hard for the grocery owner. However, this type of job is not a good substitute for school, because in this job *El Burrito* does not learn anything, except how to carry groceries.

Object Relations

The boy's parents care very much about him. Both his father and his mother try very hard to convince him to continue going to school and to remain with them in the house because, some day, they want him to get a good job. However, Burrito is very stubborn and decides to go off on his own.

Once he leaves, he gets along well with the owner of the grocery. He also gets along with two streetwise persons, Mr. Fox and Mr. Dog. However, the Burrito is very naive and knows very little about people's motivations.

Reality Testing and Judgment

El Burrito shows himself to be a very immature boy, with poor judgment. He is unable to anticipate the consequences of his behavior, that is, how bad it is going to be for him once he leaves his home and goes to live on the outside.

However, very soon, he learns that living on the outside is no fun; he has to work very hard, much harder than he worked at home and in school; and he does not earn very much. He earns just enough to live. Therefore, he starts feeling guilty and regrets having left his home and having dropped out of school. So, he decides to return home, but he is ashamed to go back home without any money, so he stupidly accepts the invitation of Mr. Fox and Mr. Dog, who tell him that he can earn good money in a short time.

The boy again shows poor judgment. He does not realize that one cannot earn a lot of money without working very hard. He does not realize that Mr. Fox and Mr. Dog were using him to steal money.

Moral Judgment

El Burrito does not know that his two accomplices are going to rob a house. When he sees the house, he realizes that there is no abandoned house, but that maybe the two are going to steal money from a rich family's house. However, again, the two sly persons convince him that he is wrong.

However, Burrito is guilty by association. He goes along with two professional thieves and helps them steal, albeit unwittingly. Because of his poor ego development, he is also immature in moral development: He cannot recognize unethical situations.

He is arrested because he is caught with the stolen money. He claims he is innocent but the police take him to prison. Fortunately, Mr. Fox and Mr. Dog admit that they stole the money and that Burrito was so stupid that he did not know they were stealing money. Therefore, he is set free.

Personal Relations

Living alone is very hard. When El Burrito realizes that other people used him and manipulated him, he also realizes that his parents really love him. So, he wants to return home to his parents. He also realizes that he loves his parents and that he is going to obey them from that day on.

Reality Testing and Judgment

Burrito shows good judgment at the end of the story. He wants to return home to his parents and wants to return to school. He has learned a good lesson.

Evaluation of Treatment Outcomes

Anxiety Outcomes

With regard to immediate posttest anxiety ratings, treatment groups differed significantly only at the first-grade level. The adapted cuento group reported significantly less frequent anxiety symptoms than the other groups, with moderate to large effect sizes (SDs = .63–1.22). The original cuento group reported anxiety symptoms significantly less often than the no-treatment control group (SD = .33), but did not differ significantly from the art/play control group.

Analysis of the follow-up data indicated that treatment effects were stable after 1 year for all grade levels. The adapted cuento group reported significantly less anxiety than the two control groups ($SD = .34-.68$), but did not differ significantly from the original cuento group. The original cuento group differed significantly and moderately ($SD = .48$) from the no-treatment control group, but did not report significantly less anxiety than the art/play control group.

Thus, the evaluation of anxiety symptoms as a treatment outcome revealed a complex pattern of findings. Immediate treatment effects were evident only with younger children in the first grade; in this specific subgroup, the cultural modeling intervention based on folktales adapted to bridge Puerto Rican and American cultures had the strongest impact on reduction of anxiety symptomatology. However, treatment differences were uniform (regardless of grade level or sex) after 1 year. Adaptations of the folktales once again had substantial impact on anxiety symptoms relative to the control conditions, but the difference between the two cultural interventions was not confirmed. Anxiety reduction, achieved by introducing cultural sensitivity into modeling therapy with Puerto Rican children was consistent with the treatment outcomes reported in earlier studies using social learning techniques with nonminority populations (see Costantino et al., 1986). This treatment outcome is especially prominent because anxiety is a core symptom in many other types of more severe psychopathology. Because Puerto Rican children generally may be classified as a high-risk population, and because the children screened for participation in this study were already experiencing behavior problems at school and at home, cuento therapy may serve a preventive mental health function.

Social Judgment

Treatment effects on social judgment (WISC-R Comprehension subtest) were significant only in the analysis of immediate posttests. Reconsidering the potential preventive mental health value of cultural interventions, the lack of stability of cognitive outcomes after 1 year suggests the need for provision of supportive follow-up services. The promotion of adaptive social judgment among children is especially critical for the prevention of the development of conduct disorders, particularly in the case of minority children who often lack adaptive social and academic role models and instead are exposed to maladaptive peer models, which reinforce delinquency, truancy, and even criminal behavior.

HERO/HEROINE THERAPY WITH ADOLESCENTS

Interviews with the older (third grade) children participating in the cuento therapy study, combined with small-sample pilot studies on adolescents, revealed their tendency to view the folktales as juvenile and the characters as cartoon-like (Costantino, Malgady, & Rogler, 1988b). In conjunction with the anxiety outcomes specific to the younger children in the cuento study, these findings inspired the development of a somewhat different approach to the introduction of cultural sensitivity into modeling therapy. Following the promising treatment outcomes from the evaluation of the cuento therapy study, the program of research was extended to an adolescent Puerto Rican population, basing the storytelling modality on "heroic" adult role models.

Adolescence is considered to be a turbulent period in the psychosocial development of most youngsters, and the weight of evidence suggests that Puerto Rican adolescents may be at increased risk of mental disorder. According to national figures (U.S. Bureau of the Census, 1980), 41% of Puerto Rican families are single-parent households headed by women, and estimates specific to Puerto Ricans in New York City are even slightly higher (44%, reported by Mann and Salvo, 1985). Moreover, according to the National Puerto Rican Forum (1980), about 9% of Puerto Rican households are headed by adolescents and young adults under 24 years old. The frequency of young, single-parent households—typically a result of the father's absence—indicates that Puerto Rican adolescents often lack appropriate adult role models with whom they can identify, and therefore also lack adaptive values and behaviors to imitate during adolescence (Lash, Segal, & Dudzinski, 1979). It has also been suggested that the identity crisis of Puerto Rican adolescents is compounded by strong intercultural and intergenerational conflicts (Lewis, 1966). Consequently, Puerto Rican adolescents appear to be suitable candidates for a modeling therapy that fulfills their need for adaptive adult role models in a culturally sensitive manner.

In the second study, Malgady, Rogler, and Costantino (1990b) developed a modeling therapy that used biographical stories of heroic Puerto Ricans to bridge the identity, bicultural, and intergenerational conflicts faced by Puerto Rican adolescents. This modality sought to enhance the relevance of therapy for adolescents by exposing them to successful adult models in their own culture, thus fostering ethnic pride and identity as a Puerto Rican, and by modeling achievement-oriented behavior and adaptive coping skills to deal with the stress common to life in the Puerto Rican community. The contents of the biographies embodied themes of cultural conflict (e.g., expression of cultural pride juxtaposed with experiences of discrimination), with group discussion and imitative role-playing drawing on members' personal experiences in Puerto Rico and the United States. Hence, this approach to cultural intervention represented an attempt to bridge cross-cultural conflict in much the same manner as the adaption of folktales in the previous study.

Methods

The hero/heroine therapy was implemented in group sessions with 40 male and 50 female Puerto Rican eighth and ninth grade adolescents (mean age = 13.67), who were screened from among more than 300 students for behavior problems by teacher rating on the Conner's Behavior Rating Scale and classified as having secondary risk status. All households were of low SES, 64% were receiving welfare benefits, and 71% were headed by women. The major difference from the children participating in the cuento study was that these adolescents were all U.S.-born and English-dominant. The adolescents were randomly assigned to either the hero/heroine intervention group ($n = 70$, with 9 dropouts) or an attention control group ($n = 40$, with 11 dropouts). The intervention group participated in 18 weekly, 90-minute therapy sessions; the attention control group participated in 18 weekly discussion sessions. Each session was led by male and female Puerto Rican therapists in a public school within the Hispanic community. Attendance at the sessions averaged 68% in the intervention group, and 84% in the control group.

A research panel selected and compiled biographies of nine male and nine female heroic role models from various periods of Puerto Rican history. The role models were chosen on the basis of their significant achievements (in politics, sports, arts, and education) and adaptive coping to overcome adversities such as poverty and prejudice. A different male or female biography was presented in each session.

The intervention sessions were conducted in three stages. First, the group members read the biography and the therapists led a discussion of the source of stress and the behavior that reflected ethnic pride, positive self-concept, and adaptive coping strengths. Second, to promote identification with the model, the therapists led the group through structured questioning, comparing group members' experiences with the model's biography. The therapists verbally reinforced group members' self-reported behavior that was consistent with the model and explored alternatives to maladaptive behavior. Third, the group members dramatized an open-ended skit related to the biography, with instructions to resolve the conflict posed. Peer reinforcement of adaptive resolutions was encouraged and also verbally reinforced by the therapists.

Thus, the intervention sought to promote adolescents' identification with the heroic role models through ethnic and cultural similarity, and also by comparison with stressful experiences. Group discussion and imitative role-playing then provided a forum for the reinforcement of appropriate target behaviors.

Measurement of Treatment Outcomes

Adolescents were pre- and posttested individually with a battery of measures by Puerto Rican examiners blinded to treatment assignments. Testing was conducted largely in English.

The models in the therapy intervention displayed a positive self-concept and strong ethnic identity. Therefore, these outcomes were targeted using the Piers–Harris Self-Concept Scale (0 = low self-concept, 1 = high self-concept) and a 17-item Puerto Rican Identity rating scale (1 = very Puerto Rican, 5 = very Anglo); (Costantino, Malgady, & Rogler, 1988b; Malgady, Rogler, & Costantino, 1990a). The models also were selected for emphasis on adaptive coping with stress; thus, anxiety and symptom distress were also targeted as treatment outcomes. Anxiety symptoms were measured by the Trait scale of the State–Trait Anxiety Inventory, described in the cuento study. Symptom distress was measured by the SCL-90-R (Derogatis, 1983), which was scored for the Global Severity of Mental Health Index across symptom dimensions (0 = no distress, 4 = extreme distress).

Hero/Heroine Therapy Session Format

Hero/heroine modeling therapy in general followed the cuento therapy format; however, the group therapy was conducted with boys and girls without the participation of their mothers. Adolescents, who are in the process of establishing their own self-identity, shy away from situations, especially emotionally laden situations, when a parent is present. In the modality, there was a group leader and a group co-leader, usually of the opposite sex. Six to eight adolescents participated in a given group. The intervention was short term, consisting of 26 sessions patterned around the school year. Short biographies of significant historical and contemporary figures were read, discussed for semantic understanding, and analyzed for ego functions. The participants were encouraged to talk about their own life experiences as compared with those of the role modeling of the biographies. The following is one protocol of hero/heroine biography and its analysis used in the role modeling sessions.

Biography

Angelita Lind

Angelita Lind was born in 1959 in the town of Patillas in Puerto Rico. She had six brothers and sisters and is one of the fastest runners in the history of Puerto Rico's sports world.

Angelita had a strong need to make friends ever since she was a youngster. In school, she realized that the best students had the most friends, but she was only an average student. So, she decided to be the class clown in order to make friends. Every morning she asked her mother to braid her hair into a lot of little braids and during recess in school she would undo the braids and muss up her hair and pretend to be a monster. Soon, she also realized that playing a monster was not the right way to make friends, so she decided to look for another way to make friends—to become a star in the sports field.

It was not until she was in the seventh grade, and she began to take part in the athletic contests in school, that Angelita began to think seriously about becoming an athlete. When she would leave school at noon, she would run to her house, leave her books on the table, change her clothes, and run as fast as she could to her grandmother's house—three miles away! There, her grandmother would have lunch ready for her. Angelita would stuff the lunch in her pocket and run back to her own house—another three miles!

But Angelita did not neglect her studies. She found time to study when she was not running, and she got good grades—better grades than when she was undoing her hair and playing the clown.

And that is how Angelita became a runner. Her family was too poor to buy her a pair of sneakers or running shoes, so Angelita ran barefoot. She took part in all the running events in school competitions and, by the time she graduated from high school, she was an excellent athlete. The Interamerican University recruited her for their athletic team and gave her a scholarship.

University life was one of the most difficult stages in Angelita's life because she had to separate herself from her family and live in the university dormitory. She missed her family, but she rarely found time to visit them because of her athletic activities. Both she and her family knew that she had to train very hard to come out well in the competitions. It was only thanks to this hard training that Angelita won all the university competitions she participated in and graduated with a degree in Physical Education. She was now a well-known athlete in Puerto Rico and began to participate in international sports events. Angelita represented Puerto Rico in the Central American Youth Games in 1977 and 1978, which were held in Mexico and Colombia, respectively. In 1979, she represented Puerto Rico in the Panamerican Games held in San Juan, the capital. In 1982, she participated in the Central American and Caribbean Games in which she had the honor of carrying the flag at the head of the Puerto Rican delegation. Here, she won a silver medal in the 800-meter race and a gold medal in the 1500-meter race.

Something unexpected happened in the 800-meter race. From the start, Angelita expected to win this race and get a gold medal. Instead, she came in second, but won the 1500-meter race, something she had never dreamed would happen. Angelita fought to win the 800-meter race to the finish. For most of the race, she was well ahead, but when there were only 50 meters left to go, Angelita turned her head to see where the other runners were. Because of this, Angelita, lost her balance and the runner behind her knocked against her elbow and both fell to the ground. So, Angelita, who thought for sure she would win, came in second. Her first reaction was to think, "This can't be, I knew I would come in first." She had spent months training for this race and now she was second. Then Angelita paused and thought of God and it came to her that second place was not bad at all. She learned from this failure, so when she ran the 1500 meters, she did not make the same mistake of looking back, and she won the gold medal.

In 1983, Angelita went to the Panamerican Games in Caracas, Venezuela. She got sick there, but even so she competed, this time without winning a medal. When she returned to Puerto Rico, she felt that she had let her country down and said to herself, "I am going to show everybody that I can win." She then began the most intense training of her life and it paid off. Angelita went to the Central American and Caribbean Games in Santo Domingo and came back with one gold medal and two silver medals.

In addition to her sports achievements, Angelita has reached many of her personal goals. Through sports, she achieved something she had yearned for when she was a child: being popular and having lots of friends. She also achieved a university degree and a professional career, for she is now a trainer at the Interamerican University. And last but not least, Angelita was able to buy a new house for her family.

The keys to Angelita's success were her determination, her persistence, and her hard work. She came to realize that she could learn not only from her successes but also from her failures. Her philosophy of life is, "You cannot have success without suffering and everyone who wants to get to the top has to overcome a number of obstacles first. There is an invisible wall in front of us all the time, but we have to be strong enough to knock down this wall little by little to get what we want."

Angelita's sports career has given her many joys and successes, many tears, and much suffering, but she does not plan to retire just yet. She still has one goal to reach—a gold medal in the Olympics.

Main Points of Story

This cuento makes several points:

1. When she was a child, Angelita wanted to make friends and to become popular with her classmates. She tried to do this by becoming the class clown. It was not until later, when she began to participate in sports events, that she found friends and became popular.

2. Angelita participated in school events. This opened the door for her not only in terms of having friends and becoming popular, but also in terms of showing her where her talents were and of developing those talents.
3. To excel in sports, Angelita had to undergo hard training. She had to prepare herself for each race and never lose sight of her goals.
4. She persevered, even when she lost a race or when she was sick.
5. She was willing to overcome the obstacles in her way. Before you can overcome an obstacle, you first must want to overcome it.

Pivot of Discussion and Role-Playing Situation

Angelita's statement is that "there is an invisible wall in front of us all. . ." What was Angelita's invisible wall? What is yours?

Relate Main Points of Story to the Adolescents' Lives

- Do you engage in any sports in school? Outside of school?
- Why was Angelita's way of making friends not the best way? What is the best way?
- Do you take part in any school activity: science club, drama club, school band, etc.?
- Did you ever win an award or a medal for a sports contest, or get a very good mark on a hard test? What did you have to do before that to obtain that distinction?
- Have you ever persevered in something, even when you did not feel like it, or when you were sick—even going to school and attending classes when you did not feel like it?
- Do you know what you want? Is it a high school diploma? Do you know how to obtain this goal?

Role-Playing

1. Ask one student to imagine him- or herself in elementary school, feeling lonely, inadequate, and isolated in the middle of a playground. The student wants to make friends, and to do this he or she starts playing the clown. The other students play the part of his or her classmates. Elicit responses to the "clown's" behavior; explore the clown's feelings as it becomes clear to him or her that he or she is not being accepted and valued the way he or she wants to be.

2. Ask one student to be a runner in the 1500-meter race in the Central American and Caribbean Games. A second student plays the part of the coach; the rest of the students play the part of members of the Puerto Rican sports delegation. The coach and the athletes of the Puerto Rican delegation are reviewing with the runner his or her performance, the wins he or she has had as well as the losses. Elicit the runner's reactions to triumph and loss, his or her evaluation of what went wrong and how to cope with disappointment. Explore also the other students' ability to be objective and supportive, and their feelings as they do this or as they resist being either objective in evaluating the runner or being supportive.

Evaluation of Treatment Outcomes

Treatment main and interaction effects were significant in the analyses of anxiety, self-concept, and ethnic identity symptoms, but not in the analysis of symptom severity.

Anxiety Outcomes

The analysis of anxiety outcomes revealed a treatment by grade level interaction in which treatment groups differed significantly only at the eighth-grade level. The intervention group reported significantly less frequent anxiety symptoms than the control group, with a modest effect size ($SD = .39$).

The grade-level-specific finding in the evaluation of anxiety symptoms as an outcome of the hero intervention is consistent with the earlier cuento study, but is somewhat weaker in effect size. However, it is not entirely clear why cultural modeling of heroic biographies would be less effective among an older group of adolescents. One clue is provided by feedback from the therapists and informal interviews of the participants after the study. After about half of the sessions, the 14–15-year-old participants were somewhat jaded by what they perceived as repetitive themes in the biographies. Thus, as their interest waned, they became less responsive to the therapeutic message. This may also explain the poorer attendance rate in the hero study compared with that in the cuento study.

Nevertheless, this treatment outcome supports the preventive mental health value of cultural intervention for younger adolescents and invites the development of new cultural modalities that can capture and maintain the interest of an older population. It may be that anxiety symptomatology of older adolescents should be treated with very short-term interventions.

Self-Concept and Ethnic Identity Outcomes

Overall, there was no significant main effect of treatment intervention on self-concept, but a moderate main effect on ethnic identity. The hero intervention group evidenced significantly greater Puerto Rican identity than the control group ($SD = .54$). However, unexpected interaction effects involving treatments were evident with regard to both self-concept and ethnic identity, as a function of sex and father-presence in the household.

Treatment outcomes did not differ significantly for girls in father-absent families nor for boys in father-present families. However, boys from father-absent families showed significantly and substantially greater ($SD = 1.15$) Puerto Rican identity in their intervention group as compared to the control group, although a similar effect ($SD = .87$) was apparent among girls from intact families. Girls from father-absent households generally had stronger Puerto Rican identities than their male counterparts, and this was not augmented by the therapeutic role models, perhaps because the girls already strongly identified with their mothers. Similarly, boys in intact families identified ethnically with their fathers (i.e., no male identity gap needed fulfillment), but their female counterparts may have experienced intergenerational or cultural conflict with their fathers, which was ameliorated by the intervention.

The therapeutic role models promoted increased self-concept, significantly more so for adolescent girls ($SD = .56$) than boys ($SD = .36$). Consistent with the ethnic identity outcomes, boys from intact families did not enhance their self-image as a result of exposure to therapeutic role models. However, there was a significant and large ($SD = 1.29$) negative treatment effect among adolescent girls from intact families.

This unexpected negative treatment outcome may derive from the same source implicated in ethnic identity. Although adolescent girls from intact families became "more Puerto Rican," their self-image diminished in the process. A two-fold explanation of this process seems plausible. The role models idealized in therapy may have aroused conflict about their own parental models, and through identification with their parents, led to feelings of personal inadequacy. This process may have operated among girls only because the therapeutic female role models typically represented nontraditional female sex-roles (e.g., professional athlete; mayor of San Juan, Puerto Rico; lawyer). Thus, ideal–real parental conflict and female sex-role conflict may account for the negative treatment outcomes among adolescent girls.

The unexpected interactions impacting on treatment outcomes call attention to the importance of adolescents' social context in considering the preventive mental health value of cultural interventions. This implicates the need to investigate both the integrity and quality of intrafamilial relations not only as potential mediators of treatment outcomes, but in the development of interventions for populations with special mental health needs.

LIMITATIONS, GENERALIZABILITY, AND FUTURE DIRECTIONS

Perhaps the most fundamental question that should be faced by culturally sensitive psychotherapy research is whether or not the consideration of culture is consequential to treatment outcome. In a review of two decades of cross-cultural psychotherapy research on ethic minority populations, based primarily on Blacks, Sue (1988) identified two competing conclusions pertinent to this issue. The first is that ethnic or cultural mismatch between client and therapist decreases the likelihood of favorable therapeutic outcome. The second suggests that cultural differences are largely irrelevant to therapeutic outcomes. According to Sue, the research literature on this fundamental issue apparently is equivocal and riddled with methodological flaws. Although studies specific to Hispanics are scant, our research on cuento therapy and hero modeling therapy shows that culturally sensitive interventions produced more favorable outcomes on some behavioral and emotional problems than standard play therapy intervention and no-therapy intervention, thus lending support to the conclusion that the consideration of culture in psychotherapy is consequential. In the tradition of psychologists who have proposed a narrative conceptualization of human thinking, Howard (1991) suggests that storytelling, as in the relation of cuentos and heroic biographies, is fundamental to the development of one's identity, which he calls "life-story construction." Psychopathology occurs when life stories go awry; hence, the effectiveness of culturally sensitive storytelling techniques may correspond to Howard's view of psychotherapy as an "exercise in story repair." This reasoning may explain the age-specific effects of the cuento and hero modalities: Storytelling is associated with the self-identity that is appropriate for a given age. As children mature, the complexity of their stories increases from folktales about fictional characters to biographies of historical characters. Moreover, cognitive complexity may enhance this developmental process, as a physical/pictorial modality may be most effective with young children followed with greater maturity by a verbal/written modality. Cultural sensitivity in psychotherapy, then, might be viewed as the composition and narration of an age-appropriate story fitting the functional demands imposed on ethnic minority youngsters to repair their own dysfunctional stories.

Limitations and Generalizability

Unfortunately, studies of therapy outcomes with Hispanics, especially with child and adolescent populations, present a fragmented picture of the extent to which the goal of culturally appropriate treatment services has been realized. In this regard, cuento therapy research is exemplary in providing a test of the effectiveness of cultural interventions compared to a standard therapy control group. On the other hand, hero therapy research provides evidence that cultural intervention is more of a therapeutic than a nontherapeutic intervention. However, the more rigorous question of whether cultural intervention promotes outcomes superior to standard treatments remains unanswered. Specifically, culturally sensitive treatments such as cuento and hero therapy need to be compared in effectiveness with family and cognitive–behavioral therapy as alternative interventions.

Methodologically, treatment outcome research has been limited not only by the absence of therapeutic comparisons or appropriate control groups, but also by the failure to specify the precise psychiatric disorders of the children or adolescents who are the targets of these interventions. Thus, we do not know whether positive treatment outcomes are limited to particular disorders such as depression, conduct, and anxiety. Essentially, treatment-by-disorder interaction effects are presently unknown. A serious limitation in treatment outcome research with ethnic minority populations is the choice of measurement techniques. Although multimethod–multitrait designs are highly desirable, they are time consuming, costly, and unwieldy to implement with large samples of research participants, especially in naturalistic settings such as schools and mental heath clinics. Similarly, the choice of measurements poses special concerns for this research, inasmuch as the validity of standard psychological assessment techniques for ethnic minority children has been challenged for decades (e.g., Rogler et al., 1989).

Finally, a limitation of interventions such as cuento and hero therapy is that their feasibility of implementation in a clinical or school setting has not been explored. The practical aspects of delivering such culturally sensitive mental health services to the Hispanic community, such as training therapists in the field, have not been addressed in our programmatic research. This is an issue of growing importance because current projections are that ethnic minorities will constitute about 40% of the mental heath clientele by the year 2000, yet the number of corresponding minority providers is lagging far behind (Cross, Bazron, Dennis, & Isaacs, 1989). Therefore, the effectiveness of culturally sensitive therapeutic services may be limited if they can be administered only by ethnically matched therapists.

The treatment outcome research conducted on cuento and hero therapy has focused on low SES, urban-dwelling Puerto Rican children and adolescents of specific age ranges in the northeast. As with any research findings, generalizability across other variables should be made with caution. Our own program research is currently expanding to include new groups who are immigrating rapidly into the northeast, such as Dominicans, Mexicans, and Central and South Americans. There is considerable diversity between the major Hispanic subgroups, particularly socioeconomically, which needs to be taken into consideration in determining where culturally sensitive services have differential outcomes across these nationalities (Malgady, Rogler, & Costantino, 1990a).

Research in progress in other cultural settings has replicated cuento therapy with American Indian children in the northwest (La Fromboise & Fink, 1990). In addition, hero therapy has been replicated with Black adolescents in South Africa (Woutres, 1990). A related issue of generalizability is whether culture-specific interventions enhance treatment outcomes in the cultural target population or different racial groups, for instance, limiting our research to Puerto Ricans who are of mixed heritage (European White, Caribe Indian, and African Black), with individuals displaying a spectrum of skin colors and racial identities. The hero therapy protocols were chosen to capture this racial diversity to ensure their generalizability across groups.

Similarly, in practical settings, racial, socioeconomic, acculturative, and language factors should be considered in clinical decisions about whether to assign a Hispanic child or adolescent to culturally sensitive or mainstream services. For instance, White, second generation, middle-class, English-dominant Hispanic children might be more appropriate candidates for mainstream treatment services.

Future Directions

The limitations and issues of generalizability discussed here are obvious targets of research efforts on culturally sensitive treatment interventions, not only with Hispanics but with other ethnic minority groups as well. Less evident is the need to uncover the theoretical underpinnings of how cultural considerations operate in therapy. Sue and Zane (1987) advance an interesting question regarding whether culturally sensitive or ethnic matching of client and therapist has a proximal or direct effect on therapeutic outcome, or a distal or indirect effect by way of facilitating the therapeutic process. This is a topic that has been virtually neglected in empirical studies of interventions with minority children and adolescents. To our knowledge, no therapy process research has been conducted with Hispanic children or adolescents, but some recent work by Sue and his colleagues (personal communication, 1994) have studied process variables (e.g., saving face, gift giving) among Asian Americans.

Another direction for further research is to determine what specific cultural elements influence treatment outcomes. Carefully controlled experimental studies are needed to study the independent and possibly interactive effects of ethnic matching of client and therapist, the conduct of bilingual sessions, and the introduction of cultural elements into treatment, and to determine how much variance each contributes to treatment outcomes.

REFERENCES

Amato, A., Evans, R., & Ziegler, E. (1973). The effectiveness of creative dramatics and storytelling in a library setting. *Journal of Educational Research, 67,* 161–162.

American Psychiatric Association. (1987). *Diagnostic and statistical manual of mental disorders* (3rd ed., rev.). Washington, DC: Author.

Amor, R. (1969). *Afro-Cuban folktales as incorporated into the literary tradition of Cuba.* Unpublished doctoral dissertation, Columbia University.

Anderson, J. C., & Johnson, W. H. (1971). Stability and change among three generations of Mexican-Americans: Factors affecting achievement. *American Educational Journal, 8,* 285–307.

Arbuthnot, M. H. (1976). *Anthology of children's literature* (4th ed.). New York: Lothrop Publishers.

Aspira, Inc. of New York. (1983). *Racial and ethnic high school dropout rate in New York City.* New York: Author.

Bandura, A. (1977). *Social learning theory.* Englewood Cliffs, NJ: Prentice-Hall.

Bandura, A., & Walters, R. H. (1967). *Social learning and personality development.* New York: Holt, Rinehart & Winston.

Bettelheim, B. (1977). *The uses of enchantment: The importance and meaning of fairy tales.* New York: Vintage Books.

Bruner, J. (1986). *Actual minds, possible worlds.* Cambridge, MA: Harvard University Press.

Canino, I. A., Earley, B., & Rogler, L. H. (1980). *The Puerto Rican child in New York: Stress and mental health* (Monograph No. 4). New York: Hispanic Research Center, Fordham University.

Canino, I. A., Gould, M. S., Prupis, M. A., & Shafer, D. (1986). A comparison of symptoms and diagnoses in Hispanic and Black children in an outpatient mental health clinic. *Journal of the American Academy of Child Psychiatry, 25,* 254–259.

Conners, C. K. (1973). Rating scales for use in drug studies with children. *Psychopharmacology Bulletin* (Special Issue: Pharmacotherapy of Children), *9,* 24–84.

Costantino, G. (1980). The use of folktale as a new therapy modality to effect change in Hispanic children and their families. Grant No. 1-RO1-MH33711, National Institute of Mental Health.

Costantino, G., Malgady, R. G., & Rogler, L. H. (1985). *Cuento therapy: Folktale as a culturally sensitive psychotherapy for Puerto Rican Children.* (Hispanic Research Center, Fordham University: Monograph No. 12). Maplewood, N.J.: Waterfront Press.

Costantino, G., Malgady, R. G., & Rogler, L. H. (1986). Cuento therapy: A culturally sensitive modality for Puerto Rican children. *Journal of Consulting and Clinical Psychology, 54,* 639–645.

Costantino, G., Malgady, R. G., & Rogler, L. H. (1988a). Folk hero modeling therapy for Puerto Rican adolescents. *Journal of Adolescence, 11,* 155–165.

Costantino, G., Malgady, R. G., & Rogler, L. H. (1988b). *Technical manual: The TEMAS test.* Los Angeles: Western Psychological Services.

Cross, T. L., Bazron, B., Dennis, K. W., & Isaacs, M. R. (1989). *Toward a culturally competent system of care.* Washington, DC: Georgetown University, CAASP Technical Assistance Center.

Derogatis, L. R. (1983). *SCL-90-R administration, scoring, and procedures manual—II for the revised version.* Towson, MD: Author.

Emslie, G. J., Weinberg, W. A., Rush, A. J., Adams, R. M., & Rentelmann, J. W. (1990). Depressive symptoms by self-report in adolescence: Phase 1 of the development of a questionnaire for depression by self-report. *Journal of Child Neurology, 5,* 114–121.

Faro, S. (1939). *El folklorismo y su función social y politica* [Folklore and its social and political functions]. Buenos Aires, Association Folklorica Argentina.

Fisher, R. I. (1974). A study of non-intellectual attributes of children in a first grade bilingual–bicultural program. *Journal of Educational Research, 67,* 323–328.

Freyberg, J. (1973). Increasing imaginative play in urban disadvantaged kindergarten children through systematic training. In J. L. Singer (Ed.), *The child's world's of make-believe* (pp. 129–154). New York: Academic Press.

Gardner, R. (1971). *Therapeutic communication with children: The mutual storytelling technique.* New York: Science House.

Garrison, C., Jackson, K., Marsteller, F., McKeon, R., & Addy, C. (1990). A longitudinal study of depressive symptomatology in young adolescents. *Journal of the American Academy of Child Adolescent Psychiatry, 29,* 581–585.

Howard, G. S. (1991). Culture tales: A narrative approach to thinking, cross-cultural psychology and psychotherapy. *American Psychologist, 46,* 187–197.

Jilek, A. L. (1976). The Western psychiatrist and his non-Western clientele: Transcultural experiences of relevance to psychotherapy with Canadian Indian patients. *Canadian Psychiatric Association Journal, 21,* 353–359.

Klosinski, G. (1978). Report of a painting and fairy-tale therapy with a female anorexia nervosa patient. *Praxis der Kinderpsychologie und Kinderpsychiatries, 27*(6), 206–215.

La Fromboise, T. M., & Fink, S. (1990). *Use of traditional Chippewa storytelling with "at risk" elementary students.* Unpublished manuscript, Stanford University, Stanford, CA.

Langner, T., Gersfen, J., & Eisenberg, J. (1974). Approaches to measurement and definition in the epidemiology of behavior disorders: Ethnic background and child behavior. *International Journal of Health Services, 4,* 483–501.

Lash, T., Segal, H., & Dudzinski, D. (1979). *Children and families in New York City: An analysis of the 1976 survey of income and education.* New York: Foundation for Child Development.

Lewis, O. (1966). The culture of poverty. *Scientific American, 215,* 19–25.

Madrid, M. A. (1953). *The attitudes of Spanish-American people as expressed in their coplas or folk songs.* Unpublished doctoral dissertation, Teachers College, Columbia University, New York.

Mair, M. (1989). *Between psychology and psychotherapy.* London: Routledge.

Malgady, R. G., Rogler, L. H., & Costantino, G. (1990a). Culturally sensitive psychotherapy for Puerto Rican children and adolescents: A program of treatment outcome research. *Journal of Consulting and Clinical Psychology* (Special Series on Treatment of Children), *58,* 704–712.

Malgady, R. G., Rogler, L. H., & Costantino, G. (1990b). Hero/heroine modeling for Puerto Rican adolescents: A preventive mental health intervention. *Journal of Consulting and Clinical Psychology, 58,* 469–474.

Mann, E. S., & Salvo, J. J. (1985). Characteristics of new Hispanic immigrants to New York City. *Research Bulletin* (Hispanic Research Center, Fordham University, No. 1–2), 8.

Martinez, O. (1987). Minority youth and crime. *Crime and Delinquency, 33,* 325–328.

National Puerto Rican Forum. (1980). *The next step toward equality.* New York: Author.

New York City Board of Education, Office of Research, Education and Assessment. (1990). *The Cohort Report.* New York: Author.

New York City Department of City Planning. (1994). *City planning report.* New York: Author.

New York State Office of Mental Health. (1994). *Primary diagnoses of all children in CDF database.* Albany, NY: Author.

Padilla, A. M., Ruiz, R. A., & Alvarez, R. (1975). Community mental health services for Spanish-speaking surnamed population. *American Psychologist, 30,* 892–905.

Piers, E. V. (1984). *Piers–Harris Children's Self-Concept Scale: Revised manual.* Los Angeles: Western Psychological Services.

Pumariega, A. J., Swanson, J. W., Holzer, C. E., Linskey, A. O., & Quintero-Salinas, R. (1992). Cultural context and substance abuse in Hispanic adolescents. *Journal of Child and Family Studies, 1,* 75–92.

Roberts, R. E. (1992). Manifestation of depressive symptoms among adolescents. *The Journal of Nervous and Mental Diseases, 180,* 627–633.

Rogler, L. H., Malgady, R. G., Costantino, G., & Blumenthal, R. (1987). What do culturally sensitive mental health services mean? The case of Hispanics. *American Psychologist, 42,* 565–570.

Rogler, L. H., Malgady, R. G., & Rodriguez, O. (1989). *Hispanics and mental health: A framework for research.* Melbourne, FL: Krieger.

Rooth, A. B. (1976). *The importance of storytelling: A study on field work in Alaska.* Stockholm, Sweden: Almqvist & Wiksell International.

Saltz, E., & Johnson, J. (1973). *Training for thematic fantasy play in culturally disadvantaged children: Preliminary results.* Detroit, MI: Wayne State University, Center for the Study of Cognitive Processes.

Singer, J. L. (1973). *The child's world of make believe: Experimental studies of imaginative play.* San Diego, CA: Academic Press.

Smilansky, S. (1968). *The effects of sociodramatic play on disadvantaged preschool children.* New York: Wiley.

Spielberger, C. D., Edwards, C. A., Lushene, R. C., Montuori, J., & Platzek, D. (1973). *Preliminary manual for the State–Trait Anxiety Inventory for children.* Palo Alto, CA: Consulting Psychologists Press.

Sue, S. (1988). Psychotherapeutic services for ethnic minorities. *American Psychologist, 43,* 301–308.

Sue, S., & Zane, N. (1987). The role of culture and cultural techniques in psychotherapy: A critique and reformulation. *American Psychologist, 42,* 37–45.

U.S. Bureau of the Census. (1991). *1990 Census of Population and Housing* (Summary Tape File 1A, Data User Services Division). Washington, DC: Author.

U.S. Bureau of the Census. (1994). *Current Population Reports, Population Characteristics.* Washington, DC: Author.

Vega, W. A., Zimmerman, R. S., Warheit, G. J., Apospori, E., & Gil, A. G. (1993). Risk factors for early adolescent drug use in four ethnic and racial groups. *American Journal of Public Health, 83,* 185–189.

Warren, R. (1994). *Estimates of the unathorized immingrant population residing in the United States, by county of origin and states of residence.* Paper presented at the California Immigration 1994 Conference, Immigration and Naturalization Service, Statistic Division.

Wechsler, D. (1974). *Wechsler Intelligence Scale for Children—Revised.* New York: Psychological Corporation.

Weimer, S. R. (1978). Using fairytales in psychotherapy: Rapunzel. *Bulletin of the Menninger Clinic, 42,* 25–34.

Westone, H. S., & Friedlander, B. Z. (1974). The effect of live, TV and audio story narration on primary grade children's listening comprehension. *Journal of Educational Research, 68,* 30–34.

Woutres, A. (1990). *Folk hero modeling with Black South African adolescents.* Unpublished manuscript, Vista University, Pretoria, South Africa.

28

FAMILY INTERACTION PATTERNS: STRUCTURAL FAMILY THERAPY WITHIN CONTEXTS OF CULTURAL DIVERSITY

WILLIAM M. KURTINES and JOSÉ SZAPOCZNIK

A major concern of families in the 1990s is the prevention and correction of endemic antisocial problem behavior in adolescents. This chapter describes a structural approach for working with Hispanic families that evolved as part of more than two decades of research at the Spanish Family Guidance Center at the University of Miami. The structural approach to working with Hispanic families described in this chapter is a direct outgrowth of our efforts to develop and investigate novel, theoretically based, and culturally appropriate interventions that can be used in the prevention and treatment of behavior problems and drug abuse among youth.

This work was funded by grant 3481 from the National Institute of Mental Health, grant DA5334 from the National Institute on Drug Abuse, grant 1H86 SPO2350 from the Center for Substance Abuse Prevention, grant 1 HD7 TI00417 from the Center for Substance Abuse Treatment, grant 90CL1111 from the Administration for Children, Youth, and Families, and grant 90PD0211 from the Administration for Children and Families, Department of Health and Human Services to Dr. José Szapocznik; by grant 1 P50 DA07697 to Dr. Howard Liddle; and by grant 85-JS-CX-0021 from the Office of Juvenile Justice Delinquency Prevention, Department of Justice to the National Coalition of Hispanic Health and Human Services Organizations. Correspondence concerning this chapter should be directed to Dr. William M. Kurtines, Department of Psychology, Florida International University, Miami, FL 33199.

PROGRAM DESCRIPTION

In 1972, the Spanish Family Guidance Center was established in Miami, Florida, to provide services to the local Hispanic community. In 1975, the Center adopted structural family therapy (SFT) as its core approach, and SFT has been at the heart of all of our efforts to develop interventions for use in culturally diverse contexts (Szapocznik & Kurtines, 1993). The core of the approach presented in this chapter is thus based on SFT as practiced at the Center for Family Studies/Spanish Family Guidance Center.[1] As our program of research evolved over the past two decades, we extended this approach in two important directions.

First, although our work began with Cuban families, as our program of research evolved, we expanded our focus to include drug-abusing and behavior problem youth from a variety of cultural backgrounds. Our interest in extending the use of SFT grew out of our experience in working with families in the context of cultural diversity. In working with our families we found it necessary to extend the conventional approach to family therapy to permit us to work with these families in ways that more truly represent the cultural reality in which they are embedded, namely, a culturally pluralistic milieu. Consequently, STF, as described in this chapter, assumes that many of the core concepts, methods, and procedures used in working with families (Hispanic or from other ethnic or cultural groups) are transcultural, and that working with culturally diverse populations requires the culturally appropriate adaption of the generic features of SFT to specific cultural content.

In addition to extending our approach for use in culturally diverse contexts, we also expanded our structural interventions to include the multiple systems that have an impact on youth and family. Thus, although our work began with a focus on the family as the basic context for child functioning, as our program of research evolved we became more directly concerned with the impact of other systems on the child (e.g., school, peers, community), and on the relationship between these systems. We have come to recognize more fully that the structural orientation that provides the foundations for SFT also provides a tool for understanding within and between systems interactions. That is, that our focus for intervention should be on the repetitive patterns of interactions that occur within *and* between systems. Hence, in its latest development our work has become

---

[1]There are two important original sources for more extensive information on how we have adapted SFT for use with behavior problem youth, which are recommended readings for a more comprehensive presentation of the work described in this chapter: *Breakthroughs in Family Therapy with Drug-Abusing and Problem Youth* (Szapocznik & Kurtines, 1989), and *Preventing Juvenile Delinquency Among Hispanic Adolescents: A Structural Family Therapy Approach* (Szapocznik & COSSMHO, 1993).

more multisystemic as well as structural. This structural multisystemic, family-focused approach based on Structural Ecosystems Theory (Szapocznik et al., in press) now pervades our work at many levels, ranging from clinical interventions to neighborhood- and school-based interventions.

This chapter has two basic goals. The first goal is to illustrate some of the ways in which we have adapted the core concepts, methods, and procedures of SFT for use in working with families in contexts of cultural diversity. In the United States, this is a population that has increasingly come to include virtually all families, regardless of cultural or ethnic origin. The second goal is to illustrate some of the ways in which we have been responding to the changing needs of families by extending the core of SFT to the structural ecosystems theory, which includes interventions targeted at the multiple social ecosystems that impact on families.

STRUCTURAL FAMILY THERAPY

From the structural systems theory, we adopt the view that the interdependence between the parts of a system can be understood in terms of the repetitive patterns of interactions between the parts. The family is a system whose structure is defined by the repetitive patterns of interactions between family members. From such a perspective, the goal of family therapy is to identify and to change maladaptive patterns of interactions (by *maladaptive*, we mean those patterns of interactions that keep the family from achieving its goals). We also adopt the three basic change-producing procedures associated with the SFT tradition: joining (entering the system), diagnosing (identifying maladaptive interactions), and restructuring (changing maladaptive interactions). In SFT, treatment is designed to help the family shift from one set of interactions that are problematic to another set of interactions that will cause the problem symptom to disappear or to be reduced to an acceptable level. This approach is based on reaching a clear understanding of the nature of the interactions in the family that are maladaptive; understanding how these interactions are related to the symptoms that the family is experiencing; and intervening in a very deliberate manner to modify those interactions that are maladaptive, while choreographing opportunities for more adaptive and successful interactions to occur.

The power of the family can be nearly irresistible when the family learns how to behave in ways that will cause a child to change to more adaptive behaviors. Typically, a family member, particularly a child or adolescent, will readily respond to the family system's pull to behave adaptively provided that the family knows how to pull in the proper direction.

The goal of SFT is to help the family find the correct manner for achieving its goals.

USING SFT WITH FAMILIES WITHIN THE CONTEXT OF CULTURAL DIVERSITY

In adapting SFT to work with families in contexts of cultural diversity, we continuously look for ways to take advantage of the generic features of the structural systems approach that are transcultural, while at the same time adapting SFT's concepts, methods, and procedures for use in specific cultural contexts. This section illustrates some of the ways in which we have adapted specific SFT concepts, methods, and procedures for working in contexts of cultural diversity.

Joining

The first step in working with a family is to establish a therapeutic relationship. The therapist and the family need to form a new system: a therapeutic system. In the therapeutic system, the therapist is both a member and its leader.

To become the leader of the therapeutic system, the therapist has to earn his or her way into the leadership role. He or she does so by accepting, respecting, and earning the trust of the family. Joining the family is an essential part of establishing a therapeutic system in all cultural contexts—it can, however, be rendered more useful in joining a particular family if it is adapted for use in a culturally specific context. For example, *respeto* (respect) is always particularly important with a Hispanic family and an understanding of this cultural concept facilitates our joining Hispanic families. To earn a position of leadership we must show respect for each family member and, particularly, for powerful family members.

The process of joining the family (i.e., of establishing a therapeutic relationship) involves all those maneuvers and movements that demonstrate to the family and all of its members that the therapist respects and accepts them; and by respecting and accepting them, the therapist eventually earns the family's trust and becomes accepted as their leader.

In the case of a Chinese family, the second author joined by recognizing and accepting that a "best family friend," who was brought in by the family when the therapist asked them to "bring in your family," functioned in the traditional role of "second wife." By accepting and respecting the relative roles of first and second wife, a therapeutic alliance was established, built on common understanding.

Diagnosis

Informal Diagnosis of the Structural Family Systems Ratings (SFSR) Dimensions

Joining is the proverbial "foot-in-the-door;" it gives us an entry into the family. It also provides an opportunity for making a diagnosis. In research settings, we use the SFSR to make a formal assessment of the family's functioning (Szapocznik, Rio, et al., 1991). In clinical work where we do not have the opportunity for conducting a formal assessment, we use the joining process to facilitate making a less formal "clinical" assessment (Szapocznik & Kurtines, 1989). In the process of joining, we encourage the family to act and interact as it usually would when we are not present. This provides us with the opportunity to observe the family's usual patterns of interacting and, in turn, allows us to assess and diagnose the interactive problems in the family along the dimensions that define the SFSR.

In SFT, diagnosis refers to the identification of interactional patterns (structure) that are not working for the family (i.e., creating symptoms). We are thus interested in the nature and characteristics of the interactions that occur in the family that cause the family the fail to meet its own objectives, which are defined by the family as "getting rid of an undesirable symptom."

We examine in detail five aspects of a family's interactions when making a diagnosis. We developed a measure for assessing family interaction: the Structural Family Systems Ratings (SFSR; see Szapocznik et al., 1991 for a more detailed discussion of the psychometric properties of the measure, and Hervis, Szapocznik, Mitrani, Rio, & Kurtines, 1991; Szapocznik & Kurtines, 1989, for a more detailed discussion of the clinical application of the SFSR). Based on the theoretical work of Salvador Minuchin (Minuchin, 1974; Minuchin & Fishman, 1981; Minuchin, Rosman, & Baker, 1978), five Likert scales were developed to provide ratings of (a) structure, (b) resonance (enmeshment and disengagement), (c) developmental stage, (d) identified patienthood, and (e) conflict resolution. Ratings are obtained by asking the family to interact with each other on three of the Wyltwick standardized tasks (Szapocznik et al., 1991): (a) deciding on a menu for a meal, (b) telling what pleases and displeases them about other family members, and (c) describing the most recent family fight or argument. A trained rater observes videotapes of the family performing these tasks and records specific categories of interaction on a rating form. These clinical ratings are then scaled (5-point Likert) for each of the five dimensions. As we will next illustrate using several of these dimensions, we use the SFSR to assess both transcultural and culture-specific dimensions of family functioning.

Structure

Structure refers to the organization of the interactional patterns within the family system. Like all of the definitions of each of the SFSR dimensions and the variables by which we define them, structure has both transcultural and culture-specific dimensions. The structure dimension of SFSR is transcultural in that in all cultural contexts the SFSR is used to evaluate the subsystem organization, particularly the executive subsystem that provides leadership within the family. The pattern that defines a particular family, however, has to be evaluated in a culturally specific context. For example, in a conventional nuclear family model, the individuals in the parent roles (usually the biological parent or parents) are expected to provide leadership to the family. In the context of a mainstream cultural framework that adheres to a value on the nuclear family, intrusion from extended family members is viewed as dysfunctional.

However, using the SFSR to examine executive systems across cultures, and in particular in cultural contexts that value the kinship network or extended family over the nuclear family, we have found executive system organizations that involve the parent figure as well as extended family or kinship network members that are culturally and functionally adaptive. Examples of families with extended family members adaptively functioning in executive roles can be found in African American and Hispanic families with a single mother living in the grandmother's home. In these cases, if the mother is sufficiently old to parent, a functional executive system may be composed of a mother and her own mother (the child's grandmother) who coparent. Hence, from the perspective of a culture that values nuclear families, parenting by an extended family member might be evaluated as dysfunctional in that it undermines parental authority. From the perspective of a culture that values involvement of the extended family, however, coparenting by mother and grandmother might be evaluated as adaptive, so long as the coparenting relationship was functional.

Why this latter caveat? Clearly, coparenting relationships, whether comprised by two biological parents or by a parent and a grandparent, can be functional or maladaptive. In a functional coparenting relationship, there is shared decision making, and the parental figures support each other with regard to rules and consequences. In a maladaptive relationship there might be a struggle for power between the parental figures, an inability to establish joint parental decisions, as a consequence of which rules and consequences are unclear and unpredictable. In such a maladaptive case, the child may be triangulated in the executive system conflict.

Thus, from a transcultural perspective, we define adaptive executive systems in a similar way as consisting of cooperation and collaboration. However, from a culture-specific perspective, we define the participation of certain sets of individuals as adaptive or maladaptive according to the cultural norms.

Another example of how family structure is influenced by cross-generational intrusions that are highly culture-specific can be found in Asian American families. In some Asian American families, the husband's mother is highly involved in giving her daughter-in-law direction for proper behavior, both with her husband as well as with the husband's family of origin and family of procreation. From a culture-specific perspective, the expectation is that the husband's mother will help shape her daughter-in-law's behavior because the latter is viewed as a member of her husband's family. The husband and his mother, in turn, remain quite close as a means of securing care for the mother when her own husband dies (Sue, Zane, & Young, 1994).

Resonance

Resonance is another dimension in which it is important to be sensitive to transcultural as well as culture-specific differences in using the SFSR. For example, in the resonance dimension, the amount of closeness that is found in a Hispanic family is much greater than that found in an Anglo family. Some of our markers for closeness in assessing resonance, such as the variables of interruptions, simultaneous speaking, and "continuations," are all more typical of Hispanics than of White Americans from Boston, the midwest, or California. White Americans have come to value individuation and separation more than Hispanics. As such, we find that relative to one another, Hispanics are more enmeshed and many White Americans are more disengaged.

Are either of these adaptive or maladaptive? Well, it depends. If a daughter or son in a Hispanic family rebels because he or she is not allowed to individuate, then the tendency for greater emotional and psychological closeness in this particular Hispanic family is related to the emergence of symptomatic behavior. As such, it needs to be addressed even though it is culturally syntonic for the parents.

In the same way, let us consider the case of a father in a family from a culture that encourages individuation, who told his 17-year-old daughter that she was expected to go away to college, and the daughter attempted suicide as a way of communicating that she was not ready to separate. Hence, culture syntonic behavior of a parent may produce a symptom in an already troubled child.

Developmental Stage

The rate at which children are expected to take on responsibilities in a family not only varies considerably from family to family, but also from culture to culture. Thus, the use of the SFSR to assess developmentally appropriate roles varies considerably across cultures, and has to be sensitive to both transcultural and culture-specific differences. For example, in a Hispanic migrant family, it might be expected that an 8-year-old girl would miss school during crop time to work with the family in the fields. Yet, in an urban context of some Latin American cities, a 16-year-old girl may not be allowed to date unchaperoned. By contrast, in some Asian cultures, children are committed to each other for marriage at an early age, and marriage may occur as early as the onset of puberty.

In many Western cultures, if a child acts as the emotional support of his or her mother, such a burden might be considered developmentally inappropriate in that the child is being asked to perform in a burdensome role more appropriate to an adult. Yet, in some Asian cultures, a son may be expected to provide emotional and material support to his mother in the long term, and thus may show signs of growing in this direction early in life (Sue et al., 1994).

Conflict Resolution

Conflict resolution styles also vary considerably across cultures and consequently it is another dimension of family functioning in which it is important to be sensitive to the transcultural as well as culture-specific differences in using the SFSR. In the mental health culture, for example, full conflict emergence with resolution is valued. In contrast, some Hispanic groups make frequent use of conflict diffusion, and in some "refined" groups, conflict diffusion is considered an enviable art.

Restructuring

At this point, we are ready to develop a treatment plan. We must plan carefully how to get from point A to point B: How do we intervene to help the family move from its present way of interacting, and the undesirable symptoms that it produces, to a more adaptive and successful way of interacting that will eliminate these symptoms?

Those interventions aimed at helping the family move from point A to point B are called *restructuring*. In restructuring, we orchestrate change in the family's patterns of interactions—that is, we change the family's structure. In bringing about these changes, we encourage the family to behave differently. We do so by using a broad range of techniques, four of which are described in this section: (a) working in the present, (b) reframing, (c) working with boundaries and alliances, and (d) tasks. As in all interactions with families, in using these techniques we are sensitive to both transcultural and culture-specific dimensions.

Working in the Present

Although some types of counseling focus on the past, SFT focuses primarily in the present. However, even our definition of present needs to be clarified because our focus is not on hearing verbalizations about the present, but rather on the present interactions that occur among family members in front of the therapist. The initial step is typically to create within the counseling situation the experience that usually occurs in the family: an enactment. That is, to get the family to interact in the office in the usual way it would at home.

To change the family's patterns of interactions, initial work is directed at orchestrating new interactions for the family within the therapy session. Thus, the focus of the therapy is to create new interactions in the here and now in the presence of the therapist. Later, once the family has learned to behave in a more successful way within the therapy session, we will ask them to try it out at home (tasks described below).

It is important to remember that in this kind of therapy, we are not as interested in having the family "talk about" behaving differently as we are interested in getting the family to behave differently within the therapy situation. This requires that the counselor remain decentralized. The counselor needs to make every effort to have the interactions occur among family members. When the counselor attempts to change the nature of these interactions, he or she has to make sure to remain decentralized so that the new interactions occur among the family members.

Reframing

Perhaps one of the most interesting, useful, and certainly subtle techniques used in SFT is *reframing*. Reframing means to create a different sense of reality; to give the family members the opportunity to perceive their interactions or their situation from a different perspective or, to use our jargon, in a different "frame." For example, in working with a Hispanic family in which an adolescent son is rebellious and oppositional, the parent may be angry and act angry and injured. The typical interaction is one in which the parent berates the youth: "You are a no good; I wish you were not my son. . ."

The parent feels frustrated at his or her inability to guide the son down the "right" path and as a result, frustration gives way to anger. The son, in turn, experiences an uncaring and rejecting parent. The feeling of the interaction is one of fighting with an enemy. Both parties feel that the other is an adversary. Thus, all possibility for genuine dialogue has vanished.

How to break this impasse? Create a new "frame," a different sense of reality. For example, the counselor might say to the parent: "I can see how terribly worried you are about your son and your son's future. I know you

care an awful lot about your son, and that is why you are so concerned."
With this intervention, the counselor modifies the parent's own perception
of him- or herself from anger to concern. Typically, most parents would
respond by saying: "I am very worried. I want my son to do well and to
be successful in life." When the son hears the parent's concern, he feels
less rejected. In fact, the parent, instead of communicating rejection, is
now communicating concern, care, and support for the child. Hence, by
creating a new sense of reality, the counselor is able to transform an adversarial relationship between parent and child, orchestrating opportunities
for new channels of communications to emerge.

Beyond the illustration of how reframing might work, this intervention also highlights a very central aspect of our therapy model: One major
goal of all restructuring interventions is to create the opportunity for the
family to behave in new ways. That is, when the family is stuck, when it
is behaving in a rigidly repetitive fashion, when it is unable to break out
of its maladaptive interactions, the therapist's job is to create the opportunity for the family to behave or interact in a new way.

Working with Boundaries and Alliances

There are some simple rules about what kind of family organization
will be more successful in preventing and controlling behavior problems.
Whenever the authority figures in the family—let's say the parents—are
allied with each other, they will be in a better position to exercise effective
control over undesirable behaviors. However, the moment that a rigid alliance forms between a parent and one of the children against the other
parent, we have the perfect formula for trouble—particularly the antisocial,
out of control, behavior problem type of trouble.

How can alliances be harmful? Because a son who is allied with an
authority figure has himself a great deal of authority within the family
system, he has been placed in a role of strength. Conversely, according to
the simple but true rule of divide and conquer, whenever the parents or
authority figures (parent(s), grandparents, probations officers, teachers,
etc.) are divided on parenting issues, the child has conquered and will do
as he or she wishes. Therefore, it would be difficult to place limits on his
or her antisocial behavior.

Shifting Boundaries. Maladaptive alliances such as those that occur
across the generations (parent–child) are reorganized by the therapist; this
is called *shifting boundaries.* An alliance basically denotes a subsystem. Any
subsystem has boundaries around it. To change the nature of the alliances,
we shift the boundaries that tie some family members together and that
keep some family members apart.

For example, a common case is that of a family in which a mother
and her children have an alliance with each other against a "no good

stepfather" who is emotionally and psychologically distant from the whole family. In this case, the stepfather has argued for setting limits on the oldest son, and the mother has argued that the stepfather was a brute. For years this son has usually gotten away with all kinds of unacceptable behaviors because he had his mother's protection and his father's uninvolvement. And, if the father ever attempted to intervene, the mother would take the son's side against the father, often because the stepfather's intervention with the son may occur as part of a complicated set of interactions that might also include "getting back at Mom." This is in fact a very typical pattern of family interactions with acting out, drug-abusing, behavior problem boys.

Now the youth is 14 years old and starts getting into serious trouble. He is in a gang whose members use and sell drugs, vandalize, carry weapons, and, in general, make a mockery of prosocial behavior. Now the mother, by herself, is no longer powerful enough to control him and is going to need all the help that she can get. The counselor's job is to shift the alliances that exist in the family, to restore the balance of power to the parents—to empower them to bring their "out of control" son back under control.

When the family is referred to therapy by a probation officer, much of the power belongs to the antisocial youth who is doing as he pleases. To join this family, the first step is for the therapist to join the youth, who appears to have the most power. Then the therapist must convince the son that he should come into counseling with the family, emphasizing that there is something in it for him. Once the family is brought into counseling and it becomes clear that the problem is one of inappropriate alliances, then we can begin to make a plan for restructuring the alliances in the family.

At the end of counseling, we will want to have the mother and father (as well as other authority figures, such as probation officers) allied around all issues pertaining to how they will control the behavior of their son.

These are delicate politics that require the therapist's best political and strategic skills. Rather than confronting the alliance of the mother and son directly, we may begin by encouraging the stepfather to establish some form of an interaction with the son, perhaps using some excuse about boys at this age needing their fathers. First, we would encourage some kind of an interaction to get the stepfather and son to communicate (communication is *process*, what they talk about is unimportant because it is *content*) in the session, and then we would shift the communication to their making plans to do something together outside the session (process)—and for this we may need to resort to all kinds of excuses or reasons (content) for why we would want them to do something together. As a relationship develops between the father and the son, the strength of the bond that held the mother and son together is somewhat weakened, because the son now has alliances with both parents.

Once the rigid alliance structure that kept the father out of the family has been weakened,[2] the therapist can move to the next step of encouraging the mother and father to do some things together (process) about the problem that they both agree they have with their unruly son (content or excuse used to bring about the desired process/interactional change). In a case like this one, we recommend tracking the family's content (problem with son) as a maneuver to change the nature of the interaction between the father and mother from that of an adversarial relationship to a relationship in which they agree on something.

Once the mother and stepfather are brought to the negotiating table, we are ready to begin the tough work of helping these spouses negotiate their deep-seated resentments and grievances against each other. Because ours is a problem-focused approach, we do not attempt to resolve all of the problems encountered by the marital couple, rather, we attempt to resolve only those aspects of the difficulties between the spouses that are interfering with their ability to approach the problems of their son.

If we manage to help the parents work together around the problems they are having with their son, we have now shifted the boundaries that existed in the family by breaking up the mother–son alliance and creating a mother–father alliance—at least around how to begin to control the adolescent's behavior.

In the case of single parents, several different situations can occur. One is the case of the single parent who is truly alone, has difficulty with adequate and consistent consequencing, and does not feel capable of doing this work alone. In these cases, in working with Hispanic or African American families, we would seek a member of the extended or kin network that could assist in occasional coparenting, thereby providing support to the single parent. Another problem that occurs with single parents is that co-parenting is occurring but that the coparents are at odds with each other. In this case the problem is addressed just as it was in the prior example with a two-parent family. One exception to this rule is that in the case of the single parent there is the option of working toward moving

---

[2]It should be noted that, from a systems perspective, everyone in the family would have to contribute to maintaining the family's organization in which the stepfather was excluded from family life, including the mother, stepfather, and children. Hence, it is not our intent to suggest that it was the mother who was keeping the stepfather out, but rather that both the mother and stepfather as well as the children must have contributed by their behaviors to keeping the stepfather out. The stepfather, for example, may have behaved erratically, encouraging the mother's instinct to protect the children; and the stepfather may have enjoyed the freedom of being psychologically and emotionally distant from the family. Of course, there also may have been negative consequences for all family members because of such an arrangement, such as a feeling of alienation and constant conflict at home when the stepfather was present.

a bothersome extended family member out of the coparenting arrangement, leaving the single parent in a stronger position alone.

Tasks

The use of tasks is central to SFT. Tasks are used both inside and outside the counseling sessions. Tasks are the basic tool for orchestrating change. Because our emphasis is in promoting new behaviors and interactions among family members, the assignment of tasks is one of the most important vehicles through which we, in fact, choreograph the opportunities for the family to behave differently.

In the example above where the mother and son were initially allied, and the stepfather was left outside of this alliance, we initially assigned to the stepfather and son the *task* of doing something together in which they would have a mutual interest. Later on, in attempting a rapprochement between the father and mother, we assigned the mother and father the *task* of working together at defining some rules about what type of behavior they would permit, and what contingencies they would assign to their son's behavior and misbehavior.

As a general rule, a task always should be first assigned within the office where we have an opportunity to observe, assist, and facilitate the successful conduct of the task. It is important to attempt to give the family an experience of success by assigning tasks that are doable. Tasks are more likely to be doable if they are assigned in small increments. A second general rule with regard to tasks is to never assign a task to accomplish at home until you have helped the family to do it in the session. For those tasks that can only be done out of the session, mock rehearsals are used within session.

Summary

The basic intervention strategies that we have described in this part of the chapter focus on the kinds of interactions that occur in families that may encourage, maintain, or permit undesirable behaviors. We consider our SFT approach a family empowerment as well as a family preservation approach in that families are given the skills to interact in new, successful ways to bring about the outcomes that they desire (such as the prevention or elimination of problem behaviors in youths). In this way, rather than taking the *problem person* out of the family, this approach encourages taking the *problem* out of the family. The therapist's work is intended to identify the interactions that are not working for the family, and to orchestrate the opportunity for the family to behave in new ways that will achieve the family's desired outcomes.

Thus far, our focus has been on how we have adapted SFT intervention strategies for use in our clinical work. These strategies were developed and refined as part of our clinical and research efforts at the Spanish Family Guidance Center. The Center has conducted large-scale funded clinical, research, and demonstration projects using the SFT approach in the Miami area uninterruptedly since 1975. In this section, we briefly describe some of the SFT research that we have conducted, and in the following section we describe some of the research that we have conducted that extends basic SFT concepts to specialized applications.

When we began our work at the Center in 1972, one of the first challenges we encountered was to identify and develop a culturally appropriate and acceptable treatment intervention for our population, problem-behavior Cuban youths. In 1975, to define the Cuban culture and to develop a better understanding of how it resembled and differed from the mainstream culture, a comprehensive study on value orientations was designed based on the pioneer work on worldviews by Kluckhohn and Strodtbeck (1961). The major study on value orientation (Szapocznik, Scopetta, Aranalde, & Kurtines, 1978) that ensued determined that a family-oriented approach in which therapists take an active, directive, present-oriented leadership role matched the expectations of our population. This finding was the first indicator that a structural and systemic approach to family therapy was particularly well suited for this population (Szapocznik, Scopetta, & King, 1978).

To investigate the effectiveness of a family-oriented intervention with Hispanic families, a series of pilot research studies (Scopetta et al., 1977) was conducted comparing individual and conjoint family ecological interventions. These pilot studies provided evidence that SFT was compatible with the issues and problems of our Hispanic population. Since 1975 we have conducted a large number of funded studies on SFT and on its specialized application.[3] We confine our discussion here to a brief description of some of our work developing specialized applications of SFT to address issues and challenges that emerged in the family therapy literature.

Specialized Applications

Acculturation, Biculturalism, and Multiculturalism

Our first efforts at developing specialized applications of SFT sought to address the challenge that the impact of immigration and acculturation

---

[3]Two reviews providing more extensive information on the SFT research that we have conducted are recommended for a more comprehensive presentation of the research foundations of SFT. Specifically, we recommend Szapoznik, Kurtines, Santisteban, and Rio (1990) and Szapocznik, Kurtines, et al. (in press), which not only review our work in detail but also illustrate the complex interplay of theory, research, and application that took place in the evolution of our approach.

had on families. In working with recent immigrant Hispanic families, we came to realize how profoundly the process of immigration and acculturation could affect the family as a unit as well as each of its individual members. It became evident that for a subset of families these clinical/cultural issues required an intervention designed specifically for this constellation of problems. As a result of this experience, we developed and tested an intervention specifically designed to address the constellation of immigration/acculturation stressors that this population was facing and the clinical problems this constellation of stressors was producing. More specifically, we developed an intervention, Bicultural Effectiveness Training (BET), to enhance bicultural skills in all family members.

BET is an intervention specifically designed to ameliorate the acculturation-related stresses confronted by two-generation immigrant families. Although BET is based on SFT concepts, it is delivered as a psychoeducational modality. BET is based on a strategy that provides families and family members with skills for effectively coping with the acculturation stress and conflict that confronts families living at the interface of manifestly conflicting cultural values and behavioral expectations. In its application, BET is a package of 12 lessons described in more detail in Szapocznik, Santisteban, Kurtines, Perez-Vidal, and Hervis (1984).

A randomized clinical trial study[4] was conducted to investigate the relative effectiveness of BET in comparison with SFT (Szapocznik, Santisteban, et al., 1986). An experimental design was achieved by randomly assigning 41 Cuban American families with behavior-problem adolescents to either the BET or SFT conditions. The results (Szapocznik, Santisteban, et al., 1986) indicated that BET was as effective as SFT in bringing about improvement in adolescent and family functioning. These findings suggested that BET could accomplish the goals of family therapy while focusing on the cultural content that made therapy attractive to Hispanic families.

Subsequently, we combined SFT and BET into a package called Family Effectiveness Training (FET; Szapocznik, Santisteban, et al., 1989). A large-scale randomized clinical trial prevention/intervention study[5] was conducted to investigate the effectiveness of FET (Szapocznik et al., 1989). An experimental design was achieved by randomly assigning 79 Hispanic American families and their preadolescents to the FET or minimum contact control conditions. Considerable work went into designing not only the experimental condition (FET) but also a control condition that would minimize the amount of therapeutic interactions while keeping the family safe and under professional supervision. The results of this study (Szapocznik et al., 1989) indicated that families in the FET condition showed

[4]This study was funded by grant MH31226 from the National Institute of Mental Health.
[5]This study was funded by grant 1E0702694 from the National Institute on Drug Abuse.

significantly greater improvement than did control families on independent measures of structural family functioning, problem behaviors as reported by parents, and on a self-administered measure of child self-concept. Thus, the intervention was able to successfully improve functioning in both the areas of child and family functioning. Furthermore, the results of the follow-up assessments indicated that the impact of the FET intervention was maintained at 6 months follow-up.

More recently, the complexity of our cultural context has changed considerably. When we developed BET and FET in the 1970s, our Cuban-born families lived in a cultural context that was dominated primarily by Cuban immigrants and mainstream White Americans. However, by the 1990s the cultural context of Miami changed to become a complex melange including Cuban Americans, Cuban immigrants, mainstream White Americans, as well as Latin Americans from nearly all countries in the hemisphere, African Americans, and Haitian immigrants. Consistent with these contextual changes, we recently redesigned our BET intervention into a Multicultural Effectiveness Training (MET; Mancilla, Szapocznik, & Kurtines, 1994) program that assists non-Cuban Hispanic parents in developing an understanding of the complex cultural context in which they are embedded. In MET, for the first time we incorporate interventions that consider the complexities and threats involved to non–Cuban Hispanic families who find themselves in a cultural context that is heavily influenced by Cuban Americans.

One-Person Family Therapy

As the family therapy movement grew in momentum, we extended our basic SFT concepts to address other challenges that arose in the field. One such challenge was how to treat families in contexts in which it was not possible to get entire families into treatment (i.e., the challenge of developing a procedure that would achieve the goals of family therapy—changes in maladaptive family interactions—without having to have the entire family present).

To meet this challenge, we developed one-person family therapy (Szapocznik & Kurtines, 1989; Szapocznik, Kurtines, Foote, Perez-Vidal, & Hervis, 1983, 1986). The one-person modality of SFT differs from conjoint family therapies in that it attempts to achieve the goals of family therapy (i.e., the reduction or elimination of problem behaviors in the youth and the development of more adaptive family functioning) while working primarily with only one family member.

What made one-person family therapy possible was the novel application of the principle of complementarity (Minuchin & Fishman, 1981). What is novel about the one-person modality is the deliberate and strategic use of this principle in directing the identified patient in therapy to change her or his behavior in ways that require an adjustment in the behavior of other family members toward the identified patient. A large-scale randomized clinical trial study[6] was conducted comparing the conjoint versus one person modalities of SFT (Szapocznik, Kurtines, et al., 1983, 1986). An experimental design was achieved by randomly assigning 72 Hispanic American families with drug-abusing adolescents to either the conjoint or one person modality. Both conditions were designed to use exactly the same theoretical framework (SFT) so that only one variable (conjoint versus one person) would differ between the conditions. Considerable work was done to develop a treatment manual and modality guidelines for both the one person (Szapocznik, Hervis, Kurtines, & Spencer, 1984; Szapocznik, Kurtines, et al., 1983, 1986) and the conjoint (cf. Szapocznik & Kurtines, 1989) conditions to ensure standardization and replicability of the study. The results (Szapocznik, Kurtines, et al. 1983, 1986) indicated that one-person family therapy was not only as effective as the conjoint modality in bringing about significant improvement in behavior problem/drug abuse in the youths, but also that it was as effective as conjoint in bringing about and maintaining significant improvements in family functioning.[7]

Engaging Hard-to-Reach Families

The final specialized application that we describe in this section addressed the challenge of hard-to-reach families who seek treatment but are never engaged into therapy. The approach that we developed, Strategic Structural Systems Engagement (Szapocznik & Kurtines, 1989; Szapocznik, Perez-Vidal, Hervis, Brickman, & Kurtines, 1990) is based on the premise that whatever the initial presenting symptom may be, the initial obstacle to change is "resistance" to coming into treatment. When resistance to coming into treatment is defined as the symptom to be targeted by the intervention, SFT allows for a redefinition of "resistance" as a manifestation or symptom of the family's current pattern of interaction. Therefore, the same systemic and structural concepts that apply to the understanding of family functioning and treatment also apply to the understanding and treatment of the family's resistance to engagement (Santisteban & Szapocznik, 1994; Szapocznik, Perez-Vidal, et al., 1990).

Our work on Strategic Structural Systems Engagement was made possible by the findings that came out of our research on One Person Family Therapy. In developing our specialized engagement procedures we drew from One Person Family Therapy techniques designed to bring about

---

[6]This study was funded by grant DA0322 from the National Institute on Drug Abuse.
[7]These findings are particularly compelling when contrasted with other studies that compared family structural with nonfamily modalities (Szapocznik, Rio, et al., 1989; Szapocznik, Santisteban, et al., 1989) in which changes in family functioning were not achieved by nonfamily modalities. Hence, the changes in family functioning in one person appear to be specific to the family orientation of this modality.

changes in family interactions through one person. Typically, initial contacts requesting treatment for problem-behavior and drug-abusing youths are made by a parent. However, in the vast majority of these families either a parent is unwilling to become involved in therapy on a conjoint basis, or more frequently the problem youth refuses to come into treatment.

Having defined resistance to treatment as an undesirable problem or symptom to be overcome, SFT holds that the solution to overcoming the undesirable "symptom" of resistance is to restructure the family's patterns of interaction that permit the symptom of resistance to continue to exist. It is here that One Person Family Therapy techniques become useful because in fact the person making the contact requesting help becomes our "one person" through whom we can potentially work to restructure the family's pattern of interaction that is maintaining the symptom of resistance.

A large-scale randomized clinical trial study[8] was conducted to test the effectiveness of Strategic Structural Systems Engagement (Szapocznik, Perez-Vidal, et al., 1988). An experimental design was achieved by randomly assigning 108 Hispanic families of behavior-problem adolescents (who were suspected of, or who were observed, using drugs) to one of two conditions: Strategic Structural Systems Engagement or engagement as usual (the control condition). In this control condition, the clients were approached in a way that resembled as closely as possible the kind of engagement that usually takes place in outpatient centers. Considerable work was done to develop a manual for the experimental condition (Szapocznik & Kurtines, 1989; Szapocznik, Kurtines, et al., 1990) and to describe modality guidelines for both conditions to ensure the standardization and replicability of the study. The results (Szapocznik et al., 1988) were dramatic. Over 57% of the families in the control condition failed to be engaged into treatment. In contrast, only 7.15% (four families) in the Strategic Structural Systems Engagement condition were lost to treatment, $\chi^2(4, N = 1{,}108) = 29.64$, $p < .0001$. The differences in the retention rates were also dramatic. In the control condition, dropouts represented 41% of the cases that were engaged, whereas dropouts in the Strategic Structural Systems Engagement condition represented 17% of the engaged cases. Thus, of all of the cases that were initially assigned, 25% in the control condition and 77% in the Strategic Structural Systems Engagement condition were successfully terminated, $\chi^2(N = 1{,}108) = 26.93$, $p < .0001$. For families that completed treatment in both conditions, there were highly significant improvements both in the problematic adolescent's functioning $F(1,57) = 39.83$, $p < .0001$, and these improvements were *not* significantly different across the engagement conditions. The critical distinction between the conditions was in their differential rates of engagement and retention.

[8]This study was funded by grant DA2059 from the National Institute on Drug Abuse.

These results are stunning (see Liddle & Dakof, in press) in the adolescent substance abuse literature.

A second large-scale randomized clinical trial study[9] was conducted to replicate these engagement findings and to further explore the mechanisms by which the intervention efficacy is achieved was recently completed (Santisteban et al., in press). This study was designed to provide for a more rigorous controlled experimental test of the engagement interventions by using a larger and more multicultural sample, more stringent criteria for successful engagement, and two control conditions instead of one. The results of this study were also dramatic. Analyses of the overall effectiveness of the specialized engagement interventions showed that they were extremely effective. Highly significant differences were found between the experimental engagement condition and the two control conditions for rates of engagement and retention.

FUTURE DIRECTIONS: STRUCTURAL ECOSYSTEMS THEORY AND PRACTICE

With changing times and the changing needs of families, the theoretical and clinical work of the Center continues to evolve. In particular, expanding our program of research to respond to the declining social conditions in the inner city and the multiplicity of problems with which Hispanic families present, and to respond better to the complexity of contextual factors that impact on problem behaviors have become our most recent and important challenges. In response to these challenges, we have begun to refine a more fully articulated Structural Ecosystems Theory (Szapocznik et al., in press) for working with families in contexts of cultural diversity.

For this extension of our basic SFT approach, we have turned to the work of Bronfenbrenner (1977, 1979, 1986) and others (Hawkins & Weis, 1985; Henggeler & Borduin, 1990; Henggeler, Melton, & Smith, 1992; Newcomb & Bentler, 1989; Newcomb & Felix Ortiz, 1992; Newcomb, Maddahian, & Bentler, 1986). Bronfenbrenner was particularly interested in the complexity of contexts, and especially in the complex relationship that exists between various aspects of the context of an individual. In doing so, he identified and defined *microsystems* as those systems that have direct contact with the child, such as family, school, and peers. He defined *mesosystems* as those systems that occur when microsystems interact. One example of this type of system occurs at the interface between parents and school. Another example is the type of system that occurs at the interface between parents and peers (e.g., do parents organize and supervise peer activities?). He defined *exosystems* as those systems that affect family mem-

---

[9]This study was funded by grant DAO 5334 from the National Institute on Drug Abuse.

bers, and through their impact on family members have an impact on the child. Examples of exosystems are a mother's place of work, or her indigenous support network. Finally, Bronfenbrenner defined *macrosystems* as the cultural blueprints, as well as the more formal aspects of the social structure, that impact the family through rules and policies. Included among the macrosystems are the government of a country, the laws of the land, cultural traditions, and the international sociohistorical events (politics, economics) that shape the lives of Hispanic families.

In addition to the complexity of contexts such as the ones already mentioned, we have been acutely aware of culture as a context. As Szapocznik and Kurtines (1993) have argued, the concept of culture has been overly simplified because of a lack of understanding of the complexity of the cultural streams that permeate the various aspects of the contexts that affect a family. For example, in reading the literature on Hispanics, there has been a preoccupation with understanding the culture of origin. However, in our work with Hispanics in the United States (Szapocznik & Kurtines, 1979; Szapocznik, Kurtines, & Fernandez, 1980; Szapocznik, Scopetta, Kurtines, & Aranalde, 1978), we do not find a single Hispanic whose context is purely an idealized culture of origin. Rather, a Hispanic family in America, even in a very Hispanic region like Little Havana, is embedded in a complex melange of cultural influences that include the culture of origin that exists in the living memories, values, and behaviors of the older members of the family. However, this cultural melange also includes the hybrid culture in which the children are immersed both in school and with acculturating peers. Moreover, the clash of cultures that occurs when parents and schools (the mesosystem) come together represents another aspect of cultural context; a cultural context that represents not the culture of origin, but rather a clashing of cultures. Yet, at another level are the exosystems, those systems that include the parents but not the child. Some of these contexts are very authentically Hispanic, typically the support systems; whereas, in other instances, they may be alien to Hispanic culture. Finally, there are the rules that govern the social structure that in Hispanic cultures, for example, may be highly personal, whereas in the life context of the Hispanic family in America may be more impersonal. It is in this context that we have extended our basic structural approach to include the multiple systems that impact on families.

Three Structural Ecosystemic Programs

Three of our currently ongoing studies reflect this complex, ecological contextual perspective, and are described briefly here. Our structural ecologic approach extends our basic structural orientation by building on: (a) the theoretical work of Bronfenbrenner at the most general level, (b) the theoretical and empirical work of Hawkins and colleagues in the drug abuse prevention area, and (c) the work of Hengeller and colleagues in treatment of drug-abusing adolescents.

Although our work does not disagree with any of the basic multi-systemic postulates of Bronfenbrenner and Hengeller, our work does add another dimension not found in the work of these authors in that our work is intrinsically structural in nature. Structural, as in structural family therapy, means that we conceptualize the nature of the interdependency of systems from an interactional perspective. Thus, we are interested in promoting those repetitive patterns of interactions within and between systems that are linked to adaptive behaviors and in transforming those repetitive patterns of interactions within and between systems that are linked to maladaptive behaviors.

Shenandoah in Action is a school-based prevention intervention study[10] evaluating the effectiveness of our structural ecologic approach in enhancing adaptive behaviors and reducing risk for drug abuse and other antisocial activities. This study involves a quasi-experimental design in which one experimental elementary school and two control elementary schools are located in a single feeder pattern for a middle school. Thus, the long-term impact of the intervention will be evaluated by comparing the children, once they reach middle school, who attended the one experimental and two control elementary schools.

The intervention is organized along the social ecologic framework of Bronfenbrenner, with restructuring interventions aimed at strengthening the adaptive interactions and correcting the maladaptive interactions in the microsystems of family, school, and peers; in the mesosystems of family–school, and family–peers; and in creating exosystem parental support networks. The intervention seeks to redirect participants out of conflictive or nonsupportive interactions into a supportive network of interactional processes, using structural intervention techniques. The Shenandoah in Action program intervenes not only with individual children directly in the microsystems, but also through interventions at the mesosystem level to create a network that will foster positive developmental outcomes.

Little Havana Parent Leadership is a large-scale randomized clinical trial study[11] investigating the effectiveness of a neighborhood-based, parent-focused approach (cf. Mancilla, Szapocznik, & Kurtines, 1994) to prevent gang involvement in high-risk youth, as compared with existing modes of intervention provided by other community-based programs. The study targets Hispanic immigrant families of behavior-problem adolescents who reside in the inner-city community of East Little Havana. The youth, referred for services by school counselors, are considered at-risk for gang involve-

[10]This study was funded by grant 1 H86 SPO 4927 from the Center for Substance Abuse and Prevention.
[11]This study is funded by grant 90CL1111 from the Administration for Children and Families.

ment due to factors such as academic failure, chronic truancy, multiple suspensions, and aggressive behavior. One half of the families are randomly assigned to a control condition, "treatment as usual," and referred to agencies that represent the range of professional services usually utilized as referrals by the source schools. One half of the families are randomly assigned to the experimental condition, the East Little Havana Family Leadership Program (Padres Líderes de la Familia Hispana). Using concepts derived from the Structural Ecosystems theory, the program is intended (a) to restructure relevant exosystems by creating a strong social network—a system for change—made up of multiple neighborhood families, that will in turn foster change in the community conditions that lead to gang involvement in youth; and (b) to restructure the family microsystems by providing parents with the skills, and access to resources, that they need to take leadership of their families and their communities. In the process of designing and implementing a series of supervised activities for their youth, parents have an opportunity to develop and rehearse family and community leadership skills.

This intervention is designed to restructure the social ecology of the family by working at the level of the youth's mesosystems and exosystems. At the level of the mesosystem, parents become directly involved with their adolescent's peer group as they organize field trips and team sports for youth. At the level of the exosystems, parents develop supportive social networks among themselves (change interactional patterns of isolation) and become involved in activities on behalf of the larger community. For example, families are collaborating with the City of Miami Police in activities to promote cross-cultural understanding and to prevent crime. The ultimate goal is to restructure the nature of the interactions that occur among the various components of the family's social ecology in the same manner that SFT restructures interactions among individuals in a family.

Human Ecology Treatment Program for African American and Hispanic drug-abusing adolescents is a large-scale randomized clinical trial study[12] investigating the effectiveness of the Human Ecology Treatment when compared with a "treatment as usual" condition, the latter defined by referrals to several community treatment services that offer drug abuse treatment for minority youth. The experimental intervention, Human Ecology Treatment, uses the structural ecosystems approach to organize the life context of the drug-abusing youth. That is, the structural techniques of joining and diagnosing are used to identify maladaptive patterns of interaction in the microsystems that comprise family, peers, and school.

More specifically, interactional patterns within the family microsystem are evaluated with respect to the basic dimensions of family functioning (e.g., structure, resonance, developmental stage, identified patienthood,

---

[12]This study is funded by grant 1 HD7 TI00417 from the Center for Substance Abuse Treatment.

and conflict resolution). In addition, the interactional patterns in the school microsystem are evaluated (e.g., the interactional patterns between the youth and school authorities). Finally, the interactional patterns of the peer microsystem are evaluated (e.g., the extent to which the child's peers are pro- or antisocial). At the mesosystem levels, the relationships between parents and school, parents and peers, and parents and the justice system are evaluated. At the mesosystem level, the focus of diagnosis is on the extent to which interactions between the component systems support or are in conflict with each other. For example, in the parents–school meso-system, do parents and school support each other? In the parents–peers mesosystem, do parents know the peers? Do parents organize supervised peer activities?

Restructuring interventions occur in the life-context of the youth and of the family (i.e., home and community based), targeting those interactional patterns that are most significantly linked to the youth's problematic behavior. Our experience to date suggests that it is possible to affect the youth's observable problem behavior syndrome (conduct problems at home and school and school adjustment) separately from the youth's drug-abusing behavior. It appears that the former requires correction of maladaptive interactional patterns in the microsystems of family and schools, and the mesosystem of family–school; whereas the latter requires correction of maladaptive interactions within the microsystem of peers (antisocial vs. prosocial peers) and the mesosystem of family–peers.

CONCLUSIONS

Our work began in the 1970s when we adopted SFT in an effort to address an issue of growing concern: behavior and drug-abuse problems among our community's Hispanic youth. Since then, SFT has provided the foundation for our program of research that, in turn, provided a solid foundation from which to pursue new approaches. We think that, in its evolution, our work has reflected the growing "wisdom of the field" and in this sense the direction that our work has taken us also speaks to the broader issue of future directions in supporting families.

With changing times and the changing needs of families, work in the field needs to continue to evolve toward addressing the multiplicity of problems that families will continue to confront. This means that our efforts will have to continue to extend outward in the direction of having an effect on the complex set of systems that impact families. Our ongoing and continuing efforts operate under the assumption that it takes a village to raise a child. It is necessary to both create a village that can be supportive of healthy child development as well as modify policies and systems in the provision of services to the community. Bronfenbrenner (1979) wrote that "Seldom is attention paid to the person's behavior in more than one setting or to the way in which relations between settings can affect what happens within them" (p.18). He suggested that an individual's social ecological environment comprises a complex set of nested structures. As mental health professionals, we cannot help but to be concerned with the broad contextual issues of the social and cultural structures in which our families are embedded.

From our earliest work, then, one of our concerns has been with applying this approach in working with youth and their families in contexts of cultural diversity. In describing our work, we have sought to contribute to the wisdom of the field by sharing some of the knowledge that we have acquired in such contexts. This work has implications that extend beyond the particular population that has been the focus of our work. The need to develop psychosocial interventions that can be used in contexts of cultural diversity takes on a larger significance in view of the broader social, political, and historical trends that are taking place. This is especially the case as we, in America, become an increasingly culturally diverse society.

REFERENCES

Bronfenbrenner, U. (1977). Toward an experimental ecology of human development. *American Psychologist, 32*, 513–531.

Bronfenbrenner, U. (1979). *The ecology of human development.* Cambridge, MA: Harvard University Press.

Bronfenbrenner, U. (1986). Ecology of the family as a context for human development: Research perspectives. *Developmental Psychology, 22*, 723–742.

Hawkins, J. D., & Weis, J. G. (1985). The social development model: An integrated approach to delinquency prevention. *Journal of Primary Prevention, 6*, 73–97.

Henggeler, S. W., & Borduin, C. M. (1990). *Family therapy and beyond: A multisystemic approach to treating the behavior problems of children and adolescents.* Pacific Grove, CA: Brooks/Cole.

Henggeler, S. W., Melton, G. B., & Smith, L. A. (1992). Family preservation using multisystemic therapy: An effective alternative to incarcerating serious juvenile offenders. *Journal of Consulting and Clinical Psychology, 60*, 953–961.

Hervis, O. E., Szapocznik, J., Mitrani, V. B., Rio, A. T., & Kurtines, W. M. (1991). *Structural Family Systems Ratings: A revised manual* (Technical Report). Miami, FL: Spanish Family Guidance Center, Department of Psychiatry, University of Miami, School of Medicine.

Kluckhohn, F. R., & Strodtbeck, F. L. (1961). *Variations in value orientations.* Evanston, IL: Row, Peterson.

Liddle, H. A., & Dakof, G. A. (in press). Family-based treatment for adolescent drug use: State of the science. In E. Rahdert & D. Czechowicz (Eds.), *Adolescent drug abuse: Clinical assessment and therapeutic interventions* (NIDA Research Monograph No. 156; NIH Publication 95-3908, pp. 172–189). Rockville, MD: National Institute on Drug Abuse.

Mancilla, Y., Szapocznik, J., & Kurtines, W. M. (1994). Multicultural effectiveness training (MET) for Hispanic/Latino parents. In J. Szapocznik (Ed.), *A Hispanic family approach to substance abuse prevention*. Rockville, MD: Center for Substance Abuse Prevention.

Minuchin, S. (1974). *Families and family therapy*. Cambridge, MA: Harvard University Press.

Minuchin, S., & Fishman, H. C. (1981). *Family therapy techniques*. Cambridge, MA: Harvard University Press.

Minuchin, S., Rosman, B. L., & Baker, L. (1978). *Psychosomatic families. Anorexia nervosa in context*. Cambridge, MA: Harvard University Press.

Newcomb, M. D., & Bentler, P. (1989). Substance use and abuse among children and teenagers. *American Psychologist, 44,* 242–248.

Newcomb, M. D., & Felix Ortiz, M. (1992). Multiple protective and risk factors for drug use and abuse: Cross-sectional and prospective findings. *Journal of Personality and Social Psychology, 63,* 280–296.

Newcomb, M. D., Maddahian, E., & Bentler, P. M. (1986). Risk factors for drug use among adolescents: Concurrent and longitudinal analyses. *American Journal of Public Health, 76,* 525–531.

Santisteban, D. A., & Szapocznik, J. (1994). Bridging theory, research and practice to more successfully engage substance abusing youth and their families into therapy. *Journal of Child and Adolescent Substance Abuse, 3,* 9–24.

Santisteban, D. A., Szapocznik, J., Perez-Vidal, A., Kurtines, W. M., Murray, E. J., & Laperriere, A. (in press). Engaging behavior problem drug abusing youth and their families into treatment: An investigation of the efficacy of specialized engagement interventions and factors that contribute to differential effectiveness. *Journal of Family Psychology*.

Scopetta, M. A., Szapocznik, J., King, O. E., Ladner, R., Alegre, C., & Tillman, W. S. (1977). *The Spanish drug rehabilitation research project: Final report*. Miami, FL: University of Miami Spanish Family Guidance Center.

Sue, S., Zane, N., & Young, K. (1994). Research on psychotherapy with culturally diverse populations. In A. E. Bergin & S. L. Garfield (Eds.), *Handbook of psychotherapy and behavior change*. New York: Wiley.

Szapocznik, J., & COSSMHO. (1993). *Preventing juvenile delinquency among Hispanic adolescents: A structural family therapy approach*. Washington, DC: COSSMHO.

Szapocznik, J., Hervis, O. E., Kurtines, W. M., & Spencer, F. (1984). One-person family therapy. In B. Lubin & W. A. O'Connor (Eds.), *Ecological approaches to clinical and community psychology* (pp. 335–355). New York: Wiley.

Szapocznik, J., & Kurtines, W. M. (1979). Acculturation, biculturalism and adjustment among Cuban Americans, In A. Padilla (Ed.), *Psychological dimensions on the acculturation process: Theory, models, and some new findings* (pp. 139–152). Boulder, CO: Westview Press.

Szapocznik, J., & Kurtines, W. M. (1989). *Breakthroughs in family therapy with drug-abusing and problem youth.* New York: Springer.

Szapocznik, J., & Kurtines, W. M. (1993). Family psychology and cultural diversity: Opportunities for theory, research and application. *American Psychologist, 48,* 400–407.

Szapocznik, J., Kurtines, W. M., & Fernandez, T. (1980). Bicultural involvement and adjustment in Hispanic American youths. *International Journal of Intercultural Relations, 4,* 353–366.

Szapocznik, J., Kurtines, W. M., Foote, F., Perez-Vidal, A., & Hervis, O. E. (1983). Conjoint versus one-person family therapy: Some evidence for the effectiveness of conducting family therapy through one person. *Journal of Consulting and Clinical Psychology, 51,* 889–899.

Szapocznik, J., Kurtines, W. M., Foote, F., Perez-Vidal, A., & Hervis, O. E. (1986). Conjoint versus one-person family therapy: Further evidence for the effectiveness of conducting family therapy through one person. *Journal of Consulting and Clinical Psychology, 54,* 395–397.

Szapocznik, J., Kurtines, W., Santisteban, D. A., Pantin, H., Scopetta, M., Mancilla, Y., Aisenberg, S., McIntosh, S., & Coatsworth, J. D. (in press). The evolution of a multisystemic structural approach for working with Hispanic families in culturally pluralistic contexts. In J. Garcia & M. C. Zea (Eds.), *Handbook of Latino psychology.* Needham Heights, MA: Allyn & Bacon.

Szapocznik, J., Kurtines, W. M., Santisteban, D. A., & Rio, A. T. (1990). The interplay of advances among theory, research, and application in treatment interventions aimed at behavior problem children and adolescents. *Journal of Consulting and Clinical Psychology, 58,* 696–703.

Szapocznik, J., Perez-Vidal, A., Brickman, A., Foote, F. H., Santisteban, D., Hervis, O. E., & Kurtines, W. M. (1988). Engaging adolescent drug abusers and their families into treatment: A Strategic Structural Systems approach. *Journal of Consulting and Clinical Psychology, 56,* 552–557.

Szapocznik, J., Perez-Vidal, A., Hervis, O. E., Brickman, A., & Kurtines, W. M. (1990). Innovations in family therapy: Overcoming resistance to treatment. In R. A. Wells & V. A. Gianetti (Eds.), *Handboook of brief psychotherapy* (pp. 93–114). New York: Plenum Press.

Szapocznik, J., Rio, A. T., Hervis, O. E., Mitrani, V. B., Kurtines, W. M., & Faraci, A. M. (1991). Assessing change in family functioning as a result of treatment: The Structural Family Systems Rating Scale (SFSR). *Journal of Marital and Family Therapy, 17,* 295–310.

Szapocznik, J., Rio, A., Murray, E., Cohen, R., Scopetta, M. A., Rivas-Vasquez, A., Hervis, O. E., & Posada, U. (1989). Structural family versus psychodynamic child therapy for problematic Hispanic boys. *Journal of Consulting and Clinical Psychology, 57,* 571–578.

Szapocznik, J., Santisteban, D., Kurtines, W. M., Perez-Vidal, A., & Hervis, O. E. (1984). Bicultural effectiveness training: A treatment intervention for enhancing intercultural adjustment. *Hispanic Journal of Behavioral Sciences, 6,* 317–344.

Szapocznik, J., Santisteban, D., Rio, A. T., Perez-Vidal, A., Kurtines, W. M., & Hervis, O. E. (1986). Bicultural effectiveness training: An experimental test of an intervention modality for families experiencing intergenerational/intercultural conflict. *Hispanic Journal of Behavioral Sciences, 8,* 303–330.

Szapocznik, J., Santisteban, D., Rio, A. T., Perez-Vidal, A., Santisteban, D. A., & Kurtines, W. M. (1989). Family effectiveness training: An intervention to prevent problem behaviors in Hispanic adolescents. *Hispanic Journal of Behavioral Sciences, 11,* 4–27.

Szapocznik, J., Scopetta, M. A., Aranalde, M. A., & Kurtines, W. M. (1978). Cuban value structure: Clinical implications. *Journal of Consulting and Clinical Psychology, 46,* 961–970.

Szapocznik, J., Scopetta, M. A., & King, O. E. (1978). Theory and practice in matching treatment to the special characteristics and problems of Cuban immigrants. *Journal of Community Psychology, 6,* 112–122.

Szapocznik, J., Scopetta, M. A., Kurtines, W. M., & Arnalde, M. A. (1978). Theory and measurement of acculturation. *Interamerican Journal of Psychology, 12,* 113–130.

VIII

EPILOGUE

29

FROM IVORY TOWER TO CLINICAL PRACTICE: FUTURE DIRECTIONS FOR CHILD AND ADOLESCENT PSYCHOTHERAPY RESEARCH

PETER S. JENSEN, EUTHYMIA D. HIBBS, and PAUL A. PILKONIS

As a benchmark for the degree of interest in and progress toward developing effective child and adolescent psychosocial therapies, we find the many research programs outlined in this volume heartening, even inspiring. The progress in the past decade is impressive, and effective treatments are either on the horizon or already safely in the harbor (albeit not yet fully "tied down," unloaded, and disseminated) for most childhood psychopathologies. Yet, although the degree of progress is impressive, as researchers and clinicians, we must take heed that our efforts do not fall into the "same-old, same-old," methodologically rigorous but intellectually sterile efforts that (in our opinion) have constrained many areas of the psychotherapy research field (Weisz, Donenberg, Han, & Weiss, in press). Although the field of child psychotherapy research tends to lag behind the larger psychotherapy field by a number of years, this does not constitute sufficient reason to follow systematically the missteps taken by our colleagues who have studied adult psychotherapies. In fact, the relative newness of the child and adolescent psychotherapy research field and awareness of the limitations of the findings from the broader psychotherapy research field should provide sufficient opportunity to plot a course less encumbered

The opinions and assertions contained in this paper are the private views of the authors and are not to be construed as being official or as reflecting the views of the Department of Health and Human Services or of the National Institute of Mental Health.

by obstacles. Particularly for child and adolescent clinical researchers, our experiences in research and clinical settings with children has honed our appreciation of children's sensitivity to contextual factors and heightened our awareness of the give-and-take between a growing child and a nurturing environment. These considerations must fully inform our theories of therapy and the actual operationalization of our treatments into manuals. If thoughtfully done and well explicated, the child and adolescent field can provide new avenues for progress for adult psychotherapy researchers as well. So, what are these research constraints, and what are the possible alternative considerations?

RESEARCH AND CONCEPTUAL CONSTRAINTS

Internal Versus External Validity

In what some may regard as heresy, we suggest that, in our attempts to be methodologically rigorous, we have been fooled too often by the misleading characterization of our research efforts as being focused either on internal validity or on external and ecological validity. Although arguing against either of these utopian goals would be akin to raising questions about the value of air versus that of water for life, many of the actual steps that we have taken in the course of researching our treatments have proceeded as if internal validity were paramount and, once established, external validity then could be developed simply by tweaking the rigorously developed, internally valid methodology. Too often, approaches that start from the other vantage point (treatments that are optimized to be sensible, feasible, and palatable) are seen as too complex, intrinsically unreliable, or otherwise not replicable. We suggest that this implicit assumption that has guided much of the field is conceptually limiting (variously termed *methodolatry* or *scientism*) and will set an upper limit on the empirical benefits that will ever be demonstrable from these treatment research programs.

Palatability and Acceptability to Parents and Children

Overemphasis on specific methods and procedures sometimes occurs at the expense of taking fully into account the issues of palatability to parents and children. In some instances, this emphasis does violence to the actual nature of the relationship between families and the treatment staff, and vitiates one of the potential core ingredients in the therapeutic process. Such factors, often termed *nonspecific*, may actually be highly specific and may reflect most human beings' need to have a hand in shaping their fates and to feel trust in those persons to whom they allow some control in influencing their lives. Yet in essence, in many of our models, children and families are asked to hold still while we treat them. Relatively speaking, we assume an active, somewhat authoritarian role as we attempt to deliver a product or agent to them, and they must receive it more or less passively. Resistance or noncompliance are perceived as the difficulties.

An extension of this same conceptual limitation is the fact that many of our models imply or ascribe a degree of blame to the child's caretakers. Although responsibility, guilt, and reparation are at times necessary ingredients in successful treatment, we have been insufficiently aware of the complex web of interacting etiologies that combine to bring a child and family to clinical attention. Most often, the interpersonal styles and conceptual approaches embodied in our treatments should communicate that these childhood conditions are nofault disorders.

Limited Conceptualization and Assessment of Outcomes

Another limitation that characterizes much of the child (and adult) treatment research has been the narrow range of outcomes studied. Too often, the simple reduction of behavioral symptoms or remission of a clinical condition is the principal outcome. The child's functioning in home, school, and community settings is understudied and seldom targeted as a critical outcome of treatment (*functional* outcomes). Even more rarely considered as outcomes are the child's interactions with the larger environment (*environmental* outcomes), the family perspectives on outcomes (e.g., consumer satisfaction, quality of life, family burden, etc.; *consumer* outcomes), or outcomes that assess the larger service system and economic factors associated with treatment (*services/system* outcomes). A comprehensive model of outcomes to guide child and adolescent treatment research is very much needed (Hoagwood, Jensen, Petti, & Burns, in press); unfortunately, only a handful of studies have addressed this range of outcomes (Jensen, Hoagwood, & Petti, in press).

Generalizability and Transfer to Clinical Practice

The critical issue of the lack of generalizability of our research findings to actual clinical settings is captured in the title of this chapter and has been the major scope of this book, as we have asked each of the authors to address specific details of their treatment and manuals, as well as what was known about the generalizability of the described treatment to diverse populations and settings. Yet, the problem is more complex. As well documented by others (Cohen, Sargent, & Sechrest, 1986; Morrow-Bradley & Elliott, 1986), clinicians usually do not apply research findings to their day-to-day clinical practice. Part of the difficulty stems from the clinicians' well-justified suspicions that patients treated in research settings are unlike those treated in clinical practice, because researchers often exclude complex, comorbid conditions or noncompliant parents from the research protocol. In their defense, clinicians explain that most research is not applicable to the problems of clinical practice, is frequently focused on esoteric or irrelevant questions, and fails to consider crucial factors (Howard, 1986). From a clinical perspective, it is difficult to apply research findings to individual patients because research studies use selected subjects and tightly constrained methods, and individual differences are rarely considered (Barlow, 1981a, 1981b; Morrow-Bradley & Elliott, 1986).

One Size Fits All

Much of the previous research seems to follow the "one size fits all" approach to the design of therapies. Although this suits treatment research approached from the vantage point of internal validity, it has divorced much of our treatment research from developmental theory, ignored individual differences and developmental trajectories, and is roundly criticized by clinicians for seeming nonsensical and failing to take into account what they feel they know about the individual children and families. Furthermore, such prepackaged approaches may be less palatable to families (a plausible but untested hypothesis). Of course, it is very sensible to develop new treatments by testing single components, then adding new components in a step-by-step fashion to handle previously unaddressed problems. However, on its own, such an approach is insufficient and should, instead, complement other treatment development approaches that embed therapies in developmental theory and ecological perspectives. Such considerations must take into careful account whether an intervention should (a) be implemented in a single setting or must cross multiple settings (e.g., home and school); (b) focus on one or multiple domains of function (e.g., self-concept, parent–child behavior management, and peer relationships); (c) incorporate the families' values and inputs in treatment design and selection; and (d) tailor the treatment to the specific clinical and developmental needs of the child.

Short-Term Versus Long-Term Perspectives

Most treatment studies have been time limited and, as we have documented in Jensen, Hoagwood, and Petti (in press), there are literally less than two dozen studies of psychosocial treatments that have examined children's outcomes at periods of 6 months or more after treatment. Part of the difficulty in conducting such longer-term studies is due to the fact that long-term studies with placebo or attention control participants may be unacceptable on ethical grounds and not feasible and not palatable to families. Yet, such information is going to be increasingly critical to establish parity for mental health treatments coverage and inclusion by third party payers and benefits managers. This requires researchers to explore alternative research strategies, particularly those which address the other constraints discussed earlier.

FUTURE CONSIDERATIONS

Accentuate External Validity in Study Design

To grapple more effectively with the issues of internal versus external validity, we suggest that researchers begin with different end points in mind as they design future treatment studies. Investigators must begin with the goals of developing therapies and treatment trials that are *feasible*, *sensible* (e.g., face valid whenever possible), and *palatable*. Primacy should be placed on these first three parameters and, only then, should additional methods be applied to ensure the internal validity of the trial. As these new therapeutic approaches are envisioned and tested, researchers should attend to input from clinicians and families in discriminating sense from nonsense. For example, although long-standing notions about what is therapeutic (and what is not) continue to guide our narrow conceptualizations of treatment, families in the service system, when asked to identify the most helpful aspect of treatment services, describe *respite care* for their child as the single, most valued component. Ignoring such feedback risks rendering our treatment approaches ineffective, unappreciated, unreimbursed, or some combination of all three (not to mention extinct!). Early in the course of treatment definition, development, and testing, feedback from these most valuable allies is critical to the success of our research efforts.

Parents and Families as Partners in the Therapeutic Process

To address concerns about the palatability to families of our therapies and the clinical trials that purport to test our treatments, we must strengthen our relationship with the children and families to that of *partners*. Therapies that fail to build this principle into the approach to families are likely to miss a critical component of treatment effectiveness. Unlike more traditional biomedical procedures that are presumably active once the intervention has been delivered or ingested (e.g., medications), the psychotherapies are inextricably intertwined with the psychopathologic conditions to the extent that both are embedded in behavioral patterns of human social exchange. Without the full enlistment of all critical family members in using their behaviors to change the child's behaviors, success is dubious. This recruitment of family effort is possible only to the extent that the therapy itself represents an interpersonal partnership between therapist and family participants and to the degree that the therapist communicates this principle effectively and convincingly to these would-be therapeutic partners. Such a partnership cannot progress fully if it is not consonant with the family members' values and world views. To be credible to family members, this therapeutic partnership perspective must rest on the principles of an ethical compact between family members and psychotherapist, as they jointly work to understand the child's and the family's difficulties, and assist all family members in developing necessary skills within a human, social, and caring context. The maxim "I don't care how much you know until I know how much you care," although simplistic, is likely to be valid and must be better operationalized into our treatment approaches. We must take very seriously the organizing function of positive attachments in terms of how they structure cognition, memory, and behavior.

Can such an approach be taught and outlined in a manual? Probably, but we are unaware of any systematic efforts in this regard. Much rests on the actual nature of the therapists and their values and on the degree of native skill in communicating these principles, within an interpersonal context, to the family members. Yet, the difficulty of this task does not constitute a reason not to seek means to develop our therapies so that they better fit an individual child's and family's world view. Interestingly, in this regard, the National Institute of Mental Health is seeking means to increase the involvement of families as participants and partners, including seeking their early input in treatment research design, developing more sensible terminologies, and crafting better plans for research dissemination. Of note, some National Institutes of Health clinical trials have used designs in which participant choice is actually one of the "arms" to which participants are assigned randomly. As noted, if such participatory models are realized more fully, we clearly need to expand our models for assessing outcomes. Consumer satisfaction, quality of life, family burden, and other consumer perspectives may be much more central than we have heretofore acknowledged.

Taking Better Advantage of Clinical Wisdom

As we improve our efforts to work with families, we must make similar efforts to learn from experienced clinicians. The best of clinical insights need to be taken seriously if we are to understand why some treatments are only modestly or not at all effective for some individuals or subgroups. One means of obtaining more systematic clinical input might be through the use of research design workshops that encourage the participation of more experienced clinicians and in which their input can be obtained; yet, such approaches have been widely underused.

Furthermore, research efforts need to begin with difficulties as perceived from the clinicians' perspective and for which clinicians would most like answers. If questions are framed from the perspectives of the immediacy of clinical needs, the likelihood that research results will be useful and actually applied in clinical practice is enhanced. Moreover, the best clinical insights are likely to provide testable hypotheses embedded in an understanding of children within a developmental context. To the extent that these insights can be incorporated into the treatments, greater specificity of treatments targeted to individuals becomes possible.

Treatment Strategies and Clinical Decision-Making Algorithms

In our view, almost no areas of medicine use a "one size fits all" approach to the treatment of pathology: Medication dosages are adjusted to body size or surface area, the pace and order of cancer chemotherapies are adapted to the individual patients' type and severity of side effects, and even surgical procedures are modified for better toleration by frail or compromised patients. Likewise, a good psychotherapist does not continue with a tightly focused cognitive–behavioral didactic approach with parents, if significant dissension between the parents threatens to scuttle the entire therapeutic enterprise; nor does a competent therapist continue to apply his therapeutic skills to a family if overarching issues of trust/distrust or like/dislike appear to undermine the family's confidence in the therapist's abilities. Yet, too many of our research-based treatments proceed as if these issues were not paramount to the integrity of the treatment. Too many research-based treatments attempt simply to follow a set program, needed or not, with little attention to the particular needs of the individual patients.

To take such considerations seriously, designers of research-based treatments should proceed only if

1. they possess a clear understanding of the principles of treatment (e.g., what are the necessary though not sufficient elements of change in this treatment paradigm);
2. given these therapeutic principles, what are the types of person- or family-specific obstacles that may hamper the delivery and effectiveness of the treatment (including the family's commitment to the therapeutic partnership; and
3. they know which modifications in pace, ordering, and timing of treatments must be accommodated to avoid minimizing the effects of these potential obstacles on the active components of treatment.

For example, an overarching hierarchy of therapeutic principles (based on the clinicians' best wisdom) might be constructed that supersede (or must precede) the implementation of an effective psychosocial intervention. Such principles might include the family's or parents' need for control or autonomy in directing family affairs, the apparent consistency of an intervention with the family's values, sufficient marital harmony so that both parents can actively support the intervention, trust or liking for the therapist, the apparent sensibility and credibility of the intervention to the family, the fairness of the intervention to family members affected by it, the family partners' ability to attend to and learn the intervention, and the presence of appropriate and sufficient emotional reserves and equilibrium in those who must deliver and receive the intervention.

The presence of these factors, coupled with elements and principles of change, might *together* constitute the necessary and sufficient ingredients to deliver a reasonably effective psychosocial intervention with an active treatment component. Yet, in a therapeutic partnership, it is likely that some autonomy must be surrendered to the partner–therapist (if change is to occur), but this occurs best in the presence of trust, liking, and confidence in the therapist. If the intervention is inconsistent with family values, seems unfair, or simply "does not make sense" from their perspective, it will take a very high degree of trust before such an intervention can proceed (if at all), and the differences in therapist and family values and treatment rationale must be fully adjudicated. Likewise, the presence of marital difficulties, preoccupation with other problems, or severe emotional distress (sadness, anger, anxiety) in any of the therapeutic partners must be monitored. Just as the cancer chemotherapist delays the delivery of more antitumor agents when the platelet levels drop too low, the psychotherapist monitors these core emotional levels within the family therapeutic partners and, at critical junctures, addresses these issues directly, all in the service of providing the most effective psychotherapy for the child's identified difficulties.

To develop such sensible treatments, it will be necessary to construct a hierarchical decision-making tree that incorporates individual modules that can be used if and when needed. Measures and sensible thresholds for critical aspects of the family climate related to the therapeutic partnership must be developed and operationalized, and these must be tested. Such strategies need not be complex initially and may address only a few of the potential obstacles that emerge in the course of treatment. Such strategies might address not only the person- and family-specific obstacles noted above, but should also incorporate other principles of learning and behavior change, such as selection of the optimal modes of learning (e.g., experiential vs. cognitive–didactic), appropriate change mechanisms (e.g., relational, insight-oriented, new skill acquisition, etc.), and flexible vs. static. These concerns all point in the direction of the need for therapeutic process-oriented manuals, rather than manuals that focus exclusively or principally on didactic content.

Have such decision-making strategies and clinical algorithms been successfully used in any clinical trials? The Multimodal Treatment Study of Attention Deficit Hyperactivity Disorder (the MTA study) has incorporated these types of algorithms into each of its treatment arms, including a psychosocial-only arm, a medication arm, and a combined treatment arm. This has yielded more sensible clinical approaches that allowed adaptations in the ordering, pacing, and intensity of several psychosocial components within a specified range, based on the families' particular needs. Similar adjustments are specified and allowable in the medication-only and combined treatment arms (Greenhill et al., in press). When made, these adjustments are also measured and are accomplished within the overarching framework of a random assignment, controlled clinical trial. Although such approaches have limitations and cannot answer every question, coupled with the incremental, step-by-step testing of various combinations of treatment components, they can provide powerful and complementary scientific evidence to bridge many of the knowledge gaps left by the more traditional treatment research approaches.

Efficacy Versus Effectiveness Studies

Elsewhere, we (Hoagwood, Hibbs, Brent, & Jensen, in press) have elaborated a three-dimensional model of the differences between efficacy versus effectiveness studies. Any strict dichotomization of these two approaches is highly artificial and glosses over the many intricacies of study designs employed by different investigators. Yet, to accept the dichotomy briefly, we suggest that too much emphasis has been placed on the traditional, short-term efficacy studies that principally assess symptoms and disorders. By far, too few studies have been conducted examining the long-term outcomes of treatments, surveying the broad range of potential outcomes—clinical, functional, environmental, consumer-oriented, and systemic. These types of studies are particularly needed for children in whom the possibility of disorder chronicity and adverse long-term outcomes must be countered with the potential for developmental plasticity, behavioral change, and growth. Yet, as we have tried to establish in this chapter, such long-term studies cannot be mounted effectively (for both pragmatic and ethical reasons) if the issues of feasibility, palatability, sensibility, and real-world flexibility (e.g., algorithms) are not thoughtfully incorporated into the research design. Failure to deliver these abilities (see Whalen, 1991) in future studies will result in researchers' defaulting on yet three more abilities: replicability, generalizability, and transportability. From a scientific perspective, we suggest that if researchers do not increase their abilities in these areas, in the long run, their scientific contributions risk remaining limited in appeal, restricted in conceptual approach, and incapable of providing strong tests of developmental theory.

CONCLUSION

Researchers, clinical practitioners, and family partners must work closely together to bridge the gaps between treatment research and treatments in clinical settings, and between traditional treatment strategies and family-centered treatment approaches. Such efforts will enable us not to simply translate findings into practice but also to determine the actual mental health needs and most effective treatments for children and families in real-world settings—the "proving ground of experience" (Barlow, 1981a, 1981b; Burke, Pincus, & Pardes, 1986; Hoshmand & Polkinghorne, 1992, Weisz et al., in press). Bridging these gaps will require the development of new assessment tools that can be used more readily in day-to-day clinical practice and are palatable and feasible in such settings (e.g, Jensen, 1991; Jensen, Irwin, et al., in press), and the development of sensible clinical algorithms and decision trees that are testable and comparable with other alternatives.

Over the past decade, great progress has been made in the development of assessment tools, manualized therapies, and research designs. These changes, although significant, pale against the backdrop of the heretofore almost unimaginable changes in our mental health care systems, economic and reimbursement structures, and newly empowered families who have a critical hand (and stake) in shaping our shared future. These changes must be realized, understood, accepted, even embraced, if we are to maximize the effectiveness of our therapies for the next decade. The pressing, increasing problems of children will require nothing less and will likely demand much more.

REFERENCES

Barlow, D. H. (1981a). On the relation of clinical research to clinical practice: Current issues, new directions. *Journal of Consulting and Clinical Psychology*, 49, 147–155.

Barlow, D. H. (1981b). A role for clinicians in the research process. *Behavior Assessment*, 3, 227–233.

Burke, J. D., Pincus, H. A., & Pardes, H. (1986). The clinician–researcher in psychiatry. *American Journal of Psychiatry*, 143, 968–975.

Cohen, L. H., Sargent, M. M., & Sechrest, L. B. (1986). Use of psychotherapy research by professional psychologists. *American Psychologist*, 41, 198–206.

Greenhill, L., Arnold, L., Cantwell, D., Conners, C., Elliott, G., Hinshaw, S., Hoza, B., Jensen, P. S., Kraemer, H. C., March, J., Newcorn, J., Richters, J., Severe, J., Swanson, J., & Wells, K. (in press). Medication treatment strategies in the MTA Study: Relevance to clinicians and researchers, *Journal of the American Academy of Child and Adolescent Psychiatry*.

Hoagwood, K., Hibbs, E., Brent, D., & Jensen, P. (in press). Efficacy and effectiveness in studies in child and adolescent psychotherapy. *Journal of Consulting and Clinical Psychology.*

Hoagwood, K., Jensen, P. S., Petti, T., & Burns, B. (in press). Outcomes of care for children and adolescents: Part 1. A conceptual model. *Journal of the American Academy of Child and Adolescent Psychiatry.*

Hoshmand, L. T., & Polkinghorne, D. E. (1992). Redefining the science–practice relationship and professional training. *American Psychologist, 47,* 55–66.

Howard, G. S. (1986). The scientist–practitioner in counseling psychology: Toward a deeper integration of theory, research, and practice. *Counsulting Psychology, 14,* 61–105.

Jensen, P. S. (1991). The research database in clinical practice. *Journal of Child and Adolescent Psychopharmacology, 2,* 375–380.

Jensen, P. S., Hoagwood, K., & Petti, T. (in press). Outcomes of care for children and adolescents: Part 2. Application of the CFCES model to current research. *Journal of the American Academy of Child and Adolescent Psychiatry.*

Jensen, P. S., Irwin, R. C., Josephson, A. D., Davis, H., Bloedau, L., Ness, R., Xenakis, S. N., Mabe, A., Lee, B., Traylor, J., & Clawson, L. (in press). Data-gathering tools for "real world" clinical settings: A multi-site feasibility study. *Journal of the American Academy of Child and Adolescent Psychiatry.*

Morrow-Bradley, C., & Elliott, R. (1986). Utilization of psychotherapy research by practicing psychotherapists. *American Psychologist, 41,* 188–197.

Weisz, J. R., Donenberg, G. R., Han, S. S., & Weiss, B. (in press). Bridging the gap between lab and clinic in child and adolescent psychotherapy. *Journal of Consulting and Clinical Psychology.*

Whalen, C. K. (1991). Therapies for hyperactive children: Comparisons, combinations, and compromises. *Journal of Consulting and Clinical Psychology, 59,* 126–137.

AUTHOR INDEX

Numbers in italics refer to listings in reference sections.

Jackson, D. N., *130*
Jackson, K., 640, 667
Jackson, K. L., 188, *203*
Jackson, N. F., 350, *367*
Jacob, T., 192, *203*
Jacobson, D. S., 147, *152*
Jacobson, G., 147, *152*
Jacobson, N. S., 117, 119, *130*, 272, 277, 284, 447, 458, *470*, *471*
Jacobson, R. R., 410, 413, *431*
James, L. S., 526, *548*
Jamieson, B., 574, 582, 585, 586, *587*
Jarrett, R. B., 139, *154*
Jefferson, J., *101*
Jennings, P., 554, *571*
Jensen, P., 703, 704, 709, *711*
Jensen, P. S., *308*, *368*, 710, *710*
Jenson, W. R., 189, *203*, 231, *237*
Jilek, A. L., 643, *667*
John, K., 149, *152*, *154*, *206*
Johnson, J., 527, 528, *548*, *550*, 643, *669*
Johnson, M. J., *183*
Johnson, R., 149, *153*, *205*
Johnson, W. H., 666, *669*
Johnston, C., 269, *284*, 363, *367*
Johnston, H., 96, *101*
Joiner, T. E., 208, *238*
Jones, E., 631, *636*
Jones, E. E., 158, *183*
Jones, R. R., 501, *517*
Jones, R. T., 415, 421, *431*
Josephson, A. D., 710, *711*
Jouriles, E. N., 442, *470*

Kafry, D., 409, 410, 413, *431*
Kahn, J. S., 189, *203*, 231, *237*
Kain, C. D., *183*
Kaiser, A. P., 555, 569, *570*, *572*
Kalikow, K., *100*
Kandel, D. B., 138, *153*, 159, *183*, 188, *203*
Kane, M., 27, *37*, *38*
Kane, M. T., 30, *37*
Kane, R., *37*
Kaneko, W. M., 539, *551*
Kanner, L., 159, *183*, 535, *549*
Kanter, F. H., 288, *307*
Kaplan, B. H., 159, *185*
Kaplan, N. J., 159, *183*
Kaplan, T., *205*
Kashani, J. H., *61*, 139, *153*, 159, *183*
Kaslow, N. J., 207, 208, *237*, *238*

Kasvikis, Y., *101*
Kaswan, J. W., 442, *471*
Katic, M., *204*
Katz, L. F., *470*
Katz, S., 283, *336*, 342, 343, *366*
Kaufman, J., *154*, *205*
Kaufman, K. F., 269, 283, 343, *366*
Kayser, C. S., 342, *366*
Kazdin, A., 96, *100*
Kazdin, A. E., 11–14, *17*, *61*, 79, 193, *203*, 231, 293, *307*, 312, 315, 327, 331, *336*, *337*, 373, 378–381, 383–385, 388, 390–403, *404–407*, 409–415, 420, 422, 425, 427, *431*, *432*, 436, 467, *471*, 498–500, 502, 508, 514, *517*, 619, 620, 637
Keane, S. P., 604, 605, *617*
Kearney, C. A., 65, 69, 79, 80
Keetz, A., 555, 569, *570*
Kehle, T. J., 189, *203*, 231, *237*
Kellegrew, D. H., 568, *571*
Keller, M. B., 139, *153*, 188, 193, *203*
Kelly, J., *61*
Kelso, J., 413, *431*
Kendall, P., 84, 86, 96, *101*
Kendall, P. C., 21, 23–25, 27–36, *37*, *38*, 40, *61*, 208, 210, 219, 220, 228, *237*, *238*, 460, *471*, 497, 508, *517*, 625, 637
Kendler, K., *61*
Kennedy, C. R., *61*
Kennedy, H., 621, 628, 636, 637
Kennedy, K., 476, *490*
Kennedy, R., *636*
Kenniston, 597
Kent, R. N., *132*, 331, *336*
Kernberg, P., 630, 637
Kerr, M., 556, *572*
Kessler, R. C., *61*
Keysor, C. S., *100*
Kim, R., *61*
King, J., *154*
King, O. E., 684, 695, 697
King, R., *102*
King, R. A., 87, *102*
Klein, D., 283
Klein, D. F., 311, *336*, 342, 348, 366, 367
Klein, R. D., 529, *552*
Klein, R. G., 286, 287, *307*, 341–343, 360, 365, *367*

Lerner, M., 308, 368
Lerner, M. S., 189, 197, 204
Lester, D., 202
Levin, H., 484, 490
Levin, M., 32, 38
Levitt, E. E., 11, 17, 18
Lewinsohn, P. M., 106, 109, 110,
    112–115, 117–122, 125–127,
    128–134, 134–135, 140, 153,
    166, 183, 187–191, 202, 204,
    231, 447, 471
Lewis, K., 208, 238
Lewis, O., 655, 668
Liard, R. A., 198, 205
Libet, J., 115, 132, 183
Licht, B. G., 339
Liddle, H. A., 689, 695
Liebert, D., 608, 616
Liebowitz, M. L., 61
Lillenfield, S. O., 460, 471
Lindholm, L., 139, 152
Linn, J. D., 208, 238
Linskey, A. O., 640, 668
Livingston, R., 208, 237, 238
Lloyd, M., 379, 405
Lochman, J., 88, 101
Lochman, J. E., 316, 326, 336, 337
Locke, B. Z., 152
Loeber, R., 299, 307, 351, 366, 400, 407,
    408, 426, 433, 435, 436, 471
Loeber, R. L., 471
Lollis, 602
Lollis, S., 61
Long, J. S., 526, 550
Long, N., 385, 405
Long, P., 15, 18, 407
Lonigan, C., 572
López, S. R., 158, 160, 183
Lovaas, O. I., 15, 18, 526, 531, 535, 550,
    569, 571
Love, L. R., 442, 471
Lubetsky, M., 416, 430
Luborsky, L., 204
Lukens, E., 154
Luria, A. R., 288, 307
Lushene, R. C., 648, 669
Lushene, R. E., 133

Mabe, A., 711
Maccoby, E. E., 484, 489, 490

MacDonald, J. P., 34, 38
MacDonald, J. T., 313, 335
MacGuire, M., 208, 238
MacPhillamy, D., 131
MacPhillamy, D. J., 117, 118, 132, 134
Madanes, C., 415, 432, 500, 517
Maddahian, E., 689, 695
Madrid, M. A., 643, 668
Mahoney, M. J., 603, 615
Main, M., 622, 637
Mair, M., 642, 668
Maletic, V., 96, 101
Malgady, R., 592, 640, 641, 646, 655,
    657, 665, 667
Malgady, R. G., 158, 160, 183, 668, 669
Mallinger, A. G., 407
Malloy, P., 343, 367
Malsheen, B., 563, 571
Mancilla, Y., 686, 691, 695, 696
Mandanes, C., 432
Mann, E. S., 655, 668
Mannarino, A. P., 616
Mannino, F. V., 162, 183
Mannuzza, S., 286, 287, 307, 311, 337,
    343, 366, 367
March, J., 83, 85–88, 91, 96–98, 101,
    102, 710
March, J. S., 22, 365
Marchione, K. E., 616
Marciano, P. L., 395, 407
Margolin, G., 119, 130, 447, 470
Marín, G., 162, 184
Markell, R. A., 608, 614
Markman, A., 470
Marks, D., 339
Marks, D. A., 284
Marks, I. M., 66, 80, 84, 86–88, 101,
    102
Marlatt, G. A., 120, 132
Marlowe, D., 119, 129
Marlowe, J. H., 386, 404
Marshall, P. T., 415, 432
Marsteller, F., 131, 640, 667
Marsteller, F. A., 203
Marten, P. A., 60, 61
Martin, D., 360, 365
Martin, G., 315, 317, 337
Martin, J., 150, 153, 204, 489
Martin, P., 203
Martinez, O., 640, 668

Martínez, S., 161, 180, *184*
Marton, P., *204*, 288, *305*
Maser, J. D., 117, *132*
Mash, E. J., 269, 284, 363, *367*
Matier, K., 290, *305*
Matkoski, K. M., *429*
Matson, J. L., 109, *132*, 231
Mattes, J., *283*, 336, 343, *366*
Mattoon, G., *636*
Mayes, L. C., 622, *637*
Mays, V. M., 158, *183*
Mazure, C., *100*
Mazurick, J. L., 385, 395, 406, *407*
Mazza, J., *101*
McArthur, D., 537, *548*
McBurnett, K., 286, 289, 308, 317, 320, 338, 368, 408, *433*
McCandrews, M. M., *430*
McCarthy, D. A., 576, *586*
McCarthy, M., 210, *238*
McClaskey, C. L., 360, *366*
McConnell, S., 350, 368, *617*
McConnell, S. R., 585, *586*
McCord, J., 484, 489, *617*
McDaniel, S., 180, *185*
McDonald, B. A., *489*
McDonald-Scott, P., *203*
McDowell, J. J., 488, *489*
McEachin, J. J., 15, *18*
McEachran, A. B., *407*
McGee, R., 60, *61*
McGoldrick, M., 158, 160, *184*
McGonagle, K., *61*
McGonigle, J. J., 529, *552*
McGrath, P., 269, 284, 415, *432*
McGuire, K. D., 596, *616*
McHale, J. P., 290, 299, 306, *307*
McHugh, T. A., 401, *404*
McIntosh, S., *696*
McKain, B., 188, *202*
McKay, G. D., 503, *516*
McKeever, J. M., *430*
McKeon, R., 640, *667*
McKeown, R. E., 188, *203*
McKeown, S., *203*
McKinley, J. C., 119, *130*
McLaughlin, P. M., 414, *430*
McLellan, A. T., *204*
McMahon, R. J., 269, 284, 315, 318, 329, 335, *337*, 351, *366*, 385,

407, 442, 458, 470, 471, 501, 516
McNees, M. P., 352, *367*
Meadowcroft, P., 483, *489*
Meichenbaum, D., 224, 225, *237*, 447, *471*
Meichenbaum, D. H., 287, 288, *307*
Mellins, C. A., *183*
Mellott, K., *414*
Melnick, S., 304, *307*
Melton, G. B., 12, *17*, 689, *694*
Mendelson, M., 112, *128*, *202*
Mentis, M., 545, *549*
Merikangas, K., 139, *152*
Merikangas, K. R., *154*, *206*
Mermelstein, R. M., 118, *131*
Metz, G., 149, *151*
Meyer, E. C., 412, *432*
Michelsen, L., 315, *337*
Michelson, L., 596, *616*
Miezitis, J. L., 231, *237*
Milich, R., 287, *305*, 312, 318–320, 323, 326, 335–339, 342, 365, 460, *471*
Miller, C. L., 316, *335*
Miller, D., 144, 145, *152*, *153*
Miller, G. E., 331, *337*, 385, *407*, 478, *490*
Miller, J., *284*, 339, 628, 630, *636*
Miller, J. M., *637*
Miller, P. M., 596, *616*
Miller, S., *205*
Mills, J. I., 527, *552*
Minuchin, S., 241, 258, 275, 284, 415, *433*, 675, 686, *695*
Miranda, J., 166, *184*
Mischel, W., 119, *131*
Mitrani, V. B., 675, 694, *696*
Mize, J., 599, *616*
Mock, J., *202*
Mock, J. E., 112, *128*
Moes, D., 538, 550, 568, *571*
Moffitt, T. E., 400, *407*
Mohammed, Z., 198, *205*
Moilanen, D. L., *202*
Molina, B. M., *340*
Monroe, C., 350, *367*
Monteiro, W., *101*
Montgomery, L. M., *18*
Montuori, J., 648, *669*

O'Leary, K. D., *132, 269, 288, 295, 305, 307, 308,* 312, 315, 316, 321, *336, 337,* 343, 351, 368, 442, *470, 471,* 529, *548*
O'Leary, S. G., *283,* 312, 317, 321, *336, 337, 339, 361, 365, 366*
Ollendick, T., 38, 39
Ollendick, T. H., 415, *431,* 529, *552*
O'Malley, S. S., 198, *206*
O'Neill, M. E., 342, 347, *366*
O'Neill, R. E., *526–528,* 545, *548–551,* 560, *571*
Ort, S. I., *102*
Orvaschel, H., *61,* 149, 153, 159, *183,* 188, 192, *205*
Osborne, S., *365*
Osgood, D. W., 476, *490*
Ostrow, L., *205*
Otero-Sabogal, R., 162, *184*
Owens, S. E., *340*

Padian, N., 139, *155*
Padilla, A. M., 641, *668*
Paez, P., *202, 429*
Pagan, A., *181, 365*
Pakiz, B., *205*
Paluchowski, C., *284, 339*
Panas, J., *37*
Panichelli, S., 32, *38*
Pantin, H., *696*
Paolicelli, L. L., 290, *305*
Pardes, H., 710, *710*
Parke, R. D., 597, *616*
Parker, J. G., 287, *307,* 596, *616*
Parkhurst, J. T., 597, 602, *615*
Parks, D. R., *549*
Parloff, M. B., *129, 152*
Parrish, J. M., 410, *433*
Parrone, P. L., *203*
Parry, P., 288, *305*
Parsons, B. V., 195, *201,* 239, *258*
Partridge, F., *61*
Patterson, C. J., 529, *551*
Patterson, G. R., 119, *133,* 239, *259,* 288, *307,* 312, 317, 318, 321, *335, 337,* 380, 384–386, 400, 401, *404, 407,* 408, 436–438, 442, 446, *471,* 479, 484, *490,* 497, 498, 500–503, 509, *516–518*
Paul, D., *340*
Paul, R., 554, 555, 557, 560, *571*
Paulauskas, S. L., 153, 188, 203, *204*

Pauls, D. L., *101*
Pausoff, B. A., *206*
Paykel, E. S., 139, *154*
Pear, J., 315, 317, *337*
Pearce, J. K., 158, *184*
Pearlin, L. I., 118, *132*
Pearson, G. S., 620, *638*
Peck, C. A., 556, *571*
Pederson, A., 596, *614*
Pedulla, B. M., 12, *17*
Pekarik, E., 608, *616*
Pelham, W. E., 264, 269, 286–289, 291, 293, 302, *307, 308,* 311, 312, 314, 316–321, 323, 324, 326–328, 330, *335–340,* 342, 343, 347, *365, 367, 368*
Pelham, W. W., *284*
Peplau, L. A., *133*
Pepler, D. J., 381, *408*
Peradotto, D., 269, *283*
Perel, J. M., *407*
Perez-Vidal, A., *685–687, 695–697*
Perlman, R., 274, *283*
Perlman, T., 341, 343, *367, 368*
Perper, J. A., *202*
Perrin, S., *61*
Perry, D. G., 602, *616*
Perry, L. C., 602, *616*
Perry, S. W., 409, *429*
Petersen, A. C., 158, *184*
Peterson, R. A., 65, *80*
Petti, T., 703, 704, *711*
Petti, T. A., 231, *237*
Pfiffner, L., *308*
Pfiffner, L. J., 317, *339*
Phillipson, S. J., *433*
Physician's desk reference, 318, *339*
Piacentini, J., *205*
Piaget, J., 545, *551*
Pickles, A., 139, *152,* 188, *203*
Pickrell, E. P., 413, *433*
Pierce, K., 541, 546, *551*
Piercy, F. P., 198, *205*
Piers, E. V., 180, *184,* 362, *368, 668*
Pilkones, P. A., *152*
Pilkonis, P. A., *129*
Pilowsky, I., 118, *132*
Pincus, H. A., 710, *710*
Pisterman, S., 269, *284*
Piug-Antich, J., *204*
Platt, J. J., 316, *340,* 442, 460, 472, 502, *517*

Rio, A. T., 675, 694, 696, 697
Risley, T. R., 555, 567, 569, *570*
Ritchey, W. L., 596, *616*
Ritvo, E. R., 527, *548*
Rivas-Vasquez, A., *408*, 696
Rivers, R. Y., 157, *181*
Robbins, D. R., 140, *154*
Robbins, F. R., *550*
Robbins, P., 316, *335*
Roberts, D., 556, *572*
Roberts, N., *204*
Roberts, R. E., 109, 111, 112, 114, *131,*
132, 640, 668
Robin, A. L., 109, 119, *132, 133,* 192,
195, 205, 239, 241, 249, 251,
252, 259, 275, 284, 498, 502,
508, *517*
Robins, E., 189, *202*
Robins, L., 109, *133*
Robins, L. N., 9, *18,* 378, 379, *408*
Robinson, D., *154*
Robinson, E. A., 441, *472*
Rock, A. F., 426, *430*
Rodgers, A., 11, *17,* 394, 397, 406, *407,*
425, *431*
Rodick, J. D., 476, *490*
Rodriguez, O., 640, *669*
Roehl, J., 409, 415, *430*
Roff, M., *617*
Rogers, T., 446, *470*
Rogler, L. H., 158, 160, *183,* 641, 646,
647, 655, 657, 664, 665,
666–669
Rohde, P., 110, 112, 113, 118, 122, 125,
130, 131, 133, 134, 188, *204*
Ronan, K., 34, *37, 38*
Ronnei, M., *339*
Ronnel, M., *284*
Rooth, A. B., 642, *669*
Rorty, R., *80*
Rose-Krasnor, L., 381, *408*
Rosenbaum, A., 288, *307,* 316, *337*
Rosenbaum, M., *131*
Rosenberg, M., 118, *133*
Rosenberg, T. K., 139, *153*
Rosenfeld, S., 624, *637*
Rosman, B. L., 241, *258,* 675, *695*
Ross, 602
Ross, A. O., 317, *340*
Ross, R., 415, *429*
Rosselló, J., 106, 161, 164, 180, *184*
Roth, C., *202*

Rothberg, P. C., *202*
Rotheram-Borus, M. J., 190, 194, *205*
Rounsaville, B. H., 137, *153*
Rounsaville, B. J., 149, *155,* 173, *183*
Rowden, L., 596, *615*
Rowe, D., 529, *552*
Rowe, M., 34, *38*
Rubin, K. H., *61,* 381, *408,* 460, *472,*
596–598, *615*
Rubin, Z., *617*
Rubio-Stipic, M., *181,* 341, *365*
Rudel, R. G., 348, *367*
Ruiz, R. A., 641, 668
Runco, M. A., 527, *551, 552*
Rush, A., *37, 40*
Rush, A. J., 117, *128,* 139, 140, *154,*
155, 166, *181,* 190, 194, 197,
202, 205, 206, 227, 237, 640,
667
Russell, D., 119, *133*
Russell, G. F. M., 256, 258, *259*
Russo, D. C., 543, *551*
Russo, M. F., *408,* 425, *433*
Rutter, M., 9, *18,* 139, *152,* 188, *203,*
205, 379, *408,* 442, 467, *472,*
535, *551,* 630, *637*
Ryan, N., *204,* 233, 237
Ryan, N. D., 138, 139, *154, 205*
Rzasa, T., 318, *335*

Sabogal, F., 162, *184*
Sagotsky, G., 529, *551*
Sailor, W., 545, *548*
Salt, P., *202*
Saltz, E., 643, *669*
Salvo, J. J., 655, *668*
Samoilov, A., 150, *153, 204*
Sams, S. E., 308, 312, *336, 338*
Samuelson, H., *203*
Sánchez-Lacay, A., *181*
Sanchez-Lacay, A., *365*
Sancilio, M. F. M., 574, *587*
Sanders, M. R., 352, *366,* 401, *404,* 446,
469
Sandler, I. N., 119, *133*
Sandler, J., 628, *637*
Sansbury, L. E., 478, *490*
Santisteban, D., 685, *697*
Santisteban, D. A., 687, 689, *695,* 696
Santmeyer, K., 244, *258*
Santogrossi, D. A., 598, *616*
Saraaf, K., 342, *366*

Singer, J. L., 645, 669
Siqueland, L., 27, 33, *37*, *38*, *61*
Sisson, L. A., 585, 586
Sloman, J., 597, 598, *617*
Small, R., 476, 490
Smallish, L., 274, 311, *334*
Smilansky, S., 644, 646, 669
Smith, B. H., 321, *340*
Smith, L. A., 12, 15, *17*, 689, *694*
Smith, R. E., 317, *340*
Smith, T., *18*
Smith, W. D., 157, 162, *185*
Smoll, F. L., 317, *340*
Snyder, D., 568, *572*
Soltys, S. M., *433*
Somberg, D. R., 381, *405*
Sotsky, S. M., *129*, *152*
Sparrow, S. S., 535, *552*
Speilberger, C., *62*
Spencer, E. K., 139, *152*
Spencer, F., 687, *695*
Spiegel-McGill, P., *586*
Spielberger, C., *38*
Spielberger, C. D., 118, *133*, 648, 669
Spitalnik, R., 295, *305*, 529, *548*
Spitzer, R. L., 193, *202*, 362, *368*
Spivack, G., 381, 408
Spivak, G., 316, *340*, 442, 460, *472*,
    502, *517*
Sprafkin, J., 290, *305*
Sprague, J. R., 560, *571*
Sprague, R. L., 343, *368*
Sprich, S. E., 341, *365*
Sprince, M., 624, *637*
Spurlock, J., 158, *182*
Stabb, S. D., 316, *335*
Stafford, M., 210, *238*
Stahmer, A. C., 543, *552*
Stalai, J., *204*
Stallings, P., *102*
Stark, J., 535, *548*
Stark, K., 210, *238*
Stark, K. D, 207, 208, 233
Stark, K. D., 109, *133*, 209, 216, 228,
    231, *237*, *238*
Stawar, T. L., *433*
Steele, H., 622, 636, *637*
Steele, M., *636*
Steele, P., 436, *472*
Steinberg, L., 119, *133*
Steinmetz, J., 119, *130*
Steinmetz, J. L., 112, *131*, *133*

Steinmetz, S. L., 447, *471*
Steinmetz-Breckenridge, J., 114, *130*,
    166, *183*
Steltz-Lenarsky, J., 188, *206*
Stemmler, M., *184*
Stern, M., *616*
Stewart, E. S., *489*
Stewart, M. A., 410, 413, *431*, *433*
Stewart, S., *258*
Stierlin, H., *185*
Stock, J. R., 575, *587*
Stoel-Gammon, C., 563, *572*
Stokes, G. S., *433*
Stokes, T. F., 321, *340*, 529, *552*
Stolar, M. J., 395, *407*
Stolmaker, L., 66, *79*
Storey, K., 560, *571*
Stouthamer-Loeber, M., 408, 426, *433*
Stowitschek, J., 582, *586*
Strain, P. S., 436, *472*, 522, 574,
    582–585, *586*, *587*
Strauss, C., *38*, *41*
Strauss, C. C., *62*
Strayhorn, J. M., 363, *368*
Strober, M., 138, 139, 149, *154*
Strodtbeck, F. L., 684, *694*
Stroul, B. A., 477, *490*
Strupp, H. H., 198, *206*
Sturge, C., 467, *472*
Sturges, J., 320, *339*
Sue, S., 157, 158, 160, 161, *185*, 663,
    665, 669, 677, 678, *695*
Sugai, D., 315, *337*
Sugai, G., 529, *552*
Suh, C. S., 198, *206*
Sullivan, H. S., 159, *185*
Suomi, S. J., 573, *587*
Sutherland, M., *205*
Sverd, J., 290, *305*
Swanson, J., *710*
Swanson, J. M., 286, 289, 293, 308, 363,
    368
Swanson, J. W., 640, *668*
Swathing, S., *202*
Swedo, S., 83, 98, *101*
Swedo, S. E., 83, *101*, *102*
Szapocnik, J., *695*
Szapocznik, J., 158, *185*, 398, 408, 592,
    672, 673, 675, 684–691, *694–697*
Szatmari, P., 285, *308*
Szmukler, G. I., 256, *259*

Tabrinzi, M. A., *202*

SUBJECT INDEX

BET (Bicultural Effectiveness Training), 685–686

BFST. *See* Behavioral family systems therapy

BHS (Beck Hopelessness Scale), 192

Bicultural Effectiveness Training (BET), 685–686

BMT (behavior management training), 275–278

Booster sessions, in treatment of depression
cognitive–behavioral approach to adolescent depression, 120–121, 122–123
suicidal depression, adolescent, 199–200

Boundaries, and structural family therapy, 680–683

Bronfenbrenner, U., 689–690, 693–694

Buddy System (summer treatment program for children with ADHD), 316, 321

CAADC. *See* Child and Adolescent Anxiety Disorders Clinic

CAPP (Childhood Anxiety and Phobia Program), 64–65

CBCL. *See* Child Behavior Checklist

CBQ (Conflict Behavior Questionnaire), 192

CBT. *See* Cognitive–behavioral therapy/ treatment

CD. *See* Conduct disorders

CDI. *See* Children's Depression Inventory

Center for Epidemiological Studies-Depression Scale (CES-D), 111, 127

Center for Family Studies, 672

Center for Stress and Anxiety Disorders (CSAD), 44–45

CES-D (Center for Epidemiological Studies-Depression Scale), 111, 127

CGAS (Children's Global Assessment Scale), 149, 631

Child and Adolescent Anxiety Disorders Clinic (CAADC), 23–24, 30, 31, 33, 35, 36

Child and Adolescent Services System, 477

Child and Family Psychosocial Research Center (Florida International University), 64

Child Behavior Checklist (CBCL), 40, 179, 192, 254, 327, 609–610
Anxiety Scale (CBCL-A), 34
Parent Report Form, 51, 391
Teacher Report Form, 41, 391

Child-deficit hypothesis, 460

Childhood Anxiety and Phobia Program (CAPP), 64–65

Children's Depression Inventory (CDI), 39, 49, 50, 179, 180

Children's Global Assessment Scale (CGAS), 149, 631

Children's Social Skills Program (University of California, Los Angeles), 598

Child's Perception of Therapeutic Relationship (CPTR), 34–35, 39

Chronic-care model (treatment for conduct disorder), 399

Classroom environments, in summer treatment program for children with ADHD, 317–318

Clinical practice, transfer of research to, 703–704, 706–707

Clinical samples, 14

Clinicians. *See also* Therapist(s)
control exercised by, with autistic children, 555–556
gap between researchers and, 4–5

Clinician Severity Rating (CSR), 49, 58

CNEQ (Cognitive Negative Errors Questionnaire), 192

CNS stimulants. *See* Stimulant medication therapy, for treatment of ADHD

Coached play, in treatment plan for socially rejected children, 603–604

Coalitions, family, and treatment of conduct disorders, 499–500

Coercion hypothesis, 437

Cognitions, maladaptive, 221–222, 224, 227–228

Cognitive–behavioral therapy/treatment (CBT), 4, 12
ADHD, for treatment of, 287–290, 343–344
anxiety disorders, for treatment of childhood, 23–36
assessment, 26

Cultural/ethnic issues (*continued*)
joining, 674–675
present, focus on, 679
reframing, 679–680
restructuring, 678–683
tasks, use of, 683
Culturally sensitive psychotherapy,
641–642. *See also* Cuento
therapy; Hero/heroine therapy
future research, directions for,
665–666
generalizability of, 664–665
limitations of, 663–664
CWD-A (Adolescent Coping With
Depression Course), 110,
114–115, 116, 134–135

Daily Mood Scale, 167
Daily report cards (DRC), 296, 352
DBD. *See* Disruptive behavior disorders
Dental-care model (treatment for
conduct disorder), 399–400
Depression
in adolescents, 187–191. *See also*
subheadings below
course of depression, 188
onset, 188
psychopharmacologic treatment,
190–191
psychosocial interventions,
189–190
recurrence, 188–189
risk factor research, 189
anxiety, comorbidity with, 31
cognitive–behavioral approach to
treatment of adolescent,
109–128, 189–190, 193–194
Adolescent Coping With
Depression Course (CWD-A),
use of, 110, 114–115, 116,
134–135
applications, treatment, 126–127
booster sessions, 120–121,
122–123
comorbidity issues, 110–111
conflict resolution skills, 119–120
depressotypic cognitions,
reduction of, 117
effectiveness, 121–125
formerly depressed, characteristics
of, 112

future depression, risk factors for,
111–112
limitations, 125–126
measures (table), 118–119
parent participation, 115
planning skills, 120
pleasant activities, 117
psychosocial problems, related,
111
Puerto Rican adolescents,
166–173
rationale, 113–114
relaxation training, 117
school-based prevention as
alternative to, 127–128
social skills training, 115
and suicide attempts, 112
holistic approach to treatment of, in
children and adolescents,
207–237
behavior, maladaptive, 221
cognitions, maladaptive,
221–222, 224, 227–229
disturbances and corresponding
treatments (table), 213
effectiveness, 231–234
family interactions, 231
family intervention, 209–210
generalizability, 235
group therapy format, use of,
210–212
initial sessions, 212, 215–217,
219
limitations, 234–235
multifaceted interaction, 208
parent training, 209, 229–231
problem-solving set, adoption of,
219–221
program outline (table), 214–215
rationale, 210–211
social skills training, 208–209
workbook forms, 217, 218, 223,
225, 226
interpersonal psychotherapy as
treatment for adolescent,
137–151, 190
clinical trials, 149–151
development, 138–140
goals, 140
grief, 143–144

McCarthy Scales of Children's Abilities, 576

MCDD (Multiple Complex Developmental Disorder), 620

MDD. *See* Major depressive disorder

Measures. *See* Assessment

Medication, treatment with. *See* Psychopharmacology

Mental health services, minority representation in, 157–158

Mentalization, 621

Mental processes, in children with developmental difficulties, 622, 623, 627

Mesosystems, 689

Methylphenidate, 301–302, 319, 343–349

MET (Multicultural Effectiveness Training), 686

Microsystems, 689

Minorities
    representation of, in mental health services, 157–158
    research focusing on, 15

Modeling and modeling therapy. *See also* Cuento therapy; Hero/heroine therapy; Videotape modeling, for treatment of oppositional-defiant disorder and conduct disorder
    for obsessive–compulsive disorders, 87
    structuring of, 645

Monkeys, remediation of social deficits in, 573–574

Montreal Children's Hospital, 333, 345

Motivation
    to communicate, in autistic children, 555
    in Pivotal Response Training for children with autistic disorder, 527–528, 530–531, 537–540

MTA. *See* Multimodal Treatment Study for Children with ADHD

Multicultural Effectiveness Training (MET), 686

Multimodal therapy, for children with attention deficit hyperactivity disorder, 344–364
    academic skill training/remediation, 352–354
    control treatments, 356–358

attention control, 356
conventional stimulant treatment group, 358
delivery of treatment, 355
effectiveness, 358, 364
family counseling, 352
future research, directions for, 359
generalizability, 359
goals, 345
instruments used (table), 360–363
and medication withdrawal feasibility, 358
method, 345–348
parent training, use of, 351–352
psychotherapy, use of, 354–355
report card system, use of, 352
social skills training, 349–351, 355
stimulant treatment, 349

Multimodal Treatment Study for Children with ADHD (MTA), 293–294, 302, 359, 364, 709

Multiple Complex Developmental Disorder (MCDD), 620

My Standards Questionnaire-Revised, 228–229

NASSQ (Negative Affectivity Self-Statement Questionnaire), 34, 40

National Institute of Mental Health (NIMH), 23, 24, 57, 65, 69, 148–149, 293, 333, 477

Necessary thinking, 167

Negative Affectivity Self-Statement Questionnaire (NASSQ), 34, 40

Negative reinforcement, 87

Negative self-evaluations, 228–229

Negative thinking, 168, 224

NIMH. *See* National Institute of Mental Health

NIMH Global Obsessive-Compulsive scale, 96, 97

Non-directive Support Treatment (NST), 197–198

Nortriptyline, 191

OADP (Oregon Adolescent Depression Project), 109–112

Schedule for Affective Disorders and
Schizophrenia for School-
Aged Children—Parent
Version (K-SADS-P), 192
Schneider Children's Hospital, 345
School(s)
clinical samples taken from, 14
cognitive–behavioral treatment of
adolescent in, 127–128
conduct disorders and school setting,
467
parent management training and
child's performance in, 387
social skills training in, 598
SCL-90 (Symptom Checklist), 149
Self-concept, effect of hero/heroine
therapy on, 662
Self-control
anxiety disorders, transfer of control
approach in treatment of,
67–68, 76–78
as aspect of ADVANCE parent
training videotape modeling
program, 447
Self-evaluation
development of skills for, in ADHD
treatment program, 295–296
negative, 228–229
Self-initiated queries, in communication-
oriented treatment for autistic
children, 557, 558–559,
563–564
Self-instruction, 224, 288–289
Self-management
ADHD, as strategy for treatment of,
291–304
anger management training,
utilization of, 296–297
effectiveness, 300–302
future research, directions for,
303–304
generalizability, 303
goals, 291
limitations, 303
outcome measures, 297–300
participants, study, 293–294
previous studies, 292–293
procedures, study, 294–295
self-evaluation skills,
development of, 295–296

autism, in communication-oriented
treatment for children with,
557, 562, 565–566
autism, in Pivotal Response Training
for children with, 541–547
advantages, 528–529
generalizability, 546–547
limitations, 545–546
parental implementation,
feasibility of, 544
severely handicapped children,
effectiveness with, 542
steps in training, 531–533
Self-monitoring, 50
Self-Perception Profile for Children, 326
Self-reports
anxiety disorders,
cognitive–behavioral group
treatment for, 50–51
socially rejected children, in
treatment plan for, 608
Self-statements, of anxiety-disordered
children, 27, 32
Separation anxiety disorder, 25
Session structure
anxiety disorders,
cognitive–behavioral group
treatment for, 53–56
childhood firesetters, treatment
outcome study on, 420–421
conduct disorder, treatment for
parent management training,
386–387
problem-solving skills training,
382–384
depression, treatment for
holistic approach to treatment of,
in children and adolescents,
212, 215–217, 219
interpersonal psychotherapy as
treatment for adolescent,
140–143
developmental difficulties, treatment
of children with, 628
hero/heroine therapy, 657
obsessive–compulsive disorders, for
treatment of, 95–96
socially anxious adolescents,
cognitive–behavioral
treatment for groups of, 53–56

Speech intelligibility, improvement of, as
    component of
    communication-oriented
    treatment for autistic children,
    557, 562–563, 566
Sports skills training, in summer
    treatment program for
    children with ADHD,
    316–317
SSRS (Social Skills Rating System), 608
STAIC. See State-Trait Anxiety
    Inventory for Children
Standardized research approaches, 704,
    707–709
State-Trait Anxiety Inventory for
    Children (STAIC), 40, 49,
    50, 648, 657
State-Trait Anxiety Inventory for
    Children—Modification of
    Trait Version for Parents
    (STAIC-P), 41
State University of New York at Albany,
    44
STIC tasks, 27–29
Stimulant medication therapy, for
    treatment of ADHD, 268
  assessment issues, 318–319
  with behavioral–cognitive
    interventions, 286
  family-based treatments as
    alternative to, 274
  follow-up studies, 342–343
  limitations of, 289, 290–291,
    311–312
  multimodal intervention, as
    component of, 349
  withdrawal feasibility, 358
Stimulus overselectivity, 531
STOP model, 68
Storytelling. See also Cuento therapy;
    Hero/heroine therapy
  and cultural history, 642–643
  as therapy modality, 643–644, 663
STP. See Summer treatment program, for
    children with attention deficit
    hyperactivity disorder
Strategic Structural Systems Engagement,
    687, 688
Structural Ecosystems Theory, 673,
    689–693
  Human Ecology Treatment program,
    application in, 692–693

Little Havana Parent Leadership
    Program, application in,
    691–692
Shenandoah in Action, application
    in, 691
Structural Family Systems Ratings
    (SFSR), 675–678
Structural family therapy (SFT), 672–694
  ADHD, for treatment of adolescent,
    275–277
  diagnosis, 675–678
  future research, directions for,
    689–693
  joining in, 674–675
  restructuring in, 678–683
    and alliances/boundaries,
      680–683
    present, working in, 678
    reframing, 678–679
    tasks, use of, 683
  specialized applications of, 684–689
    acculturation, 684–686
    hard-to-reach families, 687–689
    one-person family therapy,
      686–687
  and structural ecosystems therapy,
    689–693
Subjective units of distress scale (SUDS),
    50, 51, 56, 57, 91–92, 96
Substance abuse, among Hispanic youth,
    640
SUDS. See Subjective units of distress
    scale
Suicidal depression in adolescents
  occurrence of, 112
  psychosocial interventions for
    treatment of, 191–201
    assessment, 192–193
    booster sessions, 199–200
    cognitive–behavioral therapy,
      193–194
    design, study, 191
    distinctness/flexibility of
      treatment, 198–199
    effectiveness, 200–201
    family psychoeducation, 193
    interventions, choice of, 191–192
    non-directive support treatment,
      197–198
    parents, treatment of, 200
    removal from study, 199
    sample, 192

ABOUT THE EDITORS

Euthymia D. Hibbs, PhD, is head of the psychosocial treatment research, childhood schizophrenia, and eating disorders programs at the Child and Adolescent Disorders Research Branch, Division of Clinical and Treatment Research, at the National Institute of Mental Health (NIMH). She has authored and coauthored a number of research articles, book chapters, and edited books on the topic of mental disorders in children and families. Dr. Hibbs has received several professional and civic awards.

Peter S. Jensen, MD, is chief of the Child and Adolescent Disorders Research Branch, Division of Clinical and Treatment Research, at NIMH. Formerly, he was with the Walter Reed Army Institute of Research. In addition to his continuing studies of military families, Dr. Jensen is the lead NIMH investigator on a six-site study of multimodal treatments of attention deficit hyperactivity disorder funded by NIMH and by the U.S. Department of Education and is also an investigator on other NIMH multisite studies. Dr. Jensen serves on a number of editorial and scientific advisory boards and is the author of many scientific articles and book chapters. He has received numerous national awards, including the Norbert Regier Award from the American Academy of Child and Adolescent Psychiatry and the Agnes Purcell McGavin Award from the American Psychiatric Association.